PRAISE F(... VGER

The most haunting murde ... y during the 20th
century has finally been sol
—Stephen I   ... County Head Deputy District Attorney

"Los Angeles is the construct of its mythologies good and bad, fact and fiction. The legend of Elizabeth Short is one of the most enduring. Hodel's investigation is thoroughly and completely convincing. So too is this book. As far as I am concerned, this case is closed."
—Michael Connelly, *NYT* Bestselling author of *Harry Bosch novels*

"Crime was rampant as musicals in Los Angeles in the postwar years-this is the age of Bugsy Siegel, the founding of Las Vegas, Mickey Cohen and gun battles on Sunset Boulevard....and it's the age of film noir....George Hodel, I think is fit company for some of noir's most civilized villains-like Waldo Lydecker in *Laura*, Harry Lime in *The Third Man,* or even Noah Cross in *Chinatown.*"
—David Thomson, *New York Times Book Review*

"[Steve Hodel] gives us a fascinating family psychodrama; we watch his image of his father morph from flawed but lovable ladies' man to monster."
—*Newsweek*

"Fascinating."

— Johnny Depp

"[Hodel] has written an intensely readable account....So what's the final verdict on *Black Dahlia Avenger?* Its accounts of cover-ups and civic corruption are all too believable, and much of the circumstantial evidence it presents against George Hodel is persuasive....Has Steve Hodel solved the case? I think so."
—Jon L. Breen, *The Weekly Standard*

"A Must read."

—*New York Post*

"The book has been described as 'Hannibal Lecter meets L.A. Confidential meets Chinatown,' but even that Hollywood characterization doesn't do it justice. Former Los Angeles police detective Steve Hodel has written one of the most compelling true-crime books of all time."
—*Seattle Weekly*

"An ex-L.A. cop uncovers a painful answer to the notorious 1947 Black Dahlia slaying...Hodel appears to have solved one of the most sensational murders in the history of Los Angeles."
—*People Magazine*

"[Hodel] makes a strong case that the Black Dahlia was part of a larger series of ritual murders that went on for years. This unsparing, chilling account of the actions of a perfect psychopath grips to the end."

—*Toronto Globe and Mail*

"Hodel tells the story well and with incredible objectivity . . . A real-life tale of a Dr. Jekyll and Mr. Hyde."

—*Richmond Times-Dispatch*

"This remarkable book will keep readers riveted from the first page to the very last."

—*Citizen*

"In this 2003 case study, Hodel declares the case is solved. He offers irrefutable evidence piled fact upon fact as only the mind of a professional detective can present. The Black Dahlia Avenger is packaged as neatly as a court deposition."

—*St. Augustine Record*

"Black Dahlia Avenger is a fascinating and horrifying tale of 1940s Los Angeles-as Steve Hodel says, a real-life *L.A. Confidential*."

—*San Jose Mercury News*

"The story boasts all the glamour and sinister mystique of film noir."

—*The Daily Telegraph (London)*

"Readers must hang on tightly as Hodel hurtles along on his compelling parallel journeys of discovery-a return to the melodramatic days of old Hollywood and a simultaneous plunge into the dark roots of his own family tree."

—*London Free Press*

"*Black Dahlia Avenger* is the best nonfiction book about L.A. crime I have ever read. Former LAPD detective Steve Hodel's journey into the heart of a brutal crime and into the dark places of his soul stayed with me after I read it. Black Dahlia Avenger has it all: suspense, intrigue, bizarre sex, moral ambiguity, all set against a backdrop of the L.A. of Mickey Cohen, Bill Parker, and Tony Cornero. The words 'compelling' and 'riveting' though accurate do not do justice to this nonfiction tour de force."

—Gerald Petievich, author of *The Sentinel* and *To Live and Die in L.A.*

ABOUT THE AUTHOR

Steve Hodel was born and brought up in Los Angeles. Now a private investigator, he spent almost twenty-four years with the LAPD, most of them as a homicide detective-supervisor. During his tenure, he worked on more than three hundred murder cases, and had one of the highest "solve rates" on the force. He currently resides in the Los Angeles area. *Black Dahlia Avenger: A Genius for Murder,* published in 2003, became a *New York Times* bestseller.

Steve's Black Dahlia investigation and related books have been featured as full-hour segments on: *Dateline NBC, CBS 48-Hours, A&E Bill Kurtis Cold Case Files, Discovery Channel "Most Evil"* and *The Truth about the Black Dahlia on NBC Universal (France)*

Visit his Web site at www.stevehodel.com

Irony or Synchronicity?—Photo of author's original LAPD detective badge. It was the custom back then to have one's police badge set in a block of heavy brass showing their years of service. Note the appointment of February 4, 1963 and the official retirement of July 29, 1986. Thirteen more years would pass before the author would learn the name of Elizabeth "Black Dahlia" Short and that her birthdate was—July 29th.

Black Dahlia
Avenger
II

Black Dahlia
Avenger
II

Presenting the Follow-Up Investigation and Further Evidence Linking Dr. George Hill Hodel to Los Angeles's Black Dahlia and other 1940s LONE WOMAN MURDERS

STEVE HODEL

Thoughtprint Press

Second Edition, Published March 2014
ISBN-13: 978-0-9830744-3-4

Published in the United States of America by Thoughtprint Press
Los Angeles, California
www.thoughtprintpress.com

Interior formatting by Aubrey Hansen

For the victims, living and dead,

and

For Roberta McCreary—*Constant and True*,
Who believed and has been at my side since '95

Roberta and Steve, Mulholland Drive, Los Angeles, California 2005

Contents

Introduction

TWELVE YEARS AND THREE MONTHS HAVE NOW PASSED since I received that fateful 1 a.m. phone call from my stepmother on May 17, 1999.

"Steve, this is June in San Francisco. Your father is dead! The paramedics are here. Come down now."

As a career homicide cop with LAPD, most of my three-hundred plus murder investigations began with a call just like that, but, always from the Hollywood Watch Commander.

Not in my wildest dreams could I have imagined that a personal death notification would become the most difficult murder investigation of my career.

But, it did and it has.

Since the spring of '99, seemingly, each month has brought a new twist to the investigation. New witnesses have surfaced, new cold case victims were discovered, and new evidence was found.

It has taken over a decade for the public perception of the investigation to transition from "strong circumstantial" to "solved."

The Black Dahlia murder, for obvious reasons, has stood out as the most challenging criminal investigation in my forty-three years of working cases.

Surprisingly, my biggest challenge did not come from within. It wasn't, as you might imagine, from being confronted by the fact that the prime suspect I was pursuing was my father.

No, rather, it came from without: when I found myself for the first time in my career having to deconstruct the evidence.

What do I mean?

Prior to the Black Dahlia, without exception, all of my previous murder investigations had always been a *tabula rasa*—a clean slate. You start with a blank field notebook and move forward as you begin to build your case.

Not so with the Dahlia. As I began my investigation, I discovered that the "facts" of the case were a briar patch of misinformation, constructed from fifty-years of legend and lore.

Never was the oft-quoted cinematic line from the 1962 classic, *The Man Who Shot Liberty Valance,* truer than in the Black Dahlia murder:

"This is the West, sir. When the legend becomes fact, print the legend."

As if to underscore this, within three short years from the time of her murder, we have Elizabeth Short's legend appear on-screen, as a laugh line, in the 1950 Hollywood classic, *Sunset Boulevard.* [Ironically, the words are spoken by a young Jack Webb, who, the following year, will begin his career in his new television show, *Dragnet,* starring as LAPD Sergeant Joe "Just the Facts" Friday.]

In *Sunset Boulevard,* Webb plays the part of Artie Green, a young film producer, who, at his New Year's Eve party, introduces his writer friend, Joe Gillis [William Holden] to the guests with the following line:

"Fans, you all know Joe Gillis, the well-known screenwriter, uranium smuggler, and Black Dahlia suspect." [Much laughter]

With the publication of this, my third book on Elizabeth Short and the related 1940s Los Angeles Lone Woman Murders, I believe that I have been able to replace most of the hype and *faction* [hack writers' hyperbolic mix of fact and fiction] with the truth from the official Los Angeles District Attorney's Black Dahlia secret files. These records contain many of the original summaries from the LAPD's 1947 Black Dahlia investigation.

Here, in *BDA II,* I present separate chapters detailing the Black Dahlia's three major myths. (1) The Black Dahlia was a stand-alone crime, (2) Elizabeth Short had a "missing week" and (3) the case was never solved.

None of these "urban legends" was ever true and I present the evidence which proves them false.

In explaining and exposing the third myth—the case was never solved—I now have confirmation coming from within the LAPD, from most of its top commanders, past and present.

The last official word from LAPD on the Black Dahlia case status came from self-professed gatekeeper, Detective Brian Carr, who, before retiring in May 2009, informed the public:

"I don't have time to prove or disprove Hodel's investigation. All the physical evidence from the Dahlia investigation has disappeared, so we can't do any DNA and so we can't solve the case."

Nevertheless, on my side of the law enforcement ledger, I now have many officers who agree that the Black Dahlia murder is solved.

They include four of the original top-ranking command staff: two former LAPD police chiefs, as well as the original DA's investigators; a LASD undersheriff, an LASD commander, and the 2004 LAPD chief of detectives.

Also voicing his strong support was a then-active head deputy district attorney who, in 2003 and again in stronger terms in 2006, informed the public that based on the evidence he would have charged Dr. George Hodel—if he and witnesses were still alive—with two murder counts ["Black Dahlia" Elizabeth Short and "Red Lipstick" victim Jeanne French]. He was confident he'd "win a conviction in both cases in a jury trial."

But it is you, my readers, who have followed my ongoing investigations and served as dedicated jurors in the court of public opinion, and have been my biggest supporters.

The many letters and thousands of e-mails I have received from you over the past decade indicate that most of you have found the evidence not just compelling, but "beyond a reasonable doubt," meeting the legal criteria for establishing a guilty verdict.

Within the following chapters, you will find much that is new.

Chapter Two, "Maganda," deals with the controversy of the photographs found in my father's private album. I was able to prove myself wrong on what I formerly believed was solid forensic evidence. It was not. And by following the truth of it, and correcting my error, it led me to new and important proofs.

That is what truth does. It opens doors and keeps on opening them until the case is made.

In a criminal investigation, one of the surest signs that one might well be on the wrong track is when the doors start to close and no more open. Generally speaking, when one hits that dead-end, it is advisable to either turn around or to back out and drive down another alley.

Probably the most dramatic new investigative finding came in 2008 with the linkage of new physical evidence to the actual Black Dahlia crime scene. That evidence is presented in these pages.

Finally, there are the *Huston Letters*—private, highly personal correspondence between my mother and her former husband, famed film director/writer/actor, John Huston.

They span the years 1948–1957 and give us a real-time understanding of the absolute terror and horror my mother was suffering as she struggled to keep us together—just to survive. Her struggle was literally week by week during those dangerous post-Dahlia months from 1948 to 1950. Reading those letters, which contained her desperate pleas to John for help, leave no doubt that our father was a psychological time bomb about to explode.

I have included all of the letters not only because of my mother's dramatic first-person descriptions of the desperate conditions at the Franklin house, but also because in the later years they documented an exchange of ideas between John and Dorothy that will interest many readers, historians, and cinephiles.

Personally, these hitherto unknown and unpublished letters make me exceedingly grateful for John's overwhelming generosity.

Time and again, my mother's letters show John repeatedly sent emergency dollars that kept the sheriff at bay and fed and housed us during those difficult gypsy years.

I would like to acknowledge a few close friends who have been of tremendous help. First, as always, there is Roberta McCreary, my confidant who has been with me from the start, and remains constant and true.

Also much thanks goes to my good friend, Hermann H., for providing encouragement and suggestions, and to Dennis Effle, my resident Hollywood historian, amigo, and researcher extraordinaire! Kudos to Kevin Knoblock for his many suggestions and critique. And finally a sincere "well done and thank you" to my good friend, journalist and bestselling author, Ron Franscell, who has served as my editor for this 2014 updated edition. Ron is a man of true grit and his literary contribution to this revision cannot be overstated.

Steve Hodel
Los Angeles, California
March, 2014

1
Madi Comfort, Duke Ellington's Original "Satin Doll"

"We all knew that he (Dr. George Hill Hodel) had done it. There was no doubt!" —Madi Comfort, June 2003

THE YEAR WAS 1942. The cigarette girl at the Hollywood Casino Club on the Sunset Strip was a knockout. Just eighteen, she had a perfect figure, satin-soft skin, and jet-black hair. Mattie Hodge (at Duke Ellington's suggestion, she would later change the spelling to "Madi") was the bar crowd's favorite. A few whispered complaints might have come from the chorus-line girls who knew they couldn't compete with Mattie's natural beauty.

From the contacts she made on The Strip, Mattie's public persona would go on to include: model, singer, film actress, and, later in life, she would school herself in painting and become an accomplished artist. Mattie also had a secret—a big one. A secret so big that all of Los Angeles wanted to know it. For fifty-five years, she kept it hidden and planned to take it with her to the grave. But in the last ten days before her death, fate or happenstance whispered in her ear, "Share it." She did. This is Madi's secret.

THE LEAD

I've been a detective all my adult life. Born and raised in Los Angeles, I am sixty-eight, and this is my forty-seventh year in conducting criminal investigations. Working LAPD's Hollywood Division Homicide in the 1970s, my hot leads came to me in one of three ways: (1) from a jailhouse snitch, (2) someone "dropping a dime" and calling me with information, or (3) a "walk-in" where the witness would come to the police station with a "Here's what I know..."

Detective work is much different today. Twenty-first century tips now generally come to me by email. That's how this one arrived. It was from Lynelle Lujan, the office manager at the Whittier Historical Society Museum. It read:

August 20, 2010

"Dear Mr. Hodel,

I don't know if you remember me. I sent you a *Whittier Daily News* article about 3 months ago. I'm writing you today for a different reason however. While lending my boss [Myra Hilliard, the Museum's Executive Director] your first book, she recognized Madi Comfort's name, whom she knew briefly before her death.

We have since made contact with Madi's longtime companion and mentioned your book and the connection of your father with Madi. His name is George and he is willing to meet with you. He remembers the time that your father died, and that Madi made several phone calls and seemed agitated.

If you would like to meet with George, we can offer the Whittier Museum as a private meeting place, perhaps before or after your October 12th speaking engagement at the Whittier Public Library.

Sincerely,
Lynelle Lujan

MADI COMFORT—HER BACKSTORY

Madi returned to her roots, Whittier, California, in 1970. The small town, just twelve miles southeast of Los Angeles, was originally a Quaker community and is now famous for its "urban forest," magnificent tree lined parkways providing a country lifestyle for its city dwellers.

Madi had been featured in a number of local articles over the years, and former Whittier Mayor Allan Zolnekoff proclaimed February 3, 2002, as Madi Comfort Day "...for the historical precedent set by her family of pioneering African-Americans to settle in Whittier and overcoming racial unwelcome; her achievements as an artist, her contributions to the Whittier Community, and her dedication to the arts and music in Whittier."

Sixteen months later, Madi suffered a heart attack and died in Whittier on June 20, 2003, at age seventy-nine.

She was born Mattie Hodge on November 19, 1923. Her mother, not wanting to raise her newborn daughter, allowed her to be adopted by Whittier's first black citizens, Mr. and Mrs. Mark Huff. But when the time came to turn the child over, her mother changed her mind and decided to keep her daughter. She would, however, give the baby Mrs. Huff's given name, "Mattie."

Mattie's mother was abusive, and her childhood was difficult, compounded greatly by the hard times of the Great Depression.

As a young woman, Mattie's natural charm and exceptional beauty drew her west, from Whittier to Hollywood, where in 1942, at age eighteen, she was offered a job as a cigarette girl at a Sunset Strip nightclub. Her popularity at the club and regular contact with Hollywood celebrities won her modeling jobs, some singing gigs, and a few small movie parts.

Mattie met and fell in love with Joe Comfort, a young soldier who would become a well-known L.A. bassist who played with Lionel Hampton, Nat King Cole, and Frank Sinatra in the 1940s and '50s. Joe and Mattie married in Los Angeles on May 13, 1943. Just nineteen, Mattie soon found herself in an abusive relationship with Joe and ended the marriage several years later.

Mattie and Joe Comfort, Wedding Day, May 1943
Dancing at the Plantation Club, 108th and Central, Watts

MADI AS EBONY MAGAZINE'S 1955 COVER GIRL— *KISS ME DEADLY*

Mattie's most memorable film role was a small part in the 1955 film noir, *Kiss Me Deadly*, a Mickey Spillane-adapted classic. She plays a blues singer in an L.A. jazz club where hard-boiled P.I. Mike Hammer (played by actor Ralph Meeker) enjoys a few drinks as she sings, *"I'd Rather Have the Blues than What I've Got."* In the film, Mattie lip-syncs the song by popular Central Avenue vocalist Kitty White, although the film's producer would reportedly later tell her, "If I'd known you sang as well as you do, I'd have had you sing the piece in our picture."

Screen shots from the 1955 film noir, Kiss Me Deadly – Left: Mattie singing Right: Mattie with star of film, Ralph Meeker and unidentified male

One of Mattie's major claims to fame was that she inspired the 1956 hit song *"Satin Doll,"* by Duke Ellington, Billy Strayhorn and Johnny Mercer.

Ellington, who was once Mattie's boyfriend, called her his "satin doll" and suggested that she change the spelling of her name. "My Dear," Ellington told her, "you should really spell your name M A D I, because you really are the Mad One, you know." She followed his advice and Mattie became Madi.

This excerpt from a book about Charlie Mingus, another bass player, offers more insight into the Madi anecdote. ["Knepper" is Jimmy Knepper, who was Mingus' trombonist.]

From: *Myself When I Am Real: The Life and Music of Charles Mingus* by Gene Santoro (2001, Oxford University Press):

One night during the Hollywood gig, Mingus started riding Knepper onstage in front of women friends. One of them was one of Duke Ellington's girlfriends, Mattie Comfort, wife of Mingus' Watts friend and fellow bassist Joe Comfort. Mattie looked like Lena Horne, and was sitting with Pat Willard, a white Duke fan, in the front row.

Mattie called out, "Hey, Mingus, leave that white boy alone, he loves you." He rasped, "You're not black enough to talk to me like that." She said coolly, "You're lighter than I am, Mingus."

Mingus spotted Knepper with the women in the lobby. When Mattie left to get her car, he followed her into the parking lot, then took out a thick pen filled with a charge to shoot pepper. He had no pepper, just charges. He had taken to firing it off in the club during his shows, but now he shot it off in her face.

Mattie was still shaking when she picked up the other two. In the rearview mirror, she watched Mingus follow them up Sunset Boulevard in the Cadillac. She turned right on Vine, right on Hollywood, and headed for the police station. No cops, no cop cars, and Mingus was right behind them. So she made a right on N. Bronson and ran a red light at Sunset, where a police cruiser parked there stopped them.

To the puzzled cop, Mattie explained that Knepper worked for Charles Mingus, who was chasing them. When the cop looked up, the limo wheeled into a U-turn and sped off. The cop shrugged, and let Mattie off with a warning. Relieved, they drove to Pat Willard's house and listened to Ellington records.

THE DA SECRET FILES

Black Dahlia Avenger originally published in April 2003. Breathless and extensive media coverage of my story led to full hour episodes of *NBC's Dateline, CBS 48 Hours Mystery, A&E Court TV*, and Bill Kurtis' *Cold Case Files.* New interest in the Black Dahlia led Los Angeles District Attorney Steve Cooley to give *Los Angeles Times* columnist Steve Lopez an interview and access to some previously secret DA files that had been locked in the county vault, unexamined, for over fifty years.

In two back-to-back L.A. *Times* articles, Lopez revealed some of the contents of these never-seen DA files. To the absolute shock of both LAPD and Angelenos in general, the reports fully documented the DA's separate investigation into the original Black Dahlia murder and named Dr. George Hill Hodel as the prime suspect. This was huge news because it was a totally independent and external confirmation of my own findings.

A month later, in mid-May, I approached DA Steve Cooley and requested permission to view those secret files. He agreed and I spent a full day copying all the relevant Hodel-Black Dahlia documents, some 600 pages that hadn't been seen since 1950.

Over the next several months, I wrote two new chapters for the 2006 paperback edition of *Black Dahlia Avenger*.

Among the new material was proof of the DA's 1950 electronic surveillance and "bugging" of Dr. Hodel's Hollywood home.

It began on February 15, 1950, when DA Detective Lt. Frank Jemison and his partner arranged to interview my father at their office in the downtown Hall of Justice.

While they questioned him, officers from both the LAPD and the DA's sound lab broke into Dr. Hodel's private residence by shimming the front door. They installed microphones inside the walls in the living room/home office and the master bedroom. A hard line was then run from the basement of our home, to Pacific Bell telephone lines that led straight to the basement listening post in the *Hollywood police station* two miles away. There, live conversations in the house were monitored and recorded by detectives around the clock. [It is important to understand that these microphones were picking up "live conversations" and were not simply phone bugs.]

A task force of eighteen detectives, including officers from both the DA's Office and LAPD, conducted the 24/7 stakeout for forty days. They collected over forty spools of wire tape recordings, including statements from my father admitting to killing the Black Dahlia.

The DA tapes also contained admissions by George Hodel to committing the 1945 barbiturate overdosing of his personal secretary, Ruth Spaulding. That crime, while originally listed as an undetermined death and possible "suicide," was actively investigated by LAPD as a suspected murder some eighteen months before the Dahlia crime. The Spaulding investigation was suspended when Dr. Hodel temporarily left the country in February 1946 to become chief medical officer in Hankow, China, while working for the United Nations. He would unexpectedly return to Los Angeles and resume his medical practice in September 1946, four months before Elizabeth Short's murder.

Several weeks into the surveillance, one of the bugs captured Dr. Hodel admitting to performing abortions at his privately owned venereal disease clinic in downtown Los Angeles. "This is the best payoff between law enforcement agencies that I've ever seen," he says to a confederate at one point, according to the transcripts. "You do not have the right connections made. I'd like to get a connection made in the DA's office."

Later he brags, "I'm the only person who knows how all these things fit into the picture."

Detectives who were listening to another live conversation reportedly overheard a crying woman attempting to dial a telephone operator. Then heard George and a second man walk downstairs to the basement. After the sound of a pipe striking an object, the woman cried out. More blows, and she cried out again. Then silence.

Detectives then heard a brief discussion about "not leaving a trace"—then only silence. Inexplicably, these two on-duty officers, listening to what might have been a serious felony assault or, worse, an actual murder in progress, were just two miles away and alerted nobody.

Much more is contained in the 146-page transcripts, which I have attached unaltered, and in their entirety, as an addendum to this book.

The stakeout ended in late March 1950, only because George Hodel had been informed by his ex-wife(and my mother)Dorothy that the detectives had some damning evidence and photographs, and she was sure that he was about to be arrested. Spooked by that information, my father immediately left town.

Sample page of DA Transcript of Surveillance Tapes (1 of 146 pages)

LAPD Hollywood Division Basement. Detectives are monitoring live conversation from the Hodel residence, 5121 Franklin Ave, Hollywood, California. DA investigators Hronek & McGrath on duty. Verbatim transcript of Spool #2:

February 18, 1950
7:35 pm- Conversation between two men. Recorded. Hodel and man with a German acent [sic] had a long conversation; reception was poor, and conversation was hard to understand. The following bits of conversation, however, were overhead.

Hodel to German:
"This is the best payoff I've seen between Law Enforcement Agencies. You do not have the right connections made. I'd like to get a connection made in the DA's office."

"Any imperfections will be found. They will have to be made perfect. Don't confess ever. Two and two is not four." Much laughter. "Were just a couple of smart boys." More laughter.

Hodel to German:
"Supposin I did kill the Black Daliah. [sic] They couldn't prove it now. They can't talk to my Secretary anymore because she's dead."

MATTIE COMFORT—THE DA'S SECRET BLACK DAHLIA WITNESS

As I continued my careful review of the previously secret Hodel DA Files, a new name surfaced. A name that had never appeared in any police reports, newspaper account, or the volumes of lore and mythology—*Mattie Comfort*.

BACKGROUND

During the 1950 investigation and before installing any microphones at my father's Frank Lloyd Wright Jr.-built home in Hollywood, DA Lt. Frank Jemison and his partner, Lt. Sullivan, contacted a young ex-sailor named Joe Barrett.

They picked-up the twenty-five-year-old Navy veteran from his day job and brought him to their office for questioning. At the time of the interview, Barrett was a struggling artist. Since 1948, he'd been renting a room at the north end of our home. His space was large and open, with great lighting that served as both his apartment and art studio.

"Lt. Sullivan laid it on the line with me," Barrett told me in 1999. "He came right out and said, 'We think Dr. George Hodel killed the Black Dahlia. You live there and we need your help. We want you to be our eyes and ears.'" Simply put, they wanted Joe Barrett to be their mole, their informant. With his free, inside access he could be invaluable. He agreed to help.

With that as background, let's examine a scanned excerpt from the police report exactly as found in the DA files:

Camarillo. Joe Barrett, a roomer at the Hodel residence cooperated as an informant. A photograph of the suspect in the nude with a nude identified colored model was secured from his personal effects. Undersigned identified this model as Mattie Comfort, 3423-1/2 South Arlington, Republic 4953. She said that she was with Doctor Hodel sometime prior to the murder and that she knew about his being associated with victim.

Actual scan of original DA documents referencing Mattie Comfort

Barrett eventually gave police several stolen photographs of Dr. Hodel. Not just ordinary portraits. In these, Dr. Hodel appeared completely naked in the company of a "nude colored model," later identified as Mattie Comfort.

Detectives later noted, *"She [Mattie Comfort] was with Doctor Hodel sometime prior to the murder and that she knew about his being associated with victim. [Elizabeth "Black Dahlia" Short.]"*

Had Mattie Comfort seen Dr. Hodel and Elizabeth Short together, as the report suggests?

Take a closer look. I realized in 2003 that an unknown writer at an unknown date and time altered the report by inserting the word "nothing" in that sentence. This simple act was obviously an attempt to reverse the meaning of the statement, which now reads, *"She said that she was with Doctor Hodel sometime prior to the murder and that she knew **nothing** about his being associated with victim."*

Enlargement showing word "nothing" inserted by hand

Based on Lt. Jemison's report, what we know for sure is that Mattie Comfort and George Hodel were on intimate terms sometime in the 1940s.

Was this document deliberately altered years or possibly decades later? Clearly, Lt. Jemison would not have allowed his typed final investigative report to be filed away uncorrected. Who changed it and when? What was the truth of it?

LT. JEMISON INTERVIEWS DOROTHY HODEL—"ON THE RECORD"

Left: Dorothy Huston Hodel, 1946
Right: Later photo of Mattie Comfort, circa 1954

On March 22, 1950, while the stakeout and bugging continued at my father's home, Jemison and a DA stenographer went to my mother's private apartment on Santa Monica Pier and conducted a follow-up interview.

This six-page transcript was placed in the secret files and only came to light in 2003, some fifty-three years later. I should note that while my mother, my two brothers, and I continued to live on-and-off with my father at the Franklin house, well into 1950, my parents had been legally divorced in 1944.

While there is much of interest in the transcript, I will just include those portions about the separate photographs that Lt. Jemison showed to Dorothy Hodel. It should also be noted that at the time of this interview, Jemison had apparently not yet identified the "nude colored model" as Mattie Comfort. And it became clear that he was hoping Dorothy would be able to identify her. (I will attach the complete interview as addendum.)

Excerpts from Lt. Jemison/Dorothy Hodel 3.22.50 Interview transcripts:

Page 2:

Lt. Jemison: I will now show you a photograph of Beth Short, Santa Barbara No. 11419 and ask you whether or not you have ever seen that young lady in your life?

Dorothy: No, I never have.

Elizabeth Short "Black Dahlia" booking photo shown to Dorothy Hodel

Lt. Jemison: Did you have a conversation with Dr. Hodel about the murder of Beth Short?

Dorothy: No, unless we mentioned it when it was in the papers, but I don't like to read about things like that. I can't say for sure that I have never mentioned her name to him, but it may have been in passing.

Lt. Jemison: Did he ever tell you, "They can't pin that murder on me?"

Dorothy: No, to the best of my knowledge he didn't and doesn't know her.

Lt Jemison: On or about the date of her murder, January 15, 1947 do you remember being out until 4:00 in the morning with George

Hodel and coming in slightly intoxicated? Now, that's three years ago.

Dorothy: Well, I think I explained before we never went on drinking parties because I don't drink because of certain tendencies to drink too much and particularly if I were near him I would not drink because from a medical point of view he does not approve of my drinking and I don't know that I understood that question.

Page 3:
Lt. Jemison: Well, the information that I have is that he was quite intoxicated himself and at that time on that occasion stated that they couldn't pin the Black Dahlia murder on him. [Note: In Lt. Jemison's follow-up investigation and final report prepared in 1951, he corrected George Hodel's quote to read, "They will never be able to prove I did that murder."] [Black Dahlia]

Dorothy: No. No, that isn't true.

Lt. Jemison: Do you remember ever telling Tamar that? [Note: Tamar was my then twelve-year-old half-sister and George Hodel's daughter by another woman.]

Dorothy: No.

Lt. Jemison: Did you ever tell Tamar that Dr. George Hodel was out the night before the murder with Beth Short at a party?

Dorothy: No, I was living at my brother's house at the time. We were not living at the same house. I wouldn't know what he was doing.

Page 5:
Lt. Jemison: Now in view of the fact that the District Attorney's office is interested in contacting all persons that might know something about whether or not Dr. Hodel had anything to do with this murder, I now show you a photograph of a nude girl and ask you if you recognize who that girl is. In other words, we want to know her name and where we can contact her?

Dorothy: There is something familiar about her face. I think she may have been some model or something.

Lt Jemison: Would you say she is a colored girl or half Indian, do you know?

Dorothy: No.

Lt. Jemison: I show you another photograph of the same girl with a man. Do you recognize that man in that photograph?

Dorothy: I would say that was Dr. Hodel.

Lt. Jemison: Do you know the person who owns the cat that they are holding between them?

Dorothy: No, I don't.

Lt. Jemison: In other words, I am sincerely interested in contacting this girl for information.

Dorothy: No, I don't know her I have seen her face. I have seen photographs that George has of her.

Lt. Jemison: Would you have any idea where we could find her?

Dorothy: No.

Lt. Jemison: I show you the third picture. Dr. Hodel and the colored girl. You still can't place any person that might know where I can find her?

Dorothy: No, I don't know. I can't think.

Lt. Jemison: Let me advise you that we do have information that he [George Hodel] did associate with Beth Short... [Emphasis mine]

Entries by detectives in the surveillance transcripts reveal that my mother went directly to George's home the day after this interview and told him of being questioned by Jemison, and gave him all the questions she'd been asked. Most importantly, she said she'd been shown photographs of both Elizabeth Short and Mattie Comfort. While my parents' actual conversation was apparently out of microphone range and not recorded, we know that she told him everything based on the following conversation, which was recorded.

DA TRANSCRIPTS—FRANKLIN HOUSE

March 23- 7:45 pm- Hodel came in with Dorothy. (Phone rang, recorded) ...

March 25 11:10 pm
Hodel and Baron (man with accent) came in talking low (can't hear) ...Sounded like Hodel said something about Black Dahlia. Baron said something about F.B.I. Then talked about Tibet. Sounds like Hodel wants to get out of the country. Mentioned passport. Hodel giving Baron dope on how to write to Tibet. Hodel talking about Mexico. Going down and take pictures and write a story. Hodel seems afraid about something. Hodel says his Sanitarium, if he gets it started in Mexico would be "Safe."

March 26 12 a.m. (spool 39)
Spool ran out. Changing. Talking about woman. Hodel says "he wants money and power. "Talking about China. Talking about selling some of Hodel's paintings or something. Hodel talking about picture police have of him and some girl-thought he had destroyed them all- (wire quit at 50-new one going on) Not much talk.

This was the final night of the surveillance tapes. The next day, George Hodel left town, leaving the DA and LAPD detectives in a lurch, literally sitting there with their microphones up his walls. Jemison was forced to terminate the stakeout.

In the final hours before George Hodel left L.A., Dorothy Hodel has made him aware that the police now had photographs of Mattie Comfort ["I thought I had destroyed all of them"]. And despite Mother's best efforts at withholding her name, the cops were sure to discover it in short order. The stakeout detectives referenced that "Hodel seems afraid of something." Hodel mentioned the "Black Dahlia," "the FBI," and, the following day, he is in the wind.

Upon reading the Jemison/Dorothy Hodel transcript for the first time, I knew my mother was lying and stonewalling. I knew that Mattie Comfort was my mother's close friend. One night in the 1970s, my mother called to ask if I could give her a ride out to the Sunset Strip, where she wanted to attend a party being thrown by some friends. So I accompanied her to an apartment house. At the door, Mother briefly introduced me to a beautiful woman, simply saying, "Steven, this is Mattie, a good friend from the old days. Mattie, meet Steven." The beautiful "Satin Doll" smiled at me. We shook hands, and I left.

But Mattie Comfort's face is not a face one forgets.

THE WHITTIER MEETING

I asked Lynelle Lujan and Myra Hilliard to contact Madi's boyfriend, "George" to see if he was available to meet with us at their office at the Whittier Historical Museum on September 11 2010 at 10 a.m. He was.

"George" is George Parkington, a gentle, intelligent carpenter with the look and manner of an artist.

George had met Madi in1997. The two of them became very close and spent the last six years together before her death in 2003.

As the four of us sat down to talk, George spoke first:

> I want to say something to you right away. When your book came out, there was a big article and photos of you in *People Magazine*. Madi always read *People*. And as soon as she read the piece, she called me. She was so excited. I couldn't believe it. Madi said, "George, you've got to come home right now." I drove home immediately, and she was ecstatic...thrilled because this [the Black Dahlia connection] was a secret she'd always held inside her. And now it was in the open.

In the week after my book published, *People Magazine* interviewed me and on June 2, 2003, ran a feature story complete with photos. It was entitled, *"Accusing His Father: An ex-L.A. cop uncovers a painful answer to the notorious 1947 Black Dahlia slaying."* Madi Comfort never got to read my book as she died from a sudden heart attack eighteen days later, on June 20, 2003.

My first question to George was the obvious one. "Did Madi ever discuss with you what she knew about the Black Dahlia murder? Did she ever provide any specifics?"

George responded:

> Here's what I will tell you. Madi told me that she and everybody else were sure that it was your father that killed the Black Dahlia. They had no doubt. She told me, "We all knew that he had done it." Now, who the "we" was I'm not sure, but there are some people still around from way back then. I'll try and dig on that a little bit and see if there is someone you can speak with. Most of the people I know were more like from the fifties, so I'm not sure there is anybody I can locate from that exact era.

As we listened to George share his memories of Madi, it was obvious that the man had been deeply devoted to her. When he spoke her name, his words were filled with a deep love and a great sense of loss.

A half-hour into our talk, George reached into his briefcase and removed a stack of papers. Handing them to me he explained:

> Madi has written a book. It's in rough form and unpublished and runs about twelve-hundred pages. It's her autobiography. The title

is: *Madi Comfort: The Original Satin Doll*. I think Madi started writing it sometime in the seventies or maybe later. In it she mentions and writes about both your father and mother. What Madi writes about them is explicit, but I thought you would want to have everything about them. There may be other references because her writings are scattered, and she jumps back and forth in time. But, for now, I wanted you to have these pages that talk about your parents.

I reached for the papers and asked, "Had Madi mentioned Elizabeth Short in her book?"

George replied:

I don't think so. I don't think, even all of these years later, that she wrote about that. That is why she was so excited when your book came out. My sense of it was that she was still protecting people she cared about even though they were dead. She would have been like your mother. She would have protected anybody she cared about. She would have protected even somebody that she didn't care about.

Our meeting lasted nearly two hours. It ended with a handshake and the assurance that the four of us would keep in touch. George and I exchanged phone numbers with the hope and promise to together try and search deeper into the mystery of Madi and how she was further connected to my father, Dr. George Hill Hodel, now known and identified as the "Black Dahlia Avenger."

DOROTHY HUSTON HODEL—"DORERO"

George Parkington had warned me that Madi's writings about my parents were "explicit." He was right.

Before opening Madi's manuscript, a little background on my mother is in order:

Dorothy Jean Harvey was born in New York (Central Park West) on April 15, 1906. Her parents moved to Los Angeles sometime in the teens with two children, Dorothy and her younger brother, Eugene. Dorothy was exceptionally precocious, as well as strikingly beautiful—a dangerous combination. Ever the free spirit, she was named Elysian Park's, "Queen of the May" in 1917. As a teen in high school, she dabbled in acting and began dating. Dorothy dated a teenager named George Hodel who, though only fifteen had a stratospheric IQ (186) and was enrolled in Pasadena's prestigious California Institute of Technology. (Caltech) Another couple who dated with them included a beautiful young woman named Emilia Lawson, who worked at the newly opened Los Angeles Public Library, and her lean, lanky boyfriend John Huston, the son of one of Hollywood's brightest film stars, Walter Huston.

At some point in their double-dating, John and George switched partners. John and Dorothy discovered that they were in love. In about 1926, the two teenagers found a Justice of the Peace who married them.

They eloped to New York and decided to play house in Greenwich Village. There they began socializing with a very Bohemian crowd of artists, actors, and musicians—free spirits all. John and Dorothy partied with George and Ira Gershwin and many of the Algonquin Round Table types. Lots of drinking, lots of lovemaking. It was the Roaring '20s, and they were in full roar.

Left: Stage and screen star, Walter Huston, meeting his son, John and new bride Dorothy at L.A. train station, circa 1926.
Right: Dorothy Harvey Huston, age eighteen, circa 1924.

John and Dorothy returned to Los Angeles and both became screenwriters for the film studios. They traded Bohemian New York's red wine for Hollywood's martinis—very dry.

By 1934, after seven years of a very bumpy marriage, John and Dorothy had become serious alcoholics and both were freely sleeping around.

In about 1936 Dorothy, with her beautiful actress-lover, Greta Nissen in arm took a cruise to Europe where she continued to drink and play. (In his well-researched 1989 book, *The Hustons*, author Lawrence Grobel gave a fine account of how John went to England, rescued Dorothy from an almost certain death from alcoholism, and brought her back to the U.S., where she made a full, albeit temporary, recovery.)

Dorothy was very open about her bisexuality. She was proud of what she called her "paganism" and wore it on her sleeve in defiance of conventionality.

Around 1938, Dorothy reunited with her former boyfriend, George Hodel, who had graduated from medical school. After completing his internship at San Francisco General Hospital, he was hired as a logging camp surgeon in Arizona and then took a temporary appointment as a U.S. Health Department public-health doctor in the Southwest, treating Hopi and Navajo Indians on the reservation.

George and Dorothy fell back in love. George returned to L.A. and Dorothy immediately got pregnant. My older brother, Michael, was born in July 1939. They married in Mexico in 1940 and my twin "John" and I were born in 1941, followed by my younger brother Kelvin just eleven months later.

Our father was hired by the L.A. County Health Department to treat venereal disease and he was quickly promoted to chief VD officer for all of Los Angeles County.

Father, a believer in the importance and symbolism of names, christened his new wife, "Dorero," replacing her given name of "Dorothy." To all who would listen, he explained that his inspiration came from combining two words: "Dor," meaning "a gift of" and "Eros," the God of sexual desire. Hence, to him, "Dorero" was a gift of sexual desire.

This quick overview brings us to about the point in time when, according to Madi's manuscript, she met my parents. So, I will let her take over the narrative from here with her own very unique perspective. With the exception of some minor spelling corrections, Madi Comfort's writing and words are presented here exactly as they appear in her manuscript. I have changed nothing. These are her verbatim descriptions, written some twenty or thirty years past.

I have, however, inserted in bold my own comments to help the reader understand or to clarify a specific person, place, etc.

SKH Note- One further explanation is needed. What we are reading here are Madi's personal reflections as dictated directly into a tape recorder and then transcribed to paper. So, they are not actually her "writings" so much as they are a conversational storytelling of her life, which was then transcribed into a 1,200-page rough draft manuscript. The following excerpted pages, which directly relate to Madi's association and memories of my parents, George and Dorero Hodel, were provided to me by her boyfriend, George Parkington.

MADI COMFORT: THE ORIGINAL SATIN DOLL— (ROUGH DRAFT)

Page 28 (bottom):
Well, I was introduced to Dr. George and Dorero [Dorothy] Hodel by Suzette Harbin, who was one of the chorus girls in the show. Dorothy posed for the great photographer Man [The artist, Man Ray, a close personal friend of my parents and our family photographer] with Suzette. What a beautiful photograph! Dorero's white delicate face profile together with Suzette's rich beautiful brown skin was such a beautiful contrast, yet there was such a oneness.

Page 29:
George and Dorero lived in this tremendous mansion in Pasadena. Once entering the driveway one would wind, in this case I would wind with George and Dorero in their ... [in their car up the driveway]...last to be made after or before the war. It was a gorgeous black Lincoln Continental convertible with a wheel on the back. It was pure gorgeous. Round and round and up and down for what seemed like blocks to this four-story mansion. The top floor was a ballroom; the third floor was a nursery for their three gorgeous children. The second was their bedroom quarters. I guess I should say playground because that's where we played. They were both completely sensuous. George a very handsome polished tall lean born rich man indulged and adored by his father. George had beautiful black hair with a sophisticated wave in front, a classic nose with a perfectly trimmed mustache and very nice lips.

George would smile at a person with such charm and sweetness as well as elegance in his perfect clothes with such sincerity. George could turn around and be as cold as ice, yet complete composure in his superior authoritative voice, become this strange distant in charge person. He was a doctor.

George and Dorero led me gracefully and pleasurably, into sharing their joys in many exciting ways of the art of making love. It was all done so tastefully and made us very close friends. We liked very much bringing such joy and pleasures to one another's life, yet we all maintained our dignity and self-respect.

Dorero's first husband had been John Huston. Her father-in-law, Walter Huston. Dorero had been a writer. She once told me that John and George and she were good friends. George stole her away from John. Dorero was so soft and lovely as well as feminine. I loved the way she pronounced words. Her father told me she had once been a schoolteacher. Her father also told me her name was Dorothy. She certainly had her own style.

George and Dorero had me over to their home for dinner quite often. They would take me out, come all the way to Willowbrook to pick me up. ... Dorero was having guests for dinner who had arrived from New York. They had both been put under contract. Their names were Van Heflin and Vincent Price. Actually we were having hors d'oeuvres and cocktails at their [the Hodels] home first then we were going to Chinatown for dinner afterwards. Chinatown was fairly new (remodeled) then and quite fancy and intriguing. It was a fun evening. Van and Vincent were both very charming and witty and they talked about New York and the theater. I just mostly remember what nice down-to-earth gentlemen they were.

One morning around ten a.m. or so I was lying in bed and I hear this crash and Dorero crying. I ran into the bathroom. Dorero was in the bathtub, crying. George cool as you please explains to me Dorero is an alcoholic and has "sneaked a drink." He was reprimanding her for her own good. I'm protesting. "You could break her neck! George I cannot stand to see you knocking poor Dorero around like this. Please don't treat her like this." Meanwhile, I'm busy trying to pull Dorero out of the tub. We were all stark naked.

Left: Dorero Hodel, 1942
Right: George Hodel, circa 1950

The photo on left was taken in October/November 1942. It shows Mother holding her newborn son, my younger brother, Kelvin, as I look on while standing on the fencepost. Based on the timing, this photo would have been taken at the hilltop "tremendous mansion" described earlier by Madi. (I have no memory of this location, but my half-sister, Tamar, recalls the home, and specifically remembers seeing our father "physically abusing Dorero by pulling her around by her hair in the large open driveway."

Page 31:
I truly enjoyed my job, and loved walking around meeting people, being constantly complimented. I shared the dressing room when I changed with the chorus girls. ... Here comes Joe Comfort on his

first furlough from Camp Rucker, Alabama. What a thrill. ...Joe proposed marriage. I naturally said, "Yes." There was a problem.

One had to wait three days after getting your license at City Hall plus the blood test. Well, Dr. George Hodel solved that problem for me. He pulled strings at City Hall and we got our marriage license in one day. Off we went with my sister, and Joseph's sister, Laura, as witnesses, to the preacher.

Page 39:
I married him **[Joe Comfort]** on May 13, 1943. I missed him so much when he left and went back to Alabama. I couldn't sleep. I cried most of the time. They said, "You can't go to the South with all its prejudices." ...George and Dorero Hodel bought me a ticket and put me on the train. Dorero gave me some advice about pleasing my new husband. She suggested that I should before kissing and sucking Joe's penis, I should gargle or drink some very hot water so my mouth would be steaming hot. She said that would drive Joe crazy. She said, better yet for me to chew some of those red, dried chili peppers and that would really send Joe into pure ecstasy. ...When I tried to kiss Joe's penis he had a pure fit. He snatched his penis out of my mouth and asked, 'Where did you learn that?' I told him Dorero had told me about it, and Dorero had said, 'you'd be in pure heaven.' 'Well, I'm not in pure heaven. I don't want my wife doing things like that.'

SOME FINAL THOUGHTS

Madi's unpublished manuscript with its candid and highly explicit narrative is a remarkable historical find. Because it surfaced posthumously, there is no breach of Madi's personal code of silence, only confirmation. Madi's excited call to her boyfriend, George, came on June 2, 2003—the very day the *People Magazine* article informed the world that George Hodel was the Black Dahlia killer. The day and the time it became public knowledge, permitted her—in Madi's mind—to reveal her fifty-six-year-old secret to George Parkington. She could now finally, in good conscience, relieve herself of a terrible burden and tell her closest friend her darkest secret., "We all knew that he had done it," she said.

Two weeks later, she was gone. But look at what she has left us. Madi's memoir, written decades ago, just like the DA's secret files, have now presented us with new evidence and new confirmation into what the DA and the LAPD knew back then.

*Madi Comfort's boyfriend, George Parkington at a 2010 meeting
with author at Whittier Museum*

*Whittier Daily News, September 27, 2010, announcing Madi Comfort's
connection to the Black Dahlia*

Madi passed away in Whittier, California on June 20, 2003, just
two weeks after revealing her fifty-six-year-old secret to her boyfriend,
George Parkington.

*Left: Madi Comfort
Right: Self-portrait done in acrylic*

2

"Maganda"

"This anatomical anomaly [identical freckle on left eyebrows] is as distinct as a tattoo, and proves beyond any doubt that they are one and the same woman." —Steve Hodel, 2005, *Black Dahlia Avenger,* page 546

ONE OF THE THINGS I ENJOY MOST about being my own P.I. is that I get to wear all the hats. I am the gumshoe "in the field," knocking on doors and taking routine witness statements, and the detective supervisor sitting behind the desk, reviewing his/my own reports for accuracy.

In this chapter, I will present my own reinvestigation of my initial claim that Elizabeth Short and Photograph No. 1 in my father's album (the woman standing by the horse statue) were the same person.

Over the years, readers have questioned whether the two photographs were the same women. They were correct.

By following new evidence, I proved myself wrong. My identification of Photograph No. 1 as Elizabeth Short, despite the fact that both women have what appears to be an identical freckle in the approximate same location on their left eyebrows, was incorrect.

In September 2006, within two weeks of discovering that the woman in my father's photo album *was* not Elizabeth Short, I publicly disclosed it in a televised interview on CNN News with journalist Anderson Cooper. The eight-minute interview also discussed the surrealist aspects of my father's crime, as well as Head Deputy DA Steve Kay's reconfirmation that, in his opinion, "the case was solved and the evidence and proofs go way beyond the question of the photographs."

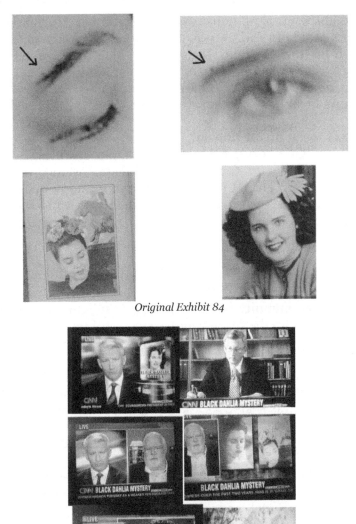

Original Exhibit 84

September 18, 2006 CNN AC-360 interview

Two weeks later, I interviewed the woman in the photo and published an investigative summary on my website. In 2006, to protect the woman's privacy, I simply called her, "Maganda," which in Tagalog (she is Filipina) means, "beautiful one."

Three important people helped me get it right:

First and foremost, my half-sister, Tamar, believed the woman in Photo No. 1 appeared to be Asian, and vaguely remembered seeing her as a child at the Franklin house. My ex-stepmother, Hortensia Starke, also believed Photo No. 1 was an Asian acquaintance of George Hodel's from the Franklin house days. Finally, Elizabeth Short's surviving sister apparently remarked that "the woman was not Elizabeth, as she never wore flowers in her hair in that fashion." My further investigation, some six years later, has proven each of you correct.

So how was it finally proven?

In September 2006, CBS News replayed its previously aired program, *Black Dahlia Confidential*. By happenstance, a channel-surfing woman recognized Photo No. 1 as her grandmother. After the show, she contacted both the network and me, which led to my immediate follow-up.

MAGANDA'S STORY
(As originally reported on my website in 2006)
On Monday, October 2, 2006, the fog had lifted early, leaving the small coastal community bathed in bright sunlight. As I pulled my Ford Crown Vic into the restaurant parking-lot, I felt high excitement, knowing that the fog surrounding a sixty-year-old mystery photograph was also about to be lifted.

Maganda (not her real name, but one I have selected to protect her privacy, means "Beautiful One" in Tagalog, the native language of the Philippines) was seated at a large open table covered with white linens and fine china. Her two granddaughters were seated on either side of her there to protect and support their ninety-one-year-old "nanny."

Polite introductions were exchanged and Maganda's older granddaughter explained to her that I was the author of a book written about Dr. George Hodel, and was also-his son. Her eyes brightened as she spoke, "You are the son of Dr. Hodel?" I nodded and smiled. "Oh, give me a hug. It was your father who I have to thank for starting me in my career as an actress."

I would spend the next five hours with Maganda, as she shared her incredible life story. Maganda would tell me about her life in Manila, where she and her family were held captive in a Japanese prisoner-of-war camp. She told me how, in the mid-1940s, she and her family were freed with the liberation of Manila and hastily escorted directly to a Navy transport ship, which brought them to America.

She narrated how, soon after her arrival in Los Angeles, she met my father, George Hodel, and their five-year association. She also told me how, in the early 1950s, she decided to leave the bright lights of

Hollywood and the brand new medium of television so she could devote herself full time to raising her beautiful children.

Now in her nineties, Maganda remains alert and happy. She has been kept strong and nourished with the familial love from both grandchildren, who held "Nanny's" arms as we conversed. After the introductions, Maganda slowly reached into the cardboard box on the table and handed me two large pictures from the group. One was framed, the other was not. She smiled and said, "Here are the two pictures your father took of me at his beautiful home in Hollywood. These pictures were on your father's desk, and they are what got me started in motion pictures."

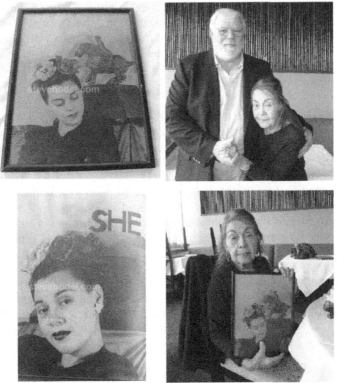

Top right: "Maganda" and author, October 2006
Photos on left (top and bottom) taken by Dr. George Hodel
at the "Franklin house" circa fall or winter, 1945

What follows are selected, relevant excerpts of Maganda's incredible story, told in her own words.

EARLY LIFE:

I was born in the Philippines. My mother was Filipina and taught Spanish. My father was an American missionary. When he first saw my mother, he said, "I'm going to marry that woman." My parents' romance was love at first sight.

During World War II, my husband, who was American, and I and our children were kept in a Japanese prison-of-war camp in Manila. We were there almost six years. Then American soldiers came and freed us. I had my young daughter and my newborn son. They took us straight to the Navy ship and we boarded and came to America. The ship was originally going to go to dock at San Francisco, but there was a world conference, so they came to Los Angeles, to San Pedro harbor instead. (Note: The San Francisco Conference was held on April 25, 1945. Delegates from fifty nations met in San Francisco for the United Nations Conference on International Organization. The delegates drew up the 111-article Charter, which was adopted unanimously on June 25, 1945 in the San Francisco Opera House.)

MEETING DR. GEORGE HILL HODEL

I met your father through a woman that was raising money for the War Chest to send donations to the Philippines after the war had ended. She was connected somehow with the mayor's office, and also owned a modeling agency. The woman knew George Hodel and suggested that he might want to meet and photograph me. She sent Dr. Hodel a note. And later, we met and he photographed me and took these two photographs along with some others. On the one, he had me close my eyes and tilt my head downward. I don't know why?

Your father's home was filled with many of these art objects (Maganda pointed to the Chinese horse statue in the background of photo) and he wanted to photograph me with each separate art piece. There were many such objects, but it never happened and we just photographed this one.

I don't recall how many times your father took photographs of me. It was a number of times, but my husband was always there. He waited in the interior courtyard, or in his car. Your father and my husband liked each other. My husband was chief engineer for a large aircraft company, and your father and he enjoyed talking to each other.

I never attended any parties at your father's house. I was only there during the photographic sessions. Your father was always professional and never said or did anything that would be considered out of line. My husband was always present.

It was because of these two pictures that your father took that I became an actress and got into motion pictures. The pictures were in a frame on a desk at your father's house. Your father had two important men, patients of his, who he was seeing at his house. He was treating them for some illness or something. The men were high up in the government of a foreign country.

They saw the pictures of me and said, "Who is this? She is perfect for a part in the film we are making." George told them that he had taken the pictures and who I was, and the next thing I know; I had a small part in their film. From there, I went on to make many more films and was one of the first actresses to be involved in a television series.

ON MEETING TAMAR HODEL

I never met your mother, or you boys. But, I did meet his daughter, Tamar. She actually stayed with me overnight. It was quite strange. Here is how I recall what happened. Your father called me one night and his voice was quivering. He sounded very upset. He said to me, "Are you alone?" I told him I was. He went on to say, "There has been some trouble and would you mind if my daughter, Tamar, stayed with you for some time?" I told him she could, and he sent her over in a taxi cab.

Tamar was a young girl, maybe twelve or thirteen? She arrived in the cab and was crying. She said, "My daddy was bad to me," but wouldn't tell me what had happened, so I didn't ask anything further.

I asked her if she was hungry and she said, "Do you have any milk?" I gave her the milk and put her to bed. I was rubbing her arm, comforting her on the bed, and she said, "It's nice to have a mommy." And I told her, "Well, I can be your mommy." I told her that anytime she had trouble, she could talk to me."

George called me early the next morning and told me that "Tamar has to go to school" and for me to, "send her to school in a cab." Tamar refused to go to school, so I told George that I was sending her back to him instead. I then sent her home.

FRANKLIN HOUSE CONNECTIONS

I met a few people and recognized some names that you mentioned, but I never really met any other girls at your father's house. Fred Sexton and Joe Barrett sound familiar. There was an artist friend of your father's that gave me a large wooden sculpture of a pelican. He had made it for some important person in Brentwood, but they decided they didn't want it, so he gave it to me. I still have it at home. It is very large, all carved from one piece of wood. It was quite modern. (Note: The artist was most likely Fred Sexton, who as we know, sculpted in wood and carved "The Black Bird" for his friend, John Huston, which John used in *The Maltese Falcon* in 1941.)

I remember that your father had told me that "he had gotten into some trouble and was going on a long trip." I asked him, "Are you going to get out of it?" He told me, "Oh yes, one of these days I will." Shortly after that he left for the Philippines.

The last contact I had with your father was very strange. He called me from Manila. I was still living in Los Angeles. He asked me, "Do you know of any young women here in the Philippines that I could take pictures of?" I told him, "No, I don't." It was a very strange call, and I felt a bit uncomfortable about it. That was the last I ever heard from your father. No, I never was invited to any of the parties. No, I never met Hortensia.

MAGANDA IDENTIFIED

More than five years have passed since my original interview with Maganda and I have decided now to reveal her true identity. I break no confidence since she never asked me to keep her name private and I believe she deserves just credit and recognition for helping us better understand the truth of what occurred in the mid- to late 1940s.

Based on Maganda's statements, it became obvious that she had unknowingly become an important witness related to the July 1949 sexual molestation by George Hodel of his then fourteen-year-old daughter, Tamar.

We learned that George telephoned Maganda and told her, "There has been some trouble and would you mind if my daughter, Tamar, stayed with you for some time?" She agreed, and he immediately sent Tamar by taxi to the residence, where, upon arrival, Tamar was crying and immediately told Maganda, "My daddy was bad to me." (Had the DA's office known about these actions and statements, Maganda certainly would have been called to testify as an important prosecution witness at George Hodel's December 1949 criminal trial.)

Maganda's real name is Marya Marco, aka Mary Marco, aka Maria San Marco. Her acting credits include both screen and television. To name just a few of her early films: *Anna and the King of Siam (1946), Song of the Thin Man (1946), Intrigue (1947), Tycoon (1947), Sleep, My Love (1948),* and *The Clay Pigeon (1949).*

Marya Marco publicity photo from Intrigue (1947)
Film starred George Raft and June Havoc

Left: Marya in scene from Song of the Thin Man *(1947)*
Right: Sleep, My Love (1948), star Bob Cummings in scene with Marya

George Hodel bought the Sowden/Franklin house in 1945. He likely took the Marya photographs that same year—probably in the spring or winter of 1945—sometime after she arrived in the US and prior to his departure for China in February, 1946.

In my interview with Marya, it became clear that she had no knowledge or suspicions that my father had been the DA's prime suspect in the Black Dahlia investigation, nor did it appear that she was even aware of his 1949 arrest by LAPD for child molestation and incest. Her only reference to George was him telling her just before his departure from the US that he "was in some trouble and was leaving the country and expected one day to get out of it." Then, at the close of our talk, she mentioned that her final contact with my father was "a strange and uncomfortable telephone phone call" she received from him from Manila, where George asked her if she could provide him with the names of any girls in the Philippines that he could photograph.

DR. GEORGE HILL HODEL—ONE DEGREE OF SEPARATION

During her acting career, Marya Marco came in contact with many well-known actors. One of them was the handsome lead actor, Robert Cummings, who gave her the below autographed photograph circa 1948. As shown in the previous clip, Marya and Bob worked together in the 1948 film, *Sleep My Love*.

"To my dear friend Maria, beautiful, exotic, charming, and I mean very, your friend, Robert Cummings"

As detailed in BDA, Robert Cummings was also friends with actress Jean Spangler, and was one of the last persons known to have seen her alive. He had a conversation with Spangler at the studio on October 5, 1949, just two days before her date with an unidentified new boyfriend. Spangler at that time told Cummings, "I have a happy new romance and am having the time of my life." [Note: Refer to BDA, chapter 24, for the linkage of victim Spangler to George Hodel, as being this probable "new boyfriend."]

I showed a photograph of Jean Spangler to Marya, who indicated "she looked familiar," and thought she might well have seen her on the studio lots back in the forties, but did not personally know her.

The new information received from Madi Comfort informed us that George Hodel was personally acquainted with actor Vincent Price, as Madi was present at the Hodel residence when George and Dorero hosted Price and Van Heflin. Afterward, the five of them dined in Chinatown.

Jean Spangler's last movie, *Champagne for Caesar,* was filmed in Hollywood in 1949, just weeks before she was murdered. One of the stars of that comedy was Vincent Price, George Hodel's acquaintance and former dinner guest. I strongly suspect that Jean Spangler knew and was dating my father in October 1949, and was the same "Jean" whom Duncan, my then [1949] twenty-one-year-old half-brother, met at the Franklin house as one of our father's dates. Duncan described her as, "a drop-dead gorgeous actress by the name of Jean."

What we do now know for sure is that with both the Robert Cummings-Marya Marco and the Vincent Price connections, we again have just one degree of separation between *Lone Woman Murder* victim, Jean Spangler, and George Hodel.

HOLLYWOOD'S DIRTY BIG SECRET

Who was the "we" that Madi Comfort spoke of as knowing that George Hodel had killed Elizabeth Short? Clearly, some were from her inner circle of friends from the late 1940s.

That would include many of Hollywood's literati, as well as actors, artists, dancers, and politicians, many of whom visited George and were entertained at his lavish Frank Lloyd Wright Jr.-built Mayan temple in the heart of Hollywood. Film stars like Walter and John Huston; Tim Holt; the surrealist artist and our family photographer, Man Ray; author Henry Miller; and Beat poet Kenneth Rexroth. And there were lesser luminaries, with the beautiful but yet-undiscovered wannabes who, like pilot fish, can always be found swimming close by.

Also in attendance at the Franklin house parties were "The Girls," mostly current or former patients at George's First Street VD clinic, very likely working double shifts on loan from Madam Brenda Allen. Brenda, known as Hollywood's "Queen of Hearts," was the Heidi Fleiss of her day. Before her arrest for pandering in 1948, Brenda had 114 girls working in her stable, and was making sizeable weekly payoffs to LAPD's vice squad and brass.

As the head venereal disease control officer for all of Los Angeles County, Dr. George Hill Hodel was powerful and connected ...

basically "untouchable." If you were a studio exec [like two producers Marya told us visited Dr. Hodel at his private residence for medical treatment], a politician, or a cop with a girlfriend "in trouble," Dr. George was the go-to guy in 1940s L.A., a true *bon vivant* and a man who could be trusted with any confidence.

Many of Hollywood's elite must have whispered the secret. Power and information go hand in hand. But it was like a low-burning grass fire, which must be smothered before it spreads. There was simply too much at risk to allow this secret to become public knowledge. This was not difficult in 1947 Los Angeles, which was a real-life *LA Confidential*, where corruption was the rule rather than the exception.

Practically on the very day of the *Black Dahlia* murder, Hollywood novelist turned screenwriter, Steve Fisher—who wrote *I Wake Up Screaming, Destination Tokyo, Song of the Thin Man,* and *Winter Kill* for MGM in 1947—had just finished adapting a screenplay for Raymond Chandler's, *Lady in the Lake.*

One of L.A.'s largest dailies, the *Los Angeles Herald Express,* asked Fisher to ponder this true whodunit. On February 3, 1947, just over two weeks after the Dahlia murder, in a *Herald Express* article headlined, **"Noted Film Scenarist Predicts 'Dahlia' Killer Will Soon Be in Toils,"** Fisher complied.

He opened the article by saying:

"After writing this I am going to leave town, and I will not return until the killer of the 'Black Dahlia' is under lock and key."

Fisher went on to provide readers with a long-running scenario on how the fictional detective, Nick Charles, "The Thin Man," would have conducted the investigation. He suggested:

"I'd have him [sleuth Nick Charles] "rig" a phoney [sic] killer, one the police would give credence to, and have him use the phoney as bait to bring the real culprit in." [Note: Incredibly, the *Herald Express* newspaper took Fisher's suggestion to heart, and, just one week later, "rigged a phoney confessor as bait."]

Their headline in six-inch letters read:

"CORPORAL DUMAIS IS BLACK DAHLIA KILLER."

The police, going along with the ruse, initially gave it credence, despite knowing that the false confessor was innocent and had already established that Dumais was on his east coast military base on the date of the murder. Did the *Black Dahlia Avenger* respond by turning himself in? No, but their ploy did provoke him to act. He went out the following night *and killed again*, writing his response in lipstick on his new victim, Jeanne French's strangled and bludgeoned body. It was his direct and very public reply to the press and police department's attempt to try and trap him. In large bold letters, he wrote across her nude torso, **"FUCK YOU - BD."** This savage killing, known as *"The Red Lipstick Murder,"* occurred just three weeks after Elizabeth Short's and is the second murder count that Head Deputy DA Steve Kay indicated he would file against George Hodel, based on the accumulated evidence.

Fisher ended his 1947 piece with these startling comments:

"I think I know who the killer is, and think the police do also, and in a very short time will have his name. When the killer's name is published I think a lot of his friends will be very surprised and terrified. ... I believe the police right now have a definite 'line' on the real killer. Look for a thriller finish to this case."

Apparently, Fisher didn't get the "Don't Tell Memo." For those who might wonder just exactly where Fisher would have obtained this "inside information," I would offer the following:

At the time Steve Fisher wrote his article, Dorothy "Dorero" Hodel, a fellow studio screenwriter, though still living with George Hodel, was working for and having an ongoing affair with the iconoclastic writer and rebel film director, Rowland Brown. (*Quick Millions, Blood Money, The Doorway to Hell, What Price Hollywood, Angels with Dirty Faces, Nocturne*).

Rowland would remain close to Dorero until his death in 1963. Dorero knew George had overdosed his personal secretary, Ruth Spaulding, in 1945. And the later DA files revealed that she knew he had killed Elizabeth Short. Obviously, my mother would have shared this knowledge with her then current lover, Rowland.

At that time, Rowland was a close friend of and collaborator with fellow screenwriters Steve Fisher, Ben Hecht, and Gene Fowler. [Brown co-wrote the screenplay of *What Price Hollywood* with Gene Fowler. Fowler's son, Will, was one of the first news reporters to arrive at 39th and Norton Avenue, and obtained his own private set of photographs of the Black Dahlia crime scene, which most certainly would also have also been circulated to many of Hollywood's "insiders."]

In addition to Steve Fisher being a close friend of Dorothy Hodel's then part-time lover, Rowland Brown, we also have a second direct link of Fisher to George Hodel, again, by way of George's friend and actress, Marya Marco. As we have seen from her filmography, Myra had a small part in the 1947 film, *Song of the Thin Man* starring

William Powell and Myrna Loy. Who was the screenwriter for that film? Steve Fisher.

3

Marion Herwood Keyes & Ruth Spaulding

Marion Herwood Keyes circa 1947
1940s personal secretary to Vincente Minnelli and Dr. George Hill Hodel

MARION HERWOOD was born in Greenfield, Massachusetts, on January 25, 1904, and died in Sequim, Washington, on July 4, 2009, at the remarkable age of 105.

In his excellent book, *A Hundred or More Hidden Things: The Life and Films of Vincente Minnelli* (Da Capo Press, 2010) author Mark Griffin confirms that in the late 1930s, Marion was personal secretary to Vincente Minnelli. But Griffin's research indicates the Minnelli-Herwood relationship might well have been more than just business.

On pages 30-31 Griffin writes:

Just as Vincente's relationship with Lester Gaba had everybody guessing, so did his association with a striking, modishly attired young woman named Marion Herwood. As Minnelli recalled, "The work at the Music Hall was getting so involved that it was decided that I should have a secretary. I hired Marion."

Each time Minnelli made the move from Broadway to Hollywood (first for a brief stint at Paramount in the late '30s, then with MGM for keeps) Herwood went with him. It was during Vincente's second attempt at breaking into the movies that his faithful assistant was dealt a devastating blow. Without explanation, Vincente suddenly shifted his attention from Herwood to MGM's resident showstopper. [Judy Garland]...After Herwood recovered from her broken engagement and the breakdown that followed, she would resume her work as a costumer on such MGM classics as *The Picture of Dorian Gray* and *The Postman Always Rings Twice.* And she would eventually marry an investment banker.

Based on the timing of her breakup with Minnelli, it would appear that Marion was then almost immediately hired by Dr. George Hill Hodel to be his personal secretary at his privately owned, downtown Los Angeles First Street VD clinic.

During the war years, Marion was obviously wearing two hats: George Hodel's girl Friday, as well as being a highly talented A-list costumer for Hollywood film studios.

Marion was a co-worker and close friend of Ruth Spaulding, another secretary at the First Street clinic. In the early to mid-1940s, Ruth had an ongoing, intimate affair with George Hodel.

As summarized in the "Aftermath" chapter of *BDA,* we now know that Ruth was the previously "unidentified secretary" that George Hodel admitted to killing in the 1950 DA tape recordings. Here is a partially excerpted section from those original DA transcripts where George was speaking in conversation with his close confidant, "The Baron," in the living-room of the Franklin house:

"Supposin I did kill the Black Dahliah [sic]. They couldn't prove it now. They can't talk to my Secretary anymore because she's dead."

"...They [LAPD] thought there was something fishy. Anyway, now they may have figured it out. Killed her. Maybe I did kill my secretary. ..."

Ruth's forcible overdose occurred in May 1945, just eighteen months before the Black Dahlia murder. And it is believed that Marion Herwood Keyes quit as George Hodel's secretary shortly afterward.

Here is a summary of Marion's amazing filmography from the years 1944-1948:

1944: *Gaslight, Mrs. Parkington, The Thin Man Goes Home, Marriage is a Private Affair.* 1945: *Between Two Women, The Picture of Dorian Gray, Keep Your Powder Dry, Without Love, Her Highness and the Bellboy, Weekend at the Waldorf, Adventure, The Clock*, and *The Valley of Decision*. 1946: *Easy to Wed, The Hoodlum Saint, The Postman Always Rings Twice, A Letter for Evie*. 1947: *The Other Love, Body and Soul*. 1948: *No Minor Vices* and *Arch of Triumph*.

Marion Herwood Keyes's last credited film, *Arch of Triumph* (1948) starred Ingrid Bergman, Charles Boyer, and Charles Laughton.

In the secret DA files, I discovered that Lt. Frank Jemison had interviewed two of Elizabeth Short's personal acquaintances, Ann Toth and Connie Star, both would-be starlets who frequently played bit parts in Hollywood. Ann Toth, a part-time actress, was the girlfriend of Mark Hansen, owner of the *Florentine Gardens*, a popular restaurant and nightclub with a popular nude revue. I am quite certain that my father both knew and frequented Mark Hansen's nightclub on a regular basis because (1) he loved burlesque and nude shows [on the DA Bugging Tapes, he bragged about taking some visiting dignitaries from China to a local burlesque house] and (2) Hansen's *Florentine Gardens Club* was just one mile from the Franklin house.

In her interview with Lt.Jemison, Connie Star recalled seeing Elizabeth Short with a young boyfriend at Mark Hansen's home on Carlos Avenue, at the rear of his club, on January 11, 1947, just four days before Short's body was discovered.

Lt. Jemison determined that both Connie Starr and Ann Toth worked together as studio extras for the film *Arch of Triumph*. Marion Herwood Keyes, George Hodel's former personal secretary, was the costume designer on that film, so the three women most certainly would have come in contact with each other during the shoot. Just another example of the seemingly unending one-degrees-of-separation.

The DA's Hodel-Black Dahlia files also contained Lt. Jemison's original handwritten notes, including his George Hodel "To Do List." Below is a scan from the files where we discovered that on March 2, 1950, less than two weeks after George Hodel's taped "confession" to his secretary's murder, that Lt. Jemison is reopening the original 1945 LAPD Spaulding death investigation with plans to re-interview all the original witnesses. He listed six items for follow-up on the Hodel investigation, No. 4 being:

"#4- all witnesses – In Re. to Ruth's death- Sec. to Hodel."

Lt. Jemison's re-interviews of all of the original 1945 witnesses would most certainly have included Ruth's then co-worker and closest friend, Marion Herwood Keyes.

DA Lt. Jemison

Section of Note referencing
Dr. Hodel's secretary, Ruth

RUTH SPAULDING—MOTIVES FOR MURDER

On the back of the thick brown envelope, the handwritten note read, **"NOT TO BE TAMPERED WITH OR OPENED BY ANYONE EXCEPT -------."**

The writer, a young, distraught married woman had sealed the packet in March 1945. She left instructions that it was not to be opened until after her death. Sixty years later, the personal and highly confidential contents of this package would find their way to me to help establish, at least in part, the probable motive for my father's murder of his personal secretary, Ruth Spaulding.

Ruth Spaulding was George Hodel's secretary at the First Street Clinic. She died of an overdose of barbiturates on May 9, 1945. The facts were suspicious and LAPD investigated George Hodel as her possible killer. LAPD learned that they were having an affair and that George had recently broken up with Ruth. As a woman scorned, Ruth had written detailed information about George Hodel's activities and was about to reveal them. My father, in a late night telephone call from Ruth's apartment, summoned my mother to the residence and gave her Ruth's writings, ordering her "to burn them." LAPD investigated, but the evidence was insufficient to charge him with the crime. Five years later [February 1950] in a confidential conversation with "The Baron," which was captured on the DA surveillance recordings, George Hodel admits to the Spaulding murder. "They thought there was something fishy. Anyway, now they may have figured it out. Killed her. Maybe I did kill my secretary..."

Part of the Spaulding puzzle has been previously examined and discussed. We know that had Ruth survived the forced overdose, she could have most probably linked George Hodel to dating and possibly treating Elizabeth Short as his patient. Hence, his recorded statement, "Supposin' I did kill the Black Dahlia, they couldn't prove it now. They can't talk to my Secretary [Ruth Spaulding] anymore, because she's dead." But my father's statements came after the fact. They did not provide a motive for Ruth's 1945 murder. We know that my father killed Ruth to keep her silent, but about what?

These sixty-year-old private letters and documents might well answer at least part of that question.

It appears that Ruth Spaulding was about to expose and make public the fact that Dr. George Hill Hodel, head venereal disease control officer for the Los Angeles County Health Department and chief-of-staff of his privately-owned First Street Clinic, was intentionally misdiagnosing patients, then fraudulently billing them for unwarranted laboratory tests, prescriptions, and medical treatment. What patient in 1945 Los Angeles would even think to question or consider a second opinion after hearing the diagnosis of "syphilis" or "gonorrhea" coming from the mouth of L.A.'s top VD doctor? Imagine the headlines and scandal that would have resulted from Ruth Spaulding's revelations:

"HEAD OF COUNTY HEALTH CHARGED WITH MALPRACTICE"

Here is the back story and documentation.

In 1945, Mrs. X, a married woman, met and fell in love with a dashing young naval officer. They had a brief affair. Mrs. X became worried that she might have contracted a venereal disease. And her lover, to reassure her, suggested that she go and see Dr. George Hodel at his First Street Clinic. Dr. Hodel examined the young woman and ordered lab tests. Shortly after, she was informed by Dr. Hodel that "she has contracted gonorrhea" and he treated her accordingly. Mrs. X was billed and paid $75 in services. [Approximately $750.00 in today's dollars.] Upon returning to her home state, the distraught woman obtained a second opinion and was advised that she never had a gonorrhea infection. Mrs. X contacted Dr. Hodel's clinic secretary, Ruth Spaulding, who then rechecked the lab reports and determined that they "were negative" and confirmed to Mrs. X that she had never contracted a venereal disease.

Ruth Spaulding sent Mrs. X the laboratory reports, signing the letter with, "cordial personal regards." [Note: This is hardly a business salutation and to my thinking is suggestive that the two women could well have had additional correspondence or personal contacts of which we are unaware.] My father's secretary further personalized her letter by adding an apologetic, "P.S., I am required to send the enclosed bill."

EXHIBIT A

A   COPY OF MRS. X 1945 TYPED/SIGNED LETTER TO BE OPENED ONLY AFTER HER DEATH

(I have redacted personal names and identifying information)

Wednesday, June 27th, 1945.

I, ▓▓▓▓▓▓▓, being of sound mind and memory hereby testify and certify that i never had a Gonococus infection (Gonorrhea) despite the alleged findings of laboratory worker ▓▓▓▓▓▓▓ who was employed by Dr. C. Hill Hodel and that the said ▓▓▓▓▓▓▓ findings were true and incorrect and that Dr. Hodel guided himself by these erroneous reports. It is quite possible the said ▓▓▓▓▓▓▓ falsified the report and then again it is probable he made an honest mistake.

The above statement can be verified and proved by contacting ▓▓▓▓▓▓▓ ▓▓▓▓▓▓▓

It is true I had and have ▓▓▓▓▓▓▓ which was my only condition when i first called end Dr. Hodel and which was my only condition during the horrible peri od when I was told of the veneral disease l was alleged to have.

This horrible time cost me dearly in nervous strain, mental anguish and monetary expenditures.

I make this statement so that in the event of my death I am leaving an honest and true picture of the occurrence.

When I arrived in ▓▓▓▓▓▓▓ on March 9th and then learned that it was utterly impossible for me to have contacted in any form or manner such an infection, that this was definitely and satisfactorily proven to me, I wanted to take up the matter then and there with Dr. Hodel and Staff, but
because of the embarrassment involved and the/still shaky condition/of my natural reluctance to go thru any more upheavals I did not press the matter.

If it weren't for my friend ▓▓▓▓▓▓▓ of Los Angeles i doubt if I could have so bravely faced the then (alleged and supposed) situation.

l hereunto set my signature and verify and swear that all the above is true.

▓▓▓▓▓▓▓

*Copy of Mrs. X 1945 typed/signed letter to be opened only after her death
(Personal names and identifying information redacted)*

EXHIBIT B

B COPY OF 1945 LETTER RUTH SPAULDING MAILED TO MRS. X

(Dated and signed *just sixty-days* prior to her death by "barbiturate overdose")

FIRST STREET CLINIC
C. HILL HODEL, M.D. AND STAFF
369 EAST FIRST STREET
LOS ANGELES 12
24-HOUR TELEPHONE: MICHIGAN 2697

March 9, 1945

Dear Mrs. ▬▬▬:

The following are the reports which you requested.

3/5/45 Urethral & cervical smears:
    Moderate amount of pus cells.
    Moderate amount of gram negative diplococci,
      extracellular, and diplo-bacillus.
    No gram negative diplococci seen which are
      typical of N. gonococcus.
    Smears are negative for gonorrhea.
The culture was grown under reduced oxygen tension.
    The oxydase reaction was negative.
    The culture was negative for gonorrhea.

3/6/45 Urethral and cervical smears:
    Few pus cells seen.
    Many gram positive rods.
    No gram negative diplococci seen.
    Smears are negative for gonorrhea.
The culture was grown under reduced oxygen tension.
    The oxydase reaction was negative.
    The culture was negative for gonorrhea.

Cordial personal regards!

                Sincerely,

                Ruth Spaulding
                Clinic secretary

P.S. I am required to send the enclosed bill.

Copy of 1945 letter that Ruth Spaulding mailed to Mrs. X
(Dated and signed just sixty days prior to Spaulding's death by "barbiturate overdose")

EXHIBIT C

Mrs. X's 1945 *First Street Clinic,* billing receipt

C

FIRST STREET CLINIC
G. HILL HODEL, M.D. AND STAFF
369 EAST FIRST STREET
LOS ANGELES 12
24-HOUR TELEPHONE: MICHIGAN 2697

TO ▬▬▬▬

FOR PROFESSIONAL SERVICES 5/1/45

Consultation, examination,
and medication

75.00

Paid in full

Mrs. X's 1945 First Street Clinic billing receipt

EXHIBIT D

Mrs. X's Public Health V.D. prevention pamphlet provided by George Hodel

D

a booklet on the

prevention
of **syphilis**
and **gonorrhea**

VD Bulletin No. 95
FEDERAL SECURITY AGENCY
UNITED STATES PUBLIC HEALTH SERVICE
WASHINGTON, D. C.

☆ U. S. GOVERNMENT PRINTING OFFICE : 1942   16—36665-2

Price . . . . 5 cents

for distribution in clinics
and by private physicians

Mrs. X's Public Health VD prevention pamphlet provided by George Hodel

In addition to Ruth Spaulding's knowledge of the above malpractice, I can now add a second, equally compelling reason, why my father would have wanted his personal secretary dead. In her secret writings intended to expose my father, it is likely that Ruth had also included her firsthand knowledge of the fact that her ex-boyfriend/boss was regularly performing illegal abortions at his downtown First Street Clinic.

How do we know this? It came directly from George Hodel's own mouth—his own recorded statements and admissions. Overlooked in 2005, I discovered them during a careful review of the District Attorney's 1950 Hodel Surveillance Transcripts.

The date was March 19, 1950 [Day 31 of electronic surveillance at the Franklin house]. As we know, the detectives were recording and monitoring the conversations two miles away in the basement of LAPD's Hollywood police station. Below is a scanned copy of page 133 (my numbering). Between 2 and 2:30 p.m., George Hodel and "a colored woman" are at the Franklin house, discussing the possibility of the woman being provided a room in exchange for her maid service. Father tells her he is a doctor. They discussed medicine, and she mentioned having had a *"currettement"* (abortion) in 1944. Father informed her that he owned the First Street Clinic, located downtown at First and Central. Incredibly, he went on to tell her he "has done lots of them (abortions)." [Note: The transcript shows the word as "currettement." This is the shortened term for a 1940s abortion procedure known as a "D&C", or dilation and curettage. The patient was first administered an anesthetic and then the physician performed a surgical abortion, where, after dilating the cervix, he used a curette (sharp metal instrument) to scrape the uterus. In modern times, this scraping has been replaced with a suction technique to reduce the chances of heavy bleeding and infection. My half-sister Tamar's 1949 abortion by Dr. Ballard was a "D&C," and, according to Tamar, "resulted in a large amount of blood loss."]

Before I discovered these statements, I had speculated that at least part of my father's power and influence came from sensitive information he had locked in his First Street Clinic VD files—medical records that documented the sexual and moral indiscretions of well-connected film, police, and politicians.

Now, with absolute certainty, we can add criminal behavior. In 1950, abortion was a felony, punishable by prison time. Anyone (including a police officer, deputy mayor, or film director) who brought his pregnant girlfriend or mistress in for a quick cure was guilty as an accessory or accomplice. Once the procedure had been performed, the patient and her partner were at the mercy of the doctor they had trusted. From 1938 through March 1950 at the First Street Clinic, that was Dr. George Hill Hodel.

EXHIBIT E

E Dr. Hodel 1950 Electronic Surveillance Transcript page 133

133

HODEL FILE - 114 / 3 3

1:45P	Hodel answers door bell, lets in woman - he talks to her about renting her a room in return he will knock off the rent - any work she does for him such as cleaning and taking care of his quarters. Negro woman has her minor daughter with her.
1:50P	Phone rings - Hodel says "Mrs Hodel is out - I can take message. He said he is going down to the beach about 4 PM today - talks about renting room.
2:00P	Hodel again talking to negro woman. Hodel asks her daughter where she goes to school - the girl says-a catholic school.
2:10P	Colored woman and child leaving. woman is going to think it over - about renting room. Woman then starts talking about Doctor's-Hodel tells her about his clinic at 1st and Central Woman said she had a curettemat (curettement ?) in 1944. Hodel said he has done lots of them. Hodel and woman continue to talk about doctors, sickness, and other medical subjects. (Hodel seems to be acting overly nice to this woman He must be trying to talk her into renting the room, or ?) Hodel tells her that Dr. Hill, a colored Doctor, lives next door.
2:30P	Woman leaves
2:50P	Phone rings 2 times, must have been answered in another room. Hodel moving about desk.
3:15P	Hodel leaves room - all quiet.
3:45P	All quiet.
SPOOL 38 4:00P	Hronek, D.A.'s office, on duty.

Dr. Hodel 1950 Electronic Surveillance Transcript page 133

In 2003, LAPD reluctantly confirmed to the press that George Hodel was a suspect in his secretary's overdose. In 1949, the LAPD detectives interviewing my sister Tamar in juvenile detention also revealed their suspicions:

"We [LAPD] found her death [Ruth Spaulding] suspicious, and suspected George Hodel was involved in her overdose, but didn't have enough evidence to prove it."

In May 1945, secretary/girlfriend Ruth Spaulding's secret writings, which would have revealed George Hodel's malpractice and criminality, cost her life.

Five years later, in January 1950, Lillian Lenorak, after perjuring herself a second time at the trial of Dr. Francis Ballard and Charles Smith, made similar threats to George Hodel. She told George that she was "going to the DA and inform him of her twice perjured testimony and that in truth, she had witnessed Tamar's abortion performed by Dr. Ballard and his assistant, Charles Smith." This almost cost Lillian her life, too. She escaped George Hodel's wrath with only an assault, drugging, and his staged "attempted suicide." [He used a scalpel to inflict superficial cuts to her wrists while she lay unconscious.] Father's actions were apparently effective enough to at least temporarily discredit her as being "psychologically distraught."

These latest posthumous revelations from Mrs. X, supported by her original 1945 letters, along with my father's admissions that he "had performed abortions, lots of them" at his First Street VD clinic, established powerful motives for the Spaulding overdose-murder and reinforce what my investigation has demonstrated time and time again: In 1950 Los Angeles, Dr. George Hill Hodel was untouchable.

4

Lillian Lenorak & John Farrow

THE BACK STORY

I FIRST INTRODUCED LILLIAN LENORAK to the public in a 2004 update of BDA after I discovered a letter written by Santa Barbara police officer Mary Unkefer, a former acquaintance of Elizabeth "Black Dahlia" Short. The Unkefer Letter—buried deep in the district attorney's secret files—documented, confirmed, and greatly expanded upon a verbal report first made by Joe Barrett.

In 1950, Joe Barrett was a young artist renting a room at our Hollywood home. In a 2003 ABC *Dateline* interview, Barrett recounted witnessing an incident at the Franklin house: When he returned home one day in early 1950, our agitated maid Ellen warned him that Lillian Lenorak was waiting in George Hodel's bedroom, threatening to shoot the doctor when he came home.

Barrett found a hysterical Lenorak in the bedroom, armed with a rifle belonging to George Hodel. Lenorak was screaming, **"He is going to pay for what he has done. He has to pay for it. I'm going to kill him."** Barrett claims he calmed her down, and took away the rifle. When asked by reporter Josh Mankiewicz what Lenorak meant, Barrett replied, **"It was about the fact that Lillian knew that George had killed Elizabeth Short. Lillian knew Elizabeth and had met her at the house, and said that George had to pay for killing her."**

Barrett continued: "When George came home, I told him about what happened, and that Lillian was going to shoot him, and George's response was, 'Why didn't you let her?'" (In the DA's Hodel bugging transcripts in March 1950, George Hodel confirmed Barrett's account and was overheard saying, "She [Lillian Lenorak] was going to shoot me and then kill herself."

From *Black Dahlia Avenger: A Genius for Murder* page 479:

Unkefer-Short-Hodel-Lenorak Connections

On January 16, 1947, the day "Jane Doe Number 1" was identified by the FBI as Elizabeth Short, Santa Barbara policewoman Mary Unkefer was one of the first important witnesses contacted by LAPD in the Black Dahlia investigation. Why? Because Officer Unkefer had direct and extended contact with Elizabeth Short after Elizabeth's September 1943 arrest for "minor possession." The L.A. *Daily News* of January 17, 1947, under the headline: "Identify Victim as Hollywood Resident," detailed Officer Unkefer's connections:

She (Elizabeth Short) had been a clerk at the Camp Cooke post exchange near Santa Barbara and was picked up for drinking with soldiers in a cafe there.

Policewoman Mary Unkefer of the Santa Barbara police department took the girl to her own home to live with her for nine days...

"We put her on the train for her home, and several times later she wrote to me from there" Miss Unkefer recalled. One of her letters said: "I'll never forget you. Thank God you picked me up when you did!"

Incredibly, we only now discover that Officer Mary Unkefer—who in 1943 had been directly responsible for rescuing Elizabeth Short from a dangerous environment—in January 1950 drove from Santa Barbara to Dr. Hodel's Franklin Avenue residence and there removed another young female victim from harm's way.

Officer Unkefer, after safely returning Lenorak to Santa Barbara, typed a letter to Los Angeles DA investigators, describing Dr. Hodel's involvement in multiple crimes, including subornation of perjury and felony assault.

Through other DA documents, we learned that Lillian Lenorak, a 1949 defense witness at the Hodel incest trial, was an acquaintance of George Hodel. And when photographs of Elizabeth Short were shown by DA investigators, she identified her as Hodel's girlfriend. Miss Lenorak was preparing to recant her previous sworn testimony and admit that she perjured herself at the incest trial. Lenorak's perjury at the Hodel trial had to do with the fact that she was present at Dr. Ballard's office with Charles Smith when Tamar, George Hodel's fourteen-year-old daughter, was "examined" but no abortion occurred. She was now going to admit the truth that, in fact, an abortion was performed on Tamar.

[Note: It is my belief that the "rifle incident" occurred in late January 1950, and was the event that immediately precipitated my father's "staging Lillian's attempted suicide." Lillian Lenorak, under pressure from George Hodel, had perjured herself twice in the preceding weeks. First, at his incest trial in late December 1949, and then again on January 15, 1950, at the abortion trial of Dr. Francis Ballard and Charles Smith. Lillian testified as a defense witness that she had been present with Tamar at Dr. Ballard's office when she was examined, but lied and informed the court "that no abortion had occurred." Her perjury resulted in Dr. Ballard and Smith being found "not guilty" by the judge hearing the case.]

Lillian Lenorak was now threatening to reveal the truth and to inform the DA that she was present and witnessed Tamar's abortion. George Hodel had to either kill her or discredit her. With Barrett as a witness, he couldn't kill her. So, he took the next best step—try to set her up as a "mental case." He then drugged her and staged her "attempt suicide" as described in policewoman Unkefer's letter to the DA. We even have the dramatic corroboration from Lillian's three-year-old son, John, who witnessed George Hodel's assault on his mother.

Enroute to Santa Barbara with his mother and officer Unkefer, the child told the policewoman, **"He [Dr. Hodel] hit mommy and knocked her down. He made her cry hard."**

In 2003, with the post-publication discovery and release of the DA's secret Hodel files, we first learned that Lillian Lenorak met with DA Lt. Frank Jemison and made a positive identification of Elizabeth Short as being a sometime girlfriend of George Hodel.

Before that, Lillian Lenorak's name had surfaced only as an acquaintance of George Hodel and as one of the "defense witnesses" in his December 1949 incest trial. Lenorak also appeared as a defense witness three weeks later, on January 15, 1950, on behalf of Dr. Francis Ballard and Charles Smith who had both been arrested by LAPD and were on trial for performing the actual abortion on fourteen-year-old, Tamar Hodel.

After the discovery of the Unkefer/Lenorak letter, I now know that Joe Barrett was not completely candid with me regarding all of the facts and his further involvement in this Lenorak incident at the Franklin house.

Barrett withheld all of the critical information that followed in the immediate aftermath of Lenorak's confrontation with Dr. Hodel at the Franklin house. He didn't tell me he helped Officer Unkefer transport Lillian to Santa Barbara after she had been drugged and had her wrists superficially cut and bandaged by George Hodel. This staged "attempt suicide" was my father's way of anticipating and going on the offense should Lillian follow through with her threats to inform the DA of her perjured testimony. By branding her "distraught and suicidal" in advance of any allegations she would make against him, he could make anything she said "sound, unreliable." For the most part, it worked.

However, what George Hodel had not anticipated was the Unkefer letter.

It corroborated Barrett's, Lenorak's, and her three-year-old son John's versions of what occurred at the Franklin house in the day(s) and hours immediately following the Franklin house incident.

Here is a brief recap of excerpts from Officer Unkefer's report, which she mailed to Lt. Jemison at the DA's office on January 30, 1950, immediately following her contact with the three witnesses. [For a complete review of the Lenorak-Unkefer investigation, see BDA "Aftermath" chapter, pages 479-484.]

Re. Lillian Lenorak

...She [Lillian] told me she had witnessed an abortion performed on his [George Hodel] little girl [Tamar, age 14] He had threatened to have her child [John Lenorak, age 3] taken away from her if she did not testify in his favor in Court. She said that she had never attempted suicide and that she had never cut her wrists or her hands. She said that the Dr. constantly gave her drugs and that when she wakened the cutting had been done. There were scratches and bruises on her forehead and arms. Lillian stated that she had a very guilty mind after the trial and told Hodel that she was going to tell the DA that she had lied on the witness stand and that Dr. Hodel told her if she squealed that he would name Charles and the other doctor [Smith and Ballard] as being the ones who performed the operation. [Tamar's abortion] Lillian said she would like to tell me all the true facts concerning the doctor's activities, but knew that he [Hodel] would have her done away with as well as her baby. ...she was just PLUMB SCARED to tell for fear he would carry out his threat to have her Boy taken from her and to have her committed to an insane institution.

Re. John Lenorak [Lillian's three-year-old son]

Her three-year-old baby told me that "the doctor knocked his mommie down and made mommie cry hard."

Re. Joe Barrett

He stated emphatically that there was nothing wrong with Lillian except what had been brought on by the cruel treatment received from Dr. Hodel. He stated that he knew Lillian had perjured herself at the trial because the Dr. had her under his influence. He stated that the relations between the Dr. and his Child [Tamar] were terrible and were worse than I had any idea. He stated that Dr. boasted that the $15,000.00 the doctor paid Jerry Giesler [his criminal defense attorney] was used to influence the DA and that

BLACK DAHLIA AVENGER II | 54

was how the doctor was cleared of the charge against him. Barrett described Dr. Hodel as being "A REAL NO GOOD GUY."

Officer Unkefer had originally responded to Dr. Hodel's residence to pick up Lenorak and her son, John, at the specific request of Lillian's mother, Mrs. Hamilton, a prominent resident of Santa Barbara.

Unkefer, after arriving at the Franklin house, insisted that Dr. Hodel call an adult female friend to accompany Lillian on the ride back home. George Hodel called, Karoun Tootikian, a dance instructor at the Ruth St. Denis Studio, who rode with Joe Barrett and Officer Mary Unkefer to Santa Barbara. [Note-Tootikian would remain with the St. Denis Studio for the next twenty years and eventually become a director and head of the Oriental Dance Department.]

On their arrival in Santa Barbara, the toddler was dropped off at his grandmother's home, and Lenorak, due to her drugged and distraught mental condition, was driven by Unkefer to the psychiatric evaluation unit where she was examined and initially admitted for "72-hour observations." [Note: The subsequent hospitalization likely would and could have been avoided had Mrs. Lillian Hitchcock Hamilton been willing to take Lillian into her custody. But due to a "falling out" between mother and daughter, she refused. Mrs. Hamilton died five years later in 1955.]

Officer Unkefer's January 30, 1950, letter to the DA's Office offers more information:

This morning I went to the hearing at the Psycho Ward and it was determined that she [Lenorak] was mentally upset. The Dr. said a great deal of the condition was brought about from the strain of the trial. Both Drs. stated that they felt she should have medical care. So she is to be taken to Camarillo State Hospital for treatment.

My personal opinion is that if the feeling between her and her Mother was not so strained, she might have been given a chance to go home & be taken care of by her Mother. There seems to have never been love between these two. The Mother takes the attitude that she is going to MAKE Lillian do things the way she (Mother) wants them & the Girl seems just as determined that she is not going to be always treated as a Child. Hence there is fireworks between them.

George Hodel (center) December 1949 at the L.A. Courthouse awaiting trial charged with incest and sexual molestation of his fourteen-year-old daughter, Tamar. Lillian Lenorak will, by her own admissions, provide perjured testimony in behalf of Dr. Hodel, and, just one month later in January 1950, will repeat her perjury at the felony trials of abortionists Dr. Ballard and his assistant, Charles Smith, resulting in the case being dismissed by the judge. Within days of that dismissal, Lillian would confront George Hodel at his Franklin house at gunpoint and threatened to recant her testimony and admit she was present during the abortion. These actions and threats resulted in Dr. George Hodel's drugging her and staging her "attempted suicide," as well as threatening to have her son, John, taken from her, and to harm him should she go to the police.

LILLIAN LENORAK AND FILM DIRECTOR JOHN FARROW

As previously documented in 2003, with the post-publication discovery and release of the secret DA Hodel Files, we learned that Lillian Lenorak met with DA Lt. Frank Jemison and made a positive identification of Elizabeth Short as being a sometime girlfriend of George Hodel.

Lillian was an extremely intelligent and attractive woman, as well as a talented dancer with the famed Ruth St. Denis studio.

In the mid-1940s, Lillian met and had an affair with the well-known Hollywood film director John Farrow, who at that time was married to actress Maureen O'Sullivan. [Note-John Farrow 1904-1963. Credited with directing forty-seven films, including: *Two Years Before the Mast* (1946), *The Big Clock* (1948), *Where Danger Lives* (1950), *Hondo* (1953), *Around the World in Eighty Days* (1956), and many more.]

From this relationship, John was born and three years later, in January 1950 he would witness George Hodel's brutal assault on his mother at the Franklin house.

In the DA Hodel Surveillance Transcript (page 114), there was a reference to my mother knowing and having met John Farrow.

Exhibit F is a scanned extract from that page. The date was March 11, 1950. The police log showed the time to be 1:59 p.m. My mother was at the Franklin house. She dialed and spoke with a secretary, "Elsie," then to a person identified only as, "Bob." She talked about "John getting her a job." [Here she was referring to John Huston, her ex-husband, not John Farrow.] She then went on to mention a story idea for a screenplay she thought might interest John Farrow.

EXHIBIT F

DA Hodel Surveillance transcript (scanned excerpt) pg-114

EX F

1:59P   Woman dials phone. Sounded like she said, "This is Elsie".
Talked about Vincent Price. Also, about M.G.M. Talked abou
John getting her a job. "Say Bob", I found a story. A stor
of a black saint, a negro. Do you know John Farrow? I
thought of him because of his Catholicism. I met him years
ago. I have the babies down at the beach. But, I'd love
to see you. (t must be Dorothy talking) You're at home
all day. Oh, wonderful darling" then "I'll get to see you"
2:05P   End of conversation.

DA Hodel Surveillance transcript (scanned excerpt) page 114

At the same time the DA/LAPD was bugging and staking out on our home, director John Farrow was completing his noir film, *Where Danger Lives,* to be released in July 1950. The story involved a woman who attempted suicide [Maureen O'Sullivan], a young doctor who falls in love with her [Robert Mitchum], a murder, and their attempt to escape to Mexico. But the irony doesn't stop there. Cast in a bit part in the film was an attractive Eurasian actress by the name of Kiyo Cuddy, the ex-lover of George Hodel and future wife of then nine-year-old Steve Hodel.

John Lenorak would not discover that his actual biological father was film director John Farrow until adulthood. As fate would have it, the disclosure did not come from a relative, but rather from his mother's 1940s acquaintance and former Franklin house tenant, Joe Barrett.

The two men had a chance meeting in the late 1970s. John had no memory and Joe Barrett made no mention of the January 1950 Franklin house assault by George Hodel on his mother. Their discussion centered strictly on Barrett informing John that he was the son of film director John Farrow.

Subsequent to receiving this information, I was told that John contacted and met his half-sister, Mia Farrow, and was accepted into the Farrow clan. John, after verifying the truth of it, then changed his name to John Lenorak Farrow.

THE PALM SPRINGS MURDER

Lillian Hamilton Lenorak was murdered on November 8, 1959. She was just forty-two.

She was living in Hollywood and dating Dr. Frank Back, a wealthy physicist and businessman who had an office at Hollywood's *Crossroads of the World*. Dr. Back designed and manufactured movie camera lenses and had become world famous for his development of television's Zoomar Lens.

Dr. Back picked Lillian up at her Hollywood home for a weekend getaway on Saturday, November 7, 1959. They drove from Hollywood to his vacation home, two hours away, in the desert community of Palm Springs. They had known each other for about one year.

After spending the day at Dr. Back's home, the two dressed for dinner and at about eight p.m., left for the Rivera Hotel. En route, an argument erupted in the car and Lillian decided to go back to Los Angeles immediately. She asked Dr. Back for the keys to his house so she could pick up her clothes, but he refused.

The quarrel escalated and Lillian demanded that he let her out of the car. He stopped in front of the El Mirador Hotel and she walked away. Dr. Back then drove home. When Lillian didn't show up by the next morning, he collected her clothes and drove back to Hollywood alone.

On Sunday morning, just six hours after she stormed away from Dr. Back's car, a passing motorist found Lillian's body lying just off the highway on the north side of Palm Springs. The autopsy showed that her skull had been crushed, and she had been bludgeoned to death with the butt of a rifle.

Lillian's identity remained unknown for several days until Dr. Back, having read the article and her description in the newspaper, contacted several of her friends who, in turn, called Palm Springs authorities. Three days later, on November 10, Frank Back returned to Palm Springs and positively identified the body.

FRIEND — Dr. Frank G. Back, optical physicist, who said he quarreled with desert murder victim.

SLAYING VICTIM — Lillian Lenorak, above, described by a friend as a "girl of many romances," was found beaten to death on a lonely road near Palm Springs, Calif., Sunday morning. Police are seeking some of her many men friends for questioning. (AP Wirephoto.)

Dr. Frank Back and Lillian Lenorak

Lenorak's murder was solved within a week.

Her killer was Tord Ove Zeppenfield, age twenty-one. A troubled young man, Tord lived with his mother who owned a motel not far from where Lillian got out of the car. Tord saw Lillian walking down the highway and approached her in his car. When she refused to get in, he abducted her at gunpoint and killed her. Here is his excerpted confession of what happened, as printed in the *Los Angeles Times* on November 18, 1959, just eleven days after the murder:

> "He was sitting in his room when he saw Mrs. Lenorak walk past. ...He followed her in his mother's car and offered her a ride, which she refused.
>
> He threatened her with a sawed-off rifle and she got into the car. Then he drove to the north limits of Palm Springs, hit her once with the gun, dragged her from the car and struck her repeatedly."

On March 2, 1960, in a plea bargain to avoid the death penalty, Tord Zeppenfield pled guilty to killing Lillian Hamilton Lenorak.

Los Angeles Times November 18, 1959

Top: John and Lillian Lenorak, circa 1956
Bottom: A younger Lillian as a Ruth St. Denis dancer

At the time of Lillian's murder, her son, John, was thirteen years old and attending Elsinore Military Academy.

Larry Harnisch, a copy editor for the *Los Angeles Times* and a self-described "Black Dahlia expert" has, for the last fourteen years, been claiming to be writing his own theory with his own "surgeon-suspect." In 2009, using McCarthy-like tactics, Harnisch wrote an article questioning both Lillian's morality and her mental stability. Choosing to post his article specifically on the fiftieth anniversary of Lillian's murder, he went so far as to publicly "blame the victim" and advised his readers to be skeptical of Lillian Lenorak, her three-year-old son John, and Officer Unkefer's statements as originally reported. Harnisch, appointing himself as a defense witness for Dr. George Hodel and sounding like he belonged right back in the sexist Fifties, had this to say regarding the DA reports and the murder victim, Lillian Lenorak:

> "Keep in mind as you read these letters that this lady [Lenorak] is not a typical, well-grounded middle-class suburban housewife but a chronic patient of mental hospitals and adjust your skepticism accordingly."

How's that for a sexist slam! Apparently, in his mind, any woman who might dare to consider stepping outside the role of "a typical, well- grounded suburban housewife" can forget about being the victim of a crime. Outrageous!

Mr. Harnisch's statement that Lillian was "a chronic patient of mental hospitals" is totally unsubstantiated and has no basis in fact.

Other than the one George Hodel/Franklin house incident, which clearly was "a set-up" to my knowledge, there is no record of Lillian Lenorak ever having been admitted for "mental problems" at any other hospital or psychiatric facility.

The fact is that Lillian Lenorak was a bright, fully functioning hard-working mother who loved her son. She was well liked and admired by her co-workers, and, at the time of her murder, was working as a film editor at General Film Laboratories in Hollywood.

A single mother, she also worked a second job as an actress using her maiden name of Lillian Hamilton. Her filmography credits show that she worked in both films and television, receiving separate bit parts every year from 1949 until her untimely death in 1959.

Lillian Hamilton Filmography:
1950- *Outrage-* Mrs. Walton 1951- *On the Loose-* Miss Druten
1952- *Week-End with Father*
1952- *Phone Call from a Stranger-* Nurse 1952- *The Unexpected* (TV series) 1953- *Sweethearts on Parade-* Mother
1954- *The Pride of the Family* (TV series) 1956- *Storm Center-* Mrs. Banning
1957- *The Joseph Cotton Show-* On Trial (TV series) Mrs. Bagby
1957- *Sheriff of Cochise* (TV series) Mrs. Conley, Bisbee National Bank 1958- *Whirly Birds* (TV series) First Nurse
1960 *Men in Space* (TV series) Mrs. Bennett (filmed in 1959, but aired after her murder in 1960)

In 1949-1950 Lillian worked on the then controversial film, *Outrage*, directed by Ida Lupino, which starred Mala Powers and Tod Andrews. *Outrage* was one of the first films to take an honest and sensitive look at rape and how society's attitudes impact a young rape victim's life. [Note-Prior to making this film, Mala had just completed sharing equal billing with Jose Ferrer in her role as Roxanne in the Hollywood film classic, *Cyrano de Bergerac*, which was also released in 1950.]

In *Outrage*, Lillian Hamilton Lenorak plays the mother of the rape victim, Ann Walton (Mala Powers).

Lillian Hamilton Lenorak and Mala Powers in a clip from Outrage (1950)

POSTSCRIPT

On October 16, 2010, I received an e-mail from Rosanna Wilson Farrow informing me that her husband, John, had passed away the previous Saturday. John was in Fort Bragg, California, and died suddenly from an unexpected heart attack. He left behind his wife, Rosanna Wilson, and their two daughters, Kyla and Acacia.

John passed away at a relatively young age of sixty-four.

REST IN PEACE JOHN LENORAK FARROW
1946-2010
(Photo courtesy of Rosanna Wilson Farrow)

5
The Scene of the Crime

"I am confident that the murder [Black Dahlia] occurred in some permanent place of abode, rather than some hotel, rooming house or auto court. It is doubtful that such a crime could be perpetrated in cramped quarters with nearby neighbors." —Captain Jack Donahoe, LAPD Homicide Division *Los Angeles Times*, January 23, 1947

Sowden/Franklin house, 5121 Franklin Avenue, Hollywood

THE LINK

SIXTY-TWO YEARS AFTER THEY WERE WRITTEN, documents preserved at *UCLA's Special Collections Department* literally establish a "paper trail" connecting Dr. George Hill Hodel to the Elizabeth Short "Black Dahlia" crime-scene, the vacant lot at 3815 South Norton Avenue.

BACKGROUND

On January 22, 1947, a coroner's inquest into the death of Elizabeth Short began at the downtown Hall of Justice. After hearing the testimony of sworn witnesses, as well as the deputy coroner, the coroner's jury ruled that the victim died from "blunt force trauma to the head and face caused by person or persons unknown." Elizabeth Short had been brutally murdered.

One of the witnesses that morning was Lt. Jesse Haskins from LAPD's University Division. He was one of the first officers to arrive at the crime scene.

Lt. Haskins testified about the condition of the body. He said the murder had been committed elsewhere and the dismembered body transported by car to the vacant lot. [Note- Apparently, several large, empty paper sacks were used to prevent spillage in the car and to then transfer the body parts from the car to the curbside]. In more than sixty years since the murder, these facts have never been in doubt and are supported by the original crime scene photographs.

Elizabeth Short crime scene, January 15, 1947
[Top] LAPD crime photo showing empty paper sacks used by killer to transfer body parts from his car to curbside. A portion of victim's upper body is seen posed at bottom of photo.
[Bottom] Crime scene enlargement showing blood on paper sack.

LLOYD WRIGHT-GEORGE HODEL LETTERS UCLA SPECIAL COLLECTIONS LIBRARY

In October 2008, some five years after the publication of BDA, I learned that famed architect Lloyd Wright had donated many of his personal papers to UCLA's Special Collections Department. I also discovered that within these papers, there was a Hodel File containing documents and correspondence between Wright and my father, Dr. George Hill Hodel, covering the years, 1945-1947.

Here is what they established:

1) From 1945-1947, Wright was engaged by George Hodel to oversee construction repairs and renovations at the Sowden/Franklin house. [Note- Originally designed and built by Lloyd Wright in 1926 for John Sowden, and later purchased by Dr. Hodel in 1945.] Most of the repair work was to be done during George Hodel's temporary assignment as United Nations chief regional medical officer in Hankow, China between February and September, 1946.

2) In an April 1946 letter George Hodel mailed from China to Wright, father advised the architect that he had "made inquiries into the possibility of your being brought to China for city planning work." Father's letter went on to provide several names to Wright, suggesting he contact them for potential jobs

3) Included in these papers were receipts showing that cement work and repair was performed at the Hodel residence, requiring ten (10) fifty-pound bags of cement. The work was completed on January 10, 1947.

These receipts circumstantially link physical evidence connected to Elizabeth Short's murder directly to George Hodel and the Franklin house, and from there to the vacant lot at 3815 South Norton Avenue.

According to LAPD and the DA investigative reports, Elizabeth Short reportedly "disappeared" on January 9, 1947 after meeting a man in front of L.A.'s downtown Biltmore Hotel, at Fifth and Olive, just three blocks from Dr. Hodel's medical office.

Police surmised that the victim was taken to an unknown private residence, held captive, tortured, then bisected by a man "with medical finesse" who, in their (and the coroner's) opinion, was most likely a skilled surgeon.

In a public statement to the press, eight days into the investigation, LAPD Homicide Capt. Jack Donahoe confirmed that the victim had not been slain at the vacant lot, adding:

"I am confident that the murder occurred in some permanent place of abode, rather than some hotel, rooming house or auto court. It is doubtful that such a crime could be perpetrated in cramped quarters with nearby neighbors."

LAPD confirmed that her body parts were placed on top of several fifty-pound empty cement paper sacks and transported by car from the actual murder location to the vacant lot where they were posed, with the bloody cement sacks left nearby the body.

THE CEMENT SACKS

The below document is a scanned copy of the original receipt.

It showed that Lloyd Wright contracted with a Mr. J.A. Konrad and had him perform renovations at Dr. Hodel's Franklin house in January 1947. The cement work was completed on January 9-10, 1947.

According to the receipt, the work performed at the Franklin house required a total of ten (10) sacks of cement. Eight (8) were used on January 9, 1947, and two (2) sacks were added the next day, January 10.

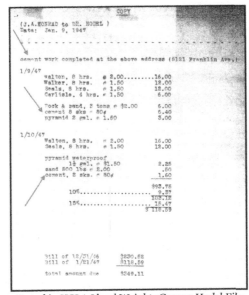

Found in UCLA Lloyd Wright–George Hodel File
"J.A. Konrad to Dr. Hodel January 9, 1947
Cement work completed at the above address." [5121 Franklin Ave]

In addition to the cement-bag link, there was more in the UCLA Wright-Hodel Letters.

Below is a scan of the envelope mailed to Wright by George Hodel from China in April 1946. The address is typed. But on the envelope, George Hodel has hand-printed the word **"Registered,"** which I readily identify as my father's handwriting.

Note his unusual letter "D" compared to the letter "D" written in lipstick on the body of L.A. *Lone Woman Murder* victim, Jeanne French, who was slain in February 1947, just three weeks after the

Black Dahlia murder and four months after George Hodel's return from China.

The same identical characteristics are clearly visible in both. In the letter "D," we see the curved, overextended horizontal lines with the vertical line unconnected to either the top or bottom in both samples. These are some of the same characteristics that document expert Hannah McFarland used to positively identify George Hodel's handwriting in other known samples—as well as in the Jeanne French, "Red Lipstick Murder."

Unusual hand printed letter "D" written in lipstick on nude body of Jeanne French "Lipstick Murder" 1947

Unusual hand printed letter "D" written by George Hodel in letter to Lloyd Wright sent from China, in May, 1946

George Hodel envelope mailed to Lloyd Wright from China in 1946

The envelope contained the below letter written to Wright. In it, George Hodel mentioned his "promise" to check out architectural design potentials for Wright while in China.

From this we learned that the two men obviously had some personal discussions prior to George leaving the US for China in February 1946.

We also learned that as of May 1946, it was Dr. Hodel's intention to remain in China at least until "the spring of 1947." His UN personnel papers in my possession show that just four months later, in September 1946, he suddenly "resigned for personal reasons" and quickly returned to Los Angeles.

We will likely never know his reason for resigning. Was it under duress for conduct unbecoming? Did he commit a crime in post-war China's Wild, Wild East? Did he receive a letter from Elizabeth Short mentioning or hinting at her suspicions of his possible connections to the 1945 Chicago Lipstick Murders?

The secret DA files documented that Elizabeth was actively investigating those crimes in Chicago in June-July 1946, just a month after George wrote this letter to Wright. The DA files went so far as to provide names and addresses of several different Chicago reporters that Elizabeth was sleeping with, apparently in hopes of obtaining inside information related to the murder investigations.

UNITED NATIONS
RELIEF AND REHABILITATION ADMINISTRATION
Anlee House,
Sze Wei & Han Chung Roads,
Hankow, China.
20 April, 1946.

Lloyd Wright,
858 Doheny Drive,
Los Angeles 46,
California.

Dear Mr. Wright:

In pursuance of my promise, I have made inquiries as to the possibility of your being brought to China for city planning work. I am informed that a firm request has been made by the Chinese National Relief and Rehabilitation Administration for at least two city planning experts, and that the Washington headquarters of United Nations Relief and Rehabilitation Administration may soon be recruiting these specialists.

If you are interested, it is suggested that you write to Franklin Ray, Director, Far Eastern Division, UNRRA, Dupont Circle Building, Washington, D.C.

It might also be well to write to Ha Shiung-Wen, Vice-Minister, Ministry of the Interior, Nanking, China. I know Mr. Ha, but did not discuss your interest in China with him because I was not aware, during the occasions on which I spoke with him, that he was in charge of city planning work.

I expect to remain here until the spring of 1947. It would be a pleasure to hear from you, and I am naturally very much interested to know how my house is coming along.

With cordial personal regards, I am

Sincerely yours,

G. Hill Hodel, M.D.,
Chief Regional Medical Officer,
Hankow Regional Office, UNRRA.

George Hodel Letter to Lloyd Wright mailed from China, dated April 20 and postmarked May 5, 1946

A MIXED BAG—MORE CRIME SCENE EVIDENCE

"Roll Call, Kuster, O'Steen, Mannocchia, Souza, Jones, Everheart ..."

As an occupation, nothing tops police work. It is never routine. Every day brings something new and exciting. Working homicide guarantees that there will always be a new *whodunit* just around the corner. It might come tonight, tomorrow, or next week. You don't know when, but you do know it's coming. (I think my old partner and I still hold the record at Hollywood. We were called in and investigated three separate unrelated murders on one weekend standby.)

It's especially good when you're teamed up with a savvy, street-smart partner. During my career, I was luckier than most and had more than my share of the best.

Since the publication of BDA, I've learned that you don't have to wear a gun or carry a badge to be a good detective.

In the past ten years, thanks to the power of the Internet, I've heard from scores of armchair detectives. Their real day jobs? Secretary, librarian, bus driver, history professor, medical doctor, and electrician—John and Jane Q. citizens all.

Many of these men and women possess an uncanny ability to think like a veteran detective and have provided invaluable insights into my ongoing investigations. Here is just one more example, an e-mail from Tom Davis, a patent-illustrator with a keen eye and photographic memory.

Tom wrote:

Steve,

...

A photo I have seen clearly shows yet another type of empty bag at the body site.

The bag says BANDINI which is a brand of fertilizer. It is just possible that a bit of garden and lawn repair was done to the Franklin property in addition to any architectural work, and this empty bag was discarded on 39th street along with the cement bags.

Tom goes on to say:

And there is yet another little mystery this fertilizer bag may clear up. The autopsy of Elizabeth's body noted a mysterious "green granular material" inside her stomach. Could this stuff have been left over steer manure that she was forced to eat as part of an act of sado-humiliation? It's my personal hunch. Such an ordeal may also have been meant to add a bit of surrealist wit to her death. It was a message: "This woman is/was full of bullshit."

As a former art student I learned that the surrealists sometimes expressed visual puns and this would have been a perfect example.

Tom Davis

After reading my June 11, 2009, blog post [*Architect Lloyd Wright Letters at UCLA Link Dr. Hodel to Dahlia Crime Scene*] Tom sent me a new e-mail the following day, which in addition to complimenting me on my newly designed website, pointed to what he believed was an important error on my part, having to do with one specific paper bag. I quote verbatim from Tom's second e-mail:

> "I also found one new exciting detail. On your website you show an enlarged portion of a photograph that you call a cement bag. In fact, if you study this blow-up very carefully you can just make out the letters "URE" as in "MANURE." If I'm correct, and this bag is indeed a FERTILIZER bag, then you now have ABSOLUTE PROOF that BOTH cement AND fertilizer bags were used in the transport of Bette Short's body to the dump site. Please look into this as I think it is of extreme importance. No longer can ANYONE pass the existence of these two types of bags at the scene as coincidence. Taken along with your own research into renovations at the Sowden House, it STRONGLY points to Hodel driving directly from the Sowden House to the dump site."

Let's now re-examine several of the original crime scene photographs in light of what Tom Davis has pointed out.

First, in the crime scene photos we see what appears to be three separate paper sacks. The one on the extreme left is enlarged and does appear to read "URE" as in MAN**URE**. This is the sack I originally labeled as Lt. Haskins' "cement sack" which appears to have watery blood stains on it. Based on the evidence before us, it becomes obvious that Tom is correct and this bag contained manure, not cement.

What happened? Re-examination of additional LAPD photographs gave us the answer. The detectives, after photographing the original cement sack lying just inches from Elizabeth Short's extended right hand, then moved it out of the way [collecting it as evidence] and reshot the crime scene from a different angle. Here are the proofs.

The above photograph was obviously taken first and shot from north to south. It shows a different bag, probably, Lt. Haskins' "cement bag" left by the killer just inches from Elizabeth Short's extended right hand.

Seen kneeling on sidewalk are the primary LAPD detectives Finis Brown and Harry Hansen and reporter Will Fowler. (Man on right was not identified. It was possibly criminalist Jones from LAPD Scientific Investigation Division.)

This photo was taken standing south of the body looking north and showed that the original "cement" sack had either been collected as evidence and removed from the scene or was one of the three sacks seen in this photo, which had been moved north, away from the body.

In this third photo, we no longer see three bags above the body, but just two. The third had either been collected or removed from view; or possibly, it was moved eastward and was the sack seen close to the curbside.

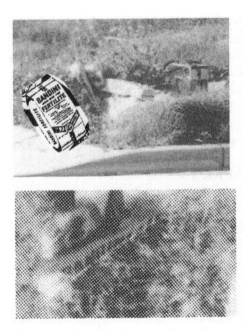

Photo above shows an enlarged area to the right of driveway. Clearly visible are the photographer's equipment box and an empty paper bag which appears to read "BANDINI." [Rotated in lower photo for easier readability.] I have also inserted in the photo an *L.A.Times* display showing a 1947 bag of "Bandini Fertilite."

Bandini Steer Manure/Bandini Fertilite

The above display ads were copied from the *Los Angeles Times* newspaper showing pictures of fifty-pound Bandini fertilizer sacks as they appeared for sale in 1947. The Bandini lettering on the side of the bag is similar to the brand labeling seen at the crime scene.

Based on the photographic evidence we can now confirm that both large cement and Bandini Steer Manure paper sacks were found at the crime scene. (By my count, at least three separate sacks, possibly more?)

A SECOND PAPER TRAIL

Included in the UCLA Lloyd Wright-George Hodel Papers were additional receipts for renovation work completed between 1945-1947. Below, we'll find an itemized billing list which includes, "Gardening-$230" and "Flower Box & bank planting-$60.00." [Nearly $300 just for landscaping, a sizable amount equal to approximately $3,000 in today's dollar value.]

Granted, unlike the cement bag receipts, which connected the cement work to the exact time of Elizabeth Short's murder, the below receipts were presented a year earlier in December 1945. However, the gardening needs would have been ongoing and the receipts establish that there existed a large demand for fertilizer due to the extensive landscaping.

Lloyd Wright receipts dated November 1945
including $330 for "landscaping/planting" expenses at "Dr. Hodel Residence."

"GARDENING TOM OGA--$270.00"

"FLOWER BOX & BANK PLANTING $60.00"

Photos from a 1949-1950 sales brochure prepared by Dr. George Hodel for the sale of his
"Shangri-La," Franklin house. Note the heavily landscaped interior and exterior gardens.

Is it relevant that manure sacks and cement sacks were both used to transport the body? To fully understand, we must venture deeper into the absolute horror of this crime.

"LA'S MOST HORRIFIC MURDER EVER"—THE SIGNATURE OF A MASTER SADIST

The murder of twenty-two-year-old, Elizabeth "Black Dahlia" Short lives in infamy because it was a torture-murder of the highest order. Her killer was a sophisticated sadist who went to extremes to make sure the public would both be horrified and outraged. Her killer wanted to ensure his crime would be forever remembered as a masterpiece of the macabre. He succeeded.

These specific acts of sadism are so extreme and the signatures so unique that they set this killer totally apart from your "average sexual psychopath."

Below is a list of what we KNOW occurred during the killer's drawn-out ritualistic torture-slaying of Elizabeth Short in the early morning hours of January 15, 1947:

1. Bound feet and hands with rope or wire ligature
2. Strangulation to neck leaving ligature marks
3. Blunt force trauma to face and head
4. Scalpel lacerations (five distinct incisions to her upper lip)
5. Surgically rounded scalpel lacerations to both sides of mouth
6. Tic-tac-toe scalpel cuttings to the right thigh
7. Scalpel laceration/incision (two inches) near the left nipple
8. Scalpel lacerations and some cutting away of pubic hair and insertion of hair into anus
9. Cigar or cigarette burns to the back [at least eight separate burn marks]
10. Incision from umbilicus to supra pubic in imitation of a hysterectomy (four and a half inches)
11. Scalpel incision and removal of large section of left thigh and insertion of it into vagina
12. Surgical removal of right breast. (Not believed recovered at autopsy. Possibly retained by killer as "trophy.")
13. Sexual anal-rape using unknown object. (Sodomy)
14. Surgical bisection of body (hemicorpectomy]) by incision through the intervertebral disks between the second and third lumbar vertebrae. [Note: To date, four separate surgeons have viewed the autopsy photographs and provided their expert opinions that "only a highly skilled surgeon could have performed the bisection without leaving any "hacking" marks and would have known that only by dividing between the second and third lumbar vertebrae can a body be bisected without the use of a saw.]
15. Washing and scrub down of the body parts using a coconut fiber brush

The most shocking act of sadism was revealed in the transcripts of Chief Autopsy Surgeon Dr. Frederick Newbarr's testimony before the coroner's inquest. Short was forced to ingest feces.

From the surgeon's testimony at the coroner's inquest of January 22, 1947:

> "The stomach was filled with greenish brown granular material, mostly feces and other particles which could not be identified."

[Note: Some self-professed "Dahlia experts" have claimed that the feces in the stomach was there "due to natural digestion and as a result of her being bisected."]

Asked about this, Dr. Doug Lyle M.D., a recognized forensic expert, said:

> True feces is produced in the lower portions of the bowel. And the bowel doesn't move stuff backwards so there is no way feces can get from the colon to the stomach—unless some connection between the two was made at the time of the bisection, but that would be obvious. If the stomach was found intact with feces inside it got there some other way.

Bottom line: Elizabeth Short, during her extended torture, suffered the ultimate humiliation of being forced to swallow feces.

Having reviewed the many acts of known torture, it takes very little imagination to speculatively add to that list the forced feeding of *Bandini Steer Manure or Bandini Fertilite* from a nearly empty bag of fertilizer—perhaps recently used by the gardener in the inner courtyard landscaping at the Franklin house.

Certainly, this fertilizer would match the coroner's description of the stomach contents as a "greenish-brown granular material, mostly feces and other particles which could not be identified."

Based on all the previous evidence, which was supported by the crime scene photographs and the Wright documents and receipts, it is my firm belief that Dr. George Hill Hodel, in the hours before her death, drugged and held Elizabeth Short captive at the Franklin house.

[Note- As previously noted, the DA files from 2004 established that father was alone at the house as my mother and we, three sons, were temporarily staying with her brother, our Uncle Gene, some three miles away in the Silver Lake District of East Hollywood.]

TIME LINE AND CRIME SCENE REENACTMENT
JANUARY 14, 1947 3:00-4:00 P.M. [APPROXIMATE]

LAPD policewoman Myrl McBride was the last person to see Elizabeth Short alive. Officer McBride stopped and spoke with Elizabeth Short on two separate occasions in the hours just prior to her disappearance. The first was at approximately 3 p.m. when a frightened Elizabeth ran up to her and claimed, "A man, a former suitor, just threatened to kill me." McBride accompanied her back to a bar and the man was gone and Elizabeth retrieved her purse. The second encounter came about one hour later when the officer watched Short leave a second bar in the vicinity of Fifth and Main Street.

Officer McBride said Elizabeth was accompanied by "two men and a woman." McBride asked Elizabeth, "Are you okay? Elizabeth nodded that she was and told McBride she "was going to the Greyhound Bus station to meet her father." At the time, the bus depot was just two blocks away.

I believe these two males and one female were the same three people who were looking for Elizabeth at the Dorothy French residence in San Diego just one week earlier. A neighbor reported to the police about seeing three individuals, "two males and a female," on January 7, knocking at Dorothy French's door. After a few moments, the witness saw them run to their parked car and "they hurriedly drove away." I believe that one of the males was likely George Hodel, possibly accompanied by either Fred Sexton or the man later described on the DA tapes as "The Baron." So far, we have no clue as to the woman's identity.

JANUARY 14-15, 1947—SOWDEN/FRANKLIN HOUSE

The newly discovered paper sacks link the Franklin house to the vacant lot and confirm our earlier suspicions that it was the original crime scene.

The extended torture and subsequent "surgical operation" (a hemicorpectomy), would probably have required a minimum of three (3) hours to complete, according to several forensic and medical experts.

I suggest that the murder unfolded this way:

Elizabeth Short was initially drugged with either chloroform or an injection of a strong sedative, likely by Dr. Hodel.

She was then bound and trussed with rope, tortured with non-lethal scalpel cuts to the body, sodomized with an unknown object, and then subjected to the ultimate sadistic humiliation of being forced fed with *Bandini* steer manure.

Franklin House Master Bathroom tub

She was taken to the master bathroom tub, where the torture continued, and she was eventually slain. [Note-Time of death, based on the coroner's estimate, would have been at approximately 2:00-3:00 a.m. in the early morning hours of January 15, 1947. This time is also substantiated by the fact that officers and the deputy coroner at the crime scene at 10:00 a.m. noted that rigor mortis had not yet stiffened the body, which normally begins at eight to twelve hours after death.]

The body was then cut in half and drained of blood before being scrubbed with a coconut fiber brush and washed clean. (Fibers from the brush were found on the body during the autopsy.)

The two halves were likely towel-dried and each placed separately on top of a large empty paper sack, which was readily at hand and left over from the recent construction and landscaping work. [Note: Each half, having been drained of fluids, would likely have weighed no more than fifty-five pounds.]

Franklin House Diagram
[Arrows mark: probable route from master bathroom to car]

The victim's separate body parts were carried from the master bathtub through the house to the rear garage and placed in George Hodel's black sedan. They could have been placed either in the trunk or on the backseat of the car. Additional cement and/or fertilizer sacks were likely placed over them to cover and conceal the butchery.

As seen in the above diagram, all of these actions, including placing the body parts in the car, would have been conducted within the privacy of the home and at no time would George Hodel ever have been exposed to public view.

On January 16, 2011, I reenacted the drive from the Franklin house garage to 3815 South Norton Avenue. Departing from the rear alley at 6 a.m., I arrived at the location of the vacant lot at 6:32 a.m., which is the same time that witness Robert Meyer claimed he first saw a black sedan pull up and stop at the curbside.

Meyer observed a lone male get out and indicated that the vehicle remained at the location for approximately four minutes. It was dark, he was nearly a half-block away, and his view was partially blocked by grass, so it would have been impossible for Mr. Meyer to see exactly what the killer was doing.

After waiting four minutes, I then drove from 3815 South Norton to the 1100 block of South Crenshaw Boulevard, where the killer had placed Elizabeth Short's purse and shoes atop a trashcan outside of a local restaurant. I arrived at 6:50 a.m. and daylight had just begun to break. [This location is approximately halfway between the vacant lot and the Franklin house.] The drive from Crenshaw Boulevard back to the Franklin house added another twenty minutes, and I arrived back at the rear alley at 7:12 a.m.

I offer the foregoing reenactment not as fact but as a *possible* scenario.

We will likely never know what exactly occurred. While I suspect that my father was one of the three people seen leaving the Main Street Bar with Elizabeth, he might not have been. The three could have brought her to the house and then departed.

Another question: Did George Hodel perform these horrific acts by himself or were others present? Again, we will probably never know the answer. But in at least one of his taunting mailings to the police after the murder, he did claim to have an accomplice:

> ... A certain girl is going to get the same as E.S. got if she squeals on us. We're going to Mexico City—catch us if you can.
>
> 2K's

[Note: Does the signature "2K's" after the "us" and "we" stand for "Two Killers"?]

We have multiple motives. The most likely is inside the DA's secret files.

It would appear that Elizabeth Short might have unwittingly signed her own death warrant by inadvertently making known to her ex-boyfriend, George Hodel, that she had gone to Chicago and was investigating the *1945 Chicago Lipstick Murders.* [Note-I would refer my readers to my sequel, *Most Evil: Avenger, Zodiac and the Further Serial Murders of Dr. George Hodel,* Dutton 2009 for full details of that investigation.]

In a later 1947 hand mailed taunting note to authorities the *Black Dahlia Avenger* writes:

...“Dahlia Killing was justified”

GEORGE HODEL ALBUM—PHOTO NO. 2—FRIEND OR TROPHY?

“Eyewitness misidentification is the single greatest cause of wrongful convictions nationwide, playing a role in more than 75% of convictions overturned through DNA testing.” —The Innocence Project

I have no desire to reopen the 2003 George Hodel photo album controversy.

In my 2006 CNN interview, I was personally able to publicly rule Photograph No. 1 in my father's album as not being Elizabeth Short. As summarized in Chapter 4, we now know that the Franklin house photo was my father's friend, Marya Marco.

Whether the second photograph in my father's album is Elizabeth Short, no longer matters. Its initial relevance was to address the question of whether George Hodel and Elizabeth Short had ever met.

Thanks to the 2004 post-publication discovery of the secret DA files and transcripts, that question has become a moot point. We now have independent confirmation from both law enforcement documents and new witnesses that George Hodel both knew and admitted killing Elizabeth Short.

Over the past seven years, I have received dozens of varying opinions on who Photo No. 2 might be. Many believe the photo is Elizabeth Short.

Dr. George Hodel
photo album

Elizabeth Short
crime scene, 1947
(lacerations airbrushed)

Photo No. 2 compared to Elizabeth Short photo at crime scene (airbrushed)

Others suggest the photo looks more like the 1949 *Lone Woman Murder* victim, actress Jean Spangler, whose purse was found just a half-mile from the Franklin house. Miss Spangler vanished on October 7, the day after George Hodel bailed out of jail on the child molestation charges. Jean was last seen seated at a table at a Hollywood restaurant, engaged in a late-night argument with two men, one of them described as "dapper-looking" who closely fit George Hodel's description.

Daily News 1949 Jean Spangler headlines
suggesting killer might be linked to 1947 Black Dahlia Murder

Jean Spangler comparisons to George Hodel's Photo No. 2

Jean Spangler rt/ear

Hodel photo rt/ear

Jean Spangler and Photo #2 enlargement

Jean Spangler

Jean Spangler

Was this the "drop-dead gorgeous actress named Jean" whom my half-brother Duncan recalled was dating our father and whom he met at the Franklin house parties in 1948-1949?

George Hodel photo No. 2 nude compared to "Showgirl" Jean Spangler nude

Still others offer the possibility that Photo No. 2 could have been the unidentified woman/victim eavesdropping cops heard crying and dialing the telephone operator from the Franklin house on February 18, 1950. Later that same evening, in the transcript, the stakeout detectives described hearing George Hodel and his confidant, "The Baron," go downstairs to the basement. Then beating sounds and blows were heard, which detectives described as "sounding like a pipe striking an object," immediately followed by a woman crying out several times, then silence.

Setting aside speculation about who appears in Photo No. 2, let's take a closer look at the actual photo.

In the top photograph below we see George Hodel sitting on top of the desk in his home/office/living room. This photo was taken circa February 1950. Displayed on the north wall are forty-nine (49) separate Chinese and Tibetan art objects which GHH, using his "diplomatic immunity," sent to himself from his UNRRA base in China before unexpectedly resigning and returning home in September 1946. Also, note his preference for mixing the old with the new as demonstrated by the modern art painting [enlarged, artist unknown] hanging on the wall behind his desk.

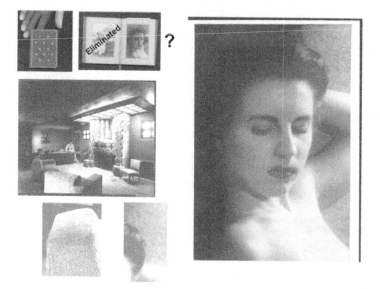

GHH album, Photo No. 2

When I initially viewed this photograph, I assumed that the woman was lying on a carpeted floor. However, in closer examination, it becomes obvious that she is not.

Based on the downward slope of her breast line, it appears that her head and shoulders are braced against a vertical object, with her left arm bent and propped behind her head.

In the living room, we see two upholstered chairs. The lower-left photo shows a close-up of the chair material in comparison to the material in Photo No. 2. To my eye, they look similar. I would suggest that the nude woman's back was braced against one of these fabric chairs when this photo was taken.

The woman in the photo, with eyes closed, is either feigning sleep, drugged unconscious, or worse ... she might be dead. Could this be one of George Hodel's "trophy" photographs?

Her lipstick is heavily applied and appears to have been smeared on, possibly by someone else.

Lipstick and lips were a regular and repeating theme seen in many of the surrealist art works of that time period.

In one of Man Ray's later photographs, believed taken shortly before his death, he was seen holding a photograph of a large pair of lips identical to the Photo No. 2 enlargement shown below as he winks directly into the camera. Behind him, hanging on the wall in plain view, we see one of his paintings—a bisected body.

In addition, in Photo No. 2, we also have the suggestion of the surrealist's *Minotaur* theme, with the woman's arm bent at the elbow and extended above her head. Could all of this add up to another George Hodel post-mortem homage to his Dadaist Master and good friend, Man Ray?

Photo No. 2 lipstick enlarged

Regardless of who this woman was ... Short, Spangler, Jane Doe in the basement, or someone else ... we cannot discount the very real possibility that she might have been another one of George Hodel's victims, drugged, posed, and about to be or already slain.

As we know, drugging his victims was an important part of the doctor's methodology. We already know of at least three drugging incidents: Ruth Spaulding, Lillian Lenorak, and his teenage granddaughter, Deborah Hodel [Tamar's daughter] who, after being drugged while having dinner with him, reported awakening to find herself nude and spread-eagled on his hotel room bed with George snapping pictures of her.

The fourth probable drugging, based on a reading of the 1950 DA transcripts, was the Jane Doe victim who was assaulted and possibly slain in the Franklin house basement on February 18, 1950.

SOWDEN/FRANKLIN HOUSE PHOTOS-1969

In August 1969, the National Park Service undertook a project to both survey and photograph the Sowden/Franklin house.

This "Historic American Building Survey" CA-1940 and the photographs taken in connection with it were made public and I am here including those 1969 photographs.

George Hodel sold the house in 1950. It's believed the new owners moved in but left after a few years, and the home remained vacant during the 1950s and '60s. Later, in the early 1970s, the owner's grandson and his wife moved in and lived there until selling the home in 2002.

[Note- In BDA Chapter 20, "The Franklin House Revisited," I refer to the owners as "Mr. and Mrs. Bill Buck" to protect their privacy.]

These survey photographs show that by 1969, the interior courtyard had become overgrown and the home had fallen into disrepair due to being vacant for more than a decade.

I am including these photographs from the '60s as they have best captured the look and feel of the Franklin house—as it was in 1947. A little landscaping and some pruning would restore it to its 1940s look.

5121 FRANKLIN AVENUE, HOLLYWOOD, CALIFORNIA.

It is 1947. A warm starlit night and the sweet smell of jasmine fills the air. Imagine you are one of the invited guests, standing on the polar bear rug, sipping an ice-cold gin-and-tonic, as the handsome, dapper doctor approaches with a charming smile and his most sincere, "Good evening. So glad you could make it tonight."

HISTORIC AMERICAN BUILDINGS SURVEY-NATIONAL PARK SERVICE SOWDEN HOUSE PHOTOGRAPHS, 1969

(Full text and diagrams attached as Addendum)

Left: Entrance, oblique view; Right: Entrance, axial view

Left: Entrance gate; Right: Entrance gate, detail view

Left: Living room, distant view, looking west to study
Top Right: Living room, close view, looking west to study
Bottom Right: Study, fireplace

Left: Glazed opening, living room, looking towards court
Right: Court, looking north from living room terrance

Left: Entrance to studio at north end of court, from court
Right: Entrance to studio, close view

Left: View in courtyard, looking south to living room
Left: Living room, close view from courtyard

Left: Colonnade, looking through door
Right: Colonnade, beyond door

Left: Bathroom, tub; Right: Bathroom, sink

6
The DA's Hodel-Black Dahlia Transcripts

AS YOU BEGIN TO READ THE FOLLOWING SUMMARIES, It is important to understand that the detective's entries that make-up these 146-pages of transcriptions are nothing more than *their personal log*. In these files, [with a few fortunate exceptions] we are only reading brief "headlines" as to what was contained in each of the separately recorded conversations.

The officers entries, made in real time, summarize only *bits and pieces* of each conversation. Consequently, we are only receiving a few sentences of a total conversation.

Unfortunately, the actual 41 wire recordings have "disappeared" from LAPD custody and it is almost certain that the missing recordings containing the complete conversations were destroyed and will never become available.

It is also important to understand that the modern day LAPD had nothing to do with the original investigation *and had no idea that Dr. George Hill Hodel was ever named as a suspect, let alone that he had confessed on tape to committing the crimes. Today's LAPD first learned of both Dr. George Hodel's existence and these transcripts only AFTER the publication of BDA in 2003.*

Today's LAPD had no knowledge that these DA Transcripts existed. All of the evidence connecting George Hodel to the crimes as well as these transcripts was removed from LAPD files a long time ago, probably in the 1950s or 1960s.

Like, LASO Undersheriff, James Downey had told his Chief of Detectives, Gordon Bowers, when speaking about George Hodel and LAPD solving the case, **"...it will never come out."**

Also, keep in mind as you read these transcripts that we owe their existence solely to one honest [and very cautious] detective.

It was Lt. Frank B. Jemison who was assigned by the 1949 Grand Jury to reinvestigate the Black Dahlia and other *Lone Woman*

Murders. He did it and he solved it. When he was then ordered by his superiors to "shut it down and turn over all the files, tape recordings and transcripts to LAPD's Chief of Detectives, Thad Brown, he did that too.

But, it was Lt. Jemison's final act that ultimately changed the course of history and permitted the public to ultimately discover the truth.

Prior to turning over all the materials to LAPD, as ordered, Lt. Jemison made a copy of his complete investigation, including the Hodel transcripts, and secretly locked all of the documents away in the DA's vault, where they remained unopened and untouched for six-decades. This was his insurance. Unbeknownst to all the top brass in both the DA's office and the LAPD, *Lt. Jemison kept a second set of books.*

Here then, thanks to an honest and careful cop, are those books!

Note- In the pages that follow I have reduced the 146-pages down to just 15 for easier readability. Included in those pages are extracts of what I consider to be the most relevant statements and admissions.

For historical purposes and the hardcore researchers, [and in case I have missed something that an eagle-eyed armchair detective might find] *I have included the complete unedited Hodel- Black Dahlia Transcripts in the Addendum.*

LOS ANGELES DISTRICT ATTORNEY

BUREAU OF INVESTIGATION

HODEL – BLACK DAHLIA CASE FILE

ELECTRONIC SURVEILLANCE TRANSCRIPTS OF GEORGE HILL HODEL M.D.

DA Case No. 30-1268
Title- Elizabeth Short
Suspect: Dr. George Hill Hodel
Inv. Assigned: Lt. Frank Jemison
Charge: Murder
Case: ACTIVE

The following fifteen-page annotated summary was prepared by retired LAPD Homicide detective Steve Hodel. It contains the verbatim statements and entries of both DA and LAPD detectives as found in the original 1950 DA Case File.

The statements and admissions made by Dr. George Hill Hodel are also verbatim, taken from the pages of the DA's transcription of the secret wire-recordings.

The tape-recordings were obtained during a joint DA/LAPD Task-Force stakeout comprised of 18 detectives. The electronic surveillance was ongoing 24/7 over a five-week period from February 15, 1950 through March 27, 1950 (1872 man hours) and was terminated only because Dr. Hodel after being tipped-off then fled his residence.

As of that date, detectives had recorded 41 wire spools of Dr. Hodel's personal conversations. The DA's original summary resulted in 146-pages of transcription. In the pages that follow, I have left the original timeline intact, and included only those statements relevant to criminal activity, payoffs to law enforcement, and which make specific references to the Black Dahlia Murder investigation. *The complete and unedited 146-page transcript is included as an addendum to this book.*

ELECTRONIC SURVEILLANCE INSTALLATION
DR. GEORGE HILL HODEL RESIDENCE —5121 FRANKLIN AVE, HOLLYWOOD
2/15/50

D.A. Hodel/Black Dahlia File

"INVESTIGATOR'S PROGRESS REPORT"

The handwritten report (above) is a copy of the one found in the D.A. Hodel – Black Dahlia File.

The verbatim typewritten copy at the right includes all spellings and punctuations as they appear in the above original.

Case No. 30-1268   Date: 2/27/50
Title: Short, Eliz.
Suspects: Dr. Geo. Hill   Inv. Assigned Jemison
Charge: Murder
THIS CASE IS: ACTIVE
BRIEF STATEMENT AS TO RESULTS TO DATE: (Indicate present status if being brought to trial at this time.)

"On Feb. 15, 1950 the undersigned investigator, working with Sgts Stanton & Guinnis from the LAPD crime lab, installed two microfones in the home of Dr. Geo. Hodel. The microfones were connected to a wire recorder located in the basement of the Hollywood Station of the LAPD thru telephone lines leased from the Pac. Tel. & Tel. Co. Trouble was not rectified until approx. 2:00, Feb. 18. No intelligible conversation was heard over the system until that time."

Signed—David E. Bronson

DA/LAPD MICROPHONE INSTALLATION LOCATIONS

Two microphone (M) "bugs" installed in main level walls of Dr. Hodel's residence. Based on surveillance transcripts we know they were hidden in the West Office Library, and Master Bedroom. Because of its placement. the bug in George Hodel's bedroom was able to pick-up and record the Feb. 18 assault and possible murder that occurred in the basement. Below floor plan diagrams basement which was located directly below the Master bedroom.

16°-37° AERIAL DIMETRIC
FROM SOUTHWEST

SOWDEN HOUSE

BASEMENT FLOOR PLAN

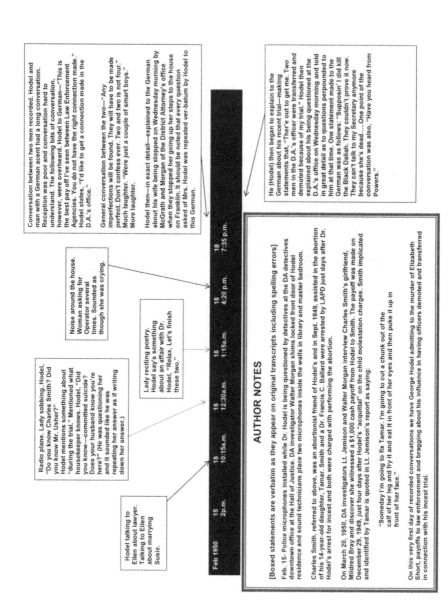

Conversation between two men recorded. Hodel and man with a German acent had a long conversation. Reception was poor and conversation hard to understand. The following bits of conversation, however, were overheard. Hodel to German—"This is the best pay off I've seen between Law Enforcement Agencies. You do not have the right connection made." Hodel states, "I'd like to get a connection made in the D.A.'s office."

General conversation between the two—"Any imperfections will be found. They will have to be made perfect. Don't confess ever. Two and two is not four." Much laughter. "Were just a couple of smart boys." More laughter.

Hodel then—in exact detail—explained to the German about his wife being stopped on Wednesday morning by McGrath and Morgan of the District Attorney's office on Franklin. It should be noted that every question asked of Mrs. Hodel was repeated ver-batum by Hodel to this German.

He (Hodel) then began to explain to the German about his recent trial—making statements that, "There out to get me. Two men in the D.A.'s officer were transferred and demoted because of my trial." Hodel then explained about his being questioned at the D.A.'s office on Wednesday morning and told in great detail as to questions perpounded to him at that time. One statement made to the German was as follows: "Supposin' I did kill the Black Daliah. They couldn't prove it now. They can't talk to my Secretary anymore because she's dead.....One point of the conversation was also, "Have you heard from Powers."

Radio plane. Lady sobbing. Hodel, "Do you know Charles Smith? Did you know Mr. Usher?" Hodel mentions something about "during the trial." Mentioned what housekeeper knows. Hodel, "Did you know—committed suicide? Does your husband know you're here?" (He was questioning her and it sounded like he was repeating her answer as if writing down her answer.)

Noise around the house. Woman asking for Operator several times. Sounded as though she was crying.

Lady reciting poetry. Hodel say's something about an affair with Dr. Hodel. "Relax, Let's finish these two."

Hodel talking to Ellen about lawyer. Talking to Ellen about marrying Susie.

Feb 1950 | 15 2p.m. | 18 10:15a.m. | 18 12:30a.m. | 18 1:15a.m. | 18 4:20 p.m. | 18 7:35 p.m.

AUTHOR NOTES

[Boxed statements are verbatim as they appear on original transcripts including spelling errors]

Feb. 15. Police microphones installed while Dr. Hodel is being questioned by detectives at the DA detectives downtown office at the Hall of Justice. DA investigator Walter Morgan shims locked front door of Hodel residence and sound technicians place two microphones inside the walls in library and master bedroom.

Charles Smith, referred to above, was an abortionist friend of Hodel's and in Sept. 1949, assisted in the abortion of his 14-year-old daughter, Tamar. Smith and Dr. Francis C. Ballard were arrested by LAPD just days after Dr. Hodel's arrest for incest and both were charged with performing the abortion.

On March 20, 1950, DA investigators Lt. Jemison and Walter Morgan interview Charles Smith's girlfriend, Mildred Bray and discover she witnessed a $1,000 cash payoff from Hodel to Smith. The payoff was made on December 29, 1949, just four days after Hodel's "acquittal" on the child molestation charges. Smith implicated and identified by Tamar is quoted in Lt. Jemison's report as saying:

"Someday I'm going to fix Tamar. I'm going to cut a chunk out of the calf of her leg and fry it and eat it in front of her eyes and then puke it up in front of her face."

On this very first day of recorded conversations we have George Hodel admitting to the murder of Elizabeth Short, payoffs to law enforcement and bragging about his influence in having officers demoted and transferred in connection with his incest trial.

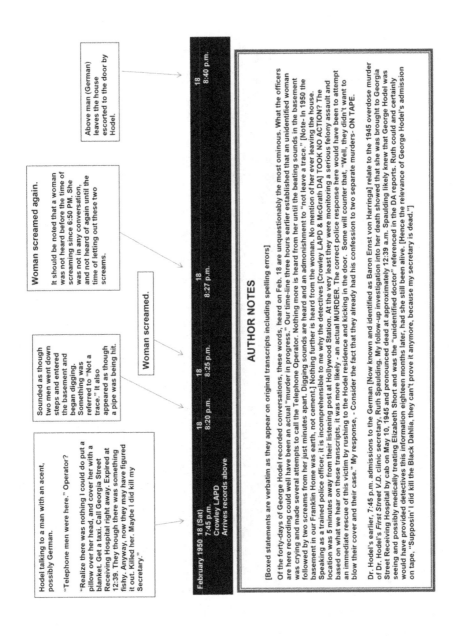

Hodel talking to a man with an acent, possibly German.

"Telephone men were here." Operator?

"Realize there was nothing I could do put a pillow over her head, and cover her with a blanket. Get a taxi. Call Georgia Street Receiving Hospital right away. Expired at 12:39. They though there was something fishy. Anyway, now they may have figured it out. Killed her. Maybe I did kill my Secretary."

Sounded as though two men went down steps and entered the basement and began digging. Something was referred to "Not a trace." It also appeared as though a pipe was being hit.

Woman screamed.

Woman screamed again.

It should be noted that a woman was not heard before the time of screaming since 6:50 PM. She was not in any conversation, and not heard of again until the time of letting out these two screams.

Above man (German) leaves the house escorted to the door by Hodel.

February 1950 18 (Sat)
7:45 p.m.
Crowley LAPD
Arrives records above

18
8:20 p.m.

18
8:25 p.m.

18
8:27 p.m.

18
8:40 p.m.

AUTHOR NOTES

[Boxed statements are verbatim as they appear on original transcripts including spelling errors]

Of the forty-days of George Hodel recorded conversations, these words, heard on Feb. 18 are unquestionably the most ominous. What the officers are here recording could well have been an actual "murder in progress." Our time-line three hours earlier established that an unidentified woman was crying and made several attempts to call the Telephone Operator. Nothing more is heard from her until the beating sounds in the basement followed by two screams from her just minutes apart. Digging sounds are heard and an admonishment to "not leave a trace." [Note- In 1950 the basement in our Franklin Home was earth, not cement.] Nothing further is heard from the woman. No mention of her ever leaving the house. Speaking as a trained police officer, it is incomprehensible to me why the detectives [Crowley LAPD & McGrath DA] TOOK NO ACTION? The location was 5 minutes away from their listening post at Hollywood Station. At the very least they were monitoring a serious felony assault and based on what we hear on these transcripts, it was more likely - an actual MURDER. The correct police response here would have been to attempt an immediate rescue of this victim by rushing to the Hodel residence and kicking in the door. Some will counter that, "Well, they didn't want to blow their cover and their case." My response, - Consider the fact that they already had his confession to two separate murders- ON TAPE.

Dr. Hodel's earlier, 7:45 p.m. admissions to the German [Now known and identified as Baron Ernst von Harringa] relate to the 1945 overdose murder of Dr. Hodel's First Street V.D. clinic secretary, Ruth Spaulding. My follow-up investigation into her death showed that she was brought to Georgia Street Receiving Hospital by cab on May 10, 1945 and pronounced dead at approximately 12:39 a.m. Spaulding likely knew that George Hodel was seeing and possibly medically treating Elizabeth Short and was the "unidentified doctor" referenced in the DA reports. Ruth could and certainly would have provided detectives this information eighteen months later, had she still been alive. [Hence the relevance of George Hodel's admission on tape, "Supposin' I did kill the Black Dahlia, they can't prove it anymore, because my secretary is dead."]

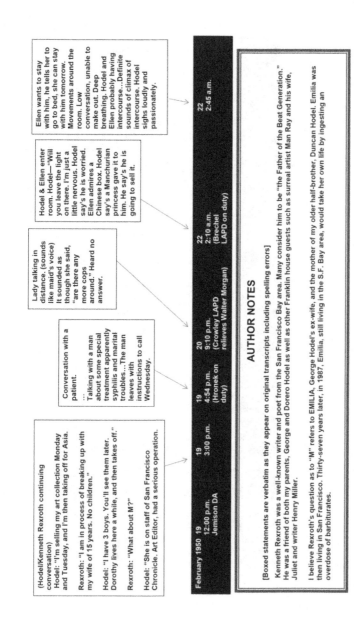

(Hodel/Kenneth Rexroth continuing conversation)

Hodel: "I'm selling my art collection Monday and Tuesday, and I'm then taking off for Asia."

Rexroth: "I am in process of breaking up with my wife of 15 years. No children."

Hodel: "I have 3 boys. You'll see them later. Dorothy lives here a while, and then takes off."

Rexroth: "What about M?"

Hodel: "She is on staff of San Francisco Chronicle. Art Editor, had a serious operation."

Conversation with a patient.

...

Talking with a man about some special treatment apparently syphilis and marital troubles...The man leaves with instructions to call Wednesday.

Lady talking in distance. (sounds like maid's voice) It sounded as though she said, "are there any more cops around." Heard no answer.

Hodel & Ellen enter room. Hodel—"Will you leave the light on there. I'm just a little nervous. Hodel say's he is worried. Ellen admires a Chinese box. Hodel say's a Manchurian princess gave it to him. He say's he is going to sell it.

Ellen wants to stay with him, he tells her to go to bed, she can stay with him tomorrow. Movements around the room. Low conversation, unable to make out. Deep breathing. Hodel and Ellen probably having intercourse...Definite sounds of climax of intercourse. Hodel sighs loudly and passionately.

| February 1950 19 12:00 p.m. Jemison DA | 19 3:00 p.m. | 19 4:54 p.m. (Hronek on duty) | 20 9:10 p.m. (Crowley LAPD relieves Walter Morgan) | 22 2:10 a.m. (Brechel LAPD on duty) | 22 2:45 a.m. |

AUTHOR NOTES

[Boxed statements are verbatim as they appear on original transcripts including spelling errors]

Kenneth Rexroth was a well-known writer and poet from the San Francisco Bay area. Many consider him to be "the Father of the Beat Generation." He was a friend of both my parents, George and Dorero Hodel as well as other Franklin house guests such as surreal artist Man Ray and his wife, Juliet and writer Henry Miller.

I believe Rexroth's question as to "M" refers to EMILIA, George Hodel's ex-wife, and the mother of my older half-brother, Duncan Hodel. Emilia was then living in San Francisco. Thirty-seven years later, in 1987, Emilia, still living in the S.F. Bay area, would take her own life by ingesting an overdose of barbiturates.

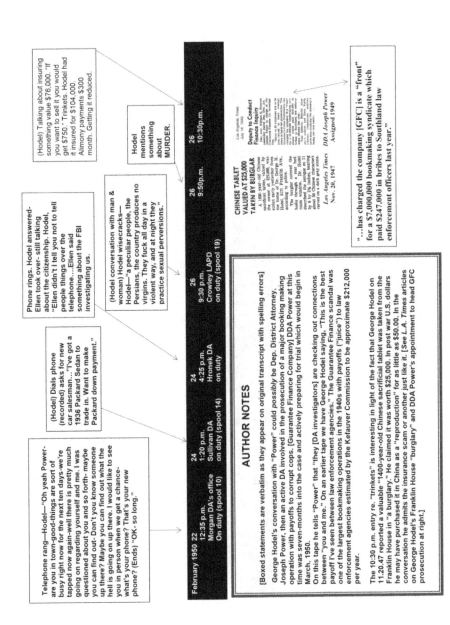

Telephone rang—Hodel—"Oh yeah Power- are you in town-good-things are sort of busy right now for the next ten days-we're tapped now again-well there is pretty much going on regarding yourself and me. I was questioned about you and so forth- maybe you can find out- Don't you know someone up there? Maybe you can find out what the hell is going on up there. I would like to see you in person when we get a chance-what's your phone? That's your new phone? (Ends) "OK- so long."

(Hodel) Dials phone (recorded) asks for new car salesman…"I've got a 1936 Packard Sedan to trade in. Want to make Packard down payment."

Phone rings. Hodel answered-Ellen took over- still talking about the citizenship. Hodel, "Ellen didn't I tell you not to tell people things over the telephone….Ellen said something about the FBI investigating us.

(Hodel conversation with man & woman) Hodel wisecracks—Hodel—"a peculiar people, the Persians, the country produces no virgins. They fuck all day in a violent way, and at night they practice sexual perversions."

Hodel mentions something about MURDER.

(Hodel) Talking about insuring something value $76,000. "If you want to sell it you would get $750.' Trinkets. Hodel had it insured for $104,000. Alimony payments $300 month. Getting it reduced.

February 1950 22	24	24	26	26	26
12:35 p.m. Morgan DA's office On duty (spool 10)	1:20 p.m. Sullivan DA on duty (spool 14)	4:25 p.m. Hronek DA on duty	9:30 p.m. Crowley LAPD on duty (spool 19)	9:50p.m.	10:30p.m.

AUTHOR NOTES

[Boxed statements are verbatim as they appear on original transcript with spelling errors]

George Hodel's conversation with "Power" could *possibly* be Dep. District Attorney, Joseph Power, then an active DA involved in the prosecution of a major booking making operation with payoffs to corrupt cops. [Guarantee Finance Company] DDA Power at this time was seven-months into the case and actively preparing for trial which would begin in March, 1950.

On this tape he tells "Power" that "they [DA investigators] are checking out connections between "you and me." On an earlier tape we have George Hodel saying, "This is the best payoff I've seen between law enforcement agencies." The Guarantee Finance scandal was one of the largest bookmaking operations in the 1940s with payoffs ("juice") to law enforcement agencies estimated by the Kefauver Commission to be approximate $212,000 per year.

The 10:30 p.m. entry re. "trinkets" is interesting in light of the fact that George Hodel on 11.20.47 reported a valuable "1400-year-old Chinese sacrificial tablet was taken from the Franklin House in "a burglary." He claimed it was worth $25,000. In post war U.S. dollars he may have purchased it in China as a "reproduction" for as little as $50.00. In the conversation he admits the insurance scam or another just like it. [See *L.A. Times* articles on George Hodel's Franklin House "burglary" and DDA Power's appointment to head GFC prosecution at right.]

Los Angeles Times
July 14, 1949

Deputy to Conduct Finance Inquiry

DDA Joseph Power
Assigned 1949

CHINESE TABLET VALUED AT $25,000 TAKEN BY BURGLAR

Los Angeles Times
Nov. 20, 1947

"…has charged the company [GFC] is a "front" for a $7,000,000 bookmaking syndicate which paid $247,000 in bribes to Southland law enforcement officers last year."

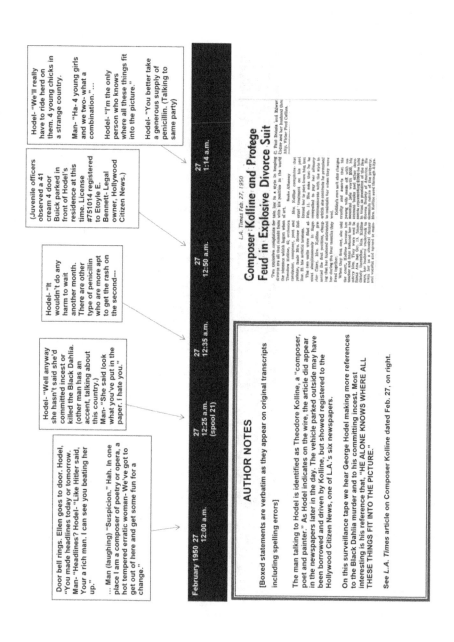

Box 1 (12:00 a.m.): Door bell rings. Ellen goes to door. Hodel. "You made headlines today or tomorrow." Man- "Headlines? Hodel." "Like Hitler said, Your a rich man. I can see you beating her up."

... Man (laughing) "Suspicion." Hah. In one place I am a composer of poetry or opera, a hot tempered erratic woman- We've got to get out of here and get some fun for a change."

Box 2: Hodel- "Well anyway she hasn't said she'd committed incest or killed the Black Dahlia. (other man has an accent, talking about this country.) Man- "She said look what you've put in the paper. I hate you."

Box 3: Hodel- "It wouldn't do any harm to wait another month. There are other type of penicillin who are more apt to get the rash on the second—"

Box 4: (Juvenile officers observed a 41 cream 4 door Buick parked in front of Hodel's residence at this time. License #751014 registered to Etoyle E. Bennett- Legal owner, Hollywood Citizen News.)

Box 5: Hodel- "We'll really have to ride herd on them. 4 young chicks in a strange country." Man- "Ha- 4 young girls and we two- what a combination." Hodel- "I'm the only person who knows where all these things fit into the picture." Hodel- "You better take a generous supply of penicillin. (Talking to same party)

February 1950

| 27 12:00 a.m. | 27 12:25 a.m. (spool 21) | 27 12:35 a.m. | 27 12:50 a.m. | 27 1:14 a.m. |

AUTHOR NOTES

[Boxed statements are verbatim as they appear on original transcripts including spelling errors]

The man talking to Hodel is identified as Theodore Kolline, a "composer, poet and painter." As Hodel indicates on the wire, the article did appear in the newspapers later in the day. The vehicle parked outside may have been borrowed and driven by Kolline, but showed registered to the Hollywood Citizen News, one of L.A.'s six newspapers.

On this surveillance tape we hear George Hodel making more references to the Black Dahlia murder and to his committing incest. Most interesting is his reference that, "HE ALONE KNOWS WHERE ALL THESE THINGS FIT INTO THE PICTURE."

See L.A. Times article on Composer Kolline dated Feb. 27, on right.

L.A. Times Feb. 27, 1950

Composer Kolline and Protege Feud in Explosive Divorce Suit

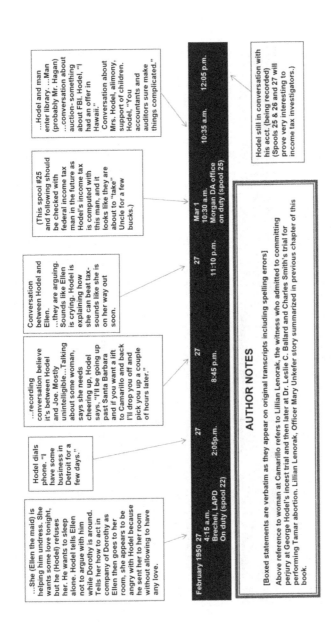

...She (Ellen the maid) is helping him undress. She wants some love tonight, but he (Hodel) refuses her. He wants to sleep alone. Hodel tells Ellen not to argue with him while Dorothy is around. Tells her how to act in company of Dorothy as Ellen then goes to her room, she appears to be angry with Hodel because he sent her to her room without allowing to have any love.

Hodel dials phone. "I have some business in Detroit for a few days."

...recording conversation believe it's between Hodel and Joe. Mostly unintelligible....Talking about some woman, says she needs cheering up. Hodel says, "I'll be going up past Santa Barbara and if you want a lift to Camarillo and back I'll drop you off and pick you up a couple of hours later."

Conversation between Hodel and Ellen. ...they are arguing. Sounds like Ellen is crying. Hodel is explaining how she can beat tax- sounds like she is on her way out soon.

(This spool #25 and following should be checked with federal income tax man in the future as Hodel's income tax is computed with this man, and it looks like they are about to "take" Uncle for a few bucks.)

...Hodel and man enter library. ...Man (probably Mr. Hagan) ...conversation about auction- something about FBI. Hodel, "I had an offer in Hawaii." Conversation about Mrs. Hodel, alimony, support of children. Hodel, "You accountants and auditors sure make things complicated."

Hodel still in conversation with his acct. (being recorded) (Spools 25 & 26 and 27 will prove very interesting to income tax investigators.)

February 1950 27   27   27   27   Mar 1   10:35 a.m.   12:05 p.m.
4:15 a.m.   2:05p.m.   8:45 p.m.   11:10 p.m.   10:30 a.m.
Brechel, LAPD   Morgan DA office
On duty (spool 22)   on duty (spool 25)

AUTHOR NOTES

[Boxed statements are verbatim as they appear on original transcripts including spelling errors]

Above reference to woman at Camarillo refers to Lillian Lenorak, the witness who admitted to commiting perjury at George Hodel's incest trial and then later at Dr. Leslie C. Ballard and Charles Smith's trial for performing Tamar abortion. Lillian Lenorak, Officer Mary Unkefer story summarized in previous chapter of this book.

Phone rang. Hodel answered. Whoever he was talking to he said, "Don't say anything over the phone- it is tapped- said he had there phone number, and would call tomorrow-said he would have to go out to call- said if he said phone number, "They" would be out and bother them- that is what "They" always do. When Hodel hung up, Ellen asked him how he knew- Hodel said he was just talking.

Hodel and Ellen have conversation is Spanish. They are in bedroom having sex intercourse or something, probably perversion. Sounds like he got another blow job.

...Conversation between Hodel and Woman. Woman, "I owe 4 times 75.00, that's 300.00 (possibly his wife)" "I have to pay my rent or get out." Conversation with woman continues. Relative to her expenses and the childrens. ...Conversation with wife resumed. Hodel, "I've lost money every year." Talking about what money she's earned. Hodel discusses his lossess of that year. Now I must sell the house. Hodel, something about penitentirary. Noises in background.

Conversation with woman. (wife) She's talking about the children. Hodel talks about having wife and children with him again.

Phone rings. Hodel answers (recorded) "You're talking over a tapped line. Oh yes, it's been tapped for a long time. I'll be home for the next hour. Be sure and come.

Man still talking – (recorded) talking to Hodel about some woman. Mentions Barbara Sherman, Dorothy Black (?) Something about Santa Barbara. Hodel- "She called me this morning. She's coming over this P.M."

Man- "You had pretty good success with some of those dames I fixed."

Hodel to man, "In about 2 or 3 weeks I'll probably be on way abroad."

L.A. Times Feb 1, 1950
Probation Given in Morals Case

Barbara Sherman given probation ordered not to see/associate with Dr. Hodel.

March 1950	1	3	3	3	4	4	4
	11:37 p.m.	4:10 a.m.	12:07 p.m.	1:11 p.m.	1:21 p.m.	2:45 p.m.	3:26 p.m.
	Meyer, LAPD	Brechel LAPD (spool 21)	Sullivan DA				

AUTHOR NOTES

[Boxed statements are verbatim as they appear on original transcripts including spelling errors]

Based on above response it is obvious George Hodel was just guessing that his phone was "tapped." When maid, Ellen, asks him "how he knows?" he responds by saying, "he is just talking." Hodel's reference to "they" obviously refers to, LAPD & DA detectives. Clearly, he has no suspicion that the rooms have concealed microphones and are "wired for sound."

Barbara Sherman [Shearman] was a star witness in the 1949 incest trial and present in the bedroom when Hodel & Sexton had the sex acts with George's 14-year-old daughter, Tamar. Shearman testified at the preliminary hearing to being present and seeing the sex acts. She then refused to testify at the later Superior Court trial and was arrested for perjury, based on her previous sworn testimony. On Feb. 1, 1950, she was allowed to plead guilty to a lesser charge [Contributing to a Minor] and as the L.A. Times article indicates, was given straight probation.

What is of particular interest here is the conversation between Hodel and the unidentified male caller on March 4th. The conversation centers on Barbara Sherman and despite the judge's order to "keep away" Hodel tells the man that "she is coming over this PM." [Sounds like he is talking about Sherman?] Then the man reminds Hodel that he had "good success with some of those dames I fixed." One has to wonder based on the earlier conversation if the "fixed" refers to their witness testimony? [The DA Files mention a $15,000 payoff-bribe paid by Hodel through his attorney to secure an acquittal.]

George Hodel, true to his word, leaves later that month [March 28] leaving the surveillance teams "staked out" on an empty house.

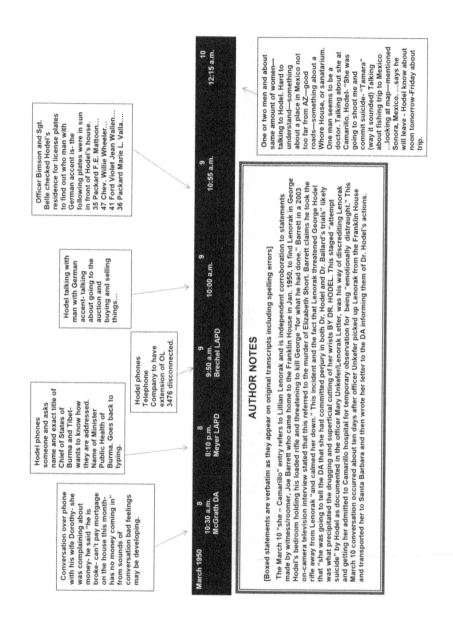

Conversation over phone with his wife Dorothy - she was complaining about money - he said "he is broke - can't pay mortgage on the house this month - has no money coming in" from sounds of conversation bad feelings may be developing.

Hodel phones someone and asks name and exact title of Chief of States of Burma and Tibet - wants to know how they are addressed. Name of Minister Public Health of Burma. Goes back to typing.

Hodel phones Telephone Company to have extension of OL 3476 disconnected.

Hodel talking with man with German accent - talking about going to the auction and buying and selling things....

Officer Bimson and Sgt. Belle checked Hodel's residence for license plates to find out who man with German accent is - the following plates were in sun in front of Hodel's house.
35 Packard F.E. Mattoon...
47 Chev. Willie Wheeler...
41 Ford Violet Jean Wallen....
36 Packard Marie L. Valla....

One or two men and about same amount of women—talking to Hodel. Hard to understand—something about a place in Mexico not too far from AZ—good roads—something about a Whore House, or sanatarium. One man seems to be a doctor. Talking about she at Camarillo. Hodel- "She was going to shoot me and commit suicide-"Tamara" (way it sounded) Talking about fishing trip to Mexico ...looking at map—mentioned Sonora, Mexico. ...says he will leave - Hodel know about noon tomorrow-Friday about trip.

March 1950					
8	8	9	9	9	10
10:30 a.m.	8:10 p.m.	9:50 a.m.	10:00 a.m.	10:55 a.m.	12:15 a.m.
McGrath DA	Meyer LAPD	Brechel LAPD			

AUTHOR NOTES

[Boxed statements are verbatim as they appear on original transcripts including spelling errors]

The March 10 "she – Camarillo" entry refers to Lillian Lenorak and is independent corroboration to statements made by witness/roomer, Joe Barrett who came home to the Franklin House in Jan. 1950, to find Lenorak in George Hodel's bedroom holding his loaded rifle and threatening to kill George "for what he had done." Barrett in a 2003 on-camera television interview stated that this referred to the murder of Elizabeth Short. Barrett claims he took the rifle away from Lenorak "and calmed her down." This incident and the fact that Lenorak threatened George Hodel that "she was going to tell the DA that she had committed perjury in both Dr. Hodel and Dr. Ballard's trials" likely was what precipitated the drugging and superficial cutting of her wrists BY DR. HODEL. This staged "attempt suicide" by Hodel as documented in the officer Mary Unkefer/Lenorak Letter, was his way of discrediting Lenorak and getting her admitted to Camarillo hospital for temporary observation for being "emotionally distraught." This March 10 conversation occurred about ten days after officer Unkefer picked up Lenorak from the Franklin House and transported her to Santa Barbara and then wrote her letter to the DA informing them of Dr. Hodel's actions.

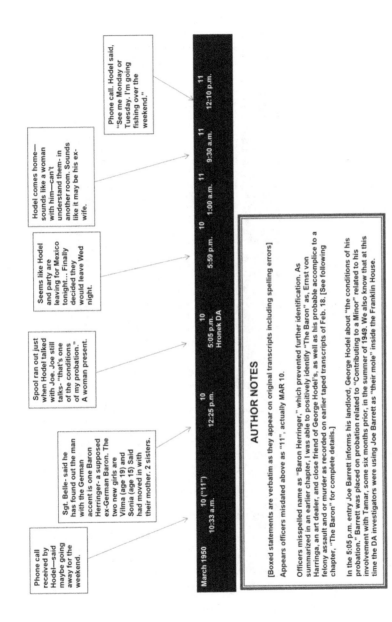

Phone call received by Hodel—said maybe going away for the weekend.

Sgt. Belle- said he has found out the man with the German accent is one Baron Herringer- a supposed ex-German Baron. The two new girls are Vilma (age 19) and Sonia (age 15) Said had moved in with their mother. 2 sisters.

Spool ran out just when Hodel talked with Joe. Joe still talks- "that's one of the conditions of my probation." A woman present.

Seems like Hodel and party are leaving for Mexico tonight... Finally decided they would leave Wed night.

Hodel comes home—sounds like a woman with him—can't understand them- in another room. Sounds like it may be his ex-wife.

Phone call. Hodel said, "See me Monday or Tuesday. I'm going fishing over the weekend."

March 1950   10:33 a.m.   10 ("11")   12:25 p.m.   10   5:05 p.m. Hronek DA   10   5:59 p.m.   10   1:00 a.m.   11   9:30 a.m.   11   12:10 p.m.   11

AUTHOR NOTES

[Boxed statements are verbatim as they appear on original transcripts including spelling errors]

Appears officers misdated above as "11", actually MAR 10.

Officers misspelled name as "Baron Herringer," which prevented further identification. As summarized in an earlier chapter, I was able to positively identify "The Baron" as, Ernst von Harringa, an art dealer, and close friend of George Hodel's, as well as his probable accomplice to a felony assault and or murder as recorded on earlier taped transcripts of Feb. 18. [See following chapter, "The Baron" for complete details.]

In the 5:05 p.m. entry Joe Barrett informs his landlord, George Hodel about "the conditions of his probation." Barrett was placed on probation related to "Contributing to a Minor" related to his involvement with Tamar, some six months prior, in the summer of 1949. We also know that at this time the DA investigators were using Joe Barrett as "their mole" inside the Franklin House.

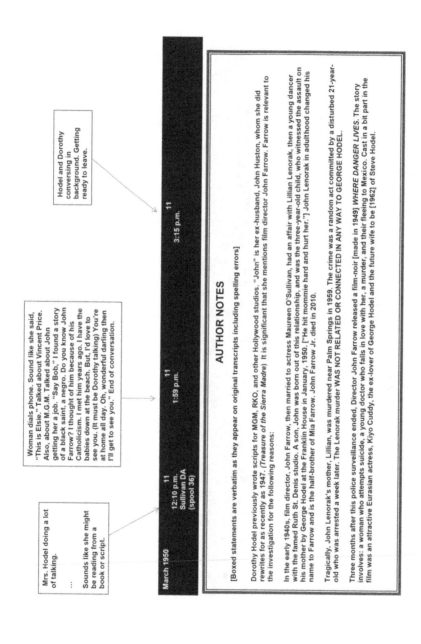

Mrs. Hodel doing a lot of talking.

...

Sounds like she might be reading from a book or script.

Woman dials phone. Sound like she said, "This is Elsie." Talked about Vincent Price. Also, about M.G.M. Talked about John getting her a job. "Say Bob," I found a story of a black saint, a negro. Do you know John Farrow? I thought of him because of his Catholicism. I met him years ago. I have the babies down at the beach. But, I'd love to see you. (It must be Dorothy talking) You're at home all day. Oh, wonderful darling then I'll get to see you." End of conversation.

Hodel and Dorothy conversing in background. Getting ready to leave.

March 1950		
11	11	11
12:10 p.m. Sullivan DA (spool 36)	1:59 p.m.	3:15 p.m.

AUTHOR NOTES

[Boxed statements are verbatim as they appear on original transcripts including spelling errors]

Dorothy Hodel previously wrote scripts for MGM, RKO, and other Hollywood studios. "John" is her ex-husband, John Huston, whom she did rewrites for as recently as 1947. (*Treasure of the Sierra Madre*) It is significant that she mentions film director John Farrow. Farrow is relevant to the investigation for the following reasons:

In the early 1940s, film director, John Farrow, then married to actress Maureen O'Sullivan, had an affair with Lillian Lenorak, then a young dancer with the famed Ruth St. Denis studio. A son, John was born out of this relationship, and was the three-year-old child, who witnessed the assault on his mother by George Hodel at the Franklin House in January, 1950. ["He hit mommie hard and hurt her."] John Lenorak in adulthood changed his name to Farrow and is the half-brother of Mia Farrow. John Farrow Jr. died in 2010.

Tragically, John Lenorak's mother, Lillian, was murdered near Palm Springs in 1959. The crime was a random act committed by a disturbed 21-year-old who was arrested a week later. The Lenorak murder WAS NOT RELATED OR CONNECTED IN ANY WAY TO GEORGE HODEL.

Three months after this police surveillance ended, Director John Farrow released a film-noir [made in 1949] *WHERE DANGER LIVES*. The story involves: a woman who attempts suicide, a young doctor who falls in love with her, a murder, and their fleeing to Mexico. Cast in a bit part in the film was an attractive Eurasian actress, Kiyo Cuddy, the ex-lover of George Hodel and the future wife to be [1962] of Steve Hodel.

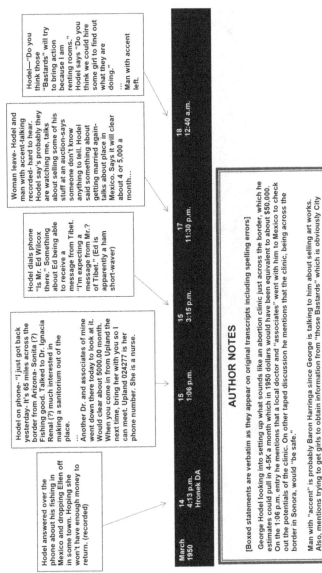

March 1950

14 — 4:13 p.m. — Hronek DA

Hodel answered over the phone about his fishing in Mexico and dropping Ellen off in some town. Hoping she won't have enough money to return. (recorded)

15 — 1:06 p.m.

Hodel on phone- "I just got back yesterday- It's 65 miles across the border from Arizona- Sonita (?) Fishing good. Talked to Dr. Ignacia Renal (?) much interested in making a sanitorium out of the place.
...
Another Dr. and associates of mine went down there today to look at it. Would clear about 5000.00 month. When you come in from Upland the next time, bring her with you so I can meet. Upland 024277 is her phone number. She is a nurse.

15 — 3:15 p.m.

Hodel dials phone "Is Mr. Ed Wilcox there." Something about Ed being able to receive a message from Tibet. "I'm expecting a message from Mr. ? of Tibet." (Ed is apparently a ham short-waver)

17 — 11:30 p.m.

Woman leave- Hodel and man with accent-talking recorded- hard to hear. Hodel say's probably they are watching me, talks about selling some of his stuff at an auction-says someone don't know anything to tell. Hodel said something about getting married again-talks about place in Mexico. Says it will clear about 4 or 5,000 a month...

18 — 12:40 a.m.

Hodel—"Do you think those "Bastards" will try to bring action because I am renting rooms." Hodel says "Do you think we could hire some girl to find out what they are doing."
...
Man with accent left.

AUTHOR NOTES

[Boxed statements are verbatim as they appear on original transcripts including spelling errors]

George Hodel looking into setting up what sounds like an abortion clinic just across the border, which he estimates could pull in 4-5K a month which in 1950 dollars would have been equivalent to about $50,000. On the 1:06 p.m. entry he mentions that a local doctor and "associates" went with him to Mexico to check out the potentials of the clinic. On other taped discussion he mentions that the clinic, being across the border in Sonora, would "be safe."

Man with "accent" is probably Baron Harringa since George is talking to him about selling art works. Also, mentions trying to get girls to obtain information from "those Bastards" which is obviously City authorities.

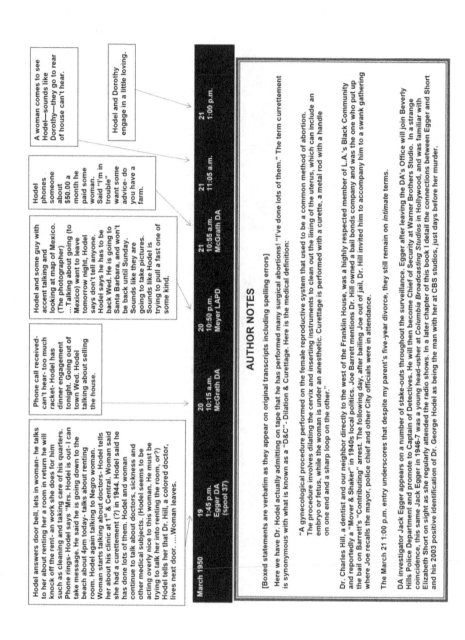

Hodel answers door bell, lets in woman- he talks to her about renting her a room in return he will knock off the rent- an work she does for him such as cleaning and taking care of his quarters. Phone rings- Hodel says "Mrs. Hodel is out- I can take message. He said he is going down to the beach about 4pm today- talks about renting room. Hodel again talking to Negro woman. Woman starts talking about doctors- Hodel tells her about his clinic at 1st & Central. Woman said she had a curettement (?) in 1944. Hodel said he has done lots of them. Hodel and woman continue to talk about doctors, sickness and other medical subjects. (Hodel seems to be acting overly nice to this woman. He must be trying to talk her into renting the room, or?) Hodel tells her that Dr. Hill, a colored doctor, lives next door. …..Woman leaves.

Phone call received- can't hear- too much racket- Hodel has dinner engagement tonight. Going out of town Wed. Hodel talking about selling the house.

Hodel and some guy with accent talking and looking at map of Mexico. (The photographer) …Talking about going (to Mexico) want to leave tomorrow night, Hodel says don't tell anyone. Hodel says he has to be back Wed. He is going to Santa Barbara, and won't be back until Sunday. Sounds like they are going to take pictures. Sounds like Hodel is trying to pull a fast one of some kind.

Hodel phones someone about $50.00 a month he paid some woman. Said "I'm in trouble" want some advice- do you have a farm.

A woman comes to see Hodel—sounds like Dorothy—they go to rear of house can't hear.

Hodel and Dorothy engage in a little loving.

March 1950						
19	20	20	21	21	21	21
1:45 p.m.	10:15 a.m.	10:50 p.m.	10:55 a.m.	11:05 a.m.	1:00 p.m.	
Egger DA	McGrath DA	Meyer LAPD	McGrath DA			
(spool 37)						

AUTHOR NOTES

[Boxed statements are verbatim as they appear on original transcripts including spelling errors]

Here we have Dr. Hodel actually admitting on tape that he has performed many surgical abortions! "I've done lots of them." The term curretement is synonymous with what is known as a "D&C"- Dilation & Curettage. Here is the medical definition:

"A gynecological procedure performed on the female reproductive system that used to be a common method of abortion. The procedure involves dilating the cervix and inserting instruments to clean out the lining of the uterus, which can include an embryo or fetus, while the woman is under an anesthetic. Curettage is performed with a curette, a metal rod with a handle on one end and a sharp loop on the other."

Dr. Charles Hill, a dentist and our neighbor directly to the west of the Franklin House, was a highly respected member of L.A.'s Black Community and reportedly a "Mover & Shaker" in 1940s local politics. Joe Barrett mentions Dr. Hill owned a bail bonds company and was the one who put up the bail on Barrett's "Contributing" arrest. The following day, after bailing Joe out of jail, Dr. Hill invited him to accompany him to a swank gathering where Joe recalls the mayor, police chief and other City officials were in attendance.

The March 21 1:00 p.m. entry underscores that despite my parent's five-year divorce, they still remain on intimate terms.

DA investigator Jack Egger appears on a number of stake-outs throughout the surveillance. Egger after leaving the DA's Office will join Beverly Hills Police Department and promote to Captain of Detectives. He will then become Chief of Security at Warner Brothers Studio. In a strange coincidence, this same Jack Egger in 1946-7 was a young head-usher at Columbia Broadcasting Studios in Hollywood, and was familiar with Elizabeth Short on sight as she regularly attended the radio shows. In a later chapter of this book I detail the connections between Egger and Short and his 2003 positive identification of Dr. George Hodel as being the man with her at CBS studios, just days before her murder.

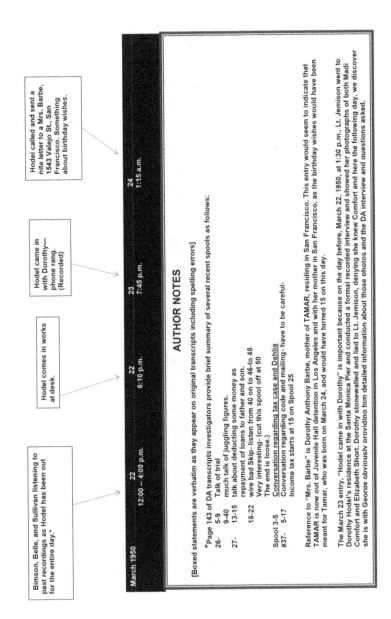

Bimson, Belle, and Sullivan listening to past recordings as Hodel has been out for the entire day."

Hodel comes in works at desk.

Hodel came in with Dorothy—phone rang. (Recorded)

Hodel called and sent a nite letter to a Mrs. Barbe, 1543 Valejo St., San Francisco. Something about birthday wishes.

March 1950

22	22	23	24
12:00 – 4:00 p.m.	6:10 p.m.	7:45 p.m.	1:15 a.m.

AUTHOR NOTES

[Boxed statements are verbatim as they appear on original transcripts including spelling errors]

*Page 143 of DA transcripts investigators provide brief summary of several recent spools as follows:

26-   Talk of trial
5-9   much talk of juggling figures.
9-40   talk about deducting some money as
27-   repayment of loans to father and son.
13-15
       wire bad Skip- listen from 40 on to 46-to 48
18-22 Very interesting- (cut this spool off at 50
       The end is loose.)
Spool 3-5   Conversation regarding tax case and Dahlia
#37-   5-17   Conversation regarding code and mailing- have to be careful-
       Income tax starts at 15 on Spool 25

Reference to "Mrs. Barbe" is Dorothy Anthony Barbe, mother of TAMAR, residing in San Francisco. This entry would seem to indicate that TAMAR is now out of Juvenile Hall detention in Los Angeles and with her mother in San Francisco, as the birthday wishes would have been meant for Tamar, who was born on March 24, and would have turned 15 on this day.

The March 23 entry, "Hodel came in with Dorothy" is important because on the day before, March 22, 1950, at 1:30 p.m., Lt. Jemison went to Dorothy Hodel's residence at the Santa Monica Pier and conducted a formal recorded interview and showed her photographs of both Madi Comfort and Elizabeth Short. Dorothy stonewalled and lied to Lt. Jemison, denying she knew Comfort and here the following day, we discover she is with George obviously providing him detailed information about those photos and the DA interview and questions asked.

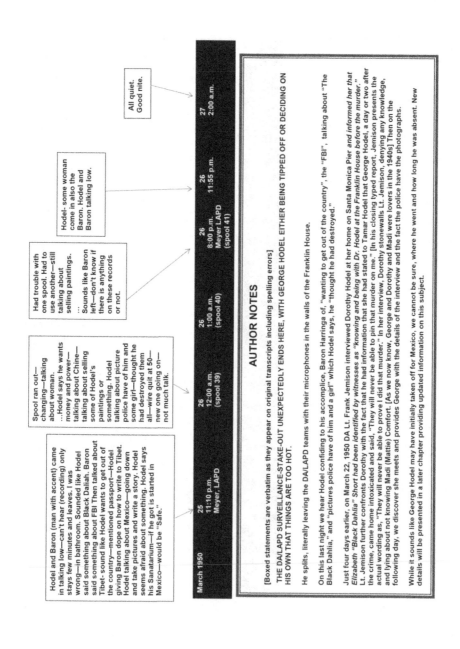

March 1950

25 11:10 p.m. Meyer, LAPD

Hodel and Baron (man with accent) came in talking low—can't hear (recording) only stays few minutes and leaves. I was wrong—in bathroom. Sounded like Hodel said something about Black Daliah. Baron said something about FBI Then talked about Tibet- sound like Hodel wants to get out of the country—mentioned passport—Hodel giving Baron dope on how to write to Tibet. Hodel talking about Mexico—going down and take pictures and write a story. Hodel seems afraid about something. Hodel says his Sanatarium—if he got is started in Mexico—would be "Safe."

26 12:00 a.m. (spool 39)

Spool ran out—changing—talking about woman. ...Hodel says he wants money and power—talking about selling some of Hodel's paintings or something. Hodel talking about picture police have of him and some girl—thought he had destroyed them all—wire quit at 50—new one going on—not much talk.

26 1:00 a.m. (spool 40)

Had trouble with one spool. Had to use another—still talking about selling paintings. ... Sounds like Baron left—don't know if there is anything on these records or not.

26 8:00 p.m. Meyer LAPD (spool 41)

26 11:55 p.m.

Hodel- some woman come in also the Baron. Hodel and Baron talking low.

27 2:00 a.m.

All quiet. Good nite.

AUTHOR NOTES

[Boxed statements are verbatim as they appear on original transcripts including spelling errors]

THE DA/LAPD SURVEILLANCE-STAKE-OUT UNEXPECTEDLY ENDS HERE, WITH GEORGE HODEL EITHER BEING TIPPED OFF OR DECIDING ON HIS OWN THAT THINGS ARE TOO HOT.

He splits, literally leaving the DA/LAPD teams with their microphones in the walls of the Franklin House.

On this last night we hear Hodel confiding to his accomplice, Baron Harringa of, "wanting to get out of the country", the "FBI", talking about "The Black Dahlia," and "pictures police have of him and a girl" which Hodel says, he "thought he had destroyed."

Just four days earlier, on March 22, 1950 DA Lt. Frank Jemison interviewed Dorothy Hodel at her home on Santa Monica Pier *and informed her that Elizabeth "Black Dahlia" Short had been identified by witnesses as "knowing and being with Dr. Hodel at the Franklin House before the murder."* Lt. Jemison further confronts Dorothy with the fact that he had information that she had stated to Tamar Hodel that George Hodel, a day or two after the crime, came home intoxicated and said, "They will never be able to pin that murder on me." [In his closing typed report, Jemison presents the actual wording as, "They will never be able to prove I did that murder." In her interview, Dorothy stonewalls Lt. Jemison, denying any knowledge, and lying about not knowing Madi (Mattie) Comfort. [As we now know, George and Dorothy and Madi were lovers in the 1940s] Then on the following day, we discover she meets and provides George with the details of the interview and the fact the police have the photographs.

While it sounds like George Hodel may have initially taken off for Mexico, we cannot be sure, where he went and how long he was absent. New details will be presented in a later chapter providing updated information on this subject.

7

"The Baron"

IN FEBRUARY 2009, almost fifty-nine years to the day after the "Baron" is first overheard by detectives speaking in conversation with my father on the DA Hodel-Black Dahlia transcripts, he has been identified.

Previously, all LAPD and DA detectives knew about the mysterious "Baron" was that he had a German accent. And according to the 1950 transcript, his possible last name was "Herringer."

Over the years, several possibilities arose, but I was never able to confirm "The Baron"'s identity. And none of the later police reports in my possession ever indicated the authorities tried to learn his identity either.

Then on February 9, 2009, I received the following e-mail from genealogist/researcher Jil Anderson, who succeeded where the rest of us had failed:

Dear Steve,

After having read all of your website, I forgot to mention that I think I may have discovered the identity of "Baron Herringer," not that it will make any difference, but thought you might be interested to know what popped up on a genealogy website. (I have frequently done "random acts of genealogical kindness" for people searching their ancestry; and likewise, people have helped me with discovering my own family tree.)

Maybe you already know about him, but your intriguing statement that no one knew who he was, made me wonder if I could locate him in the genealogical databases. Since he was German, and I know that families wanting to express nobility frequently use the name "von" in their names, I looked him up that way. The fact that he was called "Baron" makes me think that was a nickname, leading people to believe him to be of noble heritage. So I have attached some records of one "Ernst Von Harringa" who emigrated from

Germany, via Chungking China, to the United States. He applied for naturalization 5 times and wed an American in 1939. (Actually he had changed his name from Ernst Franz Meyer which was his name in Germany.) He was a writer and an art dealer and married a socialite by the name Alene.

Also in a book about Aleister Crowley, titled *The Unknown God,* there is a mention of "Baron Ernst Von Harringa."

I've attached these documents . . . the extent of my suspicion of who "Baron Herringer" was.

Best, Jil Anderson

I spent the next two months conducting a background investigation and further research on the name provided by Jil, and my findings proved her "suspicions" to be correct.

Baron Ernst von Harringa, aka Ernst Meyer, was in fact the same man tape-recorded by law-enforcement and overheard in multiple conversations with Dr. George Hodel at the Franklin house in February and March 1950.

WHO WAS "BARON" ERNST VON HARRINGA?—A TIMELINE

Here is what my follow-up research to Jil Anderson's identification has produced so far:

Born Ernst Franz Meyer in Netteln, Germany on March 4, 1899.

Fought as a soldier in WWI, during the Second Reich (Weimar Republic 1919-1933)

Worked as a "banker" in Chungking, China

Meyer sailed from Shanghai, China to San Francisco on the vessel *Taiyo Maru* and entered the US on August 21, 1925

On November 4, 1931, Von Harringa was arrested by LAPD for "attempted extortion." The victim was Dr. H. Clifford Loos and his former wife, Mrs. Anita Johnson. The charges alleged that "Von Harringa" demanded $5,000 from Dr. Loos and Mrs. Johnson under threats of defaming their character in published articles." Baron Harringa was found guilty of the charges, but then, the case was later overturned on appeal. *[Dr. Clifford Loos was the older brother to then popular Hollywood author/screenwriter Anita Loos. Dr. Loos with his partner, Dr. Donald E. Ross, founded the Ross-Loos Medical Group in Los Angeles in 1929.]*

Los Angeles Times, NOVEMBER 4, 1931

Asserted Threats Lead to Complaint

CHARGE IN EXTORTION CASE FILED

German Accused of Plot to Obtain $5000 From Physician and Ex-Wife

Ernst Von Harringa, 32 years of age, German, yesterday was charged with attempting to extort sums from Dr. H. Clifford Loos and his former wife, Mrs. Anita Johnson, in a complaint issued by Thomas P. Menzies, deputy District Attorney, in charge of the complaint department.

The defendant was arrested last Friday in Mrs. Johnson's home at 1590 Laurel avenue by Detective Lieutenants Taylor and Loudis. The officers charge that Von Harringa demanded $5000 from Dr. Loos and Mrs. Johnson under threats of defaming their character in published articles. It also charged that the defendant made threats of attacking the character of Mrs. Johnson's young daughter.

Dr. Loos told Dep. Dist.-Atty. Menzies that he first met Van Harringa on a fishing trip in Owens Valley three years ago. Later, he said, he introduced the man to his wife. Recently, the physician said, he had a disagreement with the man and told him not to call at his home again. Shortly thereafter came the telephone calls and threats, according to Dr. Loos.

Both Dr. Loos and Mrs. Johnson declare they knew of nothing Von Harringa could use against them to cause them embarrassment. Although separated for more than a year, both the complaining witnesses still appear to be the best of friends, posing for photographs together.

Dr. Loos has offices at 1561 South Grand avenue.

Prisoner and Accusers

Above—Dr. H. Clifford Loos and Mrs. Anita M. Johnson. Below—Ernst Von Harringa.

Ernst von Harringa, 1931 Extortion Arrest

On December 11, 1932, "The Baron" wrote a lengthy article for the *Los Angeles Times,* entitled, "I FOUGHT AMERICANS—But, they healed my hate." "My first contact with them was on the battlefields," his introduction began, "and they were such good sports I decided to become an American citizen myself—which I've just done." *[His entire article was a blatant attempt to help him gain citizenship, which was denied.]*

On April 2, 1933, "The Baron" wrote a second lengthy article which was also published in the *Los Angeles Times* entitled, "I WAS A BANKER IN CHINA." He wrote, "Far in the interior, near the Tibetan border, I ran into strange customs—forty-course banquets, ninety kinds of currency, bandits who robbed one politely... and business methods, which will make you smile."

Baron von Harringa Los Angeles Times articles 1932-1933

He legally changed his name to "Ernst Von Harringa" and on a 1933 "Declaration of Intention" the document lists his physical description as: Male, White, age 34, 5'10", 175, blonde hair, blue eyes, occupation: "Writer"—Residence, 947 Parkview St., Los Angeles, California. Marital Status: Single.

In 1935, Los Angeles artist Robert McIntosh created a portrait of Ernst Von Harringa entitled, "The German Art Dealer." *[At the time I was conducting my background investigation on Baron Harringa, the oil painting was on display at the Trigg Ison Art Gallery in West Hollywood with an asking price of $30,000].*

In 1937, Baron von Harringa opened his art gallery in the posh Oviatt Building and received a write-up and opening announcement in the *Los Angeles Times* from then art critic Arthur Millier, who had this to say about Baron Harringa's gallery:

NEW GALLERY
Los Angeles Times, May 9, 1939

Good clothes and good pictures consort well together. So we have the Oviatt Galleries, just opened by Ernst v. Harringa in the well-known clothier's establishment downtown.

Some excellent pictures by older masters are in this first showing, among them two exceptionally fine "Scenes Galeantes" by Pater of eighteenth century France, a very pure "Madonna," attributed to Luis de Morales, the great sixteenth century Spanish religious painter; a fine anonymous Flemish "Bearing of the Cross," done about 1820; Joseph Highmore's, "Portrait of a Gentleman," better than many an alleged Gainsborough; an exquisite small circular river scene by Herman Saftleven, pupil of Van Goyen, a portrait by Rembrandt's pupil, Levecque, and canvases by Gillis van Tilborch, Charles Le Beran, Berne-Bellecour, Charles Hoguet and an anonymous Spanish painter of "St. Francis." The choice of works shown inspires confidence in the future of this enterprise.

The Oviatt Building, 617 South Olive Street, is still standing and is a striking Art Deco. Built in 1928, it remains one of L.A.'s finest architectural structures. The clothier with its clock-tower restaurant was popular with Hollywood's rich and famous. The building and Baron Harringa's art gallery was less than one block south of the Biltmore Hotel and just three blocks from Dr. George Hill Hodel's then private medical practice at Seventh and Flower Street.

Here is how the Art Deco Society described the Oviatt Building for a 2008 lecture and film screening:

> Through lecture and film screening, here is the untold story of downtown Los Angeles' first Art Deco jewel: the 1928 Oviatt Building and its opulent penthouse. Virtually a second home to Clark Gable, Errol Flynn and other male stars of Hollywood's Golden Age; the Oviatt Building housed L.A.'s finest haberdashery and catered to filmdom's titans. For eight decades, its glamorous and controversial history has been shrouded in mystery and clouded by misinformation...until now. Full of long-lost archival images and long-forgotten events, this myth-busting documentary spans more than a century and interviews the men and women who shaped the Oviatt Building's turbulent history.

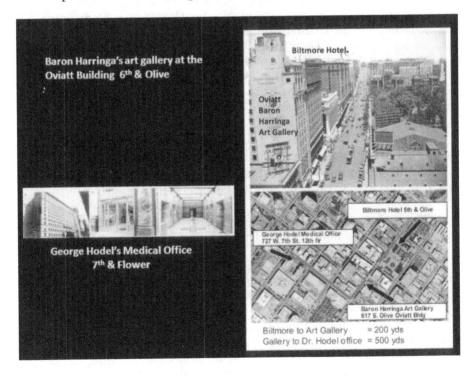

In his 1939 petition for naturalization, Von Harringa provided additional information: a residence address listed as 946 Arapahoe Street Los Angeles and occupation as "Art Dealer."

He claimed he was married to Alene von Harringa on January 14, 1939, in Calabasas, California, declaring his wife to be a US citizen with a birth date of May 12, 1912. He listed her residence as, "3747½ W. 27th St., Los Angeles." Additional documents indicated Harringa had previously requested, but was denied, citizenship in 1931.

In November 1952, Harringa reportedly left the US "for a job building dams in India."

BARON HARRINGA AND W.T. SMITH—CHURCH OF THELEMA CONNECTIONS

In my further search for information on Baron Harringa, I found very little personal information but did find some important insights in the book mentioned by Jil Anderson in her email, *The Unknown God: W.T. Smith and the Thelemites (Teitan Press, November 2003)* written by Martin P. Starr.

An excerpt from the publisher's description of the book reads:

The first documentary study of Aleister Crowley's contemporary followers in North America, told through the life of their de facto leader, Wilfred Talbot Smith (1885-1957). ...To promulgate the Crowleyan teachings, in 1934 Smith incorporated his own "Church of Thelema"—known to Los Angeles newspaper readers as the "Purple Cult." The following year he initiated OTO activity in Los Angeles which attracted its own cast of occult characters.

It turns out that Wilfred Talbot Smith and Baron von Harringa, according to author/researcher Martin Starr, were close friends in Los Angeles. In his book, Starr included some brief but quite remarkable insights into Ernst von Harringa and his personality:

The Unknown God, page 322-323:
In the hiatus, Smith had befriended Baron Ernst von Harringa (b.1899), a naturalized German art dealer and importer who worked as the director of the Oviatt Galleries in Los Angeles. Von Harringa had studied in Count Hermann Keyserling's "School of Wisdom" which had been founded in Darmstadt, Germany in 1920; he also claimed the passing acquaintance of Theodor Reuss. However, he knew nothing of Crowley's work prior to his friendship with Smith. The Baron was a lover of Chinese art and bestowed many prize objects of virtu on Smith and Helen. Calling on his training as a cabinetmaker, he had Smith construct replicas of Asian furniture for sale in his gallery. Helen cheerfully waited on

her two "big boys" as they spent long hours drinking tea and sharing their ideas. Given von Harringa's level of understanding, Smith considered him the equivalent of an Exempt Adept; Jane, too, was impressed by his person, thinking him a second Crowley, but changed her mind after she read several analyses of the Baron's horoscope, including one prepared by Phyllis Seckler. Von Harringa was an extreme individualist and he felt that any effort for humanity was a waste, in view of the catastrophe that he believed was just around the corner. ...

Smith felt himself loved and understood by von Harringa, who left California in November 1952 for a job building dams in India and never saw his friend alive again. Helen and Smith kept up a regular correspondence with the Baron, and frequently lamented his absence from their lives. To his intellectual soulmate Smith revealed his thoughts on politics, gender roles and the future of humanity, sometimes all rolled into the same paragraph:

"We are headed for a radical social change; which among other things, will ultimate in the ladies fulfilling the function nature (not man) adapted them to better grace, and less intrusion into spheres of activity they are so unsuited to occupy. Men will find them at hand when they are needed and in the interim enjoy tranquility and peace, or the company of an intellectual, wise, and understanding companion." (Smith to Ernst von Harringa, June 28, 1954, WTS Papers.)

WHAT WAS THE GEORGE HODEL—ERNST VON HARRINGA CONNECTION?

By identifying "The Baron," we might have created as many questions as we have found answers, which is frequently the case.

Did George Hodel and Ernst von Harringa's friendship in L.A. trace back to the Baron's arrival in the mid-Twenties? Probably.

As a high-profile art dealer, did Ernst Harringa know and possibly even represent George Hodel's close friend, artist Fred Sexton? Very likely. At the very least, they must have known each other—perhaps much more?

Was Baron Harringa associated with many of the L.A. artists listed in Mark Nelson and Sarah Hudson Bayliss's book, *Exquisite Corpse: Surrealism and The Black Dahlia Murder* with its extensive listings and map: *Los Angeles 1935-1950, A Web of Connections?*

We have established that Baron Harringa and George Hodel's L.A. offices were within three blocks of each other and, in their chosen professions as art dealer and physician, both socialized with the rich and famous, including city politicians and men in power.

It is obvious that the two men were kindred spirits. Both loved art and enjoyed intellectually stimulating conversation. Both shared a burning desire to travel and had been to many of the same locals in China, including Chungking and Shanghai. Both were extremely eccentric and from what we know from the bugging tapes, were politically connected and at the very least were involved in payoffs to law enforcement as well as being accomplices together in the assault or possible murder of a female victim at the Franklin house. "We're just a couple of smart boys. Don't confess ever."

What other crimes had the two men committed? It is likely we will never know. But now, thanks to Jil Anderson's efforts, we know "The Baron"'s identity and have gained some fairly good insights into his background.

DA LT. JEMISON'S RESPONSE

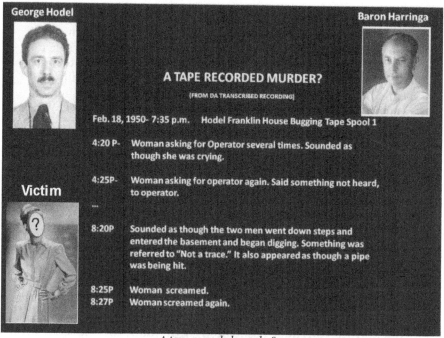

A tape recorded murder?

Within days of recording the February 18, 1950, conversation between George Hodel and "The Baron," Lt. Jemison ordered his men into action.

While we don't know the full extent of what was done, I found three separate investigative documents in the DA file that relate directly to the February 18 Hodel-Harringa conversations. And that confirmed that detectives definitely suspected a murder might well have occurred.

The first document prepared by DA investigator James McGrath and submitted to his direct supervisor, showed that detectives immediately tried to find potential witnesses who could substantiate any signs of digging or makeshift graves in the Franklin house basement.

The report says that a day or two after the February 18 "assault," George Hodel called a plumber to the home to unclog a drain. McGrath located the plumber—Mr. Stokes, an employee of Sonntag Co. 5156 Hollywood Boulevard—and asked whether he had seen evidence of fresh digging or anything unusual in the basement.

The plumber responded that he had been in the basement, unclogged the drain, but really hadn't paid much attention to anything but his work. While McGrath wrote both of these reports in late March 1950, the investigations obviously occurred in the days following the suspected "foul play." McGrath's surveillance log is dated February 23.

[Note: For those thinking "forensics" in 2002, prior to the publication of BDA, during major renovations of the Franklin house, much of the basement area was cemented over and a home office was constructed. It remains highly doubtful that any trace evidence from sixty years past would still be accessible.]

Detective McGrath's "Elizabeth Short Murder Report" is reproduced on the following pages and is a scan of the original.

The second DA document confirms that in addition to the ongoing electronic bugging of the Franklin house, just four days after the Hodel/Harringa admissions, Lt. Jemison ordered that a physical surveillance be placed on Dr. George Hodel. Detectives James McGrath and Walter Morgan took up the surveillance. On the following pages is their original two-page typed report about what they observed of George and Dorothy Hodel on February 23, 1950.

30-1266   James F. McGrath   March 24, 1950

          Elizabeth Short   Murder

          Unknown

          I contacted the H. A. Sonntag Company, 5156 Hollywood Blvd., a
plumbing organization, and spoke to Mr. Francis W. Stokes, who is the
manager of the firm. This person was questioned as to whether or not
he was one of the parties who did plumbing work last week for Dr. George
Hodel, 5121 Franklin Avenue, or if he was familiar with the work done.
He stated that he was one of the men who entered the basement and
opened up a clogged drain. Upon further questioning, he stated that
he did not notice any fresh diggings in the basement, or anything of
an unusual nature, however, he did assert that at the time he was not
looking for any fresh earth. Investigation has revealed that over the
last two years this plumbing firm has done quite a bit of work for
this subject. Records were checked and it was found that numerous
calls were made to the suspect's residence in the past. Either Dr.
Hodel or his wife, Dorothy, had signed the work slips but for the
following exceptions: on February 4, 1947, a person by the name of
L. S. Burgeon signed the work slip; on April 25, 1947, one Floyd C.
Hagan signed the work slip; March 25, 1948, it was signed by Mrs.
E. M. Walker; on April 20, 1948, a Katherine Dawn signed the slip,
and on May 18, 1948, a Connie Coahram, or Cochram, signed the work
order. No further information was obtained from this informant.
He was requested by the undersigned not to discuss this visit with
him, and the purpose of it, with the suspect, Dr. Hodel.

                    _____
                         James F. McGrath

DA investigator James McGrath follow-up report March 24, 1950

30-1268   REPORT BY James F. McGrath   DATE March 27,1950

        Elizabeth Short   Murder

        Unknown

    Information regarding Dr. George Hodel, 5121 Franklin Avenue,
Hollywood, California.

    February 23, 1950, in company with investigator Walter Morgan of
this office, I placed the subject under surveillance. The following
is a route of his actions of this date:

    12:00 noon   I took position of surveillance in vicinity
                   of house; no further action until 3:05 P.M.
    3:05 P.M.   A Packard car, bearing license number 3N 2948,
                   arrived at the house. This car was driven by
                   a man whose description is as follows: male
                   Caucasian, 42 to 45 years of age, 5'7", 160 lbs.,
                   stocky build, wearing a dark blue hat, gray
                   shirt, dark blue pants. These license plates
                   belong to a 1936 Packard coupe registered to
                   W. G. Holland, 1221½ West 1st Street, Los
                   Angeles; legal owner, John F. Casey, mother's
                   address, 1036 South Figueroa Street, Los
                   Angeles.
    3:15 P.M.   Subject came out of his residence, and ac-
                   companied by this man, drove this car to the
                   vicinity of Western and Franklin, where they
                   parked the car and both seemed to enter into
                   a general discussion about the car, walking
                   around it and looking it over as if the sub-
                   ject was contemplating buying it. They then
                   left and drove south on Western, where they
                   parked between 6th Street and Wilshire Blvd.
                   on the west side of Western. They remained
                   in the car approximately 15 minutes talking.

    3:55 P.M.   They left this location and drove to the corner
                   of 3rd and Union, where subject let the other
                   man out. This other man walked to the Taxi
                   Driver's Social Club, located at 3rd and Union.
    4:07 P.M.   Subject drove alone to Hollywood and Sycamore
                   Streets, arriving at 4:30 P.M. Sitting on
                   a bench at this corner was subject's ex-wife,

*DA Investigators McGrath & Morgan Physical Surveillance Report
of Dr. George Hode, 3.27.1950*

Dorothy Hodel. She got in the car, and they parked same on Sycamore Street just north of Hollywood Blvd., where both of them got out of the car, proceeded to the rear of the house, and looked at an old Stutz automobile. They then both entered the car and drove to Wilshire and La Cienega Blvd. in Beverly Hills, where subject entered the Orient Art Galleries.

4:55 P.M.   Subject left the art galleries, entered car and drove to the Frank Perl's Art Galleries, arriving at 5:20 P.M. These art galleries are located on Camden Drive north of Wilshire in Beverly Hills. Subject and his wife remained in this art gallery until approximately 5:35 P.M., when they both left. With subject driving, they proceeded in a westerly direction on Wilshire Blvd. Agents then dropped surveillance, inasmuch as subject was proceeding to the vicinity of his ex-wife's residence in Santa Monica, and because of the fact that this surveillance was instituted because of information received that subject was contemplating getting $1,000.00 on this date, which we now have reason to believe was from the sale of paintings at these art galleries.

James F. McGrath

*Author prepared diagram showing route and stops
of February 23, 1950 surveillance by Investigators McGrath & Morgan*

1. 5121 Franklin Avenue, George Hodel's Franklin house residence
2. Western and Franklin Avenue
3. Western and Sixth Street
4. Third Street and Union
5. Hollywood Boulevard and Sycamore Avenue
6. Wilshire and La Cienega Boulevard
7. Wilshire and Camden Drive
8. Wilshire and Beverly Glen [terminated vehicle surveillance at 5:40 p.m.]

The third Hodel-Harringa document is written in Lt. Jemison's own hand. They are his personal notes and list his "To Do's" relating to George Hodel.

Jemison's notes are dated March 2, 1950, and relate to the need to interview various friends and acquaintances of George Hodel.

No. 4 on that list is clearly the result of the Hodel-Harringa conversations and confessions.

Here we see that Lt. Jemison, now obviously convinced that George Hodel killed his personal secretary, Ruth Spaulding, has decided to reopen the original Spaulding death investigation and re-interview all the witnesses.

Lt. Jemison's note to himself reads:

March 2, 1950 handwritten notes of DA Lt. Frank Jemison
"3/2/50 Interview-... 4. –all witnesses In re: Ruth's death—Secretary to Hodel."

A PERSONAL MEETING WITH BARON VON HARRINGA

In mid-January 2010, I personally met and shook hands with Baron von Harringa.

Baron von Harringa (his given name) is the grandson of Ernst von Harringa. Baron is a handsome young eighteen-year-old. He too was looking for answers.

We met at one of my favorite breakfast spots, Art's Deli in Studio City. Both of us were there with the same hope—Baron wanting to learn more about his mysterious grandfather and I wanting to discover additional background on my father's old friend, confidant, and possible accomplice to murder.

Our talk lasted nearly two hours, but provided little new, "hard" information for either of us. Here is what I learned from the grandson:

1) Von Harringa family rumors say his grandfather, Ernst von Harringa, aka Ernst Meyer, might have been related to nobility in Germany, but there's nothing to support the contention and no actual names.

2) Ernst von Harringa apparently returned to the US (possibly from India) in the mid-1950s and supposedly died in Los Angeles circa 1960. I have yet to find a death certificate or obituary.

3) The grandson met his grandmother, Alene Valla Von Harringa, several times before she died in 2001 and he had heard that her family (Valla) had owned large land parcels in Orange County in the early days, possibly around the turn of the century.

4) Baron gave me the following photograph of his grandfather, believed taken sometime in the 1940s or early '50s.

Baron Ernst von Harringa circa 1949
[Courtesy of grandson, Baron von Harringa]

8
The Huston Letters

"Back again at George's after two weeks away. ... It is acutely dangerous for the children to be here. There is a growing threat of no control and physical violence..." — Excerpt from Letter No. 6 from Dorothy to John, mailed from Franklin house, 1950

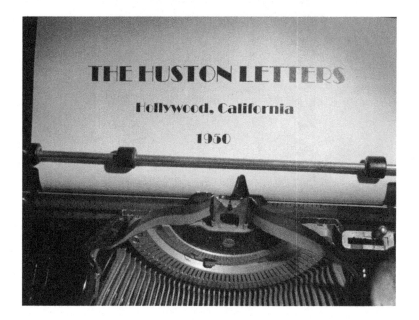

THE FOLLOWING HIGHLY PERSONAL LETTERS were written by my mother, Dorothy Huston Hodel, to her ex-husband, film director John Huston.

The letters span nearly a decade, from 1948 through 1957.

All are highly personal and reflect the tremendous stresses, both psychological and financial, that our mother was under before and after our father's arrest for incest.

The letters shine new light into a very dark period of Dorothy's life where she was trying to be the family's sole breadwinner while raising three young boys aged 6, 7, and 9.

I am going to let my mother's own words, written in confidence to John, recreate what can only be described as her personal horrors. Her letters capture the very real fear and terror she was experiencing when her ex-husband, our father, George Hodel, was about to harm both her and us.

The first letter to John [April 1948] was written a little over a year after the Black Dahlia murder. The tension builds up to and through our father's 1949 LAPD arrest for child molestation and incest where, according to Mother, he was becoming increasingly unhinged and dangerous. The peak of her personal terror came in the spring and summer of 1950, just after the DA ended his surveillance of the Franklin house as George Hodel was preparing to leave the United States.

My discovery of these letters was pure happenstance. I came across them while browsing through the John Huston Files at the Academy of Motion Pictures Arts and Sciences, Margaret Herrick Library in Beverly Hills, California. There, I found an index labeled, "Dorothy Huston." It contained these original letters written by my mother to John.

LETTER NO. 1

2313 Bushrod Lane
Los Angeles 24
April 7, 1948.

Dear John,

This letter really should begin: "Stranger, you ask me why I am so sad..." Its precipitating cause is a check I didn't get. I wrote a radio script dealing with a romantic and lovely <u>Russian</u> princess, which was accepted with a perfunctory "Charming" and has remained in the producer's archives since November. When I timidly asked for a check, he recoiled in horror. In view of the Russian Situation and his job, the script can't be produced. <u>No</u> Russian, even one long dead, can be permitted on the air in a glamorous light. And so, so close is the margin on which the babes and I exist, no food, no rent paid, George hasn't given us any alimony for months, and in view of his mental difficulties, I don't want to be unpleasant. I'm really having a tough time, since both the boys and earning a living are a full time job. There aren't enough hours. So many things take time: like listening to a neighbor elucidate Technocracy, so he'll be won over and let Mike ride his pony. Something's always cropping up! We're very happy, and life is good; difficult, but good.

I've got eight radio scripts assigned, but I can't get them out fast enough, or get paid for them fast enough to meet this emergency. Listen...

Two boys in bed with fever and virus x.
Third slightly lacerated from aforementioned pony.
Mother out of hospital after major operation, with us,
Needing medicine and nursing.
No rent paid.
No electric bill paid.
No grocery bill paid.
No bills paid.
No bank balance.
I'll be forty two next week

STRANGER, YOU ASK ME WHY I AM SO SAD.
If you could loan me, and I mean loan, about five hundred dollars (or even five!) I could repay it within six months. This epidemic can't last forever. I finished a script by working all night last night, rushed it by messenger to the producer today, only to discover I can't get paid for it for at least three weeks. Gandhi could have weathered it, but not the boys! I did a washing this morning, cooked, cleaned, took three temperatures, all too high, placed a cool hand of three fevered brows in rapid succession, and ironed until eleven tonight. If this letter sounds flippant or gay, it's only because I'm frightened. I've done everything I could, and it isn't enough
If you're able to help, please do.

Dorothy

Author Notes: *Based on the return address, this letter indicates we are living in a rental several miles north of Sunset Boulevard in Beverly Glen Canyon. The home was called, "Robber's Roost." Immediately behind the house, there were some high caves set into the mountain. According to legend, these caves were used as a hideout for banditos at the turn of the century. Literally in our own backyard, we three brothers would climb up and into them to hangout and "make our plans."*

George and Dorothy were separated in 1944 and formally divorced in 1945.

In this April 1948 letter, Mother referred to our father's "mental difficulties" a full eighteen months before his October 1949 arrest for incest and child molestation, which informs us that they were pre-existing and ongoing.

"Mother" was Dorothy Harvey, our maternal grandmother who, in 1948, would have been in her late sixties.

LETTER NO. 2

5121 Franklin Ave
Los Angeles 27
October 24, 1949

Dear John,

I'm sending you this because I think it is the kind of story you would like. Please let me know how you like it. It is a pattern that particularly fascinates me: one that Bierce used first, and later Conrad Aiken used in a beautiful tale called "Mr. Arcularis." In your opinion is it too slight for a motion picture?

I'm working at General Service Studios with Rowland Brown. Call me there if you can – GR 3111- or at home OL 3476.

Dorothy

Author Notes: While there is no mention of George Hodel in this letter, he had been arrested for incest/child molestation on October 6, just eighteen days before it was written.

"Bierce" is Ambrose "Bitter" Bierce, one of Mother's longstanding HEROES. [She wrote a screen or radio play about the journalist's mysterious disappearance called, "Occurrence at an Unknown Bridge."]

As mentioned previously, Mother was having an ongoing affair with film director Rowland Brown. And here we learn that Rowland had hired her to work/write at his office.

LETTER NO. 3

410 Santa Monica Pier
Santa Monica, Calif.
February 2, 1950

Dear John:

Thank you very much for the needed $$$$. They averted famine and the sheriff. I feel a certain hesitancy about calling you at home and there are two matters to ask you about.

I saw George's attorney yesterday. He thinks it will be about six months before the house and antiques can be sold and a trust fund set up. George has sent out about a hundred letters to find work in outlying parts of the world. My problem is to keep the children alive for the next few months. As I told you I have various scripts out and something may happen at any time. It's the uncertainty!

Could you help to keep the children going until affairs straighten out? $200 a month will do it. I have no claim on your generosity and this is a difficult letter to write. I have lived so close to terror and disaster; and it is impossible to conceal this entirely from the children.

I went to an employment agency down here and got some work—night work at a hotel for a couple of nights. But I can't do that and take care of the children too. The certainty of a sum of money on the first of the month would make it possible to plan and budget and work out a way of life. I'm sure I can repay it soon. But if you feel hesitancy about doing it, and cannot for any reason, please say no.

The second thing whether or not Horizon Pictures is interested in acquiring outside money for making pictures. There are Philippino [sic] business interests (friends of George) who want to put money ($250,000 up to a million) in a motion picture. They don't want any voice in the making of it; they would like a part to be done in the Philippines.

They want an Academy award director; they care less about name actors. John Ford was going to do it, but his recent removal to Republic gives him no time for a year to do anything outside, and they want to act sooner. If this interests you, why don't you call George at Normandy 2-7464.

They've given him full power to act; and he doesn't know anything about pictures. It might be a chance to do something really good– Hardy's Return of the Native? If it's not the sort of thing you care about, maybe you could suggest someone?

Please let me hear from you. I've started work on the cowboy Hamlet. Do you honestly think it might get a production?

Dorothy

Author Notes: *This was written on February 2, 1950, from the apartment on Santa Monica Pier. Two weeks later, the DA/LAPD secretly installed the microphones at the Franklin house and began* *recording George Hodel's conversations. Lt. Jemison will interview Dorothy at this address in March.*

The Filipino "money connections" could well be Hortensia Laguda who, in two years, would become George's wife. Hortensia met my father after responding to a personal advertisement he had placed in the Saturday Review Of Literature *magazine requesting to correspond with "an Oriental woman of sensitive tastes." In 1949, Hortensia, who was taking some classes in New York, responded to the ad and followed up with a visit to George at the Franklin house where she met George, Dorothy, and Tamar, and attended several social parties.*

LETTER NO. 4

410 Santa Monica Pier
Santa Monica, Calif
June 13, 1950

Dear John,

I have the impression that you are very busy and it is difficult for you to get away. It might be a short cut to put down a plan:

1. I could start working on a treatment of THE MYSTERIOUS STRANGER.

2. I could submit one-page suggestions for stories. I read enormously and have run across a great deal of material: To do SERENA BLANDISH as a musical. MGM owns the rights. I think it would be better than GENTLEMEN PREFER BLONDES.

To do a picture like QUARTET: one whose subject matter concerns children. The beautiful mood story of Conrad Aiken's SILENT SNOW...FALLING SNOW together with MY OLD MAN of Hemingway's, and perhaps one other. The Jose Allonada story.

3. I could finish a novel I have 100 page start on. It isn't one you have seen. It is experimental and candor compels me to admit it has more in common with New Directions than with Bessie Smith. Still if you would care to gamble on the royalties....

I'm afraid you were right about George...several jobs were offered and then withdrawn when they found out about the recent trial. He will work out something, but right now I feel as though we were walking a tightrope. Kelvin is ill (aftermath of mumps, he almost had encephalitis) and I don't even have carfare to take him to the doctor's. I literally don't know where the children's next meal is coming from. It takes $250 to cover the monthly necessities. I don't know if you can afford to gamble that much on my accomplishing anything; I imagine your responsibilities are heavy. Please let me know what you want me to do, what would be most useful for your purposes. It is a situation that calls for the Marines!

Why don't you send Pedro down to stay with us for a week or two when school is out?

Dorothy

LETTER NO. 5—THE TELEGRAM

JOHN HUSTON – MGM AUG 4, 1950 9:49 A.M.
YOUR HUNCH ABOUT GEORGE TRUE CAN YOU HELP CHILDREN AND ME GET OUT OF HIS HOUSE TODAY IF POSSIBLE OLYMPIA 3476
DOROTHY

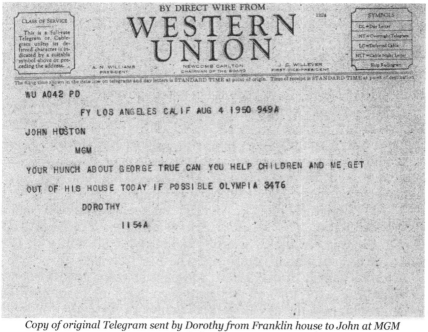

Copy of original Telegram sent by Dorothy from Franklin house to John at MGM on August 4, 1950

Author Notes: *It doesn't get any more ominous than this. We can only guess at John's "hunch about George." Had he heard that George was the Black Dahlia killer? Another murder? Whatever it was, it is clear that Mother was confirming that John was correct and believed that she, and we, her three sons, were in imminent danger and must immediately flee the house for our safety. [More* *information on what John might have known is presented at the end of this chapter.]*

LETTER NO. 6

5121 Franklin Ave
Los Angeles 27
August 23, 1950

Dear John:

Back at George's again, after two weeks away – nothing to eat, nowhere to go. It is acutely dangerous for the children to be here. There is danger from two sources: George (I won't go into that one! – except to say there is a growing threat of no-control and physical violence;) the second source is from neighborhood hostility towards everyone connected with George's house, which centers on the children because they are the only ones who have contact with the neighbors. I have had to keep them entirely indoors after one woman heaped the most unspeakable abuse on them because they were their father's children! The boys were completely bewildered, because they know nothing of the trial at all. They shouldn't know anything about a world like that.

The children and I went to Palm Springs Sunday. (Steve was looking for a horned toad and a mirage. I was looking for a house, in which to live a less frenzied future – (possibly a mirage, too!) I found one, built in the modern charming desert fashion – 4 bedrms, 2 baths, and large grounds for $85 a month, furnished....by the year. Palm Springs is probably as safe a place to be as any if people start exploding bombs—(Duncan has just been inducted, by the way) and anyhow I love the desert, and it's a fine place for the children...(but there were no horned toads)!...bombs or no bombs, it gives them room to expand and a horizon to see. The schools there are excellent.

I would have to take it right away – this weekend, because rents there start soaring, and they won't hold it longer. They could probably get 200 for it during the season. It would require 170 dollars for 2 mos rent on the year's lease, and something for utility deposits. George will give me 100 on Sept 5, and 200 every month hereafter, he says. He is working at Ross-Loos clinic. If you could (as Mark suggested) put me on your payroll for 100 a month starting Oct (and I will work on Mysterious Stranger) –I think I can just make it.

I have 6 prospects of jobs – mostly television; they can be worked out there with occasional commuting... the Greyhound bus is a block from the house.

So all our future depends on you, and if you can send enough now to get in the house – 200 for that and about 50 more for groceries and moving. And a hundred a month after, which I will do my best to earn.

Darling, I know you have immense responsibilities. I hate piling mine on top of you. But there is no one else I can go to; and the danger to the children is very real. I'll keep my fingers crossed and wait to hear from you.

Dorothy
Olympia 3476

Author's Notes: *A couple of new points are contained in Mother's letter of August 23.*

The first is that George Hodel is back in town *and has taken a temporary job with Ross-Loos clinic. Perhaps his presence was necessary for the sale of the Franklin House. We know that he will be gone in six to eight weeks and relocate to the Territory of Hawaii, where he has accepted a professorship at the University of Hawaii and will begin teaching a course in Abnormal Child Psychology, as well as counseling the criminally insane in the prisons.*

Secondly, are the comments regarding the neighbors coming down hard on us three boys for father's actions? While I have no memory of this, I do recall that my brother Kelvin and I, at about this time, lit an empty cardboard egg carton on fire and threw it into the next door neighbor's garage. The garage caught fire, requiring the fire department to put it out. There was minimal damage. In later years, when I asked Mother why we did that, she responded that we claimed, "We simply wanted to see the fire trucks roll," which made very little sense. Based on what was revealed in these letters, I have to believe our motive was to get even with our neighbors for "the bad things they said about our father." [I guess I can clear my conscience on this now, since there is only a three-year statute of limitations for committing arson.]

John must have "come through again with the money" because mother rented the house and we moved to Palm Springs that fall. [Actually, Rancho Mirage, where we lived very close to Rowland Brown, his wife, and their son Steven.]

Duncan is my older half-brother, born to Emilia and George Hodel in 1928.

Again, Mother referred clearly to the threat of physical danger to her and to us from Father. As we know from earlier chapters, Mother suffered physical violence from George. I suspect quite a lot.

While the remaining series of letters have no direct bearing on my investigation, I am going to include them here due to their historical value and interest to film buffs, historians, and the general reading public. I must confess a second motive, which is to put on display the absolute elegance of my mother's intellect and her remarkable ability to communicate.

LETTER NO. 7

754 Locust St.
Pasadena, California
June 10, 1954

Dear John,

I have a wonderful – although startling suggestion to make. Let's do Ulysses. You've told me you think I have talent, and you'd like me to write something, and I think you mean it sincerely. Who except you and I could do such a picture? I am sure we are the only two people in the world who have ever read it through twice <u>aloud</u>. If it came off it would be the greatest picture ever made. The freshness and vitality of the book and of the language, the panorama of Dublin from dawn through the night; the changes of style in story-telling from girly-girly Gertie on the beach to the drunken dreamlike sequence of the whores—there has never been a picture like it. Ulysses remains for me after countless readings the most exciting and living book ever written.

Please let me try! I should like to begin right away. I am still working in the real estate office, because I can't find a job that pays more. Of course it would be ideal if you could keep me on salary while I wrote the picture. But if that isn't feasible I could work on it nights. George isn't sending me anything, so all I have is my salary, and I do loath the work. I am revoltingly good at it. Please let me know right away!

The boys are getting very grown-up. They are really wonderful. I am trying to model them on you, because you remain the man in the whole world I most admire, probably because you caught me young and made so deep an impression upon my malleable nature! I came upon a photograph of you as a child—do you remember that very beautiful one your mother wrote a verse on? Twice I have carried it to the post office to send to you thinking you would probably like to have it, and then brought it back home because I didn't want to part with it. It should belong to your children, I suppose. Perhaps I can have it copied.

Let me know right away about Ulysses. If you think it is not feasible, I would also like to do Mr. Gilhooley. But Ulysses is all I can think about at the moment!

Love,
Dorothy

LETTER NO. 8

754 Locust St.
Pasadena, Calif
November 9, 1954

Dear John,

An English poet and bullfighter wrote once a description of our bullfighter, Manolete:
"Andalusian art reach the summit of its expression in the style of the bullfighter Manolete. He was ornate yet severe like Seneca. He was called 'the tower of Cordoba'. He personified opposite extremes at one and the same moment contrasting, in one being the austerity, coldness and hardness of a statue with the softness and warmth of a flower: for while his brain, his muscles and his sword were dedicated to the clear and icy geometry of death, yet with his crimson cape and his scarlet mulete he sculptured to the imagination of the full-blown corollas of magnolias, roses, and camellias."
This sums up; it seems to me, the whole essence of what we should try to do in the picture. Therefore, your suggestion of using the rigid pattern of the bullfight as frame for the story, and keeping it within the confines of the ancient stole of La Maestranza is exactly right. The story is a duel between Life and Death enacted almost as a ritual dance between the superb overflowing vitality of the matador and the cold shadow of Absence, while each augments and enhances the stature and mystery of the other. A towering spiral—Lorca's "spiral of whiteness" in which the two forces contend in a sort of ecstasy. I hope this doesn't sound too high flown or too abstract. I have to think this way! If I get clear sure feeling of the bones of the story, in this case the bullfight, then I get a fine feeling of freedom in describing the flesh on the bones, the whole glorious exhuberance [sic] and sound and smell of life and its great careless profusion thrown into relief by the Shadow.
So now I am trying to translate all this into words and scenes. I confess to stage fright since I want this to be so very good, and it will inevitably fall way short. I hope you will not be disappointed in it. It is

good to be working at writing again. The papers here say Ferrer is planning to direct and act in Matador with Aubrey [sic] Hepburn. Does this affect anything? Hope not!

I'm working hard and hope to send you some scenes soon.

Love,
Dorothy

(The children send love and want to know how soon can they see Moby Dick? It is their most favorite story.)

LETTER NO. 9

754 Locust St.
Pasadena
Jan 10, 1955

Dearest John,

You will never know what your Christmas gift meant to the children. It arrived at the psychological moment on Christmas Eve. It was the only gift they received, except the things I gave them, so it had a special and unexpected magic about it. It set in motion one event....It seems that Kelvin, who is 12, has been harboring a passion for paint. As the messenger left the door, Kelvin was demanding $33.33 immediately! (He waived the 1/3 cent). He made a beeline for the art store 2 blocks away, and came back loaded down with easel and paints. He set up the easel and hasn't stopped painting since. I am sending you his first efforts. His mind is made up. He is merely marking time until I (who in his eyes can accomplish any miracle) make the arrangements to go to Paris. His teachers are a somewhat paint smeared copy of Goya reproductions, and a very smeared copy of Picasso reproductions. I got them the Metropolitan Museum reproductions—have you seen them? —but he ignores all other painters. He is a gifted child, but what direction he will go needs time to see.

He is now acting out the story he told me when he was three: "Blood and brains were going for a walk and they met a skeleton. Blood said, "Can I have a ride on you?" Brain said, "Let me ride on top!" The skeleton said, "All right!" "But it was the WRONG BODY!" – This beautiful little parable, which he has forgotten he told me, is now being demonstrated. Whether painting is his particular skeleton I don't know. I think all one can do is to praise and admire and wait. The paintings are his way of thanking you.

Too bad about MATADOR – but we'll find something better. Paul wishes to talk to me about BRIDGE OF SAN LUIS REY. We've been delayed getting together. First he had flu, and then the children in pitiless succession for the last two weeks. When a germ reaches our house, it ceases to be a sickness and becomes an epidemic! I am enclosing a clipping I found. What about this—as a hot jazz musical? It is your St Louis.

I'd love to have an indication of what you'd like me to do. I'm dying to get started earning this money you are giving me!

All my love and the childrens.
Dorothy

I found the perfect story for you: BRIDGE OVER THE RIVER KWEI. [sic] Got terribly excited and wrote the publisher about the rights. Found they were already sold to guess who?—Sam Spiegel! Have you a way—guile or force—to get it from him?

Author Note: Mother's intuition was spot on! Sam Spiegel produced the film and it premiered in Los Angeles in December 1957. It was a huge hit, winning seven Academy Awards (Oscars).

LETTER NO. 10

754 Locust
Pasadena
May 7, 1955

Dear John,

I read in the paper yesterday that Bogeaus has signed Barbara Stanwyck to do THE BRIDGE OF SAN LUIS REY and has a cameraman scouting out locations in Lima. So for the second time in the last six months I pulled a page out of the typewriter rolled up a useless bundle of MS and threw it in the deepest drawer of my desk. What rotten luck! – wasted money and wasted time. To interpolate a gentle criticism, that bastard Paul might have checked on ownership. Bogeaus did produce it before.

I feel I still owe you a script for the money you sent me. As you know, it was the desire to write a good script that prompted my letter to you. I'll follow my original hunch and do an original story, probably a book. But it will belong to you. I hate the feeling of all that unearned money. Most of all I want to give a good concrete reason for the completely irrational belief you have always had in my talents! And how important that belief has been to me you will never guess.

I have been thinking about a story of a little boy and his mother, loosely based upon you and your mother and that kind of gay, piratical gallantry she had, and Gram, rooted so solidly in the soil of the country. I saw them, I think, in a way that no one else did; they lived vividly and recreated their lives for me. Their own and that of your great-grandfather, and your grandfather' (you must resemble him a little). I feel a kind of nostalgia for that breed which seems to be dying out; I despise the small cautious people who have taken their place. Their story is one of trains, of constant journeying, of precariousness; of that curious deep-seated love of horses which your mother had – remember the kind of funeral she wanted? It should have the mood of a lazy summer day in a small town, so quiet you can hear the buzzing of flies and the switching of horse's tails, but with a thunderstorm brewing on the edges of the town; never breaking, but just about to. It should be told very simply, with a little of the feeling of Sherwood Anderson, only different. If you come right down to it, it's a story you should write.

Anyhow, thank you for everything, darling. I'm sorry the other things didn't work out. All my love, as always.

Dorothy

LETTER NO. 11

Courtown House Kilcock
County Kildare Ireland
4th June, 1955

Dear Dorothy:

I am ever so sorry, dear, that things turned out the way they did on Matador. However, whatever you read about the *Bridge of San Luis Rey* was inaccurate. The story has not been sold and I think it would be a good idea for you to do a screenplay of it – that is if it is sufficiently attractive to you.

I love the drawings you sent me. The photograph of "The Artist as a Young Man" does everything to explain why you are so proud of him...you might tell him that I am too.

I very much like your idea about the novel, but it would be my suggestion that you do the screenplay first.

I might be paying a fast visit to California during the next few weeks, and when I do I want very much to see you and the boys.

BLACK DAHLIA AVENGER II | 140

Meanwhile...

All my love,
John

LETTER NO. 12

1014 Milan St. South
Pasadena
[Nodate]

Dear John,

I am completely at the end of my rope and I don't know what to do—for the first time in my life. I was in the hospital for three days (they suspected cancer, but this I couldn't tell anyone) – The possibilities of that are pretty well eliminated, I think. Steven brought me a letter to the hospital which said we had to be out of our house in three days. That means we should have been out today. I called my employer today and he said since I had used company money ($500) he was going to proceed on embezzlement charges unless it was paid back this week. Of course I left the hospital immediately. Steve gave me the dispossess notice, without notifying my doctor or anything. I seem to fail at everything I attempt. If it were not for the great and generous love of the children, and of you, I would not care to live. But this love obliges me to go on.

I am in such fear about the children I even cabled George asking him if I could send them to him. This is the last thing I want for them, and in any case he will probably politely refuse. What will happen to them? They are so wonderful, and I am so afraid for them. It isn't your problem, but I feel like someone who is drowning. I called Morgan today and explained a little of this, although being in the accountant's office I couldn't say much. If the 500 is returned I can go back to my job (not that I want to) but it is a living. We are homeless, and tomorrow I have called in a second hand man to buy what things we have. I have 25¢ at the moment. I was supposed to be in the hospital for another two weeks, but I have medicines which I think will enable me to go on working. The doctor does not believe there is anything wrong with me except complete physical and nervous exhaustion. It has been a long hard pull for the last twelve years, and I suppose it's finally catching up with me, in my old age. The job plus washing, ironing, cooking and cleaning is hard, but when I'm well I can do it. Don't you think the children are fine? But now, when in some ways they need me the most, I seem to be giving out.

It will only be a few years more that they need me. If only I could be strong just a little longer!

I'm not throwing this problem in your lap. But I would appreciate some advice.

Love,
Dorothy

Author Notes: I have serious doubts that Mother ever actually sent a cable to our father, asking if she could send us to him in the Philippines. Her whole life was about trying to keep the four of us together until we "became of age." It is dramatic and I'm sure John responded by sending the necessary money to help keep mother and children together.

LETTER NO. 13

JOHN HUSTON
KATEL ITO JAPAN- NOV 14, 1957

DOROTHY HODEL INFORMED ME ONE SON IN HOSPITAL RENT DUE OTHER OBLIGATIONS PRESSING SHE DESIRES 300 DOLLARS IMMEDIATELY YOU ALREADY ADVANCED HER LAST NINETY DAYS IN EXCESS OF 1,000 DOLLARS. CABLE INSTRUCTIONS

MARK

MARK COHEN
9606 SANTA MONICA BLVD.
BEVERLY HILLS CALIFORNIA - NOVEMBER 14, 1957

IS HODEL KID REALLY SICK OR ANOTHER DODGE ACT ACCORDING YOUR OWN JUDGMENT.
REG RDS
JOHN

Author Notes: These sets of telegrams were the last two "letters" in the Huston File.

Mark Cohen was John's long time agent/business manager. Most of Dorothy's "emergency pleas for money" went through Mark. Here we see Mark relaying an urgent request from Dorothy to John and his reply, with eyes wide open, wanting to know if Mark thinks it

Black Dahlia Avenger II|142

is "real" or just another ploy (in his words, "a dodge act") from Dorothy?

After seeing these letters for the first time, my personal respect for John has gone way up. While he might have been known in filmdom as a genius and a monster, it is clear from these many letters that he continually threw lifesaving dollars our way throughout the 1950s. Without his aid, it is doubtful that we would have been able to stay together as a family, and for this I would like to offer a most sincere, thank you, John.

It was in 1958, only two years after this letter that I joined the Navy as soon as I turned 17.

JOHN HUSTON—WHAT DID HE KNOW? WHEN DID HE KNOW IT?

Earlier, I alluded to the fact that I believed that John Huston's "hunch" was that he either knew or strongly suspected that George Hodel killed Elizabeth "Black Dahlia" Short, and possibly other victims.

We have already examined reasons why I believe this. Here is a quick review:

1) John and George had been close friends since their teens.

2) Both were geniuses who looked at life and shared a slightly different wiring than most of us mere mortals. Both men listed the Marquis de Sade high on their list of heroes, and were recognized as having "sadistic natures."

3) Both were in competition for and shared the mind, heart, and body of a truly remarkable woman, Dorothy Huston Hodel.

4) John, as a Hollywood A-list filmmaker, knew and associated with screenwriters: Rowland Brown [also a paramour of Dorothy Hodel] Gene Fowler, Steve Fisher, Ben Hecht, as well as being a close personal friend of Peter Viertel, whom John hired in 1950 to write the screenplay for one of his greatest films—*African Queen*.

Keeping in mind what we've learned from the newly discovered "Huston Letters," let's now consider some new information.

PETER VIERTEL—AFRICAN QUEEN-*WHITE HUNTER BLACK HEART*
Collier's, June 13, 1953

The natives' shoulders tipped back and forth. The drumbeat grew faster. Then Wilson waved his hat, and they screamed with joy

White Hunter, Black Heart

By PETER VIERTEL

John Wilson had become a violent and ruthless man. Now he was obsessed with a crazy urge to kill—to kill the greatest beast in the jungle—and perhaps destroy himself

Excerpt from Collier's introduction of Viertel's novel:
John Wilson is a man of limitless energy, determination and creative artistry. His reputation as a motion-picture director is tremendous. As a human being, he is unsuccessful—selfish, cynical, loveless and cruel. His projects are destined for great success or doomed to spectacular failure: for him, there is no middle ground, no mediocrity.

White Hunter, Black Heart is the story of the filming of a movie. It is also the story of Wilson's growing compulsion to destroy, at any cost, a creature nobler than himself. It is the story of a great talent gone haywire.

Peter Viertel, the author, worked with John Huston on The African Queen in the Congo in 1951. His novel, of which this story is the final section, will be published soon by Doubleday & Company.

In 1952, screenwriter/author, Peter Viertel wrote an absolutely riveting novel, *White Hunter, Black Heart*. [Doubleday & Co. Garden City, NY, 1953]
Its subtitle read:

**A NOVEL OF BIG-GAME HUNTING
IN THE BELGIAN CONGO
AND ONE MAN'S OBSESSION WITH IT.**

A *roman a clef*, Viertel simply changed a few names, calling John Huston "John Wilson" and himself "Peter Verrill." In a spectacular fictionalized narrative, Viertel documents his close friendship with John and the events surrounding the *1951* making of the *African Queen*, and gives us a full—and in my opinion—fair view of the real Huston. We see and hear both sides: Huston's shining genius along with his dark-sided views of life, which gained Huston the well-earned reputation for being both a genius and a monster.

Having had a father of similar character—with tremendous strengths and weaknesses and who was both generous and sadistic—I felt I better understood Viertel's expressed love and disgust for Huston after recently re-reading the "novel."

John was a serpent who hypnotized his prey with charm and humor, then struck quickly and sank his fangs deep into his victim's flesh.

In the light of what is now known about George Hodel, a number of quotes attributed by Peter Verrill [Viertel] to John Wilson [Huston] take on a much deeper meaning. As you read the first comments on Huston's view and attitude on testing "friendship," keep two things in mind. First, George Hodel and John Huston were friends since high school. Second, John's observations are made circa 1950-1951, just after George Hodel was about to be arrested and decided to flee the country. As we now know, George was fleeing arrest for a cold-blooded, premeditated murder. [Several actually.]

Here are Huston's comments on "Real Friendship."

White Hunter, Black Heart, page 64:

...
"No, it's not. To try and find out who your real friends are is very important. "How would you propose to go about doing that, John? Randsome asked.

"Well, I don't know. It's kind of difficult. I think the perfect test would be to go to your friends and tell them you've just committed a murder, a cold-blooded, premeditated murder, and that you want to escape. There are no extenuating circumstances. All you want is help. The people who'd stick to you and help you escape without asking any questions would, I believe qualify as real friends."

The following comments related to my mother, Dorothy, John's first wife. They were married for seven years. The "I'd done something wrong" refers to Mother walking in and catching him in bed with another woman fairly early on in their marriage.

White Hunter Black Heart, page 214:

...
"I believe in the signs, you know. I've met them too often in my life to doubt them. In everything I've ever done. Work, or women, or gambling. Everything." "How do you mean?"

"Well, when I broke up with my first wife for instance. I knew I'd lost the best dame I was ever likely to meet, and I'd lost her because I'd acted like a horse's ass. And it turned out that way. I'd done something wrong and I had to pay for it, and so every time I fell in love again after that, I knew the disenchantment would ultimately turn up. And it did. Never failed. Because you get one good chance at everything in life, and that's all."

Finally, I believe the following excerpt captures John's true psychology.

It is dangerous, over the edge, and guaranteed to fill one's life with excitement, adventure, and, in all likelihood, misery and disappointment. I make no moral judgment here. Those, like John Huston and George Hodel, make the choice with eyes wide open. Their thinking compels and propels them forward into the Abyss.

The below conversation was between Peter Viertel and John Huston [Peter Verrill and John Wilson]. They were in Africa and far behind schedule on the filming of the *African Queen*. A screenwriter and close friend of Huston's, Peter Viertel was attempting to dissuade Huston from going on an elephant hunt.

White Hunter, Black Heart, page 295-296:
Verrill [Viertel] say's:
"Well, in order to kill one of them, you're ready to forget the rest of us, and let the whole goddam show go down the drain. It's not a passion this time that's guiding you, that's pulling you away from your responsibility. A passion would be an excuse. This time it's a crime. Because it's a crime to kill an elephant. And in order to commit this crime you're willing to ruin everyone else. If you were running out on the picture because of a woman, or a better offer, or because you'd suddenly gotten bored with the whole thing, I'd go along. But this way, it's even too rough for my taste."

Wilson looked intensely serious for a minute. He drew reflectively on his cigarette. I knew something I had said had made an impression on him. Most of it, I realized, had gone past him into the warm African night, but something had struck him in the strange way it occasionally did, had pierced into his armor-plated process of thought. He was pausing now to give his answer weight. I knew him so well, I thought.

"Kid," he said, after a long pause, "you're wrong. It's not a crime to kill an elephant. It's bigger than that. A crime....what the hell, that isn't much. And that isn't it. It's a sin to kill an elephant, you understand, a sin. As basic as that. The only sin you can buy a license for and then go out and commit. And that's why I want to do it before I do anything else. You understand?"

Thirty years later, Peter Viertel, by then long married to actress Deborah Kerr, wrote another book which I highly recommend, *Dangerous Friends: At Large with Hemingway and Huston in the Fifties.* [Nan A. Talese/Doubleday, New York, 1992]

Viertel's recounting of his time shared in the 1950s with both of his "dangerous friends," Huston and Hemingway, gives us a fascinating behind the scenes look into both men's personalities.

I will close this chapter with a short excerpt from a full page letter written by Hemingway to his good friend, Peter Viertel in 1958. [Viertel adapted two of Hemingway's novels for film, *The Sun Also Rises* and *The Old Man and the Sea.*]

In reading Hemingway's letter, it becomes obvious that a bitter Papa has nothing but contempt for Hollywood film-making and its hacks, and he would like to see Viertel—whom he believed had genuine talent—give up his day-job as a screenwriter and throw himself full-time into real writing—novels.

The letter to Viertel was written on May 1, 1958, from *Finca Vigia* [Lookout Farm], Hemingway's home near Havana, Cuba.

...Wish to Christ you would write and not do that picture shit. Leave that to swine like Irwin and Hecht....Last winter I re-read all your books. The only one that is worthless is Line of Departure which is much worse than when I read it. But the Africa one [*White Hunter Black Heart*] in spite of carelessness re-reads very damned well.

Go ahead and write your damned book. But don't think you can keep jerking yourself off for pictures and then command any fee at stud...in writing they can't yank you when you lose your stuff. What the hell. You get it back the next day or the next week. What if they knock the shit out of you? You can cut that out and go on when you have your stuff going again.

Excuse bad letter. Now I have gotten rid of this lousy bitterness about the pictures will write you good and cheerful next time.

...

Love from us both,
Papa

["Us both" would include his wife, Mary Hemingway. Three years after writing this letter, Hemingway, back in the United States and being treated for severe depression, committed suicide in Idaho on July 2, 1961.]

9

DA Investigators Jemison & Morgan

Lt. Frank Jemison

ONE OF THE FEW MEN IN THE BLACK DAHLIA INVESTIGATION who it can be said was actually wearing a white hat was Lt. Frank B. Jemison of the Los Angeles District Attorney's Bureau of Investigation.

From everything that I've seen, he did his job, solved the case, and was just about to make the arrest when the powers that be pulled his plug. We can speculate all day about why. The reasons are many and varied.

However, what is not in dispute is The Order. Lt. Jemison, in his final closing report, made it crystal clear that he had been removed from the case [later independently confirmed in a 2004 television interview of DA investigator Walter Morgan] and ordered to hand over his investigation, interviews, and all his evidence, which included the wire recordings and transcripts, directly to LAPD Chief Thad Brown.

As I said in an earlier chapter, Lt. Jemison's saving grace was to copy his original investigation, complete with the Hodel-Black Dahlia

File, and secure it in the DA's vault, where it would remain hidden for the next fifty-three years until finally being opened and revealed.

Los Angeles Hall of Justice
210 W. Temple Street, Los Angeles

The above photo taken by the author in 2008 shows the downtown Los Angeles Hall of Justice at the corner of Temple and Broadway Streets. The HoJ built in 1925, has a long, colorful, and macabre history. Most of L.A.'s famous trials were held in this courthouse. The building served as a jail detention facility for prisoners awaiting trial, as well as housing the L.A. County Sheriff's Department, Coroner and District Attorney, including Lt. Jemison's office in the Bureau of Investigation.

The HoJ was within easy walking distance of all three of Dr. George Hodel's medical facilities: Health Department in Chinatown, First Street VD Clinic at First and Central, and his private medical office at Seventh and Flower Street.

The building has direct connections to our investigation.

1) In the early 1940s, Dr. George Hill Hodel's Health Department office was inside this building [1938-1942];

2) In 1947, the autopsy on Elizabeth "Black Dahlia" Short was performed in the Coroner's morgue in the basement of the HoJ, and the inquest into her death was held in a courtroom of the building; and

3) In 1949, Dr. George Hodel was arrested and booked into the jail facility here and was later tried in Superior Court on the lower floors of the premise. On February 15, 1950, George Hodel was detained and questioned by Lt. Jemison here, while at the same time, LAPD and DA sound technicians and detectives broke into the Franklin house to install the microphones.

Dr. Hodel was free to go only after Lt. Jemison got the "all clear" call from detectives as they exited the Franklin house, having "wired it for sound."

Charles Manson and the rest of his "Family" were tried and convicted here. So were RFK assassin Sirhan Sirhan, mobsters Bugsy Siegel and Mickey Cohen, actor Robert Mitchum, as well as most of L.A.'s historic bad boys and *femme fatales*. In addition to Elizabeth Short, this was also the morgue where the autopsies on Marilyn Monroe and Robert Kennedy were performed.

The building was deemed "unsafe" after the 1994 Northridge earthquake and has been vacant for nearly two decades. With such a distinguished history, hopefully, it will be saved from the wrecking ball, updated to current codes and preserved.

Dr. George Hill Hodel's four downtown L.A. medical office locations:
(1) Health Dept. Chinatown;(2) Health Dept., Hall of Justice [1938-1940
(3) His privately owned, First Street VD Clinic; and (4) His private practice at Roosevelt Bldg.

Upper Left: GHH Chinatown office; Upper Right: First Street Clinic
Bottom: Dr. Hodel's private practice on 12th floor at Seventh and Flower

A FAMILY SECRET

"The Dahlia murder suspect was a doctor and we know who did it, but we couldn't put him away." —Lt. Frank Jemison Hall of Justice Summer, 1951

In mid-October 2006, I was contacted by a close surviving relative of District Attorney investigator, Lt. Frank B. Jemison. For privacy's sake, I will simply use his initials, "J.F." He advised me that he was Jemison's nephew [Jemison's sister's son], a medical doctor, and a retired Air Force colonel. Here in his own words is his description of his Uncle Frank, and one very important meeting he remembers from 1951:

Family background:
Frank was my mother's brother, the only son of a Methodist minister. He seemed a little eccentric to me. Every two years, he and his wife would fly to Detroit, pick up a new Cadillac, and drive through Ohio unannounced to visit his three sisters. If they weren't home—too bad, until two years later. He had not followed his father Dave's advice and entered the ministry and after graduation from Ohio Wesleyan College, he took off for the west coast. I thought he had a Law degree. Family rumor has it that he earned a good bit of money in real estate and as a financial advisor prior to his career as a DA investigator.

I know he was proud of his fortune, which was, at least in 1951, over one million dollars. While there was some family friction with Uncle Frank, he was always described as a person of impeccable personal integrity. I surmise that this integrity plus the fact that he had already made his fortune made him an excellent choice as investigator in the midst of apparent corruption. At his wife's death, the estate was left to Ohio Wesleyan.

The Black Dahlia Murder Case:
When I was 12 years old in the summer of 1951, I accompanied my family to a medical convention in San Francisco and we stopped in L.A. for three days, my only extended contact with Uncle Frank. At dinner, he asked if my father, a family physician, and I would like to see where he worked. At that time, the Hall of Justice was one of the, if not the, tallest buildings in LA. My father and Uncle Frank sat in the front seat and I sat in back. As they drove, Dad turned and said, "You know your Uncle Frank was the investigator for the Black Dahlia case." I liked the name but it didn't mean much to me. They explained that it was a famous murder case. I didn't listen too hard to the conversation until they said the body was cut up. Then I was all ears. Uncle Frank described the cuts, etc., and asked Dad what he thought. My father said he thought it had to be the work of a surgeon. Uncle Frank agreed and said that "We know who did it but we didn't have enough to put him away." For some reason, my twelve year old mind couldn't understand that. I wondered why, if they knew who did it they couldn't arrest him. I never thought of that case from that time, but the name "Black Dahlia" remained stuck in my mind. Just thought this might be interesting to you as background information. Really have enjoyed your book!

Sincerely Yours,
J.F. M.D. COL USAF (ret)

Dr. J.F.'s "background information" is much more than interesting. With what we already know, his family reflections are extremely illuminating, especially because of his certainty as to when Uncle Frank met with him and made these statements. It was the summer of 1951!

Let's briefly review Lt. Jemison's investigative chronology:

1) **October 1949**—Grand Jury appointed Lt. Frank Jemison to take over the Black Dahlia and other L.A. Lone Woman murder investigations. George Hill Hodel became DA Lt. Jemison's prime Dahlia suspect.

2) **February 15-March 27,** 1950—Jemison established an eighteen-man task force assigned to twenty-four-hour electronic-surveillance of Dr. Hodel's Franklin house.

3) **March 28, 1950**—George Hodel was tipped about surveillance. Realizing he was about to be arrested, he fled the residence. DA Lt. Jemison forced to remove surveillance equipment and shut down operation. After that, Lt. Jemison and police never again have contact with prime suspect, Dr. George Hill Hodel.

4) **February 1951**—Lt. Jemison ordered to close Dahlia case and turn all investigation and evidence and Hodel surveillance recordings and interviews over to LAPD. He complies, but locks away a "second set of investigative files" in the DA vault, where they remain untouched and unexamined until 2003.

5) **July 1951**—Lt. Jemison brought his vacationing brother-in-law, a medical doctor, and his twelve-year-old nephew, "J.F." to his office at the downtown Los Angeles Hall of Justice and informed them that "the Dahlia murder suspect was a doctor and we know who did it, but we couldn't put him away."

On August 15, 1967, some seventeen years after solving the Black Dahlia murder and locking his secret away in the DA vault, Frank Jemison died in Beverly Hills, California. He was sixty-eight.

He died a rich man. His will gave some of it to his alma mater, Wesleyan College in Ohio. The rest of his assets, after his wife Jane's death, were placed as a trust fund for the Los Angeles District Attorney's Office.

In 1979, the Frank Jemison Award was established from his bequest for the purpose of selecting and acknowledging "excellence in public service."

Every year since then, the award has been given to two outstanding employees selected from the DA's Office. One of the recipients is a DA investigator, and the other from the DA's support staff. Each Jemison Award Winner receives $5,000 cash.

DA INVESTIGATOR WALTER MORGAN—THE LAST COYOTE

"I guess there's not too many left in the hills in the city—least near where I live. So whenever I see one, I get this feeling that it might be the last one left out there. You know? The last coyote. And I guess that would bother me if it ever turned out to be true, if I never saw one again." —Detective Harry Bosch, from Michael Connelly's *The Last Coyote*

The following is based on an obituary I wrote for DA Investigator Walter Morgan when he died in 2007.

September 8, 2007
Los Angeles

DA INVESTIGATOR WALTER MORGAN, BLACK DAHLIA MURDER'S LAST COYOTE DIES AT 92
1915-2007

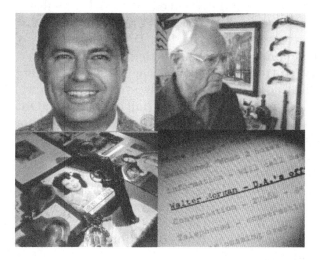

Walter Morgan, the Los Angeles District Attorney's Bureau of Investigation "old school" detective and the last surviving member of the 1950 Black Dahlia DA Task Force, in the final years before his passing, linked Dr. George Hill Hodel to the 1947 murder.

In a 2004 CBS *48 Hours* crimespecial, Morgan publicly acknowledged bugging the doctor's private home. He also confirmed the existence of secret surveillance tapes and transcripts, and that the DA's 1950 task force was unexpectedly and summarily shut down. In a surprisingly candid on-air response, Morgan acknowledged that he and his fellow officers suspected that the shutdown was the result of a payoff and cover-up.

For me, it ended as it began with this morning's call from my half-sister, Tamar Hodel. "Steve, I just heard from my daughter, Fauna. Walter Morgan died this morning."

In my book, *Black Dahlia Avenger: A Genius for Murder,* published in 2003, here is how I originally described my introduction and first meeting with Walter Morgan, then an eighty-seven-year-old retired L.A. district attorney investigator.

Page 449:

My INVESTIGATION HAD BEEN COMPLETED for some four months. I was working on the final editing of the manuscript when on April 24, 2002, my phone rang. It was my sister Tamar. "Steven," she said, "I have the most amazing news. Fauna [her eldest daughter] has just spoken with a man named Walter Morgan." (I immediately recognized his name as a district attorney investigator, Lieutenant Jemison's partner from the 1950 investigation, and swallowed hard at hearing his name come from her lips.) "He was a private detective or something back in the 1940s," she said. "He was involved in investigating, guess who: *Dr. George Hodel!* He told Fauna that they put a bug in the Franklin House to listen in on Dad's conversations. Can you call Fauna and find out what this is all about?"

I assured Tamar I would check it out immediately. Contacting Fauna, whom I had not spoken to for ten years, I learned she was working in the San Fernando Valley and had been visited in her place of work by a casual acquaintance, Ethel. In her seventies, Ethel was with her boyfriend whom she introduced as Walter Morgan. Walter shook Fauna's hand and said, "'Hodel?' That's an unusual name. I once worked a murder case on a Dr. Hodel. Any relation?" Fauna and Walter compared notes, and quickly learned that Morgan's suspect and Fauna's grandfather were one and the same.

Two days later, on April 26, I called Walter Morgan and told him my name was Steven Hodel, the uncle of Fauna Hodel, and the son of Dr. George Hill Hodel, who had died in 1999 at the age of ninety-one. I also informed him that I had retired from LAPD after working most of my career as a homicide detective in Hollywood Division.

Morgan greeted me warmly, in that unspoken bond that exists cop to cop, and proceeded to reminisce about the Hodel story.

Morgan, now eighty-seven, said he had worked for the sheriff's department from 1939 to 1949 on radio car patrol, in vice, burglary, and in other details. Then he left LASD and became a DA investigator in 1949, where he remained until retirement in 1970. He worked homicide on temporary assignment for a few months back in 1950. He was sent over to help out Lieutenant Frank Jemison, who he said "had picked me to be his sidekick."

Walter Morgan remembered well the day they had installed listening devices at the Franklin House, which he authoritatively informed me "was built by Frank Lloyd Wright." (As we know, the true architect was his son, Lloyd Wright.) Morgan continued:

"We had a good bug man, a guy that could install bugs anywhere and everywhere. He worked in the DA's crime lab. So the chief assigned me to take him over to the house on Franklin, and he was going to install a bug system at the Hodel residence. My chief at the DA's office had me take him over there and we met the LAPD at Dr. Hodel's house. It was during the daytime and nobody was home. I remember there were some ranking LAPD officers outside, and no one could figure out how to get in. I suggested, "Well, have any of you officers tried a card to see if it would open the door?" They laughed, so I pulled out my wallet, and took out some kind of a credit card or whatever card I had, slipped it through, and the front door popped right open! They couldn't believe it. Anyway, our man went in and installed some bugs there. That was our job, to get the bugs installed so we could listen in."

Based on Walter Morgan's confirmations that my father was the Black Dahlia suspect and our Franklin house was bugged and secret tapes obtained, I closed the chapter (written in 2002) by publicly asking the following questions:

BDA page 454:
Standard operating procedure would have been to make transcripts of these conversations, as well as investigative follow-up reports documenting the findings. *Where are these transcripts? Where are these reports? What do they say?*

A month after publication (May 2003), those questions were answered.

Los Angeles District Attorney Steve Cooley granted me access to the locked and vaulted *Hodel-Black Dahlia Files*, which had remained unexamined for over fifty-years, and, as they say, "the rest is history."

In June 2004, the five-decade-old surveillance transcripts and investigative reports, along with photographs and copies of the DA files, were released to the public by way of a new chapter, "Aftermath," added to the BDA's HarperCollins paperback edition.

DA LIEUTENANT WALTER MORGAN—BIOGRAPHY

- 1939- Appointed a deputy with the Los Angeles Sheriff's Department. Highly skilled in firearms, became one of the sheriff's department's "crack shots" after qualifying as a "Distinguished Expert" marksman.
- 1940-1949- L.A. deputy sheriff for nine years. Assignments included: patrol car, vice, and detective bureau (Burglary Detail).

- 1949- Left the sheriff's department and appointed a detective with the Los Angeles District Attorney's Office, Bureau of Investigation.
- 1950- Selected by Lt. Frank Jemison to assist him in the Grand Jury ordered reinvestigation of the Black Dahlia case.
- February 15, 1950- Morgan, ordered by Lt. Jemison to coordinate a meeting between DA crime lab electronics' expert and LAPD detectives for the specific purpose of surreptitiously installing microphones inside the Franklin house residence of Dr. George Hill Hodel. Morgan accompanied by "bug men" and "high ranking LAPD officers" proceeded to 5121 Franklin Avenue and personally "shimmed" the front door of Dr. Hodel's residence. [To prevent him from walking in on them, the "installation" was coordinated and done at the same time George Hodel was being detained for questioning by DA investigators at the Hall of Justice.]
- March 1970- Morgan retired from the DA's Office.
- April 2002- Interviewed by me about the Black Dahlia investigation and for the first time in fifty-two years, confirmed George Hodel as the prime suspect and the "bugging of the Hodel residence."
- May 2004- Interviewed on CBS *48 Hours*, where he publicly acknowledged that he "shimmed the front door" of Dr. Hodel's residence, and "electronic experts placed bugs in the walls." Morgan confirmed that he and Lt. Jemison were unexpectedly removed from the case and it was returned back to LAPD for further investigation. In an on-camera statement, Morgan indicated that in 1950, "a cover-up and payoff was suspected."
- September 8, 2007- Morgan fell ill and passed away in Los Angeles.

In several meetings with Walter Morgan after our introduction in 2002, I became acutely aware that he was a man of many moods and many secrets, most of them from a long time ago.

In his prime, Morgan lived and breathed *Chinatown* and *LA Confidential*. He *was L.A. noir*—only this gumshoe was no celluloid fiction—he was the real deal. As you will read below, he was Philip Marlowe (before Marlowe got fired from the DA's Office for insubordination) and Dirty Harry rolled into one. And in 1944, a couple of street thugs would "make his day."

In the mid-1940s, Morgan was close to the power that influenced and ran Los Angeles: gangster Mickey Cohen, Florentine Gardens' owner Mark Hansen, and his "Mr. Show Business," M.C. Nils Thor Granlund, better known as-"N.T.G."

In 1945, Morgan married the Florentine's lead showgirl, Tanya "Sugar" Geise. Best man at his wedding was no less a luminary, than L.A. County's top-cop, Sheriff Eugene Biscailuz. Tanya was good friends with Lavonne Cohen, Mickey Cohen's wife, who also attended the wedding. Mickey Cohen was Bugsy Siegel's lieutenant who, in two short years, would take over as L.A.'s *Numero Uno* gangster after his boss was gunned down in Beverly Hills.

Below I've included just a few press clippings from Morgan's Feisty Forties, to give a sense of the man in his time.

In 1944, while still a deputy sheriff, Morgan was parked in a car with his fiancée Sugar Geise on the Sunset Strip. The couple was approached by two armed robbers.

Excerpt from L.A. *Times* article on September 30, 1944:

Dead-Shot Deputy Foils Two Asserted Bandits
...
Suddenly one of them (Gallentine) shoved a pistol through a partly open window, rapped on the glass, and said, "O.K., give us the dough and the jewels"

Let "Jewels" Go

"I (Morgan) stepped out and said, "O.K., here are your jewels—and let go eight 'little jewels' from my automatic."

SHARPSHOOTER—Deputy Walter Morgan, sheriff department champion shot, shows Dancer "Sugar" Geise gun with which he shot two bandit holdup suspects.

Dead-Shot Deputy Foils
Two Asserted Bandits

ARRAIGNED—Manuel Riofrio, left, and Joseph Gallentine, charged with attempting to hold up deputy sheriff and fiancee Sept. 28, shown at their arraignment.

Men Who Picked on Deputy
as 'Soft Touch' Arraigned

Florentine Gardens singer/dance Sugar Geise with mother

Florentine Gardens Showgirl Tanya "Sugar" Geise

June 8, 1945 Los Angeles Times

Sugar Geise Wed to Deputy Sheriff

Dep. Sheriff Walter Morgan and Tanya (Sugar) Geise, Florentine Gardens night-club singer, whom he once saved from two bandits, yesterday were married in Superior Judge Edward R. Brand's court chambers.

Best man at the double-ring ceremony was Sheriff Biscailuz, with Mrs. Sam Katzman, wife of the R.K.O. producer, acting as matron of honor.

The couple met two years ago while Miss Geise was the star attraction at the Florentine Gardens,. Last September, while Morgan was escorting her home, two bandits attempted to hold them up. Morgan leaped from the automobile and wounded both men in a blazing gun battle. Later they were convicted of robbery and sentenced to San Quentin.

"That convinced me I had met the right guy," Sugar declared yesterday after the wedding. She gave her age as 28 and Morgan admitted to being 30.

Other attendants at the wedding were Sugar's father, Harry (Pop) Geise, Lt. John Law, Morgan's immediate superior officer,

Times photo

THREE'S A CROWD—Dep. Sheriff Walter Morgan, about to kiss his bride, Tanya (Sugar) Geise, night club singer, following wedding ceremony yesterday, apparently intends to push Sheriff Biscoiluz, best man, out of picture.

and Mrs. Lillian Cohen and Miss Pauline Davis, friends of the bride.

Immediately after the ceremony the couple left for a honeymoon trip which will include San Francisco and Reno.

Walter Morgan weds Sugar Geise in June 1945
Sheriff Biscailuz "Best Man"

2004- 48 Hours Black Dahlia Confidential
CBS investigative reporter Erin Moriarty questions Walter Morgan
regarding the Black Dahlia case being closed down and turned back to LAPD

Morgan: The only thing I can think is that some money must have transpired between people.

Moriarty: It sounds like you think it may have been a cover-up of some sort?

Morgan: Well, everybody thought that.

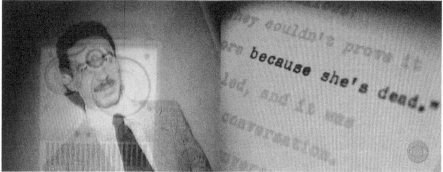

Dr. George Hill Hodel Surveillance Transcripts 40 days--(146 pages)

To DA investigators Frank Jemison and Walter Morgan: I want to personally thank both of you for your service to the City of Angels and its people. Thank you for your honesty and integrity. You did what others could not. One of you preserved the truth and the other told it.

May you both rest in peace.

DA investigator Walter Morgan in 1952 walking across the street from his office at the Hall of Justice. [Federal Court in background.]

10

Hollywood Roomers

TREE OF LIFE, **1948**

IN 2001, after my relocation to Los Angeles, I contacted an ex-roomer—perhaps lodger is more *apropos*—who had lived for several years at the Franklin house. For privacy's sake, let's call him Chris D. Chris was an artist who, in 1948-49, shared the rent in the north-wing studio with his friend and fellow painter Joe Barrett.

I phoned Chris, who was living with his wife in a beach community several hours north of Los Angeles. We agreed to meet next time he came to L.A.

Some months later, Chris called. He said he was in town and stopped by with his wife for a visit. We talked about "the old days" for about four hours, but nothing of any real consequence surfaced. Since my investigation at that time was *sub rosa*, naturally I made no mention of the "Black Dahlia" or any other suspected criminality. It was obvious that Chris was saddened about my father's passing and his memories of the man were seemingly filled only with fondness and respect. After listening to Chris talk about Dad for a number of hours, my sense was that he considered George his mentor.

I had no further contact with Chris for about two years. By then, my book had been published. In 2004, he sent a letter saying he had read BDA and found it difficult to believe that the George Hodel he knew could have committed such crimes. He remained highly skeptical.

Enclosed in his letter was a photograph of some of the 1948 roomers then living at our home. The photograph was entitled "Tree of Life—Shangri-LA, 1948." Chris identified each individual in the photo by hand-writing their names next to their "branch" on the tree.

"Tree of Life-Shangri-LA, 1948"

Franklin house tenants from top down:
1. Suzanne D'Albert
2. Gladys Krenek
3. Dorothy Bowman
4. Fuji Walker
5. Tony Walker
6. Chris D
7. George Hodel
8. Ellen Taylor
[1948 tenants: artist Joe Barrett and actress Carol Forman not in photograph.]

I have very few specifics on the various roomers living with us back in the late Forties. I know that Dad did not begin to rent out any rooms until 1948, which was at least one full year after the Black Dahlia murder.

I believe that most of the above named tenants were gone either before or soon after George's arrest for incest in October 1949. We know that Joe Barrett is still there in February 1950, and that George was interviewing prospective tenants as late as March 1950. But based on the transcripts, it sounded as if conditions might have prevented any new occupancy.

I am going to provide a very brief and limited sketch of some of the named tenants because I think it is important to understand that George Hodel, in addition to being connected to Hollywood's elite—A-list writers and directors—also had direct "in-house" connections to its working actors and artists, which might well provide us with some future linkage.

Let's start at the top of the "tree" and work our way down.

SUZANNE D'ALBERT

Suzanne D'Albert, circa 1949

Suzanne D'Albert was born in France on May 12, 1927, and would have been just twenty-one when she moved into the Franklin house. She was reportedly discovered by Paramount mogul Hal B. Wallis. Suzanne spoke five languages (French, English, German, Russian, and Spanish.) Her filmography credits her with twenty-seven acting parts in film and television. Tragically, she died from an apparent suicide from an overdose of sleeping pills in Paris in 1971 at the age of forty-three.

In the photo below, we see Suzanne posing with seven other young women, including Marilyn Monroe and Enrica "Ricky" Soma in a 1949 *Life Magazine* article featuring up-and-coming Hollywood starlets. Monroe, at the time this photo was taken, was in Los Angeles shooting a small part as "Angela" in John Huston's *Asphalt Jungle*. Ricky Soma would marry John Huston that same year and became his fourth wife. Bizarrely, this photo with Suzanne D'Albert appeared in the October 10, 1949, edition of *Life Magazine*, which was George Hodel's forty-second birthday. [He had been arrested for incest just four days prior.]

(1) Marilyn Monroe (2) Laurette Luez (3) Lois Maxwell
(4) Suzanne D'Albert (5) Ricky Soma (6) Dolores Gardner
(7) Jane Nigh (8) Cathy Downs

GLADYS NORDENSTROM-KRENEK

Gladys Norenstrom was born in Mora, Minnesota, on May 23, 1924. I have little information on her life. She was an accomplished composer and shortly after living at the Franklin house, married world-renowned Austrian composer, Ernst Krenek in 1950.

DOROTHY BOWMAN

At the time Dorothy Bowman was renting a room at the Franklin house, she was twenty-one and was already a recognized Los Angeles artist. Her works had been shown at galleries throughout the Southland and she most certainly would have been a friend and acquaintance of fellow artist and regular houseguest Fred Sexton and his wife Gwain.

Dorothy attended L.A.'s Chouinard Art Institute, where she met fellow painter Howard Bradford. The two also studied together at the Jepson Art School in Los Angeles. This is the same school where Fred Sexton was an art instructor and was fired, because according to Joe Barrett, who also attended the school, "He [Sexton] was hitting on all the young girls and half the class left, so Herb Jepson fired him."

Dorothy Bowman and Howard Bradford relocated to the California coast of Big Sur around 1950, where they became part of that community and befriended writer Henry Miller, another famous Franklin house visitor. The two artists eventually married. Both Dorothy and Howard became internationally respected and their paintings and serigraphs can be found in museums throughout the world.

Dorothy Bowman art shows, 1950
[Los Angeles Times]

FUJI AND TONY WALKER

I have no biographical information on Fuji or her son, Tony but I'm sure, like all the others, there's is a story just waiting to be told.

ELLEN TAYLOR

Ellen was the maid. I am not sure exactly when she began working for Dad. Perhaps in mid- to late 1947. From the photograph, we know she was there in 1948 and remained until the spring of 1950.

We also know from the DA tapes that she was a "full-service maid." Sex with George was—from the sound of the explicit recordings—a part of her regular duties. To quote the eloquence of the detective's log, "Sounds like Ellen just gave George another blow-job." It is also clear from the tapes that she wanted and demanded sex and became very upset when George told her, "No, not tonight."

In BDA, in the chapter, "The Franklin House Revisited," I mentioned an interview I conducted with "Bill Buck" [not his real name] who owned and had been living in the house for thirty years, and whose father, a medical doctor, bought the home from Dad in 1950.

It's worth retelling here since I am sure his descriptions, coupled with Joe Barrett's separate comments, clearly suggested that the person described was Ellen Taylor.

BDA page 263:

Another strange incident: Buck told me about the appearance of a "bag lady" who came to the door back in the 1970s or early '80s. "She looked quite old," he said, "but with street people it's hard to tell." I spoke with her and she said, 'This house is a place of evil'." He said that normally he would have simply dismissed her, but then she continued to describe the interior of the house. "It was very scary," he said. "She obviously had been inside this place before we owned it. She described in detail to me: the great stone fireplace, and your father's gold bedroom, and the all-red kitchen that your father had painted. No question that she was very familiar with the house when your dad had lived here. She looked at me and said again, 'This is a house of evil.' God knows what connection she had with this place. She left, and I never saw or heard from her again."

Based on a conversation I had with former tenant Joe Barrett, it is my belief that the person Buck described as a "bag lady" was most probably our former maid, Ellen Taylor, Father's live-in housemaid/girlfriend, who lived at Franklin House from 1945 to 1950. In later years, Joe Barrett had run into Ellen on the street in downtown Los Angeles and discovered that she had been in and out of mental hospitals. Joe Barrett described her as "living on the fringe, delusional, claiming she had had affairs with a number of prominent and locally famous personages." (Knowing what we now know, perhaps Ellen was not as delusional as Barrett thought.)

While we cannot be positive that the "bag lady" was Ellen, all the pieces fit together quite well. The discovery and reading of the DA files established that Mother and we three boys were not at the house during the weeks before and after the murder of Elizabeth Short. But now a new question arises—was Ellen? She was questioned by DA investigators in 1950 but unfortunately, hers and many other interviews of George Hodel's acquaintances were not among the DA papers secured in the vault. And, as we know, LAPD's copies have all "disappeared."

CAROL FORMAN

Carol Forman was also a roomer at the Franklin house; she was just not at home when the *Tree of Life* photo was taken. (Unless she took it.)

Carol was born June 19, 1918, and would have been thirty at the time she was renting a room there. According to her filmography, her first part was in the 1946 RKO film, *From this Day Forward*. That same year, Carol had a bit part as a secretary in the *noir*-thriller, *Nocturne*, a story written by Rowland Brown, who, in 1946, was involved in an ongoing romance with my mother, Dorothy Hodel.

In 1947, Carol played Sombra in *The Black Widow*, establishing herself as a leading villainess. True to form, in 1948, she starred as Spider Lady, taking on mild mannered reporter Clark Kent [Kirk Alyn], in Columbia's big screen serialization of *Superman*.

Carol Forman secretary scene in Nocturne (1946)

1948 clips of Carol Forman as Spider Lady in Superman

As if written for a Twilight Zone episode, Carol Forman was selected and appeared on this January 1947 calendar, which was the same month Elizabeth "Black Dahlia" Short was brutally murdered at George Hodel's Franklin house. Then one year later, the unsuspecting actress rented a room and moved into and resided at the crime scene.

CAROL, TIM HOLT, AND MY BRO

My younger brother, Kelvin "Kelly" Hodel, was born in October 1942, just eleven months after the birth of my twin, John and I. He would be Dorothy and George's fourth and final son. Kelly, from an early age, "loved the girls," and believe me—the girls loved him. This 1949 Franklin house anecdote is appropriate:

At the time Carol was living with us at the Franklin house, she was dating film star Tim Holt. The two actors had worked together in a number of B-westerns, including the 1947 *Under the Tonto Rim* and again in 1948 on *Brothers in the Saddle*. Tim Holt, who had just received huge critical acclaim for his role as the down-on-his-luck drifter Bob Curtin in John Huston's *The Treasure of the Sierra Madre*, naturally visited Carol at the house regularly.

Brother Kelly, then aged six or seven, had a terrible crush on Carol. And whenever Tim showed up to take her on a date, Kelly would object, informing Holt in no uncertain terms, "She's my girlfriend." Finally, Holt could take it no longer and took Kelly into the center courtyard, *mano a mano,* and made the following suggestion:

"Look Kelly. You're too young to be with Carol now. I will date her only until you get old enough. And then you and Carol can get married. And I will get on my horse and ride off. Fair enough?"

Kelly agreed. Holt and Hodel shook hands, and the battle for Carol's heart was ended—without having to fire a shot to find out which was the fastest gun alive.

My brother, Kelly, [left] and I in the courtyard of Franklin house, circa 1949

Carole Forman, after appearing in more than twenty-four separate films, then turned her acting skills to television and theatre. She died in Burbank, California, in 1997.

This short peek into the lives of these five Franklin house tenants gives us a much broader understanding of just how eclectic and far-reaching was George Hodel's web of connections.

In the 1940s, his hand was either directly on or at least only one degree away from the power and the politics that was Los Angeles. As he told Baron Harringa on the DA tape:

"I'm the only one that knows how all these things fit together."

EDMUND TESKE

"Bill Buck," the former Sowden/Franklin house owner whom I interviewed in 2001, after telling me about "the bag lady," mentioned a second visitor.

BDA, pages 263-264:
Bill Buck also told me that another man who had visited the house on three different occasions over the years was a photographer named Edmund Teske, "a local photographer and sort of a fixture here in old Hollywood. He had a home just down the street on Hollywood Boulevard. He visited here three separate times over the years and told me he was a good friend of both your father and Man Ray."

In 2001, I had never heard of Edmund Teske, and his name meant nothing to me. I ignored the information for about a year until it came up again, this time from former Franklin house tenant Joe Barrett.

I was visiting Joe in his home in Ventura, California, and we were looking at some old photographs that my father had given me. One of them showed my two brothers and I standing inside the Franklin house courtyard. I had dubbed it, "The Three Musketeers."

I showed this photo to Joe and told him that I suspected it might have been taken by Man Ray.

Joe smiled. "No, not Man Ray," he said. "It was taken by another photographer friend of George's. His name was Edmund Teske. I know, because I was there when he took it. Teske was a friend of both your dad and Man Ray."

PHOTOS BY EDMUND TESKE, CIRCA 1948

"The Three Musketeers" [Left to right: Steven, Michael, Kelvin]

Second photo by Edmund Teske taken from inside the living room
[Left to right: Michael, Steven, and Kelvin]
My brothers are now holding the two black cats while I blow bubbles.

This second reference got my attention. Later, I discovered that Edmund Teske, while ever the eccentric, had a remarkable past and deep ties to Hollywood up until his death in 1996.

Here is an excerpt from the J. Paul Getty Museum on a retrospective called, "Spirit into Matter: The Photographs of Edmund Teske" that ran from June to September 2004.

> Edmund Teske (1911–1996) was one of the most significant artist-photographers active in Los Angeles in recent decades. He approached photography as a highly malleable medium, open to the artist's intervention at several points in the creative process. An inventive darkroom technician, Teske created photographs that expressed his emotional and spiritual concerns. His images reveal the power of memory and dreams to transform our perception and understanding of the visual world.
>
> ...

And from a Getty Research biography:

> ...
> In the mid-1940s, Teske relocated to Los Angeles, where he initially worked at Paramount Pictures in the photographic still department. He continued to photograph and began to exhibit his images more frequently. His increasing experimentation led to his use of the solarization technique to reverse highlight and shadow. In 1956 he detoured briefly from photography to appear in the film biography of Vincent van Gogh, *Lust for Life*. After 1960 he frequently returned to older negatives, reinterpreting them through the use of experimental printing techniques.

From the Edmund Teske Archives:

> Teske was drawn west by the allure of the motion picture industry and a desire to meet Greta Garbo. He worked in the stills department of Paramount Studios. He lived at the Frank Lloyd Wright residence of Aline Barnsdall on Olive Hill where he met Man Ray and other notable folk. He photographed actors and notable folk throughout his career. To name a few: Joel McCrea, Geraldine Page, Kenneth Anger, John Saxon, Ansel Adams, Jim Whitney, Ramblin' Jack Eliott, Will Geer, Anais Nin, Jane Lawrence, and others.

Edmund Teske, friend to Aline Barnsdall, was an artist in residence here at "Hollyhock House" in Studio B from 1944-1949.
Hollyhock House, 4800 Hollywood Boulevard, Hollywood, California

The Frank Lloyd Wright-designed residence known as "Hollyhock House" rests atop a hill at 4800 Hollywood Boulevard in East Hollywood.

It was built for Aline Barnsdall in 1921, who would later donate the home and its surrounding eleven acres to the city of Los Angeles to be preserved as a public art park.

The home is located only five blocks from the Franklin house and as a child, I have many fond memories of my brothers and I riding our bikes the short distance to play all day in "Barnsdall Park."

"SYNCHRONICITY HAPPENS"

In mid-September 2011, I received notification of the imminent closing of one of Los Angeles's oldest and most respected downtown restaurants, Clifton's Cafeteria at Seventh and Broadway. The notice also contained an invitation for those interested to meet and have a "last luncheon" before the closing and renovation by the new buyer. Although I didn't know any of the dozen or so people planning to attend, I decided to go out of respect for the original philanthropist owner Clifford Clinton, who had done so much for Angelenos in the 1930s and '40s.

The small group of us met outside at noon, introduced ourselves, then went inside to pick from hundreds of cafeteria "choices." Out of homage to the establishment, I went with the blue-plate special—traditional turkey, mashed potatoes, and gravy, which Clifton's sold during the Depression to the needy for a penny.

The brainchild for the luncheon was Steve Lamb, a residential architect from Altadena, California. Steve and I got to talking and it turned out that he had read my books. He then went on to tell me a most remarkable story that he said he had been relating to his friends for over thirty years. After hearing the story, I asked him if he could "write it up" and send it to me. He did, and here is a scan of his letter, which I received on September 28, 2011:

STEVEN S. LAMB

P.O. BOX 333, ALTADENA CA. 91001 ███████████

28 Sept. 2011

MEETING ED TESKE

Back in the late 1970's I used to volunteer at a Christian ministry to street people in Hollywood called CENTRUM OF HOLLYWOOD. Often I volunteered on our suicide prevention hot line called the Hollywood Lifeline. Before I would do my shift on the lifeline, I would go over to the Sowden house on Franklin and park my Triumph T.R. 3 in front. I'd try to park about half an hour before sunset. As the sun would set the colors and shapes of the textile blocks on the house would seem to change and I would take those wonderful moments of beauty with me as I volunteered.

One cold fall evening in 1978 I was leaning against my Triumph with my deerstalker on lighting my calabash pipe. I was looking east and I saw a tall thin man with a purple coat and a limp walking towards me. He looked like an old wino. The man came up to me and stood very close leaning over me and with a expressive voice said

"DO you like the House?"

"Why yes, Sir, it's a very important and early Lloyd Wrigh.."

"It's an E V I L place! Artist's Philosophers,accountants and politicians we all played and paid there. Women were tortured for sport there. Murders happened there. It's an E V I L place."

He walked down about half a block, spun on his heels and pointed at me like an Old Testament movie prophet and again said

"It's an E V I L place."

I thought he was just some old wino. All the street people said the Sowden house was evil. I assumed it was because the roof and balcony configuration were different, and it was kind of run down in those days, so there had to be a Hollywood legend about it. I figured this guy was just another half crazed old street person and that in any case his facts were all wrong, he was confusing this house with Fatty Arbuckle's house down the street, and whatever happened there, happened in San Francisco, anyway.

About a decade later, I was a member of both the Taliesin Fellows and the Wrightian Association. Those groups were having a combined event at the Pacific Design Center, on photographing Frank Lloyd Wright. We were doing so in part to honor a new book by Pedro Guerro, who had been Frank Lloyd Wright's personal photographer in the late 1930's, 1940's and 1950's.

In the lobby of the Auditorium there was a large U made up of several tables selling various books, ties, T shirts and photographs related to Frank Lloyd Wright. I bought a copy of Pedro's book and got it autographed and looked over the stuff for sale, most of it I had already.

At the end of the U, as far away from the entry as possible, were a collection of large sepia toned photographs, each about 16" wide and 24" long. The Photographs were mounted on brown construction paper and there were geometric Wrightian designs drawn sometimes at a corner, sometimes at a side. They were in the new gold ink paint pens that had just come out and were each signed in gold "Edmund Teske". I thought this was strange, the signature looked right, but I had assumed Teske to be long dead, since I had seen no new photographs of his in some twenty years.

As I was looking through the pile of sepia prints of Hollyhock house, a tall thin man entered the room and was warmly greeted by Paul Bogart, Eric Lloyd Wright and Pedro Guerrro. This I thought was strange, as I recognized the man as the wino who told me the Sowden house was a evil place a decade before.

The tall man walked over to where I was looking through the Sepia Prints. He stood in front of me, leaned in towards me and said

"Do You like the photographs?"

"Yes,Sir. I like them very much. They are the most beautiful photographs of any Frank Lloyd Wright building I have seen, they have captured the buildings the way Architects see them before they are built."

(He had, too. His photos were much more evocative of the spirit of the Architecture within it than any Pedro or anyone else I have ever seen has done.)

The man smiled at me and held my gaze for a very long time. He had a pride in his eyes. Incredulous, I asked him-

"Sir, are YOU Edmund Teske?"

"Well I'm Ed Teske, or what's left of him."

He said roaring as he laughed with an open mouth devoid of many teeth.

"Would you like to B U Y a photograph?"

"Sir, I would very much, but they are $300.00 and I only have $280.00 in the bank. May I come see you when I have some money and buy one?"

"Certainly."

He wrote his name and address down for me on a scrap of paper. I still keep it at the front of my address book, and like a fool, I never did go back and buy one of Ed Teske's prints. Now they are worth a cool $30,000 or so each…

This apparent chance meeting with Steve, his wife Jeanette, and a handful of his friends at Clifton's is another remarkable example of how the facts and corroborations just keep coming. All I can say is … synchronicity happens.

SOME TESKE AFTERTHOUGHTS

Edmund Teske in scene clip from MGM's Lust for Life *[1956]*
In this scene with Kirk Douglas [Vincent Van Gogh] and Anthony Quinn [Paul Gauguin] Edmund Teske, a fellow artist, is questioning Van Gogh's skill as an artist. Teske was forty-five years-old when the film was released. Quinn won an Oscar for Best Supporting Actor.

For those who would categorize this chance conversation between Steve Lamb and Edmund Teske as nothing more than the rantings of a "mad artist," a lost and delusional soul whose words were not to be trusted, consider the following—his well-documented biography.

I will pick up his bio just from 1978 forward. The conversation in front of the Franklin house occurred when Teske was sixty-six. Here are some of the highlights of his life and some remarkable personal accomplishments after that conversation:

My biographical source came from: *Edmund Teske: A Chronology* compiled by Michael Hargraves, as found in *Spirit into Matter: the Photographs of Edmund Teske* by Julian Cox, Edmund Teske, J. Paul Getty Museum. What follows is only a partial summary from Hargraves' chronology:

...

1978: Conducted workshop for the Friends of Photography and Lectures at the Society for Photographic Education National Conference, Pacific Grove, California

1979: Invited and became visiting professor of the Photography Department at California State University, Los Angeles.

1980: Led a workshop at the Victor School, Victor, Colorado. Guest speaker at Camera vision's Artist's Hot seat series, Los Angeles.

1981: One group show. Photographer or Priest maker, Ferens Art Gallery, Hull, England (followed by several other British venues).

1982: Presented slide lecture at the University of Colorado at Boulder; conducted a one-week workshop at the School of the Art Institute of Chicago.

1983: Taught a photography workshop at Otis Art Institute of Parsons School of Design, Los Angeles.

1986: Gave a workshop and seminar at the Victor School, Victor, Colorado.

1987: One group show, Los Angeles County Museum of Art.

1988: Was the subject of a two-part television film produced by Light-borne Communications, Cincinnati, Ohio.

1989: Lectured at the Santa Monica Public Library on Photographers and their Art.

1990: Teske was shot by an unknown assailant in the doorway of his Hollywood studio on Harvard Boulevard; suffered debilitating injuries to his jaw and the left side of his face.

1991: Participated in a symposium at the J. Paul Getty Museum, The Relevance of History and Theory to the Creative Process, moderated by Weston Naef, with Ralph Gibson, Jo Ann Callis, David Hockney, Gay Block, and Richard Misrach.

1993: One-man exhibition at J. Paul Getty Museum

1995: Gave a talk at UCLA at the Armand Hammer Museum of Art.

1996: Died at his downtown Los Angeles studio on November 22 of a heart attack. Memorial service was held at Hollyhock House on December 14.

These active and very dynamic eighteen years after Lamb's encounter demonstrate Teske to be a lecturing professor and world traveler, with all of his faculties completely intact.

With the further understanding that Edmund Teske was clear-headed and of sound mind in 1978, some twenty years before I even began my investigation, let us re-examine his disclosure to Steve Lamb in front of the Hodel Franklin house. Also, let's keep in mind that Teske was a close friend of both Man Ray and George Hodel, and obviously a regular visitor to the house, as well as (at least on one occasion) being our "family photographer."

> "It's an evil place! Artists, philosophers, accountants and politicians *we all played and paid there.* Women were tortured for sport there. Murders happened there. It's an EVIL place."

I have no reason to doubt or question Steve Lamb's specific quoting of Teske's words.

What Teske told Lamb some thirty-three years ago independently supports what the "bag lady" [probably our maid, Ellen Taylor] had said, as well as the words spoken by fellow insiders, Joe Barrett and Lillian Lenorak, and certainly underscore Mattie Comfort's 2003 declaration that, "We all knew George Hodel did it. There was no doubt."

For Teske to disclose these secrets to a complete stranger begs the question: who else did he tell and in what detail? Certainly, he would have shared this knowledge with at least some of his own close personal friends and confidants.

Edmund Teske, July 1996
Screen capture from YouTube video interview in tribute to Global Liberty Exhibition by Jean Ferro. Teske died just four months later in November 1996.

11

The Black Dahlia's Three Greatest Myths
Myth No. 1—"A Standalone Murder"

"The Black Dahlia murder was a stand-alone. Her killer never committed a crime before nor after her brutal murder."

LA LONE WOMAN MURDERS

IN MARCH 1947, LAPD believed a number of the recent lone woman murders were committed by the same killer, and released a written "11 Points of Similarity" summary to the daily newspapers to support their theory.

In this March 14, 1947 *Los Angeles Examiner* article, printed just eight weeks after the Black Dahlia murder, LAPD revealed its considered opinion that the murders of Elizabeth Short (January 15), Jeanne French (February 10), and Evelyn Winters (March 12) were all committed by the same killer and listed its reasons. Here are excerpts from that original article:

> **"Dahlia Case Similarities Checked in Fourth Brutal Death Mystery"**
> ...
> Checking similarities between the deaths of Miss Winters, and the Short, and French killings, police listed the following:
>
> 1) All three girls frequented cocktail bars where they sometimes picked up men.
> 2) All three were slugged on the head (although Mrs. French was trampled to death and Miss Short tortured before being cut in two).
> 3) All three were killed elsewhere and taken in cars to the spots where the bodies were found.
> 4) All three were displayed nude or nearly so.

5) In no case was an attempt made to conceal the body. On the contrary, bodies were left where they were sure to be found.
6) Each had been dragged a short distance.
7) Each killing was a pathological case, apparently motiveless.
8) In each case, the killer appears to have taken care not to be seen in company with the victim.
9) All three women had good family backgrounds.
10) Each was identified by her fingerprints other evidence of identity having been removed.
11) Miss Short and Miss Winters were last seen in the same Hill Street area.

In January 1947, the press suggested a link to four of the victims. Then by 1950, it was up to seven.

The 1949 Grand Jury issued a scathing report on the unsolved Black Dahlia and new Lone Woman Murders and ordered that the investigation of these crimes be taken away from LAPD and restarted by the District Attorney's Office.

LAPD and the L.A. County Sheriff's Department were both convinced that many of their unsolved 1940s slayings were committed by the same killer.

Posted below are two separate 1949 front page headlines where police and press both link a new killing, Mrs. Louise Springer, to the Black Dahlia's murderer and speculate that perhaps at least nine of the previously unsolved "Horror Murders" are connected.

"Mother Kidnaped, Slain; Seek Curly-Haired Man New 'Black Dahlia' Case" —Los Angeles Examiner, June 17, 1949

"Police are not overlooking the possibility that a single slayer committed all [nine] of the Los Angeles 'Horror Murders.'" —Long Beach Press Telegram, June 17, 1949

The *Long Beach Press Telegram* article provided details on the June 16, 1949, slaying of Louise Springer and then named the eight previous victims possibly killed by "a single slayer":

1. Elizabeth Short ("Black Dahlia")
2. Mary Tate
3. Evelyn Winters
4. Jeanne French ("Red Lipstick Murder")
5. Rosenda Mondragon ("Silk Stocking Murder")
6. Dorothy Montgomery
7. Laura Trelstad
8. Gladys Kern ("Real Estater Murder")
9. Louise Springer

Three months later, in September 1949, LAPD Chief of Detectives Thad Brown removed any question that LAPD suspected many of the L.A. murders were connected when he told the press his investigators were checking out a sex-strangulation murderer named Ray Dempsey Gardner, age twenty-seven, arrested in Ogden, Utah.

In the *Los Angeles Times* piece, "Alleged Garroter May Be Linked to Killings Here," Chief Brown is quoted as saying, "...efforts will be made to trace his activities in the hope of forming a connection with local murders."

The article goes on to specifically name the suspected crime victims as: "...Elizabeth Short, Jeanne French, Louise Springer, Georgette Bauerdorf, as well as other similar cases."

Alleged Garroter May Be Linked to Killings Here

A sex killer who has confessed three garroting murders at Ogden, Utah, was seen as a possible suspect yesterday in Los Angeles' long series of violent sex slayings.

Asst. Police Chief Thad Brown, chief of detectives here, dispatched a written request to the Sheriff at Ogden requesting details of the story told by Ray Dempsey Gardner, 27, in jail there on the sex crimes.

Brown said that accounts from Ogden detailed Gardner's admitted stranging of Shirley Gretzinger, 17, in Ogden last July. He also took police to the body of a second victim, Sue Horn, 30, of Montana, and yesterday said he strangled a cellmate in a North Dakota jail.

Strangling and sex motives have figured in the murders here of Elizabeth Short, Jan. 15, 1947; Mrs. Jeanne T. French, Feb. 10, 1947; Mrs. Louise Springer, June 16, 1949, and Miss Georgette Bauerdorf, Oct. 12, 1944, as well as other and similar cases. .

Brown said that if Gardner is unable to account for his movements during the times of any of the unsolved Southland murders, and if his record indicates possibility of his presence here during those times, efforts will be made to trace his activities in the hope of forming a connection with local murders.

Los Angeles Times, September 14, 1949

The fact that law enforcement suspected a serial killer from the get-go was eventually drowned out by tabloid accounts that created the Dahlia Myth. The truth was replaced by pulp fiction magazines and sexploitation novels. Hollywood dream-makers and spin doctors have never really cared about facts. Nightmares are the stuff their dreams are made of—and so it went.

By the Nineties, even the cops bought into the myths and legends. "A stand-alone crime, none before, none after." None of the "new breed" had ever read the case files or did any in depth study of the original investigation. They were simply ignorant of what their "old school" predecessors, the original Black Dahlia investigators, had suspected all along—many of the 1940s' Lone Woman Murders were serially connected to the same killer.

Lone Woman Murders—Updates

LA Lone Woman Murders 1943-1949 Category I (definites)

In my original BDA 2003 and in the updated chapters published in the HarperCollins revised editions ["Aftermath" chapter, 2004 and "New Investigation," 2006], I broke the suspected crimes into separate categories: I-"Definites" [strong *modus operandi* and signature linkage] II-Probables, and III-Possibles.

Within the Category I range, I initially listed seven (7) victims, most of whom corresponded with LAPD's suspected list of serial victims. Those original seven were:

1. Ora Murray-1943
2. Georgette Bauerdorf-1944
3. Elizabeth Short-1947
4. Jeanne French-1947
5. Gladys Kern-1948
6. Mimi Boomhower-1949
7. Jean Spangler-1949

Ora Murray—"White Gardenia Murder" Update

Sixty-seven years after the crime was committed, I believe I have found another link to the brutal murder of Mrs. Ora Murray, one of the eight "Category I (definites) L.A. *Lone Woman Murders*, which was originally summarized in my 2003 publication of *Black Dahlia Avenger*.

Below is a brief summary of the crime M.O. (For those wanting a fuller description, I suggest you read BDA Chapter 23, pages 294-306.)

On the evening of July 26, 1943, forty-two-year-old Murray and her sister Latona Leinann went out for a night of drinks and dancing at the Zenda Ballroom at Seventh and Figueroa in Los Angeles. [The dance hall was just one block from Dr. Hodel's medical office at Seventh and Flower.]

The victim, married to an Army sergeant stationed in Mississippi, was only in town visiting her sister.

At the dance hall, the two women met and danced with a man named "Paul." Ora's sister later described Paul as being "tall and thin, very dapper and a very good dancer. He wore a dark double-breasted suit and a dark fedora." Paul claimed he was from San Francisco, "just down to L.A. for a few days." After several dances, Paul offered to drive Murray on a sight-seeing tour of Hollywood. She accepted and after first driving the sister home, the couple then started their ostensible Hollywood exploration.

Some eight hours later, Ora Murray's partially nude body was found on the grass at the Fox Hill Golf Course in West Los Angeles. She had been severely beaten about the face and body and the cause of death was found to be, "constriction of the larynx by strangulation." Ora's killer had ceremoniously wrapped her dress around her body like a sarong and then carefully placed a white gardenia under her right shoulder. Based on this unusual signature, the press dubbed the crime "the White Gardenia Murder." Since the body was found just outside of the city limits, the case was handled by L.A. County Sheriff's homicide detectives.

Ora Murray- 1943 White Gardenia Murder victim

A COPYCAT CRIME—MURDER AS A FINE ART

I enjoy listening to *old-time radio* programs. In April 2010, I was reviewing an online index of the old CBS *Suspense Theatre* dramatizations, and one of the titles caught my eye: *The White Rose Murders.*

The show was originally broadcast from CBS's then relatively new Columbia Square Playhouse Studio in Hollywood, at Sunset and Gower. It starred the beautiful twenty-two-year-old actress Maureen O'Hara, and was first aired on July 6, 1943—just twenty days before the "White Gardenia Murder" of Ora Murray.

The radio mystery-play was written by a popular novelist and pulp-fiction writer Cornell Woolrich, who also used the pseudonyms William Irish and George Hopley.

During the 1930s and 1940s, Woolrich saw more than thirty of his short stories and several of his novels made into films. Two of the best known were *The Night has a Thousand Eyes (1948),* directed by John Farrow, and the Alfred Hitchcock classic, *Rear Window (1954),* which was adapted from Woolrich's original short story, *It Had To Be Murder.*

Woolrich's 1943 radio drama, *The White Rose Murders,* told the story of a homicidal maniac who frequented the city's downtown dance halls, where he danced with and picked up lonely women. The killer then lured them out into the night where he strangled them to death. As a signature of his kills the madman carefully placed a white rose next to each victim's body.

In the vernacular of the day, the police detective described him as a "chain killer." And as the story opens, the listener learns the city is gripped in terror as the unidentified strangler has just slain his fourth victim, and is about to kill his fifth.

Police called the fictional killer a deranged "avenger," a woman-hater seeking personal revenge on young women because he'd been rejected by them in his youth.

We recall that George Hodel, in his 1944 Georgette Bauerdorf murder note, informed the public that the reason he killed her was for "divine retribution." And, in his 1947 note, as the "Black Dahlia Avenger" he assured us, "the Dahlia Killing was justified."

The *Suspense Theatre* radio-plays, were hugely popular and always introduced by "The Man In Black." I am surprised that neither reporters or cops made the obvious connection between the radio show and the Ora Murray murder just three weeks later.

Those who've read my sequel, *Most Evil,* will have a fuller understanding of the importance of this newly discovered link. Why? Because in my father's later serial killings it became an important and recurring theme that he used as part of his murder-signature.

In his 1960s crimes, he expanded his *Murder as a Fine Art* from mere surrealistic mimicry of Man Ray's photography—as seen in his Black Dahlia murder—and splashed it on a much broader canvas.

In *Most Evil*, we discovered that George Hodel expanded his "masterpieces" beyond modern art and ventured into the world of music, film, and literature.

This is why this new discovery, demonstrating another example of his early mimicry of Cornell Woolrich's storytelling, is so important. It reinforces my theory that this was a signature act that George Hodel used in 1943, some four years before he imitated Man Ray's art in the macabre Black Dahlia murder.

Within two weeks of the fictional *White Rose Murders* broadcast, I submit that Dr. George Hill Hodel, as "Paul," the dapper businessman from San Francisco, made it real. He followed the original *White Rose Murders* script, seeking out and auditioning his own dance hall partner-victim, Ora Murray, for the part.

"Paul" danced with her, bought her drinks, and then wooed her out of the Zenda Ballroom with an invitation to "see Hollywood for a night-on-the-town." He then drove her to an isolated golf course, beat and strangled her, and with a final dramatic flair, carefully placed a "white gardenia" next to her dead body.

In *Most Evil*, I examined several separate murders that I believe my father "adapted from film," and used in his real life killings. One of these, Richard Connell's *The Most Dangerous Game*, was famously used by the Zodiac Killer as part of his signature M.O. and was subsequently mentioned in his letters to the press and police.

Among 1940s *Suspense Theatre* programs, *The Most Dangerous Game* was also listed as being performed at the same CBS Theatre. It aired in Hollywood on February 1, 1945, and starred Orson Welles as the psychopathic General Zaroff. (In 1969, the serial killer "Zodiac" costumed himself in the fashion of General Zaroff and terrorized the Bay area, informing the public that in committing his murders he was playing, "the most dangerous game.")

How many more of these fictional stories from literature and film might George Hodel have adapted and abridged into his real-life murders? So far we have documented four: *Charlie Chan at Treasure Island, The Most Dangerous Game, The Gold Bug,* and now, *The White Rose Murders.* I am aware of a fifth film, to be discussed in detail in an upcoming chapter of this book. I expect more will be found.

Since my last publication in 2006, based on new investigative findings, I am adding two more victims to that Category I list. I am upgrading one victim, Louise Springer, from a Category II "probable" to a definite, based on new information.

The second case appeared on my radar screen in 2009. Her name is Lillian Dominguez, slain in October 1947.

Here is a brief summary on both of these new Category I killings.

LOUISE SPRINGER—JUNE 13, 1949

"The Black Dahlia and the Louise Springer murders might be linked. Both crimes could have been committed by the same man."
— Detective Harry Hansen, LAPD Homicide, *Los Angeles Times*, June 1949

Detective Harry Hansen reviewing Dahlia Files

At about 9:15 p.m., on the evening of June 13, 1949, Laurence Springer drove his new Studebaker convertible to pickup his wife. Louise Springer met him in the parking lot on Crenshaw Boulevard, near Santa Barbara, where she worked as a beautician. As she entered the car, Louise noticed that she had left her eyeglasses inside the beauty parlor. Her husband ran inside to get them for her and also purchased a newspaper and cigarettes at an adjacent drugstore. He was gone less than ten minutes. Upon his return, both his car and his wife, Louise, were gone.

The husband immediately called LAPD, which referred him to University Division Police Station, where the desk officer advised Mr. Springer he couldn't make a missing-persons report for 24 hours. The husband tried to convince the officers that his wife would not simply drive away, and that she had to have been the victim of foul play. Sadly, his pleas fell upon deaf ears. Frustrated and angry, the husband returned to his Hollywood home to be with their three-year-old son, and hoped his wife would call.

Three days later, Laurence Springer's fears were confirmed. Louise Springer's body was found in the backseat of their car, parked on a quiet residential street about an hour after her disappearance. Here is the investigative chronology and findings:

June 13, 1949—9:15 p.m.

Victim Louise Springer, a twenty-eight-year-old female, was kidnapped, in her own car, while waiting for her husband to return from a short errand.

Within forty-five minutes, her abductor strangled her with a pre-cut clothesline rope that he brought with him, and then sodomized her with a fourteen-inch tree limb.

The killer then placed her body in the rear seat of her car and covered it with a beautician's tarp that Louise kept in the car for her work.

The kidnap location was on South Crenshaw Boulevard, just north of Santa Barbara Avenue [now Martin Luther King Boulevard] and just 500 yards southwest of where Elizabeth "Black Dahlia" Short's body parts were found in the vacant lot at 3815 South Norton Avenue some two years before.

Springer – Short crimes 500 yards apart

June 13, 1949—10:30 p.m.

Four witnesses observed Springer's vehicle, a 1949 Studebaker convertible, moving eastbound on Thirty-Eighth Street. They saw it swerve suddenly to the south curb and quickly park in front of 126 West Thirty-Eighth Street.

They later said the driver turned off his headlights and slumped down behind the steering wheel.

Seconds later, an LAPD patrol car with flashing lights pulled over a teenage driver nearby. As the witnesses watched, the Studebaker's driver sat motionless while the officers got out of their patrol car and wrote a ticket for the teenager, who was standing just a few yards away.

The officers then got back into their patrol car and drove off.

But the witnesses continued to watch. They saw the man reach toward the Studebaker's backseat, as if he were adjusting something. At that point, their curiosity was apparently satisfied and they stopped watching.

Because it was dark, they could only describe the man as "a white male with curly hair."

This all happened about forty-five minutes after the abduction, but because the witnesses were unaware that any crime had been committed, nothing was reported for three days.

On June 16, a different neighbor grew suspicious of the abandoned Studebaker and called the police.

Officers checking the license plate number determined that it was the missing Springer vehicle and they soon found Mrs. Springer strangled under a tarp in the backseat. Homicide detectives canvassed the area and found the four witnesses who described what they had seen on the night of June 13th.

The below map shows the probable four-mile route taken from the abduction site to where the vehicle was parked at 126 West Thirty-Eighth Street.

Driving directions: 3960 Crenshaw Blvd, Los Angeles to 126 W 38th St, Los Angeles

A Start: 3960 Crenshaw Blvd, Los Angeles, CA 90008-2543

A-B: 3.9 mi, 10 min

126 W. 38TH St. - 4 miles [10 minutes] from abduction location

Los Angeles Examiner—*June 18, 1949*

"Police Missed Mad Killer, in Auto with Slain Victim, Parked Near Squad Car."

The *Examiner* printed a diagram showing the relative positions of the police, the traffic offender, and the murder suspect on 38th Street.

Los Angeles Examiner, June 18, 1949

Los Angeles Examiner of June 17, read:

...

Body Violated

"And with a 14-inch length of finger-thick tree branch, ripped from some small tree, the killer had violated her body in such manner as to stamp this crime at once and indelibly in the same category as the killing of Elizabeth Short, "the *Black Dahlia*.""

LAPD Criminalist Ray Pinker called in a botany expert who identified the branch as coming from a "Bottlebrush tree."

The below photo shows a bottlebrush tree, which is indigenous to all neighborhoods of Los Angeles and the actual tree branch used by killer in the sexual assault. [Cropped by author from the original Louise Springer coroner's photograph.]

Top: Bottle Brush Tree
Bottom: photo is the actual tree branch used by suspect in the sexual assault.

This October, 1949 Booking photo of George Hodel showing his "Black, curly hair" was taken just three months after the Louise Springer murder.

Photo showing "Springer Murder Car" Article reads, "The discovery has touched off the wildest man hunt since the slaying of the Black Dahlia."

The autopsy was performed by Drs. Newbarr and Cefalu—the same doctors who did Elizabeth Short's autopsy two years before. Their examination revealed that Louise Springer suffered multiple blows to the head that would have likely rendered her unconscious. She was then strangled with a white clothesline cord, which the killer brought with him.

1949 Louise Springer autopsy photo showing pre-cut clothesline rope used by suspect.

Autopsy photo [cropped] showing clothesline ligature

SOME ADDITIONAL INVESTIGATIVE FINDINGS:

- Police suspected killer might have known the victim. Possible jealous ex-boyfriend? Detective Hansen and his partner traveled to San Francisco for a weeklong investigation into the victim's background. Newspapers of the day hinted at a "possible romantic affair." No hard evidence believed found.
- Before the murder, a male called Laurence Springer's work telephone six times over six days, always hanging up. He also called the Springers' home.
- Although LAPD continued to suspect that the Springer, Elizabeth Short and other lone woman murders could be connected, Louise Springer's sadistic killer, like the others, was never identified.

- 1949 Grand Jury demanded a reinvestigation of the Elizabeth Short and other unsolved murders and Louise Springer's photo was added to the long list of unsolved murders in this 1949 story:

"L.A. POLICE BAFFLED BY NINTH WEIRD MURDER IN 29 MONTHS" —Long Beach Post-Telegram, June 17, 1949

LILLIAN DOMINGUEZ—AN OVERLOOKED 1947 *LONE WOMAN MURDER*

Based on my examination and review of the known facts surrounding the stabbing-murder of Santa Monica victim Lillian Dominguez, age fifteen, in October 1947, I am now adding her name to the list of Category I, Los Angeles Lone Woman Murders that I believe were committed by my father, Dr. George Hill Hodel.

On the night of October 2, 1947, Lillian Dominguez, a fifteen-year-old student at John Adams Junior High, was walking home from a school dance with her sister Angie and their friend, Andrea Marquez.

As the three girls approached the intersection of Seventeenth Street and Michigan Avenue in Santa Monica, a man approached in the darkness and walked past them. Seconds later, Lillian told her sister, "That man touched me." She took a few steps and yelled, "I can't see." Lillian staggered against the fence, collapsed, and died.

An autopsy found Lillian had been stabbed in the heart with a long, thin bladed "stiletto-type knife" or icepick. The half-inch wide blade penetrated three and a half inches directly into her heart. The only description police ever got was the teenager's exclamation that it was "a man."

Santa Monica detectives had little to go on. They had a useless physical description and not motive. Lillian had no boyfriends and there was no trouble at the Garfield Elementary School dance.

AT INQUEST—Angie Dominguez, 17, left, sister of girl stabbed to death, and Andrea Marquez, 17, friend, testify at inquest for victim, where open verdict was returned.

LA Times October 7, 1947, victim's sister Angie Dominguez and friend Andrea Marquez

THE MURDER WEAPON

Stiletto type knife blade
Coroner reports stab wound
penetrated 3.5" and blade
was 1/2" in width

Stiletto-type knife or icepick used

Based on the limited information in the 1947 newspaper article, I sent an e-mail inquiry to my friend and fellow writer, Dr. Doug Lyle M.D., a forensic expert and heart specialist. Here is an excerpt from that e-mail:

May 9, 2010

Hi Doug:

...

In reviewing a press article on the stabbing/murder the info from the coroner's office printed in the paper reads:

"Dr. Frederick Newbarr, county autopsy surgeon, reported after performing an autopsy that the stab wound in the girl's left breast is 3 3/4" inches deep and a half inch wide and that it penetrated only the heart muscle, not the heart itself.

Death, he said, apparently was caused by internal bleeding. Severance of nerves could have numbed pain and caused the blindness of which the girl complained, Dr. Newbarr said."

1) Forgive my anatomical ignorance, but what is the distinction/difference between "the heart and the heart muscle?" What are they saying here?

2) Any thought on the blindness. Would that be unusual or common with the facts as stated?

Thanks,
Steve

And, here is Dr. Lyle's reply:

Howdy:

This shows you how far behind they were 70 years ago. The heart muscle is the main part of the heart and the part that would be stabbed in such an injury as this. Severing of nerves—of which there are no major ones in that area—would NOT cause blindness. Either she had some other injury or the blindness could be the hysterical type. Some people under extreme stress go blind—it is all psychiatric—and is called hysterical blindness. Or in this case she could have been in shock or her blood pressure could have suddenly dropped from the heart injury and if so the low blood pressure could cause blurred and then dim vision just before losing consciousness and dying. I'd suspect this latter is what happened since she died almost immediately after her visual complaints.

Doug

AVENGER NOTE

On the evening of October 9, 1947, exactly one-week after the stabbing, Lillian's killer left a handwritten note under the door of a Los Angeles furniture store.

The note, written in pencil on the back of a business card of a Mexican restaurant, read:

"I killed that Santa Monica girl. I will kill others."

While neither the furniture store nor the Mexican restaurant locations were identified by police, the information and threat from the killer was published in the *Santa Monica Evening Outlook* on October 10, 1947, which was George Hodel's fortieth birthday.

We do know that the furniture store was outside the city of Santa Monica and in Los Angeles. We recalled in some of the other Lone Woman murders George Hodel left or mailed the Kern and Short notes just blocks away from his downtown medical office. Was either the furniture company or the Mexican restaurant also near his medical offices?

DOMINGUEZ "AVENGER" SIGNATURE

In my 2009 sequel, *Avenger, Zodiac, and the Further Serial Murders of Dr. George Hill Hodel* [Dutton], I explored the possible connections of George Hodel to three 1946 Chicago "Lipstick Murders." In that book, I also examined the 1966 knife slaying of a Riverside student; the "Jigsaw Murder" in Manila, where my father was living at the time and where police suspected the killer was a trained surgeon; and finally, I explored and presented compelling evidence potentially linking my father to the 1968-1969 Bay Area murders committed by the killer calling himself "Zodiac."

In this review, I am only going to present one specific and highly unusual aspect of the killer's method—that being his "promise to kill more victims." That act, combined with the fact that we are dealing with a serial killer, is so unique that I believe it qualifies as a part of his actual signature.

Let's examine the photograph below, a reproduction of the separate notes left by the killer[s] in Chicago, Los Angeles, Riverside, and the San Francisco Bay Area.

The Notes

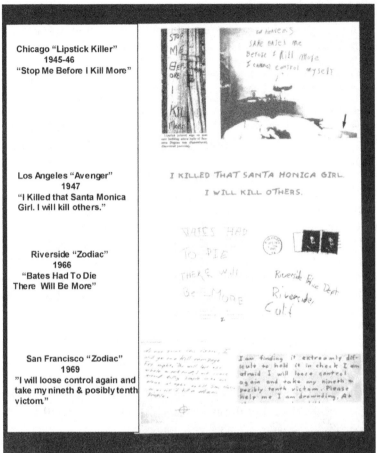

The Los Angeles Dominguez Note, "I killed that Santa Monica girl. I will kill others," was discovered after my 2009 sequel, Most Evil, *and is here presented only as a "reproduction" of what the killer wrote. Law enforcement never released a sample of the actual 1947 handwriting. The Chicago, Riverside, and San Francisco notes are all actual copies of the killer's original handwriting.*

Chicago, 1946—(written in lipstick):
"For heavens sake catch me before I kill more. I cannot control myself.
"Stop Me Before I Kill More."

Los Angeles,1947:
"I killed that Santa Monica girl. I will kill others."

Riverside, 1966:
"Bates Had To Die. There Will Be More.
"Z"

San Francisco, 1969:

...
"I am afraid I will loose control again and take my nineth & possibly tenth victom. Please help me I am drownding."

In *Most Evil*, one of my most important signature links was the fact that the killer in Chicago, Riverside and the San Francisco Bay Area was an "urban terrorist," and left notes in each of those cities, threatening to "kill more." If this was an accurate assessment then why had he excluded this important signature in his many L.A. crimes in the 1940s?

He had threatened the citizenry before and after, so why would he choose to exclude them in his hometown of Los Angeles?

Until now, we had no answer. And the absence of a Los Angeles "urban terrorist threat" weakened my hypothesis. However, with this recent discovery of the Dominguez Note, we now have an answer. Fact is, he didn't exclude L.A. The threat was always there, it was just overlooked. I didn't make the connection until discovering the note in my recent review of the facts surrounding the Dominguez Cold Case which read:

"I Killed That Santa Monica Girl. I Will Kill Others."

THE LOCATION

In the diagram below, we see that the Lillian Dominguez murder is just two miles away from another 1947 Lone Woman murder—Mrs. Jeanne French.

According to Head Deputy District Attorney Steve Kay, the French crime was committed by Dr. George Hill Hodel, and based on the evidence presented, had George Hodel still been alive and the witnesses available, he would have prosecuted the case, as a companion filing to the Elizabeth Short, "Black Dahlia" murder.

Two miles between 1947 Dominguez and French motiveless murders

AN AVENGER MOTIVE?

In the 1966 Cheri Jo Bates murder in Riverside, the victim was a teenager who had just graduated from high school.

Riverside PD investigated the possibility that her killer was a high school classmate. Detectives based their theory on a literal interpretation of a second typed note mailed by Bates' killer on the six-month anniversary of her slaying.

[George Hodel mailed in both a lengthy handwritten and a typed letter in two of his 1940s L.A. crimes: Georgette Bauerdorf (typed) and Gladys Kern (handwritten).]

In that lengthy typewritten note taunting the police and press, Bates' killer referred to his next victim and speculated on who it might be:

... "a babysitter, or maybe she will be the shapely blue-eyed brownett that said no when I asked her for a date in high school?"

In 1971, San Francisco police connected the Bates murder in Riverside to their Northern California Zodiac crimes.

Six of their seven victims were either teenagers in high-school or recently graduated. All were parked in "lover's lane" locations, reinforcing the possibility of an avenger-type serial killer exacting revenge rejections in his high-school days by some young "shapely blue-eyed brownett." (I hypothesize that George Hodel, the "super nerd," could well have been rejected numerous times by girls both in high-school and in college, since he was one of the few fifteen-year-olds at Cal Tech. He would very likely have been rejected by many college classmates because of his youth.)

The motive-less, cold-blooded killing of high school student Lillian Dominguez in 1947 fits quite well with what we know about these later crimes against high-schoolers, as well as Zodiac's stated need to avenge a youthful rebuff by a would-be girlfriend.

Based on the "hit and run" nature of the Dominguez crime and absence of any real physical evidence or witnesses, I doubt the crime is now solvable. But, it would be interesting to see the original note and compare it to George Hodel's known handwriting. Also, I am curious as to where the Mexican restaurant and the furniture company were located.

Regardless, I do think this crime might provide a missing piece in a much larger puzzle. Based on its unique signatures, location, and what is known about George Hodel's later crimes, I do believe it should be considered and included as a 1940s Category I Lone Woman murder.

Lone Women Murder Map [revised 2011]

In this updated victim map, I have added both the 1947 Lillian Dominguez murder [9] and the Louise Springer murder [10].

That makes a current total of nine Category I victims. All happened within a half-mile to nine miles from the Franklin house.

The black circles are 1940s victims where a letter or note was left or mailed by the "Avenger." This is an exceptionally rare signature act, and we find that in six of the nine Los Angeles murders (Short, Bauerdorf, Boomhower, Kern, French, and Dominguez), he taunted police with such a note or letter.

A serial killer sending taunting notes to the police in the 1940s was so rare that before the "Black Dahlia Avenger," police would have to have gone back in time some six decades to London's "Jack the Ripper" (1888) to find a similar signature.

The author of most of the Avenger notes has been independently identified by a court-certified questioned document expert as Dr. George Hodel. To date, no certified expert has offered an opinion that the handwriting is *not* George Hodel's.

In the past seven years, two separate television documentaries have claimed that "an expert contradicted my expert." In fact, he did not; he simply stated that in examining the few samples he was provided, he was unable to offer an opinion either way. He told the producers, "His findings were inconclusive. He was unable to rule Dr. Hodel in or out as to having authored the notes." I will provide further details related to the handwriting evidence in a later chapter.

Elizabeth Short and Gladys Kern letters mailed from same downtown mailbox
Killer uses same downtown mailbox to post both his Elizabeth Short (January 1947) and Gladys Kern (February 1948) handwritten notes to police. The mailbox he used was across the street from the Biltmore Hotel and just 300 yards from Dr. George Hodel's private medical practice.

1950 DA FILES REVEAL INVESTIGATORS BELIEVED CRIMES LINKED

District Attorney Lt. Frank Jemison's 1950 investigative files show that his detectives were actively investigating connections between the Lone Woman murders of Elizabeth Short, Jeanne French, Jean Spangler, Gladys Kern, George Hodel's secretary Ruth Spaulding, and the suspected felony assault or possible murder of a Jane Doe heard on tape from the basement of Dr. Hodel's Franklin house on February 18, 1950

BY THE NUMBERS

As I pointed out in my original 2003 investigation, if one takes the position that none of these 1940s Lone Woman murders were connected then, statistically, at least half should have been solved. None were.

It's now obvious these murders were not committed by eleven different sadistic sexual psychopaths all operating within the same locales and tripping over each other's bodies. The reason none were cleared was because all were committed by the same killer.

Despite the fact that sixty-years ago law enforcement did not really think in terms of "serial killings," LAPD (with a lot of help from the press) still managed to go public with their belief that many or most of these killings were serial crimes.

With the June 13, 1949, murder of Louise Springer, police reaffirmed, as they had from the very beginning, their suspicions that many if not all of the crimes were connected.

"Police are not overlooking the possibility that a single slayer committed all [nine] of the Los Angeles 'Horror Murders'" —*Long Beach Press Telegram*, June 17, 1949

Long Beach Press Telegram, June 17, 1949

The newspaper article goes on to name the nine victims they suspect are related as:

1. Elizabeth Short
2. Mary Tate
3. Evelyn Winters
4. Jeanne French
5. Rosenda Mondragon
6. Dorothy Montgomery
7. Laura Trelstad
8. Gladys Kern
9. Louise Springer

[*All of these names* are included in my original investigation; however, some are listed by me as Category II and III.]

12

Myth No. 2—"The Missing Week"

"On the evening of January 9, 1947, Elizabeth Short, the Black Dahlia, walked out of the Olive Street entrance of the Biltmore Hotel, turned right, and was last seen walking south on the sidewalk. She was never seen again, until her nude, bisected body was found six days later, on January 15, posed on the vacant lot."

ONE OF MY BIGGEST INVESTIGATORY REVELATIONS came to me late in the year 2000, when I was just completing my first full year on the case. I had spent four full months chronicling the known facts and had amassed 150 different witness interviews covering the time period from 1943-1999.

After sorting them by date, time, and location, in looking at the limited time frame of January 9-14, 1947, it became obvious that there never was a missing week. All of the original witness interviews from that time period, which law enforcement had collected independent of each other, supported the same truth—there was *no missing week*.

Apparently, no one before me, including modern LAPD detectives, had taken the time to take a look at this. That's partly understandable for LAPD because it was extremely time-intensive research that required many months to compile. But there it was!

Only now in recent years, have I come to understand why <u>modern</u>-day authors, theorists, and even LAPD have no desire to underscore the obvious. Why?

In LAPD's case, it proves that their official public position —in place for decades—is simply not true. If confirmed, it exposes the department to criticism of being inept, ignorant, or misinformed about the true facts.

No conspiracy here. The truth is simple. No modern-day LAPD detective is familiar with the facts of the case, nor have they been since the 1950s.

In the 1970s, when LAPD Robbery Homicide detectives John St. John ["Jigsaw John"] and his partner Kirk Mellecker were assigned as the official custodians of the case, they were at least honest enough to admit, they "didn't have the time to fully review the facts of the long cold case due to active case demands."

By the 1990s, when Detective Brian Carr inherited the forty-year-old case, all pretense about familiarity with the facts had been dropped. Carr quickly named himself a "gatekeeper" and said publicly "the case will never be solved" and he would "pass it on when he retired."

By 2007, Detective Carr, confronted with constant questions from the press about my investigative findings, was forced to give an on-camera interview where he simply stated, "I don't have time to prove or disprove Hodel's investigation." Carr, true to his word, "passed the case on" when he retired from LAPD in May 2009.

LAPD Wanted Information Bulletin contributed to "Missing Week" Myth

At first glance, without reading the information, the official LAPD Wanted Information Bulletin would appear to confirm a missing week between January 9-15, 1947.

However, closer examination proves that it does just the opposite. The bulletin is actually a request for information.

It was prepared and circulated just four days after Elizabeth Short's body was identified, and it is exactly what its title suggests: a wanted information bulletin.

The bulletin was originally distributed to uniform patrol officers and detectives at all roll-calls, and instructed officers to attempt to locate witnesses who might have seen her:

"Make inquiries at local hotels, motels, apartment houses, cocktail bars and lounges, night clubs to ascertain whereabouts of victim between dates mentioned."

On January 21, just five days into the investigation, LAPD officers began distributing the bulletin and asking questions if anyone had seen the victim between the dates of January 9 to 15?

Their actions resulted in twelve (12) verified reliable sightings of the victim. Elizabeth Short was seen on every day of the week from January 9 through January 14. Half of these witnesses personally knew her and could not have been mistaken.

Here are the facts:

All of the witnesses listed below made official reports directly to the LAPD. They are fresh accounts from January, 1947.

They were published in the various Los Angeles newspapers in the days and weeks immediately after the discovery of the body. [See BDA Chapter 18, pages 232-238 and page 527 for a detailed narrative of each of these 1947 witnesses' statements, and where and when they were documented.]

Witnesses Chronological Sightings During Elizabeth Short's "Missing Week"

(Name in **bold/italic** indicates witness **personally acquainted** with Elizabeth Short)

WITNESS	DATE	LOCATION
Mr. Studholme Biltmore Hotel employee	Jan. 9 (Thur) 7-10 p.m.	Biltmore Hotel 5th & Olive St. (Olive Street entrance) Downtown L. A.
"John Doe #1" (LAPD withheld name)	Jan. 10 (Fri) evening	7200 Sunset Blvd. Hollywood (street) Hollywood
Miss Iris Menuay *(Former roommate/friend)*	Jan. 10 (Fri) 8:30 p.m.	1842 N. Cherokee Ave Chancellor Hotel (lobby) Hollywood
Christina Salisbury *(Restaurant owner/friend.* *Employed victim in Florida)*	Jan. 10 (Fri) 10:00 p.m.	7290 Sunset Blvd. Tabu Club, Hollywood (street) Hollywood
Buddy La Gore *(Bartender, knew victim as a* *"regular")*	Jan. 10 (Fri) 11:30 p.m.	6818 Hollywood Blvd. Four Star Bar & Grill (bar) Hollywood
"John Doe #2" (Hotel service. station attendant LAPD withheld name)	Jan. 11 (Sat) 2:30 a.m.	9641 Sunset Bl. Beverly Hills Hotel (gas station) Beverly Hills
Mr. Paul Simone *(Maintenance man Chancellor* *Hotel)*	Jan. 11 (Sat) daytime unstated hour	1842 N. Cherokee Ave Chancellor Hotel (rear and front) Hollywood
Mr. I. A. Jorgenson (Cab driver)	Jan. 11 (Sat) afternoon unstated hour	112 W. 5th St. Rosslyn Hotel (Entered cab at front of hotel) Downtown L. A.
Mr/Mrs William Johnson (Hotel owners/on-site managers)	Jan. 12 (Sun) 11:30 a.m.	Hotel 300 E. Washington Bl. (Hotel lobby/registration desk) Downtown L. A.
Mr. C. G. Williams *(Bartender, knew victim as a* *"regular")*	Jan. 12 (Sun) 3:00 p.m.	634 S. Main St. Dugout Cafe (bar) Downtown L. A.
Mr. John Jiroudek *(Jockey/friend, knew victim from* *Camp Cooke military base)*	Jan. 13 (Mon) unstated hour	Hollywood & Highland (Street) Hollywood
Officer Meryl McBride (LAPD uniformed police officer, two contacts half hour apart)	Jan. 14 (Tues) 3:30 -4 p.m.	6th & Main St. Bus Depot(street/bar) Downtown L. A.

DIAGRAM OF LOCATIONS

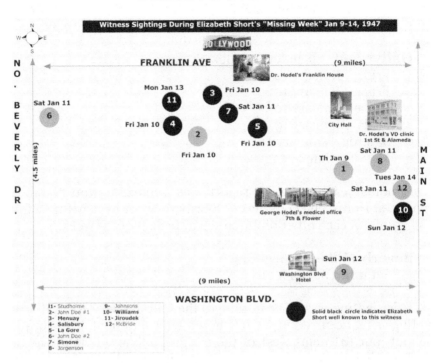

Above diagram shows the 4-mile-by-9-mile perimeter between Hollywood and downtown Los Angeles, within which boundaries Elizabeth Short was seen on twelve separate occasions during the five days (January 10—January 14) prior to the discovery of her body on January 15, 1947. Incredibly, six of these twelve witnesses were personally acquainted with the victim, so their positive identifications are not in question. (Solid black circles signify those witnesses.)

Also included in the diagram are: Dr. George Hodel's 1947 private residence, the Franklin house at 5121 Franklin Avenue, his privately owned downtown VD clinic at First and Alameda Street, and his private medical practice, at Seventh and Flower Street, just three blocks from the Biltmore Hotel [1].

Sightings of Elizabeth Short by location and day of the week during the five-day period:

Downtown Los Angeles—five independent sightings
1. Thursday, January 9
2. Saturday, January 11
3. Sunday, January 12
4. Sunday, January 12
5. Tuesday, January 14

Although each witness' report was separate from the other reports, all these downtown sightings of Elizabeth Short were within a one-mile radius of each other on four separate days of the week.

Hollywood—six independent sightings
1. Friday, January 10
2. Friday, January 10
3. Friday, January 10
4. Friday, January 10
5. Saturday, January 11
6. Monday, January 13

Although each witness' report was *separate* from the other reports, all Hollywood sightings of Elizabeth Short were within a four-block radius of each other on three separate days of the week.

Beverly Hills—one sighting
1. Saturday, January 11

This sighting was close in time to the four January 10 Hollywood sightings as it occurred just a few hours after midnight. This location is about four [4] miles west of the earlier Hollywood sightings, and was immediately west of the Sunset Strip, just inside the Beverly Hills city limits.

Los Angeles Herald-Express
Feb 7, 1947

'Dahlia' Seen in 'Lost Week'

The "lost week" of the "Black Dahlia" prior to her murder was narrowed by two days today with a report that placed her in the city on Jan. 11, four days before her body was found.

A service station attendant ... handles the gasoline pumps at the Beverly Hills Hotel "positively" identified the slain beauty, Elizabeth Short, as one of the occupants of a car that drove up for gas between 2:30 and 3 a. m. on that date.

The attendant said the "Dahlia" was accompanied by another woman and a man, and that she seemed "very upset and frightened."

The man driving the car, a 1942 tan Chrysler coupe, was described as about 30 years old, 6 (Continued on Page 10, Column 2)

LAPD Capt. Jack Donahoe was convinced that the January 11, 1947, witness sighting at the Beverly Hills Hotel gas-station was accurate and kept the "John Doe No. 2" witness' name confidential. Here is the report from the February 7, 1947, *Herald Express* article on that sighting:

> The "lost week" of the "Black Dahlia" prior to her murder was narrowed by two days today with a report that placed her in the city on Jan 11, four days before her body was found.

A service station attendant who handles the gasoline pumps at the Beverly Hills Hotel "positively" identified the slain beauty, Elizabeth Short, as one of the occupants of a car that drove up for gas between 2:30 and 3 a.m. on that date.

The attendant said the "Dahlia" was accompanied by another woman and a man, and that she seemed "very upset and frightened." The man driving the car, a 1942 Chrysler coupe, was described as about 30 years old, 6 feet 1 inch tall and weighed about 190 pounds. The other woman was dressed in dark clothing, the attendant said. Capt. Jack Donahoe ordered an immediate check on the car and its occupants.

...

During her so called, "Missing Week" [it was actually only a five-day period], Elizabeth Short was seen in Hollywood on six separate occasions by six different witnesses. *Five of the witnesses KNEW her personally and could not have been mistaken.* [The sixth might have also known her, but his name was withheld by police and released publicly only as "John Doe."] All of these Hollywood contacts were within a four square block area occurring on three separate days of the week. [January10, 11, and 13.]

Jan 10- 7200 Sunset Blvd
Jan 10- 1842 Cherokee Ave
Jan 10- 7290 Sunset Blvd
Jan 10- 6818 Hollywood Blvd
Jan 11- 1842 Cherokee Ave
Jan 13- Hollywood & Highland

HOLLYWOOD

Locations of six (6) confirmed Elizabeth Short, "Black Dahlia" sightings in Hollywood during "Missing Week"- Jan 10-13, 1947

SCALE
ONE HALF MILE

13
Myth No. 3—
"Black Dahlia Murder Never Solved"

"Since 1947, hundreds of suspects were questioned by LAPD detectives, but the killer of the Black Dahlia was never identified. The case was never solved."

LAPD, LASD, DA BUREAU OF INVESTIGATION OFFICERS PAST AND PRESENT AGREE:

"CASE SOLVED"

Despite the nearly sixty-year chasm that divides the investigation past and present, we now have statements from the four highest-ranking police officers confirming that the Black Dahlia case was solved.

These four detectives were directly involved in the original Dahlia investigation and privy to its secrets. These officers represented all three law enforcement agencies in Los Angeles: The city [LAPD], the county (LASD) and the Los Angeles District Attorney, the prosecutor for both city and county. Their statements are all the more remarkable in that they were made in absolute confidence and each is derived from a separate person, place, and time, they substantiate each other. None of these command officers' statements were ever intended to be made public. Each was a personal communication, which remained private and confidential decades after their respective deaths. All four indict the same man, "a Hollywood physician, living on Franklin Avenue, involved in abortions." They kept his name secret for over five decades.

Though never arrested, the Black Dahlia murder, according to top commanders from all three Los Angeles law enforcement agencies agree, was solved.

Now, thanks to the 2003 access and release of the secret DA files, we now know his name and address as revealed in those original reports.

OUT OF THE PAST—THE BLACK DAHLIA'S TOP BRASS:

LAPD Chief of Detectives Thad Brown, circa 1950

"The Black Dahlia case was solved. He was a doctor who lived on Franklin Avenue in Hollywood." [Statement made in the 1960s to his close personal friend, actor Jack Webb. *Dragnet's*, "Sgt. Joe Friday".]

LAPD Chief of Police William H. Parker, circa 1950

"We identified the Black Dahlia suspect. He was a doctor." [Statement made to his personal physician circa 1964.]

L.A. County Sheriff's Captain of Detectives J. Gordon Bowers, 1947

"The Black Dahlia case was solved, but it will never come out. It was some doctor they [LAPD] all knew in Hollywood involved in abortions." [Statement made by LASD Undersheriff James Downey to his chief of detectives J. Gordon Bowers circa 1961. Statement made in the presence of Downey's driver, Deputy Tom Vetter, who would later be promoted to LASD Commander.]

DA Lt. Frank B. Jemison

"We know who the Black Dahlia killer was. He was a doctor, but we didn't have enough to put him away." [Statement made to Jemison's visiting nephew and his physician brother-in-law at the L.A. Hall of Justice in the summer of 1951. Jemison's nephew grew up and became a medical doctor.]

OUT OF THE PRESENT- THE DA'S OFFICE, LAPD, AND LASD

Steve Kay, L.A. County Head Deputy DA [ret.], 2006

"Steve Hodel has taken this way beyond the pictures. It no longer depends on the pictures." [Statement in *Los Angeles Times Magazine*, November 21, 2004.]

"I have no doubt in my mind that George Hodel murdered Elizabeth Short...If the witnesses were alive today, I believe if I took that case in front of a jury, that I would convict him." [Rue 13, French television documentary, *The Truth about the Black Dahlia*, November 6, 2006.]

LAPD Deputy Chief James McMurray [ret.], Chief of Detectives

"The hardcover book was pretty compelling. Then when all the transcripts and stuff came out from the D.A.'s Office that took it over the top for me. That would have been enough for me to bring a case against Dr. Hodel." [LA Times, November 21, 2004.]

"I have told my detectives, unless that can find some major holes in Hodel's investigation—to go ahead and clear the Black Dahlia murder." [November 2004]

LASD Commander Thomas Vetter [ret.], Lt. Col. USMC [ret.]

"In 1962, I was a detective and was the driver for Undersheriff James Downey who was the sheriff department's number two man. One day, he was going to lunch with his good friend, Gordy Bowers, chief of detectives. Somehow, the Black Dahlia murder came up in the conversation. I heard Jimmy say, 'Oh, that had been solved, but it will never come out. It was some doctor they [LAPD] all knew out in Hollywood.' In my own professional opinion, Hodel has put the pieces together and solved the case." [Television interview, October 2004]

LAPD Deputy Chief of Detectives James McMurray and Chief William Bratton honor author at LAPD Author's Night function, 2004

Los Angeles Times 1947

Canyon Combed in Short Killing

Sheriff's officers yesterday searched an area in Las Tunas Canyon, near Malibu, for possible clues to the murder of Elizabeth Short after a blood-drenched man's shirt, bow tie, and a rusty, blood-caked razor blade were found inside a culvert.

Inspector Norris Stensland and Capt. Gordon Bowers, of the Sheriff's office, explored the possibility that the "Black Dahlia" was slain and her body severed in the culvert, but a search by them and four deputy sheriffs turned up nothing to bolster the theory.

Stensland said nothing definite yet linked the bloody clothes and razor blade with the Short murder. But, he added, the culvert quite possibly could be the scene of the butchery.

The clothes and razor blade were being scrutinized under microscopes to determine if the dried blood is the same type as Miss Short's.

MURDER CLUES SOUGHT—Inspector Norris Stensland and Capt. Gordon Bowers of sheriff's department search canyon culvert near Malibu for possible Short murder clues.

1947—Then Capt. Gordon Bowers "Working the Black Dahlia Case"

LOS ANGELES SHERIFF'S DEPARTMENT COMMANDER THOMAS M. VETTER

I originally met sheriff's commander Tom Vetter in 2003 at a book signing in Orange County. At that time, he was wearing a different hat and was Lt. Col. Vetter, U.S.M.C., active president of the First Marine Division. [July 2003-August 2005]

I would later discover that Tom was one of LASD's most respected command officers with forty years of distinguished service to law enforcement. His reputation as a leader in both the sheriff's department and the US Marine Corps are twenty-four carat gold.

In September 2004, Commander Vetter was interviewed by a television producer in connection with his knowledge of Black Dahlia-related events that occurred in 1962. But because of time restraints, the interview never aired.

Historically, this is a truly amazing interview that documents the then-young sheriff detective's first-person exchange with his Chinatown drinking-buddy detectives and as driver for Undersheriff James Downey, LASD's number two command officer. As Downey's driver, he was privy to a conversation wherein he learned that "the Dahlia Case was solved."

Vetter's first-person account leaves no doubt that many old-timers on both the LAPD and LASD knew who the Dahlia's killer was, that there was a cover-up, and the reasons why he was not pursued.

As a young deputy in the detective bureau, Tom Vetter was there. Listen to his words as he takes the interviewing television producer back in time to a backroom bar at Little Joe's Restaurant in the heart of Chinatown. The bar was one of the favorite watering holes for old-school cops and deputies to meet, drink, and exchange scuttlebutt.

Thank you Tom Vetter! A heartfelt thank you for your years of dedicated service to Angelenos and for your outstanding leadership as an officer and a gentleman!

THE INTERVIEW

Commander Tom Vetter (ret.)
Los Angeles Sheriff's Department
Lieutenant Colonel, USMCR (ret.)
President, First Marine Division, July 2003-August 2005
Interviewed–September 2, 2004 Los Angeles, California
(Tape transcription)

QUESTION:
Tell me a bit about yourself—how you started in the sheriff's department, and what you did there.

TOM VETTER:
I started off on the City of Bell Police Department. I was there about a year and a half. And—started there in January of '57, and—then I went on the Los Angeles County Sheriff's Department—graduated from the Academy and worked prisoner transportation, and Norwalk Station, and Lakewood Station, and—Firestone Station in the Night Detective Corps.

I went on the Academy staff as a Drill Instructor—because of my teaching ability and Marine Corps background. I spent three years there training new cadets. Then I was transferred to Detective Headquarters, and—from there I was selected to work—as an aid to Under sheriff Jimmy Downey.

I worked Headquarters Detective Division, and—I commanded the Arson and Bomb Squad, working antiterrorist investigations. Got promoted to captain, and—went to the Labor Relations Detail—commanded that. Then I commanded the San Dimas and Walnut Sheriff Station—a regional command. I was promoted to commander. I worked at our Headquarters of the Sheriff's Department, and also commanded the Training Bureau later on.

I was a field commander. Also, within patrol with the Sheriff's Department, was assigned as the night duty commander. So, I had nearly forty years law enforcement and serving the people of Los Angeles County.

QUESTION:
That's quite a resume—Tom, tell me—tell me about the Black Dahlia murder. It was a big deal back then, right?

TOM VETTER:
That was a great big deal—of course, it happened in the late '40s, but—carrying right on into the '50s and '60s, and so on. It's been a big deal, because it's been unsolved and of great notoriety, and it was always of interest—to everyone.

QUESTION:
You were how old at the time? Do you remember it at all?

TOM VETTER:
In 1947—I was twelve years old.

QUESTION:
Do you remember hearing anything about it?

TOM VETTER:
No, not at all. I was raised in Missouri and—I don't remember it being in the papers back there then.

QUESTION:
Big story here, but maybe not so much there.

TOM VETTER:
Right.

QUESTION:
But, surely when you moved out here and—joined law enforcement here, it's always been—tell me if I'm wrong, but I—I believe it's always been one of those—one of those big cases—that cops talk about.

TOM VETTER:
It's always been on the front burner. You always hear everybody talking about it. It was always a big deal case, and you—you'd—hear it being discussed every now and then by the detectives and—talking about it. It was of great interest to them.

QUESTION:
Why did they—was there ever any as to why the thing was—with all of the manpower that was put on it—why it was never—never solved? Did you ever hear that kind of scuttlebutt?

TOM VETTER:
Yeah, I have. Just—that scuttlebutt was going around and—it'd come out in the scuttlebutt that they had really solved the case, and

they knew who did it. However, he was a doctor out in Hollywood, and—fairly prominent. And—back in those days that—some of the police officials, or District Attorney officials—City officials—would take their girlfriends there for abortions. And he was doing abortions, and he had a lot of information on various people, and they—they were afraid of it.

QUESTION:
You're saying this was the scuttlebutt in the Sheriff's Department when?

TOM VETTER:
All through the '60s—usually after work we'd go down to Chinatown and—have a taste or two while we were waiting for rush hour traffic to clear. And, the Sheriff's detectives and LAPD detectives and that—we'd meet down there. We became good friends and we'd talk about various cases.

QUESTION:
Well, run this down for me again. So, there you are in Chinatown. It's—it's the early '60s—you're all having a drink after work, and what's the scuttlebutt about the Black Dahlia case?

TOM VETTER:
Well, it came up occasionally, not often, but it came up occasionally. And, usually around the time of the anniversary of her death or murder. That's when they'd start talking about it, and the scuttlebutt was going around that it was known who did it, but they were afraid of it.

QUESTION:
Why?

TOM VETTER:
He was a prominent doctor in Hollywood. He hung around public officials, and—the police officers and this and that. And, the rumor was that many of them went to him to have abortions performed on their girlfriends, or whatever. And—they were afraid he had the—the goods on them.

QUESTION:
You heard this in scuttlebutt—off-hour scuttlebutt in the early '60s?

TOM VETTER:
Yes.

QUESTION:
From the way you tell it, the sense was—as you say, he had the goods on people? It that—am I correct?

TOM VETTER:
Right. He did according to them. They were afraid of him, because they had taken—girlfriends to him to get abortions performed, and—he knew them and he had the goods on them.

QUESTION:
Was a name ever connected to this person?

TOM VETTER:
Never. I never heard a name.

QUESTION:
But it was fairly common knowledge that—that this was the story? Am I correct?

TOM VETTER:
That's true. It was fairly common knowledge that it was a doctor in Hollywood.

QUESTION:
And, in 1962, you heard a very specific conversation about this, right?

TOM VETTER:
I did.

QUESTION:
Tell me the circumstances.

TOM VETTER:
I was a detective then in 1962 and I was driving Undersheriff Jimmy Downy and—he was going to lunch with then chief of detectives—Gordy Bowers, and they were good friends. As we were driving along—somehow the Black Dahlia murder case came up in their conversation.

And, I heard Jimmy say that "Oh, that had been solved, but it will never come out. Because, it was some doctor that they all knew out in Hollywood."

QUESTION:
Any name attached?

TOM VETTER:
No name.

QUESTION:
Did he go into any more detail about it?

TOM VETTER:
No, he didn't. He really didn't.

QUESTION:
Did that surprise you? Or, did that fit in with what you had heard before to that point?

TOM VETTER:
It surprised me somewhat, yes, because at—such a high level—the undersheriff is the number two man in the Los Angeles County Sheriff's Department, and he's privy to anything going on in the area. I knew that he knew—Chief Thad Brown, the chief of detectives for the Los Angeles Police Department then. It surprised me that—he would say that.

QUESTION:
Would you presume that—he got the information from Thad Brown?

TOM VETTER:
No, I wouldn't presume that, no. But, certainly he had to hear it from someone.

QUESTION:
Set the stage for me if you will a bit about the climate back then in the late '40s in—you know, in terms of—law enforcement and how clean or dirty it was, or compromised it was? What was going on during that period?

TOM VETTER:
Of course, I wasn't active in law enforcement at that time, but—talking to a lot of my friends that I worked with in the Sheriff's Department and policemen that I met, it was a whole different atmosphere and—the Department, perhaps both departments, the Sheriff's Department and Los Angeles Police Department—had a graft problem. And—they were not an honest department at that time.

And I say—perhaps unethical, to say the least—in many ways. It was a different atmosphere. Politics was very big and everything in those days. I think you could get things done or covered up, or whatever—with a payoff.

[...]

QUESTION:
In all those years—clearly there are unsolved cases, and then there are big unsolved cases. Where—where does the Black Dahlia fit in all of that?

TOM VETTER:
Probably one of the biggest, if not the biggest. I've heard about the Black Dahlia murder case ever since I came on and after I retired. And, I read in the paper where Steve Hodel was going to speak at— one of the local book stores. And—it's always been a fascinating case for me as a professional law enforcement officer. I felt I really wanted to go up and meet him. I did and I listened to his talk, and— afterwards, I went up and talked to him a while. And—I thought, 'This guy is really on to something. He really knows what he's doing and talking about.'

QUESTION:
It had the ring of truth to you from what you knew about-- what you'd been hearing back in the '60s?

TOM VETTER:
Yes, it did. It was all fitting in—all these little pieces. It's almost like a jigsaw puzzle, and it started fitting in, and from a professional standpoint. And looking at it from the outside, I could see where it was falling in place.

QUESTION:
Once again just about the climate back then in law enforcement in the '40s that you—that you were talking about.

TOM VETTER:
The Sheriff's Department and especially the Police Department in Los Angeles—did not have a good reputation then for honesty, integrity, ethics. They had some great problems then. They were known for payoffs and graft, and what have you. And—and the atmosphere was bad. Probably stayed that way until about the early '50s when Chief William Parker came in and he really reformed the Department and cleaned it up then.

QUESTION:
Do you think—as you know, Steve has written that—that he believes that a command decision was made—that for whatever reason we're going take a pass on this. We're going to let the guy get out of the country, or, you know, kind of sweep it under the rug. Do you believe that? Is that in keeping with what you know about—about Parker?

TOM VETTER:
Not really. I just don't think Chief Parker would do something like that. He was a man of integrity and honesty, ethics—just top man. However, it might be in keeping with some of the—people at lower ranks below him.

QUESTION:
And, the conversations that you've described for us would certainly indicate that something like that did happen?

TOM VETTER
We could assume that.

QUESTION:
That there was a suspect. They knew who he was, and for whatever reasons, they either couldn't touch him or didn't want to touch him.

TOM VETTER:
I would think they probably did not want to.

QUESTION:
Because?

TOM VETTER:
Because of his political connections, it would appear. And, his personal—personal knowledge of them. You know, really back in those days, abortion was of course, a crime, and certainly if somebody got caught performing abortions, or having one done, or what have you, they were in great trouble. People would go after them. The law would go after them.

QUESTION:
Do you think this case—has been solved?

TOM VETTER:
I think so. From my own professional viewpoint. I think Steve Hodel did an outstanding job in putting the pieces together. I think it's been solved.

QUESTION:
And, when you read his book, it—tell me if I'm wrong, but it would seem that it had—again, the ring of truth about it based on what you knew and had heard forty years ago.

TOM VETTER:
Exactly, because just some of the pieces—what I'd heard were small pieces. But, when you put them all together, it's bringing the whole big picture together of the Black Dahlia murder. I think Steve solved it.

I wouldn't be surprised if that doctor kept a diary of some type or note, and—certainly he knew who these politicians and officials were in government. And—I think they were really afraid of him. I would have to think that many of them were married, and had these girlfriends or mistresses on the side.

[...]

QUESTION:
Tell me once more...what would you hear? What sorts of things would you hear—the scuttlebutt?

TOM VETTER:
They'd just start talking about her murder, and—how she'd been murdered—how they found her—how she'd been carved up. And, because of the cuttings on her—if you will, and dismemberment, it had to be done by some medical person, probably a medical doctor. And, they'd discuss that. A lot of guessing on everybody's part as to what happened.

QUESTION:
But educated guesses, apparently, right?

TOM VETTER:
Educated guesses—I was a pretty young detective during those years in—in the '60s and—these other—these other men down there—other detectives had many years' experience. So, it was interesting to listen to them and just gain knowledge from their expertise.

These guys had worked the Homicide Detail and places like that and he had—great experience, so—

QUESTION:
And once again, just putting a—putting a cap on it.... Did he ever mention—use the term "covered up," "covered over" or you know, because of the doctor's influence or power. Do you know if they ever used those terms?

TOM VETTER:
Yeah, it was a cover-up. Just the scuttlebutt going around that—they had found who had murdered—they had discovered who had murdered her, and it was really a cover-up. Somebody had covered it up.

QUESTION:
Because?

TOM VETTER:
Because they were afraid that the doctor had the goods on too many people in high places—police official and city officials—politicians and that—regarding abortions.

QUESTION:
Abortions involving what?

TOM VETTER:
Abortions involving their girlfriends—their mistresses. Many of them were married at the time, and—they just felt the doctor had a lot of goods on them and perhaps he kept a diary or notes, or something.

QUESTION:
Now, as you say, you're a young cop—a young—sheriff's deputy at this—at this point—kind of learning the ropes. Were you shocked at this?

TOM VETTER:
Yeah, a little bit. You hear things, and you know, you experience things as these cases unfold, and you go through your career, but—it was a little bit shocking. I had to adjust my thinking back to the 1945s and what type of—atmosphere pervaded the Police Department then, and the Sheriff's Department.

End of interview

14
"A Doctor Did It"

"The fact that the killer was a physician, skilled in surgery, very much limited the suspect pool." — Stephen Kay, LA County Head Deputy District Attorney

ONE OF THE RARE POINTS that *all of the professionals* involved in the Dahlia investigation—past and present law enforcement officers, district attorney investigators, coroner's experts, and FBI—agreed completely about was that the Black Dahlia's killer was a physician skilled in surgery.

ELIZABETH SHORT AUTOPSY

On January 16, 1947, the day after her body was found, Dr. Frederic Newbarr, then chief autopsy surgeon for the County of Los Angeles performed an autopsy on the victim. He determined the cause of death was "hemorrhage and shock from a concussion of the brain and lacerations of her face." It was Dr. Newbarr's further opinion that "the trauma to the head and face were the result of multiple blows using a blunt instrument."

Later sources provided this additional information:

1. As earlier described, the body had been neatly and cleanly bisected.
2. A sharp, thin bladed instrument, consistent with a scalpel, had been used to perform the bisection.
3. The incision was performed through the abdomen, and then through the intervertebral disk between the second and third lumbar vertebra.

In 1947-48, LAPD criminalists Ray Pinker and Lemoyne Snyder M.D. J.D., two of the most respected forensic experts of their day, studied the autopsy photographs and enlargements of tissue samples. They concluded the killer had advanced knowledge of anatomy and a high degree of surgical skill. (Ray Pinker had personally attended the original January 16, 1947, Elizabeth Short autopsy. And the Black Dahlia investigation was one of the first to use LAPD's newly acquired high tech equipment to obtain high resolution color photographs documenting the trauma.)

Popular crime and mystery writer Craig Rice would later devote an entire chapter to the Black Dahlia in her book, *45 Murderers: a Collection of True Crime Stories* (Simon and Schuster, New York, 1952). I quote relevant excerpts from that chapter:

> Everyone now knows that the body of Elizabeth Short was cut in two, severed at the waist, but what everybody does not know is the fact that the job was done with great precision, and with every evidence of professional skill.
>
> This fact had been noted by police criminologist, Captain Ray Pinker from the start; and his deductions were verified some time later in a joint study he made with Dr. Lemoyne Snyder, of the Michigan State Police Crime Laboratories, and a member of the editorial advisory board of *True Police Cases*.
>
> Going over the detailed photographs of the body, taken at the morgue, the two experts noted the clean knife marks made by the sharp instrument used in bisecting the body. They noted that not a single organ of the body was severed. They studied enlargements of some of the tissues, and came to the conclusion that the job showed extraordinary knowledge of human anatomy.

Dr. Lemoyne Snyder was both a medical doctor and lawyer who literally "wrote the book" on homicide investigation. His book was my bible during my early training at the LAPD Academy, and an important reference guide during my eighteen years working Hollywood Homicide.

LAPD criminalist Ray Pinker is a l s o legendary. A highly skilled scientist, he basically single-handedly brought LAPD crime-scene investigations into the Twentieth century.

Pinker was considered an expert witness in almost every field of forensics. He did it all—polygraph, chemistry, ballistics, trajectories, etc. You name it, he did it. [In the "small world category," Ray Pinker was good friends with my uncle, Charles Eugene Harvey (my mother's brother) who was a scientist, and, in the 1940s, was considered one of the leading world experts in the then-brand new field of spectroscopy. Uncle Gene worked on the Manhattan Project at Los Alamos, New Mexico, and after the war, became a college professor, taught spectroscopy, and wrote three separate text books on the subject.]

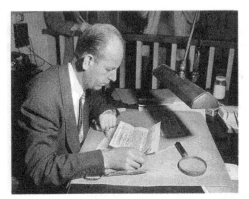

LAPD criminalist Ray Pinker, 1947, examining Black Dahlia "tip" Letter

In an hour-long documentary in October 2004, CBS' *48-Hours: Black Dahlia Confidential* sought out its own expert—Dr. Mark Wallack, chief of surgery at New York's St. Vincent Hospital—to re-examine the photographs and provide an independent opinion.

His on-air answer:

> "You don't get this kind of training where you can invade a human body unless you've had some sort of medical training. Yes, in my opinion, a doctor did it." —Dr. Mark Wallack, Chief of Surgery, St. Vincent Hospital, New York, On-air interview for *CBS 48 Hours, Black Dahlia Confidential* October, 2004

Dr. Mark Wallack, informs CBS's Erin Moriarty, in the 2006 airing of Black Dahlia Confidential *that in his expert opinion, the bisection on Elizabeth Short's body was performed by a trained physician.*

Here is a partial review of another expert's opinion, also from 2004, which was totally unsolicited. Surgeon Michael Keller's opinion was included in an updated chapter of BDA. At that time, he had been practicing and teaching surgery for over twenty years.

...

The photos of the scene and the morgue which I looked at appear to show a very clean procedure. Surgeons make bold clean incisions thru each layer of tissue with the correct amount of pressure to divide only the tissues they are attending to. The uninitiated—laypersons—usually underestimate the amount of pressure it takes just to divide skin, let alone an intervertebral disc. Their procedures often result in cuts that are serrated at the ends from going over the tissue repeatedly. We derogatorily call these "Staging Laparotomies—going thru the skin in stages." Additionally, amateurs often skive the incisions. Their cuts go thru skin at an angle to the horizontal plane so that one edge is "feathered" and the other appears peeled.

The killer here [in the Black Dahlia case] was educated enough not to attempt going through the bones of the lumbar spine. He was savvy enough to locate and divide at the disc space. An amateur would probably have left hack marks on the vertebral bodies as he "casted about" for the interspace.

Also, the willful performance of a hysterectomy which at that time [1947] would have been done through a lower vertical midline as the photos appear to show. That was a medical decision.

THE TRAUMA- CRIME SCENE AND AUTOPSY PHOTOGRAPHS

As my readers know from the inception of my investigation, now in its twelfth-year, I have always been reluctant to present photographs depicting the sadistic trauma inflicted on Elizabeth Short and other victims.

However, over the years in updated chapters, I have included some crime-scene and autopsy photographs to establish and support my points.

In this investigation, you are the jury, and I am the prosecutor's investigator, who has the responsibility of preparing the exhibits to be submitted in court.

Your need to know. Viewing these important photographic exhibits will establish the absolute fact that a skilled surgeon inflicted the trauma, so it's necessary that I include them here.

As documented in the 2004 HarperCollins revised "Aftermath" chapter of BDA in 2003, I was contacted by Judy May, the granddaughter of Dahlia detective Harry Hansen. Judy informed me that she was in possession of her grandfather's original photographs and provided me with an original full set of both the Black Dahlia crime scene and autopsy photographs. Several of these have never been previously published.

EXHIBIT NO. 1- THE HEMICORPECTOMY

In the below diagram [Exhibit 1] the arrows show us the location where the bisection was performed, which was done by slicing between the second and third lumbar discs, the only location where a body can be divided without having to "saw through bone."

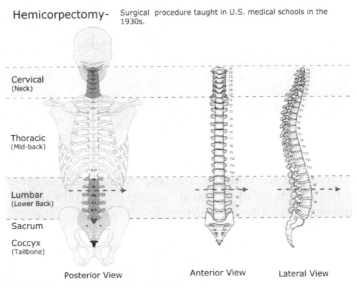

Hemicorpectomy- Surgical procedure taught in U.S. medical schools in the 1930s.

Cervical (Neck)

Thoracic (Mid-back)

Lumbar (Lower Back)

Sacrum

Coccyx (Tailbone)

Posterior View   Anterior View   Lateral View

Exhibit No. 1

Exhibit No. 2—Bisected upper torso at crime-scene

Left: Exhibit No. 3—Bisected body at Coroner's Office
Right: Exhibit No. 4—Coroner's Office

Exhibit No. 2 documents how responding officers observed the perfectly bisected body at the crime scene. Even to the untrained eye, it was obvious that this was done (in the detective's words) "with medical finesse."

Exhibit No. 3 shows the two halves removed from the crime scene and placed together on the gurney at the coroner's office before the autopsy. The crisscross incisions seen on the right hip and enlarged in the photo were clearly inflicted using a thin-bladed knife, most probably a surgeon's scalpel.

Exhibit No. 4 shows the body part as viewed from the left side. Here, we see another expertly performed scalpel incision where the surgeon has removed a small oval section of skin immediately to the right of the victim's left breast.

Exhibit No. 5—Coroner's Office

Exhibit No. 5 is a view of the large section of skin [weight approx. one pound] which was excised from the left thigh and placed inside the victim's vagina. Again, it appears a scalpel was used and we see another example of what appears to be a carefully cut out "geometric shape."

Exhibit No. 6—Crime Scene

Exhibit No. 6 shows the "hysterectomy incision" as seen by officers at the vacant lot, 3815 South Norton Avenue. Surgeon Mark Wallack described this to CBS as:

"The willful performance of a hysterectomy which at that time [1947] would have been done through a lower vertical midline as the photos appear to show. That was a medical decision."

As seen at crime scene prior to removal for autopsy

Arrows mark coroner's sutures used to close mouth

Exhibit No. 7—Crime scene comparison to Coroner's Office

Exhibit No. 7 establishes two important pieces of information. First, the top photograph was taken at the crime scene and clearly shows that the mouth wound was not a slashing but rather, like all the other trauma, an exceptionally skillful and carefully rounded incision, as if the surgeon was carving a smile into the face of the victim. The killer also made five distinct vertical incisions extending upward from the top lip.

The myth says Elizabeth's mouth was "slashed from ear to ear." Not so, and this photograph proves it. Like all myths it was born from individuals seeing the above coroner's photograph and believing that was the madman's butchery. Actually, what they are seeing is the work performed by the medical examiner. Note the black arrows I have inserted which show the four sutures that were put in place and used to stitch together the mouth for closing after the autopsy was completed.

Exhibit No. 8 shown below are the cigarette-burn marks on Elizabeth Short's back, which both the LAPD and the DA's reports claim did not exist. That would have forever remained a lie had Harry Hansen's granddaughter Judy May not given me the full set of coroner's photographs to share with the public.

Lt. Jemison wrote in his October 1949 report to the Grand Jury on two separate pages as follows:

Page 7 ...There were no cigarette burns and no tattoo marks on the body.
Page 13 ...It was found that there were no cigarette burns or other burns on her body as he had maintained.

Lt. Jemison was either (1) deliberately lying to the 1949 Grand Jury or (2) deliberately lied to by the LAPD, which wanted to keep the burn marks secret.

It is one thing to lie about facts in a criminal investigation, which is done fairly frequently in order to maintain secrets. But to put it in writing as part of your formal presentation to a seated grand jury is a wholly different matter.

For that reason, I believe LAPD deliberately kept DA Lt. Jemison in the dark about this particular aspect, which they had kept secret from everybody for three years before the grand jury reassigned the case to the District Attorney.

Exhibit No. 8—Cigarette burn marks [8 or 9] to victim's back

An independent review of the above photographs by nationally respected forensic expert and cardiologist Dr. D.P. Lyle, M.D., provided the following opinion:

> ...The lesions on the mid-back appear to be traumatic in nature. They appear to be cigarette burns, which are partially healed. They could be only hours old but are more likely 1 to 3 days old, since they seem to display some degree of healing in the central portion of each.

DR. GEORGE HILL HODEL—A SKILLED SURGEON

Over the years, a few critics have suggested that Dr. Hodel had no training in surgery and was just a VD specialist and administrator.

A&E Cold Case Files TV Host Bill Kurtis interviewing LAPD Det. Brian Carr in 2006

LAPD Detective Brian Carr, before his retirement, informed Bill Kurtis on *A&E Black Dahlia Confidential* that due to heavy case demands over the previous six years, he "didn't have time to prove or disprove Hodel's investigation."

When questioned about George Hodel's skill as a surgeon in an earlier *Court TV* interview, Carr replied, "He was not a skilled surgeon. He worked at a VD clinic."

To set the record straight, I decided to see if I could document my father's background, skill, and experience *as a* surgeon.

First, I contacted my father's medical school, the University of California at San Francisco. They provided me with his official transcripts and a list of all required curriculum and course hours in 1932-33.

Unlike today's medical training where "specialization rules," medical students in the 1930s underwent very heavy course training in surgery. All students were required to complete 744 surgical hours.

In their four years of medical school, twenty-three percent [23%] of their entire medical training was devoted to surgery. This does not include their fifth year of internship, which would require much more "hands on training."

Here are George Hodel's specific surgery courses, as listed in his personal transcripts, taken by my father during his four-years at UCSF. His totals actually exceed the required number of hours:

1. Surgery 101: 48 hours
2. Surgery 102: 64 hours
3. Surgery 103: 280 hours
4. Surgery 104: 16 hours
5. Surgery 105: 214 hours
6. Surgery 106: 64 hours
7. Surgery 107: 32 hours
8. Surgery 108: 32 hours
9. Orthopedic Surgery: 101 <u>6 hours</u>

George Hodel's Surgery total hours: **766 hours**

His UCSF transcripts further show that during his four-years, he attended and personally performed: **"53 separate surgical operations and 12 autopsies"**

His fifth year was his internship at San Francisco General Hospital, where he practiced and performed regular emergency surgeries on a regular basis for a full year.

The below photograph was taken by George Hodel in 1935 and shows students receiving surgical instruction in the operating theater at UCSF School of Medicine. These photos, along with others taken by my father, were part of a large mural on display for decades in the campus medical building.

George Hodel's classmates and physician instructors identified above as: [front row left to right] Drs. Glaven Rusk, Edwin Bruck, Leroy Briggs, Herbert Moffit, Salvatore Lucia, and Guido Milani; [back row, left to right] Urriola Goiota, Clayton Mote, and Walter Port. The lecturer was identified as Dr. Jesse I. Carr.

From **Dr. George Hill Hodel**

Dear Steve:

This is one of quite a few
photos which I took at University
of California Hospital in San
Francisco, when I was a senior
medical student, in 1935. This
one and a few others were enlarged
and put up a̷ς murals in the medical
school building (which has now been
rebuilt so that these no longer
exist).

This one shows our professors
and mentors in the front rows (now
all gone, of course), some of whom
were world-famous medical leaders.
My classmates (now also almost all
gone) are in the rows behind them.

DAD

*Note from my father to me, circa 1994,
that accompanied copy of his 1935 UCSF photograph*

After receiving his medical degree in 1936, George Hodel's first
assignment was as "camp surgeon" at a logging camp in New Mexico.
He then went on to attend and treat patients on the Navajo and Hopi
Indian reservations in Arizona and New Mexico.

12. Give a brief résumé of your activities from time of graduation to the present time, including a statement of all positions which you have held, giving inclusive dates.

Intern, San Francisco County Hospital, 1935-36.
Camp Surgeon, CCC, New Mexico, Dec. 1936 - June 1937.
District Health Officer, Second Health District of New Mexico
(County of McKinley and County of San Juan; headquarters,
Gallup, New Mexico); Chief, McKinley County Venereal Disease
Clinic; July 1937 - April 1938 (while health officer was on
leave).
Social Hygiene Physician, Los Angeles County Health Department,
in charge of venereal disease clinics at Santa Monica, Whittier,
Compton, and East Los Angeles; May 1938 - Xxbxxx January 1941.
Chief, Division of Social Hygiene, Los Angeles County Health
Department, January 1941 to present.

*George Hodel's employment application showing he was the Conservation Corps "camp
surgeon" in New Mexico from 1936-1937*

1941-1949 Documents listing George Hodel's occupation as a "Physician & Surgeon."

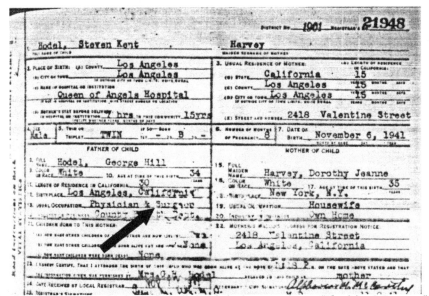

Section of author's <u>1941</u> birth certificate listing father's occupation as, "Physician & Surgeon."

George Hodel's 1942 commission as "P.A. Surgeon" [equivalent rank of military lieutenant] in US Public Health Service. Appointment signed by President Franklin D. Roosevelt on May 18, 1942.

Document above on left is Dorothy Hodel's 1944 "Affidavit for Divorce" listing husband's occupation as "Physician and Surgeon." On the right is Dorothy Hodel's 1950 DA transcript of interview where she stonewalls Lt. Jemison's question regarding her ex-husband George Hodel "using surgical tools?" While knowing full well he was a highly skilled physician and surgeon, she outright lied, claiming he has "never practiced surgery, his branch of medicine is VD and Administrative Medicine."

Note that Dorothy Hodel's Divorce Affidavit was dated and signed by Mother under penalty of perjury on November 9, 1944. This was six months before my father fell under LAPD suspicion for the murder of his secretary Ruth Spaulding from an overdose of barbiturates (1945), and some two years before the surgical murder of Elizabeth Short.

In her signed affidavit, *Dorothy Hodel vs. George Hill Hodel*, near the bottom she states the following:

"OCCUPATION OF DEFENDANT: PHYSICIAN AND SURGEON."

Finally, on page 133 of the DA surveillance tapes, we have George Hodel talking to an unidentified woman and admitting to performing curettage (D&C–Dilation and Curettage) "lots of them" at his downtown First Street Clinic at First Street and Central. This was a surgical procedure, and the 1940s *"curettement"* was a medical term synonymous with performing abortions.

HODEL FILE - ~~114~~ / 3 3

1:45P	Hodel answers door bell, lets in woman - he talks to her about renting her a room in return he will knock off the rent - and work she does for him such as cleaning and taking care of his quarters. Negro woman has her minor daughter with her.
1:50P	Phone rings - Hodel says "Mrs Hodel is out - I can take message. He said he is going down to the beach about 4 PM today - talks about renting room.
2:00P	Hodel again talking to negro woman. Hodel asks her daughter where she goes to school - the girl says-a catholic school.
2:10P	Colored woman and child leaving. woman is going to think it over - about renting room. Woman then starts talking about Doctor's-Hodel tells her about his clinic at 1st and Central Woman said she had a curettement (curettement ?) in 1944. Hodel said he has done lots of them. Hodel and woman continue to talk about doctors, sickness, and other medical subjects. (Hodel seems to be acting overly nice to this woman He must be trying to talk her into renting the room, or ?) Hodel tells her that Dr. Hill, a colored Doctor, lives next door.
2:30P	Woman leaves
2:50P	Phone rings 2 times, must have been answered in another room Hodel moving about desk.
3:15P	Hodel leaves room - all quiet.
3:45P	All quiet.
SPOOL 38 4:00P	Hronek, D.A.'s office, on duty.

DA Hodel Electronic surveillance transcript, page 133
George Hodel informs woman he has done abortions, "lots of them."

15
DAHLIAGATE: Why a Cover-Up?

"...Bosch had an idea what was coming. The fixer was here now. The investigation was about to go through the spin cycle where decisions and public pronouncements would be made based on what best served the department, not the truth." — From *Angels Flight* by Michael Connelly

OVER THE YEARS, I have been asked repeatedly whether I truly believe that there was an organized conspiracy to allow George Hodel to go free.

It's an important question and a fair one.

My short answer is yes, I do believe that there was an LAPD "cover-up." The District Attorney's "Hodel-Black Dahlia Files" have gone a long way to help me prove it.

To fully answer the question, we must ask another. Was there a logical reason *why* LAPD would do something so inconceivable?

Absolutely, but the answer cannot be found by looking at today's LAPD, which is a very different department from what it was in 1950.

Let's briefly go back to the spring of 1950. The previous year, 1949, was packed full of dynamite sticks, any one of which could have blown the lid off Los Angeles' police department and politicians. It is critical to our understanding that we take all of these historically documented events into account. Here are just a few of the wildfires threatening to burn out of control around city hall:

- Gangster Mickey Cohen had been recently shot on Sunset Boulevard, and was threatening to testify about police corruption, extortions, and payoffs.
- Crime was rampant—murders of lone women and gangland mobsters went unsolved.
- The Brenda Allen vice scandal was making headlines because of payoffs to LAPD officers.

- A corruption scandal ensnared LAPD Chief of Police Clemence "Cowboy" Horrall and Assistant Chief Joe Reed, leading both to resign or retire.

- The grand jury had ordered LAPD's Black Dahlia investigation taken away from LAPD detectives and turned over to the DA detectives for re-investigation.

- LAPD Sgt. Charles Stoker, in addition to informing the grand jury about the Brenda Allen payoffs to LAPD command, also secretly testified about a protected abortion ring involving Los Angeles medical doctors and chiropractors, all run by LAPD homicide detectives. By the summer of 1950, ten abortionists would be indicted and arrested on related charges.

- Defense lawyer Jerry Giesler had just beaten the LAPD's slam-dunk charges against George Hodel of child molestation and sexual intercourse with his own fourteen-year-old daughter. With three adult witnesses present who participated in the sex acts and the victim's testimony, along with pornography recovered from the residence, the case was considered airtight. But the jury acquitted. Documents found in the DA's files in 2003 allege that a $15,000 payoff might have gone to someone in the prosecutor's office to throw the case.

- February 15–March 27, 1950, DA investigator Lt. Frank Jemison had Dr. George Hodel's Franklin Avenue residence bugged and he is placed under both audio and physical surveillance and is the prime suspect in the Black Dahlia murder. Dr. Hodel makes damning statements and admissions about the Dahlia murder as well as other crimes. *"Supposin' I did kill the Black Dahlia. They couldn't prove it now. They can't talk to my secretary anymore because she's dead." "This is the best payoff I've seen between Law Enforcement Agencies."*

- Also during this surveillance, overheard conversations strongly suggested an actual murder might have occurred while police officers listened in. [In the actual transcripts of February 18, 1950, officers document the following: a woman was heard crying, then heard to dial the telephone operator, then screams were heard, then the sound of blows being made with a pipe, more screaming, then silence. Sounds of digging were heard in the basement and George Hodel said to a second male (later identified as Baron Ernst Harringa) something about "not a trace." Incredibly, though detectives were listening in and were

only five minutes away—they took no action! *If arrested,
George Hodel's public admission to this crime while law
enforcement listened in and did nothing, would have, by
itself, been enough to end the careers of both DA and
LAPD top brass.* At the time, George Hodel fled the
country. LAPD's William Parker was just three months
from being appointed as the department's new chief.]

- On March 27, 1950, with Lt. Jemison's team of eighteen
  detectives still maintaining a twenty-four-hour audio
  surveillance on Dr. Hodel, he slipped away. George Hodel
  left the country and was gone. After this date, he was never
  again seen or talked to by any law enforcement agency. In
  2004, today's LAPD detectives retracted earlier claims that
  "they cleared Dr. Hodel," admitting that it was the DA's
  office that had been directly involved with the Hodel
  surveillance, and a check of LAPD files resulted in no
  information on Dr. Hodel other than "a one-page memo
  mentioning his name related to some work done at his
  residence." The hundreds of pages of investigation and
  transcripts, as well as the hundreds of hours of tape
  recordings—all turned over by DA investigator, Lt.
  Jemison to Thad Brown—were nowhere to be found in
  LAPD files. All of it just—disappeared.
- In 1950, at the time the electronic surveillance was ongoing
  at the Hodel residence, LAPD deputy chiefs William Parker
  of Internal Affairs and Thad Brown, Chief of Detectives,
  were involved in a power struggle, both wanting to become
  LAPD's next chief of police. Thad Brown had the majority
  of Police Commission votes (three to two) and had been
  given the nod to become chief in July 1950. Just weeks
  before the formal vote, one of the police commissioners,
  Mrs. Curtis Albro, became ill and died unexpectedly. This
  tipped the scales back to even—and the commission was
  now divided—two votes for Parker, two votes for Brown.

So by the spring of 1950, as several scandals threatened to topple
the current administration, a new fuse was lit. If it became public, it
would certainly have been a death blow.

Just when Chiefs Parker and Brown were about to take over and
totally reform a previously corrupt LAPD, the shit hits the fan big
time.

If arrested, Dr. Hodel would further inform and make public all
that he knew of the protected abortion ring, as well as his personal
relationship to city and county officials in connection with his VD

clinic. He could very well confess to and identify the female victim of the murder that occurred during the February 1950, DA/LAPD stakeout on his Franklin residence.

So now, we have the why. It satisfies both sense and reason. In one word—survival.

Chiefs Worton, Parker, and Brown had no other options. This was a management decision. The powers that be reasoned that: (1) it was highly doubtful that George Hodel could ever be located and brought back; (2) if he was located and extradited, there were no guarantees he would be convicted [and he had just beaten a major felony beef for incest and presumably would have powerful attorney Jerry Giesler defending him again]; and (3) if he was prosecuted, he could and likely would take down and destroy everything and everybody with him. This would have included politicians, police authorities, gangsters, doctors, lawyers, and entertainers—literally, the entire heart and core of L.A.'s power structure.

The city coffers would be emptied from the civilian lawsuits that would follow as a result of the detectives' obstructions of justice, which resulted in many more murders.

Both Parker and Brown would be forced to resign, like their predecessors. If forced out, they would become powerless to "move forward to clean up and reform the department."

It would take decades for the LAPD's reputation to recover from the scandal.

No! Attempting to locate and arrest Dr. Hodel was simply not an option. It would be better to sanitize the files, remove anything and everything that connected George Hodel to the crimes and then seal the remaining files off. Lock them up forever.

And that is what was done. The Hodel friendly detectives were Thad Brown's men, and the buck stopped with him. The decision was made. Parker would be the next chief of police while Brown would remain chief of detectives. Those involved would quietly retire from the department or be transferred out of harm's way. And each officer who was present swore to take this horrible secret to their grave.

Parker and Brown were not criminals but rather Machiavellian princes who reasoned that desperate times demanded desperate actions. They fully justified their actions as being the only available choice. They reasoned that these actions were done for a higher good, for the good of the department, for the good of the city. And naturally, for the good of themselves.

We also have to keep in mind that George Hodel had extensive and long-standing connections with corrupt Los Angeles city officials.

His close friendships and *quid pro quos* within the LAPD and the DA's Office led all the way back to 1925 when he was just a young crime reporter riding with LAPD's vice and homicide detectives. Those same detectives, his former friends and "partners," were now the top brass and running the department.

I have additional information at hand that will, in time, give much stronger support to the fact that George Hodel had the city, especially its then DA and LAPD leaders, by the short hairs. With the information I possess, which will be explained and expanded on in detail in a future book, he literally was holding a gun to their heads, and the administration had no choice but to comply. He had made himself untouchable.

THE MISSING EVIDENCE AND HODEL FILES
PowerPoint Lecture, Pompidou Centre, Paris France
June 1, 2006

Author giving PowerPoint Talk, Paris, 2006

In 2004, my book was translated and published in France as, *L'Affaire du Dahlia Noir,* and became a national bestseller in that country. That same year, I was invited to Paris by my publisher, Seuil, and did a number of press, radio, and television interviews.

Two years later, in June 2006, I was invited back to Paris to speak at the Pompidou Centre.

My talk included an hour PowerPoint presentation followed by a second hour of audience Q&A. A number of subjects were explored and the entire talk was videotaped.

One of the questioners wanted to know exactly what LAPD had done as follow-up in the three years since my investigation was made public.

Here is my unedited, verbatim transcribed response. Though a bit redundant to what has just been discussed, I will include it since I believe it does add some further insights as to how it all played out.

Q: Has the Los Angeles Police Department responded to your Black Dahlia investigation?

SH: Yes, and that response has been no response. It has been very frustrating.

Because, frankly speaking, I was an honored detective highly respected. And I thought the first thing that would happen ... this was going to be a slam dunk case.

You've got DNA. They've got the envelopes. They've got the saliva where he licked the stamps. All of that. You do the DNA. It will be a slam-dunk match and there were also some proof sheet papers, if you remember from the reading. Very unique, that I felt we would make to the notes that were mailed in.

So, I never thought that there would be any kind of closing down. So, initially LAPD took the stance of, "This is an active case, we are not going to publicly talk about it."

Then, the press are the ones we really have to thank for forcing the door open to get inside the vault of the DA's office. Now, I don't know if this is clear or not, but the DA is a completely different entity, agency than the LAPD.

So, in fact, what we discovered when we got there was that it was a different set of books. I came to the suspicion, as you know in the book, that maybe they [LAPD] had sanitized it. Maybe they had removed everything from the LAPD files?

In fact, once the LAPD was backed up against the wall and had to "fess up" as we say, they said, they admitted, "Everything is gone." They don't know when it vanished? All the evidence, all the potential DNA—the hair follicles, the envelopes. Everything connected to the case, the most famous case LAPD has ever had, has vanished.

Now, they said, their excuse was, "Well, it's a long time ago, these things happen and sometimes evidence gets lost." I would agree with that. As a supervisor in homicide, I saw detectives dispose of evidence that shouldn't have been. It happens. So, I'll give them that. Maybe, although there were very few that had access to these files.

But, the bigger question is: everything that linked George Hodel to the crime from the LAPD files as missing. All of the fourteen interviews. His interview. All of the Tamar interviews. Everything that connected him. Now, these were not evidence that was disposed of...these were in a file, in a central file. Somebody had to take those and remove them. So that to me is really...and I'm not saying that it was today's LAPD. It wasn't done in modern times. This was done back then.

And the reasons for the...the reasons they did this, I take three chapters to try and explain them. I don't think we have time tonight to go into all of that. But, what it really comes down to is a management decision on the part of LAPD. I'll try. I'll just say it briefly here, as I read it.

LAPD had just overcome a major scandal about eight years before, where sixty-eight officers were fired; twenty-five high-ranking officers.

Chief Parker, who was the department's most famous chief of police, was just trying to turn the department around and be progressive and get rid of all the corruption.

And, I think what happened, in about 1950, was that a couple of....I'm not saying that Parker was involved in criminality, or Chief Brown was, but what happened I think was that a couple of detectives, Internal Affairs perhaps, came to them and said, "Look, we've got a problem. A couple of our gangster squad detectives turned away a possible suspect who was dating Elizabeth Short. A guy by the name of George Hodel. He's a doctor. As a result of that, it looks like maybe in the last couple of years, maybe he killed two or three more victims. He's now split. He's out of the country. We're not sure where he is. What do we do?"

So, I think that Parker and Thad Brown, chief of detectives looked at each other and said, "Well, let's see. We could reveal this and if we do we're out of power. The city's coffers will be emptied by the lawsuits that come from it. And LAPD's reputation will never recover. We could do that. He's out of the country. We probably can never bring him back. We might not be able to locate him. Probably have problems with prosecution. If he does come back, he's going to lay out a lot of information on a lot of different people.

"Maybe its best from a management standpoint that we just seal this off and leave it go at that." And, I think that's what happened. I think they said, "For a higher good, they needed to be a couple of Machiavellian princes, perhaps....for the higher good. And, we have evidence to support that.

We know that Thad Brown, came out with a statement to Jack Webb, who was the actor that played *Dragnet*. They had a conversation and he, Thad Brown, told Jack Webb, "Well, you know the Black Dahlia case was solved. It was a doctor that lived on Franklin Avenue in Hollywood."

Now, it may have been another that lived in Hollywood on Franklin, but I don't think so. [Laughter] So, that's a very damning statement. We have the second highest ranking officer on the Sheriff's Department, a commander, actually a deputy chief and the undersheriff who said that, "It was a doctor in Hollywood, the case was solved."

We have lots of different after the fact indications that they knew who it was, and this was an inner secret that was kept a secret. Nobody in today's LAPD knew about it. That's why when they searched the files to see and there was nothing there [about George Hodel], they felt fine in giving him a clean bill of health.

Next question?

"PARKER ON POLICE"

In 1963, as young idealistic rookie cops, my partners and I really believed we were Chief Parker's "Thin Blue Line." At police academy graduation, he looked us in the eye, shook our hand, and told us that was so. Life for me back then was literally and philosophically, "black and white."

Today, decades later, I realize that neither life nor people were ever that simple. Most of us are a combination of the two—black and white—which makes for lots of gray.

Today, with a much fuller historical perspective and understanding, I realize that my early hero, Chief Parker, was both a white and a black knight.

In May 1949, LAPD Vice Sergeant Charles Stoker was called to his second secret meeting with then Inspector William H. Parker, commander of the newly formed LAPD Internal Affairs Division.

For me, the most riveting section of Sgt. Stoker's 1951 *Thicker' N Thieves* expose on police corruption was the Parker-Stoker conversations as documented by him at the time they actually occurred.

For those who remain skeptical that Chief Parker would or could ever have been party to any kind of "cover-up," especially one that allowed a known, identified murder suspect to remain free, I answer— listen to Chief Parker's own words.

These Parker/Stoker conversations occurred in May 1949, less than one year before the George Hodel bugging tapes, which I allege became a separate—Dahliagate.

Sgt. Charles Stoker wrote this account just a few months after it occurred, and then published the full expose in 1951.

Thicker'N Thieves, Chapter 14, Grand Jury Preview page 161-162:

I appeared before the Criminal Complaints Committee on May 5, 1949, and answered each of its questions, truthfully and to the best of my ability. I told of the Brenda Allen investigations and explained in great detail exactly how they had occurred.

I was warned to say nothing regarding the fact that I had been before the grand jury.

...

About a week after my appearance before the committee, I received a telephone call from Inspector William Parker. He asked me to meet him at the same place where we had met on the occasion when he had wanted me to put Officer Jimmy Parslow of Hollywood vice in the middle. I kept the date, and Parker gave me a preliminary build-up to the effect that he and I were of the same faith, and that it was directly due to his hard work that the Catholic boys on the Los Angeles police department were getting an even break. He reminded me that we were both veterans of World War II.

After these pleasantries, Parker asked what I knew about the Brenda Allen investigation in Hollywood. When I related the story as I had told it to the grand jury, he indicated that it was as he had suspected, since he knew positively that there were two sources of corruption in the police administration.

According to Parker, one source was controlled by Chief of Police Clemence B. Horrall. Aligned with him as a lieutenant was Sergeant Guy Rudolph, his confidential aide. He then related this story concerning Rudolph, which I have never verified.

For years, while Bowron was in office, Rudolph had controlled the vice pay-offs in Los Angeles, and when Horrall held the chief's job, Rudolph was under his wing. At one time, Rudolph had kicked a colored prostitute to death on Central Avenue; and during the investigation of that incident, he and his partner had gone to a local downtown hotel where they engaged in a drunken brawl with two women. Then, while Rudolph was out of the room buying a bottle of whiskey, one of the prostitutes had been killed.

He asked me if I had heard the story. When I replied that I hadn't, Parker told me that he could prove what he had related to me. He added that Rudolph also controlled the lottery and numbers rackets operated by Chinese and Negroes, and that he had a Chinese as a partner, and maintained a business office on San Pedro Street.

According to Parker, Horrall's other lieutenant was a Captain Tucker, who was commander of the metropolitan squad, which numbers over one hundred men. He said that the metropolitan squad furnished Los Angeles police officers to act as strike-breakers in studios for so much a head. The taxpayers paid the policemen's salaries, while Horrall and Tucker collected the revenue, Parker declared.

Parker explained that this money was split with members of the city council, and that Tucker maintained a metropolitan vice division, whose only duty was to see that Chinese, gamblers and prostitutes were kept in line.

...

Parker went on to say that the other sources of corruption within the police department directly were controlled by Assistant Chief of Police Joe Reed. He explained that Joe Reed's chief aide was Lieutenant Rudy Wellpott, head of the powerful administrative vice squad, who in turn had as his assistant, Sergeant Elmer V. Jackson. Parker related that Jackson had been exempted from military duty with the police department's help and had stayed out of the war. The department's main source of revenue during this period was the "shaking down" of bar owners on Main and East Fifth Streets to allow B-Girls, a polite name for prostitutes, who are proscribed by law, to operate.

This activity constituted a million dollar source of revenue, according to Parker; and although the average cost of a liquor license was in the vicinity of five hundred dollars, a license in those areas sold for not less than ten thousand dollars during the war.

Parker said that Nate Bass, a bar owner, was middle man between the police and bar owners.

...

What ever became of this information, including the LAPD IAD investigative files that in Parker's words, "he could prove that the officers murdered the two downtown prostitutes"?

Obviously, nothing. None of the allegations of police graft, abuse of power, and even police murders, ever came to light. No officers were charged with the murders. They were simply covered up. The murder investigation on the two victims was simply, "filed and forgotten"—two more "unsolved" to add to the stack.

Any arrest of corrupt LAPD officers in 1950, especially officers who could name names and identify their partners in crime, would have resulted in too much scandal at a critical time of transition and reformation.

The involved officers retired and the department "moved forward" to deal with new problems and new challenges. Sound familiar?

William H. Parker
LAPD Chief of Police from 1950-1966

CHIEF PARKER ON POLICE INVESTIGATIONS AND *"THE LAW OF DOUBLE EFFECT"*

Earlier in this chapter, I indicated that it was my belief that Chiefs Parker and Brown reasoned that their actions relating to not pursuing and arresting George Hodel, "... were done for 'a higher good'; for the good of the department, for the good of the city, and naturally, for the good of themselves."

In short, their decision was not a legal one, but rather a moral call based on what they believed was best for the future of the department and the city.

I originally included those thoughts in BDA in 2003. I was expressing my opinion based on what I knew about the investigation and my limited knowledge of Thad Brown and Bill Parker, both of whom, as I have indicated, were my personal LAPD heroes from my 1963 academy days forward.

Never in my wildest dreams did I expect to find confirmation and corroboration coming from the man himself. But I did, and here it is in his own words.

On September 5, 2011, I found and ordered a rare book. It was one I knew existed, but had never read. *Parker on Police* was written by William H. Parker and published in 1957. (Charles C. Thomas, Springfield, Illinois)

I knew it contained his thinking on police administration, which has never particularly interested me. But I felt I should have it in my library, at least for historical reference.

I began scanning the book and came to a chapter that especially interested me, *Surveillance by Wiretap or Dictograph: Threat or Protection?*

I'll set the scene and cut directly to the chase.

It is February 1954. Bill Parker has been LAPD's police chief for three and a half years. He is testifying before the Appropriations Committee, House of Representatives in Washington, DC.

Chief Parker is arguing in support of the need for law enforcement to be able to wiretap (to listen in on telephone and telegraph lines) and eavesdrop by dictograph (to use a hidden microphone and recording device, as was done in the Franklin house.)

Parker, a licensed attorney, made various legal arguments on why it was absolutely essential to allow law enforcement to continue their crime-fighting with wiretaps and dictograph recordings, then gave the committee his closing arguments. Here is his verbatim testimony to the committee

Parker on Police, pages 111-112:

...

In a consideration of the morality of wiretap and dictograph, we may apply the principle of ethics entitled, "The Law of Double Effect." This law posits that when an action produces two effects, one good, and one bad, as long as the good effect is intended, and as long as the means are either morally good or morally neutral, *the act may be morally justified.* Thus, when this nation was faced with the ethics of warfare in the use of the atom bomb, it was obviously morally justified according to this principle. ... In the case of the wiretap or dictograph the identical rationale *may* be applicable.

We would not attempt to justify a wiretap or dictograph if the ends sought were extortion, blackmail, or like evil. If these techniques are used they must, of necessity, be rigidly controlled. But if the end is the protection of the commonwealth, then the evil effect (eavesdropping upon the conversations of the innocent) is not intended, and the action may be morally justified.

...

We are not arguing that the end justifies the means; on the contrary, we argue that the means are neutral—as is any mechanical technique, and that the use of these means is justified by moral as well as by statute law. Behind all statute law stands moral law. If an action is morally defensible, then, too, it is legally defensible. It is my opinion that the use of the wiretap and dictograph do not violate a moral precept, and that, therefore, the statute law should echo this viewpoint.

Far from being a *threat* to our freedoms, the use of modern technological devices by the police service may well be its most powerful weapon in combating our internal enemies, and a vital necessity in the protection of our nation's security, harmony and internal well-being.

Parker left no doubt about where he stood. This was a man of religion and passion who would follow his moral compass whichever direction it pointed. Be that to the heights of Heaven or to the depths of Hell.

A CONSPIRACY OF SILENCE

It is now, November, 2011. This week's headlines are just beginning to uncover what has overnight become one this year's biggest news stories—*The Jerry Sandusky-Joe Paterno, Penn State Sex Scandal.*

Former Penn State defensive coordinator, Jerry Sandusky, has just been arrested and charged with *sexually molesting eight young boys over the past fifteen year period.*

This week, PSU's president, Graham Spanier, and his legendary head coach, Joe Paterno, have both been fired from the university as a result of failing to report and take necessary action after being notified of Sandusky's criminality *more than nine years ago.*

A reading of the 2011 "Finding of Fact" transcript as summarized by the Pennsylvania Grand Jury reveals that Coach Sandusky allegedly committed serial child molestations including oral copulation and sodomy on minor boys. The offenses have apparently been ongoing for more than a decade.

The transcripts further describe a 1998 child molestation incident that was investigated by Penn State University Police, which included detectives, eavesdropping on a conversation held between one victim's mother and Sandusky. In May 1998, detectives with the mother's permission, listened in on two separate conversations and overheard Sandusky admit to the crimes committed against her then eight-year-old son wherein he stated to the mother, "I understand I was wrong. I wish I could get forgiveness. I know I won't get it from you. I wish I were dead."

The case was submitted to the then Centre County District Attorney's Office who advised there would be no charges filed and the investigating detective was ordered to "close the case" by the director of the campus police.

While this story is just beginning to unfold, early indications are that had the information been aggressively acted upon when first reported in 1998 or in the subsequent offenses in 2002, both of which should have resulted in Sandusky's arrest; *it would have prevented six or more young boys from becoming his later victims of sexual assault.*

As more information is forthcoming we will very likely discover that the motivations, the WHY of the Penn State Sex Scandal cover-up, will turn out to be for the same reasons they always are—a conspiracy of silence to protect the powerful and their institutions.

Sound familiar?

In the case of Los Angeles' 1947 Dahliagate, another conspiracy-of-silence, let's take a moment to assess the consequences that resulted from police and politicians deliberately shutting down of the Black Dahlia investigation.

What was the result of their backroom decision to not pursue and arrest Dr. George Hill Hodel, once authorities had eavesdropped and recorded his confession and positively identified him as a serial killer, in the spring of 1950?

Serial killers do not simply stop committing crimes, so if police allowed George Hodel—a known, identified serial killer—to remain free, the results were devastating.

THE CONSEQUENCES?

Just as in the case against coach Sandusky, George Hodel did not stop his predatory serial crimes after fleeing the country in 1950. The likely results:

Manila, Philippines, 1967, "Black Dahlia copycat murder" of victim Lucila Lalu, who was abducted, bound with rope; slain and according to the Manila coroner, "her body was then bisected by a skilled surgeon." After the dissection, her killer posed the body parts on a vacant lot, just three miles distant from Dr. Hodel's then residence/office on Manila Bay. The case, a copycat Black Dahlia murder was dubbed by police and press as, "The Jigsaw Murder," and forty-four years later, it remains one of Manila's most horrific unsolved crimes.

How many other Manila and Asia related crimes occurred throughout the decades will never be known. However with George Hodel home-based in the Philippines with offices in Tokyo, Hong Kong and travelling throughout Asia, Europe and the United States for forty years, the final body count could easily be several dozen more.

If I am correct that my father replaced his "Black Dahlia Avenger" sobriquet of the 1940s with "Zodiac" in the 1960s, and resumed his letter writing, city-terrorizing campaign, promising, "There will be more," then we must add, at minimum, another eight known victims to the count. They would include:

- 1966, Riverside victim, Cheri Jo Bates:
- 1968, San Francisco Bay Area victims, Betty Jensen and David Faraday
- 1969, San Francisco Bay Area victims, Darlene Ferrin and Michael Mageau (Mageau survived the attack)
- 1969, San Francisco Bay Area victims, Cecelia Shepard and Bryan Hartnell (Hartnell survived the attack)
- 1969, San Francisco victim Paul Stine

16

Grandfather Harvey

IN PHYSICAL APPEARANCE, I favor my mother's side of the family, the Harveys (UK) and the Boyles (Cork County, Ireland), from whom I also inherited my thirsty Irish genes.

I remember my grandfather, Charles Eugene Harvey, as a bear of a man, with snow white hair and a big smile, but that's about all.

Mostly, I remember my mother's stories about him. Her father was born in Pittsburgh, Pennsylvania. He was one of six brothers, four of whom worked in the coal mines. Mother would frequently tell me and my brothers the story of how these six burly brothers would walk into a turn-of-the-century bar-room and order "sarsaparillas" (a non-alcoholic precursor to "root beer"). They'd look around the room just daring anyone to make a snide remark or snicker. Tough coal miners all.

Mother was born in 1906 in New York's Central Park West. Three years later, the family moved west to Los Angeles. Grandfather got a job with the *Los Angeles Examiner* as a linotype operator.

Grandfather Harvey's second career began after he divorced Grandmother and started teaching printing at Hollywood High School in the 1920s.

Hollywood High claims over 500 "celebrity students" including a couple well known to our own investigation. To name just a few from their alma mater:

Vincent Bugliosi, Carol Burnett, Lon Chaney Jr., Judy Garland, Laurence Fishburne, Carole Lombard, Ricky Nelson, Sarah Jessica Parker, Jason Robards, Alexis Smith, Lana Turner, and Fay Wray. Both DA Head Prosecutor Stephen Kay and my half-sister, Tamar Hodel also attended Hollywood High.

First Row: Henry, Sarno, Cruse, Harvey, Snyder, Fretter, Garrison, Gray, Winchester.
Second Row: Evans, Black, Myrick, Abbott, Williams, C. S. Williams, Thorpe, Hamilton.
Third Row: Wescott, Booth, Foley, McLeod, Burleigh, Lyons, C. G. Smith, Thompson.
Fourth Row: Blair, McCausland, Staples, Johnson, De Shazo, McAfee, Hanks, Wright.

1928 Hollywood High School Year Book—Men Faculty

Photos of printing instructor, Charles Harvey in 1939 Yearbook

"Those who study printing with Mr. Harvey are given a chance to print programs, papers, and the *Crimson and White* for Hollywood."

"Mr. Harvey, printing instructor collects rare books and fine printing. In his collection he has a page from an original Gutenberg Bible." —Hollywood High Year Book 1939

At age sixty-two, after twenty years of teaching at the high school, Grandfather washed his hands of the printer's ink and donned a doorman's uniform, complete with gold buttons and epaulets, at one of Hollywood's fancy hotels.

Mother loved her father deeply. She spoke proudly of this chess-playing atheist who was a voracious reader, a liberal, a thinker, and a scholar. She affectionately described him as a lover of people and life.

My favorite anecdote about Grandfather came from his Hollywood doorman days.

As the story goes, Grandfather met a woman who was staying as a long-term guest. Each day, he would open the door for her as she came and went. The woman was a writer and they soon became acquainted. A greet, a nod, a smile, and some small talk.

One day, the woman checked out of the hotel and returned to the East.

During her stay at the hotel, she had written a play. In November 1944, it premiered on Broadway. It was a smash hit and ran for nearly five years. It won the Pulitzer Prize for Drama in 1945. The name of the playwright? Mary Chase. Her play? *Harvey*.

Based on her brief friendship and affection for Grandfather, the friendly hotel doorman, she honored him by naming her *pooka*, an invisible six-foot-six rabbit, after him.

It would be nice to end my story about Grandfather Harvey on this high note. However, like most twists and turns in my ongoing investigation, there is always something more...

A DEATH IN THE FAMILY

"I fear this means that there is some mischief afoot." —Sherlock Holmes in, *The Valley of Fear* by Sir Arthur Conan Doyle

I had never researched my grandfather's life. Especially in the past ten years, there was no real reason since nothing suggested he played any role in my Dahlia investigation.

I knew practically nothing about his life, other than my mother's few stories. I didn't know when he was born nor could I recall when he died, except it was sometime in the 1950s. In 2010, I ordered his death certificate, just to see what family information it might contain, such as his birth date, relatives, etc. Here's what I found:

Copy of Death Certificate of Charles Eugene Harvey

The facts surrounding my grandfather's death appeared clear and simple.

On a cold winter morning in December 1949, he suffered a heart attack at his residence, The Vine Manor Hotel, 1814 North Vine Street in Hollywood.

He was rushed to a nearby medical facility where he died two hours later. His attending physician arrived and indicated he had last seen his patient some two weeks before on December 9. The doctor noted a ten-year medical history of "arteriosclerotic heart disease." Obviously, the death was from "natural causes" and the doctor checked off "no autopsy to be performed" on the death certificate My grandfather's body was cremated three days later without further ceremony. End of story.

Well, not quite.

When I first saw my grandfather's death certificate, my eyes were instantly drawn to the distinctive hand-printed block lettering entered by the doctor in the cause of death section. I believed I recognized the handwriting. From there, my eyes flashed to the bottom signature line for confirmation—"G. Hill Hodel, M.D."

So, from the death certificate, we learn that not only was George Hodel claiming to be Charles Harvey's "attending physician" and was at the medical facility soon after Grandfather's initial heart attack, but he also instantly took charge of the body and ordered, "no autopsy to be conducted," ensuring cremation without any further examination or lab tests.

Bottom portion of Grandfather Harvey's death certificate

My next surprise was when I read the actual date of death—December 23, 1949. A date thoroughly familiar to me from my own investigation. Why?

Because that is the very day that Dr. George Hill Hodel was acquitted by a jury of felony child molestation and incest, charges that most people were convinced would send him to prison for a very long time.

Even my father believed he would be convicted. In a conversation with his lodger Joe Barrett, just days before the verdict, Dad reflected on prison life, saying to Joe, "It won't be so bad. I'll be able to read and perhaps work in the hospital."

LA TIMES December 24, 1949

Acquittal Won by Doctor on Morals Case

Dr. George Hill Hodel, 38-year-old physician, yesterday was acquitted of morals charges involving his 14-year-old daughter Tamar. (12.23.49)

A jury of eight women and four men returned the verdict of not guilty in the court of Superior Judge Thomas L. Ambrose after three and a half hours of deliberation.

The doctor was charged with two separate morals offenses against his daughter and the trial was featured by hotly contested points between the prosecutor, Dep Dist. Atty. William L. Ritzi, and the defense attorney, Robert A. Neeb Jr.

After the jury announced its decision freeing the physician, Dr. Hodel remained in the courtroom to shake the hands of several jurors as they left.

Some will say that these set of facts are nothing more than "coincidence." Maybe so, but I seriously doubt it. The timing, along with my father's actions in the following weeks, is just too revealing.

Consider this:

1) According to both my grandmother and mother, Charles Harvey hated George Hodel because of how Dad physically and psychologically abused his daughter, Dorothy. That being the case, he certainly would not have allowed George to be his personal physician.

2) Mother knew the truth of father's crimes and most likely had related them to the man she loved most—her father. Grandfather knew some if not all of the details and very likely was aware that Elizabeth Short had been to the Franklin house and had dated George. He would also have known that Tamar had obtained an abortion and that witnesses perjured themselves.

Despite the jury's "not guilty" verdict that very morning, Charles Harvey was still a threat to George. Perhaps hearing the unjust verdict just hours earlier, Grandfather became enraged and threatened to go to the police with what he knew.

3) As we know, George Hodel had a history of silencing those who threatened his freedom. How? By drugging them. There was Ruth Spaulding's 1945 death investigation, which LAPD was convinced was

a forced overdose by Dr. Hodel but couldn't prove it. Again, the probable motive was to silence her from revealing what she knew.

Then in mid-January 1950, just three weeks after Grandfather Harvey's death, George Hodel staged Lillian Lenorak's "attempted suicide." Again, with the same motive, he drugged her unconscious and set her up to discredit her and keep her silent from confessing her perjury. We know from his own admission to Officer Unkefer that he "gave her a sedative injection and she won't wake up for hours."

I'm also convinced that Elizabeth Short and others were drugged before he killed them.

Just weeks before Grandfather's death, there was also the mysterious circumstances of actress Jean Spangler's late-night disappearance. She was last seen in public in Hollywood at a restaurant, arguing with a man fitting George Hodel's description the very day after he bailed out of custody on his arrest for incest. This was in October 1949, just one week before George Hodel was formally arraigned on felony charges that could send him to prison for decades.

Did Jean also make the fatal mistake of threatening to reveal what she knew or suspected about him to the police?

Recall my half-brother Duncan's words, "... I remember one of the girls Dad was dating back then was a drop-dead gorgeous actress by the name of Jean."

But back to Grandfather Harvey. How easy would it have been for George to have given him a "hot shot"— maybe a large dose of an amphetamine—which, with his bad heart, would have readily induced a "cerebral hemorrhage," coma, and death?

This was followed by George's claims that Grandfather was his patient. And, within hours of the death, his filling out the death certificate as "by natural causes—no autopsy." It was followed by the cremation of the remains three days later. George, as usual, was in complete control.

The really "perfect crimes" are those that are never detected. This could well be such a case.

ALL MY LOVE AND REST IN PEACE – GRANDFATHER

17

Captain Jack Donahoe:
A Print Shop Connection

ON SATURDAY, JANUARY 24, 1947, the below cut-and-paste note was sent to the *Los Angeles Examiner,* along with a package containing Elizabeth Short's personal effects—her birth certificate, social security card, personal papers, address book with seventy-five names in it, and six personal photographs of the victim which showed her in the company of various ex-boyfriends.

This first note and the victim's personal property were sent by the killer a day after making a taunting phone call and speaking with the *Los Angeles Examiner's* city editor James Richardson. In closing his brief conversation, the killer told Richardson:

> I'll tell you what I'll do. I'll send you some of the things she had with her when she, shall we say disappeared? See how far you can get with them. And now I must say goodbye. You may be trying to trace this call.

The package with Elizabeth Short's personal effects and the note arrived a day later with the killer promising, "Letter to follow."

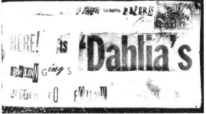

"Here is Dahlia's belongings. Letter to Follow"
Avenger posted this note to Examiner in a mailbox located just three blocks
from George Hodel's downtown medical office.

On Monday, January 26, 1947, the promise was kept. The *L.A. Examiner* received a postcard. Like the first message, it had been mailed just a few blocks from Dr. Hodel's private medical practice.

*George Hill Hodel's undisguised handwriting on a postcard
promising to "turn himself in" in two days.*

Capt. Jack Donahoe, commander of LAPD's Homicide Unit, told reporters:

> "We believe this postcard is from the killer and is legitimate and is the 'letter to follow.' The fact that the postcard was printed rather than lettered with words cut out of newspapers also supports the theory that the killer intends to turn himself in to the police, and no longer needs to take pains to conceal his identity." —Captain Jack Donahoe, LAPD Homicide Division

LAPD's Scientific Investigation Division analyzed the note and handwriting and determined it had been written with a ballpoint pen with blue ink. In 1947, ballpoint pens had only been on the market for one year and were both rare and expensive. They sold for around $12.50—equal to $125 today—so were primarily used by lawyers, physicians, business executives, and military officers.

Capt. Donahoe responded with a public message aimed directly at the killer, printed in all of the L.A. dailies:

"If you want to surrender as indicated by the postcard now in our hands, I will meet you at any public location at any time or at the homicide detail office in the City Hall. Communicate immediately by telephoning MI 5211 extension 2521, or by mail."

The Black Dahlia Avenger taunted police with several more notes, one of which demonstrated his journalistic skill in writing headlines. Some detectives voiced their suspicions that it might have been written by reporters hoping to keep the story alive. (What no one suspected was the bizarre truth of it—that the killer had actually been a journalist! George Hodel, as we know, was a crime reporter covering the police beat and had written his own headlines in the 1920s for one of L.A.'s largest newspapers, *The L.A. Record*):

"Dahlia Killer Cracking, Wants Terms"

In another cut-and-paste the next day, he wrote:

"I Will Give up in Dahlia Killing If I get 10 Years Don't try to find me"

On the morning of January 29, Capt. Donahoe, confident that the killer would actually turn himself in, positioned his detectives at all the local police stations. But by evening, it became obvious that the killer was a no-show.

The next morning, January 30, the Avenger's message addressed to Capt. Donahoe came in the mail:

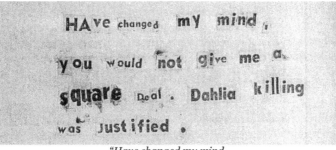

"Have changed my mind.
You would not give me a SQUARE deal.
Dahlia killing was justified."

PROOF SHEET PAPER

"At least one of the notes sent in by the Dahlia killer in that case, used proof-sheet paper, of a type commonly found in printing shops." —Captain Jack Donahoe LAPD Homicide Division

Capt. Donahoe also made public a second important link to the Avenger: He believed strongly the killer either worked for or was connected in some way to a printing company.

Why?

Because at least one of the posted notes sent in was placed on a unique proof-sheet paper, commonly used in print shops.

Proof-sheet paper was a cheap, lower grade of stock used in print shops to proofread copy before it went to press on a higher grade of paper, thus saving money.

As detailed in BDA, one of LAPD's first really viable suspects in the Black Dahlia murder was Otto Parzyjegla, a tall, thin, thirty-six-year-old linotype operator who worked at a Los Angeles printing company.

Parzyjegla had been arrested in February 1947 for the vicious murder of his employer, Swedish newspaper publisher Alfred Haij, whom he had bludgeoned to death and then "hacked the torso into six pieces and then crammed them into three boxes at the rear of the print shop."

Donahoe subsequently declared Parzyjegla to be "the hottest suspect yet in the 'Black Dahlia' killing."

On February 19, 1947, a formal lineup—called a "live show up"—was conducted by LAPD detectives at Wilshire police station. Six female victims of attempted attacks and other witnesses from both the Elizabeth Short "Black Dahlia" and Jeanne French "Red Lipstick" murders viewed the line-up. Universally, they eliminated Parzyjegla. They all said he was not the man they had seen in the Dahlia, Jeanne French, and other related crimes.

LAPD Chief Criminalist Ray Pinker also compared some of the Dahlia note's proof-sheet paper to the proof sheet paper found at Parzyjegla's printing shop. They didn't match.

GEORGE HILL HODEL—PRINTING PRESS AND PROOF-SHEET PAPERS

"Among the anonymous notes sent police in the 'Black Dahlia' case," said Donahoe, "there was one which was obviously prepared in a print shop. At the time we discounted its importance. Now, however, it may take on new significance." —Captain Jack Donahoe LAPD Homicide *Los Angeles Times*, February 17, 1947

Los Angeles Times
February 17, 1947

Publisher Slain, Body Mutilated;
Police Report Employee Confession

■ ■ ■

...ueren body.

Other Questioning Due

Capt. Jack Donahoe of the homicide detail said that Parzyjegla will be questioned about the recent mutilation murders of Mrs. Jeanne T. French, former nurse, and Elizabeth Short, the "Black Dahlia."

"Among the anonymous notes sent police in the 'Black Dahlia' case," said Donahoe, "there was one which was obviously prepared in a print shop. At the time we discounted its importance. Now, however, it may take on new significance."

Two radio patrolmen, B. H. Brown and A. J. Drobatz, made the arrest and obtained a confession in a brief two hours after other officers uncovered the crime as they sought the ...

George Hodel owned and operated his own home printing press, both before and after the 1947 murder of Elizabeth "Black Dahlia" Short.

George first used his printing press in 1925 to publish his own *avant-garde* magazine, *Fantasia,* from his father's home at 6512 Monterey Road in South Pasadena.

A Dedication

TO the portrayal of bizarre beauty in the arts, to the delineation of the stranger harmonies and the rarer fragrances, do we dedicate this, our magazine.

SUCH beauty we may find in a poem, a sketch, or a medley of colors; in the music of prayer-bells in some far-off minaret, or the noises of a city street; in a temple or a brothel or a gaol; in prayer or perversity or sin.

AND ever shall we attempt in our pages the vivid expression of such art, wherever or however we may find it—ever shall we consecrate our magazine to the depiction of beauty anomalous, fantasial.

In 1925, as editor-in-chief and publisher, he dedicated his magazine:

> To the portrayal of bizarre beauty in the arts, to the delineation of the stranger harmonies and the rarer fragrances do we dedicate this our magazine.

...

> Such beauty we may find in ....the noises of a city street; in a temple or a brothel or a gaol: in prayer or perversity or sin.

1920s vintage small printing press
similar in size to that used by George Hodel

From 1946 through 1949, the small, working printing press was in the basement of our Hollywood Franklin house where father printed advertising materials and product labels for his "Five Dynasty Tea" business.

My brothers Michael, Kelvin, and I were the "workforce" for China International Exports, 5121 Franklin Avenue, happily earning our nickels and dimes for the weekend cowboy double-features at the Hitching Post Theatre by packing Dad's fancy Five Dynasty Lapsang Souchong Tea into one-pound tins, then sticking on the freshly printed labels. From there, they were sold and shipped to many of Los Angeles' top department stores and restaurants.

Below, we see actual samples of George Hodel's original home printed labels and brochures promoting Five Dynasty Tea. Also, shown is a list of George Hodel's eighty-four separate "Accredited Retail Distributors" throughout California, which included many of the top department stores and restaurants. Local L.A. distributors included all four Brown Derby restaurants [Wilshire, Vine Street, Los Feliz and Bronson Avenue], Bullocks, Don the Beachcomber's, Jurgensen's Market, Hollywood Farmer's Market, Perino's Restaurant, and the Jonathan Club.

George Hodel used his home printing press to print these labels and brochures circa 1947 and 1948

In 1948, George Hodel advertised his Five Dynasty Tea in many of the top magazines including: Vogue, The New Yorker, and House Beautiful. Seen below [top right] is original product label for Five Dynasty Lapsang Souchong Tea printed by George Hodel on his home printing press which my brothers and I placed on cylindrical tins for distribution to stores and restaurants.

During my research, I happened upon an article written and printed in the *Los Angeles Times* on October 1, 1949, just four days before my father would be arrested by LAPD on the incest and child molestation charges.

I am including it here because it demonstrates his skill and ability as a marketing genius almost fifteen years before he would develop INRA-Asia, which became Asia's most respected market research firm.

I strongly suspect he actually wrote the following article. If not, he certainly edited it for the writer, giving his special spin, transforming what was probably a rather ordinary, albeit smoky-tasting tea into something rare and exotic, creating his own legend to turn it into a "must have" product.

Here is the original *L.A. Times* article as it appeared just days before his arrest:

Los Angeles Times October 1, 1947
Farmer's Market Today
...with Neill (Mrs.) Beek

HOW GOOD can tea be, and how do you rate as a tea taster?

Before answering those two questions, please consider the following:

The interesting study of tea, and its history, establishes that in one small district of Fukien Province, there has long been grown a tea— (Lapsang Souchong)—so superb that its use for centuries was confined to the Emperors of China, and those close to the emperors.

This noble tea—this royal tea—was for the high and mighty. Its history is ancient.

With the final fall of the Manchu Dynasty, J.P. Morgan the elder, a tea fancier, sent agents to China to acquire a supply of the tea—and in 1912 J.P. Morgan succeeded in making arrangement for the entire, and limited, output of the tea to be assigned to him.

At Christmastime he would send small chests of the tea to his friends. It became known informally, as "Morgan's Tea."

Upon J.P. Sr.'s death, the House of Morgan continued the custom. High and mighty Americans continued to receive Morgan's Tea at Christmastime, for awhile. But the custom was dropped in the late 30's, and oddly enough it was dropped while a final shipment of the rarest of all Lapsang Souchongs was in shipment. The final shipment was put in storage in San Francisco.

A certain Doctor Hodel, of Los Angeles, a tea fancier, heard of the tea, managed to sample it, and was so elated over its quality that he bought the entire supply. Hodel packaged it, and began marketing it by mail through small advertisements in the luxury magazines. Meanwhile he took steps to obtain the supplies of the tea previously absorbed by the House of Morgan. Then—Pearl Harbor!

It is only recently that Dr. Hodel has again been able to obtain the tea, which he is now marketing under the name Five Dynasty Tea.

A rather nice name. There were four Chinese dynasties wherein tea held sway. The fifth tea dynasty is made up of you and me and all the other poor people who can afford expensive tea.

The tea is sold in only a few places; Marshall Field, Bloomingdale's, B. Altman, City of Paris, Bullock's Pasadena, and Balzer's. Oh yes— and at one more place—the Farmer's Market. (Could you imagine B. Altman advertising that the Farmers Market also carries this tea?)

It is R.B. Curl's fancy groceries stall that has it in the Farmers Market.

The 120-cup tin sells for $3.75—and a tin of 25 tea bags is $2.00. That's expensive.

If you will taste this tea you will learn how good tea can be. For a mere 25c we've arranged for you to taste Fifth Dynasty Tea. We have a 3-bag sampler at 25c—and a leaflet gives the instructions for its preparation.

There is not enough Five Dynasty Tea in the world for it to become widely known. We shall not advertise it again. You may not care for Five Dynasty—but if you use tea, you should sample this brand. The Farmers Market is at 3rd and Fairfax.

Shortly after his October 1949 arrest, and while on trial for incest, Dr. George Hodel used his home printing press to prepare the sales brochure below, advertising the Franklin house as a "Shangri-La," now on the market with an asking price of $44,500, indicating that its 1949 market value was $60,000.

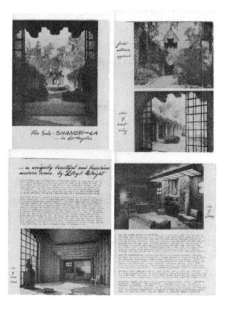

[The Sowden/Franklin home was sold in July 2011 for $3.85 million.]

PROOF SHEET PAPERS AND BLUE INK

During the late 1940s, reams of this unique "proof-sheet paper" were stored in the basement of the Franklin house. The proof-sheet paper was frequently used by my brothers and me for our childhood drawings. My father kept several of my original drawings (I was then seven years old) and after saving them for over forty-five years, returned them to me around 1995, after his permanent relocation to San Francisco.

In 2001, after two years of full-time investigation, I came to realize that these original proof-sheet papers could well be important forensic evidence. Was there a link between the proof-sheet papers mailed by the Dahlia killer and these original papers now in my possession? I was confident that a spectrographic comparison of the size, texture, and fiber content could confirm or disprove that they came from the same unusual stock.

In my 2003 post-publication briefing to LAPD brass, this was one of the first forensic comparisons I suggested. Unfortunately, both I and the senior staff officers were unaware at that time that "all the Dahlia evidence, including all the original Avenger mailings had disappeared from the locked evidence room."

Below are copies of my original child drawings drawn on proof-sheet paper from the basement of the Franklin house stock. All the handwriting on the "Chinese Chicken, Apr.1949" was written by my father—using a ballpoint pen with blue ink.

Father asked me what the drawing represented and then handwrote my response using his ballpoint pen with blue ink. It reads:

Steven Apr 1940 7-5 [my age in years and months]
"Chinese Chicken" (Mountains, Sun)
"Biggest chicken in China—they've been looking for him a thousand years."

Dad returned all of the below drawings to me around 1995. All were drawn by me using proof-sheet paper from the Franklin house basement, which also served as the Five Dynasty Tea packing and "printing office."

Of these five drawings, three contain my father's handwriting and two show my mother's handwriting. The additional four drawings read:

- [Top left] "Joe lying Down- Steven 7-6" [Handwriting of Dorothy Hodel. "Joe" would have been our then tenant/roomer, artist Joe Barrett. My age-"7-6" would convert to April 1949.]
- [Top right] "King on the Throne" Steven [Handwriting of Dorothy Hodel]
- [Middle left] "Little Me Steven" – Steven Self-Portrait 7.7 [Handwriting of George Hodel. 7.7 would convert to May 1949]
- [Middle right] "Chinese Chicken- Steven 7-3" [Handwriting of George Hodel. 7.3 would convert to January 1949]
- [Bottom center] "Chinese Chicken" - Detailed previously

In February 1947, Homicide Capt. Jack Donahoe controlled the Black Dahlia investigation. At that time, he made a number of important public statements about it. They included:

1. Elizabeth Short was most likely slain in a bathtub at a private residence.
2. The Elizabeth Short and Jeanne French murders were committed by the same man.
3. The killer wrote his "Turning myself in..." message using a ballpoint pen with blue ink.
4. The fact that it was the only undisguised note led detectives to believe the killer was actually going to give himself up to police.
5. The killer was likely connected with a printing company as some of the notes were "obviously prepared in a print shop."
6. Wrote a letter to be published in all the newspapers, offering to "meet the killer anytime, anywhere."

Shortly after making these statements, Capt. Donahoe was transferred from Homicide and placed in charge of the Robbery Detail.

Why the unexpected change in command? Were there ulterior motives in his transfer, or was it because the brass simply felt Donahoe was both grandstanding and releasing information that could compromise the investigation?

In my opinion as a homicide detective, none of the above details should have been revealed. But Capt. Donahoe's statements in both the Elizabeth Short and Jeanne French murders ultimately helped me to link Dr. George Hill Hodel to both of those crimes.

18

Handwriting Update

I HIRED COURT-CERTIFIED DOCUMENT EXAMINER HANNAH MCFARLAND to examine many of the 1947 Black Dahlia Avenger notes, as well as the lipstick handwriting on the body of Jeanne French in the Red Lipstick Murder.

In her expert opinion as a "questioned document examiner" (or QDE), it was "highly probable" that Dr. George Hill Hodel wrote at least four of the Avenger notes, as well as the writing on the body of Jeanne French. [A finding of "highly probable" is the highest finding an expert can provide as to authorship without having the original documents in their possession. It is equivalent to the forensic term of being "virtually certain."]

In subsequent examinations of other Lone Woman-related handwritings, it was also McFarland's expert opinion that it was "highly probable" that George Hodel also printed notes found on the purse of murder victim Mimi Boomhower, kidnapped in August 1949.

In a later examination of the murder note on victim Gladys Kern, McFarland found that it was "probable" that the note mailed to the police was written by George Hill Hodel. This finding is one degree below the other opinions and is defined as, "The evidence found in the handwriting points rather strongly toward the questioned and the known writings having been written by the same individual; however, it falls short of the "virtually certain" degree of confidence. [*Journal of Forensic Sciences*, Letter to the Editor, March 1991.]

In a previous chapter, I mentioned CBS' hour-long *Black Dahlia Confidential* (2006), in which the network asked its own experts to revisit several aspects of my investigation. I noted that their medical expert, Dr. Mark Wallack, chief of surgery at New York's St. Vincent Hospital, reviewed the killer's skill at bisection and stated, "In my opinion, a doctor did it."

On that same program, CBS also asked independent document expert John Osborn to compare my father's known handwriting samples to the notes written by the Black Dahlia Avenger. His inconclusive opinion caused some viewers and critics to claim Osborn contradicted my expert, proving George Hodel did not write the Avenger notes.

John Osborn gave no such finding. Here is his verbatim, expert opinion, as stated on the program:

> "There is simply not enough evidence to prove one way or the other whether his father is the writer, or is not the writer."

Osborn was likely provided with only a very limited number of known samples of Dr. Hodel's handwriting, maybe only two or three documents. As is often the case with television, he was likely only given a short time to analyze and articulate his results to the network.

Ultimately, his examination was inconclusive.

For six months, my document expert Hannah McFarland studied a couple dozen documents known to be written by Dr. George Hill Hodel.

Osborn discussed a difference in handwriting styles between Dr. Hodel and the Black Dahlia Avenger, specifically pointing to the Avenger's printed block letter "N." He showed comparative samples of both writings and demonstrated that Dr. Hodel's letter "N," in his words, was "more classic in style, whereas the Avenger's writing was much narrower."

QDE John Osborn on CBS's 48 Hours—Black Dahlia Confidential, *August 2006*

Here is a sample of the difference is the two writings of the letter "N" as pointed out by Osborn:

"Avenger letter-N"   Dr. George Hodel letter-N

Top: George Hodel
Bottom: Black Dahlia Avenger; Disguised HW

Below are additional samples of George Hodel's known handwriting that were not shown, and apparently not seen or used in Osborn's comparison (although these exact same samples were available and printed in my book.)

Note in these samples how my father writes the letter "N," as compared to the Avenger's letter "N." Though known to be written by George Hodel, it is quite dissimilar to his "Classic N," as described by Osborn and quite similar to the Avenger's style of writing the letter "N." I am confident that had their expert seen these George Hodel handwriting documents, it would have altered or at least modified his opinion regarding George Hodel's handwriting of the letter "N."

"Avenger letter-N"   Dr. George Hodel letter-N

1 & 2-   **George Hodel known handwriting**
3-   **Black Dahlia Avenger handwriting**

GEORGE HILL HODEL HANDWRITING

Those of you that have read *BDA* and *Most Evil* know that I am not a huge fan of handwriting analysis. That is not to say that I totally discredit it—I do not. It has its place and can be a very effective tool in the investigative process as long as the QDE's findings are not elevated to an absolute.

For me, handwriting analysis remains an inexact half-science. Why?

Because of its subjectivity. Handwriting analysis is like the polygraph. A useful investigative tool, but cannot and should not be relied on by itself. Two different QDE's of equal stature will and often do provide "expert testimony" that a specific questioned document "was" and "was not" written by a specific individual. Who to believe? Flip a coin. That's not science. The same is true with polygraph examiners' testimony. Examiner #1 says, "He's lying." Examiner #2, "No, he's telling the truth and was not at the crime-scene."

The same can be said of psychiatric experts. The prosecutor's doctors testified, "He's sane. He knew right from wrong when he stabbed her." The defense psychiatrist countered, "Psychotic and insane during the commission of the crime."

Because of this inherent subjectivity, one must use great caution when considering the results of any single QDE's findings. (That includes my own expert's opinions and reports as presented in *BDA* and *Most Evil*.)

With that disclaimer, let me add that as far as handwriting is concerned, I believe that in both its psychology and technical writing aspects, one cannot ignore the fact that each of us, in our handwriting, regularly and unconsciously display some unique characteristics in both our cursive and printed writing.

Consider these somewhat akin to the "points" in a fingerprint. The more unique points one finds in a HW sample, the stronger the case becomes that he or she is "probably" the writer. But unlike fingerprints where a "make," or positive match, can be scientifically verified to a certainty, handwriting cannot.

Bottom line: In my opinion, handwriting analysis and conclusions should be considered as a piece of the overall puzzle and circumstantially relevant, but these "expert findings" should never be overweighed to the point where they become the major consideration in determining an individual's guilt or innocence, especially when the handwriting is deliberately disguised.

Handwriting is such a large part of both the Avenger and Zodiac investigations that it demands major consideration. In the 1947 Avenger communications, we have about a dozen letters, and twenty years later, Zodiac's separate mailings include two dozen—over 4,000 words! That's about ten times the amount of words written in Abraham Lincoln's "Gettysburg Address."

At the end of this chapter, I will provide twenty-five separate "known" samples of my father's handwriting, which include both letters and numbers. They span a seventy-three-year period from 1925 to 1998. I offer them for your individual consideration and analysis.

1948 AVENGER KERN LETTER–1966 ZODIAC-BATES POEM—SOME COMPARISONS

Gladys Kern was one of the Los Angeles Lone Woman Murder victims. She was a real estate agent who was stabbed multiple times in the back with a long-bladed knife in 1948. Her killer, posing as a prospective homebuyer, met her at her office and requested that she take him to view a vacant Hollywood house that was for sale. Witnesses later observed two men leaving the house, but no description was made public on the second suspect.

The Hollywood murder occurred in the Los Feliz district of Hollywood, less than two miles from the Franklin house. The victim's office was just one mile from George Hodel's residence.

1948 composite drawing of Kern murder suspect [center]
Since no moustache was included in original drawing I have
airbrushed out my father's from the two photographs

George Hodel circa 1946 · Kern Murder Suspect 1948 · George Hodel 1952

1948 witness composite drawing of the Gladys Kern killer

Body found inside the vacant residence two days after the murder

Immediately after the murder, Kern's killer mailed a long rambling hand-printed letter to police at a downtown mailbox. It was at Fifth and Olive, just three blocks from George Hodel's medical office. *The mailbox was the same one used by the Black Dahlia Avenger in 1947.* The police received the killer's letter before the victim's body was discovered at the vacant house two days later.

Los Angeles 1948, Gladys Kern Letter—Her Killer's Handwriting

RIVERSIDE, CHERI JO BATES NOTES—1966

In 1966, in what the San Francisco Police Department now believes was a likely Zodiac-connected murder, college student Cheri Jo Bates was brutally attacked in the dark of night after she left the Riverside Community College library.

It was a savage attack. As in the Gladys Kern murder, Bates died of multiple stab wounds .

As in the 1947 Black Dahlia Avenger crimes, the killer taunted both police and press by telephone, and later mailed in several handwritten letters, promising "There will be more."

The investigation revealed that Bates' killer was likely "lying in wait" and wrote the sadistic "poem" below on a desktop while waiting for his victim to leave the library. The message was discovered only after the attack.

On April 30, 1967, the sixth month "anniversary" of his killing, he mailed in more sadistic notes to the Riverside police and the victim's father. One was a lengthy, typewritten letter, and the second was scribbled in his distinctive block printing. It read: "Bates had to die. There will be more—signed, "Z."

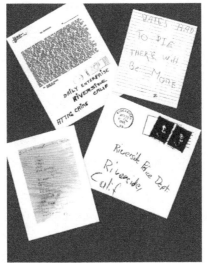

1966 Bates Desktop Poem

Bates killer's typed and hand printed letters mailed April 30, 1967

Los Angeles Times

ZODIAC LINKED TO RIVERSIDE SLAYING

In the exhibit below I have taken each letter of the alphabet and created a side-by-side comparison of the 1948 Kern killer's handwriting to the 1966 Riverside Bates/Zodiac's handwriting. Keeping in mind that twenty years elapsed between the two authors' notes, what is the likelihood that so many of the letters would be identical? I count twenty-one (21)—what is your count?

SAME AUTHOR?
1948 Avenger - 1966 Zodiac HW letter comparisons

Lower case letter comparisons of 1948 Kern letter to 1966 Bates poem

In the exhibit below I am comparing not just letters, but complete words found in both the Kern and Bates writings. The Kern words are found inside the boxes with a line connecting them to their Bates counterparts. Note the highly distinctive and uncommon use of the word "till" in both letters. The Kern killer proclaims, "I won't rest *till* I find him." The Bates killer warns, "Just wait *till* next time."

In reviewing the Kern/Bates writings, I noticed one of the most distinctive handwriting "anomalies" yet discovered. Look at the unusual letter "h" written by the killer in the 1948 Kern letter. It is found in the word "attached" and only appears once in the entire letter.

Now compare it to the letter "h" written by Zodiac in the words: "hell-hole" and "Chronicle" in his 1974 "Red Phantom" letter.

Unusual letter "h" in Avenger-Kern Note compared to Zodiac "h" in Red Phantom letter

1948 "Avenger" Kern Ltr

1974 "Zodiac" Red Phantom Ltr

Some additional Kern Letter idiosyncrasies:
Note the writing variations on the letter "M" within the same sentence.

Note the stylistic writing variations of the letter "a" (tail up then tail down) and in the letter "n" (upper and lower case [aNd vs. and) all within the same sentence.

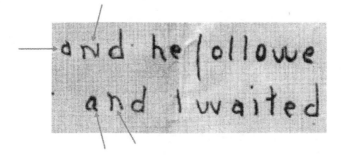

More samples of the writer's fluidity as we see a switch in the same sentence from "aNd" to "And" deviating from the previous use of—"and." Most notably, in the below sentence, he has written a backward or "mirrored" letter r. My guess is that this was not intentional on his part, but just "came out" as he wrote it—simply an unconscious writing anomaly.

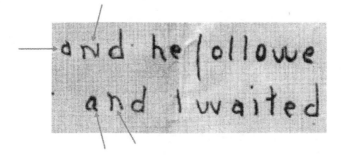

Below we see the killer changing his style of writing the letter "R" from upper case to lower—again within the same sentence and within a word.

Are these unusual writing characteristics exhibited in the 1948 Kern letter indicative of someone with high intelligence, who is simply wired differently than most of us?

We cannot know for certain, but in closing this chapter, let me offer some observations originally made in 2002 by my document expert Hannah McFarland.

After positively identifying George Hodel's handwriting as being the same as the "Black Dahlia Avenger" and providing her expert opinion that "it was highly probable that he authored at least four of the 1947 "Black Dahlia Avenger" notes," QDE McFarland went on to describe one of my father's unique and highly unusual handwriting characteristics.

I quote from *BDA I*, my chapter on "Handwriting Analysis" pages 289-290:

... In the sample below, I have enlarged my name, "STEVEN." During her character analysis of the known writing, Ms. McFarland noted a handwriting phenomenon so exceptionally rare that in her examination of documents over many years she had never come across it. This rarity related to the manner in which the three letters "TEV" in "STEVEN" were written. As Ms. McFarland explained:

It appears that all three letters were highly connected. The T bar connects directly to the top of the E. Most people lift the pen at this point to complete the E. But instead, the printer keeps going in order to form the V, and then goes back to complete the E.

She advised me that to find two connected letters was not particularly rare, but three connected was unheard of, and would indicate the type of exceptionally high intelligence and forethought that might be found in a master chess champion such as a Boris Spassky or a Bobby Fischer. Confirmation of her observation was possible because I possessed the original drawing and was therefore able to verify the three unbroken letters. Thus, in this particular instance, because we were able to view the original document, her analysis of the three connected letters was "positive" instead of highly probable.

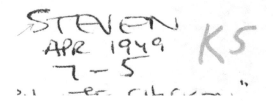

Section of George Hodel's handwriting from April 1949

Above is the sample K-5, with an enlargement of the name "STEVEN" demonstrating the printed "TEV" connected and unbroken.

I suspect that some of these other Kern handwriting characteristics we have seen and noted above would fall into a similar classification or category—handwriting authored by a mind that works quickly and functions somewhat out of the norm.

The final exhibit compares what also might be an unconscious handwriting habit.. Note that the Bates killer has used a slashmark [arrow] to divide two separate thoughts at the heading of his "poem": "Sick of living/unwilling to die." Likewise, George Hodel at the heading of his conference notes for June Hodel has also used a slashmark to divide his thoughts: "Notes/Qs [Questions]."

COINCIDENCE OR CHARACTERISTIC?

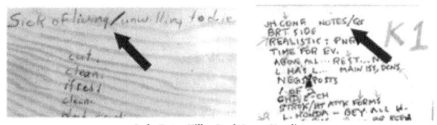

Left: Bates Killer Desk Poem Heading
Right: George Hodel Conference Notes Heading

As promised, for those interested in pursuing additional handwriting comparisons, I have here provided an additional five [5] exhibits that contain a total of twenty-five [25] separate samples of

George Hodel's handwriting, spanning some seventy-three years. As can be seen, he nearly always wrote using block printing. Most of his correspondence to me was typewritten. I am in possession of only one instant sample of his lower case cursives. [V]

HANDWRITING SAMPLES OF GEORGE HILL HODEL 1925-1997

Exhibit I

STEVEN
APR 1949
7 - 5
" CHINESE CHICKEN "
(MOUNTAINS, SUN)
"BIGGEST CHICKEN IN
CHINA — THEY'VE BEEN
LOOKING FOR HIM A
THOUSAND YEARS)

GHH
Post Office Box 913
Manila, Philippines

A-4890

EXPRESS
MAIL

VIA AIR MAIL
REGISTERED

PILIPINAS
A AIR M
PILIPINAS
PILIPINAS
PILIPINAS

DOROTHY BARBE
545 O'FARRELL ST.
APT. 111
SAN FRANCISCO, CALIF. 94102
U.S.A.

SPECIAL DELIVERY

1949	1952	1952	1952
7-5 1949	317	3, 1952	7# 602

1961	1973
1961,	3-733 261-0088

1974	1998
1974	4

Exhibit II

IMPORTANT

The person to whom ~~this passport~~ is issued must sign his name on page three immediately on its receipt. The passport is **NOT VALID** unless it has been signed.

The bearer should also fill in blanks below as indicated.

c/o DR. G~~EORGE~~ HODEL
Bearer's address in the United States
UNIVERSITY OF HAWAII
HONOLULU 14, HAWAII

317 FLORIDA ST.
Bearer's foreign address
MANILA, PHILIPPINES
IN CASE OF DEATH OR ACCIDENT NOTIFY

DR. GEORGE HILL HODEL
Name of person to be notified
317 FLORIDA ST.
Exact address
MANILA, PHILIPPINES

Should you desire to obtain a new passport after this passport shall have definitely expired, this passport should be presented with your application for a new passport.

FOR DORERO
WITH LOVE !

George Hodel

XMAS 1981

CHINESE
CHICKEN
STOVEN
7-3

RESIDENCE	18a. STREET ADDRESS (IF RURAL, GIVE LOCATION)	18b. CITY OR TOWN	18c. COUNTY	18d. STATE
	1814 North Vine Street	Los Angeles	Los Angeles	California

		19-1C. DISEASE OR CONDITION DIRECTLY LEADING TO DEATH		APPROXIMATE
SE	19-1 THIS DOES NOT MEAN THE MODE OF DEATH SUCH AS HEART FAILURE, ASTHENIA, ETC. IT MEANS THE DISEASE, INJURY OR COMPLICATIONS WHICH CAUSED DEATH.	ARTERIOSCLEROTIC HEART DISEASE	10 YRS	INTERVAL
TH	ANTECEDENT CAUSES	19-1b DUE TO		BETWEEN
	GHH-HW	ANGINA PECTORIS	5 YRS	
	MORBID CONDITIONS IF ANY GIVING RISE TO THE ABOVE CAUSE STATING THE UNDERLYING CAUSE LAST.	19-1a DUE TO		ONSET AND
		CEREBRAL HEMORRHAGE	2 HRS	
	19-II. CONDITIONS CONTRIBUTING TO THE DEATH BUT NOT RELATED TO THE DISEASE OR CONDITION CAUSING DEATH.	19-II. OTHER SIGNIFICANT CONDITIONS		DEATH
		HEMIPLEGIA	2 YRS	

TIONS PSY	20a. DATE OF OPERATION	20b. MAJOR FINDINGS OF OPERATION		21. AUTOPSY ☐ YES ☒ NO

TH TO NAL NCE	22a. ACCIDENT (SPECIFY) SUICIDE HOMICIDE	22b. PLACE OF INJURY (E.G. IN OR ABOUT HOME, FARM, FACTORY, STREET, OFFICE BUILDING, ETC.)	22c. LOCATION CITY OR TOWN COUNTY STATE
	22b. TIME MONTH DAY YEAR HOUR OF INJURY M.	22c. INJURY OCCURRED ☐ WHILE AT WORK ☐ NOT WHILE AT WORK	22r. HOW DID INJURY OCCUR?

AN'S ONER'S ATION	23a. CORONER'S: I HEREBY CERTIFY THAT I HAVE HELD AN ☐ AUTOPSY ☐ INQUEST ☐ INVESTIGATION ON THE REMAINS OF THE DECEASED AND THAT DEATH CAME AT THE HOUR AND DATE STATED ABOVE.	23b PHYSICIAN'S: I HEREBY CERTIFY THAT I ATTENDED THE DECEASED FROM 1947 TO 12/10/49 AND THAT I LAST SAW THE DECEASED ALIVE ON 12/10/49 AND THAT DEATH OCCURRED FROM THE CAUSES AND AT THE HOUR AND DATE STATED ABOVE.	
	23c. SIGNATURE ▶ George Hodel M.D. DEGREE OR TITLE	23b. ADDRESS 5121 FRANKLIN AVE., L.A.27	23c. DATE SIGNED 12/24/49

RAL TOR D TRAR	24a. ☒ BURIAL ☐ CREMATION ☐ REMOVAL	24b. DATE Dec.28/49	24c. CEMETERY OR CREMATORY Forest Lawn Crematory	25. SIGNATURE OF EMBALMER	LICENSE NUMBER 2964
	27. DATE RECEIVED BY LOCAL REGISTRAR DEC 27 1949	28. SIGNATURE OF LOCAL REGISTRAR		26. SIGNATURE OF FUNERAL DIRECTOR AND ADDRESS FOREST LAWN MEMORIAL PARK ASSN., INC. GLENDALE, CALIFORNIA	
CALIFORNIA				DEPARTMENT OF PUBLIC HEALTH	

Exhibit III

Exhibit IV

[Rare sample of George Hodel cursive HW]

o join these
with them and continue
mate their flight

Exhibit V

19

George Hodel:
Angel City Abortion Ring Link

JUST WHEN I THOUGHT IT WAS FINALLY SAFE to file away the LADA Black Dahlia-Hodel Surveillance Files the plot thickened

Re-reading some of the transcribed pages, I noted a name that seemed familiar, but I couldn't place: Dr. E.W. DeLong.

Just three days after the stakeout began, DA Investigator Walter Morgan sat at his listening post in the Hollywood Police Station and made a note in his log. On February 20, 1950, he wrote:

> 5:45 P Telephone rang – answered by Hodel – conversation about crime prevention; Delinquent accounts; Dr. E.W. DeLong's October 1948 account; Blood and spinal fluids; employment of Collector; Hodel's stock ownership in a company – maid entered conversation about time; Hodel stated that it was six o'clock, that he had to leave at seven, that he would be back at twelve- began to type.

DA Hodel File—February 20, 1950 entry re. Dr. E.W. DeLong

This log entry documents a business link between Dr. George Hodel and Beverly Hills physician, Dr. E.W. DeLong. It says George

Hodel planned to collect a debt owed to him by Dr. DeLong for work performed, apparently related to some laboratory testing. (George Hodel, in addition to his VD clinic and private practice, also owned and supervised his own private serology laboratory in downtown L.A.)

Why is that important? Dr. E.W. DeLong was a longtime friend and the personal attending physician to Dr. L.C. Audrain. And Dr. Delong had personally responded to Dr. Audrain's Hollywood Hills home, where he pronounced him dead at 3 a.m. on May 20, 1949.

Below is a copy of Dr. Audrain's death certificate in which Dr. DeLong listed the cause of death as due to natural causes—heart disease—and ordered that no autopsy be performed. Forest Lawn Cemetery picked up the body and that was the apparent end of the story. Natural death—no questions asked. Sound familiar?

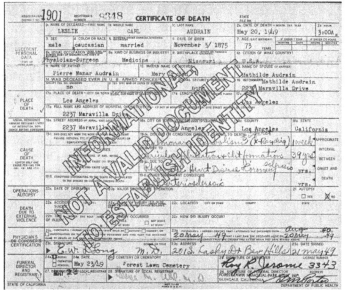

Dr. L.C. Audrain Death Certificate May 20, 1949
prepared and signed by Dr. E.W. DeLong

For those who knew, I'm sure there were many whispered questions in City Hall, in the DA's Office, and at LAPD's Homicide Division. I'm confident that the late night lamps were burning bright in all three buildings. Here's why:

WHO WAS DR. LESLIE CARL AUDRAIN?

Dr. L.C. Audrain first appeared on the Los Angeles radar screen in June 1921 when the following article was printed in the *Los Angeles Times*:

LURED BY SOUTHLAND

Dr. L.C. Audrain, who as head of the entertainment committee received the members of the local Chamber of Commerce at Mazatlan during their excursion to Mexico, is coming to Los Angeles to live. Mrs. Audrain arrived in this city a few days ago to settle in her home at the Murray Apartments, 1026 Orange Street.

While at Mazatlan a number of Los Angeles Chamber of Commerce members, including President Weaver, were entertained at the home of Dr. Audrain. There the only hospital between San Diego and the Panama Canal is located. Wound soldiers and sailors were received there during the war.

Mr. and Mrs. Audrain will make their home in the United States after a nine-year sojourn on the west coast of Mexico.

Dr. Audrain became a prominent Los Angeles OB-GYN physician and surgeon. Among others, he was the personal doctor of famed evangelist Aimee Semple McPherson, up until her death in 1944.

Records show that his wife, Mathilde Audrain, was a nurse who assisted him at his office in the Professional Building, 1052 West Sixth Street.

Dr. Leslie C. Audrain was named by LAPD Sgt. Charles Stoker in secret 1949 grand jury testimony as being the head of a clandestine and illegal abortion ring, run by Los Angeles doctors who paid protection money to LAPD detectives to keep themselves immune from arrest. Stoker said other doctors who didn't pay for police protection were often arrested, convicted, an sent to prison

LAPD SGT. CHARLES STOKER

"Stoker is the real informer in this case. Brenda Allen is just peanuts compared to what he has given us. He should be under guard. If he continues to name names and situations like he did today, he will be found dead on the curb within five days." —Harry A. Lawson, 1949 Grand Jury Foreman *Los Angeles Times*, July 8, 1949

Black Dahlia Avenger readers will recognize Sgt. Charles Stoker's name. I devoted Chapter 25, "*Sergeant Stoker, LAPD's Gangster Squad, and the Abortion Ring,*" and two following chapters in an attempt to provide a historical perspective on his critical involvement and impact in Los Angeles during two of Los Angeles's most dynamic and politically volatile years—1948-1950.

LAPD Vice Sgt. Charles Stoker, circa 1949, assigned to Vice and Uniform Patrol Right: Thicker'n Thieves originally published in 1951 and republished in 2011

Sgt. Stoker's real-time expose, *Thicker N' Thieves*, published in 1951, documented the police and political corruption of those years. He pulled no punches as he named names, dates, and locations.

Up until 2011, it had been virtually impossible to find a copy of his book. The out-of-print 1951 edition was so scarce that it was selling online for as much as $500.

In April 2011, I wrote a short foreword to a new, republished edition, now available to all as a low-cost paperback or downloadable e-book. [*Thicker'n Thieves*, by Charles Stoker, *Thoughtprint Press, 2011, Los Angeles*]

In *Thicker'n Thieves*, Sgt. Stoker laid out how the police cabal operated. He also provided critical information and answers to many of my early questions.

His book offers insights into the man, revealing an honest cop trying to do the right thing. But Stoker was a little naïve and unaware of how dangerous it was to buck the entrenched system corruption in the "City of Angles," in place for more than a quarter century.

Sgt. Charles Stoker testified secretly before the 1949 grand jury, revealing graft and corruption, and naming names twenty years before his New York counterpart Frank Serpico. But unlike Serpico, Stoker never received fame or recognition, and he died relatively young, a broken and forgotten man.

Los Angeles Times July 8, 1949

Grand Jury Chief Fears for Life of Stoker After He Testifies Again

Foreman Lawson Calls Him 'Real Informer in Case'

"Stoker is the real informer in this case. Brenda Allen is just peanuts compared to what he has given us. He should be under guard. If he continues to name names and situations like he did today he will be found dead on the curb within five days."

Harry A. Lawson
1949 Grand Jury Foreman

Los Angeles Times headlines, July 8, 1949

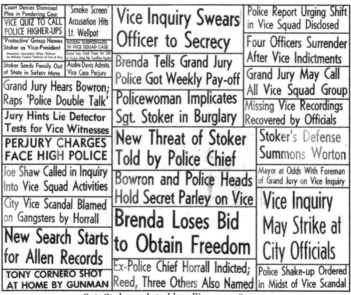

Sgt. Stoker related headlines, 1948-1949

TWENTY YEARS BEFORE SERPICO THERE WAS STOKER

Stoker's testimony opened up a Pandora's Box for L.A. politicos and LAPD. He blew the lid off most of the major corruption scandals of 1949, which included Mickey Cohen's wiretaps, Brenda Allen's prostitution ring, and her payoffs to L.A. vice cops and their bosses.

In sworn testimony earlier that year, Stoker confirmed Hollywood vice squad's intimidation and extortion of bar owners who would not pay for protection. This was in addition to systematic brutality and false arrests of bar patrons on trumped-up charges of drunkenness or lewd behavior.

As a result, the 1949 grand jury ordered a new look at the unsolved Lone Woman Murders, and ordered the Black Dahlia investigation be taken away from LAPD and re-investigated by the DA's Office. (This was an unheard-of action coming from a seated grand jury, which to my knowledge had never occurred before or after 1949.)

LAPD fumed over the grand jury's accusations of ineptitude and corruption. Stoker became a target. In 1949, he was arrested on a trumped-up burglary charge. The prosecution's "star witness" was Stoker's vice partner, Policewoman Audre Davis, to whom they promised immunity if she said she saw her partner break into an office building. They might not make the case stick, but they'd at least throw mud on Stoker's bright, shiny badge.

Sgt. Charles Stoker was defended by prominent L.A. attorney S.S. (Sammy) Hahn, who ironically also represented my mother, Dorothy Hodel in her 1944 divorce from George Hodel.

Hahn won Stoker's acquittal and later proved Audre Davis committed perjury.

Hahn was the other go-to attorney in Los Angeles from the 1920s through the 1950s. Hahn and his counterpart, Jerry "Get Me" Giesler, had nearly cornered the market on defending high-profile crimes and divorces in LA.

Many readers will also recognize Hahn's name from Clint Eastwood's 2008 film, *Changeling*. Geoff Pierson plays Hahn as the *pro bono* attorney for Mrs. Christine Collins (Angelina Jolie), the distraught mother of a kidnapped child whose testimony helped take down corrupt LAPD Capt. J.J. Jones and LAPD Chief James E. Davis.

As a side note, Attorney Hahn was found dead at the bottom of his swimming pool in 1957. The *L.A. Times,* in reporting the "mysterious death," said detectives found "a gash to the forehead and that heavy cement blocks had been tied around his neck which were holding him down at the bottom of the pool." No note was found. The *Times* article also quoted Detective Jim Wahlke as saying, "From all indications, it appears to be a suicide, but..."

BLOCKS AROUND NECK—Building blocks tied with rope were around neck of Atty. S. S. Hahn when he was found drowned in swimming pool. Here Dep. F. L. Smorgesky, left, and Sgt. Jim Wahlke, of Sheriff's homicide squad, examine them.

"Atty. Hahn Dies in Swimming Pool Mystery," L.A. Times, June 26, 1957

Hahn, like George Hodel, was a Los Angeles taproot. His connections reached deep underground and spanned four decades of L.A. politics and power.

The third leg of the legal stool in Los Angeles was Mickey Cohen's lawyer, Samuel "Mouthpiece to the Mob" Rummel, who was gunned down in front of his Hollywood Hills home in 1950.

His murder was never solved. Preliminary investigation revealed that Rummel had met with L.A. County Sheriff's Capt. Al Guasti the previous night, just hours before the shooting at his home. Though never actually tied to the shooting, Guasti was shortly thereafter indicted on major corruption charges.

As far as Sammy Hahn's "suicide," what can I say? 1950s business as usual in the "City of the Fallen Angels."

DR. AUDRAIN, DR. DELONG, AND DR. HODEL— CONNECTING THE DOTS

In *BDA*, I stated early on that I believed my father, Dr. George Hodel, participated in or knew about Dr. Audrain's abortion ring.

That belief is further supported by the DA's Hodel-Black Dahlia Files, which describe known abortionist Charles Smith and Beverly Hills Dr. Francis Ballard performing the abortion on my half-sister, Tamar.

Also found in the DA files was the documented interview with Smith's girlfriend, Mildred Bray Colby, who witnessed the early-morning $1,000 cash payoff [$10,000 in today's dollars] from George Hodel to Charles Smith, made at the Franklin house on December 29, 1949.

This cash payment was made just five days after George Hodel's acquittal on the Tamar incest/molestation charges.

Next, we had my father's statements in the DA transcripts confirming he performed abortions at his VD clinic, "Lots of them."

Add to that George's separate taped statements to Baron Herringer [Harringa] where he tells him, "I'm the only one who knows how everything fits together. This is the best payoff between law enforcement agencies I have ever seen."

And now, what does this latest discovery tell us?

1) Sgt. Charles Stoker and California Medical Board investigators sent a female undercover officer into Dr. Audrain's medical office where Audrain's nurse [not named, but probably his wife Mathilde, who worked there] told her that she was pregnant and scheduled her for an abortion. [According to state investigators and Sgt. Stoker, the sting was blown when LAPD cops warned the abortionist that a sting was pending. So when the undercover officer showed up for her appointment, she found the office locked and the doctor "on vacation."]

2) On May 5, 1949, Sgt. Stoker testified to the grand jury all that he knew about LAPD police corruption, vice payoffs to madam Brenda Allen, secret wiretaps at mobster Mickey Cohen's home involving payoffs to cops, abortion ring payoffs, and most likely named Dr. Audrain as the head of the protected abortion ring.

3) On May 20, 1949, just two weeks after Sgt. Stoker's testimony, Dr. E.W. DeLong rushed in the middle of the night to Dr. L.C. Audrain's home and pronounced his friend dead due to natural causes—"heart disease"—and ensured that no autopsy or toxicological tests would be performed before the body was removed to a private mortuary for burial.

4) Prior to Dr. Audrain's death, chiropractor Dr. Eric Kirk, who figured prominently in Sgt. Stoker's book, was arrested and was serving prison time for performing abortions. Dr. Kirk was subpoenaed by the grand jury, where he was expected to name many of the doctors in Audrain's abortion ring.

Dr. Kirk was brought to L.A. from prison in September 1949, four months after Audrain's death. His wife received death threats if her husband testified against LAPD homicide detectives, and it was unknown if he actually followed through with his promise to identify and name the corrupt cops.

5) Dr. E.W. DeLong was a personal and professional acquaintance of Dr. George Hodel. Working in Beverly Hills, he most certainly would have known George Hodel's abortionists of choice for Tamar's September 1949 abortion—Dr. Francis Ballard and his "assistant," Charles Smith.

Doctors Hodel and Audrain lived just three miles apart in Hollywood. Doctors DeLong, Ballard, Audrain, and Hodel all lived and worked within six miles of each other.

Did Dr. Audrain in fact die of natural causes at a coincidental moment? Might his death have been a suicide? Murder? We can't know now., but these newly revealed ties raise many questions.

At the time of his death, Dr. Audrain was seventy-three. If it was his wife who had falsely confirmed the policewoman's "pregnancy" and made the abortion appointment at their 1052 West Sixth Street practice, then she would have most certainly been arrested with him for conspiring to commit an abortion.

Dr. Audrain was facing a major scandal, disgrace, and almost certain imprisonment if convicted. Powerbrokers, his fellow abortion doctors, and corrupt cops would have all wanted him out of the way. His potential indictment and subsequent arrest threatened every corrupt cop and official involved.

Fortunately for them, Dr. Audrain's unexpected death eliminated that fear, at least as it related to Audrain.

GRAND JURY INDICTS TEN IN L.A.—ARRESTS CONFIRM LOS ANGELES-SAN FRANCISCO STATEWIDE ABORTION RING

In April 1950, just two days after George Hodel fled the country, a grand jury indicted ten doctors and nurses involved in what the *L.A. Times* described as "an alleged illegal surgical operations syndicate." It also began investigating alleged protection payoffs to law enforcement officers.

The article indicated that a Dr. Eric Kirk, already serving time in prison for performing abortions (and a major player in Sgt. Stoker's expose of the L.A. abortion ring) would be called as a witness and promised to "tell all." This would be additional testimony, beyond what he'd told the 1949 grand jury.

Illegal Operation Ring Broken With Six Arrests

Police Credit Discovery of State-Wide Organization to San Francisco Informer

A State-wide ring specializing in illegal operations on an assembly line basis was broken up yesterday. Los Angeles and San ... resident, was flown to the Los Angeles medical building by Dr. Schroeder and an illegal operation was performed there ...

Los Angeles Times, April 2, 1950

Jury Indicts 10 in Surgery Ring Inquiry

The county grand jury yesterday returned criminal conspiracy indictments against 10 persons in an alleged illegal surgical operations syndicate, then plunged headlong into investigation of reported protection pay-offs to law enforcement officers.

As the first step in the pay-off investigation, the grand jury requested a court order allowing three chiropractors now serving prison terms to return here to testify before the panel next Wednesday.

Chiropractors to Talk

Foreman Carey S. Hill identified the three as Samuel Collins, William H. Malone and Eric H. Kirk, all serving terms of from two to five years following illegal operation convictions.

They have indicated a desire to "tell all" concerning bribery payments, it was reported. The court order was requested of Judge Stanley N. Barnes, presiding jurist of the Superior Court criminal division.

Among the indicted persons, charged with conspiracy to perform illegal operations, were

Turn to Page 2, Column 6

Los Angeles Times, April 27, 1950

In the updated version of *BDA* (HarperCollins July 2006), I included the information related to what DA investigator Lt. Jemison referred to as, "Hodel's friend, abortionist Charles Smith." In March 1950, Smith was actively investigated for his role in the San Francisco/Los Angeles abortion ring.

On March 20, less than a month from the grand jury indictments in L.A., Jemison interviewed Smith's ex-girlfriend, Mildred Bray Colby:

"Did you know that he [Smith] has been operating girls from San Francisco for abortions?"

Colby responded, "No, But, I wouldn't put it past him."

During this same interview, Jemison referred to my half-sister, Tamar Hodel, and Smith's abortion arrest in October 1949 with Beverly Hills Dr. Francis Ballard. Miss Colby said:

> "Smith said that someday he was going to fix Tamar. He was going to cut a chunk out of the calf of her leg and fry it and eat it in front of her eyes and then puke it in front of her face."

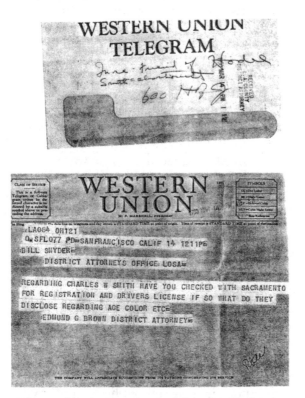

March 14, 1950, Telegram from San Francisco DA Edmund G. "Pat" Brown to Los Angeles DA's Office showing they are cooperating in "Charles Smith, abortionist friend of Hodel" investigation.

Three weeks prior to this telegram being sent from DA Brown in San Francisco to Lt. Jemison in Los Angeles, Lillian Lenorak appeared at Dr. Leslie Ballard and Charles Smith's trial and perjured herself, claiming that while she was present at Dr. Ballard's office with Tamar, "he examined her, but no abortion occurred."

As a result of Lenorak's testimony, the judge dismissed the charges in January 1950. Lenorak later recanted, admitting she lied to protect Dr. Hodel, Dr. Ballard, and Charles Smith. (The immediate cause of her lying, as we know from the officer Unkefer's letter, was direct threats from George Hodel to harm both her and her son, John, and to have her placed in a mental institution.)

LAPD CAPT. EDWIN JOKISCH (RET.)

"[Steve Hodel's] father was involved in this 1949 incest case and was apparently guilty as you could be." —LAPD Capt. Edwin Jokisch (ret.)

One of the detectives involved in the April 1950 San Francisco/Los Angeles abortion ring investigation and arrests was LAPD Sgt. Edwin Jokisch.

In the late 1940s, Detective Jokisch and his partner Lloyd Burton were both assigned to the LAPD Homicide Abortion Squad, the unit that would have normally investigated my half-sister Tamar's abortion. [In my original 2003 summary, I incorrectly attributed this detail to being under the direct supervision of the then existent, Gangster Squad. They were not. It was actually assigned to the Homicide Unit. My confusion came because during that time (1947-1949) many of the Gangster Squad detectives were working homicide, primarily on the Black Dahlia investigation.]

To this day, I have not been able to determine if Sgt. Jokisch and his partner arrested Dr. Ballard and Charles Smith in 1949, or if it was other officers assigned to their unit. If it had been Jokisch, then he should have had direct follow-up contact with George Hodel, who procured Dr. Ballard to perform the abortion; Tamar Hodel, who received it; and Lillian Lenorak, who witnessed it. [Jokisch's silence on this potential connection in recent years would seem to indicate that it was other detectives on the Homicide Abortion Squad who investigated and made the Dr. Ballard/Charles Smith arrests.]

Jokisch's career with LAPD spanned thirty-two years, from 1940 to 1972. He was promoted and retired as a police captain and passed away on August 3, 2011, at age ninety-six.

Capt. Jokisch, upon the original publication of my book in 2003, became one of the most vocal critics of my investigation. It was his belief that I was personally attacking him, as well as Chiefs William Parker, Thad Brown, and his good friend, Capt. Jack Donahoe.

Ed was mistaken, and I told him so. I didn't know that he was connected to the 1948-1950 investigation as a detective in the Homicide Abortion Detail until a year after my book was published, when he personally informed me.

Much to my surprise, Jokisch said he was the real-life "Bill Ball" and his abortion squad partner, Det. Lloyd Burton, was the same "Joe Small" named in Stoker's 1950 expose, *Thicker'NThieves*. In my original 2003 publication, I speculated that "Bill Ball" might have been LAPD Lt. Bill Burns, who at the time was head of the Gangster Squad, and who I mistakenly believed was supervising the Abortion Team.

Jokisch's 2004 admission means it was his partner, Lloyd Burton, aka "Joe Small," whom several witnesses claimed to be "on the take and receiving payoffs for protecting doctors." In an interview just a few years prior to his death, Jokisch revealed that he had never actually read Stoker's book, with its detailed allegation of police corruption in which Stoker provides specific names, dates, and locations.

Jokisch's admission also suggests Jokisch and Burton arrested Dr. Eric H. Kirk just two days before Sgt. Stoker and undercover policewoman Audre Davis coming into contact with Dr. Kirk in an attempted abortion sting operation. [For full details see *BDA I*, Chapter 25, "*Sergeant Stoker, LAPD's Gangster Squad, and the Abortion Ring.*"]

I quote from page 346 of that chapter:

> On September 17, 1949, an article appeared in the *Los Angeles Mirror* over the headline, "*Wife of L.A. Abortionist in Hiding.*" The story carried a picture of Dr. Eric H. Kirk, captioned: "He'll testify." The article said that Kirk's wife, Mrs. Marion Kirk, "a key witness in a huge abortion-payoff probe, was in hiding after it was learned that she received numerous telephone threats to "keep her mouth shut."

A year later, when the 1950 LA/San Francisco Abortion Ring Task Force arrests [in which, Det. Jokisch had also been an arresting officer], came to trial, a defendant-witness also testified to receiving multiple threatening phone calls warning him "not to testify against Jokisch and his pals."

I quote from the *L.A. Times*, September 30, 1950:

PHONE THREATS IN OPERATION TRIAL REPORTED
Telephone threats to "lay off" yesterday were featured in the trial of three persons on charges of criminal conspiracy and illegal medical operations

Henry J. Glynn, 55-year old hospital manager and one of three defendants on trial, reported to Superior Judge Thomas I., Ambrose that he had been the object of threatening phone calls since the beginning of the trial last week. [SKH Note- Judge Ambrose was the presiding judge on Dr. Hodel's three week incest trial.]
Officer's Name
Glynn said he received a call last Monday evening from a mysterious person who told him he had *"better lay off Jokisch and his pals."* [Emphasis mine]

Det. Lt. Ed Jokisch, a police officer, was one of the arresting officers in the case and currently is investigative advisor to Dep. Dist. Attys. Adolph Alexander and Albert K. Lucas.

... Hint Dropped
In early questioning of prospective jurors, attorney A.N. Chelenden, representing Oswald P. Gallardo, an osteopath and one of the defendants, hinted that a part of his defense might be allegations of official corruption and possible graft.

The third defendant, Miss Frieda Zipse, 32, a nurse, was present in the chambers hearing but made no statement.

On two separate occasions around 2004 and 2006, retired LAPD Capt. Jokisch, then in his early nineties attended my public talks. At the second one, he heatedly informed me, "Well, maybe you did solve the Black Dahlia murder, but you had no right to speak against the fine reputations of Chief Parker, Thad Brown, and Jack Donahoe. Capt. Jack Donahoe was one of my closest personal friends."

About 2009, Capt. Jokisch, at age ninety-four, gave a personal tape-recorded interview to Larry Harnisch, also one of my most vocal critics who, for the past fifteen years, has been promising to publish a book claiming that, "Dr. Walter Bayley was the probable Black Dahlia killer."

In a KFI *Crime Hunters* radio interview, when queried by the host Eric Leonard about Dr. Bayley's possible motive for the killing, Harnisch responded that the Black Dahlia murder "was rage-driven." He then speculated on-air that Dr. Bayley might have killed Elizabeth Short because of a "sustained rage over the death of his son" who, he informed the interviewer, "was killed in a traffic accident in the 1920s," some twenty-five years prior to the murder.

After Jokisch's death in 2011, Harnisch posted his taped interview on the Internet.

In it, Jokisch reflected on the memories of his time with the LAPD, vented some of his anger about the publication of my book to a sympathetic ear (Harnisch), and then surprisingly, said this about George Hodel's 1949 arrest for incest:

> "[Steve Hodel's] *father was involved in this 1949 incest case and was apparently guilty as you could be.* [Emphasis mine.] But he was found not guilty. But he had the best mouthpiece you could have in those days. He had Jerry Giesler and his partner."

"Loot Recovered"
Los Angeles Times, 1957
Det. Lt. Ed Jokisch, left, and chief of detectives Thad Brown check portion of the $88,000 worth of furs and jewelry recovered after arrest of suspects in robbery of Lauritz Melchior home.

20
Mrs. Betty Bersinger &
Detective Finis Brown

MRS. BETTY BERSINGER: "WITNESS NO. 1"

HAD THERE BEEN AN ARREST and trial in the Elizabeth Short "Black Dahlia Murder," the very first witness to be called and to testify for the prosecution would have been Mrs. Betty Bersinger.

I met and interviewed Betty in the summer of 2008. It had been sixty-one years since that fateful morning of January 15, 1947, when she strolled with her toddler daughter to the store, and chanced upon the victim's dismembered body lying in the vacant lot.

We talked for almost an hour. Betty was eighty-eight years old, exceptionally gracious, and her memory of the event remained sharp and clear. Her facts varied somewhat from those publicly reported by the press, which invariably distorts and revises them to fit what they think their readers want to hear.

My meeting with Betty was very much like my interview with LAPD Officer Myrl McBride, the last person to see Elizabeth Short alive. It was special, like stepping into a time-machine and being whisked back to 1947, as if I was one of the original detectives, taking her statement for the first time.

Here is Betty's story just as she tells it. No reporter's deadline to meet, no spin, just the facts, exactly as she recalled—in her own words.

THE INTERVIEW

"Well, I got up in the morning. I had a daughter, Anne, and Anne was about four then. I put her in her little Taylor Tot, that's what they called those things we tote the kids around in. It was a little stroller thing. And I started to walk down to Liemert Park, to the business area, and to take a pair of shoes that my husband needed to be resoled.

1940s Taylor Tot Stroller

Type of "Taylor Tot" stroller that Betty Bersinger used to take her daughter, Anne, to the shoe store.

It was early in the morning. I don't know, I assume it was about eight. Somewhere in there. I was walking by.... There's a vacant lot. I was living on South Norton. I started walking down Norton and came to the vacant lot that hadn't been developed yet. They had the sidewalks in and the streets but the lot was kind of overgrown with weeds.

I was just making my way through the clutter down Norton and I happened to look over to my side and I saw this.... It looked like a mannequin. That was the impression I had, "Oh, it's a mannequin." It was so white. It didn't register. I had never seen a dead body before anyhow. "Oh, a mannequin." It was divided in the middle, it was in two parts. I said, "Oh, dear, that's kind of strange looking." I thought, *"Well, maybe that will scare the kids as they are coming to school."* Because the kids would be riding their bikes. I thought, *"I'd better call and tell somebody to come out and clear that away."* So, that was my thought. I wasn't thinking about anything other than an old ordinary dumped mannequin.

Black Dahlia crime scene, January 15, 1947
"Mannequin-like" body as it appeared to witness Betty Bersinger

So, I kept going down on Norton to the first house I reached. I don't recall.... Anyway it was the second house that I went to, where a woman came to the door. I said, "Could I use your telephone? I just want to call the police and let them know that there is some junk up here that ought to be removed."

This map shows route taken by Mrs. Betty Bersinger from vacant lot south to private residence of DR. WALTER BAYLEY, where the doctor's wife allowed her to use the phone to notify police.

No, I didn't know it was a body. I had no idea it was a body. I thought it was a mannequin because it was so white.

So, I called the police, and Sgt. Somebody answered. And I told him my story, and he said, "Where are you calling from?" So, I looked down and gave him the number of the house where I was calling from.

Then I went on my way and went on down to Liemert Park and got the shoes into the shoe repair place. I took my time coming back. And on my way back, I think I walked up Crenshaw. Yes, that was the next block over.

And...I saw all these people around the area where I had seen the mannequin. I just thought must be something going on. I didn't know what it was. I didn't really think much about it. I went on home and it was time for my daughter's lunch and taking a nap. I didn't pay much attention; this was all before television you know. The only news we had was the papers. If there was anything really exciting, some little newsboy would be running down the street, yelling, "Extra, Extra."
So, I continued with my life. I don't think I even hardly mentioned it to anybody because it wasn't that important to me. It just wasn't

that significant. And then I saw in the paper what really was going on. It was a body. And I said, "Oh, my goodness." After that, I didn't pay any more attention. My daughter was having a lot of trouble with breathing and asthma and colds, so I was busy taking her to get help to different doctors and getting her treatment. So, my life was really filled up with her health conditions.

I think I may have called my mother-in-law who lived down on Buckingham Road up. I told her that there was a lot of activity going on; that they found a dead body here. I don't remember when I called her? That day, or maybe a few days later. There wasn't a lot of news coming out, like you get it today—every five minutes.

So, I kind of forgot about it. Then, sometime later, my husband—he worked downtown in Westlake—was going to lunch with some of his friends, and he happened to look at the newspaper stand and there was this headline, "Police looking for finder of Black Dahlia body." Then he called me up and said, "Hey, we had better go down and see the police because I think they're looking for you." I said, "Oh, my God."

As soon as my husband came home, we went down to the police. So that is what happened.

They took my picture at the station and kind of interrogated my husband. (Laugh)

On Norton Avenue, the block I lived in had houses, and then they stopped. Then I think it was one or two vacant lots, I don't remember. Then there was a street, then more houses. A woman was at the house I made the call from.

The police only asked me what number I was calling from, not my name. And I gave them the phone number that was listed on the dial. Yes, it was several houses down [south] from Thirty-Ninth Street.

No, I didn't think it was human, just a mannequin. My fear was that it might frighten the kids, because they might think it was human.

I know they made some movie where they said a man was taking his son down the street, and I said, "Well, that's not right." I think that was a television movie. I don't pay any attention to it, I know that they take liberties with the facts and do what they want.

You can take my picture. But first, let me brush my hair.

End of interview.

Mrs. Betty Bersinger seen reenacting phone call to police for reporters at University Police Station on January 23, 1947. She made the original call on January 15, 1947, from home of neighbor, Dr. Walter Bayley, at 3959 South Norton Avenue, just a short distance south of Thirty-Ninth Street.

Betty Bersinger, 2008 interview with author

DR. WALTER A. BAYLEY

Dr. Walter A. Bayley, circa 1919, wearing his WW I uniform

Dr. Walter Bayley was a former chief of staff at USC Medical Center [General Hospital] and in the mid-1940s his private medical practice was located in the Professional Building, 1052 West Sixth Street.

According to LAPD Sgt. Charles Stoker, as summarized in his expose, *Thicker'N Thieves,* this was the same building where Dr. Audrain, head of the protected L.A. abortion ring also had his practice and where Audrain's nurse/secretary [probably his wife] had scheduled an abortion with Stoker's undercover policewoman partner. Dr. Audrain was subsequently warned of the "sting" and pending raid. And when Sgt. Stoker and his partner arrived at the scheduled appointment to make the arrest, Dr. Audrain was a no-show and his "office remained closed and locked for a week."

While there is no hard evidence that Dr. Walter Bayley was performing abortions, there is a suggestion that he might have been. Clearly working in the same office building as Dr. Audrain and both doctors having long established L.A. practices, they certainly would have known each other and have been acquainted for decades.

That said, Dr. Bayley's name has never appeared in any official law enforcement report connected with either the Black Dahlia or any other criminal investigation that I have seen. Other than the 1999 reference from the one amateur Black Dahlia theorist, his name remains completely off the radar screen.

According to newspaper accounts in 1948, immediately after Dr. Bayley's death at age sixty-seven, a lawsuit was filed over his estate. In court papers, Bayley's widow alleged her husband was being blackmailed by his female associate, one Dr. Alexandra von Partyka. .

It was established that Dr. Partyka, in December 1947, had gone to the VA Hospital where Dr. Bayley had been hospitalized for over a month and was literally on his deathbed. [Bayley died on January 3, 1948.] And just weeks before his death Bayley had signed papers agreeing that she should receive half of his estate.

Widow Ruth Bayley alleged that Dr. Partyka obtained her husband's signature under duress by threatening to expose him by revealing certain medical practice secrets. Here is an excerpt from the *Los Angeles Times* article of January 19, 1948:

> Dr. Partyka represented that *she had obtained certain secrets concerning his [Dr. Bayley's] medical practice and would expose and ruin him* [emphasis mine] if he returned to his wife, from whom he had separated a year before his death.

> ... Dr. Bayley lived in constant fear that Dr. Partyka would "disgrace him in his declining years" and accordingly consented to execution of the document.

Clearly, "secrets concerning his medical practice" would suggest at least the possibility that he was either a member of the abortion ring, or perhaps simply performing abortions on his own to earn extra money.

In 1949, Dr. Eric Kirk, the Angel City abortion ring whistle-blower, agreed to testify before the grand jury. He said he would name corrupt cops, but no doctors. "I'm not going to name other doctors. I'm no stool pigeon," he told a reporter. "If all the doctors who perform abortions in Los Angeles were cleaned out, there wouldn't be many doctors left."

Obviously, despite the risk of going to prison, performing abortions remained a very common and profitable practice. And if a doctor could join a police-protected ring by paying a little "insurance juice" to avoid arrest, it was well worth it.

THREATS OF DISGRACE ALLEGED IN WILL SUIT

Charges that the late Dr. Walter A. Bayley, physician, executed his will under intimidation of a young woman colleague, Dr. Alexandra Partyka, are made in a contest filed in Superior Court by his widow, Mrs. Ruth A. Bayley.

Threats Alleged

Dr. Bayley, 67, died last Jan. 3, leaving a will dated last Dec. 22 under which he disinherited his wife and left the major part of his estate to Dr. Partyka.

Mrs. Bayley, who lives at 3959 S. Norton Ave., contends that while associated with Dr. Bayley in the practice of medicine Dr. Partyka represented that she had obtained certain secrets concerning his medical practice and would expose and ruin him if he returned to his wife, from whom he had separated a year before his death.

The widow further asserts that Dr. Bayley lived in con-

stant fear that Dr. Partyka would "disgrace him in his declining years" and accordingly consented to execution of the document.

Dr. Partyka, the widow also charges, obtained an undue influence over Dr. Bayley through "unnatural flattery and feminine wiles" and induced him to accompany her on extended trips.

Dr. Bayley's will gave his office equipment and library and half of the remainder of his estate to Dr. Partyka. It divided the other half among a sister, a brother, a sister-in-law and an adopted daughter. No estimate of the value of the estate was given except that it will exceed $5000.

Los Angeles Times
Jan 19, 1948

Los Angeles Times, January 19, 1948
Dr. Partyka threatens to reveal Dr. Bayley's "medical practice secrets."

LAPD SGT. FINIS A. BROWN—THE LEAD DAHLIA DETECTIVE

If asked what detective originally led the Black Dahlia murder investigation, most cops and reporters would say, it was Sgt. Harry Hansen. Wrong answer. Another myth.

The real lead detective was Sgt. Finis A. Brown, brother of LAPD's Chief of Detectives Thad Brown.

By all accounts, Brown did most of the leg work and pretty much all of the thinking in the important first three years of the Dahlia investigation.

Black Dahlia victim, Elizabeth Short, and lead detective, Finis Brown shared the same birthday—July 29

In December 1949, the grand jury subpoenaed a number of LAPD detectives to testify about the original investigation. Among them was, Finis Brown and Lt. William Burns, the former commander of LAPD's Gangster Squad who had loaned some of his men to the Dahlia case. Unfortunately, Gangster Squad detectives were mostly untrained in homicide investigations; they tended to be loose cannons who made messes.

At the behest of the LAPD's "department psychiatrist," Dr. J. Paul DeRiver, the Gangster Squad was persuaded to pursue the doctor's red-herring suspect, Leslie Dillon, who (much to his later regret) had originally contacted Dr. DeRiver from Florida with "some thoughts" on the case.

In January 1949, two years after the murder, Dr. DeRiver and a couple of Gangster Squad detectives lured Dillon to California "to meet and discuss his theories." After holding him "incommunicado" at various hotels for three days, they arrested him as Elizabeth Short's killer.

It made headlines after the "three-day detainee" dropped a note out of his downtown L.A. hotel window, begging someone to contact famed criminal defense attorney Jerry Giesler to rescue him.

Dillon was released several days after his arrest, although the Gangster Squad and Dr. DeRiver remained convinced that he was the actual Black Dahlia killer. For the rest of 1949, they continued to build a case against him.

In October 1949, at the request of Lt. Jemison, Sgt. Finis Brown went to San Francisco and was able to verify Leslie Dillon's alibi that he was in that city in the days before and after Elizabeth Short's murder.

The entire affair was a huge embarrassment to LAPD Homicide. Both Lt. Burns and Dr. DeRiver were called on the carpet. Burns was taken out of the Gangster Squad and Dr. DeRiver left his position as LAPD's department psychiatrist six months after the Dillon debacle.

Grand Jury Hears Two on Black Dahlia

Two police officers yesterday were called as witnesses in the county grand jury's investigation into the Black Dahlia slaying of 22-year-old Elizabeth Short.

The officers are Det. Lieut. Finis Brown of the Police Department homicide detail, who has handled investigation of the crime since the victim's nude, severed body was found in a vacant lot Feb. 15, 1947; and Lieut. William Burns, former head of the special antigangster detail operating from the office of the Chief of Police.

Testimony of the two officers was believed to include a summary of Police Department activities in the investigation. It was further indicated that the grand jury's inquiry is drawing to a close.

Los Angeles Times, December, 9, 1949

My review of the DA files included Sgt. Finis Brown's testimony before the 1949 grand jury. The transcript covered various aspects of his then three-year-old investigation; however, what I found most revealing were several questions asked of him by the grand jury foreman, Mr. Harry Lawson. These were made in the presence of Deputy District Attorney Arthur Veitch and Lt. Frank Jemison.

Here is the verbatim excerpt:

Testimony of LAPD Sgt. Finis Brown
Date: December 6, 1949
Questioned by: DDA Arthur L. Veitch and GJ
Present: 1949 grand jury members and DA investigator Lt. Frank B. Jemison

(Excerpt from page 30 of 1949 Secret Grand Jury Transcript):

Grand Jury Foreman, Mr. Harry Lawson asks Sgt. Brown
Q: Do you care to express an opinion to this Jury as to who you think killed Elizabeth Short?

Sgt. Finis Brown:
A: I can't express an opinion. I don't know. I can this: That there is over 100 pages of names cut out of this address book; also, it is

known that she was in care of some doctor. We don't know who that doctor is yet. We have never been able to find out. We do know this; that on two or three occasions a doctor identifying himself as a doctor, but refusing to give his name called the Hollywood Station and gave some information of where the information—some information might be picked up on her around Hollywood Boulevard.

```
3       Q   Do you care to express an opinion to this Jury as to who
        you think killed Elizabeth Short?
4       A   I can't express an opinion.  I don't know.  I can this:
        that there is over 100 pages of names cut out of this address
5       book; also, it is known that she was in care of some doctor.
        We don't know who that doctor is yet.  We have never been able
6       to find out.  We do know this:  that on two or three occasions
        a doctor identifying himself as a doctor, but refusing to give
7       his name called the Hollywood Station and gave some information
        of where the information--some information might be picked up
8       on her around Hollywood Boulevard.
```

Scan of excerpt from original transcript found in DA Dahlia Files

Keep in mind that this statement came just a week after Lt. Jemison's report to this same grand jury that a list of over two hundred possible suspects had now been reduced down to just five named individuals, only one of whom was a trained physician and skilled surgeon. His name: George Hill Hodel, MD.

In the following grand jury transcript, we will find that Sgt. Brown was questioned by the jurors as to his opinion of whether the bisection was done by a doctor. Here is the verbatim Q&A from page15b. Answers are coming from Sgt. Finis Brown.

Q: You have handled many murder cases, had you not, Sgt., you have seen bodies that have been dissected and bisected and so forth?

A: And otherwise mutilated, yes.

Q: Mr. VEITCH: Is this kind of cutting that occurred at all unusual?

A: Yes, it is unusual in this sense, that the point at which the body was bisected is, according to eminent medical men, the easiest point in the spinal column to sever.

Q: And he hit the spot exactly.

A: He hit it exactly.

Q: And he made clean cuts?

A: That, in my estimation, I'm still only quoting my opinion, my own pet theory, that wasn't an accident, I've seen many horrible mutilation cases, many of them, and if any of you ladies and gentlemen ever seen a case like that, and would see the pictures of this Elizabeth Short case, you could detect the difference immediately.

Q: GRAND JUROR: Could a student, that had three months training studying to be an embalmer, three weeks, could that have been possible that he could have had the knowledge to dissect?

A: My opinion would be only a layman's, I'm not a medical man, I rather think that question should be answered by a doctor, my own personal opinion is that a person whom you have just described, would not be capable of doing it.

Q: Following up your thought, you say as an individual, had you thought very much about that medical side of it, have you elaborated in your own mind where that party could be, who it could possibly be?

A: Well, this we know, the body had been thoroughly bled, and the body had been washed, common sense tells us that it couldn't be done in an automobile, couldn't be done on a bed.

Q: Had you discussed your pet theory as you call it, with any medical expert?

A: Yes, I have discussed at length with Dr. Newbarr, the County Autopsy Surgeon.

Q: And I suppose he concurs in your opinion as to the ability of one?

A: Well, he said himself, his remark, "There's a fine piece of surgery." And he said further that couldn't be done in any 15 minutes, half hour or an hour.

1 A Yes, I did.

2 Q You have handled many murder cases, had you not, Sgt., you
   have seen bodies that have been disected and bisected and so
3 forth?
   A And otherwise mutilated, yes.

4
   Q MR. VEITCH: Is this kind of cutting that occurred at all
5 unusual?
   A Yes, it is unusual in this sense, that the point at which
6 the body was bisected is, according to emminent medical men,
   the easiest point in the spinal column to sever.

7
   Q And he hit the spot exactly?
8 A He hit it exactly.

9 Q And he made clean cuts?
   A That, in my estimation, I'm still only quoting my opinion,
10 my own pet theory, that wasn't an accident, I've seen many
   horrible mutilation cases, many of them, and if any of you ladies
11 and gentlemen ever seen a case like that, and would see the
   pictures of this Elizabeth Short case, you could detect the
12 difference immediately.

13 Q GRAND JUROR: Could a student, that had three months
   training studying to be an embalmer, three weeks, could that
14 have been possible that he could have had the knowledge to disect?
   A My opinion would be only a layman's, I'm not a medical man,
15 I rather think that question should be answered by a doctor, my
   own personal opinion is that a person whom you have just
16 described, would not be capable of doing it.

17 Q Following up your thought, you say as an indivdual, had you
   thought very much about that medical side of it, have you
18 elaborated in your own mind where that party could be, who it
   could possibly be?
19 A Well, this we know, the body had been thoroughly bled, and
   the body had been washed, common sense tells us that it couldn't
20 be done in an automobile, couldn't be done on a bed.

21 Q Had you discussed your pet thoery, as youcall it, with any
   medical expert?
22 A Yes, I have discussed at length with Dr. Newbarr, the County
   Autopsy Surgeon.
23
   Q And I suppose he concurs in your opinion as to the ability of
24 one?
   A Well, he said himself, his remark, "There's a fine piece
25 of surgery." And he said further that couldn't be done in any
   15 minutes, half hour or an hour.
26

-15b-

Scan of page 15b of Sgt. Brown's testimony to 1949 Grand Jury

"There's a fine piece of surgery. That couldn't be done in any 15 minutes, half hour or an hour." —Dr. Frederick Newbarr, Chief Autopsy Surgeon, L.A. County Coroner's Office [Statement refers to the bisection of Elizabeth Short's body and was made directly to Sgt. Finis Brown]

That is one hell of a quote!

Dr. Frederick Newbarr performed the January 16, 1947, autopsy on Elizabeth Short. He was the chief autopsy surgeon for Los Angeles County Coroner's Office and had been in charge of the office for decades.

Dr. Newbarr had performed nearly all of L.A. County's high profile autopsies. For Dr. Newbarr to make that statement to Sgt.

Finis Brown, the lead detective carried tremendous weight and authority.

As stated elsewhere, though, both Jemison and Finis Brown were seemingly unaware of the identity of Elizabeth Short's "unidentified downtown doctor." With the information they had, they certainly had to consider and suspect Dr. George Hill Hodel.

The surveillance and bugging of George Hodel's residence, which resulted in his recorded confessions and admissions to payoffs to police, performing abortions, and the murders of Elizabeth Short and Ruth Spaulding, occurred just six weeks after Finis Brown's testimony which focused on a "Hollywood doctor."

Finally, there can be no doubt that Sgt. Finis A. Brown—as the lead detective in the initial Black Dahlia investigation and brother to Thad Brown, LAPD's top detective and the man who said, "We solved the Black Dahlia murder. He was a doctor, living on Franklin Avenue in Hollywood"—also had to know and took the secret to his grave.

After retirement, Finis Brown moved to West, Texas, where he died in 1990 at the age of eighty-four.

Finis A. Brown, 1906-1990
R.I.P.

Finis A. Brown, West, Texas gravesite
[Photo courtesy of bestselling true-crime author Ron Franscell]

21
Dr. George Hill Hodel:
A Surrealist Serial Killer

"People begin to see that something more goes to the composition of a fine murder than two blockheads to kill and be killed—a knife—a purse—and a dark lane. Design, gentlemen, grouping, light and shade, poetry, sentiment, are now deemed indispensable to attempts of this nature..." —The Society of Connoisseurs in Murder, from Thomas De Quincey's—*Murder Considered as One of the Fine Arts (1842)*

WITH MY SEQUEL, *Most Evil: Avenger, Zodiac and the Further Serial Murders of Dr. George Hill Hodel,* the weight of evidence that surrealism was the primary motivator of and signature to my father's three-decade long killing spree is, I believe, established beyond any doubt.

Understanding how his many crimes are linked by this most unique signature is the key to understanding both the man and his madness.

We have come a long way in exploring the surreal linkage since my early ruminations in 2002, where I first explored the possibilities in *BDA* in the chapter, *"The Final Connections: Man Ray Thoughtprints."*

In that chapter, I explored the various links both in the posing of Elizabeth Short's body in imitation of his surrealist friend Man Ray's two famous works: *The Minotaur* and *Les Amoureux, (The Lovers Lips).*

On pages 241-242, I wrote:

The killer had to make her death extraordinary both in planning and execution. In his role as a surreal artist, he determined that his work would be a masterpiece of the macabre, a crime so shocking and horrible it would endure, be immortalized through the annals of crime lore. As avenger, he would use her body as his canvas, and his surgeon's scalpel as his paintbrush

...

George Hodel, through the homage he consciously paid to Man Ray, was provocatively revealing himself to be the murderer of Elizabeth Short. Her body, and the way she was posed, was Dr. George signature—both artistic and psychological—on his own surreal masterpiece, in which he juxtaposed the unexpected in a "still death" tribute to his master, *using human body parts!*

The premeditated and deliberate use of those two photographs— one symbolizing my father and Elizabeth as the lovers in Les Amoureux, and another my father as the avenger, the Minotaur himself, the bull-headed beast consuming and destroying the young maiden, Elizabeth, in sacrifice—is my father's grisly message of his and Man Ray's shared vision of violent sexual fantasy. Given George Hodel's megalomaniacal ego, it was also a dash of one-upmanship.

I went on to enumerate the additional surreal connections to his crime.

The comparison of a 1945 Man Ray photograph, *Juliet in Silk Stocking* (showing his wife wearing a stocking mask) to the Black Dahlia Avenger's mailed photo of the teenager Armand Robles, where my father drew an identical stocking mask over his face in imitation of Man Ray's photograph.

I explored a painting George Hodel had commissioned by Manila artist Fernando Modesto, an erotic imitation of the same *Lovers Lips* painting. But in George Hodel's version, the lips appear to be dripping blood and overhead are seen three male phalluses, a vagina and spermatozoa. My father hand-delivered it to Juliet Man Ray in Paris in the late 1980s. [His good friend, Man Ray had died there a decade earlier, in 1976.]

There was more. Man Ray's 1946 photograph of George Hodel posed holding a statue of the Tibetan deity, Yamantaka, in which the god is in the "yab-yum" position, having sexual intercourse with his consort as dad looks on in what appears to be a sort of worshipful reverence.

I closed the chapter with a reference to the importance of the dream state to all surrealists. I published a 1929 group photograph of many of the major surrealists in Paris, including Andre Breton, Rene Magritte, Max Ernst, and Salvador Dali and many others, all posing with eyes closed, affirming their support and preference for the subjective dream state in defiance of the conscious and rational.

Here is what Andre Breton had to say about it in his original 1924 Surrealist Manifesto:

The mind of the man who dreams is fully satisfied by what happens to him.

The agonizing question of possibility is no longer pertinent. Kill; fly faster, love to your heart's content. And if you should die, are you not certain of reawaking among the dead? Let yourself be carried along, vents will not tolerate your interference. You are nameless. The ease of everything is priceless...

I believe in the future resolution of these two states, dream and reality, which are seemingly so contradictory, into a kind of absolute reality, a *surreality,* if one may so speak.

In *BDA*, I listed several different instances of how the importance of dreams reconnected to my father:

First, there was the description of George Hodel in the 1925 *Los Angeles Evening Herald* article, *"The Clouded Past of a Poet,"* by Ted Le Berthon in which he gives this description:

...
George drowned himself at times in an ocean of deep dreams. Only part of him seemed present.

He would muse standing before one in a black, flowered dressing gown lined with scarlet silk, oblivious to one's presence.

Suddenly, though, his eyes would flare up like signal lights and he would say, "The formless fastidiousness of perfumes in a seventeenth century boudoir is comparable to my mind in the presence of twilight."
...

Then, there are the posed photographs taken in 1946 at the Franklin house where, on two separate occasions, George photographed his subjects with their eyes closed.

In 2006, I identified the model in one photograph as his friend Marya Marco. The second depicts a model—a nude that might or might not be Elizabeth Short, and who might or might not be dead—who, like Marya, is posed with eyes closed, as if dreaming.

Thirdly, George Hodel made "dream" references at the time of his October 1949 arrest for incest and child molestation, which were published in the newspapers where he told the officers:

"We were delving into the mystery of love and the universe. These acts of which I am accused are unclear, like a dream. I can't figure out if someone is hypnotizing me or I am hypnotizing someone. If I am really here, then these things must have happened."

Finally, is Father's "Parable of the Sparrows" letter written to me in 1980, with its mystical questioning:

...

But are there only three of us? The birds, the glass, and we? Or is there a fourth? Who is standing behind our glass, invisible to us, incommunicable to us, gravely watching our brave attacks against the walls we cannot see? Is there a fifth presence, watching all the others? And a sixth, and others, hidden in mysteries beyond our dreams?

L'INCONNUE DE LA SEINE

It wasn't until the spring of 2006, just before my trip to Paris to speak at the Pompidou Centre, that I learned of *L'inconnue de la Seine* (French for "unknown woman of the Seine.")

A woman who had read *L'Affaire du Dahlia Noir*, the excellent French translation of *BDA* by Robert Pepin, contacted me by e-mail and provided me details on the story.

I say "story," but it really was much more than that. *L'inconnue* had become a mystery and legend throughout Europe, far outstripping that of our own Black Dahlia.

The body of the L'inconnue, an attractive young woman, was found floating in the Seine sometime in the late Nineteenth century, some say around 1880. Apparently, there were no signs of major trauma. So while murder could not be ruled out, most suggested she was a suicide.

As was the custom of that time, her body was laid out for public display at the Paris Morgue (behind the cathedral at Notre Dame) in hopes that she might be identified.

The open-air morgue was a macabre bazaar, a public marketplace where hundreds of the curious came daily to view the dead.

Still, the young woman remained unidentified. A death mask—a plaster casting—was reportedly made of her face and sold to the public.

By the 1920s, this mask of *L'inconnue de la Seine*, which many claimed had an enigmatic Mona Lisa smile, had found its way inside the home and onto the hearth of many Europeans. It was especially popular in France and Germany.

From there, L'inconnue found her way into literature, with many books and stories, some major best-sellers, each claiming to offer forth the secret of just how she met her fate.

One of the most famous of those works was *Aurelien,* written by novelist Louis Aragon and first published in 1944. Aragon collaborated with Man Ray, who at the time was living in Hollywood with his wife, Juliet. And both were regularly socializing with George and Dorothy Hodel.

Louis Aragon, like Man Ray, was a fellow Dadaist. In 1924, he had been a founding member of surrealism, along with Andre Breton and Philippe Soupault.

Man Ray created eight photographs of the *L'inconnue de la Seine* for Aragon's 1944 novel. A grateful Louis Aragon had this to say about Man Ray's contribution:

> "But in truth it is Man Ray who wrote the novel, playing in black and white with the mask of the *Inconnue de la Seine.*"

We can be certain that a young George Hodel knew this legend. He would have been one of the many Bohemians cum surrealists who adopted and owned the legend in the 1920s and '30s. It would not surprise me if he even owned his own mask.

In the 1940s, Dad would have discussed the legend of the *L'inconnue de la Seine* with Man Ray, Juliet, and their friends, even as Man prepared his photographs for publication for the Aragon novel.

But I suspect there was more than parlor conversation. Based on my father's photographs in his personal album, all taken by him during that time period, I believe he was obsessed with *L'inconnue de la Seine.* It might have reached all the way back to his Bohemian and surrealist teens.

In the photographs below, all found in George Hodel's album of "loved ones," we see four different women. Each taken at a different time in the 1940s. Each woman he has posed with head tilted forward and looking down with eyes closed.

Compare these to the original photograph of *L'inconnue de la Seine.* I believe it was no coincidence but a conscious, intentional posing by George Hodel to imitate her original death mask.

In some twisted, psychopathological way, Dad connected to her story. The when of it is not so important. It could have been early in his teens or as late as 1944, with the legend first introduced to him by way of his friend, Man Ray, who was then actively working, researching, and photographing the L'inconnue for Aragon's novel.

This also provides us with more dramatic circumstantial evidence and gives more weight to the theory, examined in an earlier chapter, that the nude photograph, believed to be of Elizabeth Short, could well be a "trophy death mask." George Hodel's own *L'inconnue de la Maison Franklin*.

The photograph below of the Inconnue casting was taken by portrait photographer Albert Rudomine in Paris in 1927. Rudomine, like my grandmother, was from Kiev, Russia, and also like my grandparents, fled to Paris at the turn of the century. Rudomine became a prominent portrait photographer and a number of his works now hang in the Getty Museum. He might well have known my grandparents, who lived in Paris and were close friends with the Russian count and sculptor Paul Troubetzkoy and his family.

La Vierge inconnue par Albert Rudomine (d'après le masque mortuaire de l'Inconnue de la Seine), 1927.

L'inconnue de la Seine photo of death mask
by Albert Rudomine, 1927

George Hodel photographs – An obsession with L'inconnue de la Seine?

Four women posed a la L'inconnue and photographed by George Hodel. From left to right:

1. Unknown woman, possibly Elizabeth Short, taken at Franklin house, circa 1946
2. Marya Marco, taken at Franklin house, circa 1946
3. Kiyo, George Hodel's former mistress and author's future wife, taken circa 1944

4. Unknown woman, believed to be Filipina, taken unknown date and location, possibly early fifties

EXQUISITE CORPSE

In September 2006, literally on the eve of my television appearance on CNN's *Anderson Cooper 360*, a new book was published. While I was seeing surrealist connections between the Black Dahlia murder and my father, this new book combined the genres of true crime and art history by surmising "the murder may have been directly linked to surrealist art and ideas."

The book, *Exquisite Corpse: Surrealism and the Black Dahlia Murder* (Bulfinch Press, 2006, New York) was co-written by Mark Nelson and Sarah Hudson Bayliss, two New York writers and art researchers.

The book's "Web of Connections" is an invaluable aid in mapping out George Hodel's links to the art world and fellow surrealists living in 1940s Los Angeles.

It also attempts to examine the core question of the surrealists' relationships to the Black Dahlia murder. Who knew what and when did they know it?

Did Man Ray and his close circle of friends, in the days and weeks immediately following the crime, learn that their kindred spirit and wannabe Dadaist George Hodel was the prime suspect in her murder?

Did these men with their connections to L.A.'s "inner circle," which included A-list screenwriter Gene Fowler, acquire their own set of Black Dahlia crime scene photographs?

In his book, *Reporters: Memoirs of a Young Newspaperman*, Gene Fowler's son Will Fowler described his 1947 involvement in the Black Dahlia investigation as a young crime reporter for the *Los Angeles Examiner* .

In his chapter on the Black Dahlia, Fowler described how he and staff photographer Felix Paegel were the first to arrive at the vacant lot. He claimed that with their radio tuned to the police frequency, they had heard the call and being close "were the first to arrive." Fowler details how he examined the body as Paegel snapped images with his Speed Graphic camera.

From pages 74-75 of Will Fowler's book, "Reporters":

...
While I was kneeling next to the body, Paegel took a picture documenting that absolutely no one was in the immediate area. His two principal photos showed the body alone in the barren field, and the second of me stooping beside the body. Before it was published on the front page, it was necessary for an *Examiner* artist to

airbrush a large blanket covering all but the upper arms and lower legs. He also removed the deep slashes on either side of her face.

After Paegel photographed the body, Fowler described how the first two LAPD patrol officers arrived to find the two reporters standing beside the corpse and immediately drew their service revolvers. Fowler identified himself as a press reporter and continued his narrative. Page 75:

> They [officers] gave me permission to leave the scene and I ran for a public phone. I stuck a nickel in the slot and dialed the desk, and when he heard me say, "cut in half," Richardson [Los Angeles Examiner's City Editor] told me to get the hell in with the negatives.

> The city room was already buzzing about the story as Paegel disappeared into the photo lab to develop the negatives. When he emerged, he was carrying a large dripping wet 11x14 print of the body. Several people gathered around to get a first look.

Based on my follow-up investigation and review of police reports I have found that there is much in Will Fowler's book that is simply not true.

His chapter on the Black Dahlia is filled with inaccuracies, self-aggrandizement, and hyperbole. But, it's absolutely true that Will Fowler was at the crime scene and his photographer Felix Paegel shot overall photos of the location and condition of the body. Copies of these photographs were in his possession and also easily accessible to numerous other *Los Angeles Examiner* employees.

Will's father, Gene, Fowler and his close circle of friends, including Ben Hecht,[who wrote the preface to Will's just described book], Rowland Brown [Dorothy Hodel's then lover], Steve Fisher, and many more, would have seen and very likely gotten copies of these pictures. They were simply too hot not to handle.

Were copies of these Dahlia crime scene photos given to Man Ray and did he pass them on to his closest friend, Marcel Duchamp, who would use them as the inspiration for his final, secret, twenty-year art project, *Etant Donnes*?

We cannot know, but *Exquisite Corpse* enumerated so many direct and "one-degree separations" between my father and the surrealist community that, in the end, it becomes difficult for me to believe these associates did not suspect George Hodel's involvement in the murder.

The chapter, *"William Copley: Surrealist Confidant"* introduced us to the birth of the friendship between William Copley and Man Ray that began in Los Angeles in 1946.

A wealthy art collector, Copley opened his own Los Angeles gallery and dedicated it exclusively to surrealism. He befriended many of the movement's major artists, including Man Ray, Max Ernst, Rene Magritte, and Yves Tanguy and, and displayed their work.

According to *Exquisite Corpse*, while Copley's L.A. gallery was not a financial success, his friendship with Man Ray was. In 1951, Copley and his girlfriend, Gloria de Herrera, relocated from Los Angeles to Paris with Man Ray and his wife, Juliet.

CORROBORATING THE WHO?

Looking at *Exquisite Corpse* with an investigator's eye, it is my belief that the most singularly important and circumstantially compelling contribution was the book's inclusion of a 1961 painting by William Copley entitled:

Il est minuit Dr. _____.
"It is Midnight Dr. _____."
Oil on canvas by William Copley, 1961
[permission to use painting courtesy of Billy Copley]

Exquisite Corpse, page 144:

That same year, as Man Ray was nearing completion of Self Portrait, Copley created a significant artwork. Like many of his other paintings, Il est minuit Dr. _____. (It Is Midnight Dr. _____), 1961, portrays a nude woman and a fully clothed man. The male figure appears at the upper left holding a medical bag. The woman reclines near the bottom of the canvas like an odalisque. It is a classical pose, reminiscent of Ariadne and so many other nudes in art history. She has closed eyes, a hint of a smile, and one hand resting on her forehead. Above her is an array of instruments, including a scalpel and two saws. It suggests that Copley, distanced from the crime scene by fourteen years and thousands of miles, had not forgotten it.

This painting, created some fourteen years after the Black Dahlia murder, supports the suggestion that William Copley (and, by extension Man Ray and Marcel Duchamp) might have suspected Hodel of the crime.)

Keep in mind that surrealists loved to conceal secret messages and complex cryptograms in their works—riddles, wrapped in mysteries, inside enigmas. So let's take a closer look at Copley's painting.

[Note: The following observations are not offered as "proofs." They are theoretical and speculative and were sent to me in the past few years, as e-mails, from several of my readers. I believe they might have merit and for that reason present them here for your consideration.]

Back to the William Copley painting:

To the immediate right of the doctor there are five oversized surgical tools each placed in a vertical position. Below them is a sixth instrument laid out horizontally.

In a 2009 e-mail from "D.M." he suggested the possibility that the oversized vertical surgeon's tools might conceal and actually spell out the name H O D E L.

[Compare to original William Copley painting shown previously]

To be clear, this "letter decryption" was not something presented or suggested in the Nelson/Bayliss book, but rather came from "D.M." as summarized in a website blog I wrote on September 27, 2009, *"A Letter from Dada & Moma - A Surrealist Word Game?"* [Note: In addition to the vertical letters, spelling out the doctor's name—HODEL, others have speculated that Copley might have used the horizontal tool to spell out the doctor/killer's profession as —"M.D."]

Art is totally subjective. As to whether these hidden letters exist or not, I'll leave it to the reader to make his own call. I'm open to the possibility, but would need to see further corroboration and confirmation, perhaps in the form of a "lost letter" or Copley family document.

MAN RAY LETTERS HIDDEN IN PLAIN SIGHT FOR SEVENTY-YEARS

Interestingly, I came across Abby Callard's article, *Man Ray's Signature Work*, in the November 2009 *Smithsonian Magazine*.

The article details photographer Ellen Carey's discovery of Man Ray's secret writing, hidden for over seventy years in one of his early photographs. Man Ray, unbeknownst to anyone, had concealed the letters in plain sight by reversing and disguising his signature and incorporating it as abstract lines in the photograph. Here are some significant excerpts from the Smithsonian article referencing Ellen Carey's decryption:

Artist Man Ray mischievously scribbled his name in a famous photograph, but it took decades for the gesture to be discovered.

...

In 1935, the avant-garde photographer Man Ray opened his shutter, sat down in front of his camera and used a penlight to create a series of swirls and loops. ... As a self-portrait—titled *Space Writings*—it seemed fairly abstract.

...

But now Ellen Carey, a photographer whose working method is similar to Man Ray's, has discovered something that has been hidden in plain sight in *Space Writings* for the past 74 years: the artist's signature, signed with the penlight amid the swirls and loops.

...

It might have taken seven decades and a like-minded photographer to see the disguised signature, but the evidence is clear. "Oh, it's definitely there," Carey says. "It's saying, 'Hello, how come no one noticed for 70 years? I think [Man Ray] would be chuckling right now. Finally, somebody figured him out.'"

Did William Copley, close personal friend to Man Ray, follow his mentor's lead and conceal his own secret letters? Did he create his own riddle wrapped in a real life mystery?

CORROBORATING THE WHERE?

"From the nature of the cuts the girl was probably in a semi-recumbent position in a bathtub." —Chief Autopsy Surgeon, Dr. Frederick Newbarr, January 1947 [Public statement to the L.A. Press on his Elizabeth "Black Dahlia" Short autopsy findings]

In *Chapter 5, Scene of the Crime,* we examined in-depth the evidence pointing to and linking the Sowden/Franklin House as being the probable crime scene.

In that review I also theorized that the most logical location for George Hodel to perform his "operation" was in the tub/shower in the master bathroom. [That the crime occurred in a bathtub was independently supported by the very public knowledge, printed in most of the Los Angeles newspapers, on January 22, 1947, quoting both LAPD Captain Jack Donahoe and Coroner Newbarr, "that the bisection probably was done in a bathtub."]

In a just received [November 1, 2011] e-mail question from, Jess Mayeux, one of my readers, in referencing the background squares in the Copley painting, asks: **"Could the grid represent the tiles in the master bathroom of the Sowden House?"**

George Hodel's Franklin house, tiled master bathroom as it would have appeared in 1947. As detailed in Chapter Five, this is the probable location of bisection.

William Copley, artist, art-dealer, patron and close friend of Man Ray, and Angeleno from 1946-1951, would very likely have known and socialized with Dr. George Hodel. He likely attended talks and parties at the Franklin house.

Copley probably also knew many of George Hodel's friends, including the doctor's 1950 caught-on–tape-accomplice, Baron Ernst Harringa. Copley and Harringa must have been acquainted considering the fact they separately owned two of Los Angeles' upscale art galleries within a few miles of each other.

The title of his 1961 oil painting reminded the doctor [regardless of whether Copley suspects it is Dr. Hodel or another] that, "It is midnight," the witching hour, a time for demons and devils to be about their work. By laying out the surgeon's tools, Copley suggested exactly what that work would be—an "operation."

He next introduced us to "the patient/victim." She is young, attractive and is either unconscious or dead, lying supine on what appears to be a tiled floor. She is carefully posed, with her right arm bent at the elbow.

Post-operative upper torso of Elizabeth Short [airbrushed] as actually posed by killer in vacant lot. Compare this to Copley's reclining nude [victim] on what appear to be bathroom tiles.

So many questions:

In his singular 1961 art work, *It is Midnight Dr. _____.*, has William Copley represented Los Angeles' most infamous crime, the 1947 Black Dahlia murder?

In that painting, did he reveal he suspected the "who"—Dr. George Hill Hodel—and the "where"---the Franklin house bathroom?

Had William Copley seen the crime-scene photos? Was he privy to the inner-circle's rumors and the not-so-secret knowledge, shared by Lillian Lenorak, Madi Comfort, Joe Barrett and many others? Was he part of Madi's "we" when she said, "We all knew that he had done it. There was no doubt."

At the very least we can be confident that William Copley would have known that Dr. George Hodel was on trial for incest and in

December 1949, had been publicly accused, by his own daughter of committing the Black Dahlia murder.

> "My father is the murderer of the Black Dahlia. My father is going to kill me, and all the rest of the members of this household, because he has a lust for blood. He is insane." —Tamar Hodel, December 17, 1949 [as reported in court testimony and headlined in below daily newspapers]

Girl's Story Is 'Fantasy,' Court Hears

The 14-year-old daughter o prominent Hollywood physici "plotted his downfall" with fi tastic stories, including one th he killed Elizabeth (Black Da lia) Short, his attorney, Robe A. Neeb Jr., sought to prove day.

Neeb hammered at the "fa tasies" of blonde Tamar Hod in her crossexamination at th morals trial of Dr. George H Hodel, 38.

Sex Charges

Hodel is being tried on charge of improper relations with th girl at their home, 5121 Frankli ave., in July.

Hodel, who has denied th charges, will seek to show tha

Girl accused of trying to pin Dahlia murder on dad

Tamar, loquations 14-year-old *gi*rl, helped by the girl against daughter of Hollywood physician her father.

George H. Hodel, today stood in- Atty. Robert A. Neeb Jr., in credulily accused of trying to the second day of a blistering pin the unsavory Black Dahlia cross-examination, suddenly de-murder on her father. manded of the young witness if

This told turn punctuated the she remembered a conversation trial of Dr. Hodel by a jury in with one Joe Barrett a roomate Superior Judge Thomas I. Am- at the Hodel home. brose's court on a charge of in- Neeb wanted to know if Tamar said to Barrett:

"This house has secret passages. My father is the murderer of the Black Dahlia. My father is go-ing to kill me and all the rest of the members of this household be-cause he has a lust for blood. He is insane."

On the morning of December 17, 1949, in Los Angeles, two separate articles [seen above] hit the streets. Published in the Los Angeles Daily News and the Los Angeles Mirror, both accounts reported that Dr. George Hodel had been accused by his fourteen-year-old, daughter, Tamar, of committing the Black Dahlia murder. What was not made public was the fact that Tamar, who at the time was being held in protective custody at Juvenile Hall, had been informed by the very police detectives who were transporting her to and from court, that her father "was the prime suspect in the Dahlia murder."

HENRY MILLER AND GEORGE HODEL

Man Ray and novelist/painter/surrealist Henry Miller were close friends. The two of them, along with Beat Generation poet/author Kenneth Rexroth, hung out from time to time at Miller's home in Big Sur.

During the 1940s, the three were also friends with George Hodel and visited him at the Franklin house, where they could intellectualize freely and discuss anything without bourgeois restraint.

In later years, my mother talked of Henry Miller being a family acquaintance and of visiting him often at his home in the beautiful coastal community of Big Sur in central California.

Though I was aware of Henry Miller's "Tropics" books, banned in the US until the 1960s, I had never previously read any of his writing. I only knew him through his reputation as highly unconventional, and that many considered his erotic writings both amoral and obscene.

I have no intention here of attempting to make any moral judgment on Mr. Miller's writings, either pro or con. My intent is to examine, as we have with Man Ray, how Miller might have influenced my father's thinking during that period?

A few years back, I discovered Henry Miller's *The World of Sex*. The book's first page read, "Printed by J.H.N. for friends of Henry Miller. 1000 copies printed. New York, 1940"

The passages below reflect that Miller and George Hodel were kindred sensual spirits who obviously shared similar thoughts on sex, incest, and their own unconventional sense of morality.

From what Miller revealed in his privately published book, it is easy for me to imagine the two men sharing a lively discussion at the Franklin house. Here are some selected excerpts from Henry Miller's *World of Sex*:

Page 12:
But what is normal and healthy for the vast majority leads us nowhere in seeking a clue to the rules of behavior which govern men of genius. The man of genius, wittingly or unwittingly, through his work and by his example seems to struggle to establish the truth that every man is a law unto himself and that the only way to liberation is through the recognition and the realization that he is a unique being.

Page 52:
Sex is only one of millions of ways of expressing oneself. The important thing is the expression, not what is expressed. If it would help men to liberate themselves I would recommend them to have intercourse with animals or to fuck in public or to commit incest, for example. There is nothing in itself which is wrong or evil, not even murder. It is the fear of doing wrong, the fear of committing murder, the fear of acting, or expressing oneself, which is wrong.

Page 77:
In fact, it is our dream life which affords a slight cue to the nature of that life which is in store for us. In our dream life we live indiscriminately in past and future. It is the potential, indestructible man who comes to life in the dream. For his being there is no longer a censorship; taboos, laws, conventions, customs are annihilated. In the realm of sex it is the only true freedom he ever knows. He moves toward the object of his desire unimpeded by time, space, physical obstacles or moral considerations. He may sleep with his mother as naturally and easily as with another woman. He may take an animal in the field and satisfy his desires without the slightest revolt. He may fuck his own daughter and find it extremely pleasurable. In the waking world, crippled and shackled by all kinds of fetters, everything is wrong or evil except that which has been prescribed by fear. The real, inner being knows that these things are not wrong, not evil: when he can close his eyes

he gives himself up to all these practices and pursuits which are prohibited. In his dreams he follows out his true desires. These desires are not only valid and legitimate but must be realized; if they are thwarted or frustrated the world becomes ugly and death-like.

Page 79:
A certain amount of killing, plundering, raping, and so on, inevitably occurs whenever there is a burst of freedom. Some kind of crude justice has to be dealt out when the scales are tipped and seek to return to balance. Some specimens of the human race ought, out of decency, kindness and reverence for those to come, be wiped out. Some bastards *should* be buggered and thrown over the fence for the wolves and hyaenas to finish off. Some females *ought* to be raped to death and left lying on the spot for all to see. Some mean, miserly cowards and traitors to the race *ought* to be stripped of all they possess and sent naked into the hills.

A man's prick and a woman's cunt will not need to have a name and address tied to it.

Page 83-84:
Now and then in the evenings, I pass a show window where a manikin is being dressed. The manikin is standing there nude and the window-dresser is just in the act of putting his arms around the figure to move her an inch to the left or right. Every time this happens I have the same reaction—I feel that the manikin is more alive than the man who is dressing her. Why it is I don't know, but the manikin always seems *sexually* alive. The window-trimmer, on the other hand, is just an indescribable bundle of animate flesh wrapped in meaningless clothes. His movements are utterly senseless. He is going to take the live sexual manikin and make her seductive to the passer-by by putting clothes around her and making her look like the people in the street. He makes the sexual thing dead, just as the undertaker, is ticking up a corpse, makes death look inviting. On every side I see people tampering with the natural order of things, trying to galvanize the inanimate into the semblance of life or else rigidifying the live thing into some death-like pose. Dead or alive, whatever is bare, stark, nude, frightens the shit out of them. A wax cunt in a show window can terrify them even more than a live cunt, so it seems. Even turkeys have to be dressed after the slaughter.

It is one thing to sit around drinking Bordeaux with your fellow outsiders and see which one can cast himself in the role of chief nihilist with his pen or paintbrush. But it is quite another to actually step outside the world of words and pictures and take action.

That was the danger and difference between a Man Ray or Henry Miller and Dr. George Hill Hodel.

His friends talked a good game about how there was no difference between the waking and the dream state, but when the wine wore off, they went home to their comfortable beds in the objective real world.

George Hodel did not. He drank the Kool-Aid and believed. He heard the words preached by his surrealist gurus like Andre Breton, Man Ray, and Henry Miller, and took them to heart ... and to action.

George made Breton's words real: "Kill, fly faster, love to your heart's content."

George made Man Ray's *Lover's Lips* bleed and the *Minotaur* come to life in the savage torture-sacrifice of a young woman, a surgical murder made real.

George read Henry Miller's instructions, "to commit incest," and slept with his teenage daughter. And more, through the decade of the Forties he committed horrendous acts with women, "raped to death and left lying on the spot"—all made real.

This was the method of his madness. This is what made George Hodel so dangerous and his surrealist signature crimes so unique.

SPELLBOUND

In Alfred Hitchcock's 1945 classic psychological thriller, *Spellbound,* the original movie poster shows Gregory Peck [John Ballantyne] embracing Ingrid Bergman [Dr. Constance Petersen] as he holds an open straight-edged razor in his right hand. The tag line reads:

"Will he kiss me or kill me?"

The story centers on a young amnesiac's search to find who he is and whether he has committed a murder. On a parallel track is the romance, which has him falling in love with his Freudian therapist. Pursued by the police, the two lovers flee to New York City where they seek out the aid of Dr. Constance Peterson's old school professor, Dr. Brulov [Michael Chekov] to help them with a little dream analysis, hoping to find some answers of the who and why.

Next, we are presented with what many consider the film's signature moment, a surreal dream sequence designed and choreographed by Salvador Dali.

Dali's images unfold before us on-screen as Peck describes in detail the sum and substance of his dream to the professor and Constance:

I seemed to be in a gambling house, but there weren't any walls, just a lot of curtains with eyes painted on them. A man was walking around with a large pair of scissors cutting all the drapes in half. Then a girl came in with hardly anything on and started walking around the gambling room kissing everybody. She came to my table first. I'm afraid she looked a little like Constance.

I was sitting there playing cards with a man who had a beard. I was dealing to him. I dealt him a 7 of clubs. He said, 'That makes 21 - I win.' When he turned up his cards, they were blank. Just then the proprietor came in and accused him of cheating. The proprietor yelled, 'This is my place, and if I catch you cheating again, I'll fix you.'

There's a lot more to it. Then I saw the man. He was the man with the beard leaning over the slope of a high building. I yelled at him to watch out. Then he went over—slowly—with his feet in the air. And then I saw the proprietor again—the man in the mask. He was hiding behind a tall chimney, and he had a small wheel in his hand.

I saw him drop the wheel on the roof. Suddenly I was running and then I heard something beating over my head. It was a great pair of wings. The wings chased me and almost caught up with me and I came to the bottom of the hill.

Spellbound *dream sequence clip "curtains with eyes"*

"Man with large pair of scissors cutting the drapes"

Spellbound 1945

Spellbound *dream sequence clip "the man in the mask holding a small wheel"*

Spellbound was one of my father's favorite films, and it is easy to understand why.

Not only was Dr. George Hill Hodel captivated by all things Dali and surreal. But add to the mix that he himself was just beginning to flirt with hypnosis and dream analysis. Within six years, he'd relocate to Hawaii, where he would hang out his own shingle as a Freudian psychiatrist and begin counseling to the territorial prison population's criminally insane. Psychopath to the psychopaths—perfect!

I'm convinced the dream sequence in *Spellbound* made such a powerful impression on my father that he could not resist including a reference to it and an homage to Dali as he had done with Man Ray.

I am now persuaded that Dali, like Man Ray, was also recognized with a wink and a nod in my father's Black Dahlia murder, which was committed just one year after the film's release.

Consider the following:

Man Ray's *Juliet in Stocking Mask* was created in Hollywood in *1945*, at the same time they were filming *Spellbound.*

We have examined in-depth the homage paid to Man Ray by George Hodel in imitation of his two works: The *Lovers Lips* and the *Minotaure,* as well as the many other surrealist links.

There can be little doubt that Dali met with Man Ray at his Vine Street apartment when he visited Hollywood in 1945. Though by then Man Ray had lived in Hollywood for five years, the two had previously been long acquainted as fellow surrealists in Paris. That these two masks by the two surrealists were created within months of each other, I believe, is not coincidence.

I linked the *Juliet Stocking Mask* to Man Ray in my previous investigation, and now believe that it was a co-homage to Dali and the "masked man" in his dream sequence.

Left to Right: Dali Spellbound mask, 1945; Man Ray Juliet mask, 1945; Black Dahlia Avenger mask, 1947

BEN HECHT

"I know the name of the killer and the psychology of his deed. [...] There is only one form of hatred that can equal in violence the symbolizing rage of the lunatic—and what that hatred is I will leave unsaid." —Ben Hecht, *Los Angeles Herald-Express,* Sat, Feb 1, 1947

By 1945, Ben Hecht had become Hollywood's highest paid screenwriter.

He was hired by Hitchcock to write the screenplay for *Spellbound,* and Dali was to work with Hecht in incorporating the surreal dream sequence into the film.

George Hodel admired Hecht's writing and as a young editor/publisher of his own surreal magazine, *Fantasia,* had written a review in 1925 of one of Hecht's early books, *The Kingdom of Evil.* Here's an excerpt from Hodel's review:

"...Macabre forms, more dank and putrescently phantasmal than any of Hecht's former imagining, grope blindly and crazedly in the poisonous fog out of which loom the rotting fancies that people his 'Kingdom of Evil.'"...

"With almost animate pigments has Hecht painted this monstrous dream of Mallare's, and with delicate and meticulous craftsmanship has he fashioned its cadaverous and perverse beauty." —George Hill Hodel, *Fantasia Magazine*, August 1925

A short time later, the reference from his fellow Bohemians of George Hodel's admiration for Hecht's writings, was published in the *Evening Herald* article, *"The Clouded Past of a Poet"*:

"It's not George's gloom, his preference for Huysmanns, De Gourmont, Poe, Baudelaire, Verlaine, and *Hecht* [emphasis mine] that pains us..."

Prior to writing *Spellbound*, Ben Hecht had worked with Dorothy Huston Hodel's ex-husband, John Huston, as screenwriter on both *Wuthering Heights* and *Maltese Falcon*. He also worked as a writer with Dorothy's then-lover, director/writer Rowland Brown, on two of his films, *Quick Millions* and *Angels with Dirty Faces*.

There can be little doubt that Hecht not only personally knew George Hodel and very likely socialized with the same "inner circle" of Hollywood A-list writers (including Huston, Brown, Steve Fisher, Gene Fowler, and others) but that it was George Hodel to whom he referred when, two weeks after the Black Dahlia murder, he wrote in the *Herald-Express* that:

"I know the name of the killer and the psychology of his deed."

Hecht, like his friend and fellow screenwriter Steve Fisher, knew that the police had the killer's name and was sure they would soon be making an arrest that would surprise and shock all of Los Angeles. Or, as Fisher put it in his separate article for the *Evening Herald Express*, "a lot of people who know him, and do not now suspect he has anything to do with the case, are going to be surprised and terrified."

I believe there is more. A second possible link exists to both George Hodel and his homage to *Spellbound* in another murder and another mailing that would come two decades later!

In my sequel, *Most Evil, Avenger, Zodiac and the Further Murders of Dr. George Hill Hodel*, published in 2009, I present what I believe to be compelling evidence linking my father to additional crimes.

After crimes in Chicago, Los Angeles, and Manila, it's possible that two decades after terrorizing Los Angeles as the "Avenger," George Hodel reinvented himself in the San Francisco Bay Area as "Zodiac."

I believe I have made a strong circumstantial case supporting these further series of crimes and will let the evidence speak for itself as presented in that separate investigation.

Unlike *BDA*, I am not going as far as to claim I have proven he was the killer in those crimes, but suggest that he needs to go to the top of the list of suspects. Authorities should pursue confirmed Zodiac DNA and then rule George Hodel in or out.

In *Most Evil*, I offered evidence that the killer continued his "Avenger" theme of murder as a fine art, not only in his methods but also in his mailings, where he refers to music, art, literature, and—more to the point—to specific vintage motion pictures.

I argued that Zodiac was a cinephile who stole both characters and actions from several classic films, mimicking and incorporating them into his Zodiac crime signature and *modus operandi*.

In *Most Evil*, I named two films: *The Most Dangerous Game* (1932) and *Charlie Chan at Treasure Island* (1939), and went on in separate chapters to detail the evidence and linkage to each movie.

Based on what has been presented in this chapter, I am going to offer the possibility that my father, if he was Zodiac, appears to have hidden a clue to a third classic film in his San Francisco taunts to the press: his old favorite, *Spellbound*.

Below is a copy of the Halloween taunt card that Zodiac sent to crime reporter Paul Avery at the *San Francisco Chronicle* in 1970.

On the front, the card refers to Zodiac as being reporter Avery's "Secret Pal" and promises to offer a clue to his identity. On the back, Zodiac has hand-printed the different methods by which he has or will kill his victims, writing:

"By Fire, By Gun, By Knife, By Rope"

and that they will become his,

"Slaves in Paradice"

Law enforcement, noting the strange way Zodiac wrote the message, theorized that the "clue" he was sending might be the fact the letters, as written, formed the letter **"H"** which they suggested could be a monogram clue to the killer's name.

Front and back of Zodiac's 1970 Halloween card sent to San Francisco Chronicle
Back: Letter H?

But it is the inside of this Halloween card that is on point in our current examination.

Interior of 1970 Halloween Card

In addition to writing his signature circle-and-cross, Zodiac included a strange symbol at the bottom of the card, plus a set of thirteen eyes with a threatening message to the *Chronicle* reporter Avery. "Peek-a-boo, you are doomed!"

Keeping in mind that George Hodel had a perfect photographic memory, compare Dali's hand-drawn eyes from the dream sequence in *Spellbound* to the eyes drawn by Zodiac.

Dali Dream sequence in "Spellbound"

1970 Zodiac Halloween card mailed to San Francisco Chronicle

Dali eyes [top] compared to Zodiac's hand drawn eyes [bottom] enlarged—another enigmatic clue?

George Hodel as the 1947 "Avenger" very likely paid homage to both Man Ray and Dali in his 1947 mailings to the press. Did he repeat his it two decades later as Zodiac?

22
Touch DNA

"The family of JonBenet Ramsey has been formally cleared of any role in the 6-year-old's 1996 murder, a Colorado prosecutor announced Wednesday, citing newly discovered DNA evidence." — *USA Today* April 16, 2009

THE 2009 *USA TODAY* ARTICLE went on to state:

> Boulder, Colorado—District Attorney Mary Lacy said in a statement on Wednesday that DNA evidence recovered from the child's clothing [pajamas] pointed to an "unexplained third party." Lacy apologized to the family for the suspicions that made their lives "an ongoing living hell."

> ... The new evidence, described as "irrefutable" in clearing the Ramseys, would be checked against other profiles in the national DNA database managed by the FBI.

The new physical evidence was obtained by technicians from *Bode Technology*, in Lorton, Virginia. *Bode* is considered to be one of the top forensic laboratories in the United States and is frequently the lab of choice used by the FBI, and law enforcement agencies across the nation.

The relatively new procedure used by *Bode Labs* in extracting the suspect's DNA in the Ramsey investigation is called "Touch DNA."

Touch DNA is the collection of skin cells which have been transferred from an individual's skin to the surface of items it has come in contact with, such as the grip of a gun, luggage, a car's steering wheel, a victim's clothing, or a ligature used in the commission of a crime.

The collection of the skin cells can be accomplished in various methods, such as swabbing, cutting, tape-lift, and scraping.

In the past several years, this method of collecting evidence has resulted in a number of successful murder prosecutions, as well as aiding in establishing the actual innocence of a number of wrongfully convicted individuals.

A SEARCH FOR GEORGE HILL HODEL'S DNA

In April 2009, I contacted *Bode Laboratories.* After exchanging telephone calls, letters, and e-mails with Dr. Angela Williamson, Director of Forensic Casework, we decided on the best course of action to attempt to isolate and obtain my father's DNA.

I carefully packaged and forwarded to the Virginia based lab a number of my father's personal effects, some of which had been in my possession for over forty years. They included a pair of his Bally dress shoes (size 10e) and four separate letters written by him over the past decades—all of which contained stamps and envelopes that might yield his DNA.

By July 2010, over a year had elapsed, and three of the four items, including the shoes, had none of his DNA. We were down to the last item, a letter my father had mailed to me in 1971 from Manila, Philippines.

BINGO!

Success came on this very last evidentiary item. The envelope contained his full genetic DNA profile!

George Hill Hodel Letter mailed from Manila in 1971

George Hill Hodel's DNA profile remains in my possession and upon request will be made available to any legitimate law enforcement agency to help their cold case investigations.

Locus	CCA0972-0134-E04a1
D8S1179	
D21S11	
D7S820	
CSF1PO	
D3S1358	
TH01	George Hodel full DNA profile obtained in 2010 and on file and available for comparison.
D13S317	
D16S539	
D2S1338	
D19S433	
vWA	
TPOX	
D18S51	
Amelogenin	
D5S818	
FGA	

George Hodel 1949 Booking DNA full profile now available

For those who have not read my sequel to *BDA*, *Most Evil: Avenger, Zodiac, and the Further Serial Murders of Dr. George Hill Hodel*, I will here provide only the briefest of summaries so you can understand that the following discussion about connecting George Hodel's newly obtained DNA to other crimes in other cities is not simply arbitrary. Rather, it is based on compelling circumstantial evidence provided in that book.

LOS ANGELES DA FILES—ELIZABETH SHORT—THE CHICAGO LIPSTICK MURDERS

As I reviewed the Los Angeles DA files, I discovered documents that showed in July 1946, while my father was stationed with UNRRA in China, Elizabeth Short traveled to Chicago, Illinois and began her own personal investigation into three exceptionally high-profile crimes known as Chicago's "Lipstick Murders."

The three victims—Josephine Ross, Frances Brown, and Suzanne Degnan—had made national headlines in 1945 and 1946.

The third Lipstick victim gained the most notoriety. It involved the horrific kidnap-strangulation murder and surgical bisection of a six-year-old girl, little Suzanne Degnan. Her sadistic killer had kidnapped the sleeping child from her bedroom, carried her to a basement just a few blocks from her home. There he strangled her, performed a highly skilled surgical operation known as a "hemicorpectomy," and divided the body by cutting through the second and third lumbar vertebrae—the exact same operation performed on Elizabeth Short one year later.

The killer then carried the body parts to six separate catch-basins around that north-side neighborhood. Finally, he scrawled a message in lipstick on a post in front of the "murder room" that read:

Lipstick printed sign on post near building where body of Suzanne Degnan was dismembered, discovered yesterday.

"Stop Me Before I Kill More."

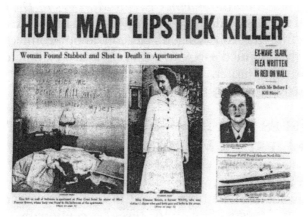

Chicago's 1945 Frances Brown Lipstick Murder

Written on apartment wall in lipstick less than one month prior to the Degnan murder:

"For heaven's sake catch me Before I Kill more. I cannot control myself"

The DA files document that Elizabeth Short spent three weeks in Chicago and slept with four separate Chicago newspaper reporters, apparently attempting to gain some inside information on the three separate Lipstick Murder investigations. She also informed the newsmen that "she knew a Chicago detective that was working the Degnan case."

The DA files also contained information indicating that the Dahlia's killer might have been an "Unknown Chicago Police Officer." Why?

The information was based on the fact that Elizabeth Short attended Jack Carson's CBS radio show in Hollywood in early January 1947, just days before being slain.

Chief Usher Jack Egger identified her as standing in line with an older "dapper male in his 30s" who identified himself to Egger as a Chicago police officer, showing Egger a police badge. Egger allowed both Short and the man to jump the line and enter the studio. Egger was familiar with Short because she regularly attended the shows, but this was the first time he ever recalled her being accompanied by a man.

Jack Egger went on to become a DA investigator, then joined the Beverly Hills Police Department, where he rose to command that department's Detective Bureau. After retirement, he became chief of security for Warner Brothers Studio in Burbank.

As detailed in my sequel, I discovered that Jack was still employed by Warner Brothers as their chief investigator, and I met with him in 2004.

After verifying the facts in his original 1950 DA interview, I then showed Chief Egger a photograph of Dr. George Hill Hodel from around 1950. He positively identified my father as being the person he saw with Elizabeth Short at the CBS studio and the same individual who had shown him a Chicago police badge.

I also possess original Los Angeles Sheriff's Department investigative reports that show LASD, in 1946, was actively investigating the possibility that their 1944 Hollywood Lone Woman Murder of oil-heiress Georgette Bauerdorf might have been connected to the later 1945 Chicago Lipstick Murders. Those reports indicate that LASD requested prints and additional information to ascertain if the crimes were linked.

Photo identification by Warner Brothers Studio, Chief Jack Egger
Left: Dr. George Hodel; Right: Elizabeth Short

JOHN F. "JACK" EGGER 1927-2010

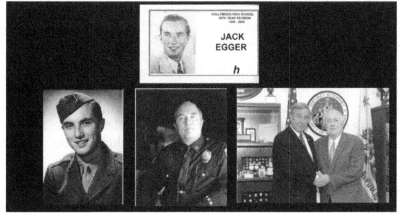

Jack Egger (top and bottom left photos, 1945-1946); Captain Egger, Beverly Hills Police Department (center); Photo right shows Jack as Chief of Warner Brothers Security with L.A. District Attorney, Steve Cooley 2006. (Photographs courtesy of Jack's son, Brian Egger)

Jack Egger passed away in Los Angeles in 2010, at the age of eighty-three. His law enforcement service spanned more than five decades and included: D.A.'s investigator for four years, from 1949 to 1953 when he transferred to *Beverly Hills Police Department*. He rose to the rank of Detective Captain. Honorably retired he then entered the private sector, and in 1979, he served at Warner Brothers Studio as Chief of Security, commanding a 400-man security force.

Up until his death he remained active in the law enforcement community. In his final years, he served as a General Board Member of POALAC (Peace Officers Association Los Angeles County.) A few of his fellow board members were: Lee Baca, Sheriff, L.A. County, William Bratton, Chief LAPD, Steve Cooley, District Attorney, Los Angeles County, Sharon Papa, Assistant Chief, LAPD.

Thank you Jack Egger for your key statements and assistance in the original and subsequent Black Dahlia investigation and for your decades of dedicated service in law enforcement to the citizens of both Los Angeles and Beverly Hills. May you *Rest in Peace.*

WHAT'S IN A NAME?—ANOTHER BLACK DAHLIA AVENGER TAUNT

In an earlier chapter, I described how I drove myself on what I believed was my father's probable original route from the Franklin house to the vacant lot on South Norton Avenue.

On arrival, I spent only four minutes at the vacant lot, just as the original witness had described it when he saw the black sedan pull up and stop on January 15, 1947.

I then resumed my drive home; again taking what I believed was my father's probable route. Driving north, I stopped halfway between the lot and the Franklin house and simulated placing Elizabeth Short's purse and shoes on top of a restaurant trash can in the 1100 block of South Crenshaw Boulevard—just where the witness had described seeing them. And then I went back home to Franklin and Normandie.

Some theorists and a few amateur profilers have argued there was a specific reason why the Dahlia killer selected the Liemert Park neighborhood. Maybe the killer had some connection to the neighborhood, they say.

In my sequel, *Most Evil*, I presented why I believe he selected that specific location. It was not because it "connects him to the neighborhood" but rather just the reverse—the placement of the body connects *her*, Elizabeth Short, to *his neighborhood*, his other crimes.

Another one of his diabolical "catch me if you can" clews, another of the Avenger's highly egotistical taunts that are, in the end, his signature. Pieced together they become his own undoing, and lead us directly to his identity.

Here is the explanation in brief.

The most direct route, the one I drove on January 16, 2011, and the one I believe was driven by my father, was: South on Normandie Avenue to Santa Barbara [now renamed Martin Luther King Jr. Boulevard], right turn on MLK for approximately two miles. He then turned right on a residential street and drove north a few blocks to the vacant lot where he stopped, carefully posed the body parts and was gone in just four minutes.

The name of the street he selected and turned right on? Degnan.

The very same name as that of his third Chicago Lipstick Murder victim.

Suzanne Degnan was the child who, just one year earlier, had been slain and a hemicorpectomy performed on her by a skilled surgeon/killer. Just as he had done with Elizabeth Short, he divided the little Degnan girl's body between the second and third lumbar vertebrae. The dissected body parts were then posed in a residential neighborhood with a taunting message written in lipstick, which was left near the body, promising, "There will be more."

I believe that Elizabeth Short had somehow made the connection of George Hodel, her "former suitor" and sometime boyfriend, to the Chicago Lipstick murders. She had gone to Chicago in June and July 1946 to investigate while he was away in China. The DA reports confirm it.

I suspect that Elizabeth later naively disclosed to George Hodel that she knew about or suspected his crimes. This might have caused his unexpected return to Los Angeles. She then fled in fear to San Diego. He pursued her. In time, she learned she had signed her own death warrant.

His choice of a dump site and the posing of her body on the street whose name related to a crime she was about to reveal was his own sardonic and macabre "poetry." It was his surrealistic homage—to add to his theme of murder as a fine art.

NORTON VS. DEGNAN

The simple fact is that George Hodel believed he had posed the body on Degnan. He likely didn't discover his mistake until reading the afternoon "extra" edition in the newspaper, which named the location as Thirty-Ninth and Norton.

What happened?

Norton/Degnan 2005 posting — Vacant Lot- Elizabeth Short's body

The above photo exhibit gives us the answer. The fact is, this street has two names—Degnan and Norton. The arrow points to the exact location where the street magically changes its name from Degnan and becomes Norton.

Driving west on Santa Barbara Boulevard [MLK Jr.], George Hodel turned right on Degnan, the street he had previously selected. He drove north on Degnan looking for just the right spot. He came to the division and bore left, thinking he was still on Degnan. He simply zigged when he should have zagged. It was a 50-50 coin toss and he lost.

The above photographs show how the streets are currently marked, not how they appeared in 1947. Back then, there was no raised island or "one way sign" just the simple choice. Bear right and remain on Degnan. Bear left and Degnan becomes Norton.

In later years, it had become so confusing that the city had to try and clarify it by adding the "KEEP RIGHT" sign for Degnan and putting in the one-way divider. Even today's Goggle maps, to try and help lessen the confusion, have the street split marked with an arrow.

Keep in mind that in his youth, George Hodel was a Los Angeles cab driver and with his perfect photographic memory, could take you to any street in the city. He knew them all.

I previously described this unique act of George Hodel by connecting his victims to a street name as one of his criminal signatures. It was, and this example is just one of many. The additional signatures can be found detailed and summarized in the sequel, *Most Evil: Avenger, Zodiac, and the Further Serial Murders of Dr. George Hill Hodel. [Dutton, 2009, New York.]*

Probable round-trip driving route from George Hodel's residence.

1. Dr. Hodel's Franklin house, 5121 Franklin Avenue
2. Vacant lot, 3815 South Norton (aka Degnan)
3. Elizabeth Short's purse and shoes left at 1136 South Crenshaw Boulevard [Halfway between body and Franklin house]

LA LONE WOMAN MURDERS—NEW TOUCH DNA
PROCEDURE POTENTIALLY OPENS DOOR TO SOLVING
MANY OF THE 1940S AND 1960S SERIAL KILLINGS

In addition to the Black Dahlia murder, as has been noted in *BDA* and reviewed again in earlier chapters of this book from 1943-1949, a number of other Lone Woman Murders occurred all in a tight geographical area between Hollywood and downtown Los Angeles.

LAPD's original on-scene detectives were convinced that many of these unsolved murders were committed by the same killer. Authorities released a summary to the press, listing eleven points of similarity.

In six of those crimes, the killer left a taunting message, just as he had in the Elizabeth Short murder. This act alone, is so unusual it raises the suspicion of linkage to the other murders.

The recent identification of Dr. George Hill Hodel's DNA profile, along with the newly developed "touch DNA" techniques improve the chances of solving many of these additional LAPD and LASD murders, or at least proving whether George Hodel was involved.

All that is required is the attempt.

It would require minimal investigative manpower. A two-person team could oversee the collection of potential evidence for DNA testing. Those profiles could then be entered into state and federal CODIS [Combined DNA Index System] for inclusion or exclusion to the known George Hodel sample, as well as providing an automatic comparison to all DNA samples already in the data banks. The DNA collected by investigators from the various Lone Woman Murders cold cases could then also be compared not only to potential suspects but to other existent crime scene DNA already in the data banks for linkage to other unsolved crimes.

The names of some of the 1940s cold cases that remain unsolved and were actively investigated and suspected of possibly being connected and could—*if tested*—potentially yield suspect DNA are:

(Listed chronologically by investigating agency)
LAPD
- Miss Elizabeth Short, January 15, 1947 [It is unclear if the victim's purse, known to be handled by the killer remains in evidence. Retired detective Brian Carr claimed all the physical evidence, letters, etc., had "disappeared" but did not specifically mention the victim's purse.]
- Mrs. Jeanne French, February 10, 1947
- Miss Evelyn Winters, March 11, 1947
- Miss Rosenda Mondragon, July 8, 1947

- Mrs. Gladys Kern, February 14, 1948
- Mrs. Louise Springer, June 13, 1949

LASD
- Mrs. Ora Murray, July 27, 1943
- Miss Georgette Bauerdorf, October12, 1944
- Mrs. Gertrude Evelyn Landon, July 10, 1946
- Mrs. Dorothy Montgomery, May 2, 1947
- Miss Geneva Ellroy, June 22, 1958
- Miss Bobbie Long, January 22, 1959

Long Beach PD
- Laura Trelstad, May 11, 1947

San Diego PD
- Miss Marian Newton, July 17, 1947

Based on my investigation of the publicly known facts of these 1940s Lone Woman Murders, it is my belief that the best chance of obtaining positive DNA would most likely come from LAPD's Louise Springer murder.

However, all of the above listed crimes are excellent potential sources for obtaining "touch DNA" due to the killer's extensive use of ligatures and the unusually rough ripping and tearing of the victim's clothing. Several included a man's handkerchief left at the crime-scene.

Cold cases in the 1940s and 1960s crimes summarized in my sequel *Most Evil* that could also potentially yield suspect DNA—*if tested*—include:

Chicago
- Miss Josephine Ross, June 5, 1945
- Miss Frances Brown, December 10, 1945
- Miss Suzanne Degnan, January 6, 1946

All three of the Chicago Lipstick Murders would offer a high probability of yielding "touch DNA."

In addition, Chicago PD hand-carried and booked into evidence at the FBI Laboratory a hair follicle found on Suzanne Degnan's body, which they insisted "had to belong to her killer." Additionally, Chicago PD detectives informed the press that victim Josephine Ross "was clutching in her hand some black hair follicles belonging to the killer which may help us in identifying him."

Does the hair follicle evidence in both the Ross and Degnan crimes still exist? Can DNA be obtained?

1945 CHICAGO "LIPSTICK KILLER" UPDATE

Attempted rape victim/witness confirmed the Lipstick Killer description as: "Tall, thin, with black hair used clothesline rope to bind her."

In a recent review of 1945 newspaper articles related to Chicago's "Lipstick Killer," specifically the June 5, 1945 murder of Josephine Alice Ross, I discovered an interesting and hitherto unknown witness/victim account, long buried and forgotten which should have had an important bearing on the later investigation. This is a new discovery, post-publication of *Most Evil*. Therefore, this was not discussed in that sequel.

This new information revealed that just a few hours before the brutal Lipstick Killer murder of Josephine Ross, another woman, Mrs. Eileen Huffman, age thirty-four was accosted in her apartment house basement by a man armed with a handgun.

Described as "tall and thin with black hair, "he tied the victim's hands with clothesline and attempted to rape her, but fled when she screamed out.

Shortly after this assault, just a few hours later, and only five blocks away, the first "Lipstick Killer" victim, Josephine Ross was attacked and murdered in her home. [See below diagram for victim locations.]

In the later, December 1945 murder of Frances Brown, the same killer used both a gun and a knife, stabbing her through the neck and shooting her twice.

Obviously, Chicago detectives made the connection between the Huffman and Ross crimes and, according to the article, delayed the murder inquest so that they could proceed with their search for a "tall, dark-haired man, wearing a light colored sweater; he was seen leaving the Ross apartment building," and closely fit the description provided by Mrs. Eileen Huffman.

*Chicgo Daily Tribune June 7, 194_*

DELAY INQUEST IN NORTH SIDE KNIFE SLAYING

An inquest into the knife slaying of Mrs. Josephine Alice Ross, 43, in her apartment at 4108 Kenmore av., was continued to June 27 yesterday as police pushed their search for a tall, dark haired man wearing a light colored sweater, who was seen leaving the building shortly before the body was discovered.

It was disclosed at the inquest that in one of Mrs. Ross' hands police found clutched several short black hairs, which may aid in identifying the slayer.

Mrs. Eileen Huffman, 34, of 650 Waveland av., told police that a man answering the description of the one seen leaving the Kenmore av. building had threatened her with a gun earlier in the day while she was in the basement. The intruder tied her hands with clothes line and attempted to rape her, but fled when she screamed, Mrs. Huffman said. Her home is five blocks from the scene of the slaying.

Two acquaintances of the slain woman, Chester Rice of Hammond, Ind., and Oscar Nordmark, 3905 Fremont st., who had been detained for questioning, were released last

"Tall, black-haired suspect" committed the Huffman and Ross crimes on June 5, 1945, just two hours and five blocks apart

Can DNA from the FBI Evidence Lab link George Hodel to Chicago Lipstick Murders?

Does the FBI laboratory still have the hair follicle DNA evidence on the 1946 Degnan "Lipstick Murder" investigation?

Original Jan 8, 1947 receipt from FBI on hair follicle booked in evidence

FBI Receipt No. PC-16339-AO Q21, dated 1/8/46

ADDITIONAL POTENTIAL SOURCES FOR TOUCH DNA

Riverside PD

- Miss Cheri Jo Bates, October 30, 1966 [Hair follicles also found in victim's hand which reportedly have been tested. Do they contain a full DNA profile? Are they available for comparison?]

Manila PD, Manila, Philippines
- Miss Lucila Lalu, May 30, 1967

Solano County S.O.
- Miss Betty Jensen/Mr. David Faraday, December 20, 1968

Vallejo PD
- Mrs. Darlene Ferrin/Michael Mageau, July 4, 1969

Napa County S.O.
- Cecelia Shepard/Bryan Hartnell, September 27, 1969

San Francisco PD
- Mr. Paul Stine, October 11, 1969

SIGNATURE CRIME

"Signature crime: (noun) any of two or more crimes that involve the use of a method, plan, or modus operandi so distinctive that it logically follows that the crimes must have been committed by the same person" —Merriam-Webster's Dictionary of Law

Modus operandi—or M.O.—is a very broad term and it is often mentioned in very general nonspecific terms when it comes to criminal investigations.

The squad-room roll call sergeant, when reading off crimes from the previous week, might say, "The suspect is a hot-prowl burglar and his M.O. is to enter upscale private residences during daytime hours."

That said, there are signature crimes and signature acts within those crimes that are so specific that they become extremely important in attempting to link serial crimes and serial killers.

In my *Most Evil* investigation, there are many such acts that I believe not only link the killer from crime to crime, but from city to city. As relates to the potential for "touch DNA" let's examine what I consider to be one of George Hodel's most significant *signature acts*—that being:

Bringing with him and use of pre-cut clothesline to either strangle or bind his victims.

Chicago's "Lipstick Killer," Los Angeles's "Black Dahlia Avenger," Manila's "Jigsaw Killer," and San Francisco's "Zodiac"—each brought and used precut sections of clothesline with them and used it in connection with one or more of their crimes.

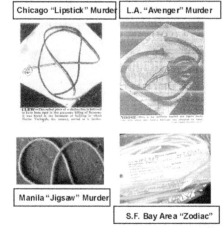

"Lipstick Killer," "Avenger," "Jigsaw," and "Zodiac" all used precut clothesline to commit their crimes.

In the 1967 bisection murder of Lucila Lalu in Manila, the killer used that country's version of clothesline rope. He bound her with "abaca," commonly known as Manila hemp. The photo seen above is a depiction and not the actual rope used in the Lalu crime. The other three photos do show the actual clothesline rope used in those murders.

Touch DNA processing could potentially result in obtaining suspect DNA skill cells on any or all of these ligatures.

DO LAPD AND RIVERSIDE PD LETTERS CONTAIN ZODIAC'S FULL DNA PROFILE?

In 2010, LAPD and DOJ teamed up to connect and solve a series of cold case murders that occurred in Los Angeles over a twenty-two-year period. [1985-2007]

The suspect, Lonnie David Franklin Jr., whom the L.A. press dubbed "The Grim Sleeper," was arrested on DNA evidence that allegedly connected him to multiple victims. As of 2011, LAPD believes he might be responsible for as many as twenty separate rape-murders over twenty years in the south-central Los Angeles area.

Based on eleven years of investigation, new evidence reported in *Most Evil,* and now in this 2012 follow-up, I would suggest that George Hodel resumed his serial killing in California twenty years after the commission of his "Black Dahlia Avenger" crimes.

Setting aside for the moment the twenty or more Northern California Zodiac letters and evidence, let's just focus on the letters he sent to the police and press in the L.A. area.

There are four letters: Two mailed in Riverside in 1967, one to the *L.A. Times* in 1971, and one to KHJ-TV in 1978.

Do these four (4) untested Southern California evidence letters contain killer's DNA? Top: Killer mailed notes to both victim's father and Riverside PD in 1967 Lower Left: 1971 Zodiac letter mailed to KHJ TV booked into LAPD as evidence Lower Right: 1978 Zodiac letter mailed to L.A. Times booked into LAPD as evidence

1971 ZODIAC LETTER TO *LOS ANGELES TIMES*

"I do have to give them credit for stumbling across my riverside activity, but they are only finding the easy one, there are a hell of a lot more down there." —ZODIAC

I believe this letter offers the highest probability of yielding actual suspect DNA. It is recognized as being a legitimate letter written by Zodiac. In it, he acknowledged and took credit for the 1966 Cheri Jo Bates murder, and informed the public that he had killed a lot more victims "down there." [Southern California]

1971 Los Angeles Times Zodiac Letter

1978 Zodiac Letter to KHJ-TV

When I first viewed this letter, I had mixed reactions as to whether this was a legitimate Zodiac letter. The handwriting in the body of the letter—though apparently disguised—seems a bit off when compared to other known writings. However, the handwriting on the envelope is much more consistent with known Zodiac samples. While focusing my attention on this letter, I have discovered what I believe to be new information that might well strengthen the case for the letter having actually been written by Zodiac. [My apologies if some of the information has been referenced elsewhere by other researchers/investigators. If it has been, I have not come across it.] Here's what I've discovered:

This letter was received by KHJ-TV in May 1978, and turned over to the LAPD. It contains death threats against five individuals: Ex-LAPD Chiefs of Police Darryl Gates and Ed Davis; singer Pat Boone; black activist Eldridge Cleaver; and Manson Family member Susan Atkins. Specifically about Atkins, "Zodiac" writes:

"And Susan Atkins—the Judas of the Manson Family. Shes gona get hers now."

THE ENVELOPE

On the outside of the envelope where the return address should be were written some backward letters and numbers. The top line reads "CIA" with the letter "C" reversed

Original 1978 envelope in LAPD custody

Below, I have reversed the original printed information, which now reads:

"1,2,3,4,5,6,7" (7 reversed)
A.G.C.G.T.H!"

HELTER SKELTER—BUGLIOSI/MANSON

Based on Zodiac's reference to the Manson Family in the text of his letter, it becomes obvious that the source of the enigmatic message on the outside of the envelope is also a direct reference to Charles Manson.

Further, it is my belief that the person who wrote this letter had also read and was familiar with author Vincent Bugliosi's, *HELTER SKELTER: The True Story of the Manson Murders*, published four years earlier. [1974]

Why?

Read this excerpt from Bugliosi's bestseller, page 294:

On May 25, I was going through LAPD's tubs on the LaBianca case when I noticed standing against the wall, a wooden door. On it was a multicolored mural, the lines from a nursery thyme, "1, 2,3,4,5,6,7—All Good Children Go to Heaven"; and, in large letters, the words "HELTER SKELTER IS COMING DOWN FAST." Stunned, I asked Gutierrez, "Where in the hell did you get that?"

"Spahn Ranch."

"When?"

He checked the yellow property envelope affixed to the door, "November 25, 1969." "You mean for five months, while I've been desperately trying to link the killers with Helter Skelter, you've had this door, with those very words on it, the same bloody words that were found at the LaBianca residence?

Guiterrez admitted they had. The door, it turned out, had been found on a cabinet in Juan Flynn's trailer. It had been considered so unimportant that to date no one had even bothered to book it into evidence.

Guiterrez did so the next day.

Photo of the Spahn Ranch door in evidence at LAPD Property
Writing on door reads, "1, 2, 3, 4, 5, 6, 7—All Good Children (go to heaven)

I believe the enigmatic reference on the 1978 envelope is classic Zodiac. He preferred to write it backwards and in code—another of his cat-and-mouse games. A new taunt from the "master criminal." Let the cops try and connect these dots.

I know for a fact that my father had read and was familiar with Bugliosi's bestseller, *Helter Skelter*, because during that time period, he expressed an interest in the investigation. On one of his regular visits with me in L.A., he told me he had read it and asked me directly, "What did you think about the book?" My response back then was, "Sorry, Dad, I haven't read it."

JOHN WALSH—ANDERSON COOPER—*MORE* ZODIAC LETTERS AND DNA?

CNN Anderson Cooper 360 "Notorious Crimes"—July 22, 2011
2011 John Walsh and Anderson Cooper discussing Black Dahlia and Zodiac cases

On July 23, 2011, CNN's *Anderson Cooper 360* aired an updated segment devoted to various "Notorious Crimes."

In September 2006, Anderson had interviewed me on the Black Dahlia murder. On air, I eliminated the one photo in my father's album as Elizabeth Short, and discussed the posing of the body and various signature connections of my father's crime to surrealism.

In the 2011 segment, Anderson updated my investigation and introduced the viewers to one of my most important new discoveries— the linking of physical evidence from my father's Sowden/Franklin house to evidence found near the body at the Thirty-Ninth and Norton vacant lot.

He presented the photographs and original receipts I had discovered at the *UCLA Special Collections Department*, linking the cement bags from the house to identical bags that LAPD determined were used to transport Elizabeth Short's body to the vacant lot. [All previously detailed in Chapter 5 of this book, "Scene of the Crime."]

In his update, he also mentioned the important fact that Dr. Hodel had fled the country before detectives were able to interview him about or arrest him for the tape-recorded admissions he made to killing Elizabeth Short and his secretary Ruth Spaulding, as well as personally admitting to "performing abortions at his VD clinic and to making payoffs to the police."

In the interview, John Walsh of *America's Most Wanted*, expressed a strong conviction that, "in my heart and in my gut from doing this for so many years, I believe it was the doctor [George Hodel]."

Here is the excerpted exchange between Walsh and Cooper regarding the Black Dahlia Murder:

AC: The Black Dahlia case. This is a case that has been fascinating Hollywood and the country for decades.

JW: Bestselling book, movie all that spin. But I do believe who killed the Black Dahlia, the main suspect they had. The doctor who is now deceased. I believe he got away with that case. They never charged him. He was a stalker. He was the main suspect. [Dr. George Hill Hodel] They never had enough to indict him. She was dismembered by someone who had great knowledge of anatomy and skills in surgery. He was the logical suspect, but back in those days, they didn't have the tools that we have now.

AC: They obviously sensationalized the case not because she was beautiful, but because of the gruesome way that she was killed.

JW: The way that he displayed her. He displayed her as a trophy, like lots of serial killers and horrible narcissistic murderers do. He displayed her in the field for the whole world to see his work.

In my heart and in my gut from doing this so many years I believe it was that doctor. [Emphasis mine]

After discussing the *Black Dahlia* case, the program then reviewed the ZODIAC murder. Here is an excerpt from that discussion where John Walsh described personally receiving multiple letters and death threats from a man identifying himself as "Scorpion," but who had identical handwriting and codes and ciphers to "Zodiac."

...

AC: The Zodiac killer's probably the most famous cold case in the US. Why do you think there is so much fascination with it?

JW: Because he terrorized and held San Francisco captive for so long. They locked down that city when he said, "If you keep looking for me, I have a sniper's rifle, I will kill the kids getting off of the buses." He claimed to have killed multiple victims. They believe he killed seven people. It actually paralyzed a city. A United States city. One low-life coward paralyzed that city. People were fascinated. He always sent this cryptic code around, and everybody analyzed it. *When I first profiled the Zodiac killer, I got a letter sent exactly like his code. Sent to me in exactly the same kind of envelope that he sent others. I had to give it to the FBI. It was signed in blood. In human blood. He said, "I will kill you. You will be the ultimate victory. I got away with it. I've committed mayhem since I murdered those other people. You will be my ultimate prize. I still have the ability to kill people. It's fascinating. We don't know if it was the Zodiac killer? Nobody knows. It fascinates people when somebody gets away with murder and they brag about it.*

AC: The Zodiac killer had seven confirmed victims. Five of them died. But he's suspected possibly to have dozens more.

Several years prior to this interview, John Walsh had published the actual letters on his *America's Most Wanted* website, informing the public that the letters and ciphers containing the death threats were sent to him in 1990. The killer signed his letters "Scorpion." [That is the same year that George Hodel relocated from Asia back to San Francisco.]

Both the hand-printing and ciphers are similar to those of the original Zodiac, and in his Anderson Cooper interview John Walsh informed us "that the envelopes were the same kind he [Zodiac] sent others."

"Scorpion Letters" mailed to John Walsh in 1990

Clearly, based on Walsh's information, these letters should be examined and processed for potential DNA.

John Walsh has been a dedicated fighter for victims' rights for twenty-three years and his success as the host of *America's Most Wanted* has resulted in more than 1,200 "solves." He has been a major force in helping law enforcement take so many vicious criminals "off the streets." His crime-fighting efforts have also resulted in an incalculable number of crimes being prevented.

He has my highest respect and personal congratulations for an outstanding job in standing up for victim's rights and his long years of assistance to law enforcement.

ZODIAC—SAN FRANCISCO PAUL STINE MURDER—SHIRT AND GLOVES

In my opinion, the best potential for hard physical evidence in the unsolved Zodiac murders can be found in the physical evidence booked in connection with the Paul Stine cabbie shooting in San Francisco.

The killer's bloodstained gloves and the section of shirt torn from the victim's body and mailed to SFPD both remain untested. Both items are highly likely to yield a full Zodiac profile, if tested.

The gloves (men's size 7) apparently contain the victim's blood splatters. They were inadvertently left behind, or maybe fell out of Zodiac's pocket before the shooting. The 1969 police and DOJ reports confirm that law enforcement believes that they were owned and worn by Zodiac.

In addition, there remain some fifteen to twenty notes mailed by Zodiac that could be retested using today's much more sophisticated techniques.

I find it incredible that no confirmed Zodiac DNA has yet been obtained. There is no Zodiac DNA entered into any state or national CODIS data banks.

The last report I am aware of from law enforcement sources dates back to 2002 and that sample reportedly is highly suspect and contains only a partial DNA profile which is insufficient to include or exclude anyone. That sample only contains three (3) out of the thirteen (13) loci found in a full DNA profile.

CALIFORNIA DOJ MEET AND THE ZODIAC DNA EVIDENCE

In November 2009, two months after the publication of my book, *Most Evil*, I met with two agents from the California Department of Justice.

The agents, I'll call them, X and Y, flew down from the DOJ San Francisco Regional Office to Los Angeles for a morning meet. I presented them with a PowerPoint summary of my overall investigation.

I focused on the Zodiac connections and what I believed were the best potential sources for obtaining Zodiac DNA with special emphasis on the size 7 gloves left by Zodiac inside the murder victim's taxi.

Both Agent Y [a retired SFPD detective] and Agent X, his supervisor, seemed impressed with my findings. Agent X said she would be back in contact with me after they had a chance to review the various written materials I had provided.

Six months later, in May 2010, I contacted Agent Y by e-mail and inquired if he had been able to test the gloves? He responded that the SFPD homicide commander "had given him permission to have them tested, and he was in the process of attempting to locate the evidence."

I re-contacted Agent Y in August 2010, and he indicated that he was hoping to meet with the SFPD detective and "track down the gloves and get the process going."

My last communication with Agent Y occurred in November 2010. In that exchange, he said he was "still trying to make contact with his contact at SFPD and continue the search for the gloves," assuring me that "at some point, this will all come together." [As a side note, Agent Y advised me that their DOJ handwriting expert "had examined and compared George Hodel's handwriting to known Zodiac documents and was unable to include or exclude him as the author of the Zodiac letters." Their Questioned Document Expert requested through Agent Y that I provide them with some additional samples of George Hodel's "lower-case handwriting." Unfortunately, I have no additional samples in my possession as my father rarely wrote in lower-case. I am currently attempting to locate additional writing samples. Despite the "inconclusive" finding, the fact that the DOJ expert could not eliminate George Hodel as the writer of the Zodiac notes and letters is, by itself, significant.]

It has now been two years since my original meeting with the two DOJ agents. It is unknown if the gloves have been found or tested, or still remain missing. In criminal investigations, "No news is bad news." We can only hope that in Agent Y's optimistic words, "this will all come together."

SFPD evidence photo showing Stine shirt and men's black leather gloves ("Size 7") at the bottom of the frame in clear plastic evidence bag. (red arrow points to gloves)

George and June Hodel Rosario Retreat, Orcas Island, Washington 1995.

Have the SFPD Stine Gloves been located and tested for DNA or is the evidence still missing?
Left: SFPD Paul Stine Evidence—Suspect's bloodstained gloves and victim's shirt
Right: George Hodel, putting on his size-7 gloves on a visit to me on Orcas Island in Washington State in 1995.

BOTTOM LINE:

I believe that the potential for obtaining the suspect's DNA on many of the 1940s unsolved Los Angeles Lone Woman Murders exists.

I believe that analysis of those samples will prove linkage, like they did in the Grim Sleeper Murders.

Once DNA is obtained, cold case detectives can enter the samples into state and federal CODIS data-banks and very possibly identify a suspect and clear many of the cases.

At the very least, detectives should make the attempt to obtain DNA from the Los Angeles area Zodiac letters booked in evidence at LAPD and Riverside to see if they *can be linked to a killer already entered in CODIS.*

With the recent advancement of "Touch DNA," I am extremely confident that the forty-year-old unsolved Zodiac serial murders can be solved.

All that it requires is just one dedicated cold-case investigator in any of the many jurisdictions to take the initiative and make a first step forward! That detective might now be assigned to any of the following: Riverside PD, LASD Homicide, LAPD Homicide CCU, Long Beach PD, San Francisco PD, Napa or Solano Sheriff, or Vallejo PD.

The solution is there, just a simple phone call away. As an old-time homicide detective who has been there and done that, I strongly urge that detective to pick up the telephone and make the call to his or her crime lab.

I'll close with a quote from SFPD Inspector Mike Maloney, who was one of the last detectives actively assigned to work Zodiac. He died in 2005, believing that DNA would one day solve the case.

In an open letter to the public, written shortly before his death, he said:

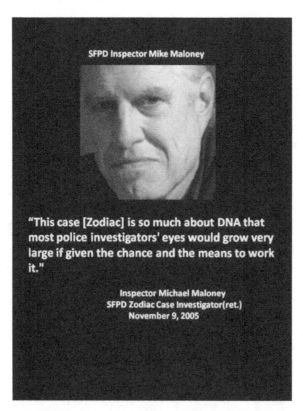

I believe Mike's assessment was absolutely correct!

REST IN PEACE MIKE!

23

LAPD Historical Society:
The New Evidence

INVESTIGATIVE UPDATES 2014

THE FIRST EDITION OF *BLACK DAHLIA AVENGER II* published on March 22, 2012. It is now January 2014.

Important new investigative findings have been developed that relate directly to the Elizabeth Short/Black Dahlia murder.

In the following chapters, I present that new evidence as it chronologically unfolded over the past twenty months.

THE LOS ANGELES POLICE MUSEUM—THE BLACK DAHLIA EXHIBIT—MAY 2012

"Steve's first book, The *Black Dahlia Avenger*, became a bestselling title. His conclusion that Elizabeth Short was murdered by his own father was supported by a significant amount of compelling evidence, and although the murder is technically unsolved it is hard to argue with Steve's solution." —Sgt. Glynn Martin (ret. LAPD), Executive Director, Los Angeles Police Historical Society, *The Hot Sheet – Newsletter No. 36 Nov/Dec 2009*

LAPD Historical Museum, 6045 York Blvd, Los Angeles CA 90042

The Los Angeles Police Historical Society Museum is in northeast Los Angeles. The historic building, affectionately known as "Old Number 11," was originally a fully functioning LAPD police station known as "Highland Park Division." (In L.A., the term *"division"* substitutes for what many readers east of the Rockies think of as a "precinct" and each has its own numerical designation. (For most of my career, I worked out of Number 6, the Hollywood Division. Since my retirement in 1986, LAPD has added three new divisions and now polices the City of Los Angeles with twenty-one separate geographic divisions.)

The non-profit LAPHS museum is open to the public. Its volunteer staff informs and preserves LAPD's history as well as being a community booster for the department's image. Over the years, it has become an increasingly popular tourist attraction, and holds an annual public fundraiser that supports special exhibitions.

In February 2012, the article "James Ellroy Presents: Elizabeth, LAPD's 65-year crusade to capture Beth Short's Killer" by LAPDHS Executive Director Glynn Martin appeared in the museum newsletter. Here are some excerpts:

> ...Long known as the "Black Dahlia" case, the museum has received materials from the investigative file to help educate the public about the investigation and further explain the incredible efforts the LAPD exerted to solve the brutal murder.

> To help us with this, long-time and loyal supporter, James Ellroy, has provided his sponsorship and will interpret the exhibit.

The article announced the exhibit—which purported to contain "original never before seen Black Dahlia documents and photographs"—would be open to the public on March 19, 2012. A special pre-exhibit tour would be led by author James Ellroy, who'd be selling signed copies of his 1987 novel, *The Black Dahlia,* for $100.

I passed on the Ellroy "guided tour" but on a quiet afternoon in May, camera in hand, I visited the exhibit. I made my way upstairs and found that the "never before seen items" were encased inside a half-dozen glass cabinets. Each cabinet contained separate photographs, investigative and booking reports, detective logs, police bulletins, etc.

It was not until I arrived home that evening and took a closer look at some of the photographs that I realized just how valuable they were, not only as additional handwriting evidence that could further identify George Hodel as the killer, but also potential DNA links between my father and the Black Dahlia murder.

After several weeks assessing the "new evidence," I wrote a letter to LAPD. Two copies were sent. The first went to Chief of Police Charlie Beck and the second to the new Commander of LAPD's Robbery/Homicide Division, Captain William Hayes.

Below is an exact copy of the six-page letter I sent to Chief Beck and Captain Hayes.

June 14, 2012

LAPD Chief of Police, Charlie Beck
LAPD Robbery/Homicide, Captain William Hayes
Los Angeles Police Department
100 W. First St. Room 1077 & 5th Floor

Dear Chief Beck and Captain Hayes:

Greetings from Los Angeles.

First, let me commend you both for your outstanding job in making our city's streets safer. The downward trend in violent crime is impressive and can certainly be directly attributed to your and the department's hard work both behind the desks and in the streets. Congratulations!

My name is Steve Hodel, and I am an honorably retired Detective III. My years of service were from 1963 to 1986. Most of my career was at Hollywood Detectives where after working all the separate tables, I settled in to work homicide (fourteen years) and personally handled over 300 separate murder investigations.

By 1982, I was the senior field homicide Detective II, working under my close friend, and longtime partner, Detective III Russell Kuster. (As you know, Russ was shot and killed in October, 1990 after being engaged in a gun-battle with parolee, Bela Marko. Marko attacked Russ while he was dining at a Hungarian restaurant in Hollywood and in the exchange of gunfire, both men were killed.)

I was promoted to Detective III in 1983 and retired three years later in '86.

LAPD Black Dahlia Murder Investigation—Background

You both are likely aware of at least some of the circumstances that unfolded and were presented to me, beginning in 1999, some thirteen-years into retirement.

I am not going to attempt to summarize all that unfolded, but will simply provide a few bullet points so that I can get to the actual reason why I am writing you.

- In 1999 at the death of my father, Dr. George Hill Hodel, certain information came into my possession that pointed to the possibility that he both knew and could have been a possible suspect in the 1947 murder of Elizabeth "Black Dahlia" Short. (At the time of the murder, he was the Head V.D. Control Officer for the entire County of Los Angeles.)

- For the next three years, (1999-2002) I followed the evidence, interviewed dozens of witnesses, collected and prepared photographic evidence and exhibits and submitted my findings in secret to one of L.A.'s most respected and a then-active Head Deputy DA, Stephen Kay. DA Kay reviewed all my materials and based on my investigation he then provided a ten-page summary which included his legal opinion, "The Black Dahlia murder was solved and Dr. George Hill Hodel was responsible for the murder of Elizabeth Short, as well as a second 1947 crime which occurred three weeks after the Dahlia Murder." (Victim Jeanne French, known as "The Red Lipstick Murder.") Kay in his written opinion stated, "If George Hodel was still alive and the witnesses available I would formally file two counts of murder and am confident I could win the case in trial."

- At my request, in 2002 Head DDA Kay contacted LAPD brass and requested a meeting with them and senior detectives from Robbery/Homicide Division so that we could brief them on the evidence and have them review my investigation. (At the time, I was confident that DNA would be found, and the case would be a "slam-dunk.")

- Between July 2002 and March 2003, LAPD scheduled and then cancelled three separate meetings with Head DA Steve Kay and myself. Despite my urging Kay to make it happen before publication of my book, his/our efforts were to no avail.

- My book, *Black Dahlia Avenger: A Genius for Murder* published in April, 2003. My investigation generated a lot of public interest, and within a month the book had become a *New York Times* bestseller. This was followed by full-hour shows on *CBS 48-Hours, NBC Dateline*, and others.

- In May, 2003 based on the publicity and press inquiries, then Chief Bratton and the powers that be agreed to meet with Head Deputy DA Steve Kay and myself. This meeting was held at Parker Center and attended by then Deputy Chief James McMurray (Chief of Detectives) and half a dozen high-ranking staff officers as well as three detectives from Robbery/Homicide Division. DA Kay and I together presented an overview briefing to all present.

- Included in the briefing was new information recently obtained from the vault of the DA's Office –the *Hodel-Black Dahlia Files*, which contained never before seen transcripts of wire-recordings revealing that Dr. George Hill Hodel was the DA's "prime suspect" in 1950 and that 18 detectives had been assigned 24/7 for five weeks on a physical and electronic stake-out after installing live microphones in the walls of my father's Hollywood residence. These transcripts contained his admissions to multiple crimes including the Black Dahlia Murder and the murder of his secretary (separately investigated by LAPD in 1945, some 18 months prior to the Dahlia murder) as well as payoffs to law enforcement and performing illegal abortions. (These DA files, the existence of which was unknown to me and today's LAPD, established his guilt independently of and apart from my own investigative findings.) In the 5th week of the DA stake-out, while detectives were still conducting the live electronic surveillance, Dr. George Hodel fled the country to avoid his pending arrest.

- Shortly after the briefing in response to questions from the press, a Robbery Homicide Detective (now retired) assigned as a self-professed "gatekeeper" to the Dahlia investigation gave a public statement indicating in checking the files he determined, "all the physical evidence connected to the Black Dahlia investigation has disappeared and because of that they are unable to proceed with any DNA testing on George Hodel."

In direct response to questions from the press regarding my investigation he went on to say, "Due to a heavy caseload on current crimes I am unable to move forward to prove or disprove Hodel's investigation."

In 2005, Chief Bratton closed the Dahlia investigation with this public statement at a book signing at *Book Soup* on Sunset Blvd:

"I just told our Cold Case Squad guys to give it [the Dahlia investigation] up. I'm more concerned about the nine murders we had last week than one going back that many years.... I know that is problematic for some people who would like to see it solved. But, what would you have to write about if it was solved? Better it go unsolved. There are more and more books being written about it all the time." [Absolute silence from the audience.]

In the seven years that have passed, I am informed that LAPD's Robbery/Homicide Cold Case Unit has adopted a new motto:

"No Case is too old or too cold."

I strongly agree!

It would appear Chief Beck that from your September 2010 public statement, you too are in agreement that "Justice, even when delayed, is still justice." I quote your words from a 2010 news article:

"MUMIFIED BABIES DNA TESTS PENDING"

"Los Angeles police Chief Charlie Beck said it was important to continue investing resources into the case, even though it was three-quarters of a century old because it could turn out the babies were homicide victims. **Justice, even when delayed, is still justice, Beck said**." —*UK Daily Mail*, September 3, 2010

Now that you have a background, let me cut to the chase and present you with the reason I am writing to you and to Captain Hayes, Commander of Robbery/Homicide Division.

I would like to schedule a meeting with whomever Captain Hayes deems appropriate from his unit.

The meeting would be for the purpose of allowing me to present a PowerPoint providing a complete overview of my updated investigation as well as a presentation of new evidence compiled from 2006-2012. (In January, 2012, on the occasion of the 63rd anniversary of the Black Dahlia Murder, I was asked and did present a modified version at the LAPD Historical museum, which was attended by Assistant Chief Michael Moore and others, but did not contain much of the newly acquired evidence.)

To list just a few of the newly discovered findings:

1.   Making available to LAPD a newly obtained (2009) and complete DNA profile on the prime suspect, Dr. George Hill Hodel. (Obtained by BODE Laboratory, one of the FBI and Law Enforcement's most respected DNA labs. No George Hodel DNA existed prior to their testing in 2009.)

2.   The connection of hard physical evidence known and identified by LAPD to have been left by the killer at the

original 1947 Black Dahlia crime-scene *to physical evidence known and documented to have been at Dr. George Hodel's residence, just four days prior to the discovery of the victim's body on the vacant lot.*

3. Most importantly, *the potential to match LAPD DNA evidence known to exist and which is currently on display at the LAPHS Museum's "Black Dahlia Exhibit" to the existing DNA profile of the original 1950 LAPD/DA suspect—Dr. George Hill Hodel.* (This brand new 2012 evidence which holds the potential to conclusively solve the case with DNA comes directly from your personal decision to green-light and allow previously unexhibited Dahlia evidence to be placed on public display.)

I anticipate my new meeting and briefing including Q&A would last about two hours.

Now, with the potential for actual DNA testing and comparison, coupled with the new evidence connecting the crime scene to Dr. Hodel's residence, it is my professional opinion that Robbery Homicide Division detectives can and will solve this crime.

Former LAPD Chief William Bratton's 2005 position and order to his Cold Case detectives was "to give it up and close the case."

I would respectfully argue that that is not, nor has it ever been the position and thinking of our LAPD. As a rookie-homicide detective in 1969 my veteran partner instructed me that, "You are standing in the shoes of the victims. Never give up. Solve the case."

Chief Beck, I believe you too believe those words. This is not about egos and territoriality. It is about a former LAPD detective wanting to work together with current detectives for the good of the victims, their families, our department and our city.

I will include a retirement letter I received from Chief Gates as part of my *bona fides.* Feel free to check my LAPD personnel file documenting my nearly 24-years of service, should you desire further references.

I am currently residing in Los Angeles and will make myself available to meet with whomever you or Captain Hayes deem appropriate.

Most Respectfully and Fraternally Yours,

Steve Hodel 11394 (ret.)
steve@stevehodel.com

Cc: Captain III William Hayes, LAPD Robbery Homicide Division
Attachment #1- Retirement Letter of Commendation from Chief
Daryl Gates, 9/4/86

LOS ANGELES POLICE DEPARTMENT

DARYL F. GATES
Chief of Police

P. O. Box 30158
Los Angeles, Calif. 90030
Telephone:
(213)· 485-3202
Ref #: 1.1

TOM BRADLEY
Mayor

September 4, 1986

Detective Steven K. Hodel
5336 Highland View Place
Los Angeles, California 90041

Dear Steve:

Although I was unable to attend your retirement dinner, I
would like to take this opportunity to offer you my most
heartfelt congratulations and sincere best wishes on the
occasion of your retirement from the Los Angeles Police
Department.

Over twenty-three years with the Department is no small
investment, Steve, however, twenty-three years of superb,
loyal and diligent service is priceless. Please know that you
have my personal thanks for all that you have done over the
years and for the many important investigations you directed.
As I am reminded daily, the fine reputation that this
Department enjoys throughout the world is based totally on the
cumulative accomplishments of individuals like you.

As you now enter the ranks of those honorably retired from the
LAPD, please accept my deep appreciation and sincere gratitude
for a job and career well done. Best of luck in any future
endeavor and let me know if I can ever be of assistance.

Very truly yours,

DARYL F. GATES
Chief of Police

AN EQUAL EMPLOYMENT OPPORTUNITY—AFFIRMATIVE ACTION EMPLOYER

BLACK DAHLIA AVENGER II|378

Two weeks later, I decided it was also appropriate for me to inform the LAPD Historical Museum's chairman and executive director of my discovery and request for a meeting with LAPD and sent them the below letter, with an enclosed copy of my original letter to Chief Gates and Captain Hayes. [SKH Note: In the letter, I mistakenly referred to my "65th Anniversary Black Dahlia Talk" at their facility. It was actually was the 63rd that I presented in 2010.]

---

29 June 2012

Mr. Robert B. Taylor, Chairman
Mr. Glynn Martin, Executive Director
Los Angeles Police Museum, 6045 York Blvd
Los Angeles CA 90042

Dear Robert and Glynn:

You will recall that in January of this year, I presented my "Black Dahlia" PowerPoint talk at your facility on the occasion of the 65th anniversary of her murder.

In May, I visited the museum and toured your "Black Dahlia" exhibit.

As you are aware, many of the items from the original investigative files had never been previously publicly displayed.

In examining the various items, I came across several pieces of evidence on display that I believe *could very possibly result in actual DNA linkage to the actual suspect.*

As a result, I have written to both Chief Charlie Beck and to Captain William Hayes at Robbery Homicide Division and expressed my desire to meet and present an overview of my updated investigation as well as the what and why of the items at your exhibit that potentially hold the key to the solution of the Black Dahlia case through DNA. (As of this writing I have not heard back from either Chief Beck or Captain Hayes)

Since your efforts and exhibit are the direct cause of this discovery, I am enclosing a copy of my letter to LAPD for your information.

Most Sincerely,
Steve Hodel 11393, Detective III (ret.)
Author of *Black Dahlia Avenger and Black Dahlia Avenger II*
Attachment: Letter to Chief Beck and Captain Hayes

Six weeks after my request to meet with LAPD Robbery/Homicide detectives, I received this response from Chief Beck and Captain Hayes:

LOS ANGELES POLICE DEPARTMENT

CHARLIE BECK
Chief of Police

ANTONIO R. VILLARAIGOSA
Mayor

P. O. Box 30158
Los Angeles, Calif. 90030
Telephone: (213) 486-6850
TDD: (877) 275-5273
Ref #: 8.6

July 30, 2012

Mr. Steve Hodel

Re: Black Dahlia Investigation

Dear Mr. Hodel:

I have received your correspondence regarding your theories concerning the Black Dahlia murder investigation and the suspect responsible for the crime. I am also aware of your request to be allowed to present those theories in a meeting with myself and other Detective Bureau Staff Officers. Unfortunately, I must respectfully decline that request. Given the fiscal constraints facing the City, and the impact on investigations assigned to my command, I do not believe it prudent that we pursue the Back Dahlia investigation at this time. I realize this is not the response you would have liked to receive, but given my responsibilities to the citizens of this City, I believe that Robbery-Homicide Division Detectives should expend their valuable skills on more contemporary investigations.

I appreciate your interest in the Black Dahlia murder investigation and wish you the best in your quest to solve this notable crime.

Should you have any further questions, please contact Captain Hayes, Commanding Officer, Robbery-Homicide Division, at (213) 486-6850.

Very truly yours,

CHARLIE BECK
Chief of Police

WILLIAM HAYES, Captain
Commanding Officer
Robbery-Homicide Division

"Unfortunately, I must respectfully decline that request. Given the fiscal constraints facing the City, and the impact on investigations assigned to my command, I do not believe it prudent that we pursue the Back [sic] Dahlia investigation at this time." ...*wish you the best in your quest to solve this notable crime.*" (Emphasis mine—sarcasm his.)

Sound familiar?

For over a decade now—since Head Deputy DA Steve Kay and I in 2003 made our original ninety-minute briefing with "the brass," which was followed with Chief of Detectives James McMurray's order to his Robbery/Homicide detectives to "Clear the Black Dahlia Murder"—*nothing has been done.*

As expressed in my letter, I hoped that a change of LAPD administration (Chief Bratton to Chief Beck) might make a difference. I was wrong.

I was wrong, and Michael Connelly's Detective III Harry Bosch was right. When Bosch in the 2002 novel, *City of Bones* addressed his somewhat naïve partner, it was as if he were speaking directly to me:

Bosch almost laughed.

The department [LAPD] doesn't care about it. The department cares about the image, not the truth. And when the truth endangers the image, then fuck the truth.

LAPDHS EXHIBIT- THE NEW EVIDENCE

According to Chief Beck, "Given fiscal restraints," LAPD is unable to spare a detective to allot an hour's time to hear and be shown the new evidence.

Is the Chief right?

It is undeniable that we are living in fiscally tough times. If an LAPD Detective II in Robbery/Homicide Division is earning around $45 an hour and my presentation could run as much as ninety minutes, that could easily cost the Department $67.50.

Let's say the detective is convinced by my evidence and sends the evidence to be tested for DNA. That would require him or her to pick-up the phone and call SID (Scientific Investigation Division) to request the property be analyzed. That additional call for investigation could easily tack on an additional fifteen minutes. That raises the bill another $11.25.

We now have a total cost to the city of $78.75.

"*Given the fiscal restraints on the city...*" (Emphasis mine, sarcasm mine.)

It's best I come directly to you, my readers, with the "new evidence." To be clear, you will be the first to see and learn the specifics of how and why I believe the 2012 LAPD Museum exhibit's evidence could forensically link my father, Dr. George Hill Hodel, to the Dahlia murder by way of DNA.

THE LETTERS

The exhibit displayed two letters that today's LAPD must have presumed were "crank letters," just a couple of samples of mailings from someone caught up in the Dahlia hysteria some sixty-plus years before.

I seriously question that. I believe at least one of the missives—possibly both—were mailed by the actual killer, Dr. George Hill Hodel.

Let's examine the evidence.

LAPD Police Museum Black Dahlia Exhibit May 2012

LETTER NO. 1

Exhibit 2.1

Exhibit 2.2

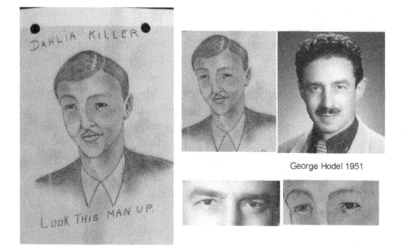

George Hodel 1951

Letter No. 1 identifies the "Dahlia Killer" with a drawing that strongly resembles Dr. George Hodel, circa 1947. The hand-printed note also appears to resemble my father's handwriting. The extended letter "D" and the dotting of the capital "I" are both consistent with George Hodel's known handwriting.

Plus, in January 1947, the legitimate "Black Dahlia Avenger" sent an altered photograph of a young male in one of his many mailings. Signing the note as "A Friend," the sender claimed the photo was a picture of "the Werewolf killer." [That photo was later identified as Armand Robles, age 17, who later came forward to inform the police that just before the Dahlia murder he had been assaulted by a man fitting George Hodel's description.]

1947 anonymous mailing of "Werewolf Killer"

Unfortunately, the photograph I took of this exhibit is slightly out-of-focus, (due to shooting it through the glass cabinet) and we cannot now read the postmark. It is unknown by me if it was sent with the original batch of 1947 "Avenger Letters" or if it was mailed later.

Either way, we see this letter was addressed to the original and primary Dahlia investigator, Finis Brown, and contains three stamps. (Placing excess postage on his mailings was a common M.O. of the Black Dahlia Avenger.)

Based on all of these factors, I believe this letter and postage should be analyzed for the presence of DNA. If a viable sample is obtained, it should be compared to the existing DNA profile belonging to my father, George Hodel.

LETTER NO. 2

Letter No. 2 [LAPDHS Exhibit 3] was mailed to sheriff's office at the downtown Hall of Justice. It reads:

Sheriff

The party that killed Elizabed Short is Manuel L. Merino.
512 South Philadelfia St.
Whitier

M.S.

It is written in the customary block printing with what I believe are deliberately misspelled words (Elizabed, Philadelfia, Whitier) that, as we know, are consistent with previous known and identified Avenger mailings.

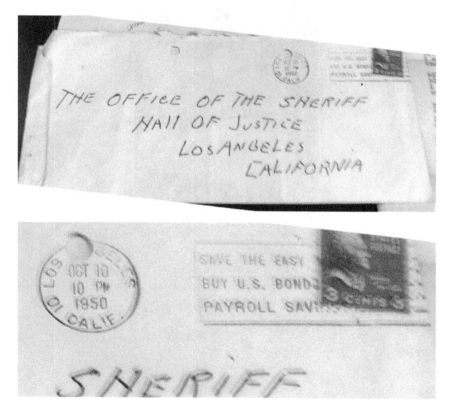

However, what really caught my attention was that this letter was postmarked in 1950, some three-plus years after the murder. Why would anyone, be they a "crank" or the legitimate killer, send in information on the Black Dahlia murder long after it had fallen from the front pages and was no longer in the public eye?

Then I looked at the date of the postmark—*October 10, 1950*—and instantly made the connection. We know the Black Dahlia Avenger had a penchant for "anniversaries" and frequently used them in connection with his taunts. Significant dates were a real part of his M.O.

Recall the 1944 Bauerdorf Letter where the Avenger's typed note to LAPD promised he would appear in person at the Hollywood Canteen (the victim's former employer) on or near October 11, and specifically called it out as "the one-year anniversary of her murder." He signed off on that note by typing, "Let the Los Angeles Police arrest the murderer if they can."

Bauerdorf Anniversary Note from her killer claiming the murder was "Divine Retribution."

Letter No. 2's postmark of October 10 is not just any anniversary. Rather, it is a specific taunt. Another "Let the LAPD catch me if they can."

October 10th is the birthday of my father, Dr. George Hill Hodel.

George Hill Hodel Birth Certificate showing birth in Los Angeles on 10.10.07

Based on our updated investigation, we know that while October,1950 had no real significance to the Black Dahlia investigation in general, it was especially time-specific to the then-prime suspect, Dr. George Hodel.

How?

Just five months earlier, as George was about to be arrested by LADA Lieutenant Frank Jemison, we know he fled Los Angeles, possibly to Mexico or to the Territory of Hawaii.

From the newly discovered Huston Letters, we also know my father was back at the Sowden/Franklin House with my mother for a brief period in August/September 1950. The reason? Maybe to collect his personal possessions and finalize the sale of the Franklin house before relocating to Hawaii and then Manila.

I believe my father mailed this birthday taunt to law enforcement as a slap in the face. Some three years later, he wanted to remind them he was still in control.

Let's examine the handwriting. Overall, it fits his usual printing style. However, there is one highly distinctive characteristic known to be used by my father that, for me, jumped off the envelope. It was the letter "c."

On occasion, George Hodel would write a lower-case "c" like a lowercase "e." Highly distinctive!

unique letter "c" written as the letter "e"

THE OFFICE OF THE SH

LAPD 10.10.50 note
(1950)

George Hodel HW
(1948)

Lipstick Killer HW
(1945)

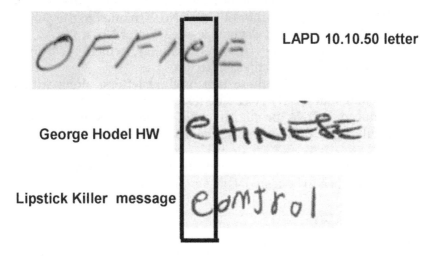

LAPD 10.10.50 letter

George Hodel HW

Lipstick Killer message

There are only three numerals on the October 10 letter—5, 1, and 2—written together as the address "512 South Philadelfia St."

Compare those to the same numbers found on a known envelope hand-printed by George Hodel in 1971. Although written twenty years apart, they look similar, especially the numeral 2.

George Hodel HW (1971)

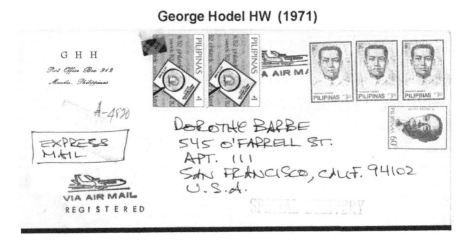

LAPD EXHIBIT HW 1950

Based on this combination of factors, it's a strong possibility that George Hill Hodel is the author of Letter No. 2, mailed to the police on his birthday and, to a lesser degree, possibly Letter No. 1, too.

Unlike the other 1947 Avenger mailings, which according to LAPD, have "disappeared," these have not.

LAPD still possesses these two original letters, along with the envelopes and stamps. They can be tested for possible DNA. If those tests produced a DNA profile, it could easily be compared to the existing full DNA profile on George Hodel to identify him as the suspect.

All that is required is for a detective to pick up the phone and order the evidence to be tested. One simple phone call.

24
Odor Mortis: The Smell of Death

JANUARY 15, 2013, WAS THE SIXTY-SIXTH ANNIVERSARY of one of Los Angeles' most notorious crimes—the sadistic torture-murder of the twenty-two-year-old Elizabeth Short, known to the world as "The Black Dahlia."

On that date I presented to the public some startling new forensic evidence that strongly suggested the historic Sowden/Franklin House, owned and lived in by Dr. George Hill Hodel from 1945-1950, was a murder scene.

In October 2012, I was contacted by a producer for *Pilgrim Productions* who was scheduling interviews for an upcoming segment of the SyFy Channel's *Ghost Hunters*, a popular paranormal/reality series that explores alleged "haunted houses."

My father's historic Sowden House was to be featured in a future episode and she was calling to inquire if I could provide some historical and personal background on the residence.

Those of you that have read my works know that I am highly skeptical about "things that go bump in the night" and have deliberately kept my criminal investigations removed from psychics, astrologers, fakirs, and all things supernatural.

Still, I recognized an interview would give me the chance to present my newly discovered evidence that suggested my father's former home was, in fact, the original Black Dahlia murder scene.

Much of the public remains unaware that items documented to be inside the house just three days before the murder have now been circumstantially linked to physical evidence recovered by detectives at the vacant lot where Elizabeth Short's bisected body was posed, some six miles south of Hollywood.

I told the producer that I was reluctant to participate. My interest was in gathering and presenting objective facts supported by science. I told her that as a child growing up in the home, neither I nor any other relative had ever experienced any "ghosts" or otherworldly activity. I simply did not believe in such things.

She countered by saying their team also remains objective and skeptical in their investigations of the paranormal, and that they were contemplating bringing in a retired police sergeant and his cadaver dog as part of the investigation.

That did it. I was sold! I immediately recognized the tremendous opportunity she presented. With the current homeowner's full permission, we would get a chance—for the first time ever—to conduct an independent forensic investigation inside what I believe to be the actual murder site.

On November 7, 2012, I met the film crew at my former home and gave an interview that included my childhood memories of living there from 1945 to 1950 (from age four to nine).

I also detailed how and where I think the torture-murder of Elizabeth "Black Dahlia" Short occurred inside the residence during the late night hours of January 14, 1947. (The 1950 secret *DA Hodel/Black Dahlia Files* established that George Hodel was alone in residence as our mother and we three sons were temporarily staying with her brother, our uncle, some three miles away.)

Based on my now thirteen-year investigation, I informed them that it was my belief that Elizabeth Short was initially drugged, posed and photographed nude in the living-room.

She was then forced to endure several hours of extended torture, possibly conducted either in the center courtyard or basement area. Her wounds included cigarette burns to her back (8), cuttings to her body face and private parts, and being force-fed fecal material (probably from the *Bandini Fertilite Manure* bag) used in conjunction with empty cement bags to transport the body parts to the vacant lot. After being sexually assaulted (anal rape) and beaten about the head with a blunt instrument, her body was most probably taken to the large tub in the master bathroom where it was surgically bisected (a surgical procedure known as a hemicorpectomy was performed) drained of blood, washed clean, towel dried and placed on top of several large, empty cement and manure paper sacks. The two sections were likely carried from the master bath through the center courtyard to the rear door, which opens into the attached garage and placed inside my father's black sedan. The body parts were covered with additional large, empty cement paper sacks then driven some six miles south to the vacant lot, where they and the paper sacks were used to transfer the body parts from the car to the lot where they were then left near the posed body.

I also related the facts as detailed in the LADA's original 1950 secret *Hodel/Black Dahlia Files*, which included the five-week (February-March 1950) police electronic surveillance and "bugging" of the Hodel house that recorded my father's admissions to police payoffs, performing abortions, and to the murder of Elizabeth Short as well as to the forced overdose of his personal *First Street* V.D. clinic secretary, Ruth Spaulding.

Concluding my interview, I detailed law enforcement's February 18, 1950, recording of what was either a serious felony assault or the actual murder of an unidentified woman in the basement of the Sowden/Franklin House by George Hodel and his accomplice, Baron Ernst von Harringa.

Author Note: The below Elizabeth Short photograph was inadvertently omitted from the autopsy photographs included in the earlier *Chapter 14, "A Doctor Did It."* I present it here because of its relevance in helping us examine the question of whether Elizabeth Short might have been slain in the Sowden House courtyard or basement?

The photograph clearly shows dirt present on the bottoms of both her right and left foot.

From an examination of the dump site at the dirt lot at 3815 S. Norton Avenue, we know the victim was not slain at that location. The body was bisected and transported there, so no possibility exists that the dirt seen on the bottoms of her feet could have come from that location.

Clearly the source of the dirt had to come after her shoes and stockings were removed prior to her death. The victim had to have been standing barefoot in what appears to be soft soil, which I expect likely preceded the extended torture and sexual assault.

We also know, based on both crime scene photographs and police and coroner reports that her body had been washed clean, with the exception of the bottoms of her feet, which her killer (s) either accidentally overlooked or deliberately ignored during his/their washdown of the body.

Based on my personal knowledge of the soil conditions at our home in 1947, it is my belief that the dirt seen on her feet is more consistent with the powdery soft soil found in the basement than that of the grassy/mixed soil known to exist in the courtyard. [That opinion is further strengthened by the fact that I was able to recover and collect actual samples of that original basement soil as will be introduced and explained in the following pages.]

Autopsy of Elizabeth Short January, 1947 showing
what appears to be dirt on the bottom of both her
right and left foot.

POLICE SERGEANT PAUL DOSTIE AND BUSTER ON THE SCENE

Two days later, on November 9, 2012, I was asked to meet again
with the film crew and to personally assist in a joint forensic
investigation. My partner would be Sgt. Paul Dostie, recently retired
from the Mammoth Lakes Police Department, and his cadaver dog,
Buster.

*K9 Buster – California State certified forensic expert
and one of the world's best trained Human Remains Detection dogs.*

PAUL AND BUSTER'S BONA FIDOS

Before getting back to the actual search for human remains and human decomposition at the Sowden/Franklin House, let me introduce you to the two experts who conducted it: Sgt. Paul Dostie and his dog, Buster.

Sgt. Paul Dostie, Buster and author in front of Sowden/Franklin House, 5121 Franklin Avenue, Hollywood, California (November 9, 2012)

Buster, a black Labrador, is casually referred to as a "cadaver Dog," but is more technically known as a *Human Remains Detection Canine*. When it comes to searching for human remains and the scent of human decomposition, Dostie says, "Buster is the most scientifically tested dog in the world due to his extensive work with forensic anthropologist, Dr. Arpad Vass."

Buster is a highly qualified court-certified expert in the field of detecting the scent of human decomposition.

Accompanied by Sgt. Dostie, Buster has performed extensive searches in Belgium, Germany and France. As a result of Buster's searches in Belgium in 2012, the remains of seven missing Americans from WWII were found and are awaiting identification at the U.S. Central Identification Laboratory in Hawaii.

Recently, Buster also found human remains and unidentified gravesites on the small atoll of Tarawa, a WWII battleground in the Central Pacific.

For many years now, Buster and Dostie have worked closely with renowned forensic anthropologist, Dr. Arpad Vass.

The clips below are from Dr. Vass's video, which describes his work and scientific research. They show Buster "in the field." In the lower clip, we see Buster next to Dr. Vass's newly developed scientific instrument, "LABRADOR" which the doctor named to honor Buster's fieldwork. LABRADOR stands for **L**ightweight, **A**nalyzer for, **B**uried **R**emains **A**nd **D**ecomposition **O**dor **R**ecognition. Once Buster alerts on the smell of human remains and or decomposition, the instrument helps pinpoint and measure the chemical gases being emitted from below ground.

TEDxYYC - Dr. Arpad Vass - Forensics

TEDxYYC - Dr. Arpad Vass - Forensics

Here is a brief bio on Sgt. Paul Dostie's impressive law enforcement experience:

Dostie has a bachelor of science degree in agriculture from Pacific Union College.

He holds Basic, Intermediate, Advanced and Supervisory California POST (Police Officers Standards and Training) certificates. He is a graduate of both the Robert Presley Institute for Criminal

Investigation with a Homicide Specialty as well as the Peter Pitchess Supervisory Leadership Institute.

After working for the Mono County Sheriff's Department for four years, Paul joined the Mammoth Lakes Police Department in 1986. During his twenty-three year career, his assignments included: Patrol, (Officer of the Year in 1987) Detectives, CA DOJ Narcotics Task Force Agent, Range Master/Firearms Instructor, Search Warrant and Chemical Agents instructor, Avalanche Dog Handler and Forensic K9 Handler and Supervisor.

Dostie is a founding member and served on the Board of Directors of the High Sierra Energy Foundation, and since 2009 has been actively involved with the History Flight American MIA Search as a member of the Board of Directors, Forensic K-9 Handler, and in Congressional Liaison.

Dostie remains actively involved as a volunteer to Law Enforcement Agencies in Clandestine Grave Detection, and he and Buster are currently working and assisting on several highly-sensitive California unsolved cold-case homicide investigations.

BACK TO "THE SEARCH"

November 9, 2012. Early afternoon.
The Sowden/Franklin House.

I met Sgt. Dostie and Buster for the first time in front of my former home. After introductions, I briefed him on the overall layout of the structure. The *Pilgrim* film crew advised us that they would simply follow our lead and videotape our investigation as it unfolded in real time.

BUSTER at the top of Sowden/Franklin House steps
waiting for his partner's command to "Search"

We began outside the house where Dostie took Buster up the steps to the entrance to the home, unleashed him, and commanded him to search.

Buster immediately took off, with the film crew in hot pursuit. He ran to a vent at the southwest corner of the property, where he "alerted," indicating to his handler that he had picked up the scent of human decomposition. This vent is on the same level and leads directly into the residence basement.

Sowden/Franklin House
Dr. George Hodel Residence
(1945-1950)
5121 Franklin Ave
Hollywood, California

N

On November 9, 2012 Cadaver Dog "Buster" along with his handler, retired Mammoth Lakes PD police sergeant, Paul Dostie, conducted a search at the Franklin House. Buster initially alerted on an exterior vent located at the SW corner of the residence and subsequently alerted to several interior locations, inside the basement. Four (4) soil samples were recovered by Sgt. Paul Dostie which are pending forensic analysis.

Diagram showing Buster's first alert

With Buster back on his handler's leash, we went inside and up one flight of stairs to enter through the doorway leading into the partially finished basement.

Dostie again ordered Buster to search. Buster ran to the west wall of the room, where he touched his nose on an electric outlet, indicating his second "alert." This outlet was at the base of a wall directly next to a door leading into the basement's unfinished dirt area, which remains essentially unchanged from its original 1947 condition.

This photo shows Buster's November 2012 search and alert in the Sowden/Hodel residence basement area. This section of basement remains unchanged from its original 1940s condition.

We followed Buster through that second door with the cameras rolling. Once inside this open dirt area Buster alerted at four (4) separate locations. The diagram below shows the basement floor plan and locations of his alerts, which are marked by black solid circles: SE1, SW2, NW3, and NE4.

Sowden House Basement Floor Plan

Based on Buster's search, Dostie and I recovered soil samples from four different locations in the dirt area, all close to the southwest side of the basement. (None of these samples were more than ten feet from Buster's initial "alert" at the exterior vent.) These samples are currently pending laboratory analysis to see if they contain chemicals common to human decomposition.

Dostie warns Buster's alerts do not necessarily indicate that a body is buried in the basement. Rather, he says Buster is alerting to the smell of the products of human decomposition, which include decomposed human blood. I strongly agree. While the presence of a body or bodies buried in the basement is a possibility, my father's presumed M.O. suggests his victims were slain in the basement where the bodies bled out and were then transported to other locations on the city streets. (As reported in my investigation, several of the 1940s *LA Lone Woman Murder* victim's bodies were never found.)

After recovering the soil samples from the basement, we searched the house's exterior perimeter.

Buster alerted once more at the base of a retaining wall on the north-side of the alley, directly behind the home.

A vacant hillside lot slopes up from this spot. In reference to this alert, Dostie informed me, "I believe that soil sample analysis from the lot above the retaining wall behind the Sowden House will indicate human burial(s). Buster's reliability around the world is exceptional." (See an aerial view of the location below.)

Two of George Hodel's suspected Lone Woman Murder victims' bodies were never found. They were Mimi Boomhower (August 18, 1949) and Jean Spangler (October 8, 1949). George Hodel was residing at the Sowden/Franklin House on both of those dates. Could the vacant lot marked in this photo contain one or both of their remains?

Photo below shows Buster on the Franklin House steps just before the search. He is wearing a bandage on his right rear leg, where Buster was being treated for an abscess.

About a week later, Dostie called to tell me a veterinarian diagnosed Buster's leg abscess as cancerous, and recommended amputation. The operation was successful, and in a recent conversation Dostie said Buster was recovering quickly and was already adapting to getting around on three legs.

"The Black Dahlia investigation was Buster's last four-legged search," Dostie said, "but he will be fine conducting future investigations on three."

No medical retirement or pension for Buster. What a dog!

November 9, 2012 Sowden House Search - Buster with bandaged leg, which required amputation one-week later due to cancer.

BUSTER'S FINDINGS MADE PUBLIC

On February 5, 2013, in an *NBC LA* television exclusive, veteran Los Angeles news reporter Patrick Healy introduced Buster and Sgt. Dostie to the public and detailed their results.

Video clips from NBC news reporter Patrick Healy's reportage of Buster's search and "alert" to human decomposition at the Sowden/Hodel residence.

Print stories followed the same night with exclusives by *Pasadena Star News* Editor Frank Girardot and *Daily Beast/Newsweek* investigative crime reporter Christine Pelisek presenting a first look at the new evidence in their separate newspapers.

Buster's discoveries were then picked up by the *AP* and major pieces on the story appeared in the *Huffington Post, Salon,* and a three-part series by journalist Kahina Sekkai in *Paris Match* magazine. From there, the story went viral on the Internet.

A few of the print stories announcing Buster's "alerts" which went on to back-ground the investigation of how and why 1940s law enforcement suspected the Sowden/Hodel residence was the original crime-scene.

LAPD FORMALLY NOTIFIED OF SOWDEN HOUSE K9 SEARCH AND FORENSIC FINDINGS

On February 4, 2013, the same date that K9 Buster's search and forensic investigation became public, Dostie personally spoke with a detective assigned to the Black Dahlia investigation at LAPD's Robbery/Homicide Cold Case Unit. The two officers then assigned the case were Detective III Rick Jackson (now retired) and his partner, Detective II Mitzi Roberts.

Here is Dostie's verbatim email memorandum received and recorded by me in my *Investigative Log and Progress Report* on February 20, 2013.

MEMO: LAPD Contact Report
TO: LAPD Det. III Steve Hodel (ret.)
FROM: Mammoth Lake PD, Sgt. Paul Dostie (ret.)
DATE: February 20, 2013 2130 hours
SUBJECT: Tel Conv. with LAPD Det. II Mitzi Roberts

Steve:

On February 4th, 2013, at about 1112 hours, I called the LAPD Robbery/Homicide Cold Case phone number listed on their website, 213-486-6810. The phone was answered by Detective Mitzi Roberts. I told Detective Roberts that I wanted to brief her on the Black Dahlia case, specifically the K9 search of the residence and surrounding area.

I described the search of the basement and the fact that K9 Buster alerted there. I also told her about the K9 alerts above the Sowden house in the alley with the source of human decomposition being above the alley on the hillside where there are several gated estates. I explained that due to the decomposition event taking place uphill from the Sowden house and draining through it, I could not say that the alerts in the basement stood alone.

I explained briefly to Detective Roberts the science behind the Gas Chromatograph/Mass Spectrometer analysis of soil samples for Chemical Compounds associated with human decomposition. I told Detective Roberts that I would advise her of the results.

She told me that soil chemistry would not clear the case. I told her that I did not expect it to clear the case, but it was powerful evidence that someone bled there.

I told Detective Roberts that I had read the letter that Chief Beck had sent to Steve Hodel regarding Steve's work on the case and it sounded condescending to me. Detective Roberts told me that it was not condescending but that the Chief would rather utilize investigative resources on more current homicide cases.

I sent Detective Roberts four peer-reviewed, published, scientific papers on the GC/MS soil chemistry. I also sent her a list of my references and gave her contact information for Dr. Arpad Vass. I also advised her that soil samples obtained from above the retaining wall might give us the answer of what is happening in the basement.

LAPD Cold Case Detectives Mitzi Roberts and Rick Jackson.
Jackson officially retired from the police department in October, 2013.

DR. ARPAD VASS: SOWDEN FOLLOW-UP INVESTIGATION

Dr. Arpad Vass is a heavyweight in the world of forensic anthropology. For over twenty-years, he has been a Senior Research Scientist at Tennessee's Oak Ridge National Laboratory as well as being an adjunct professor at the University of Tennessee (home of the famous "Body Farm") and instructor at the National Forensic Academy, Law Enforcement Innovation Center, in Knoxville, Tennessee.

Dr. Vass has a master's degree in Administration of Justice (Forensic Science) and his Ph.D. dissertation was "Time Since Death Determinations of Human Cadavers."

Put simply, Dr. Vass is one of the world's leading experts in the field of human body decomposition and analyzing and quantifying *odor mortis*—the smell of death.

In 2011 Dr. Vass was the prosecution's star witness in the Casey Anthony Murder trial, providing expert testimony as to finding evidence of human decomposition in the trunk of the defendant's car.

Expert witness Dr. Vass testifies to finding evidence of human decomposition
in the trunk of Casey Anthony's vehicle in her 2011 murder trial.

On the afternoon of September 11, 2013, I conducted a follow-up investigation at the Sowden/Franklin house where I met with Sgt. Paul Dostie, Buster, and forensic anthropologist, Dr. Arpad Vass.

A second examination of the exterior perimeter was conducted by the three of us, both at the front sidewalk level and in the rear alley directly behind the structure. Additional soil samples were recovered and given to Dr. Vass for analysis.

Buster's original "alerts" in November 2012 and again in February 2013 were at the base of a cement wall located directly behind the Sowden/Hodel residence. This is immediately adjacent to the drainage irrigation box where the soil samples were recovered. Based on this and other analysis it is believed that the best potential for finding human remains and or human bones would be on the upslope as indicated in this photo.

Soil sample recovered from this irrigation box rear alley on September 11, 2013

One month later, I received the results of the soil analysis report from Sgt. Dostie containing Dr. Vass's findings. [Reproduced in full below.]

SOIL HEADSPACE ANALYSIS

TO: Sgt. Paul Dostie (ret.)
FROM: Arpad Vass, Ph.D., Research Scientist
SUBJECT: Black Dahlia investigation (Sowden House)
DATE: October 13, 2013

On September 11, 2013, I joined Sgt. Paul Dostie (ret.) and Private Investigator Steve Hodel at the former residence of Dr. George Hill Hodel (Sowden House) to evaluate that site as a possible location of a clandestine grave. The location today is a private residence to which we did not have access, but were able to collect soil samples from in front of the home (sidewalk area by the street) and at the rear of the home (drainage irrigation box). Soil samples were collected from these two sites which I then analyzed for the presence of human decompositional chemicals (as described below).

The collection and analysis of air samples has been routinely used in many industries for over 40 years (industrial hygiene, perfume industry, environmental sampling, microbiology, etc.) with the expressed goal of determining the chemical make-up (or composition) of the odors in an air sample. Within the last decade, the chemical analysis of decompositional odors, or *odor mortis* (the smell of death), has joined this growing list. The advantage to the death investigator in considering this type of odor analysis is that the 'smell of death' lingers well past the fresh stage of decomposition (> 100 years) and, as the odor changes and migrates, can be a valuable aid to investigator in the areas of Post-mortem Interval (PMI) determinations, location of clandestine graves, and verification of decompositional events.

The production of chemicals liberated during decompositional events depends on numerous taphonomic (or environmental) factors such as barometric pressure, soil moisture and temperature. The chemical itself is also important since some are water soluble and move further down into the soil when it rains while others are nearly insoluble in water and do not move far from a decompositional event. This is one reason that certain chemicals associated with a decompositional event move in the subsurface away from a buried corpse and can be detected up to a kilometer away from the point source (the corpse) and is also one reason that cadaver locating canines will get positive alerts in areas not directly over a corpse. The research over the last decade has provided a guideline for establishing which chemicals are produced during human decomposition, their concentration range and when they should be at their maximum concentration.

Soil collected for the purpose of locating, identifying or verifying clandestine graves is best placed in 40 mL pre-cleaned glass volatile organic analysis (VOC) vials fitted with caps and a polypropylene-lined septum so that they are approximately ¾ full and quickly sealed. Depending on the type of soil, the moisture content, associated debris, and degree of compaction, this is roughly 50 g of collected soil material. The polypropylene-lined septum provides a convenient means of using a syringe to withdraw a few milliliters (mLs) of air (vial headspace) from the vial for analysis without removing the cap. It is also important to collect control samples from the area for comparative purposes (at the same depth as the test samples). These should be collected from areas devoid of obvious surface contamination, but in areas with similar soil composition as the suspect area and, if possible, parallel to established groundwater flows.

The technique selected for concentrating the sample was cryogenic trapping (cryo-trapping) which can improve the detection limit for organic constituents in an air sample by a factor of 10 times or greater compared with direct sample injection into a gas chromatograph/mass spectrometer (GC/MS). Cryo-trapping is a widely used analytical technique and has been incorporated in many analytical methods and successfully used for the analysis of fragrances and odors for many decades. Through the use of cryofocusing techniques it is possible to extract and concentrate the chemical vapor components from the headspace before injection onto the column of the gas chromatograph. The gas chromatograph then separates the individual constituents in a complex mixture and they are identified one at a time using the mass spectrometer. This process can also be used for quantification if required, but for clandestine grave detection, these analyses are usually only used to determine the presence or absence of specific chemicals and their relative abundance.

During the course of *odor mortis* research, 56 chemicals have been shown to be consistently associated with decompositional events. As previously stated, the appearance or detection of these chemicals is heavily dependent on the environment, or rather the taphonomy, associated with the human remains. It is also critical to note that the characteristics of the compound (solubility, density, molecular weight, etc.) have a profound impact on whether the compound is detected in the chemical plume (surface or subsurface) or only in close association with the corpse. Some of the taphonomic variables studied include the moisture content of the soil, the type of soil (soil texture) and whether or not the decompositional event was anaerobic (typically a deeper burial) or aerobic (typically found on the surface, a very shallow burial or loosely wrapped).

Early decomposition appears to liberate many of the fluorinated halogen compounds, the substituted benzene compounds and large amounts of very specific sulfur compounds (e.g. sulfur dioxide). These will either stay associated with the corpse (or in the general vicinity) or migrate away from the corpse in a plume depending on a host of factors which, at present, are poorly understood. As time progresses, the substituted benzene compounds become simpler in composition, more complex sulfur compounds are detected and one begins to see the appearance of aldehydes and ketones. Interestingly, older decompositional events show a noticeable increase in aldehydes with significant increases in compounds such as butanal and ethanal (among others). Also, straight chain hydrocarbons (alkanes) become more prevalent (hexane, decane, nonane, octane, etc.) as do the appearance of furans. Depending on the taphonomy (and negative control comparisons), there is a subset of compounds that appear to be consistent and commonly associated with most decompositional events. These include xylenes, 2-butanone, acetone, dimethyl disulfide, hexane, pentane, toluene, chloroform and carbon disulfide. When comparing human decompositional events with animal subsets (pig, deer, dog, cat, squirrel and sheep), carbon tetrachloride, pentane, decane and undecane appear to be human specific, the latter two only when evaluating skeletonized remains. Additionally, it was noted that when animal carcass VOCs are analyzed, 2-methyl butanal is always greater than 3-methyl butanal (this trend is also seen in animal fecal samples). This is reversed (or equal – within 10% in one instance) in human remains and is potentially a key marker to determine if the remains are human or not, especially in older gravesites. Some compounds, such as benzene, some fluorinated halogens, important sulfur compounds (dimethyl disulfide, dimethyl trisulfide), and a few aldehydes, tend to concentrate near the corpse rather than in the plume as the gravesite ages. Others, such as the xylenes (e.g. 1, 2 dimethyl benzene), chloroform and straight chain compounds (alkanes) such as pentane and octane, tend to predominate late in decomposition, but only when the conditions are predominately dry.

Results

Analysis of the drainage irrigation box sample was quite interesting and indicated not only the presence of a decompositional event, but also one that was human specific.

Expected chemical compound in soil headspace sample	Is chemical in irrigation box sample?	Comments
Alcohols (methanol, ethanol, etc.)	present	
acetone	present	
furans	present	
pentane	present	Trace amounts
Sulfur compounds	present	Dimethyl disulfide, thiobis, etc.
chloroform	present	trace amount
Aldehydes (butanal, ethanal, etc.)	present	3-methyl butanal $\geq$ 2-methyl butanal (human specific marker)
toluene	present	
Ketones (2-butanone, etc.)	present	
Hexane (sub.)	present	
xylenes	absent	
octane	absent	
nonane	absent	
Benzene (or sub benzenes)	absent	

The sample collected at the street in the front of the house showed a few decompositional products, but indicators of a human specific decompositional event were absent in that sample. Of note was that the sample collected at the front of the house consisted of very dry soil which could have affected the detection of several of the chemical compounds of interest – especially the heavier ones.

Conclusions

Chemical analysis of the irrigation box soil showed numerous markers for a decompositional event. These markers were human specific and indicates that human remains were, or are, present in the vicinity of where the soil was collected.

So here, Dr. Arpad Vass—a forensic anthropologist and one of the world's leading experts in the field of human decomposition who has studied soil samples from the likely Black Dahlia murder scene—has told us, "*...human remains were, or are, present in the vicinity of where the soil was collected.*"
But whose?

The remains could belong to any one of a long list of names that simply disappeared from what was known in the 1940s as the "Los Angeles Port of Missing Persons."

However, based on my investigation I would suggest a short list of three known *Lone Woman Murder* victims. All three disappeared within six months of each other; all were suspected of having connections to George Hodel; and none of their bodies were ever found. In chronological order, they are:

1) Mimi Boomhower, the "Merry Widow Murder."

Occurred on August 18, 1949. Victim, a wealthy heiress, disappeared from her Bel Air home while showing a potential customer her home, which she had just listed for sale. LAPD Cold Case originally investigated by WLA Division detectives. High profile case. (See full summary of case in *Black Dahlia Avenger I.*)

2) Jean Spangler, Hollywood film actress.

Occurred on October 8, 1949. Victim disappeared after last seen arguing with a man fitting George Hodel's description in front of a Hollywood restaurant and then minutes later cowering in the front seat of an open convertible at a gas station. As the male driver pulled away, she yelled to the station attendant to "call the police." Her torn purse was found at the entrance to Fern Dell Park, a quarter-mile from the Sowden/Hodel residence. This unsolved LAPD Cold Case was originally investigated by Hollywood Division detectives. High profile case. (See full summary of case in *Black Dahlia Avenger I.*)

3) Jane Doe.

Victim unknown and never publicly identified. Doubtful if her identity ever became known to police. The crime occurred on February 18, 1950 at the Hodel residence, 5121 Franklin Avenue, Hollywood. Unknown if the felony assault resulted in a murder. Only known report of this crime is documented in the 1950 DA tape-recorded transcript. Suspects identified on recording as, George Hodel and Baron Ernst Harringa. After beating victim with a pipe in the basement, they are heard to say, "Don't leave a trace." Minimal follow-up by DA investigators who checked with witness (Hodel residence plumber) to see if he had seen any digging or gravesite in the basement. No actual on-scene investigation at residence.(See Chapter 6 for a full summary.)

Buster, one of the world's best trained and court-certified Human Remains Detection Canine has confirmed what the 1950 LAPD and DA detectives suspected.

Thanks to the efforts of Sgt. Paul Dostie and Buster, we have now established, as fact, that Dr. Hodel's former residence to this very day, some sixty-six years after the murder(s), still holds the smell of death.

Dr. Vass's soil samples have captured Buster's alert, his smell of death. They have spectrographically quantified and identified it as being consistent with human decomposition. In Dr. Vass's expert opinion, there are human remains buried a short distance away from what in the 1940s was the rear attached garage of Dr. George Hill Hodel.

> "The bones came out of the ground and the hillside brush easily as if they had been impatiently waiting a very long time. ... Like their archeological counterparts who unearthed the artifacts of the ancients, the dig team used small tools and brushes to bring these bones gently to light. The process was painstaking yet it was moving at an even faster pace than Bosch had hoped for." —*City of Bones*, by Michael Connelly

VICTIM JEAN SPANGLER—LAST KNOWN MOVEMENTS—1949 TIMELINE

A few of the dozens of 1949 L.A. headlines in which LAPD and the press asserted that actress Jean Spangler was believed to be another "Dahlia Victim"

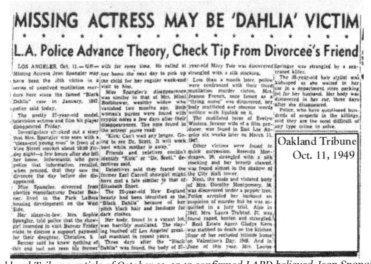

This Oakland Tribune article of October 11, 1949 confirmed LAPD believed Jean Spangler may have been a "Dahlia victim" and goes on to name nine additional women suspected of being murdered by the same killer in less than three years. (1947-1949) The Tribune names the victims in chronological order as: Elizabeth "Black Dahlia" Short (1947), Mary Tate (1947), Jeanne French (1947), Evelyn Winters (1947), Rosenda Mondragon (1947), Dorothy Montgomery (1947), Laura Trelstad (1947), Gladys Kern (1948), Louise Springer (1949) and Jean Spangler (1949).

JEAN SPANGLER BACKGROUND AND LAST KNOWN MOVEMENTS

Summer/Fall, 1949. Duncan Hodel, twemty-one-year-old son of George Hodel (and my half-brother) is a merchant seaman when he attends several parties at the Sowden/Franklin House, where he and his mates are "fixed up with girls." In a 1999 talk shortly after our father's death, Duncan told me, "I remember dad was dating a drop-dead gorgeous actress-type at the time named Jean."

Wednesday, Oct. 5, 1949, 11 a.m. Columbia Studio, 1438 N. Gower Street, Hollywood. Jean Spangler talks with friend and fellow actor Robert Cummings, tells him she has a new romance and is "having the time of her life."

Thursday, Oct. 6, 1949, 10:15 a.m. George Hodel pays $5,000 cash to bail himself out from lock-up at Hall of Justice, where he faces felony charges of incest and child molestation.

Thursday, Oct. 6, 1949 5:30 p.m. 1248 N. Vine St. Spangler is seen by known acquaintances in parking lot of the Hollywood Ranch Market. She is with a "handsome, dapper man about 35 years of age." They are standing by his black sedan, then seen walking to a nearby hot-dog stand. [SKH Note: This location is directly across the street from George Hodel's close friend Man Ray's studio apartment at 1245 N. Vine St.]

Friday, Oct. 7, 1949 *Los Angeles Times* carries following headline announcing the arrest of Dr. George Hodel: "Doctor Faces Accusation in Morals Case." On this same day, the *Los Angeles Evening Herald & Express* featured the story as, "Doctor Nabbed on Hollywood Incest Charge."

Friday, Oct. 7, 1949, 5:30 p.m. 6216 Colgate Avenue. Spangler departs her Hollywood apartment, leaving her daughter, Christine, with baby-sitter Sophie Spangler, her sister-in-law.

Friday, Oct. 7. 1949, 7:30 p.m. Spangler calls home to check on her daughter. Informs her sister-in-law that she "will be home late."

Saturday, Oct 8.1949, 1:30 a.m. Cheese Box Restaurant, 8033 Sunset Blvd. (Sunset Strip) Spangler is seated with a man at a front table. Witness Terry Taylor, the owner of the restaurant and a friend of Spangler's, describes her companion as, "male, 35 years, tallish, dark-hair, clean-cut." (George Hodel at that time was 41, but could easily pass for 35, was 6-foot-1, black hair, and had a clean-cut appearance.)

Saturday, Oct. 8, 1949, 2 a.m. Still at the same table, Spangler is spotted by entertainer Al "The Sheik" Lazar, a radio personality who broadcasts his show live from the Cheese Box. Lazar approached Jean for an interview, and saw she was arguing with two men seated at the table. As Lazar continued to approach for a celebrity radio interview, one of the men forcefully "waved him away." The Sheik said later, "I veered away, and did not attempt to conduct the interview."

Saturday, Oct 8, 1949, early morning. 8400 Sunset Blvd. (Sunset Strip). Gas station attendant Art Rodgers reports servicing a "blue-gray convertible" driven into the station by a male with a woman fitting description of Jean Spangler seated in the front passenger seat. The male ordered him to fill the tank and said, "We're going to Fresno." Rodgers went on to report, "The woman shrank down in the right side of the seat, and as the car sped off she cried out to me, 'Have the police follow this car.'" Rodgers immediately called the police, but the responding patrol units were unable to locate the suspect vehicle.

Saturday, Oct. 8, 1949, 9 a.m. Spangler fails to return home. Sophie Spangler calls LAPD and makes a "missing report."

Sunday, Oct. 9, 1949, 11 a.m. Fern Dell Park employee Hugh Anger finds Jean Spangler's purse in the park. The strap is ripped from the purse, indicating a struggle. Papers and Spangler's identification are inside, along with a handwritten note:

"Kirk,

Can't wait any longer. Going to see Dr. Scott.
Will work best this way while Mother is away."

[SKH Note: Fern Dell Park is a quarter-mile (two minutes driving time) from the Hodel residence. Police surmise from the note that Jean Spangler may have been pregnant and was possibly seeking an abortion from "Dr. Scott." See *Black Dahlia Avenger I*, pages 325-332 & 345-347 for Jean Spangler investigative summary and possible abortion ring connections.]

1. *Cheese Box Restaurant* 2. *Sunset Strip Gas Station* 3. *Purse found in park* 4. *Hodel house*

In March, 1950, DA investigators Walter Morgan and Frank Jemison—simultaneous to their covert physical and electronic surveillance of Dr. Hodel—followed up on the Jean Spangler murder and checked Hollywood area pharmacies for prescriptions written by any "Dr. Scotts." [Results of their search not included in the Hodel summary.]

Also, recorded on these DA transcripts during March 1950, just five months after Jean Spangler's abduction and murder, Dr. Hodel is recorded in conversation with a woman admitting to performing abortions at his First Street Clinic. He informs her that he has performed "lots of them."

TO SEARCH OR NOT TO SEARCH?

"I know your guys passion about this [Black Dahlia case] but we will probably not be doing anything." —Detective Tim Marcia, LAPD Robbery/Homicide Cold Case Unit, Re. K9 Buster's search of Sowden House

During both the November 2012 and the later September 2013 searches at the Sowden House, Buster alerted at the base of an uphill slope directly behind the home.

Based on their experience examining chemical distribution and "plume flows," both Dr. Vass and Sgt. Dostie believe the most likely area for finding human remains would be an area adjacent to and directly north of the Sowden House lot. (Soil samples recovered from the interior basement in the earlier 2012 Buster search and alert inside the Sowden House are still pending.)

From a strictly legal standpoint, the law is clear. Based on the evidence, ample probable cause exists that would allow law enforcement to obtain a search warrant for both the interior courtyard and the basement of the Sowden House. The known facts would also support a judge granting permission to search the level area of ground located on the property, some 60 feet north of the rear alley.

In a real-life Hollywood twist, public records show that property is currently owned by actress Laura Prepon, best known for her roles in the television series, *That '70s Show* and *Orange Is the New Black*.

Actress Laura Prepon
Photo courtesy of
http://commons.wikimedia.org/wiki/File:Laura_Prepon_crop.jpg

In November 2013, I personally contacted Ms. Prepon's attorney and provided him with an overview of the facts linking my father to the serial crimes. I also told him of Buster's recent searches and how Dr. Vass believed a likely burial site could be located in Ms. Prepon's backyard.

The attorney advised me he would contact his client and get back to me the following week.

True to his word, he called me back on November 5, 2013, and informed me that he had recommended that Ms. Prepon not grant permission for an above-ground search by Buster.

I then wrote and mailed a follow-up letter directly to Ms. Prepon. Here are a few excerpts, appealing to Ms. Prepon to reconsider granting Buster, Sgt. Dostie and myself access to conduct a brief, non-invasive examination of her backyard:

Dear Laura:

Based on my investigation it is my belief that if there is a victim buried on your property is most likely would be, Miss Jean Spangler, a twenty-six-year-old film actress, and friend of veteran screen star, Robert Cummings. She was just beginning her career and was kidnapped and slain by an unidentified "date."

Her body was never found, but her purse and identification were recovered just ¼ mile from the Sowden House, which was my father's residence at that time. A note found in her purse indicated she was most likely seeking an abortion at the time she was slain. (DA documents confirm my father was both performing and securing abortions for women just months before Jean's disappearance. Additionally, he was arrested for Incest and Child Molestation and had bailed out of jail *the day prior to* Jean's kidnap/murder.)

I am writing to ask that you reconsider and allow us to conduct a non-invasive search of the rear-yard of your property. As indicated in my letter to Mr. ————, Buster's search would only take a few minutes and if he failed to "alert" on the property *it could exclude it from being the potential burial site.*

On the other hand, if Buster did alert and was able to pinpoint the location of human remains, and those remains were found, you would be directly instrumental in helping solve one of Hollywood's most mysterious murders.

Jean Spangler, like yourself, was a young and vibrant actress who was brutally slain just as her life and career were beginning.

I have attached some newspaper articles on the 1949 crime showing that both the press and the police were convinced that Jean Spangler's abduction and murder was connected to that of Elizabeth "Black Dahlia" Short.

Based on my own findings I am convinced their original assessment was correct.

Should you have any questions, or desire to meet in person for additional information please contact me at either my email or home telephone number below.

Most Respectfully Yours,
Steve Hodel
Sherman Oaks, California

As of this writing, Ms. Prepon has not given us permission.

Nor has there been any public response from LAPD Robbery/Homicide Cold Case Unit detectives Mitzi Roberts and her partner, Tim Marcia, regarding Dr. Vass' soil analysis results. They were the first to receive his full report in October, 2013, several months before the information was made public.

Specifically addressing Buster's search, Detective Marcia informed Sgt. Dostie that "we will probably not do anything."

Echoing Chief Beck's written response to me that his detectives "should expend their valuable skills on more contemporary investigations," Detective Roberts confirmed in a May 2013 press interview there would be no further efforts to investigate the historic case. "I think [the Black Dahlia murder] may go down as one of the great Los Angeles mysteries," she said.

KEVIN STARR ON CHIEF PARKER, THE LAPD AND BLACK DAHLIA SUSPECT, DR. GEORGE HODEL

I was surprised and honored to discover historian Kevin Starr's reference to my book and my father in his *Golden Dreams: California in an Age of Abundance, 1950-1963* (Oxford University Press 2009), winner of an *L.A. Times* Book Prize. Starr was California's state librarian from 1994-2004 and is best known for his remarkable book series, *Americans and the California Dream*, documenting a hundred years of California history.

I quote from *Golden Dreams,* pages 137-8:

On the other hand, individual members of the LAPD, being human, could and frequently did succumb to payoffs from the vice culture they were expected to suppress. Working his way up the ranks, Parker encountered this corruption most painfully when he placed first in the lieutenant's examination but, having paid no one off, was placed number ten on the promotion list. By World War II, Parker held the rank of captain despite the fact that, once again, he had placed first in examinations for inspector (commander) and deputy chief. No matter; He was soon in uniform as an Army captain of military police and in 1944, as a major, he was placed in charge of all police and prison operations for the Normandy invasion. Strafed by a German plane, Parker was awarded the Purple Heart along with the *Croix de Guerre*. Further assignments took him to Sardinia, where he helped reestablish civil government, and to postwar Germany, where as a lieutenant colonel he supervised the reorganization of the police departments of Frankfurt and Munich.

Returning home, Parker once again found himself odd man out in an LAPD where the fix was in at a number of levels. Homicide for instance was a semi-autonomous enclave within the nearly autonomous LAPD, its detectives solving a crowded calendar of cases but doing it on their own terms as far as legal procedures and the use of force were concerned. This was the LAPD of the late 1930s and 1940s, whose detectives—with their overcoats and fedoras, their expensive watches and wrist bracelets, their tough talk and even tougher actions—are mirrored in the fiction and films noir of the era. Here were detectives who might or might not pursue a case, depending. Sixty years after the fact, credible evidence would surface that certain detectives had a rather strong idea of who had perpetrated the *Black Dahlia* murder but let the alleged perpetrator, a physician [Dr. George Hill Hodel] who had functioned briefly as a consultant to the LAPD during the war, skip town with no charges filed rather than have its bungled investigation—three hundred suspects interviewed, no results—come to light. In any event, a 1949 grand jury noted the evasive answers made by certain detectives when questioned regarding the *Black Dahlia* case, but the matter was never pursued.

Kevin Starr Source Note: " ...see the startling revelations in Steve Hodel's, *Black Dahlia Avenger: The True Story* (2003)

25
The KMEX-Univision Interviews

"... I actually agree with you, I think he [Hodel] has made a very compelling theory. I think there's a lot of things that looks like it and his dad could actually be responsible for the murder of the Black Dahlia." —LAPD Detective II Mitzi Roberts KMEX, *La Dahlia Negra* interview April, 2013

IN MAY, 2013, Univision KMEX anchorman Leon Krauze presented a three-part special, *La Dahlia Negra*, in which he introduced the Black Dahlia investigation to L.A.'s large Spanish-speaking community.

The news special aired in Spanish in back-to-back five-minute nightly news segments on April 29-30 and May 1, 2013.

In Part 1, Krauze reviewed the history of Los Angeles in the 1940s, along with some of the early myths connected with the infamous murder of Elizabeth "Black Dahlia" Short.

Part II re-examined some of the original potential suspects and interviewed LAPD's newest heir-apparent to the case, veteran Robbery/Homicide Detective Mitzi Roberts. (Roberts volunteered to take over the case after detective and self-professed "gatekeeper", Brian Carr, retired several years ago.)

In Part III, Krauze interviewed me about my own now 13-year Black Dahlia Avenger investigation and introduced the public to some of the evidence and linkage to my father, Dr. George Hill Hodel, as the DA's and LAPD's original "prime suspect."

Journalist Leon Krauze interviews Det. Mitzi Roberts and author on KMEX news special— "La Dahlia Noir"

LAPD Black Dahlia-related interviews are extremely rare. In recent years, Robbery/Homicide detectives have generally been reluctant to discuss the case with the media. For that reason, I was surprised to hear that they had agreed to grant reporter Leon Krauze an interview.

Perhaps the department wanted to present another changing of the guard and introduce the newest Dahlia gatekeeper, Detective Mitzi Roberts? A passing of the case from Old School to New?

Roberts was now partnered with Detective III Rick Jackson (whom I had supervised when he was a rookie-detective in Hollywood back in the '70s.) But Jackson was scheduled to retire in October 2013.

Whatever the reason, the Krauze/Roberts interview provided some dramatic new insights and revelations.

As is always the case in television, extensive interviews are cut and edited to fit into a few minutes of airtime on the nightly news.

KMEX's Hodel and Roberts interviews—which together lasted more than three hours—were no exception. It's the nature of the beast. Most of the bones and a lot of the meat from both our interviews were left on the cutting-room floor.

After the show aired, I was recontacted by the network and asked to review the full Roberts interview. They told me Detective Roberts had made several statements that seemingly contradicted my own account of events. They wanted to resolve them for a possible future follow-up segment.

What follows are verbatim excerpts from Detective Roberts recorded interview with journalist Krauze, most of which (like my own) did not make the cut. [My own commentary on her public statements are included and **bracketed in bold**.]

Detective II Mitzi Roberts
LAPD Robbery/Homicide Cold Case Unit
Reporter Leon Krauze interview, April 2013.

I think it [Black Dahlia Murder] is right out there with the Manson Murder, OJ Simpson. For sure.

In Jan. 1947, the mutilated body of Elizabeth Short was found in a vacant lot in the Crenshaw District of Los Angeles. The body had been severed, and her intestinal organs and things had been removed.

[Part of the myth. Based on the coroner's report no organs had been removed.]

A lot of doctors were looked at it at the time because the way her body was severed. It was their opinion that it took some surgical skill to mutilate the body in the way that it was left.

Yes, I think so, those taunting letters made this case so much more mysterious. The possibility that it could be the murderer taunting. Or, it could be a hoax by someone who wanted to be a part of the Black Dahlia murder.

One of the letters that was received in the initial investigation we have in the Property. There were very few items booked as evidence, but we do have one of the letters, and it was sent out just recently by the Cold Case Unit for DNA where the stamp and envelope would have been licked, but we weren't able to get a sample off that.

[This is news and the first time that LAPD has acknowledged being in possession of a letter from the "original investigation." Last public word on this came from Detective Brian Carr who informed the public "they had all disappeared."]

I think the killer would be a person that was intelligent, yet almost sadistic. To me it would seem the person would be arrogant, cocky. That he would think that he could toy with the police and get away with it. Yes, there would be some intelligence involved in that. Even the way the letters were constructed to make sure that you were not the one linked up to that letter took some thought and preparation.

There were a lot of theories back in that time and some truly believe that this murder was part of the Lipstick Murder, and Chicago and the Cleveland Torso Murders. There's never been any substantial evidence that can connect that and say that it is true.

[She apparently has not read or reviewed my "Chicago Lipstick Murders" investigation, potentially linking the crimes to the L.A. Red Lipstick Murder of victim Jeanne French and the evidence connecting the Black Dahlia to the Chicago Lipstick child murder of little Suzanne Degnan. Her statement also indicates she is unaware as reported in my investigation, that L.A. Sheriff's Office homicide investigated the 1944 West Hollywood murder of Georgette Bauerdorf as possibly being linked to the 1946 Chicago Lipstick Murders.]

As a new investigator, coming into it sixty years later and trying to go through all these files and figure out all these different theories and figure out which one is more viable.

The crime was sheer horror. Sheer horror. It scared me to think of the type of person that was capable of doing something like this. ... I'm sure she (Elizabeth Short) felt that about the person, she was with prior to what ever happened to her happened. I just think she experienced sheer horror.

You know for every Steve Hodel.... And I actually agree with you, I think he has made a very compelling theory, I think there's a lot of things that looks like it and his dad could actually be responsible for the murder of the Black Dahlia.

We have no physical evidence, at this time, sixty-six years later that we can positively link that would help solve or identify the correct perpetrator.

[Not accurate. We do have physical evidence that can potentially connect the Dahlia and the other _L.A. Lone Woman Murders_ if they were willing to test it.]

The suspect is now probably deceased or be an 80 to 90 year old. A very old man if not dead. And so, how do I justify coming out and saying, "Yes, it was Steve Hodel's father," when I have no physical evidence to back that up.

[Again, not accurate. She is seemingly unaware, or has chosen to ignore the fact that active Head DDA Steve Kay

provided a legal opinion that the "case was solved" and her own Chief of Detectives James McMurray ordered her unit to "clear the case" based on my investigation.]

If we had DNA that would be great. But, even as far as witnesses, a lot of people are deceased. There is just ... Hodel's is a great theory, but... Yes, he [George Hodel] was a suspect at the time, absolutely. But, it's not with a 100% certainty that I could say, "Yes, it's Steve Hodel's father. And we are going to clear one of the most famous cases in Los Angeles' history based on his compelling theory. Because some of his evidence checked out and some of it was also incorrect.

We have gone through it, and there is no physical evidence in this case that could help in the identification of the suspect. If there was, we'd be working it. I can guarantee that.

Steve Hodel knows that we did DNA testing. Well, he should know that? Yes, he should know that.

[No one from LAPD has informed me of any DNA testing. She apparently is unaware that LAPD has had no contact or communications with me since Head DA Steve Kay and I gave the briefing to "the brass" and Robbery/Homicide Detectives Jackson and Carr, back in May 2003.]

[*Krauze asks her if there is anything to Hodel's theory of an immense cover-up back in the 1940s*]

You know, L.A. is a...I didn't live in L.A...I wasn't even born at the time of this murder. You hear about how the Department was back then. I think a lot of it is based on fact so I couldn't say. I couldn't say for sure whether there was a cover-up or not. There is nothing in the file so far that I've read that would lead me to think that there was a cover-up. But, I've only really scratched the surface. I've not gone through every piece. I couldn't comment on that... I wouldn't feel right saying that about past officers that I know worked hard on the case. I don't have any direct knowledge. I don't think it's fair.

[Here, she makes it clear to Krauze that she is not familiar with the details of the investigation and has, so far only "scratched the surface" of what is unquestionably the Department's most complex cold case. Incredibly, she is seemingly unaware of the DA Hodel-Black Dahlia transcripts and what they contain, which is George Hodel's confession to multiple murders, police payoffs, and the cover-up of the 1950 wire-recorded felony assault and or murder of the victim by George Hodel and Baron Harringa.]

In the city of Los Angeles currently, we have over 9000 unsolved cases. And, the fact that the perpetrator of this crime would be extremely old, or most likely deceased. Most of our time in the Cold Case Unit is spent investigating contemporary crimes where there are suspects out on the loose right now that need to be taken into custody. Need to be held accountable for it. It's not fair to the citizens of Los Angeles for me to spend my time investigating a case just because it was and it is so popular.

Knowing that most likely the suspect in this case is deceased. Knowing that I have no evidence that is going to allow me to concretely even solve the case. So, yes, I think it [Black Dahlia Murder] may go down as one of the great Los Angeles Mysteries.

I don't think it's possible to solve concretely, beyond a doubt, I wouldn't feel right, just clearing it on paper. That's why I volunteered to take the case. Believe me; I think Steve Hodel has a very compelling story. I've heard a couple of others that I think are equally compelling. I can't remember, my partner Rick Jackson knows more about it.

I don't want to say for sure that he [Hodel] knows that there is no evidence, but he's been told there is no evidence. Hodel claims he saw something there. You know we did the Black Dahlia thing in Northeast, and he saw something that was evidence.

[Here Roberts is referencing the 2012 LA Police Historical Museum, Black Dahlia Exhibit. As we know, Roberts acknowledged in her telephonic conversation with Sgt. Dostie that she saw and read my letter sent to the Chief and her Captain at Robbery/Homicide Division.]

Hodel acts like he wasn't helped at all. The DNA was done; it was done years ago...

[News to me. Her statement here is confusing. Earlier in her interview Roberts mentions finding and sending out a letter which was tested, "just recently" and here she talks about DNA testing "done years ago"? It would seem there are two possibilities: 1) LAPD found and analyzed a different evidence letter from the original 1947 mailings which came back negative, that is, no discernible DNA obtained, or 2) They tested *one* of the several Police Museum letters after receiving my letter to them advising them of the possibility of DNA, in July 2012. If the latter is the case, we have no idea which letter was examined and in my request to meet and discuss the DNA potentials, I did not reference or identify any *specific letter*, which

means if they tested a letter for DNA—they were guessing on which one I was referencing.]

From Detective Roberts' interview, her own words make it clear she has just scratched the surface as far as familiarizing herself with the Black Dahlia investigation. That's understandable.

What is also true is that in regards to the Dahlia investigation, LAPD's public stance vacillates from "We never give up. No case is too old or too cold," to Chief Bratton's public statement, "I've ordered my men to close the case," to the current Chief Beck's statement to me, "I do not believe it prudent that we pursue the Black Dahlia investigation at this time."

So which is it? My interpretation is the LAPD wants it both ways. If the media calls, "We're on it." Otherwise, "Fuhgeddaboudit."

From the get-go, I have always preferred and requested a private meeting with LAPD. I approached them several times some six months before my initial 2003 publication, but they kept refusing to meet.

Based on Chief Beck's letter to me it is clear that LAPD is exercising its "right to remain silent." It doesn't want to meet nor hear any of the new evidence. So be it.

After hearing Detective Roberts's public statements in the Krauze interview, here are my responses and clarifications. Since I have been denied an opportunity to ask her privately in person, *detectivo a detectivo,* I will ask her here and now—in public.

1) In your public statements, you mention the Department tested "an original letter" for DNA, but no DNA was found. Could you tell us specifically, which letter was tested? Has the LAPD Police Museum letter dated October 10, 1950, that I suspect was written by George Hodel been tested for DNA?

2) What is your opinion regarding the fact that the DA reports place George Hodel and Elizabeth Short together and "as being acquainted" before the murder, as do multiple witnesses from that time period?

3) What is your opinion as to the 1950 DA wire recordings that contain Hodel's admissions to killing Elizabeth Short as well as his personal secretary, Ruth Spaulding, whose death was originally investigated by LAPD as a suspected "forced overdose" in 1945 some eighteen months prior to the Dahlia murder?

4) Are you aware of Hodel's taped admissions to making "law enforcement payoffs" and performing abortions ("lots of them") as well as committing subornation of perjury and threatening to kill a witness and her child if she goes to the police? (The latter being

formally documented in writing by Santa Barbara police officer Mary Unkefer, who was the same officer that handled the 1943 arrest and disposition of Elizabeth Short for "minor possession of alcohol" and allowed her to remain in [Officer Unkefer's] private residence for ten days prior to sending her home to Medford, Massachusetts.)

5) What is your opinion regarding the physical evidence—the cement sacks—confirmed by LAPD to be used to transport the body parts from a private residence to the vacant lot, which have now been connected to identical sacks documented as being at the Hodel residence two days before the murder?

6) What is your opinion as to the fact that all of the original top LAPD brass (Chiefs Parker, Thad Brown, Undersheriff Downey and DA Lieutenant Jemison) have independently confided and confirmed, "the Black Dahlia case was solved and that her killer was Dr. George Hodel, living on Franklin Avenue"?

7) What is your opinion regarding the fact that both active Head Deputy DA Stephen Kay and your own former boss and then (2004) active LAPD Deputy Chief of Detectives James McMurray publicly declared the Black Dahlia case "solved" and that Chief McMurray ordered your unit's Robbery/Homicide detectives to "go ahead and clear the case unless you can find some major holes in Hodel's investigation."

8) You stated publicly, "If there was any physical evidence available to check I can guarantee you we'd be working it." Would you be willing to meet with me and hear me out on what and why I believe there are multiple workable sources of evidence in LAPD's custody that potentially contain suspect DNA?

9) What is your opinion regarding the tape-recorded assault and/or possible murder captured on tape in the basement of the Hodel residence during the 1950 electronic stakeout by the DA and LAPD detectives? Are you aware that the detectives' transcript records a woman first trying to call the operator for help from the house, and then later she is heard being beaten with a pipe by George Hodel and Baron Ernst Harringa and heard screaming as the blows are being delivered, followed by Dr. Hodel telling his accomplice, "Don't leave a trace"?

10) Are you aware that this assault and/or murder was also corroborated in a police report in 1950 by detectives who interviewed a witness (Dr. Hodel's plumber) to see if any fresh digging occurred in the basement? And that this fact was recently corroborated by cadaver dog Buster's search and alerts to human decomposition in the basement in 2013?

11) You have been advised that I am now in possession of Dr. George Hill Hodel's full DNA profile. Are you aware that the original

LAPD and DA and Sheriff's investigators assigned the cases believed that many of the *L.A. Lone Murders* in the 1940s were serially connected and that the killer mailed in or left taunting notes in at least five of the nine murders, which could potentially be linked through modern Touch DNA analysis (mailings, clothing, ligatures etc.)?

12) The cases that your 1940s counterparts in both LAPD and Sheriff's homicide felt were possibly connected to one killer, and I believe are potentially serially connected and if tested are solvable through DNA are:

1. Ora Murray (1943) LASO
2. Georgette Bauerdorf (1944) LASO
3. Elizabeth Short (1947) LAPD (note)
4. Jeanne French (1947) LAPD (note)
5. Lillian Dominguez (1947) SMPD (note)
6. Gladys Kern (1948) LAPD (note)
7. Louise Springer (1949) LAPD
8. Mimi Boomhower (1949) LAPD (note)
9. *Jean Spangler (1949) LAPD*

26

Murder as a Fine Art:
The Hodel/Man Ray Nexus

"Violence is the Minotaur; those who survive it spend their lives threading its maze, looking for the exit." —Richard Rhodes, Winner of the Pulitzer Prize, from *Why They Kill: The Discoveries of a Maverick Criminologist*

IN JUNE 2013 I was contacted by a friend, Steve Fjelsted, and asked if I could give a talk updating my latest book, *Black Dahlia Avenger II*?

Steve F., a tall drink of water (about 6-foot-5) is an affable and erudite man. He is also the City of South Pasadena's librarian and remains a towering booster for that community. South Pasadena, a beautiful small town in the heart of our metropolis (3.4 square miles in size with a population of only 25,000) is known as "the City of Trees," and is just six miles northeast of downtown L.A. Its historic library was built in 1907 (same year as my father's birth) and during his growing-up years, George Hodel spent hundreds of hours in study at his neighborhood library while attending and then graduating from South Pasadena High School in 1922.

I happily accepted the invitation and we scheduled my talk for August 22, 2013.

In the six weeks preceding the talk, my investigation unexpectedly kicked into high-gear, presenting a dramatic breakthrough that I quickly recognized would become major news. Rather than immediately releasing the story to the press I decided to announce the new findings as an exclusive to those attending the South Pasadena Library talk.

*South Pasadena City Librarian, Steve Fjelsted
and his wife Peggy at a Rotary banquet 2011.*

THE SCOTT GANDELL ILLUSTRATIONS

Unbeknownst to me, Fjelsted contacted a well-known local South Pasadena artist/illustrator, Scott Gandell, whom it turns out, had created a number of Black Dahlia related drawings over the years. Scott volunteered to draw two original illustrations that the library could use to promote their upcoming event. [Shown below] Personally, I think Scott is one of L.A.'s most gifted artists with a truly unique style and talent.

These George and Steve Hodel illustrations are by South Pasadena artist Scott Gandell. Scott is a professional illustrator, printmaker, and an entrepreneur. He co-owns and operates South Pasadena Mercantile Company with Anneline De Croos. He is a past President of The Society of Illustrators of Los Angeles and is an alumnus of Art Center College of Design in Pasadena. Scott's work has been published in magazines, newspapers, and books. His work has also been exhibited in galleries, in the U.S. and Canada and has been acquired by clients and collectors worldwide.

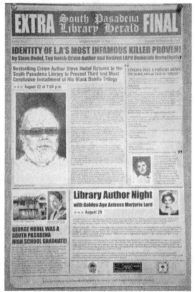

Photo courtesy of the Pasadena Public Library,
Scott Gandell and Anneline De Croos.

SOUTH PASADENA LIBRARY—AUGUST 22, 2013— THE NEW EVIDENCE

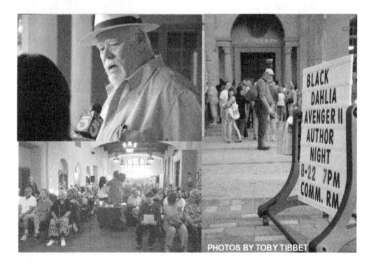

Thanks to librarian Fjelsted's promotional efforts, an audience of over two hundred showed up, along with several network news channels and local print reporters.

In a 90-minute PowerPoint presentation, I back-grounded the audience on the original crime as documented in *Black Dahlia Avenger* (1999-2005) and then presented many of the new findings as published in this book.

The final half-hour focused on a quick review of all of the visual evidence in support of George Hodel's unique signature, *Murder as a Fine Art*.

I shared all of the close connections, the one-degree-of-separations, and direct personal friendships my father had with the prominent screenwriters, artists and surrealists living in 1940s Los Angeles. As we know, those included Surrealist artist Man Ray, his wife Juliet, Salvador Dali, Marcel Duchamp, William Copley, Edmund Teske, Ben Hecht, Rowland Brown, Steve Fisher, and Gene Fowler

In chapter 21, *A Surrealist Signature,* we reviewed most of that evidence.

For the purpose of this chapter let's disregard all of the other speculative surrealist links and just focus on the following eight:

1. 1934 Man Ray *Les Amoureux (The Lovers)* photo
2. 1936 Man Ray *Minotaur* photo
3. 1944 Man Ray *L'inconnue de la seine* photo
4. *1945* Man Ray *Juliet Stocking Mask* photo
5. 1946 Man Ray/George Hodel *Yamantaka* photo
6. *1947 Armand Robles Avenger* mailing photo
7. 1947 " 'Go Slow,' *Man Killer Says Black Dahlia Case"* Avenger mailing photo
8. 1984 George Hodel *Modesto Lovers* (Man Ray homage)

Hodel/Man Ray Black Dahlia Nexus

Consider each one of these as a separate piece belonging to a larger puzzle. Do we have all of the pieces? No. But we have enough to establish what I will call the *George Hodel-Man Ray-Black Dahlia Nexus.*

Pieces of the puzzle that together make a compelling case that the wannabe artist, George Hodel, used his guru and close friend Man Ray's established works (paintings and photographs) as a cut-and-paste inspiration for his own first work. An introductory signed original. His macabre *readymade* for his fellow Dadaists to consider as George Hodel's personal application to join their club.

So far, none of this Man Ray linkage is new. I have presented and built upon this evidence in *Black Dahlia Avenger, Most Evil and here in Black Dahlia Avenger II.* With this in mind let us now view and put in place a new and hitherto missing ninth piece of the puzzle.

"There is a square pattern of superficial crisscross lacerations in the skin of the right hip." —Dr. Frederic Newbarr, 1947 Elizabeth Short Coroner's Report

Those of you who are regular readers of my web blog (blog.stevehodel.com) will recall that in a recent blog, we examined the possibility that some of the carvings on Elizabeth Short's body could be an artist's signature known as "crosshatching."

This intriguing hypothesis was first offered by a reader, architect Steve Lamb. [Lamb also met and conversed with surrealist photographer Edmund Teske, as related in an earlier chapter of this book.]

In reviewing Lamb's theory, followed by a little research on the subject, I then wrote a blog on May 13, 2013, asking the question: *"Did Dr. Hodel Sign his "Surreal Masterpiece" by Cutting an Artist's Crosshatching Marks into Elizabeth 'Black Dahlia' Short's Body Parts?"*

DAN "THE MAN" LACKEY—A EUREKA MOMENT

While I greatly appreciated Lamb's input and was convinced that he was correct that my father was undoubtedly "saying something" by leaving some kind of twisted surgical "message," I felt "crosshatching"—which appears to be more of a form of an artist's shading—was a little too generic. But since I felt it might inspire some thoughts from others, I posted the blog.

Less than seven weeks later, on July 5, 2013, I received a short email from one of my readers, Dan Lackey. Dan is fifty-one, an electrical engineer for a local utility company in his hometown of Hernando, Mississippi. He is married, enjoys Internet research, history, and music. From prior communications, I was aware that Dan had read all three of my books and possessed an unusually detailed knowledge of all aspects of my investigation. So when he spoke, I listened. Dan's discovery was his—and my—Eureka moment.

July 5, 2013

Steve,

I was looking at Man Ray's website and came across a drawing titled <u>L'Equivoque 1943.</u>

The drawing shows a nude woman, (no surprise there). To the right of the figure, it appears that there is another arm, other than the figure's arm. Instead of a head, there is some unexplained mass of what appears to be reddish colored wood. Near the center of that mass there is what looks like a yellow shield. Inside the yellow shield is a crosshatch pattern, very prominently displayed. Just like the crosshatch patterns found on Beth Short. It may be that GHH paid homage to *The Minotaur*, *The Lovers*, and *L'Équivoque*, with the Black Dahlia. When I saw that I, to use your phrase, almost fell out of my chair. I had to let you know ASAP.

Best Regards,
Dan Lackey

Attached to Lackey's email was a photo of the Man Ray painting created by the artist in Hollywood bearing his signature and the date, "Man Ray 1943."

L'Équivoque, *1943*

Autopsy photo taken January 15, 1947 showing crisscross cutting on victim Elizabeth Short's right hip. [Enlarged on right.]

L'Équivoque "surgical signature" carved into Elizabeth Short's right hip by her killer, compared to Man Ray's original.

Equivoque, also equivoke, n.
1) French equivoque, from Late Latin... 2) A pun. A double meaning. 3) To use unclear language to conceal or mislead.

Did Elizabeth Short personally model for Man Ray's 1943 painting, *L'Équivoque?*

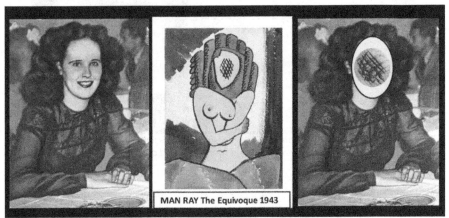

MAN RAY The Equivoque 1943

Elizabeth Short, circa 1943, as compared to L'Equivoque

I would say the chances are better than even that she might well have actually posed for the Man Ray painting.

We know Elizabeth was in both the Los Angeles and Hollywood areas during 1942 and 1943. [She was not arrested for "Minor Possession" and sent home to Medford, Massachusetts by Santa Barbara officer Mary Unkefer, until September 1943.]

We also know that in 1944, while in Hollywood, she posed for an artist, Arthur Curtis James, aka Charles Smith. [Not the same Charles Smith implicated and named as Dr. Ballard's assistant in Tamar Hodel's 1949 abortion.]

Short modeled for James in two separate artworks ("a large oil painting and a sketch") which were well-documented in an interview with James that appeared in the newspapers after her murder in 1947. [Some Dahlia revisionists and "self-appointed experts" deny this, but the facts, documents and newspaper articles speak for themselves.]

Here is an excerpt from *BDA I* where I originally referenced this back in 2003:

BDA page 155:

Arthur Curtis James Jr. (Aka Charles Smith)
Arthur James was a fifty-six-year-old artist and ex-convict, awaiting sentencing in a pending forgery charge, who first met Elizabeth in a Hollywood cocktail lounge in August 1944. "She

showed an interest in my drawings," he told police, who interviewed him in 1947 after they discovered that James had known Elizabeth Short. James told police that he was in a bar drawing sketches, and she was seated nearby. After she said she liked what James had sketched, he revealed to police that the two of them became friends. "She modeled for me, and I made several pictures of her," he explained. He corroborated his statements by giving police the names of the current owners of his artwork. "One, a large oil painting, I later turned over to a man named Frank Armand, who lived in Artesia." The second one he identified as "a sketch of Elizabeth, which I turned over to a Mrs. Hazel Milman, Star Route 1, Box 24, Rodeo Grounds, in the Santa Monica, Palisades district." James then told police that his contact with Elizabeth ended abruptly three months later in November 1944 after he was arrested in Tucson, Arizona, for violation of the Mann Act while he was using the alias of Charles Smith. The press later established that the federal charges against him, involving the "transporting of girls across a state line for immoral purposes," did not involve and were totally unrelated to the Elizabeth Short homicide.

As a result of those charges James was convicted and served two years in Leavenworth prison. After his release in 1946, he ran into Elizabeth in Hollywood that November, when he bought her several pieces of luggage. James quickly ran afoul of the law again because the check he wrote for the luggage bounced and he was arrested. At the time of his interview with reporters in January 1947, he was awaiting sentencing on those charges.

Also, note the unusual hair style in the Man Ray painting that appears identical to how Elizabeth wore her hair during that same time period. Man Ray's model appears young and trim. Elizabeth in 1943 was trim and just 19.

Elizabeth regularly visited Hollywood and could have easily met George Hodel and/or Man Ray, and after a social meet, might well have been offered money to pose for the artist at his nearby studio on Vine Street.

The DA Files document that George Hodel "was acquainted and associated with Elizabeth prior to her murder" and multiple witnesses confirm that.

I also believe the "promise is a promise" telegram sent from Washington D.C. to Elizabeth in Florida in 1944 and mysteriously signed only as "Yours" came from George Hodel, who was known to travel and make frequent trips to D.C. during those years.

If I am correct, the two (George and Elizabeth) would have met and had a relationship prior to 1944, possibly from Elizabeth being his patient and receiving treatment at his *First Street Clinic* for her STD,

"Bartholin gland cyst." This diagnosis and medical treatment was documented in the DA Files which listed the doctor as "an unknown doctor" and as one of the possible suspects. (I maintain that, in truth, George Hodel was this downtown "unknown, unnamed doctor.")

This would also explain George Hodel's tape-recorded statement which indicated that his secretary, Ruth Spaulding could have connected Elizabeth Short to George Hodel prior to her death in May, 1945. ("They will never be able to prove I did that murder [Black Dahlia]. They can't talk to my secretary anymore because she's dead.") That statement clearly implies that had Ruth still been alive in 1947—she could, in fact, "connect them" as being acquainted in 1943 or 1944.

We will likely never know if Elizabeth Short was the actual sitting model for Man Ray's painting. Obviously, after her identification as the murder victim in 1947, that is something that Man Ray and all connected to him would have kept secret and not revealed to the police or anyone else.

But setting that question aside, in viewing Man Ray's *L'Équivoque*, there can be little doubt as to what we are seeing in the marks on the Black Dahlia's corpse.

This is George Hodel ninth crime-related homage to Man Ray and, to my mind, his most significant signature.

In it, he signs his masterpiece by directly copying Man Ray's artwork *L'Équivoque*, and with a scalpel in hand, has carved his monstrous message directly into the flesh of his victim's right hip for all to see.

In so doing, he has created a double pun meant to *conceal and mislead* the uninitiated. Diabolically, he has taken Man Ray's *L'Équivoque* and used it to fashion his own.

Another taunt and clue and one-upmanship. His own *Équivoque* to be seen and recognized only by an elite circle of insiders—his fellow surrealists.

Thank you, Dan Lackey, for finding and contributing a hugely significant piece to the *Murder as a Fine Art* puzzle.

I will close this chapter with what I consider to be two highly insightful responses to the subject matter. The first is from Trenton Scott, a reader who has regularly commented on various aspects of the ongoing investigation. We have never met in person, but from his astute observations in his many emails to me over the years, it is clear he has a profound understanding of how my father's signature acts relate to all things surreal.

His most recent comment as it appears at my blogsite on the *L'Équivoque* discovery:

"I wonder how many surreal appearances are involved in this case, two dozen, more? With this latest Man Ray association, one wonders how many surrealist thought-prints remain undiscovered. How many are required before mere coincidence can be ruled out?"

"Regarding the uncertainty produced by the criminal (or criminals) involved in this crime: The bewilderment produced by the surrealist thought-prints in this case knows no bound, mystifying all involved before, during and after the murder. These surreal signatures are designed to create confusion, to destabilize the untrained eye, to conceal an inside reference or pun that only the inner circle of surrealists could fully understand. Although implanted surreal messages were often intellectual or even humorous in nature, this murder represents a homicidal instance of surreal appearance, a brutal, psychopathic act for history to witness in bafflement." —Trenton A. Scott, July 24, 2013

The second is from author/poet Jean Barrett Holloway, who recently sent me a copy of her *Black Dahlia Museum: An Installation in Four Poems* and has kindly granted me permission to publish them in this book. They are reprinted on the following pages.

BLACK DAHLIA MUSEUM:
AN INSTALLATION IN FOUR POEMS

by
Jean Barrett Holloway

THE DETECTIVE SPEAKS TO HIS FATHER

Who are the Greeks to me?
Iphigenia and her last look from the altar
into her father's eyes,
his ivory comb still in her hair.
Orestes rounds on his mother
as her boyhood gift that miniature dagger
at ease on its shelf in his old room
watches him screw up his courage.
Brother and sister to me, father,
brother and sister.

Stepmother, fresh widow, helplessly weeping
in your Nob Hill penthouse,
my fingers exploring on their own it seems,
the way lifelong skills take over in extremis,
yours into the gloved mysteries under the skin,
slipping along the edges of a tumor, a ribcage,
mine touching every speaking lipstick, pen, mirror.
And so I find Elizabeth's photograph in your album.

The old wound, stump of your absence, wakes me
and I am become professional
just when a simple phone call might have closed your affairs.
Stink of corruption, only the first I will exhume,
this photograph not the only one I'll have to look at.
First, do no harm.
Oh, Daddy.

NORTH WALL: "LE MINOTAURE"
BY MAN RAY, 1935

The curving horns are arms bent
above a headless torso,
her shadowed breasts are now his bulging eyes,
the cavity of his rapacious mouth
the dark hollow of her diaphragm stretched
across the thinness of her ribs,
cropped at her waist.
The sacrificial maiden and her monster
juxtaposed,
become one surreal ha-ha.
The artist observes his subject from a fucking point of view.
The medium is paper, the method the camera.
The hard part was getting her to hold her breath.

SOUTH WALL: "MAN RAY HOMEAGE"
BY GEORGE HODEL, 1947

The medium is body, the method the scalpel.
The hard part was getting rid of all the blood.
It's true there were not reams of girls
but there was still a good sample,
and the artist so practiced at seduction and dissection.
After all, how many men can do both?
A chortle as he bisects at her waist
observing from a fucking point of view.
The afterthought is not to waste this canvas --
a slash below the ear makes the mouth the lips
of Ray's Les Amoureux.
He leaves the piece where it is sure to be discovered.
He gets the police to take the photograph.

THE CHORUS OF THE WOMEN
(a continuously repeating video)

as if we were already hung in a gallery
were red-mouthed marionettes

as if we were squeaking pieces of fruit
weeping legs of lamb

as if we rode Chinese horses, trampled Cretan bulls
were pieces of wet

mere tunnels
as if we already hung in a gallery

27
Biometrics: New Photo Forensics

*"**Facial Recognition Software** –an application that can be used to automatically identify or verify individuals from video frame or digital images. Some facial recognition software uses algorithms that analyze specific facial features, such as the relative position, size and shape of a person's nose, eyes, jaw and cheekbones."* —Techopedia

Jane Doe Photo No. 2 in George Hodel album

IN CHAPTER 5 OF THIS BOOK, *Scene of the Crime*, I briefly re-examined Photo No. 2 (seen above) and presented some visual comparisons to several photographs of murder victim, Jean Spangler who, as we know, disappeared two days after Dr. George Hodel's October 6, 1949, posting of bail on his arrest for incest and child molestation.

Since writing that chapter, I have been presented with the new evidence confirming that in both K9 Buster and expert witness Dr. Arpad Vass' opinion that "human decomposition is or was present in or near the grounds of the Sowden/Hodel residence."

Based on the new findings in Chapter 24, *The Smell of Death*, along with the discovery of the additional circumstances pointing to the possibility that she might well be the "10th Dahlia victim," I decided to see if I could pursue some photo comparison possibilities.

To that end, I conducted some online research and made contact with Dr. Robert Frischholz, in Nurenberg, Germany. Dr. Frischholz is the chief technology officer for BioID, a firm specializing in state-of-the-art facial recognition and identification. Dr. Frischholz has been honored by Marquis Who's Who since 1998 and IBC for his outstanding contributions to science in the fields of image processing motion analysis and biometircs. With numerous publications and patents, he is considered one of the world's leading biometric experts specializing in the field of facial recognition and in 2001 was named International Scientist of the Year.

Dr. Robert Frischholz
Named 2001 International Scientist of the Year

In November 2013, I emailed Dr. Frischholz with minimal background on my investigation and requesting his assistance in attempting to see if by using his 21st century facial recognition technology, he might be able to include or exclude my father's "Jane Doe" photograph from either of the two knowns: Elizabeth Short and Jean Spangler.

Dr. Frischholz agreed to try, but first provided me with a few cautionary words of advice. Here are some extracts from his initial response to my request:

6 November 2013

Hi Steve,

Thanks for writing me. Well I actually receive many of those inquiries, and most of the time unfortunately I am unable to help. Simply because reliable face recognition requires two photos from the same viewing angle, more or less the same lighting, and not too much age difference...

Closed eyes interestingly do not disturb the process very much, since most facial recognition algorithms avoid using the eye information (yes simply because of the fact that eyes could be closed or of sun glasses used).

All of the images I ever was asked to compare never gave a good matching score – because of the reasons given above. If, on the other hand, your two images would give a high matching score, this indeed would mean that there is a strong probability that those are the same person!

So just send me the images you have, and I can run them through our company's facial recognition engine, and if the matching score is really high, you have some strong proof that it is the same person!

Nevertheless, at least here in Germany, facial recognition is not approved by law. So the result can only either confirm you in your suspicion, or raise more uncertainties. It will not undoubtedly solve your problem.

Anyway, if it helps, as said just send me the pics and I will see what results we can get.

Kind regards
Robert

11 November 2013

Hi Steve,

I got your pictures. Ok this seems to be a bit more complicated than I thought (need to correct the in-plane rotation precisely to have a fair result).

Please give me a few days on this.

Best regards
Robert

15 November 2013

Dear Steve,

Sorry that it took so long, but I wanted to make sure that all experiments I made are correct. Let me first summarize what we have: We have several photos of ID=1 called "Elizabeth Short." Then we have several photos of ID=2 called "Jean Spangler." Then we have only one photo of ID=3 called "Jane Doe."

I trained our automatic facial recognition system (let's call it AFR from now on for the sake of simplicity) with all the photos we have from ID's 1 and 2, and then tested against ID number 3 to see which matching scores we get, and whether any of those scores would mean that #3 is actually #1 or #2...

Tests against ID2: The matching scores of ID3 against ID2 are quite low. In other words, our AFR says that "Jean Spangler" is not very similar to "Jane Doe."

Tests against ID1: The matching scores of ID3 against ID1 are remarkably high. In other words, our AFR says that "Elizabeth Short" is very similar to "Jane Doe."

If the question would have been "who is more similar to Jane Doe", then our AFR would definitively say "Elizabeth Short." The matching score is relatively high. Not as high as our AFR would need it to say it definitively IS her, but high enough to say that those two are very similar.

This was surprising to me, too. As I told you earlier, I often receive similar questions, and receive two photos to match, and I never got a score as high as this one. Even though the images are not really suitable for face recognition. For most accurate results, one needs to look straight into the camera, and none of the images supplied do that perfectly.

Best regards
Robert

19 November 2013

Dear Steve,

Well to answer your two questions:

To test your images, I used the BioID engine. This engine was tested several times, especially by German institutions, and can be considered as being state-of-the-art in commercial face recognition.

Nevertheless, I am talking to you privately, so please do not assume those numbers are official numbers from BioID.

Now to somehow answer your other question, about some interpretation of that score, well I made some additional experiments and try to give more light to this:

In all biometric technologies, the test sample is compared to each trained ("enrolled") image in the training data set. This comparison gives a "score", which is usually a floating point number in the range of 0.0 to 1.0. The higher, the better. But this score is not a simple percentage – having a score of 0.7 does not mean "it is 70% sure that this one is the same person." Things are unfortunately much more complicated.

But to somehow give you some better assessment of the score of "Jane Doe," I used the score that her picture gave when comparing to the pictures of "Elizabeth Short," and made tests with some of our test sets for face evaluation today. I used a mixture of a few thousand sample images for testing, and found that the important "FAR" was 8.5%...

FAR means "false acceptance rate," that means that 8.5% of all test images were incorrectly evaluated as being a match when using the Jane Doe threshold. Or in other words, the chance of falsely identifying an image as Elizabeth Short is 8.5%.

Do not take those 8.5% too serious, this is depending on the dataset used for testing. Several hundred thousand of test images should be used to give more precise result. From my experience, I expect the FAR of that Jane Doe sample to be between 5% and 10%.

Or, being even less scientific, one could rephrase that to be: BioID's AFR rates the positive match between the image of Jane Doe and the ones supplied for Elizabeth Short as being reliable between 90% and 95%.

I hope this is somehow better understandable. 90-95% assurance seems to be quite high, but as I said it would not be accepted in a serious test. In your country, N.I.S.T. tests all face recognition engines from time to time, and currently suggests the FAR to be set to 0.1% – would mean an AFR needs to have 99.9% reliability for a positive match!

But anyway, as I wrote earlier, for such old photos, the results are astonishingly high.

Hope I was not too complicated with all those numbers. I tried to give you some feeling about the meaning of that score without going too deep into mathematics.

Best Regards,
Robert

State-of-the-art AFR (Automatic Facial Recognition) computer rates the positive match between the known image of Elizabeth Short and the "Jane Doe" photo in Dr. George Hodel's photo album as being reliable between 90% and 95%.

A very special thank you to Dr. Robert Frischholz for conducting the facial recognition comparisons.

As he points out, while the results cannot be accepted as a mathematical certainty that the Jane Doe image is in fact Elizabeth Short, the 90-95% assurance certainly lends strong circumstantial weight to that possibility.

Or let's use Dr. Frischholz prescient words prior to conducting his facial recognition examination:

"Nevertheless, at least here in Germany, facial recognition is not approved by law. *So the result can only either confirm you in your suspicion,* [emphasis mine] or raise more uncertainties. It will not undoubtedly solve your problem."

FURTHER INVESTIGATING THE ZODIAC'S HALLOWEEN WISHES

I had expected to close this 2014 updated investigation with the good Dr. Frischholz's fascinating analysis and findings on his facial recognition biometrics.

However, in late April, a new investigative door unexpectedly swung open.

During a routine check of the Internet, I noticed there was some new buzz both on Tom Voigt's website, www.zodiackiller.com which I have referred to in earlier chapters as, "Zodiac Central" as well as on the www.reddit.com *Unresolved Mysteries* blog site.

At the reddit site, a blogger known as "septicman" presented new information and publicly asked, *"Was a 1950s comic book a source of inspiration for the Zodiac Killer 'Halloween Card'?"*

Voigt's message board then examined the topic under a heading entitled, *"Found it! By Fire, By Gun, By Knife, By Rope."*

These new discoveries, combined with material I presented in the earlier *Chapter 10, Hollywood Roomers* provide us with additional circumstantial evidence pointing to the possibility that Dr. George Hill Hodel reinvented himself in 1969-70 San Francisco as the sadistic killer known as ZODIAC. Here is the 2014 updated evidence:

RED MASK, LADY DOOM AND "THE DEATH WHEEL"—THE TIM HOLT-ZODIAC CONNECTIONS

In the summer of 1952, comic book Volume 30 was published featuring the well-known "RKO Western Star," Tim Holt. It was one in a long series of stories featuring Tim Holt as the hero "Red Mask." This volume was entitled, **"Red Mask Meets LADY DOOM and THE DEATH WHEEL."**

On the cover below, we see Red Mask (Holt) bound with ropes as Lady Doom prepares to spin her death wheel, admonishing the gamblers to, "Place your bets gentlemen, you're playing for Red Mask." On the wheel behind him, we read the various potential manners of his death, to be determined by the spin: "By Rope, By Gun, By Knife, By Fire."

The Death Wheel cover featuring RKO's western star Tim Holt as Red Mask with Lady Doom. Vol. 30, published June-July 1952. "Manners of Death" on wheel read, "By Rope, By Gun, By Knife, By Fire." (Published by Magazine Enterprises)

Here we are introduced to LADY DOOM.

Now let's re-examine the 1970 Halloween card mailed to San Francisco reporter Paul Avery by Zodiac in light of this new information. The envelope with the strange Z symbol as a return address is postmarked "San Francisco on October 27, 1970" and addressed to "Paul Averly," a deliberate misspelling of the actual reporter's name. Reporter Avery had just written an extensive article on Zodiac which was published in the *San Francisco Chronicle* just two weeks prior, on October 12, 1970.

The envelope

On the front of the card Zodiac promises a clue to his name. The only visible alteration to the card is the number "14" seen written in black on the skeleton's right hand.

The front of Zodiac's Halloween Card

Full interior of card

Inside, Zodiac used a white marking pen and wrote mixed messages. On the left he wrote, "Peek-A-Boo, you are DOOMED!" He inserted the 13 "Spellbound Eyes" that we examined in *Chapter 21, A Surrealist Signature.* He repeated the "4-Teen" along with his signature zodiac sign, the letter Z, and repeated the strange symbol used as his return address on the envelope. (Also, note the spider web in the upper right portion of the card. I am unaware if this was part of the original card or inserted by Zodiac, but either way, I will consider its potential relevance as "a clue" in subsequent pages.)

Backs of card with promised "clue"

| Front | Interior | Back |

Full Zodiac Halloween card showing front, interior and back

Now let's reexamine the card based on the 2014 information we have from the Tim Holt/Red Mask comic book published in 1952.

1. The card was mailed by Zodiac as a direct personal threat to crime reporter Paul Avery, informing him "You are doomed." I believe this is Zodiac's singular use of that word in all of his several dozen mailings, and I would suggest when all the

additional factors are considered, it is a subtle reference and "clue" dating back to its use in the original comic book and to LADY DOOM.

2. In the original Halloween card, Zodiac drew a mask on the skeleton using *red ink*. Enlarged below we see the red mask in comparison to Tim Holt as the original Red Mask comic book hero. Again, a direct reference to the original comic book.

Zodiac using red ink, drew and inserted "red mask" on his card.

Zodiac Red Mask skeleton compared to Tim Holt as Red Mask

3. The "clues" left by Zodiac, to my mind, establish beyond any reasonable doubt that *the source and inspiration for Zodiac's 1970 threat came from this specific Tim Holt/Red Mask comic book.* The combination of his use of the red mask, "you are doomed," and the distinct phrase "By Rope, By Gun, By Knife, By Fire" seal the deal.

Red Mask and Lady Doom Death Wheel reproduced on Zodiac card

GEORGE HODEL-TIM HOLT—ZERO DEGREES OF SEPARATION

When I initially introduced the fact that actress Carol Forman and her boyfriend, actor Tim Holt, were close friends of my father, and that Carol resided with us a the Franklin House in 1948-1949 , I had no idea that Holt, a regular visitor to our home, would be later tied directly to evidence from the 1970 killer known as Zodiac.

Based on this new evidence, let's reread the original Tim Holt anecdote I presented in Chapter 10, originally published back in 2012.

Here, it is:

Carol, Tim Holt, and my Bro

My younger brother, Kelvin "Kelly" Hodel, was born in October 1942, just eleven months after the birth of my twin John and me. He would be Dorothy and George's fourth and final son. From an early age, Kelly "loved the girls," and believe me, the girls loved him. This 1949 Franklin house anecdote is appropriate:

At the time Carol was living with us at the Franklin house, she was dating film star Tim Holt. The two actors had worked together in a number of B-westerns, including the 1947 *Under the Tonto Rim* and again in 1948 on *Brothers in the Saddle*. Holt, who had just received huge critical acclaim for his role as the down-on-his-luck drifter Bob Curtin in John Huston's *The Treasure of the Sierra Madre*, naturally visited Carol at the house regularly.

Brother Kelly, then six or seven, had a terrible crush on Carol. And whenever Holt showed up to take her on a date, Kelly would object, informing him in no uncertain terms, "She's my girlfriend." Finally, Holt could take it no longer and took Kelly into the center courtyard, *mano a mano,* and made the following suggestion:

"Look Kelly. You're too young to be with Carol now. I will date her only until you get old enough. And then you and Carol can get married. And I will get on my horse and ride off. Fair enough?"

Kelly agreed. Holt and Hodel shook hands, and the battle for Carol's heart was ended—without having to fire a shot to find out which was the fastest gun alive.

As we have learned, in the 1940s and early '50s Tim Holt was not just a top Western movie star, but was also featured in various comic book publications for many years preceding his introduction as "Red Mask."

So, too, with Carol Forman, Holt's then-girlfriend, who lived for several years with us at the Sowden/Franklin House as "part of the family."

In addition to appearing in several Western films with Tim Holt, Carol also had her own independent career and was considered one of the top box office draws due to her multiple roles as a villainess. She starred as: *The Black Widow, Spider Woman,* and then in 1952, as the slinky foreign spy Laska in the comic book strip, *Blackhawk*, starring Kirk Alyn as "the Fearless Champion of Freedom." (Carol was also Alyn's co-star in his *Superman* series on film and in comics in the late '40s and early '50s.)

Here is Carol's short obituary from the *Los Angeles Times* in the summer of 1997 (http://articles.latimes.com/1997/jul/18).

Carol Forman; Actress in Movies, TV Series
July 18, 1997
Carol Forman, 78, a movie and television actress. She joined RKO Pictures in 1946 and played opposite Raymond Burr in the film "San Quentin." She also played Burr's girlfriend in his first film, "Code of the West." Other credits included "By the Light of the Silvery Moon" with Doris Day, as well as several westerns with Tim Holt. She appeared in the "Charlie Chan" series, was the Spider Lady in the "Superman" series and was perhaps best known as the lead in the "Black Widow" series. She is survived by three daughters, Lee Dennis, Suzy Dennis and Debbie Geiger. In Burbank on July 9 of natural causes.

Seen below is a clip from a Superman serial in which Carol is playing the part of the villainess, Spider Lady, said to be "as cunning as Moriarty and as venomous as a spider." Here, I have compared it to Zodiac's spider web, inserted in the 1970 Halloween card. Was George Hodel, in his role as Zodiac, leaving us another clue to his past? This time, not just to his friend, Tim Holt, but also to Holt's girlfriend, Spider Lady?

Carol Forman (1948) as Spider Lady. This film was made at the same time she was living in residence with the Hodel family at the Hollywood Sowden House, which we now know was the original crime scene where Elizabeth "Black Dahlia" Short was murdered, just one year before Carol moved to the residence.

This latest Zodiac linkage has most of the hardcore Zodiac researchers and armchair detectives scratching their heads. While most recognize the 1952 *Red Mask* comic book connection is undeniable, they remain confused about the how and why of it. In their chat rooms, on their blogs and message boards, they ask, "Why would Zodiac use a seemingly random 1952 cover of a Western comic book, as the inspiration for, and a "clue" to solving his serial murders some eighteen years later?"

I believe the information contained in my foregoing overview has provided THE ANSWER.

With Zodiac, nothing is random. The link to Tim Holt and his Red Mask character has *zero degrees of separation*. It is direct and personal. As I've said many times, the key to understanding Dr. George Hill Hodel and his many crimes are revealed through a knowledge of his past.

A FOGGY MORNING OVER SAN FRANCISCO BAY

Dr. George Hill Hodel, age 88, gazing across the Bay
from his 39th Floor Penthouse Suite, 333 Bush Street West, San Francisco

Epilogue

WITH THIS UPDATING OF THE INVESTIGATIVE FINDINGS as presented here in *Black Dahlia Avenger II*, I am going to "close the homicide book" on my father's serial crimes in and around the Southern California area in the 1940s.

As I indicated in my "Touch DNA" chapter, the ball is now in law enforcement's court.

Only time will tell if a detective from one of the multi-jurisdictions will decide to take a look and see if their cold-case evidence still exists, and then test it. If they do, I believe the chances are exceptionally strong they'll find a positive match to my father's existent DNA.

As for myself, after a short break, I will not move on but rather move back. I fully intend to continue my investigation and present more evidence I have collected over the past decade.

I anticipate *Book IV—George Hill Hodel—The Early Years* will complete my criminal investigations into the life and crimes of my father, and hopefully will provide some new light and additional closure to yet unsuspecting family members whose relatives were slain long, long ago.

Respectfully,
Steve Hodel
Los Angeles, California
February 2014

Addendum

Addendum A
1950 L.A. DA Hodel-Black Dahlia Bugging Transcripts

[147 PAGES, FEBRUARY 15 – MARCH 27, 1950]

HODEL FILE
FEBRUARY 18, 1950   10:00AM
SPool #1 Intermittant recordings while set was being installed.

HODSON

Spool
Time

0-3½ 10:05A   Hodel talking to Ellen about lawyer.
3½-5 10:15A   Talking to Ellen about marrying Susie.
-5½   Unable to understand.
      10:20A   Telephoning - unable to hear conversation.

BROWNSON

10:45A   7 minutes - telephone conversation pertaining to medical work
11:00A   11 minutes - telephone call Dr. Hodel makes appointment
         for 3:00 to 4:00 PM with Mr. Betty? Conversation with
         housekeeper.
11:45A   Trouble developed on phone line. Slop over - mostly did
         clicks - some occasional cross talk. Occasional dial tone.
         Trouble developed suddenly. Mikes still hot. Recording
         made at 24 minutes.
12:10P   Tone line cleared.

FRANK HUGHLY
February 18, 1950 12:00 noon
Spool #1 Log

12:31 Moving around the house.
12:36 Phone rang - answered - conversation at 5:30 PM-see someone
12:39 End of conversation.
12:54 Very bad reception
12:56 Moving around the house.
12:59 Typing

HODEL FILE
February 18, 1950
Spool #1 Log

Spool
Time

1:07   Calling someone - hello this is George Hodel.
1:09   End of conversation
1:11   Typing
1:13   Typing stopped - just moving around
1:18   Dialing - asking for at 66403   HI 3477 VA 9050
       Trying various numbers.
1:32   End of conversation - calling someone else - Betty
1:35   End of conversation
1:38   Moving around
1:43   Received call
1:45   Made call
50-55 1:47   End of conversation
1:50   Typing
55-58 2:00   Called someone
2:03   End of conversation
2:04   Talked with Ellen

HODEL FILE

FEBRUARY 18, 1950

TIME	SPOOL # 1	OFFICERS ON DUTY
		Crowley - LAPD

12:30A Radio plane. Lady sobbing. Hodel asked, "Do you know Charles Smith. Did you know Mr. Usher?". Hodel mentioned something about during the trial. Mentioned what housekeeper knows. "Did you know ? committed suicide"? "Does your husband know your here. Where were you going? (He was questioning her and it sounded like he was repeating her answer as if writing down her answer)

1:15A Lady reciting poetry. Hodel says something about an affair with Dr. Hodel. "Relax. Let's finish these two." Joe comes in room.

Sounds like objects dropping on floor. Crashing noises.

1:45A "Good night Joe".

2:00A All quiet.

2:00P	SPOOL # 2	OFFICERS ON DUTY
		F. Hronek-D.A's Office

2:10P In bathroom.

2:50P Out of bathroom.

3:26P Phone ringing four times. Picked up - not answered.

3:27P Answered.

3:31P Conversation with some lady about the house.

3:51P Conversation with the lady.

J. McGrath-D.A's Office

4:00P Noise around the house. Woman asking for Operator several times

4:20P Sounded as though she was crying.

4:22P No sound.

HODEL CASE - #   OFFICERS ON DUTY
J. McGrath-D.A.'s Office

4:25P Woman asking for operator again. Said something not heard,to operator.

4:26P No noise.

4:35P Someone walking around.

5:18P Man and woman talking. Could not understand.

6:05P Man and woman talking for a few minutes. (Approx. 2) Could not understand. They then left the room.

6:15P Man and woman talking. Garbled.

6:30P "Is Joe here. Joe is here, wait outside".

6:50P Man and woman talking. Woman asked the men a question. Unable to understand. He answered, "Haven't been able to find it yet. Must be around somewhere".

7:07P Someone using a typewriter.

7:08P Phone rang - Hodel said, "OK, right away, good".

7:15P Someone typing.

7:35P Conversation between two men. Recorded.

Hodel and man with a German agent had a long conversation; reception was poor, and conversation hard to understand. The following bits of conversation, however, were overheard.

Hodel to the German - "This is the best pay off I've seen between Law Enforcement Agencies. You do not have the right connections made." Hodel states,"I'd like to get a connection made in the D.A.'s office.".

General conversation between the two - "Any imperfections will be found. They will have to/made perfect. Don't confess ever. Two and two is not four.". Much laughter. "Were just a couple of smart boys". More laughter.

HODEL FILE - 4

OFFICERS ON DUTY
J. McGrath-D.A.'s office

5

Hodel then-in exact detail- explained to the German about his wife being stopped on Wednesday morning by McGrath and Morgan of the District Attorney's office when they stopped her going up her steps to the house on Franklin. It should be noted that every question asked of Mrs. Hodel was repeated ver-batum by Hodel to this German. He then began to explain to the German about his recent trial - making statements that "There's out to get me. Two men in the D.A.'s office were transferred and demoted because of my trial." Hodel then explained about his being questioned at the D.A.'s office on Wednesday morning, and told in great detail as to questions perpounded to him at that time. One statement made to the German was as follows:

"Suppposin' I did kill the Black Daliah. They couldn't prove it now. They can't talk to my Secretary anymore because she's dead."

As stated, heretofore, conversation was Marbled, and it was difficult to maintain a line of continuity of conversation. Hodel also referred to a woman in Camarillo. Conversation also referred to Communist. One point of the conversation was also "Have you heard from Powers". The man with the German acent then asked Hodel something about smoking. Hodel said, "I can't afford it - don't smoke". The German said, "I can get it for you Does the Name Hernandez mean anything to you". Hodel then talked to the German about a Furniture store on East 5th Street, where the cops come in and buy lengerie for twenty to fifty dollars. There was much laughter at this point.

8:20P   Sounded as though the two men went down steps and entered the basement and began digging. Something was referred to "Not a trace". It also appeared as though a pipe was being hit.

HODEL FILE - #

OFFICERS ON DUTY
Crowley, LAPD

9:25P   Maid questioning Hodel about her citizenship and what the immigration officers say in regards to her father. Hodel talking about a drunken judge in a pink shirt deciding the technicality of the law as far as her citizenship is concerned. Maids citizenship papers are fouled up (improper entry) Subject to deportation. Going to have a waver of documents (1947) They'll realize you acted in good faith. Hodel says, "are you hungry to go across the border?"

9:50P   Writing on typewriter.

10:00P   Turned on radio - unable to detect conversation.

10:45P   Walking - opened drawers. Started typing.

10:50P   Telephone rang. (Recorded)
"Hello Muriel, how are you dear? I'm not doing anything. (laught) I don't know of any amnesia that you have. I have had some since you were here. A couple of princesses dropped in. I took them to the Burbank to a burlesque-they really enjoyed the show. Why don't you drop by and talk to me about it sometime.

11:00P   Typing until 11:15 (steady)

11:15P   (Put on spool #4)
No conversation until 12:10AM. Spoke to lady. (Unable to hear what said). Apparently working at his desk, sounds of paper and drawers.

FEBRUARY 19, 1950   SPOOL #4   OFFICERS ON DUTY
Crowley - LAPD

12:12A   Typing.

12:17A   Conversing with lady few words (Did not get).

HODEL FILE - #

OFFICERS ON DUTY
Crowley, LAPD

12:25P   Walking and conversation with lady. (Recorded) (Maybe lady caller)

Spool Time
0-60 -SPOOL #4

12:35A   Radio still interfering. Unable to get any of the conversation.

12:40A   Lots of laughing and talking. "Don't make my drink too strong".

12:41A   Female voice - "Well I'll be darned." "Hodel-They are just trying ------?"

12:55A   Still talking to this lady - Recording it but radio too loud to hear conversation.

12:55A   George - Yes.

1:20A   Still recording conversation - Unable to pick it up over the interference of the radio.

1:21A   Girl - "You know my mother doesn't like it one bit".
Hodel - "Champagne creeps up on you".

1:25A   Mentions Brown Derby restaurant.
END OF SPOOL #4

SPOOL #5

1:28A   (Sounds like friendly conversation with lady friend, and nothing pertinent to investigation) "Lovey Dovey" tone of voice.

1:42A   Walking in house.

1:43A   Girl in bathroom.

1:45A   Talking in the distance. Then conversation ceases.

NOTE: Officer Brechel who relieved me came past Hodel's reside at 1:45AM. He observed a girl and a fellow (approx. 25 to 30 y leaving Hodel's house. They got in a 1936 Hudson sedan, license 19E 804, man driving, went W on Franklin. There is als a Fleetline Chevrolet about a 1946 grey or light green Ill. license 1303245 parked in front of the house.

HODEL FILE - #   9

OFFICERS ON DUTY
Brechel-LAPD

1:47A   In bathroom.

1:50A   Typing.

2:20A   Hodel says, "You better go to bed". Lady (probably maid) arguing. Hodel says, "you've been here 5 hours - You don't have to go through everything.

2:48A   Typing - He/said, "Just wipe off table by ashtray. I'll move the tobacco (someone wiping desk) more typing del

2:54A   Woman's voice. "I think I'll get everything". Hodel, "Yes please". Woman's voice. "I'll dust here too".

2:58A   Hodel. "You better go to bed Ellen". Typing stopped, radio turned off. Went to lavatory and urinated.

3:00A-3:30   Whistling, moving around, then all quiet.

3:45A   Snoring.

7:30A   Faint buzzer. Man's voice very faintly, probably outside door opened momentarily. Very loud, street noises. Hodel still asleep.

8:00A   J. McGrath-D.A.'s Office

10:20A   A.M. phone rang - talked to someone(personal) about coming over later in the day.

11:50A   Hodel up and around, noise in bathroom.

12:00P   Jemison-D.A.'s Office.

12:45P   Answered phone. "How long you going to be in town. I'm busy this P.M. How about this evening. Let me get in touch with Dorothy first".

12:50P   Typing 10 minutes.

12:55P   Hodel on phone says "This is Hodel. I'm going to stay around" and hangs up. "I'm listening to music" to woman's voice inquir "The soloist is up at Camarillo".

HODEL FILE - #   10

OFFICERS ON DUTY
Jemison-D.A.'s office

12:55P   "Do we have any extra blankets"Ellen---"No we have sheets only". Hodel - "Oh we haven't".

1:06P   Hodel on phone - "We'll work it out some way. Do you get off in Hollywood or Beverly Hills?" Balance not distinguished.

1:10P   Hodel-"He will be here tonite and may stay until tomorrow. You'd better make up a bed for him anyway".

1:45P   Phone rings - No conversation. ALL QUIET.

1:50P - 1:55P   Phone rings - Recorded. Hodel - "Where are you now. Sunset & Cornel. Then come to 5121 Franklin". "Yes, sure I'll do it". Hangs up.

2:00P   Hear conversation in distance or Hodel quoting poetry.

2:05P   S.M. 42421. Hodel asked for his number. "Hello Kenny, let me talk to Mrs. Hodel.

2:05P to 2:08P   Recorded. Conversation. Hodel and Mrs. Hodel. "Hello dear. How's everything. Kids alright. How's everything else? Oh, yes dear, I thought I'd come down and bring that to you that you asked for. Kenneth Rexrall called me today, your friend. Should I bring him down to your house this evening. Have you a snack for us. I'll be there at 6 or 6:30 with Kenneth. We'll leave here at 5 or 5:30.

2:12P   Sat down and relax "Kenny". But you can't pin that on me. So you come down to see Ryder. He's a collector that guy. He works for N.B.C.

2:14P   Recorded. Mr. Ryder is sure queer. Hodel-are you addressing a mass meeting or what? You'll have to sleep in the housekeeper's room. She's about this high. Laughter. "Oh we've had some dillys. Discusses chiropractors. "I don't think Dorothy cares. She has a great big living room.

HODEL FILE -

OFFICERS ON DUTY
Jemison-D.A.'s office

11

2:25P Jimmy Fitzsimons made notes. "Where are these things? What's
the name of the poem? Sounds of auto crash in street.

Off 2:29P Both leave and return. Kenny - Exflotus immortality. Hodel-
"What have been doing besides writing. Kenny - "traveling".

On 2:31P Hodel - "Did you get to Dine and the Orient."
Kenny - "No, went to England."
Unable to hear - laughter.

Off
2:35 Kenny - "You can make a lot of money in Paris. I was in Western
Europe about 1 year.

2:38P Hodel - "Did they pay your expenses". Laughter. "Hodel
was it hard making ends meet". Kenny-"No, not so bad". Hodel-
"He's a sexual character. Proably decayed bodies caused the
rancid odors and back ground setting in the Orient, in Hongkong"
Hodel discusses Chinese food.

2:40P Peter Chang on Sunset Strip has the best. Was big shot in China
Kenny-"You can't believe the terrible food situation in
England".

2:45P Hodel-"They gave a banquet and I had an interpreter and the
American Guard." Laughter. "It takes a couple months to
get thru to Hankow. Kenny-"I always wanted to see Central Asia,
but the war has been going on since the 30's."
Hodel-"Jean Lamb spent several years in Peiping. His
reports would be on desks of Chinese war lords as soon as on the
desk of the Ambassador. He was a staff officer. He then
was employed by a War Lord. 100's of cases of wrist watches.]
was bribery on a big scale. They had internal war. He was
ushered in and here was a yellow silk drapery. He spoke Chinese:

HODEL FILE -

OFFICERS ON DUTY
Jemison-D.A.'s office

12

2:45P perfectly. He met Prime Minister Hang Chow.

2:55P Jean became a great power and spent 7 years there. He was out
here. I tried to negotiate with him. Hodel-"They have a
special variety of pictures".
Kenny-"West"

Spool
Time
3:00-3:00P Phone rings. Recorded. Hodel-"Yes, I will", and hangs up.

Off-
3:03 3:05P Phone rings. No conversation. All Quiet.

3:15P Walking sounds

3:20P Hodel conversation with Ellen.
Ellen - "Mr. Hodel". Hodel-"Uh kughuh".

3:25P All Quiet.

3:30P Hodel and Kenny? Converse. Hodel-"Will you have tea or sherry?
Kenny - "Tea"
"Sipping of tea"sound.
Kenny-"This man is a heart special. He is Dr. Roth. I was to th
doctor in San Diego.

Hodel - "Read thru this, then we can discuss it more intelligently
Hodel laughs. "It has some coverage. I'm selling my
art collection Monday and Tuesday, and I'm then taking off for
Asia." Kenny-I am in process of breaking up with my wife of 15
years. No children".
Hodel-"I have 3 boys. You'll see them later. Dorothy lives here
a while, and then takes off". Kenny-"What about M".
Hodel-"She is on staff of San Francisco Chronicle. Art Editor.
had a serious operation.

HODEL FILE - 14
13
OFFICERS ON DUTY
Jemison-D.A.'s office

Spool Time		
On 3:45 -3:40P		Laughter.

Hodel-"How were they? They had great masses of hair
those whores. He was a
Hodel-"Rosey at 555 Hyde St., San Francisco, was a whor
but a honey."
Kenny-"I knew a tall one-black hair like Hollywood Blac
hair, pale pale gray eyes. I took her home. I thru
her in the bath tub - she was drunk. I massaged her.
rubbed her under the belly. I got 2 or 3 phone calls.
She got mixed up with some bad people. She called and
said the Psychiatrist was treating her. I guess I

Off 3:52-3:52P
am spoiled (Sounded tight) Dames I know all turn out
to be psychiatrists with pale gray eyes.
K. "Dr. Burns would object to your help but he gave
400 to 600 penicilien, but the reel help will come from

On 3:58P

3:58P
you." Hodel-Wouldn't he object to you coming to my ca
K. No, as you specialize in heart and you are my
friend. (Recorded)
Hodel-"Well alright.

4:00P

4:00P
Hronek-D.A.'s office

32-40	4:16P	Conversation with the patient.
40-44	4:30P	Another conversation with a man.
44-46	4:36P	Phone ringing - Hodel answers.
46-47	4:38	Very bad reception of conversation (3 men)
47-48	4:50P	Someone came in - a woman - Let's go in the other room

talking about the house.

HODEL FILM - 14
14
OFFICERS ON DUTY
Hronek, D.A.'s office

Spool Time		
48-52	4:54P	Talking with a man about some special treatment

apparently syphilis and marital troubles.

SPOOL #6 5:20P	Continuation of previous conversation.
0-6	
	5:37P	The man leaves with the instructions to call Wednesday.
	5:45P	Typewriter at work. Looking for something in the desk.
6-15	5:49P	Another man came in - talking about some girl.
15-21	6:03P	Phone rang - answered - continuation of conversation.
21-24	6:11P	Making a call - no answer.
24-33	6:27P	Conversation with his buddy. Mostly females.
	6:30P	Everything quiet.
	7:22P	Phone rang 9X No answer.

Crowley-LAPD

	7:45P	All quiet.
	8:45P	Dog barks.
	9:15P	Someone enters. Walking and noises in house.
	9:30P	Dog barking.
	9:35P	Walking in house - dog barking.
	9:36P	Lady talking in the distance.
	9:37P	Walking near "Mike".
	10:05P	Dog barks.
	11:00P	Telephone rings 4 times (No one answered)

FEBRUARY 20, 1950
BRECHEL-LAPD

| | 2:00A | All quiet from 11 PM until 2 AM. |
| | 2:00A-8:00A | All is quiet. |

HODEL FILE - Page 15

SPOOL #6   OFFICER ON DUTY
J. McGrath, D.A.'s Office

FEBRUARY 20, 1950

Spool Time

8:00A   No noise at all around house.

9:30A   No noise or activity.

9:40A   Phone rang 12 times - no answer.

9:41A   Phone rang 12 times - no answer.

10:40A   Someone enters - walking and noises in house.

10:48A   Phone rings 3 times - answered by Ellen. Took message - stated Hodel will be in 2 PM.

11:20A   Ellen enters - turns on radio - Mexican program.

11:35A   Much noise in room - sounds like sweeping - no conversation.

Sullivan, D.A.'s Office
12 noon

1:00P   All quiet.

1:15P   Telephone - 4 times - answered by maid - "You his father?" He went to beach last nite - said he'd be here early today". No further conversation.

1:35P   Phone - 3 times - answered by maid - no conversation.

2:00P   Quiet.

2:20P   Walking around - maid singing - banging noises.

2:23P   Quiet.

2:35P   Phone rings - 2 times.

2:45P   Someone entered - walked around very fast.

3:00P   Door bell rings - answered by Hodel.

33-42   Talking to unknown woman - Dials phone - Asks for some woman - Unable to hear name - Talk about renting rooms over phone - Attempting to get this one party to take both rooms - Hung up - Made another phone call - Wrong number.

HODEL FILE - 16

Spool Time

3:10P   Walks around house - water running.

3:12P   Phone rings - answered by Hodel - Unable to identify who he was talking to.

42-44

3:14P   Whistling and rustling of papers.

3:25P   Phone rings - answered by Hodel.

44-45   Looks for phone # TR 1252.

3:28P   Phone rings - answered by Hodel - Unable to connect conversation.

45-45½

3:30P   Phone - Answered by Hodel. Called person on other end "Baby Doll".

45½-46

3:45P   Stanton - Crime Lab here; working on set to eliminate hum.

4:00P   Talking to maid - something about post office, unintelligible- typewriter going. Machine off - being worked on by Stanton.

4:01P

4:08P   Machine back in operation - typing.

4:09P   Phone rings - "Rex Kane mentioned - Mr. Butlers name mentioned "What 2 boxes represent - Will get a little more information - Will call back".

46-50

4:15P   Walter Morgan - D.A.'s office relieves

4:20P   Conversation - 27464 - gave number of his phone.

4:21P   Telephoned - conversation unintelligible - airplane passing over.

4:22P   Talking to maid - "Close to Mexico".

HODEL FILE - 17

SPOOL #7

Spool Time		
	4:25P	Spool #7
	4:30P	Typewriter noise.
	4:35P	Unintelligible conversation with maid.
	4:48P	Telephone rang - was answered by Hodel - short conversation about price of tea.
	4:58P	Began typing.
0-1	5:05P	Conversation with maid - Typing.
1-3.5	5:08P	" " " "
3.5-5	5:14P	" " " "
5-6	5:16P	" " " "
6-8	5:18P	" " " "
8-11	5:28P	Telephone rang - answered by Hodel - conversation about "Units".
11-27.5	5:45P	Telephone rang - answered by Hodel - conversation about crime prevention; Delinquent accounts; Dr. E.M. DeLong's October 1948 account; Blood and spinal fluids; employment of Collector; Hodel's stock ownership in a company - maid entered conversation about time; Hodel stated that it was six o'clock, that he had to leave at seven, that he would be back at twelve - begins to type.
27.5-28.5	6:13P	Noise like writing on paper.
28.5-29.5	6:18P	Hodel asked maid to close door.

HODEL FILE - 17

Spool Time		
29.5-30.5	6:20P	Telephone rang - answered by Hodel - asked what the score was - ended with goodnight.
30.5-34	6:27P	Hodel asked for Sycamore 60647 (Unrecorded) - Gave operator Olympia 3476; Asked for Cris; Conversation about taking place; Hodel has another party anxious to take place - ended with "So Long".
34-42	6:23P	Dialing of phone - Hodel asked for Mrs. Montgomery - conversation about getting place in one or two days, "Just a minute, hold on", pause in conversation- Desk noise - continued conversation - ended with "Good Nigt
	6:52P	Hodel said "Already, O.K."(Not Recorded)
42-44.5	6:53P	Hodel said "Get some from _____"
	6:55P	Hodel said, "O.K. be right with you" (Not Recorded)
44.5-45	6:56P	Desk noise - Hodel walking away - door slams.
	7:20P	Stanton changed recorders.
45-45.5	7:30P	Shower noise
	8:00P	Crowley, LAPD, on duty, relieves Morgan, D.A.
	8:10P	Walking in house.
	8:18P	Walking - door slams.
	8:30P	Walking in house.
	8:35P	Loud noises in desk.
	8:40P	Someone turns radio on.
	8:45P	Crowley and Morgan note that phone # OL 3476 that Hodel charged call to at 6:27PM this date differed from # NO 27464 which he gave at 8:50PM, on 2-18-50. (He gave # 27464 to the party who was inquiring about renting the

HODEL FILE -
Spool
Time

studio, gave the address as 5123 Franklin Ave.) Morgan dialed the above OL 3476 from this telephone, and Hodel answered "Hello". (Morgan can positively identify the voice). Morgan asked, "Is this OL 3746", and Hodel answered, "No, this is OL 3476", to which Morgan replied "I'm sorry, I have the wrong number". Crowley was unable to hear any sound whatsoever from Hodel's residence during this conversation - Crowley then called Lt. Hale at Business Office, and was informed that OL 3476 is a non published secret number, registered to Dr. George Hodel at 5121 Franklin Ave.

9:00P All quiet except for radio (playing classical music).
9:07P Door closes.
9:10P Lady talking in distance (sounds like maid's voice) It sounded as though she said "are there any more cops around". Heard no answer. (Not Recorded) End of conversation.
9:49P Walking - door closes.
9:55P Walking - other noises.
10:07P Radio - stops playing.
10:25P Door closes - walking - turns radio on - changes stations then turns it off.
10:40P All quiet.
10:47P Someone moving around. Doors open - close. More walking.
11:00P Sound of someone's movements in house.

19

HODEL FILE -
Spool
Time

11:24P Door slams - someone's movements in house - goes to bathroom-urinates.
11:45P Walking in house - radio turned on.
11:55P Minneapolis Symphony orchestra playing. Station KFAC.
12:30A Door closes - radio still playing.
12:55A Walking in house.
1:05A Radio stops playing.
1:07A Loud noises in desk - walking.
1:25A Walking in house.
1:45A All quiet.
1:49A Walking in house.
1:50A Brechel, LAPD, on duty, relieves Crowley
45.5- 2:15A Loud noises. Hodel talking to maid. Hodel-"I never found
49.00   your keys. Have you looked for them?" Maid, "Yes".
Off   2:20A Hodel at desk going thru papers. cusses, to himself.
              Sorting of papers in desk.
       2:30A Still sorting papers. Closes drawer. Opens other drawer.
              Searching for something in desk.
       2:35A Hodel goes to lavatory. Urinates.
       2:40A Hodel in bedroom with someone, probably Ellen.
              Hodel - "No use working hard". Other whispered conversation
              unable to make out. Hodel goes in bathroom - runs water.
              Conversation with Ellen.
49.00- 2:45A Whispered conversation - recorded. Loud noises.
51.25   Unable to make out conversation.

20

HODEL FILE - 2   21

FEBRUARY 21, 1950

Spool Time

51.25-54.00	2:55A	Noises at desk. Hodel speaking, unable to make out due to pounding noise.
	3:10A	Sounds of numerous drawers opening and closing in different parts of the house.
	3:25A	Sounds of walking about the house.
	3:30A	Movements in house cease.
	3:45A	Alls quiet. Snoring (Hodel in bedroom)
	4:50A	Snoring ceases - alls quiet.
	5:00A	Some disconnected noises. Hodel tossing in bed or reading.
	5:45A	Hodel yawns and resumes snoring.
	6:05A	Snoring ceases - alls quiet.
	6:45A	Snoring resumes.

HODEL FILE - 2   22

FEBRUARY 21, 1950, 8:00 AM

J. McGrath, D.A.'s office on duty

Spool Time

49-50	10:55A	Telephone rang - answered by Hodel - said "Hello" then began to walk around and make a lot of noise.
50-55	11:00A	Conversation - sounds like Ellen arguing - unable to hear while recorder on.
	11:10A	Changing wire - doubt if conversation was recorded.
	11:10A	No conversation - just loud noise in house.
SPOOL 8		Started 11:15 AM
	11:20A	Conversation between Hodel and Ellen - unable to understand - not recording - can't tell if recorder is working.
	11:30A	Conversation - Hdel and Ellen.
0-4	11:30A	Telephone answered by Hodel - gave directions to other part. Attempting to rent room
4-7	11:40A	Telephone - answered by Hodel - unable to identify other party.
	11:50A	Telephone conversation - garbled.
	11:50A	Sullivan - D.A.'s office on duty
	12:00noon	Hear Hodel muttering to himself.
7-9½	12:15P	Testing by Neblo Crime Lab.
9½-10		
10-11½	12:50P	Conversation with Ellen - unintelligible - "I like potatoes".
	12:55P	Moving around - noises
	1:00P	Bad hum in set - Ellen talking but unintelligible.
10½-19		Words between Dr. and maid, "I would call American Counsel if I had money. Discussing her citizenship problems. Maid doing considerable talking - unintelligible.

HODEL FILE - 23

Spool	Time	
	1:10P	Typewriter operating.
19-22 to 22½	1:15P	Conversation by maid - much noise.
	1:20P	Conversation by maid with Hodel.
	1:30P	Noises in room - considerable hum on receiver.
22½-26	1:31P	Conversation between Hodel and Mail - regarding Mexico.
	1:40P	Sounds like water running for past 4 or 5 minutes. Can hear Hodel's voice in background but unintelligible.
	1:55P	Hodel muttering, and water running.
	2:20P	Typewriter.
26-33	2:21P	Phone - Doctor answers. - talks about architecture - talking about selling house.
33-35	2:25P	Typing
	2:55P	Conversation between Hodel and Maid. Complaining of having to do housework.
	3:05P	Typing.
	3:15P	Typing continues.
	3:30P	Hear maid talking in background - hum in set continues.
35-38	3:35P	Hodel and maid talking. Unintelligible due to hum.
38-39	3:38P	Conversation with maid (Recorded).
		Ended recording - nothing being said.
39-40	3:40P	Hodel and maid talking.
	3:48P	Typing
	4:00P	Crime lab boys here - working on hum.
	4:00P	Hronek - D.A.'s office relieving Sullivan
SPOOL 9	4:20P	L.A.P.D. lab men left.

HODEL FILE - 24

Spool Time		
0-4	4:36P	Phone rang - Hodel answers (Patient)
	4:40P	Starts typing again.
4-16	4:44P	Phone rang - Hodel answers.
	4:55P	Starts typing again.
	5:32P	Typing stopped
	5:45P	Typing resumed
	6:15P	Typing stopped - Hodel moving around in the background.
	8:00P	Lewis, LAPD, relieving Hronek (Spool time 16)
	8:17P	Phone rang twice - no one answered.
	8:50P	Radio playing - station KFAC
	9:30P	Radio - still playing - classical music.
	10:45P	Radio off
16-22	10:47P	Maid on phone wants to talk to American Consul in Mexico. Gave OL phone (Recorded)
	11:10P	Someone went toilet - No further talking on phone. Call never completed.
	11:15P	Radio started playing.
	12:10A	Radio turned off.
	12:35A	Someone walking about house.
	12:50A	Heard Hodel voice first time tonite - "Said leave that on".
	1:15A	A lady gave big "Ho-Hum" also lots of noise like slamming drawers and prying lids off of Wooden boxes. Also sawing.
	1:45A	Hodel told Maid she had better go to bed.
		5 minutes - wire used - 2 PM end watch for Lewis

HODEL FILE -
FEBRUARY 22, 1950

25

Spool Time

	2:00A	
	2:10A	Brechel, LAPD on duty
		Hodel and Ellen enter room.
22-40	2:12A	Hodel - "Will you leave that light on there, I'm just a little nervous". Hodel- "I suppose its asking a little too much". Conversation with Ellen recorded. Hodel - "What that you got there". Whistling. Hodel- "Thats a lot of nonsense". Ellen talks back. Water runnin Hodel has conversation with Ellen - asks if something is too difficult. Hodel says he is worried. Hodel - "You don't need this razor". Ellen - "Maybe you better leave it".
	2:20A	Conversation regarding cutting garment and sending it to laundry. Recorded.
	2:23A	Hodel asks if red coat is still at cleaners. Ellen thinks she sees it (apparently both are searching a closet) Conversation recorded.
7:25A	2:25A	Hodel is asking Ellen if she can stitch. Ellen replies she knows well enough. Ellen admires a chinese box. Hodel says a manchurian princess gave it to him. He says he is going to sell it. Ellen asks for taste.
	2:27A	
Off	2:29A	Ellen wants to stay with him, he tells her to go to bed, she can stay with him tomorrow.
	2:32A	Movements around room. Low conversation unable to make out
	2:35A	Deep breathing. Hodel and Ellen probably having intercourse.

HODEL FILE -
FEBRUARY 22, 1950

26

Spool Time

40-43	2:40A	Ellen says she wants to go now. Hodel says she should have gone to her room. He is pretty well tired. Sounds indicates movements on bed.
off		
43-49.5	2:45A	Deep breathing. Movements on bed. Definite sounds of climax of intercourse. Hodel sighs loudly and passionately.
	2:49A	Hodel and Ellen talking. Ellen wants him to stay with her all night. She begs him. He says no, he is tired.
Off	2:51A	Alls quiet.
	3:10A	Sounds of light snoring. Not Hodel.
	3:40A	Sounds indicate someone moving about.
	3:45A	Alls quiet.
49.5 to 51.5	7:55A	Phone is dialed. Hodel does not speak, but a female voice on phone is not distinct (recorded). This may be Ellen using kitchen phone as Hodel not up yet.
off	8:10A	Hodel arises, goes to lavatory.
	8:00A	J. McGrath - D.A.'s office on duty
	8:33A	Phone rings - Hodel answers - told someone to write to Consumers Research, Washington New Jersey, Hung up.
51.5- 53.5	8:35A	Conversation with Ellen - could not understand (recorded)
	9:08A	Very heavy breathing or gasping by Hodel as if a nervous dream. About 6 times.
53.5- 56	9:55A	Phone rang - Hodel answered - recorded. Said will borrow some money and send you $10.00. Said he would try to come down and get the fish.

HODEL FILE - 26
FEBRUARY 22, 1950
SPOOL 10

Spool
Time

10:30A   Put on Spool #10

0-10.8 10:47A   Phone call - Hodel answered - recorded - Hodel did little
talking - just kept stating, "Uh-huh" "Uh-huh" Did you
see Dr. Burns since I've see you. Does he feel I'm
interfering? hope he does not resent - talking to
Theodore - said when reports comes at 1 PM today or
tomorrow will contact you - When we won't be disturbed.

11:00A   Hodel urinated - took shower.

11:23A   Hodel typing.

11:50A   Hodel said "Let's see the phone is CR 5527 or 5537
Ellen phoned and said, are you open tonight. "Uh after 6"
Then Hodel said to Ellen you go tomorrow night, at 9 PM.

12:00noon   Horgan on duty.

12:10P   Unintelligible conversation between two men (Hodel and ?-
2 minutes).

12:21P   Hodel - "There must be something" Ellen - "There isn't
anything" Hodel- "I'm pretty sure there is something".
Recorded.

12:26P   Hodel - "Straighten up that room in there - just the way it
was before".

10.8-14.6   12:35P   Telephone rang - Hodel - "Oh yeah Power - are you in town -
good - things are sort of busy right now for the next ten
days - we're tapped now again - well there is pretty much
going on regarding yourself and me - I was questioned about
you and so forth - maybe you can find out - Don't you know

HODEL FILE - 27
FEBRUARY 22, 1950

Spool
Time

12:35P   someone up there? Maybe you can find out what .he hell
is-going-on-up-there. I would like to see you in person
when we get a chance - what's your phone? That's your new
phone? (Ends) "OK - so long".

14.6-16/8   12:58P   Telephone rang - Hodel - "Hello, yeah, yeah, yeah".
Pause - "yeah, yeah, that's the only thing to tell em -
don't say a single thing - who was it? - Sullivan?
be polite, be very nice but say you can't tell em a thing
without your lawyer's advice. O.K.".

16.8-17   Blank.

17-18.5 1:10P   Conversation between Hodel and Ellen (unintelligible)
Noise - airplane noise.

18.5-19.5   1:36P   Conversation between Hodel and Ellen (partly unintelligible)

2:00P   Hodel in bathroom - running water.

19.5-24   2:32P   Telephone rang - Hodel - conversation about sales "what
sort of a place did you find? In Santa Monica? Conversa-
tion about $1320. "I already sent him a letter - see you
maybe over the week end" (Ends "U.D. Dad")

24-25   2:54P   Telephone rang - Hodel - I can't call you back? Can you
call me from an outside phone? Call you back where you are
now in about ten minutes.

4:00P   Only sound is from radio playing, station KFAC, 4:00 PM
recorded. XXXXXXX BRUNNSON on duty, 4:00 PM
Occasional sound of a person moving about the room.

HODEL FILE - 28

FEBRUARY 22, 1950

29

Spool Time		
25	8:00P	Lewis on duty - radio playing
25-27.5	9:00P	Hodel come in room - talks to maid "Low" She wants to know what happened - he did not answer. Radio still playing (Recorded)
27.5-30.8	9:24P	Phone rang - maid answered - said Chris is here. (Recorded) No word yet. "Could hear someone whistling. Radio real loud. Could not make out what else was said.
30.6-35.8	9:40P	Phone rings 3 times - maid said call half hour - no more talking - someone in toilet - flush same. Some one walking xxxxxxx heavy and fast - radio - still playing.
35.8-37.5	10:10P	Phone rang - maid answers. (Recorded) What was said - but could not make it out as radio still very loud.
	10:34P	Hodel yelled - is that door locked. Maid answered, "No do you want to come in" Hodel said "No" Maid said, "Why did you want to know" (No answer)
	11:28P	Radio turned off - everything quiet.
	1:45A	Hodel walk about house-finally goes to toilet - after using toilet he flushes it, then walks about house again. Slams a door and is talking real low to himself (unable to understand him)
	2:00A	Lewis - end of watch.
xxxxxxxxxxxxxx	2:00A	Brechel, LAPD, on duty
	2:90A	Hodel walking about the bedroom.
	2:30A	Hodel asleep. Snoring. Alls quiet.

HODEL FILE -

FEBRUARY 23, 1950

SPOOL #10

30

Spool Time		
	8:00A	Jim McGrath-D.A.'s Office on duty
	8:55A	Phone ringing - Hodel snoring. Hodel did not wake up to answer - still snoring.
	9:07A	Someone (sounds like womans footsteps) enters room (probably living room).
	9:35A	Phone rang - no answer.
	10:10A	Phone ringing - 8 times - no answer.
	10:12A	Someone walking around - sounds like Hodel - conversation between Hodel and Ellen about going to store. Not recorded.
37-40	10:23A	Conversation with someone by Hodel. Phone did not ring, and he didn't dial, but sounded like phone conversation. (Recorded) Said she is my maid - you know she is peculiar - talked like he was asking for medical help.
40-41	10:27A	(Recorded) Hodel talking - it appears to Telephone Co. complaining about maid making long distance phone calls.
41-44	10:28A	Recorded. Hodel phoned someone asked for $1000.00 cash advance - said he was short of ready cash.
44-44.5	10:35A	Dialed phone - asked for a number - sounded like Insurance #451651.
44.5-48.5	10:41A	Telephone rings - said, "How are you Miss Montgomery - talk about getting a house. Read note he said he found on his desk. Said he will call tomorrow.

HODEL FILE - 31

Spool
Time

48.5-57 10:47A Phone rings - answered by Hodel - asks about a letter - talk about architecture - says he has been selling some antiques - says he will send some money.

SPOOL #11

0-2 11:05A Conversation with Ellen - says, "I haven't any money. I will have to sell everything".

2-12 11:09A Hodel and Ellen (recorded) in a conversation. Regarding Ellens phone calls to the Mexican Consulate. Hodel have her hell - said to write letters instead of phoning - raised hell about the bills from the Phone Company - also txixkxkxx told her to never talk over the phone.

12-14 11:23A (Recorded) Hodel phones someone (Neebs) Neebs not in.

14-14.5 11:27A Phone rang - Hodel answered, said "Yes, I'll be there at :

14.5-16 11:33A Hodel and Ellen - talk regarding a form she received about a street car accident - told her to say she did not see anything - throw the form away. (Recorded)

11:55A Hodel typing.

12:00noon Snyder-Sullivan. D.A's office on duty.

12:15P Hodel still typing.

12:50P Hodel calls Ellen (recorded) Unintelligible.

12:52P Quiet.

12:55P Typing.

1:00P Phone rings - Hodel answers (recorded) tables and chairs to go - asks for address - expects to give someone money by Wednesday - selling tea.

HODEL FILE - 32

Spool
Time

1:05P End of telephone conversation.

23-24 1:10P Talking to Ellen (recorded)

1:11P Hodel typing.

1:20P Phone rings - Hodel answers - short - wrong number.

1:25P Phone rings - apparently in remote part of house. Could barely hear it.

1:30P Hodel talks to Ellen - unintelligible - very few words.

1:33P Someone moving furniture around - hell of a racket - (P.S. not recorded)

Someone climbing down and up stairs.

24-25.5 1:42P Hodel talks to someone (Recorded)

25.5-27 1:45P Order a suit of blue - talk by a Charlie China type 5121 - conversation by Hodel (recorded) Delivery in about a week.

27-28 1:48P Hodel calls Department of Commerce - calls information.

1:50P Hodel calls on phone (recorded) Will be out 5 or 6 PM (Recorded)

1:52P Hodel dials phone - calls Mr. Neeb - wants to go to offic Will not be able to this week (not recorded)

28-32 1:55P Hodel dials phone - Department of commerce (recorded) in regards selling car in Mexico.

32-33 2:05P Hodel dials phone - car to Mexico City - talks to F.B.I. (recorded)

33-35.5 2:07P Hodel dials phone - in regards purchase of Packard car (recorded) (P.S..he wants to go to Mexico City) RO 2-7454.

35.5-37 2:12P Phone rings - Hodel answers - in regards Packard car. (recorded)

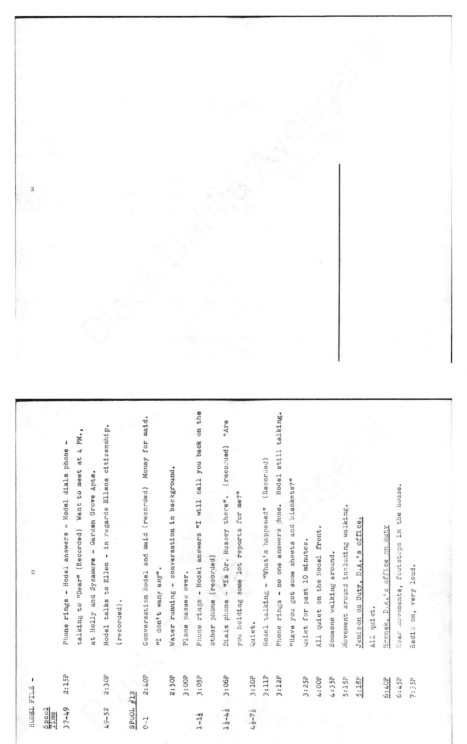

MODEL FILE -

Spool
Time

37-49   2:15P   Phone rings - Model answers - Model dials phone - talking to "Dear" (Recorded) Want to meet at 4 PM., at Holly and Sycamore - Garden Grove Apts.

49-52   2:30P   Model talks to Ellen - in regards Ellens citizenship. (recorded).

SPOOL #12

0-1   2:40P   Conversation Model and maid (recorded) Money for maid. "I don't want any".

2:50P   Water running - conversation in background.

3:00P   Plane passes over.

1-1½   3:05P   Phone rings - Model answers "I will call you back on the other phone (recorded)

1½-4½   3:06P   Dials phone - "Is Dr. Hussey there". (recorded) "Are you holding some lot reports for me?"

4½-7½   3:10P   Quiet.

3:11P   Model talking - "What's happened" (Recorded)

3:12P   Phone rings - no one answers phone. Model still talking. "Have you got some sheets and blankets?"

3:25P   Quiet for past 10 minutes.

4:00P   All quiet on the Model front.

4:35P   Someone walking around.

5:15P   Movement around including walking.

5:13P   Jemison on Duty, D.A.'s office.

6:40P   Kronek, D.A.'s office on duty.

6:45P   Rear movements, footsteps in the house.

7:35P   Radio on, very loud.

HODEL FILE -

35

Spool Time		
26-28.5	10:36P	Someone knock - Hodel said, come in - some man entered unable to understand conversation.
28.5-59.5	10:44P	Hodel and some man sounds like talking about going fishing or about pictures of fish - lot of noise. Talking about fastest bird - animal and fish and hos fast they are. Hodel - "Were going to try to get the big house out here. Skid-row - Pasadena - case of Bowron - Dug out - can't stay forever. Don't know - Well "Tom" - Police Department My moving from house - 3 very large bedrooms - There are twelve bedrooms. Pasadena - Santa Monica - (Talking about houses) 25,000 - 30,000. The grounds are kind of deteriorated. I have to use the car.
	11:30P	Radio playing.
	12:05A	Walking-noises at desk.
	12:35A	Typing - radio playing.
	12:46A	Hodel and maid speak a few words - cannot understand.
	1:02A	Radio turned down. (Volume)
	1:15A	Walking - Hodel and Ellen in conversation (distance)
	1:25A	Walking
	1:45A	Hodel and Ellen talking (unable to hear) Something about a model.
	1:51A	Typing.

HODEL FILE -

36

Spool #13

Spool Time		
0-1.5	1:55A	Lewis, LAPD on duty.
	2:15A	Hodel and maid talking. Hodel asked, "Did you look in the little box in there.
	2:20A	Hodel using typewriter - radio playing.
1.5-3 Wire broke	2:25A	Phone rang - Hodel "Yes Dear, How are you, what trouble Tell me all about it. I can't understand it. I guess tha finishes it, impossible, see you later.
new wire	2:30A	Hodel says to Maid - You going to bed dear. Hodel now typing.

Spool #14

0-1	2:50A	Hodel to maid, "Come on - you better go to bed". Hodel still typing.
	2:55A	Hodel - "You had better go bed now." Maid said, "OK" Hodel said, "Good night sweet". Everything quiet. No more typing.
	3:10A	Door opened - Hodel says "Aren't you going to bed for Chri sake - Hodel yells "O Manuel" Now quiet again.
	3:45A	Hodel snoring.
	6:00A	Everything still quiet.

HODEL FILE - 37

FEBRUARY 24, 1950
SPOOL #14

Spool	Time	
17-19	1:20P	Sullivan, D.A.'s office on duty

Dials phone (recorded) asks for a new car salesman. What is that car for $1587.00 - How much more with seats in back - $75.00. I've got a 1936 Packard Sedan to trade in. Want to make Packard down payment No chance - Will see you Mr. Shington.

1:25P Talking to maid - having lunch - maid talks about fix Hodel asks for lemons.

19-20 1:30P Phone rings - Hodel answers (recorded) "I'll be ther in 15 minutes. Let me come anyway".

1:31P Phone rings. Hodel answers (No conversation)

1:34P Talks to maid "I got to leave right away".

1:48P Phone rings - maid answers - Hodel tells her to tell party be just left.

1:55P Phone rings - maid answers - "He will be back in abot 1½ hours".

20-24 2:35P Someone enters - sounds like maid - answered phone - unable to hear conversation.

2:38P Ellen dialed information - asked for number of immigration office - dialed phone - asked to speak to Mr. P----- Apparently out - asked person on phone to have him call her back on NO 27464.

HODEL FILE - 38

Spool	Time	
	3:15P	Quiet.
	3:25P	Phone rings once - answered apparently in some other part of house.

3:40P Phone rings several times - hear no answer.

3:41P Phone rings several times - hear no answer.

3:50P Phone rings twice - hear no answer.

24-28½ 3:55P Hodel and maid talking - (Recorded). About her citizenship.

4:00P Hronek, D.A.'s office on duty

28½-30½ 4:02P MU 9077 - Hodel dials over - Is Marian there. Hello desk.

31-34 4:05P Tries to dial - phone rings - Hodel answered

34-35½ 4:07P Phone rings - Hodel answered. I'd love to have you when it'd be - around 9 or 10? Operator AT 66402

35½-36½ This is OL 3476

4:11P Hello, Mrs. Clark?

4:20P Hodel starts typing.

36½-51½ 4:25P Phone rings - Hodel answered - Ellen took over - still talking about the citizenship, Ellen, didn't I tell you not to tell people things over the telephone. Hodel ordered Ellen not to answer any questions over the telephone - Hodel calls NO 27464. Ellen argues with Hodel that lots of people cross the border without papers. Hodel orders the maid not to let anybody in the office. Then starts typing again. Ellen said something about the FBI investigating us.

HODEL FILE = 39

39

Spool Time		
	4:44P	Hodel dials and out to some Mr. Blumfield.
	4:50P	Start Spool #15
	4:50P	Typing
	6:14P	Phone rings, stops before Hodel lifts the receiver.
0-1	6:26P	Hodel dials - asks for Lyn report.
1-2½	6:28P	Hodel - Hello Margaret - are you with the patient. I would like for you to stop by - Maybe next week.
2½-8½	6:32P	Hodel dials - What's the number of Hojas & Cuttle 7100 Beverly Blvd? Talks about car. What's your name? Anderson - That's easy to remember. Hear Hodel moving around the house.
	7:10P	Meyer, L.A.P.D. on duty
	8:00P	
8½-9½	8:58P	Phone rings. Ellen answers - unable to understand wt or what she says.
9½-31	10:18P	Some girl introduced Hodel to some girl named Mickey talking unable to understand, said something about China tea, two drinks, another man around.
	10:28P	Phone rings - Hodel answers - couldn't understand too well. Come over tomorrow - call before you come after supper some time - have a pencil handy. OL 3476. Good - so am I - will you do that? I will try to keep tomorrow open. (Bangs up) Hodel talks- She graduated from school in Detroit with top honors- what did I have for desert?
	10:35P	Phone rings - Hodel answers - Yes, Why? I would say Just forget it all - put some Hillbilly music on - left room, radio on.

SPOOL #15

40

Spool Time		
31-32½	10:45P	Taling about records - put more records on.
32½-33½	10:49P	Phone rings - Hodel answers - yes, sure, absolutely. I don't really care - just forget the whole thing. Talk about records again. Put more on.
33½-34.2	10:51P	
34½-35	10:55P	Talk about records again. Put more on.
35-36½	11:04P	Girls talking - I only had a glass of tea.
36½-41	11:06P	Girls talking - Hodel talking to girls - lot of noise - radio on loud.
41-42	11:11P	Talking - radio on too loud - can't hear.
42-44½	11:22P	Hodel asks girls if want fire on - turns fire on - girl asks, haven't heard anything further, have you? Someone typing.
44½-45	11:31P	Hodel - reaching for something? Radios on very loud.
45-50	11:40P	Hodel - come here a second. Hear opening desk. Othe girl enters. Girl-"Is this a private conversation? Hodel-"Boy, it is a juicy conversation, what do you want to know". Girl-"I like to be exposed gradually" Hodel-"How many did you have"? Girl-"52"
	11:51P	Spool ran out on 56. Meyer changed spool - just small talk. couldn't hear too well.

SPOOL #16

| 1-10 | 11:57P | Hodel and girl talking - unable to understand. Radio is all can hear. |

HODEL FILE - 41

Spool	Time	
10-11	12:08A	That is Shirley's work.
11-21½	12:10A	Hodel-"Did you ever hear this record?" Played recor sounded like home made, something about humanity??? Played some records of poems. Hodel had recorded.
21½-22½	12:22A	Hodel and girl talking about poems, one girl starts reading poems. Hodel says she is pretty good. Then Hodel reads a poem.
22½-27	12:30A	Still reading poems. Hodel and girl. talking about
27-32	12:39A	poems is read to each other.
	12:45A	Still talking about poems - one girl says she read better then Hodel. One girl read them finish Hodel said "Yes - H - Chrisy" then Hodel said, "I can read better setting by a beauty - noise - then Hodel reads poem.
32-32½	12:51A	Talk about poem he just read, reads some more.
32½-47½	12:58A	Hodel finishes. Girl says - "It is a morbid poem," talk about poem. Hodel says - "you read next one". Talk about records. Hodel says he has some. Girl says "go get them" Sounds like someone leaving. Talk about some onegetting a divorce. Starts reading again. Hodel - "I own 51% of the stock - talking about Asia - more small talk - played Chinese soundir music.

HODEL FILE - 42
FEBRUARY 25, 1950

Spool	Time	
47½-48½	1:16A	Talking about records - play some - sounds like a cat fight - or a bunch of wash tube.
48½-50	1:19A	Hodel says something about a sweater looking nice. More music - unable to hear talk.
50-56	1:24A	Talk about "Carrey Grey"? Hodel says, "who is that?" Bath room and radio on at same time - music - so changed spool - then talk about music.

FEBRUARY 25, 1950
SPOOL #7

0-27	1:36A	Talking about some place ideal - people from 48 stat come - a wonderful oporunity - Santa Barbara one ti I waited two years (Hard to hear them) somex other man talking - "I was guest artist one time". Girl - "you can't worry about that". Talking about China - Man - "married 4 months. That was enough". Hodel comes back in - talk about drawing. Hodel says for a beginner is pretty dam good.
27-39	2:00A	Lewis, L.A.P.D. on duty
	2:00A	Big party going on - several girls and men talking. Hard to understand but being recorded. Some girl ea "Good night Jerry". Party seems to be breaking up as everyone is saying Goodnight.
	2:12A	Everything quiet - outside of one person walking about room.
39-62	2:14A	Hodel and another man talking about a girl - use to be attorney for Barba Sherman. She is wonderful dancer - she married a Swiss Counselor. Hodel talki about taking girls to South America 3 months - they be ready for singing - light opera. I have a way ab

HODEL FILE - 43

Spool Time

me. I can arrange ti with there folks. I have so many girls I like to have a rest for awhile. Seen as though Hodel and this other man are talking about Traveling with these girls. Hodel said he like to see parent of each girl and get permission in writing from them to allow girls to travel. Made arrangement to meet again Sunday and talk further on agreements. Would like to give it a trial in Mexico City. if you have girls over Sunday have them bring photograph of themselves. Talking about they could stay in best hotels and make at least 2500 per week. Hodel- "hard job is talking to parents". Hodel says - I will be the tough guy and you be the great guy. Hode says - I will have arias. They laugh and Hodel says- let's go to bed. They leave room and everythings qu: Hodel snoring "And loud".

End Spool 17 2:35A

3:30A

SPOOL #18

6:20A Someone up - walking about house. go into bathroom and use toilet - then flush same. Then sound like knocking on a door. Person is Mr. Hodel. Identified by his cough.

6:30A Everything quet.

0-5 6:50A Hodel knocks on Ellen's door - ask "are you up". She answers "You want in?" He states, "No, I won't start nothing now - how about 12 o'clock. Huh?"
(part talk recorded)

HODEL FILE - 44

Spool Time

Spool	Time	
0.5	7:40A	Dog barking as if it had someone cornered.
	8:00A	Lewis, L.A.P.D. off duty
	8:00A	J.McGrath, D.A.'s office on duty
	10:17A	Noise around home - sounded as though someone made a phone call from rear of house. Hodel is up.
	10:28A	Hodel made phone call - asked for "Andy Anderson".
	10:40A	Some man said to Hodel - "Andy Anderson called you". Hodel said to this man - "Tell him I'll call him back
0.5-1	10:42A	Hodel phoned Andy Anderson (recorded) about a car deal of some kind. Hodel said, "Oh no, just send me back my check and I will start fresh".
1-2	11:24A	Hodel phoned (recorded) someone asked if Dr. Bussey there. Gave phone, OL 3476, to call back.
2-4	11:27A	Hodel made phone call - asked for the Simmons Co. Wrong number - said, is this (something) 7778.
	11:28A	Made another call - no answer.
	11:45A	Sullivan, D.A.'s office on duty
	1:20P	Phone rings - unable to hear conversation. Can hear talking in background.
	1:30P	Phone rings 4 times - hear no conversation.
	1:40P	Can hear some men talking in background.
	1:48P	Phone rings - sounds muffled - rang one - record no conversation.
	2:00P	Someone walking around. Maybe Hodel.
	3:20P	Phone rings 4 times - No answer.
	4:00P	Bronek, D.A.'s office - on duty

HODEL FILE - 45

Spool
Time

4:30P	No movements
5:00P	No movements
5:30P	No movements
6:00P	No movements
6:19P	Phone rings 7 times. No answer.
6:30P	No movements
7:00P	No movements
7:01P	Phone rang 10 times - no answer
7:17P	Phone rang 10 times - no answer
7:30P	No movements
7:51P	Phone rang 9 times - no answer
8:00P	No movements
6:00 PM	All Quiet Meyer, L.A.P.D. on duty
8:22P	Phone rings 6 times - no answer
9:00P	All Qdet
9:17P	Sounds like Hodel and someone returns home. Hodel says he has a lot of work to do - moving around.
6-11½ 9:20P	Hodel and woman talking and moving - woman talking about a skirt - Hodel says, leave it here
	Girl - "Have to use bath room - (and she did to)
11½-23 9:35P	Hodel and Ellen talking quite low - unable to understand sounds as though Ellen is crying.
13-13½ 9:47P	Phone rings - Hodel answers - will try to make it over later - it will be a latish party wont it? Will look at it from a distance, yes, later. Good bye - then Hodel dials phone, but no answer.
10:05P	All quiet - sounds as though Hodel is reading or going over papers of some kind.

HODEL FILE - 46

Spool
Time

13½-14½ 10:19P	Hodel dials phone - Hello, I just got back to town, hate to bother you so late, do you have report for me? 224, yes, yes, thank you very much. Hodel then uses typewriter.
10:30P	Hodel moving around house.
11:09P	Hodel moving around house.
11:15P	Ellen turns radio on. Hodel asks, can't you do any better than that? Quiet ----
11:30P	Hodel dials phone - no answer - uses typewriter.
11:35P	Hodel turns radio up not too loud - Are you tired.
	Ellen-"no" Hodel sounded as though he said he was going to start packing.
FEB. 26, 1950	
14½-20 12:01A	Phone rings, Hodel answers - "Yes, Harry, how is par asks about party, says he had people over - asks if one o'clock is too late - talks to "Baby Doll" about party. says he will be over. Hodel tells Ellen he is going out to stay up and leave Coline (See news article in Times 2-27-50, page 13, Part I) in. I want to talk to him, will be back in an hour or so. Oh hell, they are all "baby dolls" to me. Uses typewriter again.
12:13R	Hodel-"Leave Coline in tell him to wait here for me Goes out.
20-21 1:00A	Phone rings - Ellen answers - he isn't here now. Call back in 1½ hrs. will be here in morning.
1:30A	All quiet.
	LEWIS ON DUTY, L.A.P.D.

HODEL FILE - 47   47

Spool Time		
21-22	2:00A	Phone rang - maid answered, said Mr. Coline is not in. Repeated 3 times. I don't know (sound as if she was talking to Mr. Hodel) "As he had told her he was expecting Mr. Coline when he left house."
22+23,5	2:40A	Talking by Hodel and maid - Hodel says, I am very tired, I am going to sleep, and you had better go to bed too. No, No, I am very tired, I am going to sleep.
	2:45A	Radio is now playing soft music.
	3:26A	Radio - turned off. Everything quiet.
	4:00A	Hodel sleeping and snoring.
	6:45A	Still quiet - no sounds.
	7:45A	Lewis Off duty E.H. Dresbin - D.A.'s office on duty.
23:5	8:30A	Hodel snoring very loudly - no other movements.
	9:40A	Hodel moving around - seems to be awake.
	10:00A	no movements
23.5-24	10:40A	Telephone rings - awakened Hodel - said "I'll call you back". Answered by grunting - also "Yes, I'll be there".
24-25	11:35A	Telephone - answering "Yes, yes", mentioned "Caris" Said "I'll get it" apparently went back to sleep.
	12:00noon	Dresbin off duty.

HODEL FILE - 48   48

Cuncino, D.A.'s office on duty

	12:00noon	
	12:15P	Hodel coughed loudly - turned radio on to concert program - New York Symphony orchestra. KNX
25-37½	12:30P	Toilet flushes. Water faucet is turned on. Concert music makes Hodel's movements difficult to discern. Sounds like he's shaving now. Completes toilet at approx. 12:40.
	12:45P	Girl enters. Hodel calls her "Helen, of "Ellen" and asks her to take (something) out of the room. She returns. Conversation concerns the music (Beethoven's) Hodel asks for more tea.
	1:00P	Phone rings - Ellen tells Hodel it is Dr. C----- calling. Hodel answers "Yes. Right. About what tim I'll see you there. Right. Good bye".
	1:30P	Hodel dials phone number - gets busy signal. Turns radio off.
	2:05P	Hodel dials number - gets busy signal. Conversation Hodel asks girl whether she likes the smell. Girl replied "No". Sounds like he's reading newspap
	2:15P	Hodel dials - gets Miss Montgomery Tells her the artist is moving out by end of March. (Recorded) Ends conversation with series of yesses. Olympic 2476 is an unlisted number he gave Miss Montgomery. ended 2:40P
	2:45P	Is apparently talking to maid. Difficult to understand conversation. Tells her to count his woolen sox.

HODEL FILE #49

Spool Time

	3:00P	Seems to be working in a room alone. Mumbles to himself. Sounds of running water, glasses tinkling, small motor is turned on and off at intervals. Off at 4 PM.
1 37½	4:00PM	**Hroek, D.A.'s office on duty**
	4:12P	Hodel moving around the house. Hodel taking a bath, splashing and humming to himself.
	4:30P	Movements around the house.
	5:00P	Movements around the house and starts typing.
37½-40	5:26P	Hodel dials the post office - wants to know if there is a letter pickup today at Hwd. & Western Post offi.
	5:30P	Hodel instructed Ellen to take it out (the letter) and moving around.
40-42	5:53P	Ellen returns - tells Hodel mail goes out-one at 6:30, one at 9:30, (recorded) Sends her to Wilcox Post Office
42-43	6:52P	Hodel dials Operator, asks for SU 3349 - This is OL 3476. Is Harry there. Call MO 27454.
	7:00P	Hodel moving around the house.
43-44	7:26P	Ellen entered - Hodel apologized for being rude and told her he is expecting some important people 7:30 or 8:00 PM - now let's have some dinner.
44-46½	7:40P	Phone rings - Hodel answers - recorded.
46½-47	7:55P	Phone rings - Hodel answers - Yes, I'll be right out
	8:10P	Hodel returns.
		HROEK OFF DUTY

HODEL FILE - 50

	8:00P	Crowley, LAPD, on duty
	8:12P	Maid says "hear are the matches". Maid, "Isn't that away—How miserable I was.
	8:20P	Hodel answers - unable to hear, Maid "Did you have a good lunch". Hodel-"Fried eggs, and ---- These are check slips.
47-60	8:23P	Hodel talking to some men. Man "I made six programs you can try out. Talking about germicides and quantities grams 10/1000 etc. Hodel-"what is the effect of 1/10000? Let's go ahead and run our tests Man-"it will take about 50 days to do that". Hodel-"Organic material that a small percentage of the people are allergic to". Man-We won't mention that" Hodel-"And these are used for restaurant sanitation? Man-"no am for douches, clothing, etc." Hodel-"Well, how do I get it. How much per lb is——". Man-"35¢ per lb. I think it is#/——". Hodel-And the other detergent that you use?" Man-(unable to hear) (recorded)
	8:35P	End of Spool #18 during conversation.
	8:37P	Unable to get much of conversation except talking about detergents. Hodel is very much interested and getting the names of all the manufacturers. Hodel-"what are these detergents normally used for". Man-washing, car shampoos? Hodel-"Is there any dang of them conflicting with the other barbitrates?" Lady-"I could take a bath". Man-"what are you so interested in taking a bath for? "Hodel-would you like a drink"? Man-no thanks.

HODEL FILE - 51

51

8:44P   Hodel-"Let's build a fire-I'll get some wood".
Leaves.

8:45P   Installed Spool #19

8:45P   Man-"Do you want the first". Hodel-"No","sounds
of breaking wood. Hodel-"You don't know of any othe
possibilities or the key answers"?

SPOOL #19

0-60   8:50P   Hodel-of course you get much more lasting effects
from the bath. (Something about 27¢ lb detergent
wholesale) Man-but when you take a mixture like
"rice" which is a mixture of ----, and cost per lb
of the ingredients. Man-when you consider the
millions of packages they sell it is not too much.
(apparently the man is a chemist who has been doing
research work in detergents/for Hodel.) and synthetics

16   9:05P   Man-most of the perfume they have in this stuff is--
Lady-what was that dish with mushrooms in it----
It was on the Blvd. and it wasn't very far. Hodel-
I don't remember". Lady-If he didn't have legal
representation, he wouldn't even be a Doctor.
Hodel-I don't ink I have to worry anyway, at least
not this year". Lady-"It's necessary to protect you
"Career" Hodel-in other words----? Lady------
Hodel-Any felony periods. Lady-bootmaking doesn't
count? Lady-How about moral turpitude. Hodel-
something about medical profession. Something about
tea. Lady-George, you know how I talk to Joe and
you weren't home Saturday. I said to Joe, your

HODEL FILE - 52

52

24   friend in the "booby hatch" He said she not so bad.
I said, how do you know. Lady-you don't go to
Camarillos unless your dangerous to others. Hodel-
or yourself. (Something about alcoholics) Lady-
Oh goody---I'm going to get a bath after all. I smell
awfully now.

9:15P   Lady-we should have brought towels along.

9:20P   Water running in bathroom, and lady says something
about bath tub.

9:25P   Hodel-Thats almost as good as? in this tub. Lady-
I'll take a bath in it. Man-no you won't.
Lady-tha only reason I came along was to take a bath.
Man-you wouldn't want to take a bath in an
experimental deal. Hodel-It might eat all your skin
off. Lady-I wouldn't worry with a doctor around.
Hodel-wisecracks. Hodel-a peculiar people, the
Persians, the country produces no virgins. They
fuck all day in a violent way, and at night
they practice sexual perversion.

9:30P   Hodel-those walls are so thin.

45   9:30P   Water running in bathroom again. Hodel and man
talking about the ingredients (evidently experimenti
with soap in bathroom) Man-what I've seen in your
bathtub and my bathtub----? mentions sodium sulpha

9:36P   Hodel-Telephone rings. Hodel answers - I hope is do
call because the ingredients in question will be
helpful to me. I'd appreciate any information becau
I have to make this decision immediately. Thanks
Harry.

MODEL FILE - 53

9:40P	Hodel-do you want to give me the name of this dentside man. Man-Mr. Morrison.
9:45P	Hodel-your telephone. Man-OL 4373?
9:46P	End of Spool #19
9:47P	Lady talks about making reservations to go to Santa Barbara tomorrow.
9:50P	Hodel mentions something about murder.
9:51P	Hodel - place on the strip. Lady mentions Barbara and a Japanese place.
9:52P	Lady-Joe is very unfriendly toward her. I thought he'd be very unfriendly became-----Hodel-Joe is a little"punchy" you know. How much does it cost to Santa Barbara. She'll get in about 6:00. Lady- It would be so much nicer to go by car, then we could go straight to Court house.
9:55P	Put on Spool #20
0-3 10:00P	All quiet - all leave for approx. 5 minutes.
3-38 10:05P	Conversation again with same lady and man. Something about having made call. Alimony for her. Lady- I don't want to get involved, I know the poor man will have to pay the cleaning bill.
10:09P	Telephone rings - (Hear no telephone conversation)
10:15P	Talking about tea 40% or 50 lb. Hodel-the difference between green tea and black tea is------.
10:17P	Lady-If we go to Santa Barbara, are we going to see Usher? Hodel-He opened up in the county. He's a ...... --- Hodel-something about probation.

MODEL FILE - 54

	10:20P	Telephone rings twice. Hodel-hello, yes I'm home, just fine, Mr. Sheldon. Very good, anything new with you? I'll give you a ring next week. Have you bought a car yet? (Lady whispering something about Joe and Mexico) Hodel-I have some people here, I'll call you tomorrow.
ALL	10:25P	Hodel-She's subject to deportation. However, they'll never the fact about the papers. Hodel-I can't know where she'd go. Lady-Are you planning on leaving here by any chance. Lady-
RE- COR- DED		Did she ever mention it to Bob Adams. Lady- Did Bob say he would (continuous conversation. Able to pick up only bits) All recorded.
	10:30P	Talking about insuring something, value $76,000. If you went to sell it you would get $750.00 Trinkets. Hodel-Had it insured for $104,000. Alimony payments $300 month. Getting it reduced.
38	10:35P	Hodel-She looks sick - Lady-Why aren't you selling it, all over the country. Man-Says something "Could not hear" Lady-Well, you'd have to make up your mind if want to go. Will you pay 10.00 for a Hodel-I can get a car. Lady-Then, you dont have to worry.
	10:40P	Lady and man left house. (This lady seems to know an awfully lot about the legality of matters, possib an attorney) End of recorded conversation. Movements in house.
	10:44P	Movements in house.
	10:55P	Hodel typing.

HODEL FILE - 55

Spool
Time

10:57P   Hodel-arguing with Ellen - unable to understand.
Hodel-I didn't think you'd want to talk to her in front of her husband. Ellen-I'm no more than a dishwasher to you. Hodel-I'm sorry.
Noises in the distant part of house.

11:30P   Hodel-I'm adding Maid ?-----Hodel-a little later.
11:31P   Hodel-muttering at desk.
11:45P   Hodel-That's right. I don't care to ~~mixxextxxy~~ discuss it any further with you. Take it up with the immigration. Maid talking (unable to hear)
11:55P   Hodel-Was anybody else there. What do you think of it. Hodel typing.

Door bell rings. Ellen goes to door. Hodel say - Co in. Turns radio on. Hodel-Did you have a pleasant time in Palm Springs. Unable to hear other parties answer. Radio loud. Mentions "Chicoski".

FEBRUARY 27, 1950
12:00A

12:10A   Hodel - You made the headlines today or tomorrow.
38-40   12:10A   Man-I made the headlines?
12:11A   Hodel-like Hitler said.
40   12:11A   Hodel-your a rich man. Hodel-I can see you beating her up. Woman - Don't bother me. You can't bother me. Man-"(laughing) Suspicion. Bah. In one place I am a composer of poetry or opera, a hot tempered erratic woman - I've got to get out of here and get a job for a living.

HODEL FILE - 56

Spool
Time

54-60   12:25A   Hodel-Well anyway, she hasn't said she'd committed incest or killed the Black Dahlia. (other man has an accent - talking about this country) Man-
"She said look what you've put in the paper. I hate you." Man-"I've been chased around so much."
Hodel-"Whose your Doctor". Man-"On Vine Street.
Hodel-"What was the date of your premarital ----. When was your treatment started? When are you going to see him next.
End of Spool #20.

12:30A   Something about 8 units. Hodel-you may be tapering off. Mentioned 4 units.

SPOOL #21
0-27   12:35A   Hodel-"It wouldn't do any harm to wait another month. There are other type of penecillin you are more apt to get the rush on the second----". Man-"
She was Queen of Burbank. I'm warning you because I've known you 4 years" (cannot hear most of conversation).

10   12:45A   Hodel-told she ride the girls and make them work? How do you spell it?. Man-"LaOOA. I'll tell you the whole story. About a year ago ---- 4 girls-they live across from the Catholic church on Argyle. I he

20   12:50A   ... right now in Mexico City the value of the dollar ... in pesos. Secretarys work for ---- pesos.

HODEL FILE - 57

57

12:50A $500 will buy? pesos. Hodel-"You don't think
that the girls try their ----- (Juvenile officers
observed a 41 cream 4 door Buick parked in front
of Hodel's residence at this time. license
#78101h registered to Stoyle E. Bennett-Legal
owner-Hollywood Citizen News).

1:05A   Man-"A girl called named "Deva" wanted to know about
"Renee"/ Hodel-"You and the girls do solo numbers to
Man-"Acrobatic numbers, dances, etc." Hodel-"Something about a streamlined pussy". Man-Those girls
are French, they love to travel. I asked one girl
and she said of course. Coleen or Colee. Hodel-
"They are all unmarried, aren't they?" Man-"Yes".

27-48   Hodel-"The legal matters are minor. They can get
married at 18. I would merely be the backers represe
tative. It would look better.

1:1hA   Man-"This is a crucial time for both of us. I told
"Renee" several times she is the center of all my hope
Hodel-"Well really have to ride herd on them. 4 young
chicks xx in a strange country. Man-"Ha - 4 girls
and we two. - what a combination. I will be the
musical director. Someone mentions Dr "Colee".
Hodel-"I had a frieni named Prince ---- who ----
Hodel-"I'm the only person who knows where all these

48   things fit into the picture.

1:32A   All quiet except for radio.

1:35A   Hodel-"You better take a generous supply of penicilli
(Talking to same party)

HODEL FILE - 58
FEBRUARY 27, 1950

58

48-52   1:45A   All quiet except for radio and someone moving around.

1:57A   Typing;
Brechel, LAPD on duty

2:00A   Typing - radio playing - working at desk.

4:05A   Turned off radio.

52-55   4:07A   Hodel tells Ellen to go to bed, she has to get up
early as they have a lot of things to do, but he
wants to sleep late. He tells about getting a lot
of work done tonight. She says she won't sleep good.

off   She is nervous.

55-56.5   4:13A   He tells her, come on lets go to bed. They discuss
turning on heater.

56.5-   4:15A   Discuss having socks in morning. They talk of his
61.5   having a cold. She is helping him to undress. She
wants some love tonight, but he refuses her. He wants

off   to sleep alone.

4:22A   Hodel tells Ellen not to argue with him while
Dorothy is around. Tells her how to act in company o
Dorothy as Ellen then goes to her room, she appears t
be angry with Hodel because he sent her to her room
without allowing to have any love.

4:30A   Change spools - put #22 on.
Hodel retires - alls quiet.

HODEL FILE - 59
SPOOL #22 - FEBRUARY 27, 1950

Spool Time		
	8:00A	J. McGrath, D.A.'s office on duty
	9:03A	Phone rings 7 times, no answer. Hodel snoring.
	9:12A	Phone rings 8 times, no answer.
	9:15A	Ellen goes into Hodel's room, wakes him up.
	9:18A	Phone rings 3 times (if answered was in a rear room could not hear)
	11:12A	Phone rings, 12 times, Hodel finally answers but could not make out what was said.
	11:40A	Hodel at desk - typing.

FEBRUARY 27, 1950

0-2½	12:00noon	Sullivan D.A.'s office on duty
	12:10R (Noon)	Hodel dials and then flushes toilet (recorded) but barely intelligible due to water running-talks about taxes.
2½-3	12:15P	Phone rings - Hodel answers (recorded)
3-3½	12:32P	Phone rings - Hodel answers, "Yes" - (recorded) wrote to them in Washington".
3½-4½	12:45P	Water running.
	12:50P	Hodel dials phone "Is Mr ? there? (recorded) Will he be in soon? This is Dr. Hodel speaking." Something about account being worked out.
4½-5	12:52P	Hodel dials phone "Is Mr. Meet there? Dr. Hodel speaking Will you be around this afternoon?"
5-6	12:55P	Talking to maid - Cannot make out conversation (recorded)
6-8	1:00P	Hodel dials phone (recorded) No one answers-finally hangs up.
8-13	1:12P	Phone rings - Hodel answers "Oh yes, Al" (recorded)

HODEL FILE - 60

Spool Time		
	1:12P	"Series of yeses agreeing with party on other end. "That sounds pretty good. Wonderful, and his name is Morrison?"
13-14	1:40P	Phone rings - Hodel answered (recorded) "Unable to make a cash outlay at this time".
14-15	2:05P	Hodel dials phone (recorded) "I have some business in Detroit for a few days".
15-15½	2:38P	Hodel dials phone (recorded)
	2:45P	Hodel typing.
	3:15P	Quiet since 3 PM. Hodel apparently out of house.
	3:59?	Still quiet.
	4:00P	Hronek, D.A.'s office on duty.
	4:22P	Phone rings - 16 times, no answer
	4:27P	Phone rings 7 times, no answer.
	4:52P	Phone rings 5 times, no answer.
	5:00P	All Quiet.
	5:30P	All quiet.
	6:00P	All quiet.
	6:12P	Phone rings 10 times, no answer.
15-17	6:20P	Someone named Joe used the phone, hear him moving around (Recorded)
17-18	6:45P	Someone with German accent talked with Ellen - hard to understand.
18-20	6:51P	Ellen talking to someone about something.
	7:00P	All quiet.
	7:30P	All quiet.
	8:00P	All quiet - Off Duty.

61

HODEL FILE - 61

Spool	Time	
	8:00P	Bimson, LAPD on duty
	8:20P	Someone enters - no conversation - typing.
20-34	8:35P	Typing very fast - strange shuffling noises unable to identify - recording conversation believe it's between Hodel and Joe. Mostly unintelligible. Hodel says there is a possibility of a place near Washington and Normandy.
	8:45P	Mentions Finlays - says somebody started from San Francisco, should be here in a couple of days. Talking about some woman, says she needs cheering up, Hodel say I'll be going up past Santa Barbera and if you want a lift to Camarillo and back I'll drop you off and pick you up a couple of hours later.
	9:30P	Maid entered - short conversation - unable to understand.
34-36	9:40P	Scuffling noise and conversation between a man and woman - unable to understand.
38-55	11:10P	Conversation between Hodel and Ellen - Hodel asks her what she plans to do if he manages to raise some money says she has several alternatives - they are arguing Sounds of dishes and eating - Hodel tells her she can collect $10. per week social security for 26 weeks - tells her if any lady asks to tell them she has only been getting $50. per mo. instead of $100. to avoid income tax. Sounds like Ellen is crying. Hodel is explaining how she can beat tax - sound like she is cr... her way out soon.
End of Spool		

62

HODEL FILE - 62
SPOOL #23

	Time	
	11:30P	Install Spool #23
0-3	11:45P	Sends night letter to George Hodel - 249 So. Harvard. night letter sounds like double talk.
3-33	11:52P	Company arrives—Hodel says "come in Theodore." talking about a woman by the name of Renec. Theodore says all this woman can talk about is how much she love him. Sounds very theatrical. Talk about $10,000. and why he married her. He repeats time and again that she said "This is a trap". Talking of attorneys. Then reads Hodel what sounds like a divorce paper. Hodel an friend talking and laughing at Courts and legal procedu Sounds as if Hodel is putting Theodore up for night.
		Turns on radio - resumes typing.
FEB. 28 1950		
	1:40A	xxxxx Hodel says to Ellen "Why do you have your coat on? I'm buring up in here". Can't hear Ellen answer.
33-	1:55A	Conversation between Hodel and Ellen, sounds like
60		writing on desk. Ellen says "How will they treat me". Brochel, LAPD relieves Bimson.
		Hodel quotes prices of tea. He speaks Spanish with Ell
		Hodel recites poetry.
off	2:20A	Turns radio off. Walks around. Checks doors. Goes to lavatory.
0-13	2:35A	Hodel and Ellen in bedroom - not much conversation mostly whispered. Sounds indicate both in bed, probably making love.
	2:50A	Sounds indicate Hodel reading in bed.
	3:30A	Hodel snoring.

HODEL FILE - 63

FEBRUARY 28, 1950

Spool #21

	8:00A	Morgan relieves Brechel
13-16	8:20A	Telephone rang - Hodel "I've been working pretty hard father", etc. - "Do you know when these people will be there for the furniture?" etc. - ends - "OK Dad fine, goodbye".
	9:25A	Typing
16-17	9:30A	Hodel (on telephone) unintelligible conversation about rates - ends "thank you".
17-19	9:35A	Hodel (On telephone) "Uh-huh - I'll appreciate it, otherwise I'd have to buy more blankets you see, et I phoned you for the last six or eight weeks - etc. Ends "Alright thank you, goodbye".
19-21¾ 21½	9:45A	Hodel (On telephone) "Pretty good, thank you" etc. Maybe we could finish - etc. When would be a convenient time for you? Thursday I may be going to Santa Barbara - I have things pretty well worked ou already - I'll have to make a breakdown on expenses etc. I have that all tabulated - we could sit down an hour and work it out - etc. Ends - "Alright fin Very good, goodbye".
21½- 21 3/4	9:55A	Telephone rang - Hodel - "yes, etc. You just want one pound - ends "Alright, goodbye".
	10:08A	Typing
21 3/4- 22½	10:10A	Desk noise
22½- 23½	10:42A	Hodel - conversation with Ellen - unintelligible.

HODEL FILE - 64

	10:45A	Airplane noise
23½-24	10:50A	Unintelligible conversation - Hodel and Ellen
24-24½	10:55A	Unintelligible conversation - Hodel and Ellen
24½-25	11:05A	Telephone rang - no answer
25-27½	11:12A	Telephone rang - no answer
	11:13A	Ellen - "Your phone rang" - Hodel - "Find out who i is" Ellen-"Just a moment - Jimmy?" Hodel-what's the name?" Ellen-"It's Jimy (something)" Hodel- "Tell him, I'll be with you in just a minute. Just leave it there". Toilet noise - Hodel (unintellig ible conversation) ends. "Yes-Goodbye".
27½- 27 3/4	11:30A	Telephone rang - Hodel - "Hello, yes, between 10:30 and 11:00? Does she know where to meet him? I'll tell him - bye".
27 3/4- 28	11:35A	Hodel - (on telephone) "Will he be in tonight? I'll call him".
28-28½	11:55A	Telephone rang - Hodel "hello, no we don't need any help now, your welcome".
	12:00	Hodel in bathroom - filled tub.
	12:00noon	Bill Snyder relieves Morgan
28½-29	12:30P	Phone rings - (recorded) Nd such xxxxxxxxxxxxxith
29-29½	12:35P	Conversation with Ellen - (recorded)
29½-30½	1:00P	Hodel talking to Ellen - (recorded) unintelligible
30½-31½	1:05P	Hodel climbed up or down some stairs - sounds of digging or something similar. Hodel talking to Ellen - asks for blanket or something (recorded)
31½-32	1:10P	Hodel continues talking to Ellen (recorded)

Hodel File - 65

	Time	Notes
	1:30P	Sounds of pounding or hammering - Hodel has few wor[ds] with Ellen. Unintelligible - flushes toilet and breaks wind at same time. Ye Gods - what a racket (not recorded)
32-33	1:40P	Phone rings - Hodel answers - (recorded) states someone is coming to see house.
33-33½	1:50P	Phone rings - Hodel answers - very short (recorded)
	2:15P	Plenty of noise from passing cars and trucks.
	2:20P	Hodel dials phone twice - no answer. Continued hammering and pounding (not recorded)
33½-34½	2:25P	Phone rings - Hodel answers - so much noise from outside could not understand (recorded)
	2:35P	Hodel talking to himself, but hardly above a whisper - not recorded
	3:00P	Hodel does a bit of typing - no talk - not recorded
34½-35	3:15P	Hodel dials phone - recorded
35-46	3:35P	Hodel talks to someone in regards to house - (this party is female) also talks about Chinese art (recorded) conversation faded out due to Hodel and party going to some other part of house.
	4:00P	Snyder over to ~~Baxinxx~~ McGrath, D.A.'s office
	4:02P	Phone rang 8 times, no answer
46-48	4:10P	Phone call - not able to understand all parts - said he & Mrs Hodel divorced - also something about children - Hodel became very angry, said "I do not like your questions-is none of your business. I do not desire to deal with you." Hodel hung up phone (recorded)
	4:13P	Hodel typing.

HODEL FILE - 66

	Time	Notes
48-55	5:06P	Phone call (recorded) could not understand (lots of noise and static.) Sounds like trouble in receiving set - said something about 75¢ a hour all see you 12 to 6 - come on out and try it.
Spool #2½	5:40P	Changed to Spool 24
0-1.5	5:40P	Funny sounding noises (recorded) for a couple of minutes. Typing
1.5-4	5:45P	More funny noises (recorded)
4-7	5:46P	Phone rings (recorded) Hodel answers "Hello dear."
	5:47P	Things are very much status quo". Conversation som[e]what unintelligible due to noises in background. "Well definitely try to see you this week-end. Dorero. (his ex-wife)
	5:55P	Funny noises continue since telephone conversation then some typing.
	6:10P	Lt. Frank Jaminson phoned, said Hodel moving furnit[ure] out - if Bug is found or all furniture moved phone him at CR 14917. His name is pronounced (JAMINSON) any time, day or night.
7-23	6:50P	Hodel in conversation - could not make out too much noise. May have been on phone - (tried at 6453 to record some of the conversation). "Expense along that line - tell you where I see you - what date wi[ll] this be "Sat". right, shall I come alone or bring another girl - do you have enought? Also talked ab[out] going somewhere Sat. 2 blks So. of Colorado, 6 Bl. E of Verdugo - the West end of Eagle Rock "I'll just call her Jill" Have you met some of my friends - se[e]

HODEL FILE - 67

6:50P — you Saturday how are you fixed for girls? I'm too old now - it does not make any difference to me now
Did you decide to take the other room? (It seems th person may be renting or buying the house.)

8:00P — Bimson, LAPD, on duty.

8:10P — Hodel moving around - no conversation

9:30P — Hodel enters - heavy rasping noise lasts approx. 30 minutes, can't identify - no conversation-heavy breathing.

10:20P — Someone writing at desk.

23-54 / 11:40P — Conversation - talk about selling something for $60 Sounds like a car - conversation very low. Lots of interference - talking about art - believe Hodel is talking to Chris. Talking about houses and somethi about Monday the 6th. Hodel says he needs $16,000. says there is $15,000. against his house.

54-54½ / 1:20P — Hodel makes phone call - asks if he should come bac now or in the morning.

1:25P — Hodel typing - company gone.

Spool 25 / 1:30P — Change spool - put on #25

2:00A — Brechel, LAPD on duty.
Hodel working around. No conversation.

2:50A — Hodel retires. Snoring. Have not heard Ellen talk since on duty.

HODEL FILE - 68

March 1, 1950
SPOOL #25
Spool Time

0-1 / 8:00A — Morgan relieves Brechel

9:10A — Hodel(Telephoned) "She can come over about one - hav her call me - ends "Alright thank you, goodbye".

1-2 / 9:27A — Telephone rang - Hodel, "Yes Sir" - conversation abou cold tablets - "Follow directions - I hope it breaks up right away". Ends -"goodbye".

2-2.6 / 9:35A — Telephone rang - Hodel "Yes, I'll call him, will you wait just a moment pleast - Mr. Phillips would you mind calling the number again, and he'll answer it - I won't answer it you see".

9:55A — While in bathroom, Hodel said to himself "I wish I hadn't done that" (Probably blew his nose too hard - or something)

2.6-4 / 10:08A — Telephone rang - Hodel "Hello - etc (water running in tub makes voice unintelligible)

4-6 / 10:12A — Conversation (with unidentifiable man) Hodel "Are they both looking good?" (Water isn't running during conversation; however, conversation is held out of bathroom and hard to understand) Hodel "I was surprised" "Thanks" (went back to bathroom and turne water back on).

6-7.5 / 10:24A — Doorbell rang - conversation between Hodel and Ellen (something about breakfast)

7.5-8 / 10:25A — Hodel and Ellen, very short conversation.

10:26A — Hodel "He already left"(at front door)

8-12 / 10:30A — Hodel, "Say Ellen", etc. - conversation about toa - Hodel - "Go where" (Scraping noise)

HODEL FILE - 70

	11:20A	Telephone rang - Hodel, "Hello", etc (unintelligible because of loud filing noise) Conversation with Hagan about goodwill being capital gain (long pause) conversation continues about stock - about "Showing it as an advance".
SPOOL 26	11:22A	Wire changed to Spool #26
	11:30A	Morgan requested Bimson to check cars parked in front of Hodel residence.
0-end	11:32A	Hagan, "people call me Mr. Gahagan" - laughter - conversation about income tax. Hagan "Are you married now"? Hodel-"No".
	12:00	Walter Sullivan relieves Morgan
	12:01P	Telephone rang - very short conversation
	12:10P	(Bimson reports that there were two cars parked in front of Hodel's #1 - 51B392, a '47 Pontiac Convertab Sedan, registered to Floyd Hagan - 3208 Montezuma Ave. Alhambra. #2 - 9P3 938, a '47 Chevrolet Coupe, regis tered to Willie Wheeler, 4461 Town Ave., L.A.)
	12:05P	Hodel still in conversation with his acct. (being recorded) (Spools 25 and 26 and 27 will prove very interesting to income tax investigators)
	12:10P	Phone rings - Hodel answers "Yes, whose calling". Conversation regarding house (sale).
	12:12P	HO 93311 - (This conversation may be OK on recorder)
	12:17P	Phone rings. Hodel answers (recorded)
	12:35P	Discussing and checking figures with acct.
	12:45P	Hodel reading off figures and acct. either putting th in adding machine or typewriter.

HODEL FILE - 69

12toend 10:35A (This spool #25 and following should be checked with federal income tax man in the future as Hodel's income tax is computed with this man, and it looks like they about to "take" Uncle for a few bucks.)

Conversation between Hodel and Ellen (unintelligible) doorbell rang - Hodel answers - talking to some man - Hodel and man enter library - Hodel "Your fault or mine" - Conversation about radio announcer - man (probably Mr. Hagan), "She moved to San Francisco". Conversation about a wealthy man who owned five gasoli stations - Hodel "Is he a good guy". Hagan, "Yes" etc., conversation about auction-something about FBI Hodel "I had an offer in Hawaii" - conversation about tea (men sat down at desk - everything clearly recorde hereon) Conversation about making out Hodel's income tax - conversation about Mrs. Hodel, alimony, support chiluren - conversation about exemptions - conversatio about inventory - about chinese international export company - about corportations - about five hundred dollar debt owed Hodel - about corporation books - about Hodel's books - Hagan "We have no choice in the matter", etc. Hodel asked operator for Atlantic 66407 Hodel "Well alright, will you ask him to call me pleas No, this is Doctor Hodel" (End) Men check figures (Hagan reads and Hodel checks) conversation about total income-about asking for money back - Hodel - "You accountants and auditors sure make things com- plicated". Hagan, "No, we don't" etc. - about stock.

HODEL FILE - 71

	12:50P	Changing to Spool #27 - Hodel still reading off figures.
Spool 27	12:55P	Started Spool 27. Still with acct. Tabulating figures.
0-22	1:10P	Recorder stops for about 1 min. Found tiny piece of wire which seemed to be shorting recorder.
	1:11?	Working OK now.
	1:15P	Trouble on recorder. Intermittent skipping - called crime lab. and reported to Stanton.
	1:17P	Recorder off. Airplane noise. No further conversatic Apparently account left premises while recorder was giving us trouble.
22-23½	1:25P	Some conversation (recorded) Could not distinguish voices.
23½-24	1:27P	More conversation. Believe with acct. (being recorded
24-28½	1:30P	Conversation (recorded) on figures.
	1:35P	Recorder stops at about 28½
29-33½	1:36P	Started recorder again. After moving reel forward.
	1:37P	Phone rings. Hodel answers "I don't know. Unable to refer you to anyone". Much noise in background.
33½	1:38P	Phone rings, No conversation. Continues talking to acct.
	1:39P	Recorder stops again at 33½
35-36	1:45P	Started recorder again. Still jumping.
	1:46P	Tabulating figures, lots of noise.
	1:55P	Sullivan called to telephone.
		By Morgan-Recorder on the blink - further tax computations are discussed between Hodel and Hagan.

HODEL FILE - 72

	2:00P	Telephone rang - Hodel "Helo, just a moment". Telephone apparently for Hagan - Hagan "Been busy uh-huh". Conversation related to income tax problem made date for Tuesday at 4:30 o'clock - at 35 North Arroyo (not recorded) Conversation ended 2:04 PM.
	2:05P	Hodel telephoned "Hello Deak". "Albert Band who was John Huston's assistant called you this morning - call him at Hollywood 93311 - He asked for Dorothy". End 2:07P
37-39½	2:10P	Turned on recorder at 37. Still discussing income ta with acct.
to	2:11P	Phone rings. Hodel answers (recorder still working. Stops at 39½ but starts again). Unable to get any of phone conversation. Recorder stop at 41.
	2:13P	Starts again. Recorder starts and stops.
51	2:20P	"I don't want to specify. I don't want to call it to their attention that such things are going on". (Acct. makes above statement).
	2:21P	Phone rings. Hodel answers.
	2:25P	Spool runs out reading 51.
Spool #28		
64½	2:26P	Conversation between Hodel and acct.
	2:30P	Start spool #28. (Started recording).
0-3	2:31P	"Ok, George, will see you later". Hodel-"How much will this cost? Good bye."
3-4	2:41P	Conversation with Ellen (recorded) unintelligible.
	3:15P	Telephone rings answered by Hodel - said, "Hello, I'll be down right away".
	3:25P	Radio is turned on

HODEL FILE - 73

4½-5	3:30P	Radio off.
	3:35P	Conversation with Ellen.
	3:45P	Phone rings. Hodel answers. "He's already left". (Apparently refers to accountant).
	3:46P	Phone rings. Hodel answers "He just left, I'll see if I can get him". No further.
5-7	3:48P	Conversation with Ellen. (recorded) Noise in background.
7-7½	4:00P	Conversation with Ellen (recorded)
	4:00P	Frank Hronek, D.A.'s office on duty.
7½-10	4:10P	Conversation with Ellen. Much racket. (recorded).
10-22	4:27P	Hodel invites some lady in, discussing the house and furniture - sounds like a couple of women.
22-26	4:45P	Returned from examination of different rooms and furth discussion.
26-29	4:53P	Hodel talks with Ellen.
	4:59P	Hodel starts typing.
29-33	5:32P	Hodel talking with a man.
	6:00P	Moving around and typing.
	6:30P	Typing.
	7:00P	All quiet.
	7:30P	Hodel starts typing again.
	8:00P	Meyer, LAPD, on duty.
33-34½	8:10P	Hodel calls someone on phone - asks where Michigan State College is - East Lansing - Thanks them - hangs up - starts typing.
	8:27P	Hodel phones - "Is Slim there. Have him call me when he comes in."

HODEL FILE - 74

Spool	Time	
34½-35	8:37P	Ellen enters - asks if can turn radio on - Hodel says, "Sure". Hodel says something about helping Ellen bring in the table. Radio on - Hodel typing.
	9:10P	Hodel still typing.
	9:30P	Hodel around - all quiet.
	10:00P	Hodel around - all quiet.
	10:30P	Hodel around - all quiet.
	11:10P	Hodel dials phone - no answer - still typingl
	11:30P	Phone rang - Hodel answers. Didn't say anything. Ellen turned radio on again.
35-40½	11:37P	Phone rang. Hodel answered - Whoever he was talking he said, "Don't say anything over the phone - it is r tapped - said he had there phone number, and would ca tomorrow - said he would have to go out to call - checked but would not repeat number on phone. Said it is WE 1670 and he knew name of Street. Would have phone people check - said if he said phone numbe "They" would be out and bother them - that is what "They" always do. When Hodel hung up, Ellen asked hi how he knew-Hodel said he was just talking. Still typing.
MAR 2	12:05A	Hodel still typing.
	12:45A	Hodel still typing.
	1:15A	Hodel still typing and talking to Ellen - unable to understand.
	1:45A	Hodel still typing and talking to Ellen - unable to understand.

HODEL FILE - 76
March 2, 1950
Spool #28

Spool	Time	
	8:00A	Morgan relieves Brechel
	9:10A	Door-bell rang (someone walking)
42-42.2	11:32A	Typing Begins
	11:40A	Hodel, "Ellen, if you get any mail you'll have it without an instants delay".
	12:00 noon	J. McGrath, D.A.'s office on duty
42-43	@	Someone phoned - Hodel said "are you here now - yes, it just came ½ an hour ago.
	12:07P	Ellen and Hodel talking about some woman. Hodel said, "Tell her to wait, maybe she will leave it at the door.
	12:10P	Door bell rang - Hodel said to Ellen, "Be nice to her, she is an old lady". Hodel still working at his desk.
43-45	12:12P	Hodel makes phone call - (recorded) to a Mr. Overton. Hodel to Mr Overton "I was wondering about RE 4279, it is disconnected".
45-49	12:13P	(Recorded) Hodel makes another phone call - talks abou RE 4279, and WE 6126. Also about some tests of some ki
49-54	12:14P	Hodel phones the Phone company - asked to have NO 27464 disconnected. Had talk with Phone company.
SPOOL 29-12:30P		Spool No. 29 put on
0-1	12:32P	Hodel makes phone call (recorded)
1-3.5	12:34P	Hodel phone call to a Mr. Arnell (recorded) Talked about running something down - a piece of machinery or something.

HODEL FILE - 75

Spool	Time	
		Brechel, LAPD on duty
	2:00A	Hodel still typing
	2:20A	Hodel stops typing. Tells Ellen to put things away exactly as she finds them. Hodel goes out. Alls quiet except for radio.
	2:27A	Hodel returns - goes to desk - resumes typing.
	3:45A	Typing - stops - radio turned off.
	4:05A	Hodel retires - All is quiet.

HODEL FILE - 77

1:15P	Someone comes to the door - talks about 3 keys and phones.
1:55P	Hodel asks for phone number of Dow Chemical Company.
3,5-15	Hodel phones - asks for Mr. Morrison - talk about chemical for a bath soap. Asks questions regarding various chemicals.
2:16P	Reception getting bad, also appears Hodel now using pho in rear of house - hard to hear - other phone pulled ou by Telephone Company.
2:40P	Hodel makes phone call - no response.
2:41P	Phone rings - Hodel answers - says "Hello" then hangs up and dials - phone rings again. Hodel says "Hello" then hangs up.
15-21 2:42P	Called Dr. Hussey regarding atest of some kind (recorde Also said something regarding CK 15258 - could be a phone CR 15258.
4:00P	Hodel typing. -(Hronek, D.A.'s office on duty)
21-23 4:07P	Phone rings - Hodel answers.
23-28 4:24P	Hodel dials operator"BR 20666 - OL 3476. Mr. Look, th is Dr. Hodel————" Something about microscopes - abou how much do they sell for - suppose you send me some literature - can you get us a reasonable price - about 300 or 3:30PM.
4:32P	Starts typing again.
28-30 4:39P	NO 27464 - Interior Decorator.
30-31 4:49P	Hodel talked with Ellen - walked around.
5:00P	Starts typing.

HODEL FILE - 78

31-33 5:16P	Phone rings - Hodel answers - saw some notice in the paper - "I have a house which I am willing to rent - one wing anyway - (recorded) "I'll be in and out - suppose you call on me tomorrow or Saturday".
33-34 5:50P	Hodel dials - (recorded) couldn't understand.
34-35 6:12P	Phone rang 8 times. No answer. Hodel apparently out for supper.
6:30P	All quiet.
7:00P	All quiet.
7:30P	All quiet.
8:00P	All quiet - Hronek off duty.
8:00P	Meyer, LAPD, on duty.
8:30P	All quiet.
9:00P	All quiet.
9:10P	Phone rings 18 times, no one answers.
9:30P	All quiet
10:00P	All quiet
10:30P	All quiet
10:50P	Sounds as though Hodel and Ellen returned home. Some one moving around.
34-40 11:00P	Hodel calls someone - tells them had other phone disconnected and changes phone from time to time - was on phone 15 min., but didn't say much - asked what happened today and just listened.
11:30P	Hodel still around, but quiet.
3-3-50 12:00A	All quiet.
12:30A	Hodel and Ellen moving around, talk a little.
1:10A	Hodel starts typing.
1:30A	Hodel still around.

HODEL FILE - 79

79

MARCH 3, 1950

1:30A   Brechel, LAPD on duty

2:00A   All is quiet.

2:10A   Hodel enters den probably from patio. Obtains somethin
from desk - then leaves room via patio. Hodel probabl;
in studio.

2:30A   Hodel enters lavatory - runs water - urinates - talks
to himself "This is too hot". Goes to desk - writes
with pen.

2:40A   Begins typing.

3:00A   Typing stops - Hodel leaves room.

3:05A   Hodel returns to den - works at desk.

3:15A   Hodel leaves room. All is quiet.

3:20A   Very faint noise of phone ringing 5 times.

3:25A   Hodel returns to desk in den. Mumbles to himself.
Seems to be reading.

3:40A   Hodel leaves room.

4:00A   Hodel returns with Ellen - she goes to lavatory.

            Hodel - "Did it come off alright?" Answer not readabl

40-44.5 4:03A   Hodel speaks Spanish to Ellen. She answers in Spanish
She then tells him the words in English. She seems to
be coaching him on Spanish. They enter lavatory. Hod
says "You didn't come in here to wash your hands dress
in that thing". She whispers an answer. He sends her

off   out of room "to avoid hard feelings"

44.5- 4:10A   Hodel and Ellen have conversation in Spanish. They
46   are in bedroom having sex intercourse or something,
probably perversion. Sounds like he got another blow-
job.

HODEL FILE - 80

80

4:30A   Snoring begins. Hodel asleep.

8:20A   Hodel arises, goes to lavatory.

8:25A   Hodel and Ellen talking. Not much conversation. Coul
not make out.

8:30A   Ellen goes to lavatory.

HODEL FILE - 81
Spool #29

3-3-50, 8:00A		Bimson, LAPD, on duty
	10:00A	Hodel gets up - says "come in Joe" says "There is a not on the phone".
	10:30A	Hodel walking about - washes
	11:00A	Hodel still walking about - muttering to himself
	11:30A	Phone rings - Hodel says "About how soon Mr Kesler" "Very well, I'll be here".
46-47	11:35A	Woman knocks on door, says "George, may I use your bathroom". Hodel says, "Sure come on in". Conversation between this woman and Hodel - they both leave bathroom
47-55		xxxxxxxxxxxxxxxxxxxthixxxxxxx conversation - phone ri: answered by Hodel, says, "That's all right - tomorrow after 11", hangs up - sounds like he is making a medical exam. Hodel leaves - goes into library.
55-65	11:45A	Conversation between Hodel and woman - typing - converse tion regarding branch library - pounding in background. Conversation regarding a play.

Spool 30-12:00P Changing reel - Sullivan, D.A.'s office on duty.

	12:00P	Phone rings, Hodel answers, "Let me look and see".
0-6	12:07P	Lady talking (recorded) "I owe 4 times 75.00, that's 300.00 (Possibly his wife) "I have to pay my rent or get out".
	12:15P	Conversation with woman continues. Relative to her expenses and the childrens.

HODEL FILE - 82

6-10	12:16P	Conversation continues (recorded)
	12:19P	Quiet.
10-12	12:21P	Conversation with wife resumed (recorded) He talks about a job.
12-24	12:28P	More conversation (recorded) Hodel "I've lost money every year". Talking about what money she's earned. Hodel discusses his lossess "$6000;00 in 1946, "I sold the clinic to pay for the losses of that year. Now, I must sell the house. Hodel-something about pennitentia Noises in background.
	12:40P	Quiet.
	12:41P	Conversation resumed. Much racket Hodel-"I can give yo 2 or 300.00 a month."
24-28	12:42P	Started recording "what would you advise me doing?" Static - hard to understand conversation.
	12:46P	Conversation fades. Apparently parties went to some ot part of house.
	12:50P	Phone rings. Footsteps, but hear no answer.
	12:51P	A man talking to Hodel - "Anxious to get located in th area. I have my own firm. We sell yardage. Office at 610 S. Broadway. Negotiating for another office on La Cienega". "Bamboo blinds of various kinds".
	12:54P	Conversation fades.
	1:08P	Conversation with unknown man resumes. "I think I'll t: the place". Man leaves.
	1:10P	Conversation with woman (wife?)
28-38	1:11P	Started recording. She's talking about the children. "I'm not too happy about Kelvin". Much racket. Hodel talks about having wife and children with him again.

HODEL FILE - 83

	1:21P	Conversation continues. Low tones.
38-48	1:28P	Started recording. Can't make out conversation, but hope recording is getting it. Hodel reading from Mexic paper about jobs in Mexico.
	1:38P	Hodel reading to wife from some sort of manuscript.
48-49	1:40P	Hodel threw reading, resumes conversation.
	1:44P	Dials phone (recorded) Wrong number.
	1:45P	Dials phone-No conversation.
49-50	1:51P	Dials phone - "Is he there? This is Dr. Hodel. You ha n't typed my report yet? Have him call me".
	1:55P	Hodel and wife continue conversation. Talking about six their income tax. Man arrives "Dr Hodel - We'll be thr here in a few minutes". Man replies, "I'm going back to see Ellen".
	1:56P	Typing.
	2:00P	Working on her income tax.
	2:10P	Wife talking on phone. Sounded like she called party, Carol.
	2:12P	Wife to Hodel - I won't be able to go today. I'll probably see over the weekend". Much racket and typing
50-55	2:17P	(recorded) Conversation between wife and Hodel "She get some cash and hide it somewheres".
	2:24P	Max Much interference in receiving. Man talking to Hod Unable to recognize voice or his conversation very clear
55-61	2:26P	"When I came in at 6 AM, I parked the car. It was all quiet". (recorded)
	2:28P	Phone rings - Hodel answers "Yes, I know who it is". Apparently talking to tax expert. "I'm very anxious to see the flower shop. I'll see you today.

HODEL FILE - 84

2:30P	Resumes conversation with man.
2:31P	Out of recording wire. Crime lab has been notified by Belle.
2:32P	Conversation continues. Man talks about displaying the product to a woman. She finally agreed in about 30 to 60 days she'd put thru a 7 or 7 fifty order. "I had 2 - 6.00 tins, 2 - 12.00 tins, and 12 - 3.75 tins." This man is apparently a tea salesman for Hodel. "Our firm is like the Rolls Royce Firm. It's small but it's the best".
2:49P	Phone rings. Hodel answers. Again discussing his incom tax. "Take 101.00 out of the commission. That will sat her a few dollars".
2:50P	Salesman again talking. "I had 45.00 to make the trip. If you had sent me the 25.00 sooner, I'd have done a better job. The tires are only good for another 60 day. Blew 2 tires on the trip, one out of Modesto; one out o Fresno. (Lots of bull).
3:20P	Salesman still talking. nothing from Hodel. All about the tough breaks on the trip. "I'm supposed to report to Presidio Monday AM for active duty. I got .21 in my pocket and I got to get back up there. I'll work from 8:30AM to 4:30PM, and will have Saturday and Sunday off I can still handle the tea on weekend trips.
3:25P	This guy has talked continuously since 2:25PM.
3:26P	Phone rings - Hodel answers "Whose calling? "200 today Is that it? Why don't you talk to her about that?" (water running) Can't hear no more.

85

HODEL FILE - 85

3:26P — Salesman again talking. Talked about selling some ash-trays. "They found my blood-pressure at 160. They gave me some pills. Will you take my blood-pressure". Both men walk away.

3:35P — Quiet.

3:45P — Phone - "I just thought you might know something". Hodel talking to some one. "Radiator 10.00.

3:50P — Phone being dialed. "Is this Mrs. Gomez. This is the China? This is the salesman talking. The little electr stove. We got to get rid of this stuff within the next 24 hrs. Have some ply wood and some lumber. We have 3 windows and odds and ends of lumber. We need the space. Could you call this evening. No matter how late. You can sell this stuff. There is 650.00 worth of merchandi We'll take $110.00 for everything. We don't have time t run an ad. You'll come at 8 o'clock and the boss and I will be waiting for you. 8 o'clock tonight." Hung up and then Hodel and salesman had a good laugh.

4:00P — "We'd better go-to be back here by 8 o'clock, but I want you to take my blood-pressure first". Hodel "it's 164." "What are these pills". Hodel-"They look like pheno-b.

4:01P — Belle here with more wire.

4:05P — Phone call. Unable to hear conversation due to noise.

4:10P — Hodel- "HO 91234" (salesman dials) Asks about ad in papers of March, Shangarala - unusual studio rooms or apartment in luxurous modernistic home for arxiss artist writer. $40.00, 90.00, Ph. OL 3476, put it in tomorrow' paper $1.52 Dr. Geo. Hodel.

86

HODEL FILE - 86
SPOOL 31

4:20P — Hodel and salesman leave.

4:23P — Fire Department passes Hodel's home.

4:24P — Hronek, D.A.'s office on duty

4:46P — Hodel dials, Mr. Oberley - he can be there in 20-25 min

0-2 — Has a conversation with someone

5:00P — All quiet

5:30P — All quiet

5:50P — Phone rang 2 times, no answer

6:00P — All quiet

6:30P — All quiet

7:00P — All quiet

7:30P — All quiet

7:49P — Phone rang 3 times, no answer

8:00P — All quiet, Hronek off duty

8:00P — All quiet - Meyer LAPD, on duty

8:30P — All quiet, sounds as though Ellen is running the vacuum cleaner.

2-3 — 8:48P — Phone rang, Ellen answered, party must have asked for Hodel. Ellen said he wasn't home yet.

3-4 — 9:01P — Phone rang, Ellen answered, says she will give Hodel th message. He should be home soon.

4-5 — 9:07P — Phone rang. Ellen took a message for Hodel. Didn't repeat anything.

9:10P — Hodel and some man, came in - talk in other part of house Vacum cleaner going - can't hear anything.

5-6 — 9:15P — Hodel and man talk about arranging something.

6-12 — 9:23P — Hodel calls "Nickey", and asks her over - says he will r some drinks - bring some girl along, asks her if she wil read some poems - a friend is with him.

HODEL FILE - 87

12-17½ 9:26P — Hodel tells man some girls are coming over - one is 26, a legal secretary to some lawyer. Man asks if girl is going along to Santa Barbara. Talk about 3 girls comin over in about 30 minutes.

9:47P — Hodel trys to phone 3 times, no answer - tells man ne one answered.

17½-18 9:50P — Hodel and man talk about a phone number. Hodel said he wasn't sure-repeated number. HO 9442. Wasnm't sure about the 2.

18-19 9:52P — Man trys phone - asks for Miss Jackson - says HO 94140 Trys again - says HO 9442 - then repeats 24376-trys another number - no answer.

10:01P — Radio on

10:16P — Hodel asks operator number of some theater - then repeats HO 93131. Calls and asks if anyone is at ticket agency desk.

19-21 10:20P — Man asks Hodel about mailing a letter - wanted her to get it tomorrow - Man asks Hodel for a complete physica check-up. Hodel checks man's blood pressure - talks ab that - Hodel tells him he couldn't get insurance.

21-23½ 10:30P — Girls arrive - unable to understand - are in another ro Lot of laughing.

11:00P — Still in another part of house.

11:13P — Other man comes in. Hodel introduces girls as Mickey-Shirley-Judy. Talking about a deoderizing bath salt, Hodel said he just used.

HODEL FILE - 88

11:45P — Playing some kind of guessing game.

3-4-50 12:15A — Still playing same game

1:45A — Playing a new guessing game

23½-24½ 1:27A — Phone rang, Hodel answered - didn't say anything.

1:30A — Meyer off duty.

1:50A — C.L.Wean, LAPD, on duty

2:20A — Playing cards

3:30A — Playing records, can't hear conversation
Visitors left - Hodel apparently gone to bed.

8:00A — Morgan relieves Wean

24½-25 9:30A — Telephone rang - no answer

25-32 9:37A — Telephone rang - man in xxx house woke up Hodel.
Man-"Telephone, George". Hodel-"Hello" - conversation unintelligible - Hodel went to bathroom - returned to phone - Hodel "I don't know where he is. I'll be here today".

32-33 11:55A — Hodel and Ellen - unintelligible conversation.

33-33½ 11:50A — Hodel and Ellen - unintelligible conversation.

33½-34½ 12:00P — Hodel and Ellen - unintelligible conversation.

12:00P — Sullivan Relieves Morgan

12:35P — Hodel to Ellen "You got crumbs all over my bed. Will you get them off without getting them on the floor.

34½-36 12:42P — Hodel dials phone (recorded) MY 2064 (?) hangs up and dials again. No response.

36-38 12:50P — Phone rings, Hodel answers (recorded) "How are the kid and fishing". Apparently talking to his wife, Dorothy. "I'll come down this evening, around 8 o'clock.

HODEL FILE - 89

89

38-41½	1:01P	Phone rings. Hodel answers (recorded) Water running a/ conversation is unintelligible. Sounds like talking ab sale of house. Will show by appointment only. Call about 1:45 PM.
41½-44	1:21P	Phonerings. Hodel answers (recorded) "Your'e talking over a tapped line. Oh yes, it's been tapped for a long time. I'll be home for the next hour. Be sure and com
44-45	1:26P	Hodel dials phone (recorded) Asking for theater seats.
45-46	1:27P	Hodel dials phone (recorded) "I want Gittleson's". I want 2 front centers for Martha Graham." He got them at $4.80 each.
46-46½	1:28P	Hodel dials phone (recorded) Asking about seats for Martha Graham.
46½-47	1:38P	Hodel dias phone (recorded) Asks for medical desk.
	1:44P	Ellen advises Hodel party there to see house. Hodel tells Ellen to take her back and show her the rooms on other side, that he will be out in a few minutes (from bathroom)
47-48	1:58P	Hodel talking to lady about sale of house.
	2:10P	Talking to Ellen (recorded) Not intelligible.
	2:25P	Quiet.
	2:35P	Man talking in some other part of house. Sounds like t salesman who talked all thru yesterday p.m.
	2:41P	Man still talking.
48-60	2:45P	Man still talking (recorded) talking to Hodel about s/ woman. Mentions Barbara Sherman. Dorothy Black (?) Som thing about Santa Barbara. Hodel - "She called me this morning. She's coming over this P." Man-"You had pretty good success with some of those dames I fix/

HODEL FILE - 90

90

2:55P	Spool #31 runs out.
2:55P	Man continues talking about his blood pressure and goin into army.
3:05P	Phone rings. Hodel answers - "It's on Franklin near Normandie". Talked about renting apt. or apt. and a single studio room available. 75.00 for room. Wire breaks while rewinding spool 31 at time 32.
3:10?	Phone rings - Hodel answers "giving directions as to ho' to get to his home".
3:25P	Phone rings-Hodel answers "Thank you for calling".
3:26P	Hodel to man "In about 2 or 3 weeks I'll probably be on way abroad.
3:27P	Man and Hodel still talking about man getting into serv Hodel tells him if he can get even as a private who sho' He asks Hodel if he got back in and continued to handle tea around bay area if it would make his blood pressure worse. Talks a lot about "Corky" apparently wife or friend of salesman. Hodel tells man he would pay him 1000.00 if he'd sell Hodel's house. They leave to walk around the house.
3:40P	Man and Hodel again talking about blood pressure.
3:44P	Phone rings 2 times, answered in some other part of the house.
3:50P	Phone rings 2 times - answered otherpart of house.
4:00P	Quiet for past 15 minutes.
4:00P	Jim McGrath, D.A.'s office on duty.
4:00P	Salesman and Hodel talking again. Something about a $15.00 check the salesman wanted Hodel to give him - ma

HODEL FILE - 91

4:00P   out to a Joe. Which the salesman wants to show his landlady. The check - also salesman told Hodel he was broke - told Hodel how this AM he went into a restauran he always eats at and had breakfast for 55¢ - then walk over to the magazine section - looked at some magazines and left without paying - both not a big laugh out of t

Spool 32

4:11P   A Mr. Rappart phones Hodel regarding house.

5:27P   Salesman leaves

4:44P   Spool 32 on

4:57P   Someone calls (a girl) re. a room for 2 - Hodel explain house.

5:05P   Hodel shows house to some woman - said "I've rented one the rooms since talking to you."

5:35P   Phone rings 2 times, answered in another part of house. Not able to hear conversation.

5:55P   Hodel in conversation with the man with the German accen trying to record, however reception is very poor. (tried 2 min. of recording, but shut it off - can't understand)

5:58P   Conversation ends - not heard anymore.

6:02P   Hodel receives a phone call regarding the house - could not make make cut (racket and noise is the loudest ever heard) Sounds like he rented the other room - said "let me have your phone, yes 27229 - No, since there are 4 of you, it would add too much of a load on the phones." It appears 4 girls are moving in - one by the name of Miss Maxwell it sounded like.

HODEL FILE - 92

6:40P   Phone rang - Hodel to some woman (recorded) no info. obtained.

6:55P   Some man in conversation with someone on phone - not Hodel (recorded) the salesman who had dinner with Hode got some phone number 89581. Prefix not mentioned - th is the phone number of another girl - Hodel came back phone rang - someone calling re. the house - the addres of the girl is Santa Monica Blvd and Cahuenga. Motion Picture Industry Pix operator.

7:22P   Phone rings once - no conversation - must have been answered on extension.

7:25P   Hodel in conversation with one of the girls who was goin to move in-her phone number is HU 27289 - some indicati they may not take the room. Hodel is to phone in the A could not ascertain her name.

7:35P   Hodel phones party named Mickey - said he would like he to read him some poetry tonight - asked how her energy was. Started talking very low - could not make out. "I'm a easy listener". (Presume he's talking to a s can't hear clear - said would she like to be observed - frustration and complexes-mentioned something about relationship with me - I'm sure of myself - told her 2 stories.

8:00P   Meyer, LAPD, on duty

8:30P   Talking in some other room.

8:40P   Hodel talking to two women who he is trying to sell or rent house - said he would rent for $90.00 month. Two unmarried sisters-sounds as though one can't speak Engl Said he had the studio rented to some woman painter.

93

HODEL FILE - 93

8:40P One other room to some other woman, asks them to come back and look tomorrow. He won't be home, but house-keeper will. Change spool.

Spool 33
9:03P Other man came in - women still there. Hodel introduce man as his business manager - women leave. Hodel goes other part of house.

9:12P Hodel and man talking - man has accent. Hodel takes him to bedroom and talks in low voices - said something some case being cold - seemed to talk about tax or sale of clinic - can't hear too well. (Recorded-hope can hear better) Hodel gave man Two phone numbers, his OL 3476 some office TR 1252. PBX operator comes back and other man who has been around for awhile. All three ta about some business deal - can't figure it out - say something about China.

I9:40P Phone rang - Hodel answered. Didn't say anything. Talking about selling something.

9:50P Sounds as though 2 men left. Hear one person around.

10:00P All 3 back. Hodel says he knows 4 girls in Burbank Two are 19 and two are 20, who are practising oriental dances and are going to Mexican and Latin America. Hodel asks man with accent if he thinks they would go o' down there. Hodel talks as though he has a contract an will go along.

10:37P 2 men talking - one telling about place he lives, but i leaving other can have it. Didn't mention any address.

10:45P Two people talking in one room, and a lot of racket in another room. (recorded) but couldn't understand.

94

HODEL FILE - 94

10:45P 2 men leave. Hodel says he won't be home tomorrow.

11:15P Quiet, Hodel and Ellen around.

11:45P Hodel typing.

2-5-50 12:12A Phone rings. Hodel answers, "Yes honey. I am painting some furniture. I am a great lover of honesty." Talks about car other party bought. Said he would like to get one but couldn't pay cash. Asks about taking th car someplace. Break car in andyou in at same time. Talks about a poker game.

12:45A Quiet. Hodel still moving around.

1:15A Quiet. Hodel still moving around.

1:30A All quiet. Think Hodel went to bed in another part of house.

1:45A LAPD
Wean,relieves Meyer.

2:00A Apparently still in bed. No movement of any kind.

Spool 34
0- 8:00A Mronak, D.A.'s office on duty

8:30A All quiet.

9:00A All quiet.

9:30A Phone rang 2 times, didn't hear anyone answer.

10:00A All quiet.

10:30A All quiet.

10:40A Hear child's voice in background - very faint

11:19A Phone rang 3 times, child's voice in background - must answered in another room.

11:59A Hear Hodel humming and moving around the desk.

12:00P Relieved by Jack Egger, D.A.'s office.

12:05P Bathroom noises - woman humming in background.

HODEL FILE - 95

85

12:06p	Woman greeted someone at front door, could not pick up conversation.
12:15P	Conversation in background, cannot pick it up conversa- tion between Hodel and other man.
12:20P	Turned on radio, playing symphony music.
12:22P	Typewriting can be heard over the symphony - man coughi
1 PM	Radio still on (symphony) typewriting still going on.
1:25 P	Phone rang, cannot hear conversation because of radio.
1½ 1:35P	Phone rang - recorded - conversation with some one whom he told to "come over after work tomorrow".
1:40P	Typewriting resumed by Hodel.
1:50P	Knock on door, Ho el 1st woman in-Conversation ensued
3½	(tried to record but it was background)
2:00P	Hodel seems to be opening and closing drawers. Typewri resumed.
6½-7 2:10P	Hodel in conversation with man and woman, but cannot p it up very well. Too far in background - seem to be talking about photography of a surrealistic nature. Hod shows some sxx pictures of his to the two people - also talking about renting some suites of rooms in his place Man has a definite spanish accent, asked Hodel about Spanish doctors in this area. Hodel mentioned leaving in a "couple of months" Attempt to record this convers tion proved futile because it was too much in backgroun Hode again started talking about photographs with the people - part of conversation is recorded.
11½ 3:00PM	Pictures seemed to be of Japanese girls.
3:03P	The two people left.

HODEL FILE - 96

86

3:05P	Another man came in - talked to Hodel for about a red headed girl who may live there with her mother. Both seemed interested in if the girl was over 18 or not Man asked Hodel if when he went to Santa Monica if he wa going to stay there or not.
15 3:20P	Hodel called up a girl named Carol, asked herabout buyi a couch from her.
16	Hodel bought the couch from her for $35.00 and said it a deal, now you only ow me $50. and said goodby and hun up.
3:25P	Phone rang - must have been answered in other room.
3:25P	Hodel left the room - radio still on in background.
3:33P	Hodel back in room, some typing and moving about.
	No conversation.
4:00P	Relieved by Jim McGrath, D.A.'s office

Spool 35

	J. Egger had trouble with other spool No. 34, it had br took same off and replaced with #35, lost some of the s in removing.
5:30P	Hodel and salesman in conversation. "Can't make it" Salesman said, it's down in the basement locked up. Th salesman talked about his blood pressure.
6:35P	Hodel and Ellen in conversation - not understood - mumb
7:30P	Hodel and Ellen in conversation - mumbling faint - can' hear.
7:50P	Phone call to Hodel from Pat, said, "Wait a minute, I'l be with you. Hudson 27829, is her phone. Hodel to cal her in A.M.
8:00P	Meyer on duty, LAPD

HODEL FILE - 97

97

8:40P	Hodel called Joe, asked him if he didn't want the room.
8:45P	Hodel had a chance to rent it to two "sweet"young girls one goes to U.S.C., and the other is a Secretary for Prudential Life Insurance Company.
	Calls some woman and talks about renting part of house to her - says he is going abroad soon - makes appointment for 12:45 tomorrow to show house.
9:15P	All quiet.
9:45P	All quiet.
10:15P	All quiet.
10:45P	All quiet.
11:15P	All quiet.
11:45P	All quiet.
3-6-50	
12:15A	All quiet.
12:45A	All quiet.
1:15A	All quiet.
1:45A	All quiet.
2:00A	Brechel, LAPD, on duty, all is quiet.
2:20A	Several odd sounds in background, sounds like trumpet o an elephant.
2:45A	Noises in background indicate someone working around, probably in studio.
3:10A	Hodel enters from rear, part of house, goes to lavatory urinates.
3:15A	Hodel goes to bed.

HODEL FILE -
Spool 35
3-6-50

97-A

98

5:10A	Hodel gets out of bed. Goes to other part of house for a minute, then returns to bed.
8:00A	J. McGrath, D.A.'s office on duty.
9:40A	Hodel up - talking to Ellen - said come on let's get up. going. Gave her hell for being in room for 10 minutes times.
9:55A	Phone rings - Hodel answers-about renting room.
10:15A	Ordering blankets from Broadway Hollywood.
10:35A	Hodel asking for phone number of owner's Realty's Servic
10:50A	Hodel and Spanish man talking about "refiguring a job" of some kind in the house.
11:30A	Hodel phones Manlo 46516 - did not hear my conversation
12:03A	Joe comed - Hodel talked about callers in the house.
12:00noon	Snyder - D.A.'s office on duty
12:40P	Hodel calls regarding houses for sale - hangs up and raises hell with Ellen over nothing.
12:55P	Shirley Throckmorton - student - calls - talks to Hodel regarding being student in Hodel's class (whatever that is) both move to part of house where talk is un-intelligible - both return and Hodel suggests they sit in his car and talk - to which party agrees.

HODEL FILE - 98

3-6-50

No wire
No recording

Snyder, D.A.'s office on duty

1:40P	Both return to room - talk on medical problems.
1:45P	Hodel answers phone regarding Miss Davis - ?? on position with some Mr. 1/31/50 date mentioned by Hodel.
1:50P	Resumes conversation with prospect - possibly partners ? business - talk re. 2 party phone as to costs, etc. - apparently selling "lady" bill of goods.
2:30P	Phone rings - Hodel answers - not important.
2:30P	Resume talk with lady suspect "?" or prospect.
3:10P	Gal still there - conversation unintelligible. (Belle and Bimson playing back recording?)
3:25P	Hodel phones - wants specimen picked up at 3684 7th Ave.
3:30P	Gal leaves - will return.
3:55P	Hodel does some typing - also talks to Ellen - gives her some more hell for free.
4:15P	Hodel still typing - (monotonous, isn't it?)
4:25P	Phone rings - Hodel answers.
4:30P	Snyder, off duty, Eggers on, D.A.'s office
4:45P	Hodel typing
5:00P	Hodel still typing
5:05P	Hodel goes out of room - all quiet.
5:15P	Hodel back, has another man with him - background conversation cannot pick-up.
5:25P	Woman enters - still in background.
5:30P	Everyone leaves room - all quiet.
5:35P	Hodel returns to the room-opens some drawers and leaves again - all quiet.

HODEL FILE - 99

5:40P	All quiet.
5:50P	Hodel back, with woman - woman talking about Painting he kitchen.
	Hodel talked about a woman named "Tracey Racapore" who attends UCLA who is renting rooms from him. Stated that "she is about 22 years of age, very nice girl who studie most of the time".
6:00P	Conversation continues - woman talking about renting roo
6:02P	Another man enters, conversation very much in the background.
6:05P	Hodel and girl talking - girl said she "would be afraid to live alone". Hodel said he would "protect her to the best of his ability". Girl said that she "would get ove being afraid, O.K."
6:15P	Hodel shows the girl some picture of his; they seem to portraits of an abstract nature, conversation turns to photos.
6:15P	Man with accent, apparently spanish, comes into conversation.
6:20P	Everyone except Hodel leaves.
6:22P	Another woman comes in. Hodel tells her "to sit down ar take it easy for a minute".
6:30P	Hodel in background, conversation with woman.
6:35P	Woman leaves - Hodel alone working at desk. can hear occasional dog barking in background.
6:45P	Another woman enters, she and Hodel talk about renting rooms. Woman said she will call Hodel between 11 and 1? tomorrow, and leaves.

HODEL FILE - 100

7:05P — Hodel alone - working at desk - typing

7:30P — Hodel still alone - moving about room. Hodel called Menlo 46517 from operator - no answer. Hodel called another number - could not get it, told the girl his new phone number would be OL 3476, and that he was

7:45P — "keeping it secret. He asked the girl if she and "Will would come over soon.

7:47P — A woman comes into Hodel's room; he asked her "when her mother was coming over". The girl said, this event She said her mother is Mrs Alica De Varora, and her nam is Villa De Varora. Hodel stated that his type of work is Administrative Medicine, and at present he has a laboratory and has done a lot of work for the government overseas, etc.

8:00P — Egger, D.A.'s office off duty.

8:00P — Wead, LAPD, on duty.

8:10P — Hodel moving around, no conversation.

8:20P — Woman talking to Hodel. Can't understand.

8:25P — Woman leaves - man enters - talks with Hodel about moral of spanish girls. Hodel tells man he should have seen his Chinese collection which was worth $100,000.

8:30P — Man calls women on phone and tells her he is going out with Hodel - to have some drinks.

8:35P — Hodel suggests they go to a Chinese place. They leave.

9:20P — Someone enters - then could hear woman crying. Phonograph turned on. No conversation.

10:45P — Phonograph. Still playing and someone typewriting.

10:50P — Phone rings - unable to hear with music.

11:05P — Hodel tells Ellen to pack everything in a box and

HODEL FILE - 82

11:50AM — Hodel working around desk

11:55AM — Hodel said to Ellen "Take the suitcase down and have it fixed".

11:55P — Hodel started typing

12:00noon — Hodel still typing

12:00noon — Sullivan, D.A.'s office relieves Eggers

12:15P — Hodel talking to Ellen - unintelligible

0-1 · 12:30P — Hodel dials - asks for number of Santa Fe - then dials (recorded) much racket

1-4½ · 12:32P — Hodel dials S.P. Rwy. - (recorded) wants info on trains, sounds like to Arizona, to Gila Bend, Ariz. Leave 8:30 at night - asks for fare - $12.04

12:45P — Typing

12:55P — Hodel dials phone - asks about OPA regulations in LA "Does rent control still cover L.A. House was built in 192 Place has never been registered. Well, it's a big house, a I thought I'd divide it up into rooms and apartments. The name is Harvey; Owner George Harvey, 5121 Franklin.

12:59P — Hodel dials phone - asks for American Red Cross - Call me a OL 3476

1:05P — Hodel typing

1:12P — Hodel talking to Ellen - "I can take that package down and mail. Also Tomar's. Is Tomar's ready. I got to take a trip in the car and can mail the package.

1:15P — Hodel talking in a low voice to some girl. Said something about taking something to her mother. Conversation continued for about 5 minutes, but unable to get any of it due to low tones.

1:26P — Conversation resumes, but still unintelligible.

HODEL FILE - 89/102   103

	1:55P	Typing
	2:00P	Radio ch. Hodel and woman talking. Cannot understand due to radio and racket. Sounds like someone interested in house.
	2:12P	Emergency vehicle passing. Conversation with woman continues. Still unintelligible.
	2:21P	Hodel talking to a woman - radio in background and conversation unintelligible
4½-6	2:22P	Started recording. Believe woman to be Ellen
	2:25P	Conversation with Ellen continues.
	2:28P	Phone rings - Ellen answers "Whose calling - just a moment" can't hear anything further.
	2:30P	Hodel talking "I would like a check on OL 3476 - when can you get a service man out".
	2:40P	Typing - and radio still playing
	2:50P	Phone - Hodel answers - He gives his name and address
	3:15P	Quiet
	3:25P	Hodel talking, unable to understand
	3:45P	Hodel to Ellen - something about reservations. Sounds like Ellen to go to Arizona
	4:00P	Hronek, D.A.'s office on duty
	4:30P	All quiet
	5:00P	All quiet, only water running in the bathroom
	5:10P	Conversation in the background, impossible to understand
7-12	5:30P	Hodel talking with some woman (recorded) too much disturbance to understand.
	6:00P	Hear Hodel moving around - talk in the background
	6:30P	All quiet

HODEL FILE - 84/103   104

	6:57P	Hodel starts typing
	7:00P	All quiet
12-13	7:08P	Hodel dials - gets wrong number - tries again (recorded) Hodel leaves the room
	7:30P	All quiet
13-14	7:31P	Phone rings 5 times - answered by Ellen in another part of the house - couldn't hear at all
	8:00P	Hronek off duty - all quiet
	8:00P	Wean, LAPD, on duty
	8:10P	Talking in background - can't understand.
	9:05P	Talking in background - can't understand.
	10:00P	Hodel messing around in toilet - no conversation
14-30	10:30P-11:25P	Man enters - they talk, can't make out too well (recorded)
30-34	11:40P	Hodel talking about some plans, but can't make out (recorded
3-8-50	2:00A	Brechel, LAPD, on duty - All quiet. Hodel probably in bed can hear snoring.
	3:00A	All is quiet
	4:00A	All is quiet
	5:00A	Male voice in background, too far away to understand. Sound lasted about a minute then all quiet again. Hodel still snoring.
	6:30A	Ellen moving around.
	8:00A	J. McGrath, D.A.'s office on duty
	8:30A	Phone rings - Hodel answers - about the "Packard jalopy" starting hard talking to some mechanic about fixing up the car. Said "I will see you later - about 10:30A or 11 AM regarding the car - having it fixed".

HODEL FILE - 85 / 04   105

10:30A   Conversation over phone with his wife Dorothy - she was
         complaing about money-he said he is broke - can't pay
         mortgage on the house this month - has no money coming in'
         from sounds of conversation bad feelings may be developing.
         Also spoke of going to see a Mrs. La Cour. Hodel was to
         write her.

12:25P   Called Lou regarding the Packard - said would be down in
         five minutes.

12:36P   Called Postal information for information regarding pix
         postal service with the capital of Tibet.

12:36P   Snyder, D.A.'s office on duty

         All quiet - Hodel is having car repaired - apparently no or
         in house at all.

2:30?   Phone rings 9 times - no one answer.

34-39   4:00P   Hronek, D.A.'s office on duty

39-40   4:19P   Telephone conversation with someone (recorded)

         Phone Company to disconnect the extension OL 3476 - should
         have been disconnected today, tomorrow expects to work only
         12-2 PM - or Friday, he'll stay home himself.

5:10P   Hodel starts typing

40-42   5:30P   Hodel carries a conversation with another man - phone rang
                and unkn man left.

6:15P   Hodel dials, asks to have someone call him.

42-44   7:15P   Hodel dials - asks for Dr Friedner, dials another
                3787 So. Vermont - Friedner's address

7:30P   Hodel typing like mad.

8:00P   Hronek off duty.

8:00P   Meyer, LAPD, on duty

HODEL FILE - 85 / 05   106

8:10P   Hodel phones someone and asks name and exact title of
         Chief of States of Burma and Tibet - wants to know how they
         are addressed. Name of Minister Public Health of Burma -
         goes back to typing.

8:45P   Phone rang 3 times, didn't hear anyone answer - has been
         quiet for past 20 minutes.

8:54P   Phone rang 3 times, didn't hear anyone answer.

9:30P   All quiet

10:00P   All quiet

10:15P   Hodel typing

10:45P   Hodel still typing

11:15P   Hodel still moving around

11:45P   All quiet

12:15R   All quiet. Hodel snoring

3-9-50   12:45R   All quiet. Hodel still snoring

1:15R   All quiet. Hodel still snoring

1:45R   All quiet. Hodel still snoring

2:00A   Breshel, LAPD, on duty. All is quiet except for Hodel
         snoring.

6:10A   Woman - may be Ellen moving around house

8:00A   J. McGrath, D.A.'s office on duty

9:15A   Someone knocking on a door 3 times

9:35A   Phone call - couldnot make much out. Hodel asked"if you
         were going to pick that up".

9:50A   Hodel phoned Telephone Company to have extension of OL 3476
         disconnected.

HODEL FILE - 97 -/06

107

10:00AM Hodel has a male patient - gave him Methrolate to put 3 drops in each eye, one time a day. Hodel is talking with man with German accent - talking about going to the auction and buying and selling things - talking about buying paints

10:03AM Phone call - Hodel answered -- nothing said - just "yes,yes"

10:07AM Another phone call. Hodel talks to someone about selling lumber - pressure cooker, and odd and ends.

10:40AM Hodel makes phone call - for Repair Department - complained about a condenser - sputtering.

10:55AM Officer Simson and Sgt. Belle checked Hodel's residence for license plates to find out who man with German accent is - the following plates were in sun in front of Hodel's house
75 P 519 - 35 Packard F.E. Mattoon - 251 S. Lucerne, L.A.
9 P 3938 - 47 Chev. Willie Wheeler, 4461 Towne Ave., L.A.
885 420 - 41 Ford Conv. Violet Jean Kallen - 2055 N. New Hampshire, L.A.
60A8 150 - 36 Packard, Marie L. Vaila - 2212 N. Nella Vista, L.A.

11:30AM All quiet around house.

12:03PM Hodel calls a Mr. Kurst or Hurst - talking about photo-stats - said Mr. Good has pictures - also the photographers name is Ackerman.

12:15PM Phone rings - Hodel says "I love you very much. I'm at the house"or something like that. "I'll see you at 1:15."

12:16PM Hodel phones - a Margaret said "he has a 2 PM appointment."

12:20PM Sullivan, D.A.'s office on duty.

1:15PM Phone rings. No one answers. Quiet since 12:25.

1:30PM Phone rings - no one answers.

2:05PM Someone walking around.

HODEL FILE - 88 -/07

108

2:20PM Hodel talking with some man. Conversation unintelligible (much static and noise in machine).

2:25PM Water running.

2:39PM Hodel dials phone "asks for Mr. Kurst(?) "Kurst not in? I'll call back".

2:50PM Hodel talking to someone by phone about an inlay china box. Apparently trying to sell some China piece he has.

2:51PM Hodel phones. "Hello, brother, good. I'll have some of those special manhattans for you. Take my new number, OL 3476. Give me a ring and drop by around the cocktail hour. I gave it to Mr. Kirsh (?)

3:00PM Phone rings - Hodel answers "Sure, I'll be here." Conversation in very low tones.

3:17PM Hodel asks for number at 5101 Hollywood Blvd. Then dials number. "Are my trousers and shirts ready? I'll stop by for them".

3:50PM Hodel phones someone - states he is calling for a Mrs. Chajud who wants to share a luxurious apartment with some girl. He gives this party his phone number, and address.

3:51PM Hodel calls. Gives a rental listing to share an apartment. "Calling for Mrs. De Chajud(?) Mrs. C. has a 19 yr. old daughter, and she wants some one-preferably a young college student—to share apartment. Someone year who wants an artistic setup. Mrs. C. is just here from Costa Rica, but speaks good English. Mrs. De Chajud - $35.00, 5121 Franklin by appointment.

HODEL FILE - 89/08

109

44-51 3:55PM Hodel dials (recorded) - (very interesting) repetition of above about Mrs. Chajud and daughter sharing a luxurious apartment in a $160,000; house. 4:00-8:00A - Bronek on duty, D.A.'s office. A woman comes in. Hodel - "How are you". Much static. Unable to understand. Hear Hodel again on phone talking about apartment.

4:02PM

4:20PM Hodel dials phone - again talks to a rental agency. Renews his Mrs De Chajud pitch about sharing an apartment. Wants a 19 or 20 yr. old girl. Some hammering and sawing in background.

4:25PM Hodel dials phone - another rental agency.

4:30PM Call to another agency

4:35PM Another one

4:36PM Hodel dials - gets another agency

4:41PM Hodel dials - gets another agency

4:42PM Hodel calls another agency about a girl to share the apartment

4:50PM Phone rings - Hodel answers - something about a box he could use over the weekend

4:57PM Phone rang - Hodel answered. "The sooner we have that audition the better. Sunday will be a good time. Do you know of any place where I could make arrangements?"

5:05PM Talking to some woman (new housekeeper) about showing her the secret of the lock, and about going out for awhile.

6:00PM All quiet.

7:00PM All quiet.

7:30PM Phone rang 3 times - no answer

7:55PM Hodel moving around the house and bathroom.

HODEL FILE - 89/09

110

51 8:00PM Meyer, LAPD on duty

8:02PM Hodel turns radio on - low talking - unable to hear - is on phone talking to someone about a sore throat. Said something about Mexico - if she was OK - could probably leave tomorrow night

8:20PM Hodel calls Orchid 22032 - asks for Marian - then talks to someone about Marian - going to Frisco.

8:23PM Hodel calls Sunset 16510 - asks for Harry.

8:24PM Hodel calls Sunset 33419 - talks to Harry - asks if he know where he can get in touch with Jonathan Usher? Says he is a ham radio operator, and Hodel wants to receive a message from Tibet in about 2 to 4 weeks.

8:55PM Hodel talks to Harry again - same subject

9:45PM Hodel still typing and moving around

10:45PM Hodel still moving around

3-10-50 12:15A One or two men and about same amount of women- Talking to Hodel. Hard to understand - something about a place in Mexico not too far from Arizona - good roads - something about a Moore House, or sanatorium. One man seems to be a doctor. Talking about she at Camarillo. Hodel - "She was going to shoot me and commit suicide "Tamara" (way it sounded) Talking about fishing trip to Mexico 228 miles from Phoenix, Arizona - seem to be looking at map-mentioned Sonora, Mexico - other party leaves 1:15A - says he will leave Hodel know about noon tomorrow - Friday - about trip.

HODEL FILE - 9½ //0

2:00A   Wear, LAPD, on duty -

2:15A   Hodel apparently gone to bed. All quiet.

6:15A   Hodel getting up - moving around house.

8:00AM   J. McGrath, D.A.'s office on duty. All quiet.

8:45AM   Phone rang 2 times - could not hear an answer

9:00AM   Phone rang - Hodel said, "Hello - yes - how's things" hung up. Hodel is up and around.

9:10AM   Hodel and some woman in short conversation - could not understand - then they went to rear of the house.

9:15AM   Hodel makes phone call - asks for extension 372 - Mr. Kelley or Ragay - about his export business - about an order Hodel had placed - nothing else mentioned as to products, e

10:10AM   Phone call from Ted. Hodel asked "do you know a Dr. Donald, L.A. Terry, or L.A. Perez at a mission - address may be 56 Martian or Marvana Rd. Not in private practice - asked how many siamanese practitioners there were. Told Ted first chance he has to phone him to have dinner - as he wants to talk to him.

10:20AM   Phone call to Mattel - asked if Irwin was working - asked her to have him come by - also said would like to see you some- time - asked her about pains in her stomach.

10:25AM   Phoned Telephone Company to pick up some old telephone directories.

10:27AM   Phone call - something about a short stocky man picking up a deposit.

10:32AM   Hodel phones someone to pick up something - could not make out what.

HODEL FILE - 9½ ///

10:33AM   Phone call received by Hodel - said maybe going away for the weekend - said to phone him at 4 PM - he would know

11:07AM   Phone call received - Hodel answered - sounds like planning a trip - asked when can you get away - will phone you prefixes not obtained-numbers are 84435 and 81831

11:27AM   Hodel phones Orchard 22033 - no answer

11:30AM   Phone call received - something about dropping off some clothes - said again he may leave town - also asked for a book containing names and addresses

11:35AM   Hodel makes phone call-too much static and Hodel too far away to make out.

12:25P   Sgt Belle - said the has found out the man with the German accent is one Baron Herringer - a supposed ex-German - Baron. The two new girls are Vilma (age 19) and Sonia (age 15) Said had moved in with their mother. 2 sisters.

1:15PM   Burns, D.A.'s office on duty

2:00PM   Hodel returned to house.

2:20PM   Hodel talking to man about income tax with-holding, etc.

2:35PM   Hodel talks on phone (received call)-too much static.

2:45PM   Hodel received phone call "She's coming over. Does she know the name. I'll have her call you as soon as she gets here.

2:48PM   Resumed talk of Income tax, withholding-with man (unnamed)

4:10PM   Hodel called OR 27023, No answer.

4:15PM   Income taxconsultant left.

4:20PM   Hodel received call from patient about stomach.

4:25PM   Woman entered house - no conversation with her

4:45PM   Kronek, D.A.'s office on duty.

HODEL FILE - 93 //2

113

51½	4:55PM	Phone rang 2 times - answered in a whisper
	5:05PM	Conversation with a woman - distant - hard to understand - toilet being flushed 3 times in a row
41½-52		Spool ran out just when Hodel talked with Joe. Joe still talks -"that's one of the conditions of my probation." A woman present.

SPOOL #16

0-14	4:20PM	Mixed conversation - Hodel answered the phone. Hodel called Superior 84425 - Superior 81831 - conversation about a plane trip over the weekend.
14-17	5:59PM	Seems to have a woman patient. Woman - 37 45442 - seems like Hodel and party are leaving for Mexico tonight.
17-53	6:40PM	Hodel called Charles about cancelling the trip to Mexico because he can't line up 4 reliable people. Going out for supper - woman called another party - who was willing to loan his car for the trip. Finally decided that they'll leave Wednesday night. Hodel showing the map and pictures the woman.
	6:50P	The phone rang - Hodel answered "Hello Betty"- Toilet being flushed - can't understand
	7:05P	Hodel dials information "What's the number of 5101 Hollywood Blvd.
	7:20P	Phone rang 7 times - no answer.
	7:32P	Phone rang 4 times - no answer
	7:57P	Phone rang 5 times - no answer
	8:00P	Meyer, L.A.P.D. on duty. All quiet.
	8:32P	Phone rang 3 times - didn't hear anyone answer - sounds as though someone talking in another room.

HODEL FILE - 94 //3

114

	10:05P	Phone rang 3 times - no one answered.
3-11-50	1:00A	Hodel comes home - sounds like a woman with him - can't understand them - in another room. Sounds like it may be his ex-wife. Can't understand what talking about.
	1:35A	Sounds as though Hodel is at his desk.
	1:45A	Hodel starts typing.
	2:00A	Wear, LAPD, on duty
	2:15A	Hodel moving around - no conversation
	2:45A	Hodel apparently gone to bed - can hear snoring.
	7:40A	All quiet.
	8:00A	J. McGrath, D.A.'s office on duty.
	8:10A	Phone call to Hodel - who said "OK will see you at 9 AM".
	9:30A	Phone call - Hodel said "See me Monday or Tuesday. I'm going fishing over the weekend.
	10:07A	Woman phoning Santa Monica 42421 - asked how the children were, said "I went to the doctor's yesterday and I did not feel good so I stayed with George last night. He is driving down later, and I'll be down then. (Sounded like Dorothy-Hodel's exwife)
	10:40A	Hodel and German in conversation. Can't understand as woman in bathroom - running water and making all kinds of noises.
	10:50A	Hodel and German talking - Hodel wants to rent a 26 room lo near Mexcali in Mexico. Where President Comacho of Mexico built to have conference with Roosevelt. He wants to m ake a rest home 300 air miles from L.A. 500 by car.

HODEL FILE - 95-///

115

10:55A — Phone rings 2 times - answered in rear of house - could not hear the German talking to Hodel about a man with nervous troubles (the German talks as tough he is a doctor i.e., in medical terms)

11:45A — Sullivan, D.A.'s office on duty. Hodel and woman talking in background. Believe his ex-wife, Dorothy.

12:10P — Mrs. Hodel doing a lot of talking, but apparently in some other part of house. Sounds as though she might be reading from a book or script. She's been talking for the past 10 minutes.

12:15P — Woman stops her reading or talking.

12:35P — Phone rings 3 times - possibly answered in some other part of house.

1:30P — Hear woman talking in background. Sounds like a woman and child.

1:40P — Man talking in background. Sounds like the talkative tea salesman.

1:43P — Typing.

1:55P — Typing by someone - not Hodel - Not as adept as Hodel. No conversation.

1:59P — Woman dials phone. Sounded like she said, "This is Elsie". Talked about Vincent Price. Also, about M.G.M. Talked abou John getting her a job. "Say Bob", I found a story. A stor of a black saint, a negro. Do you know John Farrow? I thought of him because of his Catholicism. I met him years ago. I have the babies down at the beach. But, I'd love to see you. (t must be Dorothy talking) You're at home all day. Oh, wonderful darling" then "I'll get to see you"

2:05P — End of conversation.

HODEL FILE - 96-///

116

2:15P — Hodel talking. Unintelligible

2:25P — Typing

3:15P — Hodel and Dorothy conversing in background. Getting ready to leave.

3:55P — Quiet reigns supreme.

3:55P — Littleton, D.A.'s office relieves Sullivan

SPOOL 37

4:00P — Hodel typing

4:11P — Hodel calls "Come in" Undistinguishable conversation with woman. Typing stops.

4:13P — Woman out, Hodel walking around.

4:20P — Undistinguishable words from woman. Heavy banging sound like wood being wrenched loose, then typing resumed. More wrenching sounds after typing stops.

0-10 — Woman patient apparently. Short professional conversation.

4:24P — Phone call regarding flight by plane. Asks if party would "like to go down there tonight". Puts a woman on phone for

10-21 — conversation with caller. Hodel says he can "go tonight" on a flight. Woman tells caller that prospect of trip is "wonderful". Apparently a flight to Mexico. Undistinguish- able chatter with woman after phone hung up.

4:35P — Phone rings. Woman answers. Undistinguishable conversation because of loud wrenching noises. Bathroom sounds - running water, flushing toilet. Hodel says "we drive (or ride) all night". Her answer undistinguishable.

4:45P — Phone bell (?) rings twice. No one answers. Undistinct mummering between Hodel and woman. Woman calls, "Doctor!" General moving around in background. Undistinct conversatic Hodel and woman over wrenching sounds. He tells her that

MODEL FILE - 97-//6 117

sxm something "is in her closet". More indistinct conversation with woman in background.

5:05P Typing. Asks some woman (patient?) "let me have your address and phone number, please". Answer undistinguishabl[e] He leaves, then apparently returns after indistinct chatter with a "Merl" (?) in background.

5:10P Goes to background and calls "Ferrero(R)(?) followed by indistinct chatter like some kind of instructions. Returns and typing is resumed.

5:15P Calls "Come in, Rose (?) and get out there". Woman's voice indistinguishable, receding to background. Child's voice indistinct in background. Child's voice - indistinct.

5:25P Typing. Leaves foreground, urinates, and flushes toilet. Undistinct talk in background - Hodel and woman. Hodel say[s] "Next week - mayba make it Friday". Apparently woman patient. Hodel returns to foreground. Talk with woman undistinguishable.

5:35P Typing, whistling as he does. Someone else moving around in background. Apparently he is not typing because he is talking indistinctly in background on phone. Says, "I'll be there and get it Tuesday night. I'll be looking for you". Rest of conversation not distinguishable because of typing. Says, "That's the only reason I'm going".

5:42P Typing continuing in foreground. Outside traffic noises also interfering with conversation. Hodel and woman in background. Hodel says something about "Calexico". Woman says "Is there a road"? Hodel says, "The only road there is". Typing stops.

5:53P Indistinct conversation Hodel and woman.

6:00P Moving about. No conversation.

MODEL FILE - 98-//7 118

6:05P All quiet, except outside traffic and possible very faint conversation in background.

6:08P Conversation - man and woman in b.g. very faint and undistinguishable. Some faint movement around background.

6:14P All quiet except outside traffic.

6:37P Steady, rushing noise - possibly bath water or shower?

6:44P Noise continues.

6:50P Noise continues. Vacuum cleaner?

7:05P Noise may be defect in receiver, but if so, cannot determine same. Phoned Lt. Jemison, CR 14917, but no answer.

7:20P Noise continues. Phoned Technician Braison at OL 9807.

7:22P While talking with him, noise stopped.

7:22P All quiet. Normal signal of outside traffic noises coming through. Dog barking.

8:00P Littleton off duty.

8:00P Meyer, LAPD, on duty

8:20P Sounds like someone moving around.

10:20P All quiet.

2-12-50 2:00AM Brechel, LAPD, on duty. All is quiet.

3:50AM Someone moving around for a few minutes.

8:00AM Egger, D.A.'s office on duty.

8:15AM All quiet.

8:29AM Someone walking around, possibly upstairs, no voices.

9:30AM All quiet.

10:00AM All quiet.

11:30AM All quiet.

12:00noon Cimino, D.A.'s office on duty.

12:05P All quiet.

1:00P Radio is turned on. Someone is walking.

MODEL FILE - 99 //8

1:10P	Voice in background is unintelligible.	
	Radio is still on - music can hardly be heard.	
1:15P	Man and woman are talking, but reception is bad - can't understand.	
1:30P	Radio off - all is quiet.	
1:45P	Bathroom sounds - footsteps. Woman talks - unintelligible.	
3:00P	All quiet.	
4:20P	Cimino off.	
4:20P	Morgan, D.A.'s office, on duty	
5:45P	Telephone rang - no answer	
7:00P	Woman talking (unintelligible)	
21-23 7:30P	Man and woman conversing (about rooms in house)	
8:00P	Wean, LAPD, on duty	
8:15P	Telephone rings 2 times - stops - no conversation	
8:30P	Telephone rings - 2 times - stops - no conversation	
6:45P	Radio playing - someone moving around	
2:00A	Brechel, LAPD on duty. All is quiet.	
6:30A	Someone moving around house.	
8:00A	J. McGrath, D.A.'s office on duty	
9:40A	Phone rings 8 times - no answer	
11:45A	Phone rings 9 times - no answer	
12:05P	Phone rings 8 times - no answer	
12:05P	Snyder - D.A.'s office on duty	
12:50P	Phone rings - 7 times - no answer	
1:20P	Phone rings 6 times - no answer	
1:45P	Phone rings 6 times - no answer	
1:55P	Phone rings 8 times - no answer	
2:10P	Phone rings 6 times - no answer	
2:10P	Phone rings 6 times - no answer	

MODEL FILE - 100 //9

2:15P	Phone rings 5 times - no answer	
2:15P	Phone rings 12 times - no answer	
2:22P	Phone rings 9 times - no answer	
2:50P	Phone rings 6 times - no answer	
3:00P	Phone rings 10 times - no answer	
3:40P	Phone rings 4 times - no answer	
4:05P	Phone rings 6 times - no answer	
5:00P	Snyder off duty	
	Wean, LAPD on duty. Someone moving around.	
5:15P	Phone rang 6 times - no answer, though some women are talki in the background and moving around	
23 7:00P	All quiet	
8:00P	All quiet	
3-14-50 2:00A	Brechel, LAPD, on duty, all quiet.	
5:00A	Someone enters. Sounds indicate it may be Hodel. Goes to desk, rustling of paper, probably going thru mail. Nope, I was wrong. He was on the can, reading and grunting, then flushes toilet.	
5:30A	Hodel walking around house.	
6:00A	All is quiet.	
6:20A	Female footsteps and voice in background	
6:50A	Hodel is snoring	
8:00A	J. McGrath, D.A.'s office on duty	
8:15A	Using a pretext - determined Hodel is back from Mexico.	
9:55A	Hodel receives a phone call - can't understand too much noise and mumbling.	
11:45A	Hodel up and moving around in the bathroom.	
12:00noon	Sullivan, D.A.'s office on duty	
12:05P	Water running. Apparently Hodel in bathroom.	

HODEL FILE - 102 /2/

121

Time	Notes
12:25P	Phone rings - Hodel answers - about a rental.
1:10P	Bell ringing - sounds like alarm clock turned off.
1:15P	Man talking with Hodel - low tones - unable to understand. Conversation about 2 minutes and man leaves.
1:45P	Door bell rings. Man talking to Hodel. They apparently go to some other part of house.
1:46P	Phone rings 3 times - hear no answer. Possibly in some oth part of house.
1:55P	Hodel pays man. Gives him a check for $18.25 on a $16.50 bill. Man gives Hodel change and thanks him very much and is sorry he bothered him.
2:50P	Man talking in background.
3:00P	Someone hammering.
3:05P	Phone rings 2 times. Hodel answers, but unable to hear any conversation.
3:30P	Hodel typing.
4:00P	Hrouek on duty.
4:13P	Hodel answered over the phone about his fishing in Mexico and dropping Ellen off in some town. Hoping she won't have enough money to return - (recorded) Resumes typing.
23-30	Joe cam in - (recorded)
30-33 6:17P	Hodel makes a call to SUnset 16510 - no answer.
33 6:33P	Hodel calls SUnset 16510 again - no answer.
7:17P	Meyer, LAPD, on duty. All quiet.
8:00P	Phone rang 2 times, didn't hear anyone answer.
8:30P	Hodel and some woman came in. Can't understand conversation.
9:00P	Radio on. Hodel didn't turn it on, not his type of music - too loud.
9:15P	

HODEL FILE - 102 /3/

122

Time	Notes
9:36P	Hodel plays some records in Spanish - says were recorded during bombing of Barcalone, Spain - in spanish.
9:53P	About 3 more females enter - sounded like Mickey or Mickey and her bunch, all talking or reading spanish.
10:20P	Phone rang - Hodel answers "Hello Harry, I have been trying to get you". Females making too much noise - can't hear Hodel - said something about fishing in Mexico - radio on again.
11:00P	Females and Hodel just talking.
11:20P	Hodel telling about the place in Mexico - he talked about before - said he looked at it when he was down this last time - shows a picture of the place - showing onthe map location of place.
11:26P	Some man came in - seemed to know girls.
33-35½ 11:30P	Hodel and man go in back room and talk. Couldn't hear too well - probably receiving order - will pick it up - sounded like will see each other 4 PM tomorrow. Man leaves - man's name "Chris".
11:40P	Lot of talking and laughing.
11:44P	Phone rang - Hodel answers - talks about place in Mexico. Said he had a mexican doctor friend down there, females making lot of noise - tells about fishing in Mexico.
	Say property will be for sale or lease in two months which about right time. Climate is perfect. Says money is in fishing, about 160 miles by road. Says will try to see him before he goes down to Mexico. Sounded like said "Bob"
3-15-50 12:05A	Hodel says he can get a plane - holds 4 people beside pilot can't hear too well.
12:15A	Woman left - Hodel moving around.
2:00A	Brechl, LAPD, on duty. All quiet except for Hodel snoring.

HODEL FILE - 104/2 (?)

123

6:30A	Female moving around house.
8:00A	J. McGrath, D.A.'s office on duty.
9:30A	No noise, all quiet to present time.
9:50A	Narcotics prefix(?) Phone call - Hodel answers. Say's wait a minute - sounds like he is looking for some papers. Gave someone a phone number 32341 - could not get prefix.
10:02A	Charlotte, phones Hodel - said to phone him around 6 - just general conversation.
10:55A	Hodel and some man talking about colors. hard to understan Talking low. Also talking about plastic bottles, tops, also colors of the caps in bottles. Talking about putting liquid in caps t test them. $16.00 a 1000 for plugs. 8 oz bottles - $27.50 a 1000. $20.00 a 1000 for caps. Non breakable bottles. Hodel going to Bullocks this afternoon - he tells salesman - Hodel talked to the buyer at Bullocks.
11:20A	Salesman leaves - all quiet.
11:45A	All quiet.
11:47A	Hodel called a Mr. Ramey - not in - left a call.
12:00noon	Hodel makes phone call - asks for Department #403 - said OK - thank you. Sullivan, D.A.'s office on duty.
12:45P	Phone rings 2 extra(?) times - no answer heard. Possibly answered in some other part of house.
12:47P	Hodel talking on phone regarding Sero-logic Laboratories and bills against it. Hodel claims some mistake in bills
1:05P	Phone rings 2 times - Possibly answered in some other part of house.
1:06P	Hodel on phone - "I just got back yesterday - It's 65 miles across the border from Arizona - Sonita (?) Fishing is

HODEL FILE - 104/2 3

124

good. Talked to Dr. Ignacia Renal (?) much interested in making a sanitorium out of the place. Cost 1,000,000 pesos to build. I'd just as soon lease it. Are you a Mexican citizen? Your'e not. I got some photos. Come on over and talk about it. Another Dr., an associate of mi went down there today to look at it. Would clean about 5000.00 a month. When you come in from Upland the next time, bring her with you so I can meet. Upland 02427? is h phone number. She is a nurse.

1:16P	Phone rings - Hodel answers - caught 27 sea bass - may go down next weekend. Talks about his trip. Fine climate, etc.
1:20P	Hodel starts typing.
1:22P	Phone rings. Hodel answers, "Yes father. I was in Med so trying to work up a business down there. There have been some new develop nts that I want to tell you about. OK, lad, I'll be seeing you.
1:26P	Hodel dials phone, mail me my slip for my deposits last month.
1:29P	Phone rings - Hodel answers. Oh Joe (?) "They're working on your phone right now. How soon can she come over. I'll wait for her. I'll be glad to have her in here. Does she do day work? How much do you pay her. Oh, she's just a friend.
1:56P	Phone rings - Hodel answers. Talks about repairs to garage
2:04P	Phone rings - Hodel answers "Pretty good, Pat. I'm just going out - can you be here in 45 minutes. Maybe to-morrow then.
2:05P	Hodel dials - Inspector 372 - Mr. Andy (?) No - I'll call him back.

2:06P   Hodel dials - no conversation.

2:07P   Hodel dials - Is Dr. Barrott there. This is Dr. Hodel. I just got back from Mexico. I went on a fishing trip. We drove down. I notice we got no business on the Research Maybe on account of phone disconnections. Discusses effort to build up Laboratories business.

2:15P   Hodel dials - no conversation.

2:20P   Phone rings - Hodel answers - unable to make out conversation.

2:25P   Hodel dials - Asks for Mr. Rockey - All the letter does is to confirm that he is an independent contractor. Relative to unemployment payment to someone.

3:00P   Talking to some woman. She said something about doing some work for Hodel. Took her to some other part of house.

3:02P   Hodel starts typing.

3:15P   Hodel dials phone "Is Mr. Ed Wilcox there". Something about Ed Being able to receive a message from Tibet. "I'm expecting a message from Mr. ? of Tibet. (Ed is apparently a ham short-waver)

3:20P   Hodel dials phone - no answer.

3:28P   Phone rings - Hodel answers. "Hello, dear. How are the children. Did you find your suit-case? I'd love to come down but I can't getaway from here. Can't you come in. Try and do it.

3:36P   Hodel - "Will you see if PH 8086 is actually busy"? Hodel has been trying to reach this number ever since he

3:45P   talked to Ed Wilcox. I believe it is the phone number of another ham.

4:00P   Morgan, D.A.'s office, on duty.

HODEL FILE - 106 / -√

128

5:10P   Telephone rang - no answer

6:35P   Telephone rang - no answer

8:00P   Meyer, LAPD on duty. Some one moving around.

9:20P   Phone rang 6 times - didn't hear anyone answer.

9:55P   People moving around making lot of noise.

10:06P   Some girls around talking - phone rang - no one answered. Hodel don't seem to be around.

10:13P   Phone rang 35 times - girls still around - no answer.

10:23P   Hodel enters - says he is tired - says something about getting something to eat - all go out to kitchen.

11:00P   Hodel and girls go out to eat.

11:20P   Phone rang - no answer.

12:30A   Hodel and girls return.

2-16-50

1:00A   Girls talking about having babys and how to keep from having them.

2:00A   West, LAPD, on duty. Several women talking.

2:30A   Some women leave - Hodel now talking with two women. Radio playing too loud to hear.

3:15A   One woman leaves.

3:30A   Hodel apparently gone to bed. All quiet.

8:00A   Phone rings twice. Hodel answers - a patient with a sore said he would come see him today.

8:00A   Egger, D.A.'s office on duty.

8:30A   All quiet.

9:00A   All quiet.

9:00A   Can hear snoring - apparently hotel.

9:30A   All quiet.

10:00A   All quiet.

10:30A   All quiet.

HODEL FILE - 107 /124   127

11:00A All quiet.
11:25A Phone rings - Hodel answers talking about Mexico.
        Apparently with some woman - says he will meet her at 3 PM
        today.
11:30A Hodel moving around
11:45A Hodel still moving around - some bathroom noises
11:55A Hodel still moving around
3-17-50
12:15P Some desk noises - Hodel leaves room
        Snyder, D.A.'s office on duty.
12:55P Hodel calls Sears-Roebuck on Santa Monica Blvd, in regards
        to mattress covers. Who knows, might be a sale, eh?
        Also calls Broadway-Hollywood-same subject.
2:10P   Hodel typing, and mumbling to himself.
2:45P   Still noise of typing, among various and sundry other
        noises.
3:30P   Phone rings 5 times - no answer
3:50P   Female voice in distance - unintelligible.
4:00P   Phone rings - Hodel answers - some chatter regarding
        personal loans - also some talk about someone having
        personal cards printed - talks by selling tea wholesale.
        $12. per/retail- 40% off - 2% ten days
4:10P   Phone rings - Hodel answers - someone coming right over
        Snyder off duty 4:15PM

HODEL FILE - 108 /125   128
3-16-50
SPOOL 37
4:20P   Hodel dials Rompage Hardware Store on Hollywood Blvd. about
        some delivery.
4:35P   Someone called at suggestion of Ed Wilcox - conversation per
        taining to Ham station W6CNB (CXB?)
5:05P   Some man, woman and a little boy arrived - adults discuss th
36   CPS
6:03P   Hodel answerd the phone and promised to be right over.
6:10P   Hodel makes call to OL 5851 - couldn't get his party. Dials
        another number - "Hello Mabel - is Erwin there?" Talk about
        sending Erwin a check (Erwin Hough) for digging some thing.
7:44P   Examination of a woman patient, who is coming back Tuesday.
7:50P   Hodel is typing.
8:00P   Meyer, LAPD, on duty. Hodel dials phone - asks operator
        OL 5851 - no answer - hangs up.
8:45P   Hodel left - all quiet.
9:18P   Phone rang 6 times - no answer.
11:00P Phone rang 8 times - no answer.
11:40P Phone rang 5 times - no answer.
2:00A   Hodel apparently sleeping. Can hear snoring.
3:00A   J. McGrath - D.A.'s office on duty
9:30A   No activity
11:00A Hodel up
12:30R Around bathroom
12:00noon Eggar, D.A.'s office on duty
12:30P Hodel moving around room.
1:00P   Hodel made phone call regarding sewage disposal or some
        digging on his property. Hodel said that he was in a hurry
        to get the work done, and he would wait for the workmen this
        afternoon.

HODEL FILE - 109 /28 [129]

1:15P	Hodel moving around. Phone rings 3 times, must have been answered other room.
1:20P	Hodel out of room - can hear him talking to several men in background.
Re-corded 1 min to 36½ 1:25P	Called Miss White about placing an ad in the paper - said the ad is in the name of E.L. Marsh in the categroy of furnished rooms and apts. "Shang-ri-la" is at top of ad. Hodel wants to change ad to read; Artists and writers preferred.
1:30P	Hodel typing at desk.
1:45P	Hodel leaves room.
2:10P	Can hear some machine noises - sounds like an electric hand drill. No conversation, drill keeps going on and off.
2:20P	All quiet.
2:35P	Phone rings 4 times - no answer.
2:45P	Machine noise - off - whistling in background - some moving around.
2:50P	Can hear talking, two or three men in background, sound lik they might be in basement; cannot make out conversation.
3:00P	Can still hear muffled conversation with occasional machine noises; sawing, etc.
3:30P	Hodel or someone moving about desk - same background noises men and machines working
3:45P	Same as above
4:00P	Still some background noises as stated above.
4:15P	Same as above
4:20P	Phone rings 6 times - no answer - can hear walking around however.
4:25P	Hodel called SY 94490 - asked for Fritz. Fritz not there.
4:25P	Hronek, D.A.'s office on duty.

HODEL FILE - 110 /1-7

5:04P	Phone rings 7 times - [130] no answer.
5:25P	Phone rings 5 times - no answer.
6:19P	Phone rings 1 time - must be answered in another room.
7:20P	Hodel returns and starts typing.
7:45P	Phone rings - Hodel answered - talked to someone about his trip to Mexico.
7:55P	Meyer, LAPD, on duty. All quiet.
7:57P	Hodel and some woman came in-talking in another room.
8:00P	Phone rings. Hodel answers - talking to someone who just got back from Frisco.
8:15P	Still talking to female who came in with him-can't make out what they are saying.
8:40P	Radio on - still talking.
8:45P	Hodel on phone - radio too loud to hear - said something about 1735 No. La Brea.
11:10P	The guy with the accent came in - radio on too loud - two women, one don't seem to understand English, other translates to her (mother and daughter)
11:25P	Hodel telling about his fishing in Mexico.
	Women leave - Hodel and man with accent - talking recorded - hard to hear. Hodel says probably they are watching me, talk about selling some of his stuff at an auction - says someone don't know anything to tell. Hodel said something about getting married again - talks about place in Mexico. Says it will clear about 4 or 5,000 a month. Hodel talking about Tibet and a letter he wrote there, says it is quite a job getting a letter sent there. Radio still on - talk world aff
36-49½ 11:30P	

HODEL FILE - 114 / 30
1-18-50

12:40A — Hodel - "Do you think those "Bastards" will try to bring action because I am renting rooms". Hodel says "Do you think we could hire some girl to find out what they are doing".

12:45A — Talking about women.

1:00A — Man with accent left - Hodel turned radio off - should have done that a hr. ago.

1:15A — Sounds like Hodel going to bed.

2:00A — Breckel, LAPD, on duty. All is quiet.

6:00A — Radio turned on (Sta KHJ) must have been left turned on as there was no one up to have turned it on. The program is first of the day.

6:20A — Radio still playing - Hodel still snoring.

7:30A — Radio still playing.

8:00A — J. McGrath, D.A.'s office on duty.

9:30A — No activity - radio now off.

10:30A — Phone rings - answered in rear of home.

11:45A — Phone rings 2 times - answered in rear.

12:50P — No sound

1:00P — Egger, D.A.'s office on duty.

1:15P — Seems to be moving around in other sections of the house, but otherwise All quiet.

1:25P — Hodel in background - conversation with woman.

2:00P — Woman's voice in background.

2:30P — Phone 1 time, but could hear no one answer - all quiet.

3:30P — All quiet.

3:45P — Background noises - Hodel and woman talking.

4:00P — Morgan, D.A.'s office, on duty.

4:50P — Someone opened and closed all the drawers in the desk

---

HODEL FILE - 112 / 31
MORGAN ON DUTY /32

4:40/4:50P — (hurriedly) also sounds of paper shuffling and scrambling in another part of the room.

49½-50½ 4:55P — Telephone rang - Hodel answered - conversation regarding room rental - Hodel turned party down.

50½-54½ 5:05P — Hodel telephoned - conversation regarding rental or room wherein Hodel suggested that some part time work around place could be applied on Rental of rooms - made appointment for tomorrow about 11 AM to show place - Hodel leaving tonight at 7 PM.

5:13P — Telephone rang - no answer.

54½-55 5:20P — Telephone rang - Hodel "Yes, yes" What did you say your name is - Madeline Smith - Oh, suppose you call me tomorrow at 12". Ends "Alright goodbye".

5:23P — Hodel (I guess) dialed phone several times - no answer.

5:30P — Going through drawers again - sounds of dog whining (barks). Typing noise.

55-55½ 5:32P — Hodel and woman (sounds like Mrs. Hodel) conversing about some medical term - Hodel "There's about a millionth of an ounce in the human body", etc.

55½-56 6:12P — Hodel dialed phone - Hodel "What time does the owl show go on What time does the whole show end?" Ends "Thank you".

56½-56¾ 7:00P — Telephone rang - Hodel "She left/about ½ hour ago my place She should be there about now". Hope you can keep it under control". Ends "Goodbye".

7:15P — Hodel conversing with another woman, who he called Gladys about some engravings they were looking at. They discussed ? cursing sounded in French, Spanish, and Chinese.

HODEL FILE - 113/3 >

563/4 - 7:42P
60

7:42P Telephone rang - Hodel "Hello Jill (or something) How's everything? Under control? Etc. Are you a tea lover? I have some tea for you - some very special tea - I am abou to take off for the evening now, etc. something about an eighteen year - answering the phone, etc.

8:00P Wean, LAPD, on duty.

9:10P Phone rang once, no one answered.

9:25P Phone rang 3 times - no one answered.

9:50P A man enters house, and asks for Hodel - some woman tells hi he is gone. He leaves.

10:55P Hodel returns - phones and asks someone if they would like to hear some music. Says OK, and hangs up.

11:15P Hodel talking with eighteen year old girl - radio too loud to understand.

11:40P Hodel typing.

3-19-50
2:00A Brechel, LAPD, on duty. All is quiet except Hodel is snorin

9:30A Jamison, D.A.'s office - all quiet.

10:00A voices - not distinguishable.

11:20A All quiet.

11:30A Tapping sound.

11:55A Hodel - in bathroom - flushes toilet.

11:58A Hodel takes a bath - says "poor fish".

12:00noon Egger, L.A.'s office on duty.

12:15P Hodel walking around desk noises.

12:20P Hodel turns on the symphony on radio.

1:00P Symphony still on - no other noise.

1:30P Symphony still on; can hear Hodel talking to woman in background.

HODEL FILE - 114/3 3

1:45P Hodel answers door bell, lets in woman - he talks to her about renting her a room in return he will knock off the rent - at work she does for him such as cleaning and taking care of his quarters. Negro woman has her minor daughter with her.

1:50P Phone rings - Hodel says "Mrs Hodel is out - I can take message. He said he is going down to the beach about 4 PM today - talks about renting room.

2:00P Hodel again talking to negro woman. Hodel asks her daughter where she goes to school - the girl says-a catholic school.

2:10P Colored woman and child leaving. woman is going to think it over - about renting room. Woman then starts talking about Doctor's-Hodel tells her about his clinic at 1st and Central Woman said she had a curettement (curettement ?) in 1944. Hodel said he has done lots of them. Hodel and woman continue to talk about doctors, sickness, and other medical subjects. (Hodel seems to be acting overly nice to this woman He must be trying to talk her into renting the room, or ?) Hodel tells her that Dr. Hill, a colored Doctor, lives next door.

2:30P Woman leaves

2:50P Phone rings 2 times, must have been answered in another room Hodel moving about desk.

3:15P Hodel leaves room - all quiet.

3:45P All quiet.

4:00P Bronek, L.A.'s office, on duty.

SPOOL
38

HODEL FILE - 115/134

0

5:00P — Sounds like someone uses the vacuum cleaner.

6:00P — No sound

7:00P — No sound

8:00P — No sound. Mean, LAPD, on duty

— Woman's voice in background.

10:30P — Phone rings 3 times, can't hear anyone answer.

11:00P — All quiet.

3-20-50

12:30P — Hodel typing.

2:00A — Brechel, LAPD, on duty

0-1 2:08A — Phone rings. Hodel answers "Hello, hes yes". Short conversation is recorded. Apparently is receiving instructions, and agrees to it. "Yes, I'll do it", or "Yes, I'll be there".

— Hodel was in bedroom when he received call and must have been waiting for it as phone rang once only.

2:09A — Hodel went out of room after the call.

2:48A — Hodel returns to room.

3:25A — Hodel moving around room.

3:45A — All quiet.

8:00A — J. McGrath, D.A.'s office on duty

9:30A — All quiet, no activity.

10:15A — Phone call received - can't hear-too much racket - Hodel has dinner engagement tonight. Going out of town Wednesday.

— Hodel talking about selling the house.

10:17A — Hodel makes phone call - too much static to hear.

10:21A — Hodel makes phone call - cannot hear.

10:23A — Phone call received - lots of static

11:54A — Phone call received by Hodel - talks low - can't hear.

11:55A — Hodel makes phone call - can't make out.

HODEL FILE - 116/135

12:00noon — Snyder, D.A.'s office on duty

1:10P — Phone rings - inquiry regarding rooms or house - Hodel tells her to call back between 3:30 and 4:00. Says he is going out for afternoon.

1:15P — Hodel call UCLA - seeking information re. Burrel lives.

— Reserves 2 seats, 13th row, near aisle - did not get date.

1:50P — The doctor Hodel is taking a bath.

2:15P — Hodel leaves house.

2:50P — Phone rings 8 times - no answer.

4:00P — Hromek, D.A.'s office on duty.

6:55P — Two women and a man carry on a conversation about books and poetry - the fellow is apparently an actor - talks about himself mile a minute.

7:05P — Moved to another part of house - conversation unintelligible.

8:00P — Meyer, LAPD, on duty. Hear people talking, but unable to understand.

8:40P — Man and woman talking, not English, can't understand.

9:00P — Hodel talking to some man with an accent (not same) sounds like a photographer talking about taking pictures. Hodel shows some pictures he took.

9:12P — Radio on - not Hodel's music.

10:00P — Still playing Chinese - music worse then Hodel's music.

10:25P — Sounds like Hodel around by himself - radio off.

10:50P — Hodel and some guy with accent talking, and looking at map of Mexico. (The photographer).

11:05P — Talking about going (to Mexico) want to leave tomorrow night, Hodel says don't tell anyone. Hodel says He has to be back Wednesday. He is going to Santa Barbara, and won't be back until Sunday. Sounds like they are going to take pictures. Sounds like Hodel is trying to pull a fast one of some kind

HODEL FILE - 217 / 36

137

Time	Entry
11:05P	This other guy seems to know the country.
11:25P	Guy with accent leaves, says will call tomorrow and make arrangements about going, if they go
11:30P	Hodel moving around by himself
3-21-50 12:00A	Sounds like Hodel has gone to bed - all quiet.
2:00A	Brechel, LAPD, on duty. All is quiet. Hodel must have slep in another part of house. There were no snoring noises all morning. Music in the background all morning till 6:30A coming from rear part of house.
8:00A	J. McGrath, D.A.'s office on duty
8:45A	Phone call received - could not hear in back room
8:57A	Phone call received - emmit can't make out - ended conversation at 9:22 - could not hear anything-too much noise and static.
9:25A	Hodel made phone call - hard to hear - said something about fishing - also a test on a patient named Thomas.
9:35A	Insurance inspector calls to inspect some belongings of one of the tenants.
9:40A	Hodel makes phone call to some doctor - sounds like Barrymore
10:45A	Phone call received for someone else - Hodel said "I will have her call you".
10:47A	Someone phoned - Hodel said "I will get hold of you as soon as the stuff is here."
10:55A	Hodel phones someone about $50.00 a month he paid some woman "Said I'm in trouble" want some advice - do you have a farm.
11:00A	Phone call received - Hodel ran to back of house-answered could not hear.

HODEL FILE - 219 / 38

138

Time	Entry
12:40P	Hodel dials - "Is this Miss Mathis?" How is Dr. Nicholas? Shall I write him? I'll write him?
12:42P	Hodel is typing and hence conversation unintelligible.
12:47P	Hodel dials (Tu 4826) asks for medical desk.
1:00 to 1:15P	Hodel and Dorothy engage in a little loving
1:16P	Water running
1:20P	Hodel typing
1:55P	Dorothy dials phones asks for ? This is Mrs Rogal (?) Tell him I called.
1:56P	Hodel dials - Water running - conversation unintelligible. He's talking about a job. "I prefer part time. Is it hospit or clinic. What pay is he offering. Talks about his work as chief of staff at clinic. I'm medical director of a local laboratory, but I have too much time. Send me your contract form.
2:02P	Talking about their children.
2:10P	Phone rings. Hodel answers "I'll call you this evening about 7 or 8 o'clock. Maybe we'll go tomorrow Joe".
2:35P	Quiet.
2:55P	Phone rings 6 times - no one answers.
4:00P	Still quiet.
4:05P	Fromek D.A.'s office on duty
4:33P	Phone rang 15 times - no answer
4:45P	" " 10 times - no answer
6:52P	" " 4 times - no answer
7:40P	" " 6 times - no answer
8:00P	Meyer, LAPD, on duty. All quiet.
9:20P	Phone rang 3 times, didn't hear anyone answer.

HODEL FILE - 118 -/3

Time	Entry
11:01A	Hodel makes phone call to some one.
11:05A	A woman comes to see Hodel - sounds like Dorothy-they go to rear of the house - can't hear.
11:45A	Sullivan, D.A.'s office on duty. Can hear Hodel and woman talking but unable to understand as they are in some other part of house.
11:55A	Hodel typing
12:05P	Dorothy asks Hodel for telephone number - he gives her HO 93311 - Albert Van. She apparently called from some other part of house.
12:12P	Dorothy Hodel dials phone - asks for Mr. Holder (Said she was Dorothy Hodel) No conversation.
12:14P	Dorothy dials phone - asks for Bollin Brown - talks to him "I went down to Mexico and had a nice time fishing, that's why I haven't seen you. Fell off the pier. Told him he should have picked up some of the weights we had dropped down there. Talks about meeting Doctor in Mexico and about the place in Mexico. Talks about how George and he fly down there It's in Sonora County. It's near Otho (?) About 400 miles from here (George is prompting her) There are whore houses from here, and we visited one. George was seeing rashes all over the place (She's sure giving this guy a sales talk) Hodel is typing and hence unable to hear Dorothy's conversation.
12:26P	Dorothy finished conversation.
12:27P	Dorothy dials phone - HO 93311 charged to HO 98485 - Dorothy dials phone - This Dorothy Huston. Is Mr. Bangs (?) there. Please have him call me at OI 3476, or Santa Monica 42424. George tells Dorothy John won't call her and won't

HEL FILE - 120
3-21-50
SPOOL 38

Time	Entry
11:25 P	Sounds like Hodel just came home - at his desk moving papers.
11:40P	Phone rang - Hodel answers "Hello, Tracey - any calls for me?" That was all.
12:30A	Hodel snoring
3-22-50 2:00A	Brechel LAPD on duty - All is quiet
7:25A	Sounds like Hodel getting up - running water in bathroom
8:00A	M. McGrath, D.A.'s office on duty
8:30a	All quiet
10:40A	Phone rings 6 times - no answer
12:00P	Sullivan, D.A.'s office on duty
12:00P-4:00P	Bisson, Belle, and Sullivan listening to past recordings as Hodel has been out for the entire day.
4:00P	Egger, D.A.'s office on duty . Hodel still out.
5:00P	No noise-Hodel still out
5:00P	Woman enters, but no Hodel
5:05P	Phone rings 10 times - no answer
6:00P	All quiet.
6:10P	Hodel comes in - works at desk
6:30P	Can hear Hodel and Woman talking in background - Hodel still working around desk.
6:35P	Hodel phoning, says "This is Dr. Hodel returning your call". Too much background and line noise to make out most of conversation - something about records. Also talking about urine specimens and venerial disease. other party seems to be doing most of the talking. Conversation is along medical lines.

MODEL FILE - 121

141

6:45P	Woman comes in and calls "Doctor". Hodel is still on phone, can hear the woman walking around, humming, then leaves.
6:50P	Hodel still on phone (not talking much).
7:00P	Conversation has now turned to corporations, stocks, and bonds with Hodel doing very little talking.
7:20P	Conversation over - Hodel moving around desk.
7:30P	Hodel still moving around desk.
7:55P	Hodel still at desk - no conversation. Hodel leaves room - then comes back.
8:00P	Meyer, LAPD, on duty. All quiet.
8:22P	Hodel and some girl come in - talking - can't understand too much other noise.
8:35P	Radio on.
9:40P	Hodel by himself - typing.
10:30P	All quiet except radio on.
10:45P	Radio off - all quiet.
3-23-50 2:00A	Brechel, LAPD, on duty. All quiet.
3:00A	Hodel makes visit to lavatory; returns to bed.
8:00A	J. McGrath, D.A.'s office on duty
10:15A	All quiet.
12:00noon	All quiet.

MODEL FILE - 122
3-23-50
4:00P-8:00P Hronek, D.A.'s office, on duty

142

4:10P	Occasional movement in the background
4:30P	All quiet
5:00P	All quiet
5:20P	All quiet
6:00P	All quiet
6:30P	All quiet
0- 7:00P	Hodel comes in and makes a call - about some compound takes the address, 60E 42nd St., New York 17, N.Y. "I'm writing myself". Seres of yes, yes, yes, alright, yes, yes, that's from the U.S. Chemical News - U&I Chem News, Feb 1950 - I know, yes, yes, they have written - OK thanks, Good night.
7:15P	Phone rang 5 times - no answer.
7:35P	Door bell rang - some woman comes in - conversation in the background.
0-6 7:45P	Hodel came in with Dorothy - phone rang (recorded)
8:00P	Meyer, LAPD, on duty. Radio on.
8:02P	Phone rang - Hodel answers - said Exbrook 32473, about a phone number.
9:30P	Radio turned on - don't hear anyone.
10:30P	Some woman just came in - Hodel asks if she ever saw a certain book - talking about "Watches" (The woman is) Sounds like she designs match covers.
11:20P	The dame is still talking, boy she is sure wound up.

143

MODEL FILE - 123
3-24-50

12:15A Woman left, had been talking since 10:30P
12:40A Dame back again and still talking
12:45A Dame left again.
12:55P Hodel typing - radio off
1:15A   Hodel called and sent a nite letter to a Mrs. Barbe
        1543 Valejo St., San Francisco. Something about birthday
        wishes. Message read "My birthday wishes must go to you.
        I hope each year will make -------?-----? Am doing my best
        and will continue trying. Please leave me know how things
        are going".
2:00A   Brechel, LAPD, on duty. Hodel typing.
2:10A   Typing stops - goes to lavatory - urinates then all quiet.
2:15A   To bed - all quiet.
8:00A   J. McGrath, D.A.'s office on duty
9:45A   All quiet.
10:10A Phone call received. Hodel answers - says "Oh yes, fine
        yes, yes. Well, all right, that's good, as soon as you
        know, yeah, good," Hangs up.
10:50A Phone rings 2 times - answered in rear of house.
10:52A Hodel typing at his desk.
11:30A Phone call received - Hodel answers - for someone else.
12:20P Phone call received by Hodel "Yeah, yeah, oh that's swell.
        Yeah, yeah, oh that's good, uh huh. He will give you some
        good advice anyway -" Talking about a $1000.00 order now.
        of some kind. Interested in a merger - "all right Tom,
        goodbye".

MODEL FILE - 124

26   5 to 9 - talk of trial
        9 to 40 much talk of juggling figures.
27   13 to 15 - talk about deducting some money as repayment
        of loans to father and son.
        18 to 22 - wire bad Skip - listen from 40 on to
        46 to 48 - very interesting (cut this spool off at 50
        the end is loose).

Spool #37
3-5   Conversation regarding tax case and Dahlia
5-17   Conversation regarding code and mailing - have to be
        careful - income tax starts at 15 on Spool 25

145

HODEL FILE - 125

3-24-50

	4:00P	Hronek, D.A.'s office on duty--all quiet.
	4:30P	Hodel starts typing.
6-8½	5:00P	Call out by Taylor MU 2165, one of Hodel's associates.
8½-11	5:10P	Same person making a call and talking
	6:18P	Hodel starts typing again
11	6:41P	Hodel comes in with another guy -"sit down, let me fix us a drink -" They talk about foods and drinks of different nations - girl comes in. Hodel call Churchill 92146.
	8:00P	Meyer, LAPD, on duty. All quiet.
	8:40P	Phone rang 4 times - too much background noise - couldn't hear anyone answer.
	9:50P	Hodel comes in with some man, talking about Mexico - lots of noise in background.
11-19	10:20P	Radio on playing records - some girl around
nothing	11:15P	Radio off - Hodel playing/talking to man, hard to hear.
	11:18P	Phone rang - Hodel answers - sounded like talking to someone in other part of house - man left.
	11:50P	Hodel comes back in - starts typing
3-25	12:05A	Radio on again.
19-20	12:30A	Phone - Hodel answers - radio on - said something about having money by then.
	12:36A 1:00A 1:30A	Radio off - sounded like Hodel left. Mean, LAPD, on duty. Someone moving around and typing Hodel returns.
	2:00A	All quiet - not sure if Hodel left or is in bed
	3:30A	Phone rings 3 times - woman calls Hodel - no more conversation.
	4:30A	All quiet.

145

HODEL FILE - 126

	8:00P	Meyer, LAPD, on duty. All quiet.
20-61	11:10P	Hodel and Baron (man with accent) came in talking low - can't hear (recording) only stays few minutes and leaves. I was wrong - was in bathroom. Sounded like Hodel said something about Black Dahlia. Baron said something about F.B.I. Then talked about Tibet - sounded like Hodel wants to get out of the country. Mentioned passport - Hodel giving Baron dope on how to write to Tibet. Hodel talking about Mexico - going down and take pictures and write a story. Hodel seems afraid about something. Hodel says his Senatorium - if he got it started in Mexico - would be "Safe".

Spool 39
        12:00A
Mar 26 1950
0-50   12:07A

146

Spool run out - changing - talking about women.

Not much talk - still recording. Hodel says he wants money and power - talking about China - talking about selling some of Hodel's paintings or something. Hodel talking about picture police have of him and some girl - thought he had destroyed them all - wire quit at 50 - new one going on - not much talk.

Spool 40
3-37   1:00A

	1:00A	Had trouble with one spool. Had to use another - still talking about selling paintings.
	1:50A	Sounds like Baron left - don't know if there is anything on these records or not.
	2:00A	Hodel at his desk - all else quiet - Good night.
	3:00P	Hodel having party - about 8 people - party ends - someone listening to radio programs. Mean, LAPD, on duty.
	3:30P	Woman and Hodel talking, but radio too loud to hear.
	5:00P	

146

147

HODEL FILE - 127

37-49 6:20P   Hodel talking with woman

        6:35P   Recorded

49-50 8:00P   Phone - Hodel answers - recorded - couldn't hear too well.
                    Meyer, LAPD, on duty.

50-   10:55P   Hodel and some man came in - not sure if Baron or not -
60   guess it is (recording) talking about paintings and etc.
                    And Asia - Change records

Spool 41

C-14   11:15P   New wire on-guess both left.

14-23 11:55P   Hodel-some woman come in - also the Baron. Hodel and Baron
                    talking low - guess woman left. Woman back. Guess same
                    gabby woman that was there other nite. About matches
                    Advertising woman left again. Gabbey is back - all looking
                    at pictures and etc.

1-27   1:00A   Everyone left.

        2:00A   All quiet. Good nite.

Addendum B
1950 Dorothy Hodel DA Jemison Interview Transcript

[MARCH 22, 1950]

DA TRANSCRIPTS- DOROTHY HODEL INTERVIEW 3/22/1950

Bk 2
Pg 14

STATEMENT OF DOROTHY HARVEY HODEL TAKEN AT 410 SANTA MONICA
PIER, SANTA MONICA BY LT. FRANK B. JEMISON AT 1:15 P. M.
ON MARCH 22, 1950.

File No.
Charge: Murder   Present:
Title: Questions by: Lt. Jemison
Deputy: Reported by: Dora A. Parisho

Q What is your full name?
A Dorothy Harvey Hodel.

Q What is your residence address at the present time?
A 410 Santa Monica Pier.

Q What is your phone number here?
A I don't have a phone. There is a fishing renting place downstairs, SM 42421.

Q What is your present occupation?
A Housewife. I do a little writing, but I'm not working at the present time.

Q Were you formerly married to Dr. George Hodel?
A Yes.

Q Are you now divorced from him?
A Yes.

Q How long have you been divorced from him?
A The interlocutory decree was in 1944 and the final was in 1945.

Q Do you have any children from him?
A Yes, I have three boys.

Q Are you acquainted with Tamara Hodel?
A Yes.

Q And is Dr. George Hodel the father of Tamara?
A Yes.

Q Are you acquainted with her mother?
A Yes.

Q What is her name?
A Dorothy.

-1-

Q Where is she living now, what city?
A I believe San Francisco, but I'm not sure.

Q You are familiar, are you with the trial that Dr. Hodel just went through in connection with Tamara?
A I know about it, but I didn't attend it.

Q Do you know Lillian Lenorek?
A Yes, I do.

Q When did you first become acquainted with her, about what year?
A I think it was about 1940. Let me see, say '46. I'm not really sure.

Q When did you last see her?
A Just before she went to Camarillo and just before her mother came for her. Anyway, after she was ill all over there at George's.

Q Do you know her mother?
A No.

Q When you last saw her did you feel she was a mental case, is that what your information is?
A I felt she must be. The little boy was running around and was very distressed. Poor little kid.

Q I will now show you a photograph of Beth Short, Santa Barbara No. 1149 and ask you whether or not you have ever seen that young lady in your life?
A No, I never have.

Q Did you have a conversation with Dr. Hodel about the murder of Beth Short?
A No, unless we mentioned it when it was in the papers, but I don't like to read about things like that. I can't say for sure that I have never mentioned her name to him, but it may have been in passing.

Q Did he ever tell you, "They can't pin that murder on me?"
A No, to the best of my knowledge he didn't and doesn't know her.

Q On or about the date of her murder, January 15, 1947 do you remember being out until 4:00 in the morning with George Hodel and coming in slightly intoxicated? Now, that's three years ago.
A Well, I think I explained before we never went on drinking parties because I don't drink because of certain tendencies to drink too much and particularly if I were near

-2-

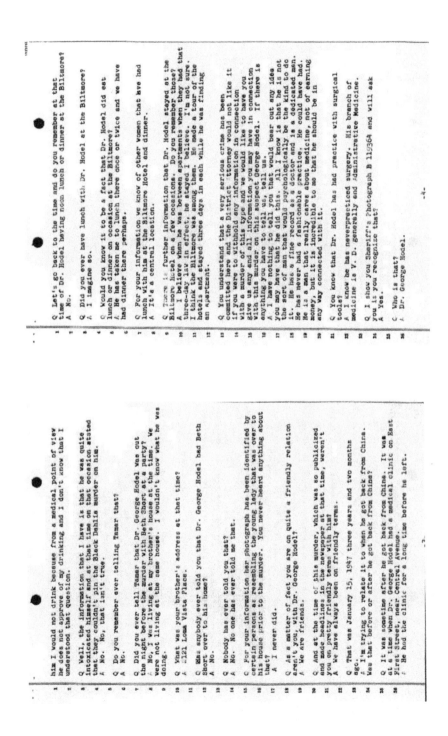

Q   Let's go back to the time and do you remember at that time of Dr. Hodel having noon lunch or dinner at the Biltmore?
A   No.

Q   Did you ever have lunch with Dr. Hodel at the Biltmore?
A   I imagine so.

Q   Would you know it to be a fact that Dr. Hodel did eat lunch or dinner on occasion at the Biltmore?
A   He has taken me to lunch there once or twice and we have had dinner there perhaps.

Q   For your information we know of other women that have had lunch with him at the Biltmore Hotel and dinner.
A   It's a central location.

Q   There is further information that Dr. Hodel stayed at the Biltmore Hotel on a few occasions. Do you remember those?
A   I believe when he was between apartments when they had that three-day law in effect, he stayed I believe. I'm not sure. I think the Biltmore was among them. He made a tour of the hotels and stayed three days in each while he was finding an apartment.

Q   You understand that a very serious crime has been committed here and the District Attorney would not like it if you were to withhold any information in connection with a murder of this type and we would like to have you give us any and all information you may have in connection with this murder on this suspect George Hodel. If there is anything you have to tell us, tell us.
A   I have nothing to tell you that would bear out any idea you may have that he did this. All I know is that he is not the sort of man that would psychologically be the kind to do it. He has a fine record as a doctor and is a dedicated man. He has never had a fashionable practice. He could have had. He is a man that really cares about medicine, not of earning money, but it is incredible to me that he should be in any way connected with it.

Q   You know that Dr. Hodel has had practice with surgical tools?
A   I know he has neverpracticed surgery. His branch of medicine is V. D. generally and Administrative Medicine.

Q   I show you Sheriff's Photograph B 119364 and will ask you is you recognize that?
A   Yes.

Q   Who is that?
A   Dr. George Hodel.

-4-

---

him I would not drink because from a medical point of view he does not approve of my drinking and I don't know that I understood that question.

Q   Well, the information that I have is that he was quite intoxicated himself and at that time on that occasion stated that they couldn't pin the Black Dahlia murder on him.
A   No. No, that isn't true.

Q   Do you remember ever telling Tamar that?
A   No.

Q   Did you ever tell Tamar that Dr. George Hodel was out the night before the murder with Beth Short at a party?
A   No. I was living at my brother's house at the time. We were not living at the same house. I wouldn't know what he was doing.

Q   What was your brother's address at that time?
A   2121 Loma Vista Place.

Q   Was anybody ever told you that Dr. George Hodel had Beth Short over to his home?
A   No.

Q   Nobody has ever told you that?
A   No. No one has ever told me that.

Q   For your information her photograph has been identified by certain persons as resembling the young lady that was over to his house prior to the murder. You never heard anything about that?
A   I never did.

Q   As a matter of fact you are on quite a friendly relation aren't you, with Dr. George Hodel?
A   We are friends.

Q   And at the time of this murder, which was so publicized and made headlines in the newspaper at that time, weren't you on pretty friendly terms with him?
A   We have always been on friendly terms.

Q   That was January 15, 1947 three years and two months ago.
A   I'm trying to relate it to when he got back from China. Was that before or after he got back from China?

Q   It was sometime after he got back from China. It was at a time when Dr. George Hodel had a medical clinic on East First Street, near Central Avenue.
A   He had the clinic for a long time before he left.

-2-

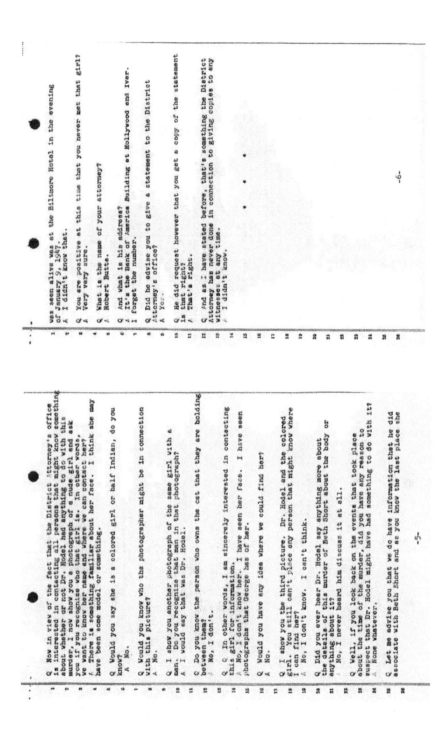

Q Now in view of the fact that the District Attorney's office is interested in contacting all persons that might know something about whether or not Dr. Hodel had anything to do with this murder, I now show you a photograph of a nude girl and ask you if you recognize who that girl is. In other words, we want to know her name and where we can contact her? There is something familiar about her face. I think she may have been some model or something.

Q Would you say she is a colored girl or half Indian, do you know?
A No.

Q Would you know who the photographer might be in connection with this picture?
A No.

Q I show you another photograph of the same girl with a man. Do you recognize that man in that photograph?
A I would say that was Dr. Hodel.

Q Do you know the person who owns the cat that they are holding between them?
A No, I don't.

Q In other words, I am sincerely interested in contacting this girl for information.
A No, I don't know her. I have seen her face. I have seen photographs that George has of her.

Q Would you have any idea where we could find her?
A No.

Q I show you the third picture. Dr. Hodel and the colored girl. You still can't place any person that might know where I can find her?
A No, I don't know. I can't think.

Q Did you ever hear Dr. Hodel say anything more about the details of this murder of Beth Short about the body or anything about it?
A No, I never heard him discuss it at all.

Q Well, if you look back on the events that took place about the time of the murder, did you have any reason to suspect that Dr. Hodel might have had something to do with it?
A None whatever.

Q Let me advise you that we do have information that he did associate with Beth Short and as you know the last place she

-5-

was seen alive was at the Biltmore Hotel in the evening of January 9, 1947.
A I didn't know that.

Q You are positive at this time that you never met that girl?
A Very very sure.

Q What is the name of your attorney?
A Robert Butts.

Q And what is his address?
A It's the Bank of America Building at Hollywood and Ivar. I forget the number.

Q Did he advise you to give a statement to the District Attorney's office?
A Yes.

Q He did request however that you get a copy of the statement is that right?
A That's right.

Q And as I have stated before, that's something the District Attorney has never done in connection to giving copies to any witnesses at any time.
A I didn't know.

-6-

Addendum C
Historical American Building Survey
National Park Service
Sowden House

[5121 Franklin Avenue, Los Angeles, 1969]

HABS No. CA-1940

HISTORIC AMERICAN BUILDING SURVEY

SOWDEN HOUSE   HABS No. CA-1940

Location: 5121 Franklin Avenue, Los Angeles, Los Angeles County, California.

Present Owner: Mrs. B. G. Mazur, 6626 Franklin Avenue, Los Angeles, Dr. and Mrs. Harold Mazur, 4821 Los Feliz, Los Angeles.

Present Occupant: Unoccupied.

Present Use: Residence.

Significance: This house, designed by Lloyd Wright in 1926, is built around a central court which originally contained an elaborate fountain. The house is entered through a cavelike opening whose textured concrete units create a striking contrast to the planar surfaces flanking it. These blocks are repeated in the central court.

PART I. HISTORICAL INFORMATION

A. Physical History:

1. Date of erection: 1926.

2. Architect: Lloyd Wright.

3. Original and subsequent owners:

   1926   John Sowden

   1930   Ruth Rand Barnett

   1936   Milton Blazier, Jr.

   1944   Romayne Goldsmith

   1945   George H. and Andree Hodel

   1950   Helen Fitzpatrick

   1951   The Mazurs

   Legal description: Book 5589, page 8, Parcel 1, lot 20, Tract 3369; and 25 feet on E. end of Lots 4, 5 and 6 of Tract 2099 (Site is 100 ft. by 175 ft.)

4. Builder, contractor, suppliers:

   W. W. Moore, Contractor

   Chevy Chase Stuff and Stone Co., textured concrete block, under direction of Mr. Paolie.

Sowden House
5121 Franklin Avenue
Los Angeles
Los Angeles County

HABS No. CA-1940

PHOTOGRAPHS

REDUCED COPIES OF MEASURED DRAWINGS

WRITTEN HISTORICAL AND DESCRIPTIVE DATA

Historic American Buildings Survey
National Park Service
Department of the Interior
Washington, D. C. 20240

SOWDEN HOUSE
HABS No. CA-1940 (Page 2)

5. Original plan and construction: Rectangular plan (64' by 125' court) around a closed 22' by 68' court with a rectangular court at center, with all rooms opening directly or by way of a corridor onto the court. Originally, there was a 32' long pool in the court, now filled in. In the pool were a pair of concrete-block pylons forming a water organ. The material is reinforced concrete block and stucco over a lathed wood frame. Originally, colored stones filled the openings in the concrete blocks in the court; these have been removed.

6. Alterations and additions: 1963: Removal of some of entrance steps with widening of Franklin. Avenue. No architects, dates unavailable; plaster box on stairs from street removed; pylons and pool removed in court; colored stones removed from pierced concrete block. Changes have been made in the kitchen and in the bathroom.

Prepared by: Esther McCoy
July 1968

PART II. ARCHITECTURAL INFORMATION

A. General statement

1. Architectural character: The Sowden House, designed by Lloyd Wright in 1926, is a city residence built around a central court which originally contained an elaborate fountain. The house is entered through a cavelike opening whose textured concrete units create a striking contrast to the planar surfaces flanking it. These blocks are repeated in the central court. The two principal rooms terminate the major axis of the house--the living room at the front, the studio at the rear.

2. Condition of fabric: Fair. The house is structurally sound although there are areas revealing deterioration of the materials, especially with regard to the textured concrete units. The interior court has been neglected and has become overgrown with vegetation. The fountain mentioned above has long since disappeared.

B. Detailed Description of the Exterior

1. Overall dimensions: 64' east to west; 125' north to south. There is one principal level. At the front (south) of the house there is a partial basement. The plan is basically rectangular, with the rooms situated around the courtyard.

2. Foundations: 8" reinforced concrete; concrete footing 1'-4" wide.

SOWDEN HOUSE
HABS No. CA-1940 (Page 3)

3. Wall construction, finish, color: 2" x 4" stud wall construction with members 16" o.c.--carried on 4" x 6" wood sills on concrete foundation. Metal lath and plaster. Exterior stucco finish in brownish tone. Reinforced concrete structural frames form the "cathedral" ceilings of studios and living room.

4. Porches, stoops, bulkheads, etc.: Entrance slab at the southern front to the house, 39'-4" away from the front of the house. Stairs up to the south front, which has an impressive cavern-like entrance passage. The entrance is on axis, but the path of entry beyond that point is indirect to the right.

There is a terrace in the central court.

5. Chimneys: A 14" x 16" flue is located on the west wall near the south corner of the house; it is finished flush with the parapet. An 8" x 12" flue is also located on the west wall just north of the midpoint. It also is finished flush with the parapet.

6. Openings:

a. Doorways and doors: Entrance passage is controlled through the use of a copper gate which has chevron-like plates on vertical bars. The front door is located atop the stairway, which is to the right upon passing through the gate. This door measures 3' x 6'-8" and has a glass light.

Sliding doors provide for passage from the courtyard to the corridor and also into the rooms of the house. They have 5 lights by 2 lights and are the same as those mentioned for interior doors.

There are sliding doors to the rear court in the northeast corner of the house. They have screen panels.

The side door (west) is 3'-8" x 7'-8".

b. Windows: Casement windows (on east side of house), double hung and hopper type windows are used. On the east and west side of the house the windows were originally covered with trellis screens. Skylights provide light into some of the interior spaces. There are large glass walls on the north and south sides of the living room, and on the south side of the studio.

SOWDEN HOUSE
HABS No. CA-1940 (Page 5)

There are six 4" risers from the patio to the studio floor level, and two 4" risers all around the court. In addition, stairs are located at the ends of the corridors on the north side.

3. Flooring: 1-1/2" oak flooring is used in all rooms except for 5-1/4" oak flooring in the living room, library, dining room, and studio; and asphalt tile in the kitchen and pantry; and concrete tile in the two major corridors (15" square with the corners off).

4. Wall and ceiling finish: Plaster; the bathroom has yellow ceramic tiles.

5. Doorways and doors: Solid wood doors in wood frames without face moldings. They are 2'-5" to 2'-8" x 6'-8" x 1-1/3" thick.

Sliding pocket doors with 5 x 2 lights (13-1/2" x 14-1/2") are used for access into the major bedroom (#2) as well as between the corridor and the courtyard.

6. Special decorative features, trim and cabinet work: The master bedroom (#2) has wood paneling on the west wall and has a heavy wood cornice. There are built-in shelves and cabinets in the library, as well as built in shelves and bureaus in the closets.

The doors have strap hinges and brass door knobs and lock plates. The front door thumb latch is also of brass.

A major decorative motif is the textured concrete block units. They are employed on all the courtyard piers and in the studio and living room. They are also used on the exterior of the house around the main entrance. The pylons in the courtyard stood 25'-4" high and also used the textured blocks.

There is a decorative skylight in the bathroom and in the dining room.

7. Mechanical equipment: There is a forced air furnace in the basement which is reinforced throughout the house by unit heaters.

There is a working fireplace in the library, on the west wall. An incinerator is located on the screen porch near the west center of the house.

The bathroom fixtures are standard, with the exception of the built in tub in the bathroom between bedrooms #2 and #3.

Lighting--coffered lighting in the living room, light panels are used in conjunction with the skylights in the dining room. bathroom and around the library fireplace.

SOWDEN HOUSE
HABS No. CA-1940 (Page 4)

7. Roof:

a. Shape, covering: Hip roof behind parapet walls. It is constructed of 2" x 4" rafters with 1" x 8" bracing. The red sand composition roofing is laid atop 7/8" sheathing.

b. Cornice, eaves: There is a plaster parapet rising about 2'-0" above the roof at the wall. 4" downspouts are used.

c. Dormers, cupolas, towers: Skylights are the only forms to rise above the roof except for the forms of the living room and studio, which peak above the primary roof level.

C. Detailed Description of the Interior:

1. Plans: Entrance is at the south end of the building on axis. After passing through the front gate, a sharp right turn is made to the stairs. Entrance is atop that stairway.

The main floor is composed of a central courtyard with the living room at the southern end and the studio at the northern end. Corridors flank the court, providing passage to the rear of the house and also providing access to the rooms opening off of them. Both corridors are single-loaded with the rooms between the passage and the exterior walls. The inner side of the corridor opens onto the court. The entrance door is at the south end of the corridor on the east side of the court. Down the corridor, opening to the right are bedroom #1 with its private bath, bedroom #2, bathrooms, bedroom #3, bedroom #4, and bedroom #5. A darkroom terminated the corridor. A small courtyard is located on the north side of bedroom #5 and accessible from it.

In the southwest corner of the house, adjacent to an opening from the living room, is the library. To the north of that room is the dining room. The western corridor begins at the northern side of this room. Adjacent to the dining room is the pantry, followed by the kitchen and the screened porch (the side entry). The corridor continues past the servants' quarters to the garage. The servants' quarters has a hall paralleling the main passage and provided access to the two servants' rooms and bath.

There is a partial basement below the living room on the south and in the southern portion of the eastern wing. Neither is finished as a useable space.

2. Stairways: 23 risers provide access to the front entrance gate of the house. These stairs are presently being altered due to the widening of Franklin Avenue and some of them are being removed. Beyond the gate, 26 risers in a scissor-type stairway provide access to the front door at the upper level. Both these stairways are composed of concrete tile treads.

HABS
CAL,
19-LOSAN,
69-

HISTORIC AMERICAN BUILDINGS SURVEY

INDEX TO PHOTOGRAPHS

HABS No. CA-1940

Sowden House
5121 Franklin Avenue
Los Angeles
Los Angeles County
California

Marvin Rand, photographer 1971

CA-1940-1	FRANKLIN AVENUE FACADE
CA-1940-2	ENTRANCE, OBLIQUE VIEW
CA-1940-3	ENTRANCE, AXIAL VIEW
CA-1940-4	ENTRANCE GATE
CA-1940-5	ENTRANCE GATE - DETAIL VIEW
CA-1940-6	LIVING ROOM, DISTANT VIEW, LOOKING WEST TO STUDY
CA-1940-7	LIVING ROOM, CLOSE VIEW LOOKING WEST TO STUDY
CA-1940-8	STUDY, FIREPLACE
CA-1940-9	GLAZED OPENING, LIVING ROOM, LOOKING TOWARDS COURT
CA-1940-10	COURT, LOOKING NORTH FROM LIVING ROOM TERRACE
CA-1940-11	ENTRANCE TO STUDIO AT NORTH END OF COURT, FROM COURT
CA-1940-12	CLOSE VIEW, ENTRANCE TO STUDIO AT NORTH END OF COURT
CA-1940-13	VIEW IN COURTYARD, LOOKING SOUTH TO LIVING ROOM
CA-1940-14	LIVING ROOM, CLOSE VIEW FROM COURTYARD
CA-1940-15	COLONNADE, LOOKING THROUGH DOOR
CA-1940-16	COLONNADE, BEYOND DOOR
CA-1940-17	BATHROOM, TUB
CA-1940-18	BATHROOM, SINK

SOWDEN HOUSE
HABS No. CA-1940 (Page 6)

D. Site and Surroundings

1. General setting: The house is located on the north side of
    Franklin Avenue, somewhat elevated above the street level. The
    main entrance is centered on the south facade. This, and the
    living room cavern-like form above it, are the only penetrations
    on the south facade. The house is inwardly oriented.

2. Historic landscape design: Originally, there was a planter box
    on axis with the house, with stairways on either side and
    merging behind it.

    The hillside was covered with ivy.

        Prepared by: Robert C. Giebner
                     Project Supervisor
                     Southern California Project II
                     August 1969

PART III. SOURCES OF INFORMATION

A. Primary Sources:

    Lloyd Wright, architect, 855 N. Doheny Dr., Los Angeles: original
    drawings in his possession; information on changes in house.

    Dr. and Mrs. Harold Mazur, owners, 4821 Los Feliz Blvd., Los Angeles,
    California: some information on change of ownership.

    Hall of Records and Assessor's Office, Los Angeles Civic Center:
    legal description.

B. Secondary Sources:

    "Lloyd Wright," Esther McCoy, Arts & Architecture, Los Angeles,
    October 1966, Vol. 83, No. 9, pp. 22-26.

    Guide to Architecture in Southern California, Gebhard-Winter, Los
    Angeles Co. Museum, 1965.

    1866-1968: Architecture in California, David Gebhard, U.C. Santa
    Barbara, catalogue, 1968, p. 75.

PART IV. PROJECT INFORMATION

This project was undertaken by the Historic American Buildings Survey in
cooperation with the Southern California Coordinating Committee for Historic
Preservation. This is the HABS-Southern California Project II, and was
undertaken in 1969.

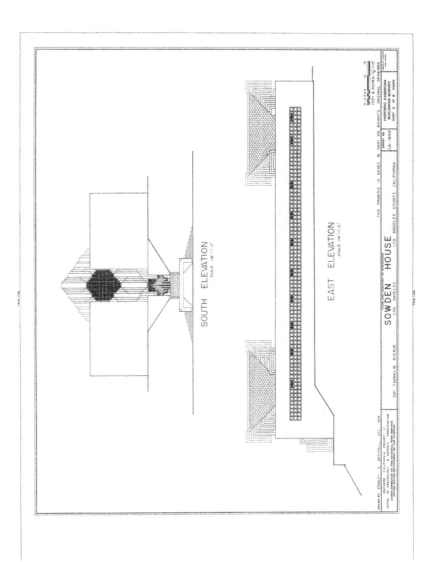

SOUTH ELEVATION
SCALE: 1/8"=1'-0"

EAST ELEVATION
SCALE: 1/8"=1'-0"

SOWDEN HOUSE
LOS ANGELES, LOS ANGELES COUNTY, CALIFORNIA

5121 FRANKLIN AVENUE

HISTORIC AMERICAN
BUILDINGS SURVEY

Sowden House Basement Floor Plan

Sowden House Basement
5121 Franklin Avenue

Dr. George Hill Hodel
Residence from 1945-1950

North

● Soil Sample Locations

SE1, SW2, NW3 and NE4
recovered from SW corner of
the basement on 11.9.12 at
approx 1530 hours by
Paul Dostie and Steve Hodel

Bibliography

Anger, Kenneth. Hollywood Babylon. San Francisco: Stonehill Publishing, 1975.

———. Hollywood Babylon II. New York: NAL Penguin, 1984.

Bonelli, William G. Billion Dollar Blackjack. Beverly Hills: Civic Research Press, 1954.

Blanche, Tony, and Brad Schreiber. Death in Paradise: An Illustrated History of the Los Angeles County Department of Coroner. Los Angeles: General Publishing Group, 1998.

Breton, Andre. Manifestoes of Surrealism. Ann Arbor: University of Michigan Press, Ann Arbor Paperbacks, 1972.

Bruccoli, Matthew J., and Richard Layman. A Matter of Crime, Vol. I. San Diego: Harcourt Brace Jovanovich, 1987.

Carter, Vincent A. LAPD's Rogue Cops. Lucerne Valley, Calif.: Desert View Books, 1993.

Chandler, Raymond. The Blue Dahlia: A Screenplay. Chicago: Southern Illinois University Press, 1976.

Cohen, Mickey. In My Own Words. Englewood Cliffs, N.J.: Prentice-Hall, 1975.

Cox, Julian, Spirit into Matter, J. Paul Getty Trust, Los Angeles, 2004

Demaris, Ovid. The Last Mafioso. New York: Times Books, 1981.

De Rivers, J. Paul, M.D. The Sexual Criminal: A Psychoanalytical Study. Burbank, Calif.: Bloat, 1949; rev. ed. 2000.

Domanick, Joe. *To Protect and to Serve: The L.A.P.D.'s Century of War in the City of Dreams*. New York: Pocket Books, 1994.

Douglas, John, and Mark Olshaker. *The Cases That Haunt Us*. New York: Lisa Drew Books/Scribner, 2000.

———. *Mind Hunter*. New York: Lisa Drew Books/Scribner, 1995.

Ellroy, James. *The Black Dahlia*. New York: Mysterious Press, 1987.

———. *My Dark Places*. New York: Alfred A. Knopf, 1996.

———. *Crime Wave*. New York: Vintage Crime/Black Lizard Vintage Books, 1999.

Fetherling, Doug. *The Five Lives of Ben Hecht*. Toronto: Lester & Orpen, 1977.

Finney, Guy W. *Angel City in Turmoil*. Los Angeles: Amer Press, 1945.

Fowler, Will. *The Young Man from Denver*. Garden City, N.Y.: Doubleday & Company, 1962.

———. *Reporters: Memoirs of a Young Newspaperman.* Malibu, Calf.: Roundtable, 1991.

Giesler, Jerry, and Pete Martin. *The Jerry Giesler Story.* New York: Simon & Schuster, 1960.

Gilmore, John. *Severed: The True Story of the Black Dahlia Murder.* San Francisco: Zanja Press, 1994.

Goodman, Jonathan. *Acts of Murder.* New York: Lyle Stuart Books, Carol Publishing Group, 1986.

Granlund, Nils T. *Blondes, Brunettes, and Bullets.* New York: David McKay, 1957.

Gribble, Leonard. *They Had a Way with Women.* London: Arrow Books, 1967.

Grobel, Lawrence. *The Hustons.* New York: Charles Scribners's Sons, 1989.

Halberstam, David. *The Powers That Be.* New York: Alfred A. Knopf, 1979.

Hall, Angus, ed. *Crimes of Horror.* New York: Phoebus, 1976.

Halleck, Seymour L., M.D. *Psychiatry and the Dilemmas of Crime.* New York: Harper & Row, 1967.

Harris, Martha. *Angelica Huston: The Lady and the Legacy.* New York: St. Martin's Press, 1989.

Henderson, Bruce and Sam Summerlin. *The Super Sleuths.* New York: Macmillan, 1976.

Hecht, Ben. *Fantazius Mallare: A Mysterious Oath.* Chicago: Pascal Covici, 1922.

———. *The Kingdom of Evil: A Continuation of the Journal of Fantazius Mallare.* Chicago: Pascal Covici, 1924.

Heimann, Jim. *Sins of the City: The Real L.A. Noir.* San Francisco: Chronicle Books, 1999.

Hodel, George Hill. *The New Far East: Seven Nations of Asia.* Hong Kong: Reader's Digest Far East, 1966.

Hodel, Steve, *Black Dahlia Avenger: A Genius for Murder,* Harper, New York, 2006.

Hodel, Steve, with Pezzullo, Ralph, *Most Evil: Avenger, Zodiac, and the Further Serial Murders of Dr. George Hill Hodel,* Dutton, New York, 2009.

Huston, John. *An Open Book.* New York: Alfred A. Knopf, 1980.

———. *Frankie and Johnny.* New York: Albert and Charles Boni, 1930.

Jeffers, Robinson. *Roan Stallion, Tamar, and Other Poems.* New York: Boni & Liveright, 1925.

Jennings, Dean. *We Only Kill Each Other: The Life and Bad Times of Bugsy Siegel.* Englewood Cliffs, N.J.: Prentice-Hall, 1967.

Kennedy, Ludovic. *The Airman and the Carpenter*. New York: Viking Penguin, 1985.

Keppel, Robert D. *Signature Killers*. New York: Pocket Books, 1997.

Klein, Norman M., and Martin J. Schiesl.*20th Century Los Angeles: Power, Promotion, and Social Conflict*. Claremont, Calif.: Regina Books, 1990.

Knowlton, Janice, and Michael Newton. *Daddy Was the Black Dahlia Killer*. New York: Pocket Books, 1995.

Lane, Brian, and Wilfred Gregg. *The Encyclopedia of Serial Killers*. New York: Diamond Books, 1992.

Martinez, Al. *Jigsaw John*. Los Angeles: J. P. Tarcher, 1975.

Morton, James. *Gangland International: An Informal History of the Mafia and Other Mobs in the Twentieth Century*. London: Little, Brown & Company, 1998.

Mayo, Morrow, *Los Angeles,* Alfred A. Knopf, New York, 1933.

Nelson, Mark and Bayliss, Sarah Hudson, *Exquisite Corpse,: Surrealism and the Black Dahlia Murder*, New York, Bulfinch Press, 2006.

Nickel, Steven. *Torso: The Story of Eliot Ness and the Search for a Psychopathic Killer*. Winston-Salem, N.C.: John F. Blair, 1989.

Pacios, Mary. *Childhood Shadows: The Hidden Story of the Black Dahlia Murder*. Downloaded and printed via electronic distribution from the World Wide Web. ISBN 1-58500-484-7, 1999.

Parker, William H. *Parker on Police,* Charles C. Thomas Publisher, Springfield Illinois, 1957.

Parrish, Michael. *For the People*. Los Angeles: Angel City Press, 2001.

Phillips, Michelle. *California Dreamin': The True Story of the Mamas and Papas*. New York: Warner, 1986.

Rappleye, Charles, and Ed Becker. *All American Mafioso: The Johnny Rosselli Story*. New York: Doubleday, 1991.

Reid, David. *Sex, Death and Gods in L.A.* New York: Random House, 1992.

Reid, Ed. *The Grim Reapers: The Anatomy of Organized Crime in America*. Chicago: Henry Regnery, 1969.

Richardson, James H. *For the Life of Me: Memoirs of a City Editor*. New York: G. P. Putnam's Sons, 1954.

Roeburt, John. *Get Me Giesler*. New York: Belmont Books, 1962.

Rothmiller, Mike, and Ivan G. Goldman. *L.A. Secret Police: Inside the L.A.P.D. Elite Spy Network*. New York: Pocket Books, 1992.

Rowan, David. *Famous American Crimes*. London: Frederick Muller, 1957.

Sade, Donatien-Alphonse-François de. *Selected Writings of de Sade*. New York: British Book Centre, 1954.

Sade, Donatien-Alphonse-François de. *The Complete Justine, Philosophy in the Bedroom and Other Writings*. New York: Grove Press, 1965.

Sade, Donatien-Alphonse-François de. *The 120 Days of Sodom and Other Writings*. New York: Grove Press, 1966.

Sade, Donatien-Alphonse-François de. *120 Days of Sodom, or the School for Libertinage*. New York: Falstaff Press, 1934.

Sakol, Jeannie. *The Birth of Marilyn: The Lost Photographs of Norma Jean by Joseph Jasgur*. New York: St. Martin's Press, 1991.

Seaver, Richard, Terry Southern, and Alexander Trocchi, eds. *Writers in Revolt: An Anthology*. New York: Frederick Fell, 1963.

Sjoquist, Arthur W. *Captain: Los Angeles Police Department 1869–1984*. Dallas: Taylor, 1984.

Smith, Jack. *Jack Smith's L.A.* New York: McGraw-Hill, 1980.

Starr, Kevin. *Inventing the Dream: California through the Progressive Era*. New York: Oxford University Press, 1985.

———. *The Dream Endures: California Enters the 1940s*. New York: Oxford University Press, 1997.

Stevenson, Robert Louis. *The Strange Case of Dr. Jekyll and Mr. Hyde and Other Stories*. New York: Barnes & Noble, 1995.

Sterling, Hank. *Ten Perfect Crimes*. New York: Stravon, 1954.

Stoker, Charles. *Thicker'n Thieves*. Santa Monica: Sidereal, 1951.

Stoker, Charles. *Thickern'n Thieves*, Los Angeles: Thoughtprint Press, 2011.

Tejaratchi, Sean, ed. *Death Scenes: A Homicide Detective's Scrapbook*. Portland: Feral House, 1996.

Terman, Lewis M. *Genetic Studies of Genius*. Vol. 1. Stanford: Stanford University Press, 1925.

Terman, Lewis M., and Melita H. Oden. *The Gifted Group at Mid-Life: Thirty-Five Years' Follow-Up of the Superior Child*. Stanford: Stanford University Press, 1959.

True Crime—Unsolved Crimes. Alexandria, Va.: Time-Life Books, 1993.

Tygiel, Jules. *The Great Los Angeles Swindle*. New York: Oxford University Press, 1994.

Viertel, Peter. *Dangerous Friends: At Large with Huston and Hemingway in the Fifties*. New York: Nan A. Talese/Bantam Doubleday Dell, 1992.

Viertel, Peter, *White Hunter Black Heart*, New York, Doubleday, 1953.

Underwood, Agness. *Newspaperwoman*. New York: Harper & Brothers, 1949.

Waldberg, Patrick. *Surrealism*. New York: Thames & Hudson, 1997.

Walker, Clifford James. *One Eye Closed the Other Red: The California Bootlegging Years*. Barstow, Calif.: Back Door Publishing, 1999.

Webb, Jack. *The Badge*. Greenwich, Conn.: Fawcett, 1958.

White, Leslie T. *Me, Detective*. New York: Harcourt, Brace & Company, 1936.

Wilson, Colin. *Murder in the 1940s*. New York: Carroll & Graf, 1993.

Woods, Gerald, *The Police in Los Angeles,* Garland Publishing Inc. New York, 1993.

Wolf, Marvin J., and Katherine Mader. *Fallen Angels: Chronicles of L.A. Crime and Mystery*. New York: Facts on File, 1986.

Weintraub, Alan. *Lloyd Wright: The Architecture of Frank Lloyd Wright Jr.* New York: Harry N. Abrams, 1998.

Work Projects Administration, *Los Angeles: A Guide to the City and its Environs,* Hastings House, New York, 1941.

MAN RAY RESEARCH–RELATED BOOKS
Foresta, Merry. *Perpetual Motif: The Art of Man Ray*. New York: Abbeville Press and the National Museum of American Art, 1988.

Man Ray. *Self Portrait*. Boston: Little, Brown & Company, 1963.

———. *Man Ray Photographs*. New York: Thames & Hudson, 1991.

Penrose, Roland. *Man Ray*. New York: Thames & Hudson, 1975.

Robert Berman Gallery. *Man Ray: Paris–L.A.* New York: Smart Art Press Art Catalog, 1996.

Butterfield and Dunning. *Fine Photographs*. Catalog, November 17, 1999.

———. *Fine Photographs*. Catalog, May 27, 1999.

NEWSPAPER SOURCES
San Francisco Chronicle: 1969-1978 *San Francisco Examiner, 1969-1970 Vallejo-Times Herald,* 1969.

Los Angeles Record, 1925.

Riverside Press Enterprise, 1966-1971 Los Angeles Times, 1941-1972.

Los Angeles Mirror, 1947.

Los Angeles Herald Express, 1945-1951 Los Angeles Examiner, 1947-1950 Chicago Daily Tribune, 1945-1950 The Manila Times, 1967.

MISCELLANEOUS
F.B.I., FOIA Files on Elizabeth Short.

Los Angeles District Attorney, Bureau of Investigation, "Black Dahlia and Dr. George Hill Hodel Files"; Electronic Surveillance Files on George Hodel, and Investigative summaries on Black Dahlia by DA Lt. Frank B. Jemison; 146-page Hodel-Black Dahlia transcripts; Frank Jemison/Dorothy Hodel 6-page interview transcripts.

Sowden House, Historic American Survey, National Park Service, Department of Interior 1969.

WEBSITES:
www.stevehodel.com

www.zodiackiller.com

www.lapl.org

www.lmharnisch.com

BLACK DAHLIA AVENGER TELEVISION DOCUMENTARIES & SHOWS
Dateline NBC, "Black Dahlia" Josh Mankiewicz (2003, twenty minute segment)

Court TV, "Who Killed the Black Dahlia?" Josh Mankiewicz (2003, one hour)

CBS 48-Hours Special, "Black Dahlia Confidential" (2004, one hour)

A&E Bill Kurtis Cold Case Files, "Black Dahlia" (2006, one hour)

NBC Universal (France), "The Truth about the Black Dahlia" (2006, one hour)

CNN Anderson Cooper-360, "Black Dahlia" (2006, eight minute author interview)

Discovery Channel, "MOST EVIL" (2007, one-hour)

OTHER BOOKS BY STEVE HODEL:

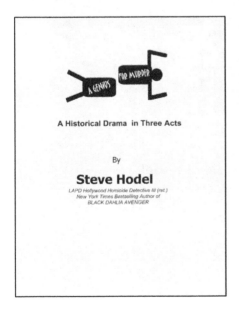

For more information, visit:

www.stevehodel.com
www.blog.stevehodel.com

THOUGHTPRINT PRESS RECOMMENDS:

THICKER'N THIEVES

THE 1950 FACTUAL EXPOSE OF POLICE PAY-OFFS, GRAFT,
POLITICAL CORRUPTION AND PROSTITUTION IN
LOS ANGELES AND HOLLYWOOD

by

SGT. CHARLES STOKER
EX-LAPD VICE-SQUAD OFFICER

Foreword by Steve Hodel

LAPD Hollywood Homicide Detective (ret.)
New York Times Bestselling Author of *Black Dahlia Avenger*